Three Generations in Twentieth Century America
Family, Community, and Nation

The Dorsey Series in American History

Three Generations in Twentieth Century America

Family, Community, and Nation

Revised Edition

John G. Clark
University of Kansas

David M. Katzman
University of Kansas

Richard D. McKinzie
University of Missouri—Kansas City

Theodore A. Wilson
University of Kansas

 1982

THE DORSEY PRESS   Homewood, Illinois   60430

ISBN 0-256-02449-9
Library of Congress Catalog Card No. 81-82915
Printed in the United States of America

1 2 3 4 5 6 7 8 9 0 ML 9 8 7 6 5 4 3 2

For our families

Preface

The response of instructors and students—at all levels and from all parts of the nation—to our effort to make the history of the United States in the 20th century come alive has been most gratifying. In carrying forward this revision of *Three Generations*, we have benefitted greatly from the encouragement, comments, and criticisms of all of you who wrote, telephoned, and, in a few cases, stopped by Lawrence, Kansas, to deliver opinions. Readers who became familiar with the first edition of *Three Generations* will note the addition of numerous photographs, a more open format in general, a bibliographical essay following each chapter, and—we hope—a tighter, more readable narrative. Those improvements are in response to sometimes vociferous recommendations from you and, as well, from us. Readers will also observe, however, that despite various pleas and demands to do so, we could not bring ourselves to expunge any of the families. Perhaps parricide will come more easily in the fourth or the fifth edition!

John G. Clark
David M. Katzman
Richard D. McKinzie
Theodore A. Wilson

Acknowledgments

Our aim has been to infuse this book with life by studying the experiences of real, unique people. We trust that the expenditure of our enthusiasm and imagination and the application of whatever scholarly abilities the authors possess have produced a book that is both enjoyable and profitable to read. The most important ingredients though have been the generosity and continuing good will of the families whose lives illustrate the central themes of this book.

As authors invariably do, we have accumulated numerous debts in the course of writing (and revising) this book. We owe most to the families who shared their stories with us. Although only one family requested that its true identity be protected, we decided to change all of the family names. That it is therefore impossible to thank them all publicly is especially distressing. We do greatly appreciate the friendly reception we were given on numerous interview trips, the frank responses they provided to questions and questionnaires, the loan of family pictures (few of the families possessed cameras during the early years), and the interest and enthusiasm with which they entered into the project. We hope that the outcome, even if not fully meeting their expectations, offers partial repayment for welcoming us into their lives.

Almost without exception, private individuals and public officials in places we investigated—librarians, gas station attendants, newspaper editors, city planners, real estate agents—willingly provided necessary data about their communities. Robert Griffith, University of Massachusetts, David Thelen, University of Missouri, Columbia, and N. Ray Hiner, University of Kansas, offered helpful criticism and numerous suggestions for improvement during the initial writing stage. We wish to thank Major Alan Osur, formerly of the Air Force Academy, and the reviewers—known and unknown—who pointed out assorted errors and helped us to take seriously the task of revision. Norma Stratemeier helped to select the photographs. We are grateful to Judith Wilson for assisting with the preparation of the revised edition. Most particularly, we thank Lois E. Clark for typing each of the many drafts of the manuscript and for serving as unofficial editor. All our own families contributed information, insights, and encouragement. Thanks Garry, Stephen, Larisa, Lois, Laura, Andrew, Judy, Sharyn, Andrea, Eric!

J.G.C.
D.M.K.
R.D.M.
T.A.W.

Preface to the First Edition

The idea for this book was conceived in response to the feeling that most surveys of 20th century America were lifeless. C. S. Lewis described the sociologist hero of his work of fantasy, *That Hideous Strength*, as a man whose education "had the curious effect of making things that he read and wrote more real to him than things he saw. Statistics about agricultural laborers were the substance; any real ditcher, ploughman, or farmer's boy was the shadow." This observation certainly applies to much of written history.

Our attempt is to present a realistic and interesting past for the fourth generation of Americans in the 20th century. Our hope is that this textbook will offer the reader a helping hand, a means of crossing the bridge between history and life, between one generation and the next, between families, communities, and the nation.

As we perceived this task, the questions of greatest intensity were: "Why am *I* like I am?" "How did *I* get this way?" "Why is *my* world the way it is?" Much of an answer to those queries lies in understanding the facts of urbanization, industrialization, expansion, bureaucratization, and their effects upon family structure, occupations, social stratification, and demographic patterns. But it is not the aggregate experience of American society in the 20th century that immediately concerns the inquisitive person. It is his own.

The history of the 20th century and the forces that produced it can be made more understandable to the fourth generation of its participants and, indeed, it can be made more relevant to their most basic questions and concerns. One solution, perhaps temporary but, we believe, viable, is to show how those forces impinged on the lives of three previous generations of American families existing in various socioeconomic-geographical situations. Therefore, we sought out a number of families and reconstructed their lives from 1900 to 1975. We also followed the "lives" of the communities in which our families resided, chronicling their growth, decay, and the changes forced upon them by internal and outside pressures.

The families through whose lives we portray American life since 1900 are not statistically typical. Needless to say, no typical families exist. The families in this book are (or were) real, comprised of actual persons whose lives we studied. We selected the Miller-Gishman, Markovich-Simich, Kurihara, Bassano, Trace, Williams-Gropper, Butler, Martinez, Nava, Reinhardt, Gale-Hart, and O'Reilly families for a variety of reasons but primarily because their experiences seemed somewhat analogous to the experience of large numbers of American families.

One major aim was to find families that comprised a rough cross-section of the population in 1900 and that would continue to reflect this relative balance while also evoking many of the changes that have occurred since 1900. Thus, we sought a mix of races, ethnicity, occupations, and income; families who lived in the country, small and large cities, and the suburbs—from New York City to Overland Park, Kansas, to a rural neighborhood in central Texas; places as disparate as a sharecropper community in Texas, a Pennsylvania steel mill town, a decaying farm community in southeastern Kansas, an upper crust Boston suburb, and working class neighborhoods in New York, Los Angeles, and Evansville, Indiana. Some would be geographically and upwardly mobile; others were to remain in the same places and situations throughout. Another factor was the willingness of suitable families to share their life histories with us. Making the final selections was one of the most difficult but also among the most satisfying aspects of the project.

The fact that the families we chose *had* histories (and all fascinating ones) stretching from 1900 to 1975 perhaps reveals a bias toward stability and success in our analysis. The problem would seem to be unavoidable, given the reasons for selection of families which had experienced the entire period. It is perhaps unnecessary to emphasize that our enterprise is not "pure" family history as that field has evolved over the past decade. The families served principally to illustrate and explain various themes of our study. Without doubt, countless other families would reveal as much about the drama and change that

have swept American society during the past three generations.

Information about the families and some data on their communities came from personal interviews with members of the various families. One or more of the authors met representatives of each of the families and visits to all the communities were undertaken. Though, as with most of us, few of the families possessed extensive written records, we did make use of available files and supplemented the interviews with questionnaires and letters. We engaged in extensive research in local libraries and archives on the families as well as the public and local records of the communities represented, including the U.S. Census.

Obviously, our purpose in writing this book was not merely to chronicle the passing of presidential administrations and to detail the activities of a political elite. We set out to provide a brief and general background regarding national and international problems and to emphasize those aspects of political, social, diplomatic, and economic history which were directly relevant to the lives of "our" families and, through them, the mass of Americans. In addition, we have attempted to describe and assess the quality of life for these families and to place their lifestyles in the context of social and cultural trends. Of course, the categories mentioned—social, political, economic, cultural—are artificial, for real lives, for better or worse, are integrated, are whole.

J.G.C.
D.M.K.
R.D.M.
T.A.W.

Contents

San Francisco, and Overland Park, Kansas. The Navas of Hidalgo County, Texas. The Groppers of Lubbock, Texas, and Decatur, Georgia. The Bassanos of Inwood (NYC), Upper St. Clair Township, Pennsylvania, and Alexandria, Virginia. The Martinezes of New York. The Butlers of Boston, Massachusetts. The Reinhardts of Evansville, Indiana. The Traces of Los Angeles, California. The Simiches of Midland, Pennsylvania. The Traces of Evansville, Louisville, Birmingham, Denver, Phoenix, Sugar Land, and Kansas City. The Harts of New Albany, Kansas. Conclusion.

Maze. Containment as Rhetoric and Religion. The Korean War. A New Departure? The Cold War at Home. New Rhetoric, Old Policies. Close of the American Century?

TABLES AND MAPS

Tables

Maps

Three Generations in Twentieth Century America
Family, Community, and Nation

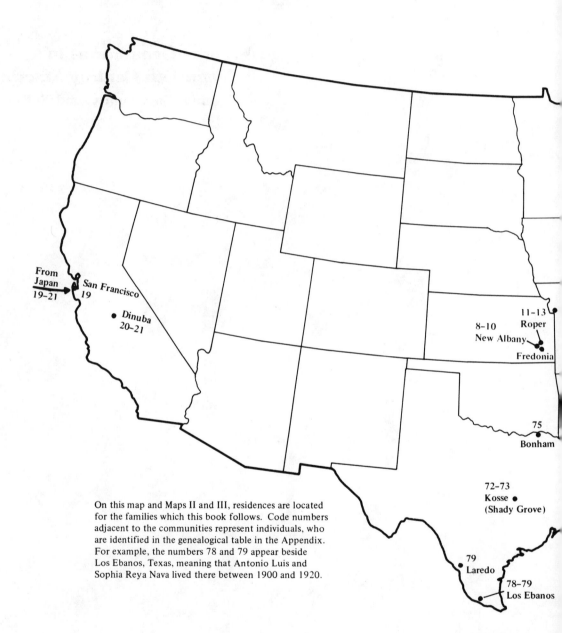

From
Japan
19–21

San Francisco
19

● Dinuba
20–21

11–13
Roper
8–10
New Albany
Fredonia

75
Bonham

72–73
Kosse ●
(Shady Grove)

79
● Laredo

78–79
Los Ebanos

On this map and Maps II and III, residences are located
for the families which this book follows. Code numbers
adjacent to the communities represent individuals, who
are identified in the genealogical table in the Appendix.
For example, the numbers 78 and 79 appear beside
Los Ebanos, Texas, meaning that Antonio Luis and
Sophia Reya Nava lived there between 1900 and 1920.

1-2
Bangor

1-7
Brookline,
34-36
(Somerville)

Providence
38-45
34-36
From Ireland

29-32
38-46
Boston
New
York

38-39 From
Russia

29 From Italy

23-24 From Germany

51-52.
54-55 From Serbia

Detroit
70-71

51-53
Midland
Primrose 54-56

23-28
61-63
Evansville and
Vanderburgh Co.

59-62
Waynesboro
and Wayne Co.

PART 1
1900-1920

1 | The First Generation

INTRODUCTION

To the delight of America's clergymen, December 31, 1899—the eve of a new year and, as many erroneously believed, a new century—fell on Sunday. Throughout the nation watch parties and church services were held to usher in the new era. At midnight, the singing of hymns at prayer meetings and the vigorous ringing of church bells proclaimed the arrival of the 20th century. More boisterous celebrants postponed their parties until the next day. In Evansville, Indiana, with the temperature a brisk 15 degrees above zero, hundreds of people, taking a work holiday, went skating at Sweetser's Pond. That evening, the fashionable set gathered for an "entre nous" party at the St. George Hotel. There the young dandies and belles of Evansville, splendidly arrayed and carefully chaperoned, danced to a program of 20 numbers provided by Gustav Schreiber's orchestra until 11:30

P.M. when a sumptuous supper was served. Smaller, more private parties were held across the city that Monday evening. The Evansville press noted the general tranquility of these affairs. The Sabbath had muted the normal jubilation associated with the passing of the old year and the start of the new.

American families, their friends, and parishioners rang in the 20th century with little nostalgia. The century just past had ended on sour notes of agricultural and industrial depression and war. They looked forward to the new century, for it appeared that good times had returned. The year ahead—1900—promised prosperity because of more favorable farm prices and rising industrial employment. Even Americans who were given over to speculative musings had little reason to expect that, within two generations, the ways most Americans lived would be radically restructured. By 1900, most Americans were caught in this process. They were moving

5

spatially—from farm to village, from town to city, from Europe to the United States—and in time—from preindustrial cultures to a modern society, from old traditions to new ones. It was a process strained by conflict and tension, especially for families in America. Time-tested ways of viewing this world and the "other world," ways of living deeply rooted in the historical experiences of both native-born Americans and foreign folk, and habitual ways of dealing with other people— all nurtured in the sanctuary of the family— came under attack by the often contrary demands of machine culture and its handmaiden, the industrial cities.

Not all were affected simultaneously nor at the same pace. But as the conflicts and tensions of adapting to a society that made ever more voracious demands on families and individuals grew more intense, the depressions and strife of the preceeding century would soon fade. Many, pulled by a dream and pushed by the realities of a harsh present and a dim future, would think of moving to the city, hoping to enter the office, shop, or factory and share in the city's wealth. Unknown to the many migrants were the hidden and high costs implicit in removal to a strange setting. The native born, workers and middle classes alike, were required to adjust to city and workplace while the foreign born, facing even greater cultural adjustments, were subjected to strident demands to Americanize. Great strain faced newcomers to city life when confronted by the industrialists' obsession with time, the intensified emphasis on specialization of labor, and the need to sacrifice cultural ties. Each individual and each family carried along those traditions and values that had worked in their home towns. This cultural baggage would have to be abandoned, wholly or in part, if these people wished to enter this new society with a fair chance of success.

Families are the basic units within American society. The historical experience of the United States is to a large measure reflected in the history of its family units and the communities within which they lived and loved and worked and played. In 1900, there were 16 million families living in the United States. Some 53 million Americans, or 70 percent of a total population of 76 million, lived in family households. Of the remaining 23.5 million, many were young adults or widowers and divorcees who would soon marry or remarry and begin new families. Native-born white parents headed between 70 and 75 percent of the families and black parents headed 11.5 percent. In 1910 (figures for 1900 are unavailable) 6 of the 20 million families, or 30 percent, were living on farms; by 1920 this figure had fallen to 28 percent while the number of families residing in urban areas (populations over 2,500) had risen from some 39 percent in 1900 to over 50 percent in 1920.

Whether one was a native-born farmer in Tennessee or Kansas, a German Lutheran Indiana farmer, a black Baptist laborer newly arrived in Detroit from Mississippi, an Italian Catholic mason living in New York City, an Episcopalian lumber dealer in Boston, an east European Jewish garment worker in Providence, Rhode Island, a Boston Irish cop, or a Serbian steelworker in Midland, Pennsylvania, the opportunities presented by American society proved irresistible. But America was so vast and so complex that none of these families experienced it totally. They encountered parts of it head-on, other parts obliquely, and still other parts not at all. The encounters could cause intense harm or bring satisfying rewards. Some remained in family-oriented communities isolated from the larger society. Others, fleeing to America for other than economic reasons, sought to transport intact the habits and traditions of their old lives. Still others thought things were and would always be just dandy. Sooner or later, however, all would discover that the path into the future was tortuous and obscure.

In the pages that follow, representative families will occupy center stage. Through their success and failures, the course of American history in the 20th century will be illuminated.

THE BUTLER FAMILY OF BROOKLINE, MASSACHUSETTS

The Butler house sprawled comfortably under a canopy of ancient elms, maples, and lindens, half hidden at the end of a steep driveway from Heath Street, a winding dirt lane that eventually merged with Boylston Pike, a principal road leading from Boston Common to Brookline and points west. George C. Butler had purchased this post-Revolutionary farm house, with its brown-red clapboard siding, white trim, and shingle roof, for his growing family three years earlier, in September 1897. To the Butlers "The Place," the familiar name for their Brookline home, provided idyllic comfort and total security. It also represented the family's acceptance into the special circle of old-line white Anglo-Saxon Protestants who comprised the social and economic elite of Boston.

George Butler had brought his wife of three years, Mary Wilson Butler, and their two infant children to Boston in 1889. George and Mary grew up in Bangor, Maine, where their families were principal citizens of that thriving lumber-commercial center. The two families (and, as well, the Carrs and Chamberlains in the maternal line) traced their ancestry to farmers and artisans who had emigrated from southern and southeastern England to the Massachusetts Bay Colony in the 17th century. "Poor but honest," as one descendant characterized them, the Butlers, Wilsons, Carrs, and Chamberlains prospered in the New World, producing large families and acquiring modest wealth. They seem to have espoused most of the Puritan virtues—the work ethic, self-sufficiency, tightfistedness in money matters, faith in education—without giving way to Puritanical sanctimoniousness and fanaticism. By the mid–19th century, their descendants were prepared to take part in larger, different spheres, moving from agriculture into industry, from the practice of law into politics, from simple obedience to the work ethic to a definition of the good life that included sports, cultural activities, and philanthropy. The effects of these changes were restrained, however, by an innate conservatism, obligations to those patterns of behavior established by the ancestral worthies, and responsibilities to Butlers yet unborn. Consciousness of place, of belonging somewhere and to something, marked the Butlers.

George's father, John Lysander Butler, became prominent in Bangor and Maine politics. After building a prosperous lumber business, he served for eight years in the state legislature. He was a loyal Republican, a close friend and supporter of Maine's most powerful figure on the national political scene, James G. Blaine. John Butler might have pursued a career in politics but he was stricken with palsy in the 1880s and was forced into semiretirement. Mary Wilson Butler's father, Franklin Augustus Wilson, was born in Bradford, Maine, graduated Phi Beta Kappa from Bowdoin College, and practiced law for some 50 years in Bangor. Through his law practice, he became general counsel, director, and ultimately president of the Maine Central Railroad. Though their parents would have shuddered at the idea that they were aristocrats (or even at the notion that such a class existed), both George Butler and Mary Wilson experienced childhoods enriched by opportunities (railroad passes, private tutors, trotting horses, summer homes) that only a few specially privileged families enjoyed in Victorian America.

Born in 1857, George Butler received the educational and other opportunities deemed appropriate for his class. He attended Phillips

Exeter Academy and then Harvard College. A gregarious, athletic young man, George pitched for the baseball team (he claimed to have been the first person to throw a curve ball in the state of Maine) and contributed poems and essays to the *Harvard Advocate*. Harvard was more noted for its social life than for intellectual rigor, and when George and most of his peers in the class of 1879 graduated, they were "young gentlemen," prepared for little else but entry into the family business or, after further education, professional careers. George possessed a secret desire to become a painter, but family pressures and, perhaps, his own conservatism precluded any such bohemian calling. After graduation, following a leisurely summer with two Harvard classmates canoeing down the great rivers of Europe, George returned to Bangor.

In the following decades, he built the family lumber business into a thriving commercial empire. Beginning with the Butler lumber holdings, he converted this small, Maine-based company into an international operation, Stetson Butler and Company, with offices in Canadian and Maine cities, Boston, and New York City. Stetson Butler and Company owned over 100,000 acres of pine and spruce forests and sold lumber, which it transported in chartered four-masted schooners, all over the world. By his 30th birthday, George Butler was a wealthy man.

George married Mary Wilson in the Bangor First Unitarian Church on June 17, 1886, and the young couple bought a fieldstone, mansard-roofed mansion that overlooked the Penobscot River. Here, their first two children were born: John in 1887 and Eliott, 10 months later. The next year, because of the expansion of the family business and his own desire to enter a larger, more stimulating social environment, George moved the family to the wealthy enclave of Brookline, five miles southwest of Boston. There in a succession of homes, Mary, attended by the local doctor, delivered three more sons: Roger in 1889, George in 1891, and, as the result of the failure of the couple's preferred birth control method, coitus interruptus, Robert in 1895.

Following Robert's birth, George Butler began to search for a permanent home. The home would have to be reasonably convenient to his office in Boston and be sufficiently large for him, Mary, the five boys, the family's cook, chauffeur, maid, nanny, Irish gardener, and guests. Another requirement was social, in order that the Butler boys have playmates of their own class and, for Mary, friends and the cultural pursuits she so enjoyed. The house at 61 Heath Street, close to shops and Brookline's Unitarian Church, was bounded by the estates of some of Massachusett's most distinguished families.

The first years of the 20th century found the Butlers settled comfortably into the life of upper-class Boston. George had so organized his business affairs that the office ran with minimal attention from him, aside from periodic business trips to Canada and New York. When at home, his routine consisted of an early breakfast (usually oatmeal with thick cream, hot buttered waffles and maple syrup, eggs, bacon, sausages, or sometimes a broiled steak, coffee, tea, and, as a rare treat, orange juice), the drive into Boston in the family's Phaeton, a few hours at Stetson Butler's offices in State Street, a leisurely lunch (where he could enjoy a good cigar and brandy, which Mary banned at home) with old friends at one of his clubs, and a return home in midafternoon. Increasingly, George spent his time at outdoor sports. He became obsessed with golf and for many years played almost daily at the country club in Brookline, the Seapui Club on Cape Cod, or anywhere the family traveled. Canoeing, hunting, and salmon fishing were seasonal pleasures.

George Butler was a devoted family man. He took special interest in the boys' athletic and school activities; however, Mary Butler was the effective head of the household, disciplining the children, dealing with servants and shopkeepers, and scheduling the family's social life. She accepted this role unquestioningly, and though she much preferred The Place's flower gardens and her club meetings, Mary took part in the yearly trips to the New Brunswick woods, to Bangor, Bar Harbor, and the Bahamas, and the almost yearly trips to Europe. Her influence on the boys, especially her youngest, Bobby, was dominant. Because she had been an only child and because of her fascination with the arts, books filled the Butler home—Dickens, Charles Lamb's *Tales from Shakespeare,* other classics, and popular juvenile books. The Everyman Library, all 100 volumes, accompanied the family each summer to its New Brunswick fishing camp. George and Mary regularly attended the Boston theatre and opera, being captivated by Sarah Bernhardt and Enrico Caruso. They received the important monthly magazines of the period, and George began each day with a searching perusal of the *Boston Globe.* For Christmas 1900, the family present was an enormous, hand-wound Victrola and a huge stack of records, mostly Italian and French operas.

Mary's influence merged with that of her husband in providing an atmosphere of attention and warmth for her sons. She inculcated an awareness of right and duty, not so much from religious convictions as from a sense of noblesse oblige, the belief that "from those to whom much is given, much is expected." There was freedom in the house on Heath Street, freedom to grow up well nourished and strong, freedom to play and explore physically and intellectually. There were, however, clear boundaries imposed by George and Mary's awareness of their special status: a code of proper behavior that required the boys to look and act adult beyond their years, an acceptance of traditional values and goals,

a view of the world outside Brookline and Boston that ignored the many signs that the larger society was pressing upon their private lives.

The beginning of the 20th century found the Butlers trapped in the very same whirlpool of events engulfing all Americans. Wealth and social status provided George, Mary, and their five sons with the means to realize the sort of life which the vast majority of Americans could only envision as ideal. There were no foolproof or unflawed paths to a fully satisfying life, but the Butlers and a few other lucky ones came as close as money could buy.

Still, for the fortunate ones like the Butlers, it was good to be alive in America in 1900 and the sheltered decades that followed. One of George and Mary's sons, later recalling a lazy summer spent near the Bonaventure River, halfway down Canada's Gaspe Peninsula, wrote:

> Here the family found its perfect flowering. The males played scrub baseball before breakfast on the cropped grass between our cabins and the river and plunged naked into the freezing morning swiftness of the Bonaventure. On Sunday all of us paddled down the river for a picnic and swim on the sandy beach of the Baie Chaleur . . . ; devoured the pink flesh of fresh-caught salmon (broiled, boiled with egg sauce, smoked in our own smoke house, and hashed with cream); and listened to the voices of Caruso and Eames and Nellie Melba pour out from our Victrola into the Quebec wilderness Italian and French operatic arias.

Contentment, leisure, security were not illusions to George and Mary and their brood.

In the next few years, George and Mary watched their sons reach adulthood and, one by one, assume the positions in upper-class Boston society to which wealth, education, and the Butler name entitled them. All five boys moved easily through prep school and on to Harvard College. The four oldest earned varsity letters in football and rowing

10

Harvard Yard *c.* 1910, during Roger and George Butler's undergraduate days

and established the Butlers as renowned athletes. The youngest, Robert, was an indifferent halfback and washout on the Harvard crew, but he excelled at intellectual pursuits. He was elected to Phi Beta Kappa his junior year, named class poet, and published a successful novel shortly after graduation in 1916. The five brothers were tapped by Porcellian, Harvard's most exclusive upper-class club—a confirmation of the family's standing. John entered a Wall Street investment firm, Eliott was first in his class at Harvard Medical School and became an internationally known surgeon, Roger launched himself into a career as ne'er-do-well and ladies' man, George de-

cided to pursue a banking career, and Robert, after a brief fling as a graduate student in English literature, was accepted by Harvard Law School.

The self-contained world the Butlers knew seemed unchangeable and eternal, but there were limits to the protection it offered. The family was forced to watch helplessly as Mary wasted away from stomach cancer. Her agony was relieved by heavy doses of morphine, but nothing could prevent her death in 1916. George Butler, depressed after Mary's death, gave up active interest in his lumber business. He continued to golf and fish and began to devote serious attention to painting.

Four of the five boys entered the armed services during World War I, and John, Roger, and Robert served in Europe.

THE GALE FAMILY OF NEW ALBANY, KANSAS

In February 1901, some 1,400 miles west of the Butlers, Cleveland Edward Gale, his wife Belle, their three daughters, and three sons prepared for the wedding of Charles Edward Gale, their oldest son. On a bright and crisp Sunday afternoon, dozens of rigs and wagons converged on the 240-acre farm located on the edge of the small village of New Albany, six miles east of Fredonia, Kansas. Securing their horses and leaving their gifts, the guests bundled up against the cold. In their Sunday best, they trooped the quarter mile to church. There, hymns, prayers, and a traditional ceremony joined Charles and Chloe Belle Packson, the daughter of a neighboring farmer, in matrimony. Chloe, dressed in a flowing white gown with yards of lace, and her husband then led the congregation to the Gale home for the reception. The pair moved into the Gale household where Charles took över active management of the farm and received one quarter ownership as a wedding gift.

The farm had been in the family's hands since the purchase of 160 acres from the original homesteader in 1865 by Christopher Gale, a Union Army veteran and later a Wilson County political leader and judge. The farm had prospered over the years: an adjoining 80 acres had been purchased; dairy and beef cattle had been added; and a tin equipment shed had been erected on the newest tract. The Gales had weathered the severe agricultural depression of the 1890s because of their diversified output—meat, grain, and dairy products. Times had been hard in ''the 90s'' but not hard enough to tempt the Gales to bolt the Republican Party and follow William Jennings Bryan or the Populists. Cleveland Gale had no money in the bank when the depression ended, but neither had he any debts. Prices rose in 1900 and 1901, crops were good, the Republicans were in office in Kansas as well, as in the federal government, and his oldest boy was soon to be married. Approaching his 68th birthday and increasingly arthritic, Cleveland looked forward to passing the responsibility and honor of land ownership to his eldest.

The Gales lived comfortably in a farmhouse constructed in the early 1890s to replace their original home, now the site of a vegetable garden. With the help of neighbors, Cleveland had laid a 30 by 40 foot limestone foundation and then quickly erected a balloon-frame structure divided into a kitchen-pantry, dining room, parlor, three bedrooms upstairs, and an unfinished attic. Two fireplaces downstairs and coal-oil burning stoves upstairs supplied heat. The family drew water from two outside wells situated a safe distance from the brick-lined pit of the ''two-seater'' privy. They filled the house with furniture and knicknacks passed down or obtained over the years. A lavender upholstered settee, other store-bought pieces, and an old family piano crowded the parlor while hand-made tables, chairs, buffets, and shelves served in the other rooms. To prepare for the wedding, Belle had ordered linoleum to lay in the kitchen and pantry from the Sears, Roebuck catalog.

Closely knit and independent, the Gales were a sociable and active family. Cleveland, while not politically inclined as was his father, was past president of the New Albany Township Grange. In addition to the Grange, which provided fun and enlightenment to all age groups, family members belonged to the New Albany Presbyterian Church and served as officers in some of its clubs. Unfortunately, the church was in trouble, for while the population of Wilson County increased between 1890 and 1900—and continued to grow until 1920—New Albany Township's population decreased by some 15 farm families. Attendance at the New Albany grade school also declined, and the school board considered closing it down and transporting the children to Fredonia. The farmers resisted because the church and the school and the social activities they sponsored were the cement of the community. Through great effort, both institutions survived.

The routine of the farm took up most of the family's time and played a role. By 1900, the children ranged from 13 to 25 years of age. Belle and her daughters were responsible for the household, the garden, and the chickens. Nearly an acre was tilled in which the women planted beans, potatoes, beets, and other vegetables. At preserving time, the men pitched in after their field work, carrying great vats of boiling water and dozens of fruit jars purchased from the Mason Fruit Jar Company plant in Coffeyville, trying to keep out of the way of the women. The livestock was a constant commitment. The profits from dairying were divided among the daughters, and the sons split the profits from the beef cattle with their father. Cleveland and the boys grew wheat, corn, oats, and made hay, selling off the entire wheat crop and the surplus of corn, hay, and oats in Fredonia. The farm was a full-time business and required expert management and increasingly large investments in horse-drawn machinery.

Cleveland and Belle both died within a year of Charles' marriage. As agreed upon beforehand, the farm passed intact to Charles with the stipulation that adequate provision be made for the brothers and sisters when they came of age or married. By 1910, all were gone, married, and independent, but none lived farther than 25 miles distant, so that visiting was common. By 1915, Charles and Chloe had five children, two boys—

Charles James and William—and three girls—Chloe Maude, Mary Olivia, and Anna Ruth. A fourth girl, Martha Isabelle, the present resident of the farm, was born in 1919.

Charles and Chloe continued many of the practices of their parents, particularly in their social and family life. Much to the delight of her husband and the children, Chloe would sit at the ancient piano in the evening playing "Maple Leaf Rag" and other Scott Joplin pieces. But elsewhere around the house and farm, some routines became more mechanized. Charles purchased a small gasoline engine to pump water into the house where it was heated in a hot-water tank. For a while he talked of buying a steam tractor but decided against it, purchasing instead another 80 acres of contiguous land and a new cultivator. The dairy shed was modernized with new stalls and milking equipment. The improvements came in installments and were purchased with cash. Charles would have preferred to use credit for everything and save his cash for the harvest labor required in late July and August, but the First National Bank of Fredonia (as was true of all other banks in the National Bank System) was only allowed to lend money on first mortgages. Implement dealers and private lenders in Independence and Coffeyville charged too high an interest rate. Charles husbanded his resources while Chloe ran a tight household, and they managed to save for future investment in their farm.

The outside world also became more accessible to the Gales. In 1904, a rural free delivery route made it possible for Charles to subscribe to a farm newspaper and to the practical bulletins of the United States Department of Agriculture. Chloe received mail from the national office of the Ladies Home Missionary Society, a magazine or two, and increasing amounts of advertisements from flower bulb distributors and other merchants.

And so the Gales flourished in a difficult vocation. Charles was occasionally upset at the vagaries of the grain and livestock markets and with Chloe's aid, contributed to the founding of the Farm Bureau Union in Wilson County. But Charles never became more than temporarily involved in the grain cooperative that opened and failed in Fredonia. As the children grew, they attended the same one-room schoolhouse that Charles had and listened to similar sermons in the Presbyterian church. Then, in 1914, the schoolmarm retired and the pastor died. It was surprisingly difficult to find replacements. City schools and churches paid higher salaries, and young professionals were not keen to accept assignments in isolated rural villages. When the township employed a new teacher, she remained only a year. So did the next one. A Fredonia preacher filled the pulpit in New Albany for two years on a part-time basis before a middle-aged minister accepted the charge.

It also became more difficult for Charles Gale to hire harvest labor because of competition from the mineral industries that developed in Wilson and neighboring counties. Moreover, freight cars were frequently in short supply because the railroads, with investments in spur lines to the new plants, gave these lines first priority. Charles normally sold his beef on the hoof in Kansas City, but car shortages in that direction at times compelled him to ship to Wichita or even Emporia where prices were less favorable. Charles and his friends complained to the railroads but without result.

With the school and church in trouble, with township population declining (and thus the tax base, too), with industry competing for labor and transportation, and with more and more goods and services offered in Fredonia, the Gales and their friends and neighbors began to shift their allegiances away from New Albany. First, the local store closed and shopping in Fredonia became habitual; then the township fair committee decided to amalgamate with the Wilson County Fair; and then

Work Projects Administration, National Archives

Horse-drawn disc of the type used before World War I on the Gale farm

the township was forced to borrow money from the county to repair several township bridges. It was the beginning of the end for New Albany as a viable community. It was also the beginning of a new relationship with Fredonia for Charles and his neighbors. It is not known whether the Gales felt any sorrow at the passing of old ties.

THE KURIHARAS OF SAN FRANCISCO, FRESNO, AND DINUBA, CALIFORNIA

Twenty one-year-old Yoshisuke Kurihara arrived in San Francisco in June 1910. Born in Japan but a resident of Honolulu, Hawaii, to which his parents had moved in 1897, he was cared for by relatives when his parents returned to Japan in 1904. In Honolulu, Yoshisuke, attended the public elementary schools but graduated from a Catholic high school. Wishing to become a physician, he decided to migrate to California, get work, and enroll in St. Ignatius College. He accomplished the first two goals, obtaining work soon after his arrival as a fruit picker in the Sacramento Valley. He became so discouraged with the racial discrimination prevalent on the West Coast, however, that he abandoned his plan to enter medical school.

Preferring to face the risks of discrimination in California to the scanty economic opportunities in Japan, Yoshisuke settled in San Francisco. He rented a room in "little Tokyo" and found work at a wholesale produce firm serving the local Japanese community. By 1916, Yoshisuke was well enough established to send passage money for his younger brother, Seito, and his family to move to California. Yoshisuke arranged for a job for Seito as a day laborer in an orchard near Fresno. Seito soon leased a small farm near Dinuba on which the family raised tomatoes, cucumbers, and watermelons for market.

Soon after American entry into World War I, Yoshisuke joined the army. He served in France and with the American occupation forces, returning to California in November 1919. He invested his army savings in a retail fruit and vegetable store in Berkeley from which he derived a good living in subsequent years. His brother Seito, seriously asthmatic, hoped to earn enough money to return and live comfortably in Japan. But the farm produced just enough to get by on. Even then, it was sometimes necessary to ask Yoshisuke for help. Seito remained an alien in a strange country.

THE BRAUER FAMILY OF VANDERBURGH COUNTY, INDIANA

For six-year-old Mathilde Brauer, who lived on a small farm just outside Evansville, Indiana, 1900 was a year of fascinating and frightening new experiences. In mid-September, Mathilde, with her two older sisters, Dorothy (14) and Anna (8), set out on the two-mile walk to White School where she enrolled in Willard Carpenter's first grade. Although she knew many of her classmates from church and family visits, and Mr. Carpenter greeted the class in the familiar *Plattdeutsch,* there were also *Englischen* children in her room, and the school books were in English rather than in the ornate German script she loved to trace. Mathilde's world had been the tidy Brauer farmstead on Red Bank Road, its 40-odd acres stretching back to the Franklin Hills and only three miles away from the whitewashed Lutheran church. Now, she was pushed into a new milieu where an alien language, different rules, and grown-ups who frowned at her held sway. Still, the conflict between the worlds of family and school was more apparent than real. The 20th century promised continuation of the sense of stability and identity which the Brauers and other members of the German community around Evansville had achieved during the years since their immigration to the United States.

Henry Brauer had come to Indiana from the rural environs of Stuttgart, Germany. The fourth son among nine children in a Lutheran farming family, he had worked as an agricultural laborer until, at 23, he sought economic independence by moving to America. After a three-year stay with an uncle in Spencer County, Indiana, he moved to Vanderburgh County in 1882. He hired out to Johann Dort, the owner of a 60-acre farm in Perry Township, and in 1884, married his employer's eldest daugher, Ruth. The Dorts had come to the United States after 1848, both settling with their families in southern Vanderburgh County. Married in the late 1850s, they raised four children in a strict Lutheran environment, clinging to their German heritage and centering family activities on the local church, which Johann helped build, and the Perry Township *Turnverein*. Ruth Dort's life in her parents' home, learning to run a farm household and raise German children, had been an effective preparation for marriage and motherhood. To hardworking, religious Germans such as Ruth Dort and Henry Brauer, this community in the outskirts of Evansville served—like the band of German settlements across southern Indiana—as an Old World sanctuary within their new homeland.

German immigrants as a group experienced a less difficult adaptation to life in America than did other immigrants. The first large wave of German migrants, following the European revolutions of 1848, adjusted so well to their adopted society that, by 1910, many were considered "old Americans" and not a hyphenate group. Similarly, the large numbers of Germans, such as Henry Brauer, who arrived in the 1880s and early 1890s were hailed as the one non-English-speaking group which assimilated rapidly and easily

through the process of the melting pot. In reality, German-Americans did not "melt" or "blend." Instead, as with other groups, their responses to American life reflected a process of cultural retention and gradual modification. Usually, rural German Protestant immigrants and both rural and urban Catholic German-Americans successfully maintained their "Germanness," the ties of culture and language, into the 20th century. Those who cited the German-American experience as proof that the assimilation/Americanization process worked referred to urban German-American Protestants. The majority's experience repeated that of Henry Brauer who followed a path—from hired hand to landowner, from bachelor to husband and father, from newcomer to community stalwart—parallel to the course his life might have taken had he remained in Germany.

In 1886, the year in which their first daughter was born, Henry and Ruth Brauer purchased a farm of their own. For $1,600, raised from savings and a loan from Ruth's parents, they bought 47 acres, three quarters tillable and one quarter woodland. They purchased the land, located four miles west of Evansville and some three miles south of the Dort farm, for less than the going price for farmland in the area because it was "bottom land," well within the Ohio River floodplain. It was flooded annually by the spring high waters, and Henry would have to delay the planting and clear off the debris deposited by the river. Every second or third year, floodwaters marooned his family. These disadvantages were outweighed by the land's low price and productivity, and its location enabled the Brauers to remain in a German-American community rather than moving farther west.

The agricultural community in which the Brauers lived was changing from subsistence to surplus farming. This meant that the farmers grew more and more crops for sale rather than for their own consumption, using the money acquired to purchase other items. At first, of course, basic requirements of shelter, survival, and the annual mortgage payments had to be met, and Henry and Ruth sought to achieve almost total self-sufficiency. They built, with the help of neighbors, their own dwelling from timber out of the farm's woodlot. Henry built a small barn and added rooms to the original log-timbered house as the family grew. In 1899, he constructed smoke and ice houses and a summer house for cooking during the hot Indiana summers. The smoke and ice houses gave the Brauers some flexibility in diet by allowing long-term storage of meat and vegetables. Pork was a family staple, served fresh, smoked, and converted into such traditional German delicacies as head cheese, blood pudding, and numerous kinds of wurst (sausage). A priceless element in Ruth's dower was the recipes for sausage passed down from generation to generation. Some corn was grown for hog feed, but the Brauers did not engage in the slaughtering of hogs for market. They canned the fruit—apples, pears, and cherries—raised on the farm as well as the vegetables grown in Ruth's garden. Neither the eggs from their chickens nor the milk and butter produced by the two Guernsey cows were sold. The only staples which the Brauers regularly purchased were flour, sugar, spices, and sorghum molasses bought during biweekly expeditions to Howell, an incorporated village on the outskirts of Evansville that housed the L&N Railroad's repair shops. In the early years, they grew everything else on the farm.

They needed money and obtained it by growing corn for market. In southern Indiana until after the turn of the century, corn served as the cash crop. The first year Henry Brauer planted some 30 acres in corn, using seed donated by his father-in-law; thereafter, he selected the biggest, heaviest ears from the previous year's crop (occasionally mixed with corn that had caught his eye at the county fair) for seed. Corn growing followed the rhythm of the seasons and the river. Henry planted his corn in April, after his land had dried out sufficiently for him to take a horse-drawn plow into the fields. Summer passed by in round after round of cultivation. In October, when the stalks turned brown and dry, Henry, his family, and two or three hired hands (often youths from the nearby black community on the river) trudged through the fields, shucking the golden ears. Then Henry hauled the corn not reserved for feed to Dogtown, a railroad junction four miles away. The elevator and mill there were owned by a local German businessman who graded and bought Henry's grain. Henry preferred this arrangement because of convenience and because the man, with whom he could dicker in German, belonged to the Brauers' church and was thought to be more fair than the high-powered grain dealers in Evansville. Despite the volatile business conditions of the 1880s and 1890s, which produced wildly fluctuating agricultural prices and industrial depression, the Brauers had achieved as much economic security by 1900 as a farmer could expect. As with the Gales, the future—measured in terms of rising farm prices—looked bright for the Brauers.

Even more important than the family's prosperity was the pattern of life that Henry and Ruth had established. Moderation and stability were their guides. The Brauers sought to continue the way of life they had known and to transmit it to their three daughters. As had been the case in Ruth's home, they spoke only German in the household, subscribed to a German language newspaper, the *Evansville Demokrat,* and, whenever possible, dealt with German businessmen. In 1890, Henry joined the local branch of the *Turnverein,* a German-American, social club which all of his friends supported. Celebrations and

Farm wagons hauling wheat from thrasher to elevator

holidays—confirmation, weddings, funerals, Christmas, Lent and Easter, Pentecost—were conducted according to old-country traditions. The Brauers' life focused on religion and church-related social activities, which fostered stability and strong cultural pride within the German-American community. Soon after Mathilde began school, the Brauers transferred from the Lutheran church in nearby Union Township to St. Paul's, a large Evangelical Church on Evansville's West Side. Most of the Brauers' neighbors attended St. Paul's, and Ruth, who was becoming active in the Perry Township *Frauenverein,* a women's sewing circle, wished to have her daughters confirmed in the higher status environment of St. Paul's. Both she and Henry enjoyed the traditional German-language services and German hymns.

Although they were not fully aware of the changes affecting their lifestyle, the Brauers' transfer to St. Paul's was part of a process that eroded their, and the German-American community's, sense of identity and brought the Brauers closer to Evansville and hence the mainstream of American society. Attendance at St. Paul's usually brought the family into Evansville twice weekly. Further, the inauguration in 1902 of a horse-drawn streetcar line from Franklin Street, one block from St. Paul's, to the western edge of Howell, just a mile from White School, encouraged them to browse in the German-owned dry goods and hardware stores lining Franklin Street. But even after an interurban system replaced the streetcars, the Brauers rarely ventured to the Main Street shopping district in the center of the city. They found the hectic, impersonal atmosphere of "downtown" distasteful, and they distrusted the German-Jewish merchants who operated many of the Main Street stores. The German enclave stretching along Franklin Street, where familiar customs and dialects abounded, seemed more relaxed and reassuring.

Even though the Brauers refused to visit Main Street, the city was reaching out to them, breaking down the isolation of the rural

Jacob Reinhardt in his confirmation suit. The services were in German.

Confirmation of Mathilde Brauer

neighborhood. Prosperity stimulated a desire for the material goods that could not be provided easily by the Howell and Franklin Street merchants or by the peddlers from whom Ruth bought vanilla, pepper, and patent medicines. As well, changing distribution and marketing patterns—advertising, the popularity of standard sizes and name brands, and the growth of general-service stores—influenced the Brauers. In 1904, Perry Township lost its only resident physician when Dr. Huessler, who traveled the country roads in a buggy, retired; thereafter, the Brauers had to travel into Evansville for medical services. Even little Mathilde, who had played happily with homemade stilts, began to ask for store-bought dolls and coconut-marshmallow candy from Sears, Roebuck for Christmas.

In 1909, Mathilde made a remarkable break with tradition by venturing into the city for employment. Soon after her 15th birthday, with her parents' permission, she began work at the La Fendrich Cigar Factory, the Evansville manufacturer of Charles Denby cigars. Although cigarmakers were skilled artisans with a strong union which had pioneered social benefits for its members, other workers in cigar factories usually were women and children, unskilled and unorganized, who did the menial jobs of picking, sorting, and cleaning tobacco. In Evansville, more than 90 percent of the cigar-factory employees were women and girls, since the work demanded nimble hands, keen eyesight, and endurance. For working 10 hours a day, six days a week in the hot, dust-filled factory, Mathilde was paid $2 a week. The only lodging she could find near the factory was in a run-down neighborhood off Division Street. The cost for room and board: $2 weekly. After two weeks at La Fendrich's, penniless, intimidated by the noise and filth of the city, and still shaking from a near collision with a runaway beer wagon, Mathilde returned to her parents' farm. Though none of the Brauers would venture again permanently into the city, they would be compelled to deal with an increasingly urban society. As Henry purchased addi-

tional land, he produced more and more for the market and correspondingly less for the family table. Ironically, the more prosperous the Brauers became the more dependent they became on a system beyond their control. This was disguised by the tranquility and quiet satisfaction with life that permeated the German-American community in Perry Township. *Mehr ist besser*—more is better—Henry observed. And so it was for people whose transplanted culture seemed to be flourishing in this lush new land.

Women's Bureau, National Archives

Women stripping and stemming leaf tobacco

Jacob Reinhardt

Jacob Reinhardt was 14 in 1900, already a man by the standards then current. Having completed eight grades at nearby White School, Jacob was working full-time on the 55-acre farm his father, Karl, had purchased in 1883, when he immigrated from Lower Westphalia to Vanderburgh County, Indiana. The Reinhardts were prosperous and influential members of the German-American community west of Evansville. Progressive and ambitious, Karl was eager to enlarge and modernize his farm (partly to ensure a livelihood for the five sons and four daughters which Providence and his sturdy wife Martha had given him). He pioneered in planting wheat as a staple crop, purchased a stall at the First Avenue Market in Evansville at which the family sold eggs, fruit and vegetables, and fresh sausage, and he pored over farm-equipment catalogs. Karl was an elder at St. Paul's Evangelical Church, where Jacob and two daughters sang in the choir, and was serving his second term as tax assessor for Perry Township. Jacob Reinhardt greatly admired his father and planned to become a farmer like him, though he realized that his older brothers, Karl and Henry, would inherit the family farm. He continued working on the family farm until his marriage, in 1914, to Mathilde Brauer.

THE BASSANO FAMILY OF NEW YORK CITY

From 1860 to 1890, approximately 10 million people, predominantly from the British Isles, Germany, Scandinavia, Switzerland, and Holland, came to the United States. Then, in the 1890s, the pace of immigration increased sharply, and the pattern of country of origin shifted from northern and western Europe to eastern, southcentral, and Mediterranean European states. In the years from 1890 to 1914, nearly 15 million persons fled poverty and persecution in the Austro-Hungarian Empire, Italy, Russia, Rumania, Greece, and Turkey, seeking economic opportunities in the United States. In 1882, the peak year of the old immigration, 87 percent of the new arrivals came from northern and western Europe; in 1907, the peak year of the new migration, 80.7 percent came from southern and eastern Europe and only 19.3 percent from "Anglo-Saxon" countries.

This new breed of immigrants generally found the transition from their native cultures, largely peasant-based, to life in America more difficult than had Henry Brauer. Partly, their adjustment was traumatic because of the suspicion, prejudice, and hostility they encountered. In 1907 Congress established the Dillingham Commission to investigate the immigration issue and evaluate its potential effects on American society. The old immigration, according to the commission report of 1911, largely consisted of families seeking a permanent home in the New World who had been quickly assimilated. The newer immigrants—Italians, Slavs, Jews, and Greeks, for example—were of undesirable stock, of alien religions and ideas, and were transients. They congregated in Eastern and Great Lakes cities. The committee blamed them for creating the many turn-of-the-century urban and industrial problems. An even more serious charge, however, was that the new immigrants were unassimilable, unable and unwilling to become good Americans through immersion in the melting pot.

Although these anxieties were hardly new, the depressions, labor upheavals, and urban tensions of the late 19th century fueled nativist concerns about the preservation of Anglo-Saxon civilization and racial purity. Except for those few immigrants who dealt with settlement-house workers, such as Jane Addams of Chicago's Hull House and Lillian Wald of the Henry Street Settlement House in New York, the newer arrivals who came to America from 1900 onward encountered antagonism and distrust at every turn. Already faced with barriers created by language, cultural differences, and their economic circumstances, they would now be forced to struggle for survival in a society hostile to their very presence. Thus, these immigrants were thrown back on their own resources and the social and economic support provided by their ethnic brethren.

Andrew Bassano, who with his mother and younger brother came from northern Italy via France to New York City in 1899, typified the experiences of northern Italian immigrants.

Jacob A. Riis, Museum of the City of New York

Backyard playground, Henry Street Settlement House, New York City, *c.* 1900

Andrew had been born in Udine Province, north of Venice, in 1876. His father had died when he was seven, and 10 years later, in 1893, his mother, almost destitute, moved the family to Paris. The Udine region traditionally was a center of terrazzo and tile production, and both Andrew and his younger brother, Phillipe, had served apprenticeships in the masonry craft. They found work as masons in Paris and brought this skill to the United States. The Bassanos had left Italy in search of greater economic opportunity, and they decided to leave Paris for America for the same reason. They had no special commitment to locate permanently in the United States. Indeed, in 1912, Andrew's mother returned to her old village of Sequals in Udine Province. Never having bothered to learn English or acclimate herself to New York's polyglot culture, she decided to retire in Italy, where she could live comfortably on her modest savings. This was not unusual; for many years during and after the First World War, more Italians returned home than entered the United States.

Andrew Bassano quickly adjusted to American ways, as did most immigrants from northern Italy. No doubt his wife Rose, whom Andrew had met and married in 1900, just a few months after the Bassanos arrived in New York City, played an important role in his rapid Americanization. Rose Gondolfo's parents had migrated to the United States from Genoa shortly before the Civil War. She was a second-generation American who, in setting up a household as a bride, wished to avoid living in a homogeneous Italian or French neighborhood such as her husband probably would have chosen. So they found a home on Manhattan Avenue, on Manhattan's Upper West Side, near the docks in an ethnically mixed area.

Before the 1880s, nearly all Italian immigrants to the New World came from northern Italy, and they founded stable, working-class Italian communities in such cities as San Fran-

cisco and New York. During the latter part of the century and the early years of the 20th century, immigration from northern Italy narrowly continued to exceed that from southern Italy; but, while northern Italians, mostly artisans and craftsmen, settled throughout the New World from Argentina to Canada, southern Italians made the urban centers of the United States their destination. Thus, the trail of the Bassano family from Italian Croatia to Venice in 1848, then to the Udine, then to France, and finally to the United States in 1899 was not an atypical migratory pattern for northern Italians.

In the apartment on Manhattan Avenue, in which the widow Bassano also lived, eight children were born: Phillip (1901), Alfred (1904), Vincent (1905), Catherine (1907), Beatrice (1908), Louis (1911), Robert (1912), and Lawrence (1915). An American doctor delivered all of the children at Rose's insistence. Normally they spoke English at home, and its use was limited only by the inability of Andrew and his mother to communicate in their new language. The older children learned some Italian, but forgot it after grandmother Bassano returned to Italy. Since the Bassanos lived in a mixed neighborhood, the children attended public school, and they practiced Catholicism only nominally, there was little reinforcement of their ethnic identity outside of the home.

The Bassanos lived in a 19th-century tenement, in a "railroad flat." The rooms ran in a straight line from parlor to bedroom with passage being made directly from one room to another. The four-room apartment had neither hot water and central heating, nor electricity. Gas lamps provided illumination and coal stoves, heat. Rose Bassano bathed her family in a washtub in the kitchen and they shared a hall toilet with other families. These conditions were hardly primitive for American cities at the turn of the century. Urban reformers fighting to improve health and sanitary standards at this time were still railing against outhouses and sanitary vaults in alleys, well water tainted by close proximity to outhouses, and unlit and unventilated rooms. The Bassanos' flat was considered safe and appropriate for an urban, working-class family. For $12 a month, Andrew and Rose considered their home acceptable.

The first four floors of the tenement on Manhattan Avenue were occupied by southern Italians, whose social life embraced their extended families and little else. No other Italians lived on the Bassanos' floor, and the family maintained a distant relationship with their neighbors. Various factors served to set apart the Bassanos and diminish their ethnic iden-

tity. Andrew's mother maintained ties with Udine Province because of the small farm she owned there, but her son had little to do with relatives; and Rose, whose family was already strongly Americanized, further encouraged him to throw off ethnic loyalties. Family friends were scattered throughout the city, and those people in the neighborhood whom Andrew and Rose came to know well were mostly the parents of their children's playmates.

Andrew found it relatively easy to find work. Many northern Italian immigrants were either skilled building craftsmen or barbers. The former group was in great demand because this was a period of enormous construc-

Tenement yard, New York City, c. 1900–1910

tion in American cities, and the latter easily found jobs as replacements for blacks who gradually were being pushed out of barbering. The building trades were well organized, and northern Italians dominated the Terrazzo and Tile Workers' Union. Andrew immediately joined the union. Since its business manager acted as an employment agent, he was freed from the kind of exploitation that unskilled and semiskilled workers faced at the hands of bosses, contractors, politicians, and saloon keepers, where kickbacks were essential to job security.

Unlike most other workers in those years, Andrew Bassano worked steadily and earned a relatively decent wage, sometimes as high as $20 per week. The terrazzo and tile workers were among that elite of American craftsmen who had won the eight-hour day. Andrew usually worked a 44-hour week, including a half day on Saturday. Most of his jobs were contracted through the union and lasted for relatively long periods of time, since they involved the setting of small tiles. During the early 20th century, Bassano worked in various churches—St. Thomas' and St. Bartholomew's Episcopal Churches—in New York, in private homes, and did some of the decorative tile work in the stations of New York City's subway, the Interborough Rapid Transit Company. In order to ensure steady work, he had to accept a job wherever it was offered, and thus he would, on occasion, leave his family for months at a time. He installed mosaics for the Wrigley family in Chicago and later the Dupont family in Delaware. Although Andrew's wages were in the highest bracket among working-class craftsmen, and he generally worked close to 50 weeks of the year, nevertheless (with six children and three adults in the family by 1911) the Bassanos' standard of living was low by the criteria of the mid-20th century.

The family ate mostly bread, potatoes, and pasta. Fresh meat, milk, eggs, vegetables, and fruit were limited not only by their relatively high cost but also by inadequate refrigeration that made them scarce items. The family had an icebox, but it could prevent spoilage of food for no more than one or two days during the summer months; thus, perishables were bought in very small quantities to minimize waste. Dried vegetables—peas and beans—in various forms were a staple, except in the summer and fall months when the fresh vegetables and fruits which the family greatly loved could be purchased cheaply.

Rose made all the children's clothes, carefully mended them, and handed them down from one child to the next. Periodically, commercially manufactured shoes were bought, but Andrew repaired them when necessary. He would purchase shoe leather from a neighborhood cobbler and cut it to size, sewing the new sole to the shoe with a curved needle and cat gut. Saturday afternoons were haircutting days, and Andrew accepted the responsibility of keeping the children's hair trimmed. Toys also were made at home.

Until the boys were old enough to work and to contribute to the family income, Andrew Bassano was the only breadwinner. Here, the Bassanos followed ethnic attitudes, for it was customary for Italian women, if possible, to remain at home, whether or not they had children. Rose never worked for pay, and one of her sons would recall many years later that his father believed it was a "disgrace" for a woman to work. American born, and with Andrew occasionally away on jobs, she was the family's financial manager. Besides, she had her special duties—bearing eight children in 14 years and, assisted by her mother-in-law until 1912, assuming responsibility for rearing the children and keeping house. She did not choose this role but accepted it as inevitable. That Rose cooperated in producing a large family was the result of her acceptance—and Andrew's—of the traditional centrality of

Italian quarter, New York City, 1930

children and family among Italians. The Bassanos could have had easy access to the birth-control devices on sale around the corner at the tobacconist's shop. Rose, indeed, read some of the tracts distributed by the radical feminist movement, led by Emma Goldman and Margaret Sanger, among others, which devoted great effort to bringing birth control to the working class. Publicity and clinics on the subject were common in New York City, but Rose was too embarrassed to attend the clinics. The close-knit family she and Andrew established was the center of her life. It eased her work, as well, since each member had household chores

and the older children cared for the younger ones. Andrew Bassano's day off—Sunday —was reserved for family outings: in the winter to the zoo or museums, in the summer to parks or a five-cent Hudson River ferry ride to the woods of New Jersey for picnics. For the children, those days were supremely happy ones.

The Bassano family may have lacked the psychological security enjoyed by their counterparts from southern Italy who inhabited the teeming "Little Italies" that grew up in almost every American city. Their standard of living far exceeded the vast majority of southern Italians or of the other new immigrants. And as the children came, the four-room apartment seemed to shrink. Andrew and Rose decided to move uptown into a more acceptable neighborhood. In 1919, they found a larger apartment with a private bath at 140th Street and Amsterdam Avenue. This move, Andrew's preferred position as a skilled craftsman, the insistence that all of the children receive an education, and the family's relative anonymity and lack of interest in ethnic contacts all reflected the ability of the Bassanos to thrive in a difficult environment. Even though Andrew's mother had retired to Sequals, that village and Italy itself were but place names for the Bassano family.

THE O'REILLY FAMILY OF BOSTON, MASSACHUSETTS

In April 1892, shortly after his 18th birthday, with just enough money to pay his passage, John O'Reilly left Ireland to come to the United States. Though he was the eldest son among 16 children, the prospect of inheriting a small leasehold in County Cork held little appeal for him, and he sought his future through emigration.

The place in American society that Irish immigrants occupied when John O'Reilly emerged from a steamship's steerage into the sunshine of Boston Harbor was in many ways unique. In common with Germans, Scandinavians, English, Scottish, and Dutch, the Irish had been journeying to the New World in large numbers since the first settlement. Then, as with other groups, the mid-19th century produced a flood of Irish immigration. Between 1846 and 1850, the worst years of Ireland's potato famine, over 870,000 impoverished tenants came to America, and by 1860 more than 1,600,000 Irish resided in the United States. Unlike other "Anglo-

Saxon" immigrants, however, most Irish lacked the financial resources to establish in America the sort of rural communities the Brauers and Reinhardts joined in southern Indiana, Dutch immigrants established in central Michigan, and Norwegians and Swedes founded in Wisconsin and Minnesota. Neither did many Irish want to recreate the life from which they had fled, for it symbolized grinding poverty and political and religious oppression. Thus, the Irish were the first large immigrant group to throng into and become identified with large American cities, piling together in tenements and shacks in such numbers that whole neighborhoods, such as Boston's North End, the "Irish Channel" in New Orleans, and New York's Five Points district, were exclusively Irish.

A society that still preached the Jeffersonian virtues of land ownership, independence, and communion with the soil would be hostile to any group that was linked with the city and its reputed vices: shiftlessness, disrespect for law and order, and libertinism. The attribution of these characteristics to all Irish, summed up in the popular sayings: "No Irishmen need apply," and "Dogs and Irishmen not allowed," was manifestly unfair but proved remarkably durable. In addition, the struggle of Irish-Americans for acceptance and economic opportunity was aggravated by their Roman Catholic faith. Protestant America mocked and feared the papacy and its adherents. Moreover, Irish clerics quickly gained control of the Roman Catholic hierarchy in America and imposed their conservative views on other, more flexible Catholic groups. The enormous growth of the Catholic Church in America caused great alarm, and the fact that 35 of the 69 American Catholic bishops in 1886 were Irish focused Protestant-nativist anxieties on the Irish.

By the time John O'Reilly reached Boston, organized opposition to the Irish, simply because they were Irish, had diminished, but they still faced various social and occupational barriers. Many Irish typically remained day laborers and domestic servants. For others, the climb up the economic ladder, frequently through municipal and public utilities jobs, was aided by increasing political clout and the arrival of newer immigrant groups. But their progress was still much less rapid than that of, say, urban German-Americans. O'Reilly's early experiences in Boston were similar to those of most unskilled, minimally educated Irish. He was welcomed by relatives in Somerville, a predominantly Irish town next to Boston. His relatives loaned John $5, enough for one week's room and board and carfare, and he found work at Squire's Slaughtering Plant, scraping hog carcasses for $1.50 per 12-hour day. He worked at Squire's for a year. Then, desiring a more secure and dignified occupation, he became a motorman with the Boston Elevated Street Railway for $12 a week and moved into another Irish neighborhood on the periphery of Boston's West End.

By this time, John O'Reilly regularly sent money to his family in Ireland and wooed a "black-haired beauty," May Quinn, whose family rented a house next to his old lodgings in Somerville. John courted May for 16 years, visiting her every week on his day off. This was not unusual for Irish men, who rarely married before their mid-30s. Besides, May kept house for her arthritic mother and was not free to marry. Although John had no desire to see Boston become like Cork, Irish family patterns of behavior dominated his personal world. With his Irish compatriots he defended the Old World custom that life should be centered around family, church, and pub.

John O'Reilly kept in touch with his parents and during his lifetime assisted two sisters and their families and two younger brothers,

Gus and Peter, to come to Boston. After the former brother's arrival on April 15, 1907, John took Gus in tow. He assumed financial responsibility for the 15-year-old lad who boarded at his sister's. Two days later, John, who had taken out citizenship papers shortly after his arrival, escorted Gus to the Boston Federal Court House to initiate the naturalization process. When Gus found work, he was on his own. His brother, however, recognizing the value of an education, contributed to Gus's tuition for an evening course at Burdetts Business College in Boston.

In the same year that Gus arrived, John realized his ambition to become a policeman. On March 16, 1907, he took the oath for the Boston Police Department, an act that provided him a secure occupation and, more important perhaps, confirmation of his status as a citizen and responsible member of Boston's burgeoning Irish-American community. A ward boss who knew May Quinn's father obtained the appointment. Three years later, John and May married in St. Joseph's Church and, after they returned from a honeymoon at Niagara Falls, set up housekeeping in a five-room house on Burke Street in the working-class suburb of Brighton. Soon after, May's father and two brothers moved in with the young couple.

Even as a policeman John continued his older associations. He participated in two Irish-American organizations, subscribed to the Irish-American *Boston Pilot,* occasionally accompanied May to mass, and frequented the local Irish pub. The pub or saloon served as the worker's club. It offered fellowship and an escape from cramped family life in small houses or apartments. For day laborers and unskilled building tradespeople it often served as a hiring hall, and for most workers it was the only place which offered them credit. John and his in-laws and Gus availed themselves of John's streetcar pass and free tickets to Boston Red Sox games on Sunday afternoons. The Red Sox have always generated fanatically loyal fans and, according to Gus, John was among the most loyal. May's life was full enough with the house to manage, four children, and four adults—to say nothing of the kin—that were in and out constantly. A devout Catholic and relatively uninterested in the world beyond her home and neighborhood, May nonetheless refused to be burdened by a constant succession of children. She regulated her sex life skillfully without forcing John into excessive periods of abstinence. The results were the wonder of the family; the methods, the happy couple's secret.

Police work satisfied John. Earning $23 per week (the officer furnished his own uniform, weapon, and ammunition), John walked the beat in Brighton, broke up an occasional fight in a saloon, refused to allow the rackets a foothold in his sector, earned respect on the street and at the precinct, and made sergeant in 1917. In that year, the placidity of the O'Reilly's life was interrupted. Gus was among the first to be drafted into the army, serving as a gunnery corporal in France. Other relatives and friends joined Gus "over there," fighting beside the English at the same time that relatives in Ireland were fighting against the English. The conflicts and tensions of the post–World War I years also caught up with John and his family. The police went on strike in Boston. Although not a member of the union and with 12 years on the force, John turned in his badge and went out with his friends. None of the strikers was rehired. John brooded about his action, about his responsibility to his family, to the public at large, and to his fellow policemen. His health declined, and in 1924 he suffered a fatal cerebral hemorrhage. By this time Gus had married a Boston Irish lass. Their first son was born on the second anniversary of John's death and was named after him.

THE MILLER FAMILY OF NEW YORK CITY AND PROVIDENCE, RHODE ISLAND

Not all newcomers hesitated about throwing in their lot with America. For example, the 2 million Jews who fled rising anti-Semitism in the Russian and Austro-Hungarian empires between 1890 and 1914 had no alternative to a permanent commitment to a new life in America. One third of Eastern European Jewry would flee during these years, most from the tyranny of the tsar, which plumbed the depths of intolerance in the 1880s. The so-called "May Laws" of 1882 prohibited Russian Jews from owning or renting land outside towns and cities and discouraged their settlement in villages. The universities and gymnasia placed quotas on Jewish students. Most importantly, violence against Jews, either officially encouraged or sanctioned, became a way of life. Pogrom followed pogrom until a day-to-day struggle for physical survival took precedence over all other concerns. Possessing as yet no homeland for *aliyah*—the people's return—Jews remained in the diaspora and searched for another secular promised land.

Jews fleeing those eastern European pogroms sought sanctuary throughout the world. Some few went to Palestine or South Africa. Most made temporary stopovers in western Europe before settling permanently in the New World—some in Latin America, Mexico, and Canada, but most in the United States. Jewish immigrants rarely looked back (except to aid others to leave), for they had never been part of secular society in eastern Europe.

In 1892, the Jaffee family in Pinsk and the Millers in Minsk were among the many thousands of Russian Jews debating the question of flight. For these two families, the decision to leave also was a decision to destroy

Rivington Street, Lower East Side, New York City

the family unit. Jacob Jaffee, a middle-class tradesman who was sufficiently prosperous to employ a domestic servant, was highly regarded as an observant member of the local synagogue. He and his wife, Leah, while encouraging their children to seek a brighter future in America, could not bring themselves to abandon the Jewish community that had been their entire life. Two daughters and one son also chose to stay in Pinsk. One son, Nathan, with help from his parents, did come to America and then brought four sisters—Ella, Ida, Esther, and Annie—to the grimy

apartment he had found in New York's Lower East Side. The five Jaffees, none speaking English, had only each other. They would never again see their parents or siblings.

In the same year, three of the children of Benjamin and Esther Miller completed the arduous journey from Minsk to New York. The Miller family was extremely poor, and thus Benjamin decided that he and Esther and the two oldest daughters would remain behind, sending Meyer, the only son, and his two unmarried sisters to America. For 22-year-old Meyer Miller, recently ordained to the rabbin-

The Jaffee sisters, soon after arrival in New York, from left to right: Ella, Ida, Annie, and Esther

Meyer and Annie Miller, 1893

ate and educated through the beneficence of a wealthy Jewish family in Minsk, the third-class ticket to New York represented a reprieve from conscription into the Russian army. If drafted, Jewish males were obligated for 25 years' service. Soon after Meyer Miller came to New York, he met Annie Jaffee, the second youngest of the Jaffee children, at her cousin's apartment on the Lower East Side. They were married in 1893 and took an apartment in the heart of the Jewish quarter on Rivington Street.

Although Meyer Miller was a rabbi, the first thing he discarded on coming to the United States was his religion. And when he and Annie Jaffee were married, Meyer insisted on a civil ceremony at City Hall. What exactly happened to transform Meyer's life was never known by his new American friends nor even by his family, for he refused to discuss the subject. Meyer's alienation was not uncommon in Judaism at this time. Jewry in eastern Europe as well as in the United States split

into differing camps. Somewhat reconciled to secular society were the observant Jews, whose life was guided by the Torah (the five books of Moses) and the Talmud and Midrashim (commentaries on the Scriptures). The Law proscribed their daily life and helped strengthen their strong sense of community and uniqueness. Opposed to them were the modernizers, proponents of *Haskala,* or Jewish enlightenment, who sought to achieve Jewish political emancipation and, at the extreme, assimilation into secular societies by reforming Judaism. Yet another element was the socialists, who were dedicated to radical change in secular society, and who (while rejecting Judaism and, indeed, all religion) sought to preserve *yiddishkeit*—Jewish culture. When he migrated to America, Meyer Miller ceased to be a practicing Jew and became a nonpracticing socialist.

Annie Jaffee Miller, however, maintained her adherence to Jewish law and culture, overcoming the pressures not only of a Christian, industrializing society but also opposition from her husband. Although she had been married in a civil ceremony, Annie and her family in the United States finally convinced Meyer Miller to repeat the ceremony before a rabbi. Thus, they signed a *ketubbah,* a Jewish wedding contract, when Annie was eight-months pregnant and faced with the possibility, according to Jewish law, of bearing an illegitimate child. Annie struggled to maintain a practicing Jewish home, following the laws of *Kashruth* relating to food and diet, keeping religious holidays, and preserving the specialness of the Sabbath. No work was permitted on the Sabbath, not even to light a gas jet or stove, and all cooking was done in advance. Meyer would walk his wife to the local synagogue and wait for her outside. Following the laws of the Sabbath, Annie refused even to carry a purse on that day. Birth-control devices were prohibited, since tradition taught that a Jewish woman's fulfillment was in having children. Six children survived infancy: Pauline (born in 1894), Jacob (1896), Betty (1900), Rose (1904), Matilda (1908), and Bertha (1912).

For observant Jews, adherence to Jewish law in the alien, often hostile American environment was extremely difficult. The earliest group of American Jews—the Sephardics who arrived in the 17th and 18th centuries—had long since assimilated. Those who came in the 19th century, mostly German Jews, had advocated *Haskala,* and, through reform Judaism, had become Americanized by abandoning the traditional law. Thus, the existing American Jewish community had already established prece-

dents for the abandonment of practicing Judaism. But pressures from non-Jewish sources were even greater. The requirements of *Kashruth* meant not only the avoidance of certain foods but also distinctive procedures for the slaughtering of animals and the handling of different types of food. Only rabbinical supervision could guarantee the pedigree of *Kashruth,* and Jewish communal institutions were to be found only in a few cities. Furthermore, observance of the Sabbath and holidays in a society where Saturday was a normal day of work and Sunday was the universal day of rest forced Jewish immigrants to confront directly the demands of economics and tradition. For most Jewish immigrants, there was no halfway house; either Sabbath, *Kashruth,* and other obligations were observed, or they were not. For Jews who chose to honor tradition, and nearly all did at first, settlement within a Jewish community was a necessity.

While much of this tradition involved the home, with the entire family sharing the joy of the Sabbath celebration and the lesser holidays—Chanukkah, Purim, and Passover—focusing on children, communal life was equally strong. The strong sense of community and ethnic identity among immigrant east European Jews pervaded not only their religious life but social, political, and economic relations as well. Religious identity combined with traditions of more than two millennia of living communally in a hostile world to bind Jews together. Although many German-American Jews viewed the new immigrants with hostility and anxiety, fearful that the newcomers would threaten their hard-won respectability, their benevolent societies aided the immigrants' settlement and adjustment. The United Hebrew Charities of New York City provided free lodgings, meals, and medical care, and even free burial for the less fortunate.

Charitable aid was limited, and the eastern

European immigrants depended more on their own limited communal resources than on aid from other Jews. Communal organizations were based on two institutions: the synagogue and the *landsmanshaft* society. *Landsmanshaft* literally means society of fellow townsmen, and it represented the transfer to American soil of secular communal institutions in eastern European villages—burial, study, sick, and employment societies. The most effective *landsmanshafts* furnished insurance, sick benefits, interest-free loans, cemetery rights, and old-age care. By 1914, there were 534 such societies in New York City, with membership ranging from 50 to 500 households each and embracing virtually every immigrant family. Charity within the family and for all Jews was a basic tenet of Judaism. Every observant home had a *pushka* or a *tzedaka*—alms boxes to collect coins for the Jewish poor or the *halukka* fund, the charity for Jewish settlers in Palestine. Even during those grim times when the Miller family had no steady income, Annie Miller contributed at least one penny a day to the *pushka* she kept on the kitchen table. For east European Jews, it was simply charity from the very poor to the destitute. For Jews as a group, however, the practice provided an important economic buttress to survival in the New World.

Community and *landsmanshaft* were also vital in securing employment for the new immigrants. Of course, language was a barrier to any job hunt, and for practicing Jews, barred from working on the Sabbath, independent work (peddler, pushcart or shop owner) or employment in a Jewish firm was critical. Those east European Jews who settled in the old East Coast and newer Great Lakes industrial centers became associated with pushcarts and the needle trades. The latter situation arose because many Jews had brought tailoring skills with them or quickly mastered them. Tailoring could be done at home, and the demand for ready-made goods skyrocketed as more and more Americans entered the market economy. But if tailoring provided a job and a path to respectability, it also guaranteed horrendous working conditions, miserable wages, long hours, and frequent unemployment.

Meyer Miller possessed no mechanical skills and spoke little English; thus, he gravitated naturally toward work in the needle trades. He found a job sewing belts by hand at an East Side sweatshop. He worked 12 hours a day at the shop and several hours every night at home. Belt making, like other needle trades, was piecework—with payment for each item completed rather than for the number of hours worked. For 10 years, Meyer pursued this "trade," though even in the rare periods of steady employment he earned only $6 or $7 per week. Most weeks brought in less and many nothing. Though Annie did everything possible to hold down their living costs, the Millers could never get ahead. Several times they had to apply for aid from Jewish welfare organizations. In 1904, Meyer was unable to find work for many months. Too ashamed to beg again for financial aid, he moved his family to Providence, Rhode Island, where Annie's sister, Ella, and her husband, a baker, lived.

In Providence, the Millers opened a small grocery store, using a moderate amount of capital provided by Ella Jaffee and a Jewish loan association. Located in a Jewish neighborhood in South Providence, the store was the kind common to cities and villages in the years between the Civil War and World War I. Made possible by special ethnic dietary requirements and the necessity for working-class families to shop daily and, often, to ask for credit, these stores served a small, local clientele, sometimes not extending more than one or two blocks. The Miller's store faced large problems, what with neighborhood competition and the Miller's inability to build up an adequate inventory. Lacking any other financial resources, the family often furnished food for the table from the small stock in the grocery. Finally, in 1908, having exhausted their credit with suppliers and Ella's patience, they closed the store. Because his creditors were threatening to jail him, Meyer went back to New York to find work in the sweatshops. His family remained in their Providence railroad flat and Meyer, having found a job and a rented room, sent whatever money he could back to them. At the same time the eldest daughter, Pauline, who had completed the eighth grade and thus satisfied the state's compulsory school attendance requirement, went to work as a shopgirl at a Woolworth's Five and Ten store. Similarly, when the other girls became 14 (Betty in 1914 and Rose in 1918), they went to work at Woolworth's. Except for some change for streetcar fares, the girls contributed all of their earnings to the household. The women provided most of the income for the family, while the only son, Jacob, continued in school. Reflecting the traditional male orientation of Judaism, in which education is a male *obligation,* the family pooled its resources to provide an education for Jacob.

In Providence, as in New York, religion, family, and community were central. The Millers continued to be a religiously observant family, keeping the laws of *Kashruth,* and, though the girls had limited religious training, Jacob attended *heder*—Hebrew school— and *talmud torah*—a school for studying the traditional law. Meyer occasionally read an English-language newspaper, but the family read Yiddish newspapers and spoke Yiddish at home. The Millers had little social life beyond the family. They were very close to their cousins, the Jaffees and their children. In New York, Meyer became active in the socialist Jewist trades-union movement and was a member of the Cloakmakers' Union. Jacob's path, as he pursued education in high school

and then as a commuting student at Brown University in Providence, was pulling him more and more away from the family goals. This dilemma seemed an inevitable consequence of the Jewish family's intense commitment to success as it was defined in America. As with the *Haskala,* where the goal of political emancipation could be achieved only by sacrificing social and religious patterns, so, too, in America could economic security be achieved, for most Jews, only at the cost of Jewish tradition.

THE MARKOVICH FAMILY OF MIDLAND, PENNSYLVANIA

Most Slavic immigrants found the process of adaptation to American society as wrenching as did Jewish immigrants. For Serbians, Poles, Croats, and other Slavs, almost all from traditional peasant, agricultural culture, coming to the United States meant a total cultural and social uprooting. Slavs moved in time as well as place, from agricultural villages that had changed little since the 16th century to the 20th century frontier of American industrialization. The circumstances in which Slavic immigration occurred dictated that they, more than any other ethnic group, would concentrate in the industrial and mining regions of Pennsylvania, New York, Illinois, Indiana, and Ohio. In these places, they would be forced to deal with a system of economic relationships and social attitudes—amounting to a new lifestyle—totally different not only from that of their parents but from that of the great majority of Americans.

Mihailo Markovich, the eldest of three children of a Serbian peasant farmer and carpenter, was born in 1888 in Primslje, a small village near Zagreb. In 1900, after attending the village school for five years, he joined his father in working the family's small farm. The

Markoviches received occasional reports of the golden life in America from a cousin who had left the village in the 1890s and had settled in Youngswood, Pennsylvania. The stories of American opportunity were personally confirmed in 1905 when the cousin returned to Primslje to find a wife. Mihailo might still have remained in the placid community of Primslje, but the following year, with the crops ruined by hail and facing a bleak future, Mihailo's father decided to send him to the United States. The Markoviches borrowed the equivalent of $60 to pay for Mihailo's long journey: by train to Le Havre, boat to New York, then train to Pittsburgh and Youngswood, where his cousin lived. Mihailo's parents recognized that he probably would never return to them, but they spoke bravely of the opportunities he would find, of the dream that Mihailo would acquire great wealth and come back.

When he finally reached the United States in May 1906, Mihailo quickly discovered that the dream of easy wealth was a mirage. His introduction to America was a nightmare of culture shock and disappointment. So many unfriendly people, so many new things, so many odd rules. When he first arrived in New York, Mihailo, overcome with happiness, stopped in the street to celebrate by playing his mandolin. A New York policeman ordered him to stop: "You can't do that here." Then, having joined his cousin in Youngswood, for six months Mihailo was unable to find a steady job. The search for work and the forced idleness had been unknown in Primslje, and Mihailo became pessimistic about his future in the United States. Finally, he and a friend, also a Serbian immigrant, learned that steel mills in McKeesport, Pennsylvania, were hiring immigrant workers. He worked as a common laborer in a McKeesport mill, earning 10 to 15 cents an hour and working a 12-hour day. Laid off after only three months, Mihailo traveled to the South Side of Pittsburgh after hearing that a plant there was hiring men. At the beginning, he worked a full six-day week, then a three-day week, and ultimately he was fired as the mill reduced its labor force. Caught in the recession of 1906 that blossomed into a full-fledged economic panic in 1907, Mihailo's next few years were a blur of temporary jobs, poverty, and disillusion. Becoming part of the itinerant Slavic labor force of western Pennsylvania, Ohio, and northern Indiana, Mihailo moved wherever work could be found. From Pittsburgh he went to Aliquippa, then Steubenville, then Kaylor, back to Steubenville, on to Gary, to Steubenville for a third time, back to Aliquippa, and finally to Midland, Pennsylvania, in 1912, where he found steady employment at the Crucible Steel Company.

Knowing only the skills of a Serbian agricultural worker, Markovich had had little preparation for the tasks he would perform as a laborer in mines and mills. Pennsylvania coal and mill operators, however, considered Slavic immigrants a desirable work force, stereotyping them as obedient, physically strong laborers with little capacity for leadership or management. The first Slavs had come in as contract workers sponsored by the operators. After contract labor immigration was forbidden by federal legislation in 1885, the employers encouraged Slavic workers to come to the coal and coke, iron and steel belt stretching from Pennsylvania to Indiana. Despite his minimal command of English, Markovich had little problem finding work when it was available. Workers themselves generally spread news of job openings by word of mouth. Mihailo learned of jobs in other towns through friends, cousins, and fellow workers in saloons, churches, and factories. This information led him from one town to another and from one job to the next.

Although immigrant labor was in demand, this did not mean that Markovich could expect decent working conditions. Few operators did anything to adjust production to stabilize the work, and hence employment fluctuated sharply week by week, month by month. Indeed, many owners and operators considered employment instability advantageous, since the resulting insecurity of the workers tended to depress wages. During his wanderings as an itinerant mill worker, Markovich's earnings ranged from 10 to 16 cents an hour. Steelworkers, largely unorganized, were unable to press successfully for a just wage. Coal mining had been organized since the 1890s when the United Mine Workers Union was formed, and miners' daily wages for an 8-hour day were from 50 to 70 cents higher than those of iron and steel workers for a 12-hour day in the first decade of the 20th century. Although Mihailo worked in non-union mines, the existence of the UMW elsewhere affected his earnings nonetheless; at Kaylor and Steubenville he received more than 25 cents an hour.

An even more serious problem was work safety. The operators expressed greater interest in the physical condition of their machinery than in the protection of the workers. The hazards of mining and mill work were legion. Miners traditionally worked until they died in mines or from a mine-related disease. While loss of life was less frequent in the mills, few could expect to work past their 40s, for either industrial accidents or physical deterioration would surely force an early retirement from the mill. Without protection on the job, and without any system of compensation for acci-

Pouring steel by hand without protective gear in a small mill, 1909

Old-time coal miner, c. 1909

dents or disease, the workers themselves, with the help of family and fellow nationals, had to bear the cost of employer negligence and exploitation.

The living conditions which Markovich encountered were equally harsh. Like Mihailo, nearly all immigrant workers were single since few would marry outside of their national church. Among Slavic immigrants, males outnumbered females by three to one. Among Serbians, the ratio was more than 25 men to each woman. Almost everywhere he went, Mihailo roomed and boarded in "bachelor barracks," most often supplied by the company. These shoddy buildings, reeking of sweat, tobacco, and the odors of the miserable food set out by company cooks, offered no privacy at all. Sometimes Mihailo slept in a "hot bed," a bunk sequentially shared with

another worker. These quarters were segregated from those of the company managers, all of whom were native born. In Midland, for instance, foreign workers were prohibited from crossing Sixth Street into the managers' residential area after dark. This was as much to protect managers' children from the diseases rife among the workers as it was to safeguard American women from the animal urges of the immigrants. The workers' area was a rat-infested, unsanitary pest hole. The streams that provided drinking and cooking water were also used for human and industrial waste, the habitations were tinderboxes, and prostitution and gambling were tolerated, if not actively encouraged, by the mill operators.

In spite of these difficulties, the primarily male Slavic society in Midland and elsewhere struggled to maintain old traditions and the familiar way of life. Most workers maintained ties with their homeland through native-language newspapers and through regular correspondence and remittances of money home. Mihailo Markovich sent money to his parents monthly until he was married. In addition, involvement in local parishes of the Roman Catholic or Eastern Orthodox Church helped to maintain links with their ethnic identity. For Markovich, brought up in the Serbian Orthodox Church, religion was more a cultural than spiritual activity. While a bachelor, he attended Sunday mass but a few times a year, although he took part in the festivals, saints' day celebrations, and the January 6 Christmas. The rare weddings and christenings in the Serbian-American communities were also treated as holidays. Beer was the major refreshment at festivals as well as on Saturday nights and Sundays when Serbian workers sought to forget their exhaustion, loneliness, and fears of the strange American environment by crowding into their own saloons, singing and dancing to national melodies, and exchanging news from home.

While the company managers welcomed the religious involvement of the workers as a stabilizing influence, they complained about absences on Serbian holidays and "blue Mondays" because of drunkenness. The problem became so prevalent that prohibitionists in western Pennsylvania made the Slavic workers a special object of their campaigns. To lonely men such as Mihailo, the camaraderie of the Serbian saloon and the holiday festivals—even with their excesses—recaptured, if only briefly, the familiar patterns of life back home. But the aftermath made clear that the activities of a bachelor society were sterile and self-defeating in this alien land.

In 1912, Markovich escaped from the narrow life of barrack and saloon by marrying a widow with three small boys, two of whom soon died of diptheria. The surviving son, Miles, was soon joined by three half sisters, the youngest, Anna, born in 1919. From the same province in Serbia as Mihailo, Maria Yaich had been running a boardinghouse since the death of her first husband in a mill accident. She married Mihailo in the Serbian church at Aliquippa a few weeks after first meeting him. Soon after, they moved to Midland, where Maria had lived previously, by mule and wagon. Mihailo found a job as a rigger at the new Midland steel mill for 15 cents an hour. The newly married couple found a company house on Pennsylvania Avenue, in the heart of the immigrant section, for which they paid 18 dollars per month—deducted from Mihailo's monthly wages of about 40 dollars. The house—occupied by the family until 1957—was new and fairly large (two stories, six rooms), but it was expensive. Maria took in several boarders, all Serbian steelworkers, to help with living expenses, and these men became almost members of the family. The economic situation of the Markoviches remained precarious, since Mihailo's job offered only unsteady employment. But he had survived, had acquired a

First family home of the Markoviches on Pennsylvania Avenue, Midland

Stanko Simich

Not all immigrants found America the promised land. Stanko Simich came to America to make his fortune and then return home rich and respected. Unfortunately, he possessed neither the necessary skill nor, it seemed, the good luck required to achieve this dream. Born in Merich, Serbia, in 1872, the only son of a tavernkeeper, he arrived in Baltimore in 1894, penniless, speaking no English, and illiterate even in Serbian. "I was like a wild animal," he later recalled, "helpless, confused, and angry."

For several weeks he floated around Baltimore, helped by some Russian and Polish boys whose language he could understand a little. Then, going up the stairs of the railroad station, he stepped on the long skirt of a matron. She called the police and Stanko was sentenced to six months in the county workhouse. The lady's irritation proved a blessing in disguise, for he was able to stay alive, save the pittance he was paid, and, most important, acquire enough English to get by. After his release, Stanko returned to the station to buy a ticket to western Pennsylvania, where he had heard gold nuggets could be picked from the ground. This time he walked into a riot (which he first thought was a parade) and was shot by a militia company and stoned by the railroadworkers whose strike was being forcibly put down. Stanko abandoned his plans to travel by train and walked, working for food and lodging, to Export, Pennsylvania, where several relatives had settled.

For the next few years, he worked as a coal miner in western Pennsylvania, never making more than subsistence wages and given up for dead by his family. Finally, in 1898, Stanko located in Primrose, Washington County, Pennsylvania, living in a company house in "ski hollow" provided by his employers, the Carnegie Coal Corporation. In 1904, he married Sasha Nikovic, a Serbian girl he had met through relatives in Export, and brought her back to Primrose. Here they would live for 32 years—until his death from a stroke—fighting off starvation, diptheria, and company goons who tried to prevent Stanko from taking part in organizing the Primrose mine. Their sole legacy would be seven sturdy children: Andrew (1905), Martha (1906), John (1907), Arthur (1911), Katherine (1914), James (1917), and Michael (1919). In 1941, Michael, employed by Crucible Steel, married Anna Markovich. The only gold Stanko found was the black gold he dug out of the Pennsylvania hills for stockholders who never knew he existed.

ready-made family to which he added, and thus a place of his own and a separate identity. The couple joined the local lodge of the Serbian National Federation, attended the federation's frequent dances, parties, and songfests, and purchased its burial and life insurance. Mihailo became secretary treasurer in 1917, cementing a family relationship with the lodge that still flourishes. In March 1913, he wrote his father to say that he would not be returning to Primslje and thus his younger brother, Arturo, should be given the family farm.

THE WILLIAMS BROTHERS OF DETROIT, MICHIGAN

An important component in the migrations that changed the face of 20th century America was internal in nature. While Andrew Bassano, John O'Reilly, Mihailo Markovich, and Meyer Miller and Annie Jaffee were entering the portals of East Coast cities, others—blacks in particular—were coming into American urban centers by the back door. Their motives were similar to those of most European immigrants: economic opportunity and social justice. But their adaptation to this rapidly industrializing, urban-centered society was quite different. In 1896, James and Henry Williams came from a Mississippi plantation to Detroit, a city soon to become the automobile capital of the world and thus symbolic of the new America. Born in a sharecropper's cabin (James in 1870 and Henry in 1872), the Williams brothers were the oldest children of former slaves. Their parents were effectively illiterate, and only one of the nine children, a surprise daughter born in 1900, received more than casual schooling. The Williams family, like the vast majority of southern blacks, could envisage little future improvement in their lot if they remained on the land.

James and Henry had worked their father George's rented land since they had been old enough to lift a hoe. The entire Williams family worked together, sharecropping, as one economic unit. Their father had survived floods, droughts, and freedom, but he was hardly nearer to owning his own land in the middle 1890s than he had been 25 years earlier when his first son was born. In the rural plantation South, opportunity was a monopoly controlled by whites. George Williams, who had never journeyed further than the village of Tecumseh, six miles from his

Bureau of Agricultural Economics, National Archives

Typical sharecropper home, North Carolina, 1910

home, had no way of knowing that many whites faced similar circumstances or that many blacks elsewhere were acquiring land. The family's view of the larger world was filtered through two sources: the plantation owner and the local Baptist church, which was served by itinerant ministers. Both helped bind and reinforce strong black communal feelings, especially the church, which gave spiritual meaning to their lives and hosted all of the black social activities on this plantation and neighboring ones. The church also served as the Williams' only regular tie with the world beyond the household and cotton fields. Coming from afar to carry messages of spiritual redemption, outside preachers also transmitted the vision of another, secular world in which blacks could obtain economic freedom. It was one of these, speaking at a tent revival, who gave James and Henry Williams the dream of a better life in a Northern city.

Joining the growing stream of migration from the South to the urban North, the Williams brothers had no idea where to go—except away. It was accidental that they ended up in Detroit rather than in one of the larger black communities in the North, such as those in Chicago, Philadelphia, or New York. Black Detroit was small in numbers in the late 1890s, with about 4,000 Negroes living there. It was receiving a steady influx of southern blacks, but at the same time, many Detroit blacks were moving on to larger black communities. Although blacks were excluded from Detroit's rapidly expanding factories, industrialization and the resultant growth in the city's population created many new unskilled and semiskilled jobs. No institutions served black newcomers, although settlement houses dotted Detroit's near East Side, where 85 percent of the city's black population lived. The long-time residents of black Detroit were equally indifferent to the needs of the new arrivals, and the Williams brothers had to

make their own way in this highly competitive, impersonal environment.

To a great extent, blacks had no other choice than to rely on their own resources in attempting to counter white racism and Negrophobia. Except for some urban social workers, such as Jane Addams and John Daniels, and some philanthropists, such as Julian Rosenwald, few whites supported black strivings for equality of opportunity. The radical stirrings of the Populists and the successful reform crusade of the progressives in their attacks on the old, 19th-century politics would nearly ignore blacks, who in most states would be eliminated from political office by the electoral changes enacted by the reformers. The Williams brothers could not look to government at any level for relief, even when they encountered discrimination and segregation in violation of the 1885 Michigan state public accommodations act. Their surest protection was to avoid situations in which their lack of real equality would become clear.

The needs of the Williams brothers and the others who had come out of the rural South to cities North or South were great. Although they had no language barrier to surmount in the way immigrants from Europe did, dialect differences still caused difficulty. In ways similar to the immigrant experience, the shift from living in one society to another required an extraordinary adjustment, especially since the demands of the new conflicted sharply with the rhythms of their old life. James and Henry had worked, played, and prayed as a family unit in the South, but in the North they found themselves, at first, totally on their own. Though literate, they had received only the rudiments of education, and "Southern" characteristics set them apart from Detroit's black community. They found it difficult to enter the network of black social and religious institutions in Detroit. In part, James and Henry caused their own isolation. Like many immigrants, the Williams brothers at first approached living in Detroit with caution and lack of commitment. They hesitated about planting roots in this strange community and kept open the option of returning to Mississippi. This, in part, explains why neither brother ever married, an unusual occurrence considering their upbringing. Work filled the vacuum created by the absence of family ties.

Lacking special skills and capital, the brothers were forced to work apart for the first time in their lives. This in itself was traumatic. More important, the rhythm of the rural South was out of time in bustling Detroit. In the North they had to adjust to the clock and work set hours, winter and summer. They had possessed an independence in their work and life that was not possible working as teamsters or construction helpers in Detroit. Back in Mississippi, their home and place of work had been the same, and they had had little contact with whites or any strangers. Detroit was huge and strange, and their work took James and Henry into all parts of the city, including places where the legend persisted that blacks were not permitted past nightfall. Like other working-class blacks, they had a strong sense of where they could and could not venture, where black people would be accepted and where they would meet with hostility. They rarely encountered rejection by whites directly because they tended to go only to places where they knew blacks were accepted.

The brothers lived in a rooming house for Negroes and purchased weekly meal tickets in a black-run restaurant. Cafes, saloons, and pool halls provided entertainment as did the southern-based fraternal order, the True Reformers, which both brothers joined in 1904. They also began to attend the Baptist church near their lodgings.

After seven years in Detroit, without families to support and free from any obligation except periodic remittances to their parents, the young men pooled their small savings and began to buy land in a working-class

suburb near the heavy industrial area and far from the black community. Eventually they erected houses on their lots, selling them to white workers. This venture led to other small contracting jobs and to a general construction business, specializing in cement work. It was fitting that these sons of a father who had dreamed of acquiring land would succeed where he had failed. It was the land that provided them the chance to work together again, as independent businesspeople, and escape the fate of almost all unskilled and semiskilled black workers in Detroit.

This urge to acquire land and their own business mirrored the fundamentally conservative outlook of most working-class and middle-class blacks at the turn of the century. Those years were retrogressive politically. Southern states barred blacks from voting, cities and states formalized in law the previously informal Jim Crow segregation, and the Supreme Court in *Plessy* v. *Ferguson* (1896) legitimatized the doctrine of separate but equal (even though not equal in fact). Monroe Trotter, the Harvard-educated editor of the *Boston Guardian,* and W. E. B. DuBois, the Berlin and Harvard-educated sociologist, historian, and journalist, sought to organize

The Williams brothers, second and third from left, and their employees.

college-educated black men and women to pursue legal equality. Booker T. Washington, on the other side, preached accommodation to the white world. Most blacks, whether or not they understood the messages of black leaders, were accommodating. The Williams brothers, like Washington, accepted the powerlessness of black people in an overwhelmingly white society—blacks were 11.6 percent of the population in the continental United States in 1900. They responded to his argument that the stigmas black people carried could be eradicated by a long-range program of self-help that centered on manual education, improvement of health standards, and promotion of black-owned businesses.

James and Henry Williams achieved substantial economic gains by migrating to Detroit. They enjoyed a higher standard of living than their parents and brothers and sisters were aware was possible. But their very success bred frustration, for the Williams brothers were not able to realize the goal of real economic power toward which their ambition and abilities drove them. The basic obstacle to realization of this dream was race, though the difficulties produced by the Williamses' color were linked with other, nonracial ones.

Certainly the work ethic was too central to the lives of James and Henry to be denied by fear of white hostility. They had come to Detroit to find economic security, and although they steered clear of whites socially, they could not afford to avoid economic relationships. Many whites viewed the mere presence of blacks as an economic threat and resented competition for work from blacks. The large factories in Detroit tended to hire ethnically homogeneous work forces—6,000 Polish-Americans worked at the Dodge Brothers plant—and employers could always use the threat of hiring blacks as a weapon against workers' discontent. Indeed, many blacks resented the ease with which recently arrived immigrants could find relatively well-paying jobs in Detroit's rapidly growing factories, and they joined the rising tide of anti-immigration sentiment at the turn of the century. Although they themselves were victimized by white stereotypes, which led to job exclusion, the Williamses, like many blacks, held similar stereotypes about the Poles, Irish, and Italians of Detroit. Typically, a black whitewasher did not think of immigrants as whites: "Many wite men in the business? No, dere's no wite men. Dere's some Polacks, but dey ain't wite men, you know." The competition for economic security turned victim against victim.

THE TRACE FAMILY OF WAYNE COUNTY, TENNESSEE

Some American families embraced the forces that were transforming America in the early 20th century. Others, like the Brauers, Bassanos, and O'Reillys, accommodated themselves rather easily to changes affecting their lives, and still others, like the Millers, Markoviches, and James and Henry Williams, merely bowed their backs and endured. For a surprisingly large number of Americans, however, the agents of change—industrialization, urbanization, technology, and centralization—had no noticeable effect on their lives. Their time would come, but so long as these families, mostly subsistence farmers and inhabitants of isolated villages, maintained their blissful ignorance of what was happening in the outside world their traditional life remained inviolate.

The Traces of Wayne County, Tennessee, belonged among those families most insulated against change at the turn of the 20th century. Traces had come from England to the colony of Virginia as indentured servants in the 1680s, and succeeding generations had been agricultural laborers in Virginia and North Carolina. In the early 19th century,

Denson Trace migrated to Wayne County in southwest Tennessee from North Carolina, establishing a homestead on good bottom land near Hardin Creek. By the 1850s, Denson's family, by now eight children and numerous grandchildren, had become sufficiently prosperous to own several slaves, but they were still essentially subsistence farmers. Wayne County was generally unsuited to agriculture, since most of the land was hill country covered with scrub pines. Only the fertile bottom land, some of which had passed down through Denson's son, Andrew James, to his son, William, produced respectable crops.

William L. Trace was born in Wayne County on April 15, 1844, the third son and youngest of five children. He attended a few grades of school in a one-room schoolhouse near the family farm, and worked on the farm until 1864. Although the Traces had been slaveholders and Will's eldest brother James had been a slave trader, the family opposed secession, voting for the Union Party in 1860. No Trace had any personal involvement in the Civil War until February 1864, when a passing Confederate cavalry patrol conscripted Will while he was working in the fields. Before he could be sworn in, however, he escaped and, in a fit of anger, went to Clifton, Tennessee, where he enlisted in the Union Army. In May 1865, he was discharged and returned to work shares on his father's farm. Three years later, Will married 17-year-old Millie Elizabeth Potts.

After their wedding, William and Millie Trace lived with Will's parents, helping with the farm on shares. Within three months, Millie became pregnant and she bore four children in her in-laws' home: James (born in 1869), Joseph (1870), William (1872), and Thomas (1874). By 1875, the Will Traces had saved enough money to buy 35 acres on the Green River, 15 miles from his parents' farm and 10 miles from Waynesboro. In this home were born Nancy (in 1876), Charles (1877),

Sallie (1879), Oliver (1880), Alice (1882), Laura (1883), Rhoda (1884), Mary (1885), Alford (1886), Margaret (1888), Cicero (1890), Benjamin (1892), and McKinley (1893). Altogether Millie bore 17 children, with only female relatives assisting. Thirteen survived childhood.

After further purchases of land, Will farmed about 75 acres to support his large family. With help from his brothers, he constructed a home from his own timber. It was originally a two-room log cabin, with the main room and kitchen-pantry connected by a covered breezeway. Later, two additional rooms were added for cooking and storage. He also built, again with the assistance of relatives, other log outbuildings: two stables, a barn for storing corn and hay, and a spring house for preserving milk and butter. Other than to raise some corn for market, all Will's efforts centered on making the farm self-sufficient. The family kept several cows for milk and butter, and barnyard fowls provided eggs and Sunday dinners. Hogs were raised and cured to provide winter meat for the family. Fruit trees offered fresh fruit and the apples and peaches were dried for winter consumption. Potatoes and turnips were stored in a root cellar white cabbage was made into sauerkraut. Other vegetables were canned. Fish from the Green River and wild game—deer, wild turkey, rabbit, squirrel, and quail—from the surrounding hills were a regular source of protein, and often Will's skill with the family rifle was needed to stave off starvation. The small cash crop of corn was sold in Topsy, a few miles away, and some of it, ground into meal, was carted back to the farm.

Life for Will Trace well into the 20th century was not much different than it had been for his parents or grandparents. While the routine on the Trace farm resembled that on the Brauer farm, location ultimately made a great difference. Wayne County was almost totally isolated from the changes besetting

American society. The American transportation revolution bypassed the Traces—no railroad would ever come through the county—and industrialization had almost no impact on their lives. Indeed, until World War II, all of Wayne County, including Waynesboro, remained without either electricity or transportation service to the outside world. Nonetheless, Will hoped to go beyond subsistence farming and enter the market economy as he understood it. He used cash reserves built up during exceptional crop years, kept at home in a strongbox, to acquire options on additional acreage, or land itself, most often in partnership with brothers and cousins. But he never crossed the line. The demands of his growing family—13 children by 1886—and the setbacks resulting from poor crop years always forced the partners to dispose of their additional land, usually at a loss. In the worst years, Will mortgaged his next year's crop to buy seed and needed implements and coffee, sugar, flour, and spices—the only food items not raised on the farm.

Kinship formed the links of the chain of social relations among Wayne County residents. Nuclear families were so large, and cousins nearby so numerous that the Traces rarely dealt with other than relatives. Work, religion, and cooperative efforts—barn raising, for instance—involved only kin. Families possessed a collective identity. When Will married Millie, it was broadcast that "a Trace" had wed "a Potts." Cemeteries were family rather than communal ones. Will chose to be buried in the Trace family cemetery near Topsy, and Millie, soon after her marriage, arranged for burial in the Potts family cemetery. Long after individuals had been forgotten, cousins could recall the family ties. Thomas, for instance, the fifth child of Will and Millie, first married "a Choate," who died while giving birth. Then he took "a Pope" as his second wife.

Although the Traces were generally made aware of dramatic events at the national level (as exemplified by naming the two youngest sons after presidents) and had an active interest in Republican party politics, the history that they knew and recounted was the personal oral traditions of kin and locality. Stories about generations of Traces and Potts, including feuds and family legends, passed on from parents to children, gave the children a strong sense of family tradition and identity, and also provided a large part of their education. None of Will and Millie's children received more than the basics of reading, writing, and ciphering. Benjamin Harrison, for example, attended the one-room schoolhouse in Topsy for only four years before beginning full-time work on the farm. There were only three books in the Trace home—a Bible, an almanac, and a dog-eared farmer's guide. Except for Sunday church services at the Baptist church four miles away, the family almost never socialized with neighbors who were not kin. Even at church, a good part of the 20 to 30 members were Traces or related to Traces.

Oral tradition played an equally important role in farming and the direction of the household. For generations, Trace children had learned to farm by working with their fathers, by listening to their parents' advice and ancient wisdom. The choice of land, selection of crops, time of planting, and practice of agronomy and husbandry were matters of experience and family lore. The farmer's manual guided them in those areas where experience was lacking. The Traces did not receive any farmers' journals, and neither seed salesmen nor implement dealers called on them. Thus, the latest innovations in farming were unknown to them. The women learned to keep house, bear and raise children, cook, and perform other assigned female roles in their mothers' households. Similarly, folk customs dictated basic medical care. Millie and her daughters took responsibility for healing and they collected and prepared the herb poultices and potions used to treat sick family members. Sallie, the first daughter to survive

Isolated country school in the hills of Tennessee, 1909

childhood, took a great interest in folk medicine and was often called upon to prescribe for kin. Will and Millie raised their brood by the rigid precepts they had learned at home, school, and church. Discipline, hard work, and simple honesty were enforced by Will's buggy whip or leather razor strop. A dour, self-willed man, he exercised a tight rein over his children. For the first 20 years of their marriage, Millie was so busy with the home and giving birth to children that she had little time or energy for those already present. The expression of affection was a luxury in the home, though both Will and Millie believed that their efforts to feed and clothe the children were sufficient evidence of their love.

As they grew up, few of Will and Millie's children thought about leaving the agricultural, tightly knit kinship society of Wayne County, Tennessee. Six sons established homes in Wayne County, four as farmers and two as farmers and livestock producers. The eldest, James, did leave home following an altercation with his father. He farmed briefly in Wayne County, then drifted into Alabama and became a law officer. James, by his own count, killed 32 men before retiring in Texas, shortly before the First World War. He would later write a colorful autobiography which began: "I first discovered America in the hills of old Tennessee." William Trace was able to help his eldest sons get a start in farming for themselves by allowing them to work shares with him and save enough money to buy farms of their own. Only a little cash was needed, since Wayne County land rarely sold for more than $20 per acre. The three oldest sons attempted to advance beyond subsistence farming, but only James fully succeeded. Joseph, the second one, traded in cattle occasionally and, in 1910, risking everything he owned, took an option on 1,300 acres of timber land. When the lumber market collapsed during the depression of 1913, he returned to farming. The younger William Trace farmed and traded cattle in Wayne County until 1897 when he was robbed and murdered after a cattle drive to Nashville. Another son, Oliver, farmed on the Green River and was stabbed to death by his brother-in-law in a dispute over wandering livestock. His widow and three small children thereafter lived with Will and Millie.

Of the three daughters who reached adulthood, two became farm wives in Wayne County. The other girl, Margaret, married William Wolfe, whose occupation, making staves for liquor barrels, took him all through Tennessee, Kentucky, and Mississippi. Margaret accompanied him and in 1913, after their first child arrived, she and her husband settled in Evansville, Indiana, where William Wolfe found work in the repair shops of the Louisville & Nashville Railroad. Within two years, Margaret was joined in Evansville by the youngest of Will's brood, Benjamin Harrison and McKinley Welch. Both obtained work at the Louisville & Nashville shops and both would soon become doughboys. Ben and McKinley left Wayne County for many of the same reasons that the Williams brothers left Mississippi: too little land and no alternative employment. Thus, before 1915, five of Will and Millie's 17 children had traveled no farther than the 70 mile trip to Nashville. The closely woven fabric of family and tradition was fraying under the weight of economic necessity and family tensions. Will and Millie continued to live as they always had, however, planting and harvesting their crops, occasionally buying "store-bought" goods from the small Civil War pension that Will received, attending church, and burying kin. Only advancing age modified the pattern of their lives.

CONCLUSION

The experiences of families in turn-of-the-century America, exemplified in the histories presented above, were so diverse as to eliminate the possibility of speaking of the "American family." Still, some general observations can be made. To a degree all Americans—the Butlers and O'Reillys in Boston, the Bassanos and Millers in New York City, Mihailo Markovich in Midland, the Brauers and Gales on Midwestern farms, the Williams brothers in Detroit, and the Traces in Wayne County, Tennessee—were affected by similar forces. In 1900, the United States was on the brink of fantastic changes that would transform the social and physical landscape of the nation. The horse and buggy would, within two decades, give way to the automobile, the wood cook stove would give way to the electric stove, and millions of men—some American— would die as world peace was shattered. In 1900, many American families were still relatively untouched by the rapid spread of industry, the national market economy, and the dynamic urban centers generated by industrialization and population growth. By 1920, few Americans were able to pursue their livelihoods in isolation, outside the system. Insofar as they understood the implications of the new urban-industrial world, Americans sought to shape its form and character. But the emerging design was too complex, and although cast in steel and concrete, too amorphous for the mind to grasp.

American families wishing to derive immediate benefit from the change, participated willingly enough in the new order even while sensing that participation meant the loss of some control over their lives. Resistance, a stance adopted by both native-born Americans and immigrants, went hand in hand with accommodation and even a grasping for the new treasures. The Butlers' successful exploitation of economic opportunities allowed them to retain a good measure of their old-family, New England lifestyle. Immigrant families, such as the Millers and Markoviches, were somewhat less fortunate. Possessed of neither economic nor political power, they sought to salvage their identities by continuing to celebrate traditional religious and national holidays in the face of demands that they Americanize. Meyer Miller and Andrew Bassano found labor unions to be of some use in attempting to control their job assignments and working conditions. Mihailo Markovich, denied the right of union participation and at the mercy of his employer, adapted when compelled to and protected the old ways at home and when among his friends. The Williams brothers, while penetrating the system more effectively than most blacks, maintained that social distance demanded by racist mores. The Gales in southeastern Kansas, living fairly comfortably and suffering from none of the sociocultural disabilities facing immigrant peoples—planting, harvesting, and selling as much as they could—knew full well that the returns from their labor were less than they ought to be.

Resistance was at best a delaying tactic. Newcomers and old families, the Brauers and Traces for example, postponed and muted adaptation and assimilation by offering alternative lifestyles to their children. For the German-Americans this was a conscious effort; for the Traces, it was simply the result of ignorance, isolation, and inertia. However, the actions taken were similar. Children remained at home within the tightly controlled milieu of the family and the ethnic community. Steps were taken to negate the socialization process to which they were exposed in schools and shops. Many immigrant families—and not a few native-born American—were suspicious of the schools as agents of assimilation, failed to see the value of formal education, or simply could not afford it. They refused to permit their children to attend school or pulled them out when they had barely acquired the rudiments of education. Others, the Bassanos and Markoviches, for example, sensed the importance of education and saw to it that their children would take advantage of what was offered. For females, the pressure to stay in the family—and ultimately marry someone like themselves—was even greater than it was for males. Still, more girls than boys went to school and remained there for a longer time. Families that feared the leveling tendencies of public schools and could afford it, like the Butlers, sent their children to private academies. Families taking pride in their ethnic origins, like the Markoviches, countered the enforced Americanization experience in schools and elsewhere by preserving their traditions at home and in ethnic clubs and churches. Whatever the families did, they found no permanent sanctuary, no secure harbor invulnerable to modernity and the processes of urbanization and industrialization. Whether reluctantly or not, all would be caught up in it, all would participate.

SUGGESTIONS FOR FURTHER READING

Valuable contemporary works include Felix Adler, *Marriage and Divorce* (1905); Katharine Anthony, *Mothers Who Must Earn* (1914); Ray Stannard Baker, *Our New Prosperity* (1900); Abraham Epstein, *Facing Old Age: A Study of Old Age Dependency in the United States and Old Age Pensions* (1922); Harold W. Foght, *The American Rural School: Its Characteristics, Its Future and Its Problems* (1910); Charlotte Perkins Gilman, *The Home: Its Work and Its Influence* (1903); Josephine K. Henry, *Marriage and Divorce* (1905); Florence Kelley, *Modern Industry in Relation to the Family, Health, Education, Morality* (1914); Frank H. Streightoff, *The Standard of Living Among the Industrial Population of the United States* (1911); Ernest L. Talbert, *Opportunities in School and Industry for Children of the Stockyards District* (1912); Marion Talbot and Sophonisba P. Breckinridge, *The Modern Household* (rev. ed., 1919); and William Graham Sumner, *What Social Classes Owe to Each Other* (1925). See also Emily S. Bouton, *Social Etiquette* (7th ed., 1894); Louise

Montgomery, *The American Girl in the Stockyards District* (1913); John Spargo, *The Bitter Cry of the Children* (1906); William Graham Sumner, *Folkways: A Study of the Sociological Importance of Usages, Manners, Customs, Mores, and Morals* (1907); Ruth S. True, *The Neglected Girl* (1914); Anna B. Rogers, *Why American Marriages Fail* (1909); and Mary Antin, *The Promised Land* (1912).

There has been an explosion of interest in family history in recent years. Among the most useful works in this area—for this chapter and for succeeding "family" chapters—are Bert N. Adams, *The American Family* (1971); Harold Seymour, *Baseball: The Early Years* (1960); Bernard Rosenberg and David M. White, *Mass Culture: The Popular Arts in America* (1957); Gilbert Seldes, *The Seven Lively Arts* (rev. ed., 1962); Robert Sklar, *Movie-Made America: A Social History of the American Movies* (1975); and Anthony Slide, *Early American Cinema* (1970). David M. Schneider, *The American Kin Universe: A Genealogical Study* (1975), and Schneider's earlier study, *American Kinship: A Cultural Account* (1968); Mary Jo Bene, *Here to Stay: American Families in the Twentieth Century* (1977); Mody Boatright et al., eds., *The Family Saga and Other Phases of American Folklore* (1958); Wyatt Cooper, *Families: A Memoir and a Celebration* (1975); Michael Gordon, ed., *The American Family in Social-Historical Perspective* (2d ed., 1978); Jerold Heiss, *The Case of the Black Family: A Sociological Inquiry* (1975); Kenneth Kenniston, ed., *All Our Children: The American Family Under Pressure* (1977); Christopher Lasch, *Haven in a Heartless World: The Family Besieged* (1977); Alice S. Rossi et al., *The Family;* and Peter G. Filene, *Him, Her, Self: Sex Roles in Modern America* (1974).

More specialized works on related topics are Joseph F. Kett, *Rites of Passage: Adolescence in America, 1790 to the Present* (1977); Robert Bremner, *From the Depths: The Discovery of Poverty in the United States* (1956); David Hackett Fischer, *Growing Old In America* (1977); David E. Stannard, ed., *Death in America* (1975); the flawed but powerful *Wisconsin Death Trip* (1973) by Michael Lesy; Charles F. Westoff and Norman B. Ryder, *The Contraceptive Revolution* (1977); James C. Mohr, *Abortion in America: The Origins*

and Evolution of National Policy (1978); Donald J. Pivar, *Purity Crusade: Sexual Morality and Social Control, 1868-1900* (1973); Gregory P. Stone, *Games, Sports, and Power* (1972); Russell Nye, *The Unembarrassed Muse: Popular Arts in America* (1970); and Donald K. Pickens, *Eugenics and the Progressives* (1968). Studies of feminism and the struggles for woman's rights include Rheta Dorr, *What Eight Million Women Want* (1910); Eileen Kraditor, *The Idea of the Woman Suffrage Movement, 1890-1920* (1965); June Sochen, *The New Woman: Feminism in Greenwich Village, 1910-1920* (1972); William Chafe, *Women and Equality* (1977); and William O'Neill, *Everyone Was Brave: The Rise and Fall of Feminism in America* (1967).

Works on the immigrant experience, as distinct from those chronicling the reactions to immigration, begin with Irving Howe, *The World of Our Fathers* (1976); Moses Rischin, *The Promised City: New York's Jews, 1870-1914* (1962); and Humbert Nelli, *Italians in Chicago, 1880-1930* (1970). Also useful are Donald B. Cole, *Immigrant City: Lawrence, Massachusetts, 1845-1921* (1963); Thomas Kessner, *The Golden Door: Italian and Jewish Immigrant Mobility in New York, 1880-1915* (1977); Josef Barton, *Peasants and Strangers: Italians, Rumanians, and Slovaks in an American City, 1890-1915* (1975); Robert E. Kennedy, Jr., *The Irish: Emigration, Marriage, and Fertility* (1973); Virginia Yans-McLaughlin, *Family and Community: Italian Immigrants in Buffalo, 1880-1930* (1977); LaVern J. Rippley, *The German-Americans* (1976); Bill Hosokawa, *Nisei: The Quiet Americans* (1969); John Modell, *The Economics and Politics of Racial Accommodation: The Japanese of Los Angeles, 1900-1942* (1977); Alexander DeConde, *Half Bitter, Half Sweet: An Excursion into Italian-American History* (1971); Carey McWilliams, *North From Mexico: The Spanish-Speaking People of the United States* (1948); Andrew M. Greeley, *That Most Distressful Nation* (1973); Mary Molek, *Immigrant Women* (1976); Gerald G. Govorchin, *Americans From Yogoslavia* (1978). *The Poles in America* (1922) by Paul Fox, is an adequate survey though outdated. The classic narrative collection, William I. Thomas and Florian Znaniecki, *The Polish Peasant in Europe and America* (2 vols., 1918-1920), is much more interesting. Also still valuable are Emily Balch, *Our Slavic Fellow Citizens* (1910); and Mary R. Coolidge, *Chinese Immigration* (1909). The several popular accounts by Stephen Birmingham are informative as well as engaging: *Our Crowd: The Great Jewish Families of New York* (1967), *The Right People: A Portrait of America's Social Establishment* (1968), *The Grandees: America's Sephardic Elite* (1971), and *Real Lace: America's Irish Rich* (1973). The experiences of black Americans are powerfully presented in Theodore Rosengarten, *All God's Dangers: A Life of Nate Shaw* (1974); and W. E. B. DuBois, *The Souls of Black Folk* (1903). There is a wealth of "I spent two days with some Indians. They sure are peculiar, those that is who survived the smallpox" books. Some

are psuedoserious, but the experience and anger of Amerindians are presented perhaps most powerfully in Dee Brown, *Bury My Heart at Wounded Knee* (1971); and Vine Deloria, Jr., *Custer Died for Our Sins* (1969).

A miscellany of memoirs includes Jane Addams, *Twenty Years at Hull House* (1910); Emma Goldman, *Living My Life* (1931); Henry Adams, *The Education of Henry Adams* (1918); Lincoln Steffens, *Autobiography* (1913); Lillian Wald, *Windows on Henry Street* (1934); and William Allen White, *Autobiography* (1946). Studies of literature and cultural history are Henry F. May, *The End of American Innocence* (1959); Alfred Kazin, *On Native Grounds* (1942); and Thomas Beer, *The Mauve Decade* (1926).

| # Communities, 1900–1920

As the family biographies reveal, Americans responded in complex ways to changing personal circumstances and to the new industrial society. In no setting was this more visible than in the places where Americans lived—in villages and small towns, in rural and urban neighborhoods.

THE SIZE OF AMERICAN COMMUNITIES

In 1913, the Ohio River and its tributaries surged out of their banks, sending people in low-lying areas fleeing for safety. Not everyone escaped—3,200 were drowned in Dayton—but among those who did were several Negro farm families in Union Township, Vanderburgh County, Indiana. Their homes, furniture, farm equipment, crops, and livestock were all swept away. Without capital to begin anew and long discouraged by the hard scrabble life of small black farmers, they headed for Evansville and a new life. Hundreds of thousands like them, the sons and daughters of farmers, black and white, whole farm families, men, women, and children from villages and towns throughout the United States and eastern Europe, crowded into America's urban centers between 1890 and 1920. The Indiana blacks, the Williams brothers, the Bassanos, the Traces, and the Meyer Millers helped to make the 20th century the age of the city.

During the period 1900–20, the urban population—in places with populations of 2,500 or more—increased by 80 percent while the rural population rose by 12 percent

Logansport, Indiana, up the Wabash River from Evansville, in the wake of the great flood of 1913

(see Table 2-1). Eight out of every 10 new inhabitants in the United States were claimed by the city. The urban trend was of long duration, reaching back to the years between 1840 and 1860 when the urban network began to assume its modern form. Cities of over 500,000 grew the fastest, attracting one of every three new urbanites during the two decades.

While cities grew at different rates, with some exceptions the largest cities in 1890 were still among the largest in 1920. Simultaneously, some regions became more heavily urbanized than others. Vast and densely populated urban areas, today called metropolitan regions, developed in the New England, Middle Atlantic, East North Central, and Pacific states. New centers such as Dallas–Fort Worth, the two Kansas Cities, and Seattle-Tacoma advanced rapidly as centers of regional economic strength while such older cities as Louisville and Charleston declined in importance, and still others lost their identities within a metropolitan district.

Towns and cities were growing at the expense of the open countryside. Although places with populations under 2,500 did increase between 1900 and 1920, this was the last period of pronounced growth for smaller villages and hamlets. In 1960, communities of under 2,500 accounted for only 800,000 more people than they had in 1920. Many of those still in the nonurban country in 1920 were about to leave it behind them.

Table 2-1
Urban Growth by Size of Place, 1890–1920 (in 000)*

	1890	1900	1910	1920
Total U.S. population	62,947	75,994	91,972	105,710
Total urban population	22,106	30,159	41,998	54,157
Percent urban population	35.1	39.6	45.6	51.2
Percent U.S. population in	7.0	10.6	12.5	15.4
cities over 500,000	(4,468)	(8,074)	(11,511)	(16,369)
Percent population in	8.3	8.0	9.5	10.4
cities 100,000–500,000	(5,229)	(6,133)	(8,790)	(11,060)
Percent population in	3.2	3.5	4.5	4.9
cities 50,000–100,000	(2,027)	(2,709)	(4,178)	(5,265)
Percent population in	9.0	9.3	10.4	11.4
cities 10,000–50,000	(5,720)	(7,138)	(9,572)	(12,109)
Percent population in	7.4	6.8	8.6	8.8
cities 2,500–10,000	(4,660)	(5,204)	(7,945)	(9,353)

* Figures in parenthesis show total population by category.

SOURCES OF URBAN POPULATION

The new urbanites came from three main sources. In 1920, immigrants from abroad added 4.8 million to the urban population. Meyer Miller, the Russian Jew, in 1892 fled Russian anti-semitism and headed west until he reached New York City. In 1899, Andrew Bassano and his mother, in Sequals, Italy, and in 1906 Mihailo Markovich, in the Serbian village of Primslje, found opportunities limited and migrated to America. Bassano and his mother, after a period in Paris, came to and remained in New York City. Markovich debarked at New York, headed for the Pittsburgh region, and finally settled in Midland, Pennsylvania. Internal migration contributed 3.5 million. The Williams brothers and Benjamin H. Trace, pushed by the scarcity of land and pulled by the hope of jobs in the city, were part of the flow. The third source, natural increase within the cities, accounted for 2.4 million. Another 900,000 persons lived in areas annexed by existing cities.

America's growing urban population surged relentlessly in several directions: from Europe to the United States with some, such as Bassano's mother and finally Andrew Bassano himself, returning to their homeland; from farm to town, from town to city, from city to suburb; and from town or city or Europe to the farm. The movement seemed to have no end. Its beginnings were the composite of millions of individual decisions, agonized over in countless obscure places, and locked securely in the memories of these seekers of a better life.

Most of the internal migration was from small to large communities in the same state. Interregional migration, a small part of the total movement, remained basically an east to west flow until the 1920s. A south to north movement became increasingly significant in the 1890s, largely between Southern and Northern states east of the Mississippi and involving both whites and blacks. The regions of exodus were the poorer and more backward agricultural areas such as Ben Trace's stomping grounds in Wayne County, Tennessee and the Jim Crow South.

The most obvious consequences of this geographical mobility were: (1) rural depopulation; (2) the concentration of foreign-born persons in the larger cities; and (3) a small but accelerating movement of middle-class urbanites into smaller and less crowded suburban areas.

From 1900 to 1920, over 40 percent of the nation's townships lost population. Aban-

doned farms were common throughout New England and other Northern states. Some of the loss was retrieved by major towns within the county or immediate region. In Vanderburgh County, Indiana, the rural population declined by some 5,700 people between 1900 and 1920 while Evansville's population

The Los Angeles business district, 1906

rose from 59,007 to 85,264. Seattle and Los Angeles were exceptions to the general rule of intraregional mobility. In 1920, 75 percent of Seattle's residents were from areas east of the Rocky Mountains or were foreign born while in Los Angeles, 55 percent of its native-born residents were born in the Northeast or Middle West. In contrast, and illustrating the general rule, over 80 percent of the native-born residents of Boston, Philadelphia, and Baltimore were born in the same state.

Immigration from abroad was the largest single contributor to urban growth, and by 1910, over 70 percent of the foreign-born population was urban. While the foreign-born population of New York, Chicago, Boston, Cleveland, and Detroit exceeded 35 percent, numerous other smaller cities, such as New England's mill towns, contained even higher proportions. Industrial communities of all sizes and places dependent upon mining and quarrying attracted the immigrant workers. Mihailo Markovich with his wife and children arrived in Midland, a town founded by Midland Steel in 1905, in 1912. He obtained work as a rigger at the Crucible Steel Company of America, the successor of Midland Steel, and retired from the company in 1955. Stanko Simich, a Serbian and the father of Mihailo's future son-in-law, wandered out to the coal mines in Primrose, Washington County, Pennsylvania, remaining in the mines until his death in 1934. Mihailo, Stanko, and other immigrants, filling the nation's need for unskilled labor, formed a disproportionately large part of the labor force in heavy industry—in 1910, over 50 percent in steel and mining.

Mihailo and Stanko, the Williams brothers, and Ben Trace all came from agrarian backgrounds and may have (Ben actually did) harbored some secret desire to return to a farm. But the opportunity to farm was just not there—even if the desire was. The number of foreign born who settled in New York City alone between 1900 and 1910 was greater than the number of new farms established during that decade. So the immigrants went where the jobs were, and the jobs were in the cities.

Blacks came to the cities, too, in increasing numbers. Suffering from worse disabilities than most Europeans, they congregated in major cities even more than European immigrants did. Black migration from the rural South to the cities of both North and South sped up in the 1890s. In 1900, some 80 percent of all Negroes still lived in rural areas but the trend was unmistakably toward the cities of both the North and the South. However, while the total black population in major Southern cities increased, it declined as a percentage of the population. Thus, the proportion of blacks fell from 43 percent in 1910 to 25 percent in 1920 in Birmingham and from 40 percent to 31 percent in Atlanta. In the North, although the movement was still but a trickle, the number of blacks slowly increased proportionate to the whole: in Detroit from 1.4 to 4.1 percent; in Chicago from 1.7 to 4 percent; in New York City from 1.7 to 3 percent; in Pittsburgh from 3.7 to 6.4 percent; and in Philadelphia from 4.9 to 7.5 percent. By 1920, 34 percent of all blacks lived in urban areas; in the South, 25.3 percent were urban, and in the North and West, 84.5 percent resided in cities. The urban black communities became cities within cities, New World ghettos.

The push off the land and the pull of the city filled up urban space, so much so that a reverse trend developed which sent those who could make such a choice to a house halfway between the city and the country. From 1910 to 1920, the population of cities over 200,000 grew by 25 percent while that of adjacent territory rose over 30 percent. Most urban Americans had not the wherewithal to escape from their communities whether large or small. The Markovich, O'Reilly, Miller, and Bassano families were compelled to cope with their communities. However hard life was in Midland, and it was hard, there was no returning to Primslje.

THE SHAPE OF AMERICAN COMMUNITIES

Main Street was everywhere. Although the extent of the central business district (CBD) and the upward reach of its buildings varied according to the size of the place, the gridiron or checkerboard pattern prevailed. Streets intersected at right angles with a city square (or numerous squares in larger places) as the nucleus. In the absence of a square, minor streets paralleled a long, ribbonlike central thoroughfare. In larger places, a variety of business districts had developed which catered to special and local needs. In most places, these districts spread out from the downtown section. Around the turn of the century, with the rapid development of electrified streetcars radiating from the center of the city, the downtown became more accessible but less livable. Downtown areas took on a similar appearance across the land: billboards and overhanging commercial signs, soon lit up garishly with multicolored bulbs and then neon lights; a vast maze of overhead trolleycar wires shooting out blue sparks in all directions and scaring the ever-diminishing number of horses that fouled the streets; freight elevators opening chasms in the sidewalk—countless physical images bombarded the eyes, to say nothing of the noises and smells that beseiged the other senses.

Economic growth and technological progress took the shape that they did because municipalities considered growth desirable and intervened only sporadically to shape its character. In places as small as Fredonia and as large as Chicago, business and industry intruded upon living space. Industrial expansion occurred without regard for the social or phys-

ical environment. Railroad tracks cut directly through residential areas in Evansville and countless other places, making life hazardous for people dwelling along those lines and filling their living quarters with smoke and soot and noise. Pigeon Creek, once a pleasant meandering stream along the northern edge of Evansville, by the beginning of World War I was thoroughly polluted with industrial and human waste. The key to city expansion, as an observer in Springfield, Illinois, remarked, was to "get the greatest number of building lots out of a given tract of land." While Americans developed an efficient high-rise technology and engineered municipal water and mass-transit systems, they were unable to engineer a pleasant social environment.

Downtown areas became specialized locations housing business, commercial, and financial institutions. They provided large numbers of jobs to people traveling daily and at approximately the same time to the CBD. Economic institutions pushed outward from the center, creating mixed residential and commercial zones in and around the periphery of the CBD. These areas were characterized by multidwelling residential units, rooming houses, restaurants and hotels, warehouses, wholesale establishments, and smaller manufacturing plants. Because housing was cheaper and close to jobs, these areas attracted many newcomers. Mathilde Brauer moved off the farm to such an area in Evansville, working in the La Fendrich Cigar Factory and living in a nearby boardinghouse until it became apparent that her earnings just covered her living expenses, whereupon she returned to the farm. On the outskirts, along railroad lines and rivers, industries frequently spawned their own industrial communities such as the Louisville & Nashville Railroad's town of Howell, Indiana, annexed by Evansville in 1916, to which Ben Trace moved. Before marrying, Mihailo Markovich lived in a succession of boardinghouses close to the steel plants in South Pittsburgh, Steubenville, Ohio, and Aliquippa, Pennsylvania.

In many cities, a changing population mix affected the stability and image of older residential neighborhoods. Affluent families frequently moved when threatened by the proximity of industry or the encroachment of poorer people. The affluent were then followed by a succession of people with lower incomes. The Oak Lake addition on the near North Side of Minneapolis, established as an exclusive white Protestant residential neighborhood in the 1880s and early 1890s, was filled up first by wealthy Jews, then poor Jews, and finally, by 1920, Negroes and light industry dominated the area. People did flee from other people. Andrew Bassano's steady movement toward uptown Manhattan was his means of escaping undesirable neighbors.

New urban transportation systems provided families in larger towns and cities with speedier means of going to their jobs and opened up possibilities for moves from one neighborhood to another. Between 1890 and 1907, the mileage of electric-powered railways increased from 1,262 to 34,000. Horse-drawn carriages and steam locomotives were replaced by subways and elevated cars and surface trolley cars. Cities such as New York, Chicago, and Pittsburgh operated over 1,000 miles of electric traction lines by 1907, Los Angeles had over 900, Boston over 700, and

Dearborn and Randolph Streets, Chicago, c. 1910

several other cities over 400 miles. In addition, New York, Chicago, Boston, and Philadelphia expanded their elevated systems and linked them with subways. Smaller cities developed trolley lines and were frequently connected with other communities by electrified interurban lines. Evansville was efficiently served by several lines by the turn of the century. In 1908, the yellow trolleys of the Steubenville, East Liverpool, and Beaver Valley Traction Company connected Midland with several nearby Ohio River towns.

The electric railroads—both inner-city and interurban—promoted expansion outward from the CBD by as much as six to eight miles, stimulating the development of residential tracts (embryonic suburbs) on the outskirts of a city as well as fostering population growth in smaller nearby villages or towns. The Markovich family and other Serbians in Midland used the interurban to travel to the Serbian church in Aliquippa, while many workers journeyed via trolley to jobs at Crucible. In southeastern Kansas, which had some 150 miles of interurban track by 1911, the electric lines extended the retail marketing areas of the larger towns into the countryside, ran branches to the major industrial plants, and carried light freight.

Within the city, rapid transit furthered the development of lower-middle-income neighborhoods whose residents were dependent upon crosstown trolley (later bus) service to reach their places of employment and other activities. The rapid transit system was crucial to Andrew Bassano because terrazzo jobs came up all over town. For many of the residents of low-income districts, however, improved transport—even with the five-cent fare prevailing—was too expensive. Indeed, to the extent that employers were motivated by such improvements to move their plants into outlying districts, beyond the walking distance of low-income people, rapid transit may have been harmful to the interests of wage earners.

Interurban service attained its peak in passengers carried around World War I and then declined rapidly, disappearing in some places scarcely a decade after completion of the system. Mass electric-transport systems suffered from the competition of buses and automobiles as well as from the development of commercial areas outside the CBD. In Chicago, in 1909, there was one auto for each 300 people. By 1920, the ratio was 1 : 20 and in Los Angeles, 1 : 6. As passengers declined after 1920, service further deteriorated when many urban areas initiated the construction of beltways and parkways to carry the mounting auto traffic.

The physical city influenced the way in which people ordered their daily lives. It was one thing to live in Brookline, Massachusetts, as did the Butlers, or in the beautifully tailored and exclusive Country Club district of Kansas City, Missouri. It was another thing to live in the new but stable white, working-class neighborhood of Howell, Indiana, an area of closely packed, single-family dwellings owned by their residents. It was quite another thing to live, as did the Bassanos, on the top floor of a five-story tenement, without hot water and sharing a bath with four other families.

Residential location had a significant influence on survival itself. In the immigrant wards of Homestead where a Carnegie (U.S. Steel) plant was located, one child in three died before reaching two years of age. The poorer districts of each city had higher rates of tuberculosis and other diseases than the wealthier sections, and within the slum sections, blacks suffered from the highest rates of all. Life opportunities were much restricted in such areas. Schools and municipal services were generally of inferior quality. Low incomes, recurrent unemployment, working mothers and untended children, drab—if not unwholesome—living conditions militated against the organization of a satisfactory family life or the chances of the child to escape. Such districts—present in Evansville as well as New

York—had the highest rates of children and women gainfully employed, the highest rates of juvenile delinquency and of illiteracy, and the highest densities of population. From 1900 to 1920, many urban residential zones suffered deterioration. Neither the open countryside nor the small rural community escaped scot-free.

Many early 20th century reformers were pessimistic as to the future of the city. While recognizing the increasing interdependence of country, farm, town, and city, they viewed the farm town as the symbol of community in America. Farm-service towns such as Waynesboro, Tennessee, and Fredonia, Kansas, both county seats with fewer than 5,000 inhabitants, conformed to most definitions of a rural place. But they offered quite different levels of services to surrounding rural areas. Fredonia was served by three major railroads providing direct connections with Kansas City and St. Louis as well as with the closer and larger towns of Independence and Coffeyville. Fredonia was also the location of a large cement plant and various agricultural industries offering employment and otherwise serving surrounding small, diversified family farmers like the Gales. Waynesboro, tucked away in wooded and hilly country, was 25 miles from the nearest rail depot. Subsistence farming prevailed. Families such as the Traces only occasionally hauled a wagon of tobacco leaf or cotton to town to trade for sugar, coffee, or nails. There was little reason to go to town. Only at the end of this period did autos and trucks open up the outside world to Waynesboro.

Many farm communities, including those of the Gales and Brauers, were located in areas with a diminishing farm population. If accompanied by the abandonment of cultivated land, as in New England, depopulation resulted in the weakening of rural institutions as well as in the economic decline of villages and towns. If the lower population was not accompanied by the abandonment of arable acreage but rather by an increase in the size of farms, then the consequences might be similar regarding rural institutions but would result in the growth of churches and schools in nearby towns. Moreover, as farm income rose between 1900 and 1918, the effects of a declining number of farm families upon retail and other farm-oriented businesses was partly compensated for by an increase in expendable income per farm family. The small village of New Albany in which the Gales originally traded declined and lost its businesses. Urban conveniences, such as rural free delivery, free parcel post, the telephone, and the more widespread ownership of automobiles contributed to the decline. But Fredonia, a few miles to the east, more than doubled its population between 1900 and 1920 and assumed the service and educational functions of New Albany. In the short run, general agricultural prosperity moderated the tendency of larger places to expand at the expense of smaller places. Agricultural villages and towns held their own into the 1920s.

Much concern was expressed over the apparent depopulation of the countryside, the disappearance of rural neighborhoods and, the various economic, cultural, and social disadvantages suffered by farmers. But the number of farm people rose slowly until the 1920s. While the exodus to cities continued, contemporaries could not agree as to its meaning. Some argued that rural migration benefited agriculture by forcing marginal farmers off the land and encouraging larger farm units. Others argued that the best, the most energetic, and the youngest were leaving while rising levels of farm tenancy presented the menace of arrested social development in the country.

Both positions represented a piece of the truth, depending upon where one looked. Increased mobility and income and more sophisticated and centralized institutional arrangements did threaten the vitality of rural neighborhoods by making traditional func-

Charles Reinhardt, on steam engine, and his brother Jacob, near the Red River Special, 1910

tions obsolete. Farm tenancy leveled off in 1910, but while most white farmers were owners and frequently tenants by choice, most black farmers were sharecroppers. A number of Traces remained on the rough lands of Wayne County, Tennessee, never used a tractor until the 1940s, and were basically subsistence farmers. Some of the best and the worst left the land while many of both remained. Among the best were the Gales, Brauers, and Reinhardts. They adopted new technologies. In 1910, the Reinhardts purchased an enormous Nichols and Shepard Company Red River Special Threshing Machine and a steam tractor to pull it to the fields. The Gales led a lively civic and social life and managed their lands with skill. The rural community of the farmer, always an amorphous structure, was expanding to encompass a wider range of life opportunities without requiring the relinquishment of his chosen occupation.

Rural areas also contained mill villages and lumbering and mining communities such as Primrose, Pennsylvania, and others scattered in the northern woods of Wisconsin or along the slopes of Colorado's Rocky Mountains. Many of those towns contained predominantly male and foreign-born populations. If the exploitable wealth, such as coal, required

long-term mining operations, a family life quickly developed. Stanko Simich brought his new bride, Sasha, to Primrose six years after he entered the mines. Families in such places lived under the constant threat of mine accidents, strikes and labor violence, and general economic insecurity. Mining ravaged the physical surroundings, and the quality of life was as poor as in any squalid slum. Loyalty to other mine families, whether Serbian, Welsh, or Belgian, sustained the Simiches. During a strike, Stanko knew that while he was away from home other men watched over his family. During normal times, Stanko and others from his shift frequently discussed the unreasonably dangerous conditions and harsh discipline that described their work. Unity existed, but it was isolated and pitted against powerful mine owners and their minions.

Americans took great pride in their traditions of local self-government. Yet for all of their experience and commitment, Americans proved themselves incapable of managing their environment. The development of cities was largely unplanned while suburbs spread haphazardly and without regard for the ecology. Towns emulated cities on a lesser scale, surrounding themselves willy nilly with residential, commercial, and industrial areas. Modern conveniences inundated the home and filled garages. Never before these decades had man seemed more in control of nature and less in control of his living space.

AMERICAN COMMUNITIES AND ECONOMIC GROWTH

Municipalities in the United States encouraged private economic progress and avoided interfering with the process. Even when municipal officials moved tentatively toward regulation, the widespread belief in private enterprise forced the best-intentioned officials to back off from rigorous enforcement. Municipalities imposed few restrictions on the use of property. Private interests pursuing economic advantages with little thought addressed to municipal welfare gobbled up valuable waterfront acreage, laced cities with steam railroad tracks, tore down housing for business purposes, and erected factories wherever they wished. In most cities, the pace and direction of growth depended on the willingness of private developers to extend utility and transportation services and to subdivide rural real estate. Developers resisted whatever stood in their way, including housing regulations and effective zoning ordinances.

Communities normally were unwilling to tax themselves for improved service. While great technological and public-health achievements such as the Chicago, New York, and Los Angeles municipal water and sewage systems should not be minimized, most places did not avail themselves of this technology. Many cities were constitutionally prohibited from raising improvement capital or carrying a bonded debt beyond some small—5 percent—percentage of the assessed value of property. But, even without such restrictions, many places carried but a small debt and demonstrated no inclination to spend to the limit. Why should they? Assumptions concerning the proper role of municipal government were narrow and restrictive. Responsibility for growth and progress was solidly lodged in the private sector of the economy.

Agriculture continued to expand physically from 1900 to 1920 but at a slower rate than during the last decades of the previous century (see Table 2–2). In 1900, 3 of 10 families earned their livings by farming compared with 5 of 10 in 1870. In 1920, when 3 in 10 families depended upon industrial employment, fewer than 1 in 4 earned their incomes on the farm. The decline in agricultural employment was more rapid than the rise in industrial employment with the difference largely absorbed in occupations related to trade and transportation. By 1920, on a national scale, more people were working in towns or cities and, within communities, more people were taking jobs in trade, transportation, personal service, and similar occupations than in manufacturing. The speed of this process varied from place to place.

Major changes occurred in agriculture, not

TABLE 2–2
Agricultural Expansion, 1870–1920

	Number of farms (000)	Acres in farms (000)	Corn acreage harvested (000)	Wheat acreage harvested (000)
1870	2,660	407,723	38,388	20,945
1890	4,565	623,207	74,785	36,686
1900	5,737	838,583	94,852	49,203
1910	6,406	878,792	102,267	45,793
1920	6,518	955,878	101,359	62,358

in where crops were raised—although cotton was moving into west Texas and would soon be grown in New Mexico and California—but in the complexity of the production and marketing processes. Machine technology applied to the land, much of it developed in the 19th century, greatly reduced the number of man-hours expended per acre of crops. Machinery, however, was very expensive. Even though prices for agricultural goods rose rapidly from 1900 into the wartime period, costs of labor and the prices of farm implements escalated even faster. Cleveland Gale and his neighbors in Wilson County, Kansas, were hard put to find and pay farm labor at harvest season. Kansas and Oklahoma alone required 40,000 or more seasonal farm workers to get the wheat in. Concurrently, the value of land skyrocketed and the average value of each farm doubled, substantially increasing the equity of those farmers holding on.

It cost more to farm, compelling farmers—already encouraged to do so by rising prices—to borrow more frequently. Thus, farm mortgage indebtedness rose along with everything else. More farmers made more numerous trips to town to obtain credit for harvest labor, equipment, seed and feed, fertilizer, and the transport of their produce. Even so, credit was difficult to arrange and costly. Banks in small towns lacked the capital resources to finance more than a fraction of farm credit requirements. Those rural banks with resources frequently sent money east where higher rates of interest were available than could be obtained by lending at home. Long-term credit for the purchase of land, dwellings, and other buildings could be obtained through a land mortgage. Although the Financial Act of 1900 expanded the National Bank System and authorized the chartering of some 2,300 new banks in small farm towns by 1912, operating capital was difficult to obtain. James Hart, whose son Austin later married Martha Isabelle Gale, complained along

with other Wilson County farmers in 1911 of leaving crops unharvested because of inability to borrow money to pay hired labor.

As the business of farming became more complex—James Hart initiated a rather sophisticated bookkeeping system around World War I—farmers went to town more frequently for credit, to sell, and to buy. With the spread of rural free delivery—from 82 routes in 1897 to 42,000 in 1911—the telephone, and then the car, the farm town and the neighbors were accessible. Cooperative organizations designed to provide marketing or purchasing economies represented an effort to strengthen the bargaining position of farmers vis-à-vis large, specialized purchasers and manufacturers. A co-op was normally located in a marketing town along with the local branch of the more politically inclined American Society of Equity, the implement dealer, and the county agricultural-extension agent. Co-ops quickly became an important factor in the institutional life of farmers in several states. The Kansas Farmers' Union represented 120,000 members by 1920 and operated 600 cooperative elevators and 200 retail stores besides offering fire and hail insurance.

The world in which farmers and their small service centers operated changed visibly from 1900 to 1920. While there were still frontier areas for small farms to move into, such as the timbered-over sections of northern Minnesota and Wisconsin, these lands and others far to the south and west demanded heavy initial capital investment. Cooperatives and other farm associations restored a measure of bargaining power for some farmers and somewhat simplified the marketing of goods but, for the most part, the larger places retained control of the marketing machinery. The boards of trade or produce exchanges in New York, Chicago, Minneapolis, Kansas City, or Duluth, and their members, the large dealers who owned many country and terminal grain elevators and the dealers' associations in hay, grain, fruit, produce, and poultry and dairy products regulated the flow of goods to wholesalers and retailers and established price patterns. The Gales and the Reinhardts took the price offered at the country elevator or held on to their crop. Few farmers could afford to hold their crops.

While most farm units remained small during this period, industry followed the opposite trend. Organizing for mass production and mass distribution, made possible by the completion of a national transportation system, was forced on manufacturers by the pressure of falling prices and intensified competition between the mid-1880s and the mid-1890s. Businessmen experimented with a variety of devices, as explained in Chapter 3, in their efforts to stabilize prices and avoid competition. But trade associations and trusts failed to provide the desired results. As prosperity returned in the late 1890s, in industry after industry the merger of previously independent companies occurred. Within a few years the most important industries in the United States were dominated by a few large corporations.

This great merger movement exploited the mass consumer market that evolved rapidly during the late 19th century. Rising expendable income for most Americans accompanied the population growth; consumer products were developed to meet the needs of an urbanizing nation. By 1900, magazines advertised electric kitchens (only the electric refrigerator was missing); new products such as the auto fostered the creation or expansion of supporting industries like rubber and glass; and improved techniques in advertising, mail-order sales, and consumer credit stimulated consumer purchases. By 1900, the Gales could have furnished their entire house and equipped much of their farm by simply writing a letter to Sears, Roebuck or Montgomery Ward.

Urbanization and industrialization went hand in hand. The New England, Middle At-lantic, and East North Central states, the most highly urbanized areas—excepting the Pacific Coast—were also the most industrialized. The value of the output of finished commodities rose from $5 billion in 1889 to $12.6 billion in 1910 and over $37 billion in 1920. In the latter year, 30 percent of the total was produced in communities located in New York and New Jersey. Only two leading manufacturing cities, Louisville and New Orleans, were located in the South.

Many cities came to specialize in one or a few industries. The Pittsburgh iron and steel district, producing 25 percent of the nation's pig iron in 1910, developed through the exploitation of the enormous veins of bituminous coal and other minerals running through the hills bordering the Allegheny and Monongahela Rivers. A few miles down the Ohio River from Pittsburgh, the steel town of Midland was developed in 1905 and by 1907 was contributing to the half-billion dollars worth of goods produced in the district. Proximity to cattle grazing country plus superb rail and water transportation were among the reasons for the location of stockyards and meat-packing complexes in Chicago, Kansas City, and Omaha. Factory-made clothing concentrated in New York City where a steady supply of semiskilled and skilled workers such as Meyer Miller was readily available within the single largest and most concentrated market in the United States.

The expanding scope, scale, and productivity of industry, matched in the commercial sector by the rise of national retail chain stores, induced important changes in numerous American communities. Corporate growth determined employment and production patterns within various communities. Evansville, a transportation hub of the middle Ohio River Valley, was the destination of large numbers of workers from Kentucky and Tennessee; the Trace family sent several of its kin to the Louisville & Nashville Railroad shops in

Evansville. Slightly more than one half of Evansville's manufacturing establishments employed almost 80 percent of all wage earners and produced almost 90 percent of the total value of products in 1920. Servel Incorporated grew out of the Hercules Buggy Company, established in Evansville in 1902 and the largest buggy manufacturer in the world. Hercules, in changing from buggies to the fabrication of automobile bodies around World War I, helped attract to Evansville other automobile manufacturers as well as metal-goods producers.

Other characteristics of industrialization, in

Illustration of an "all-electric" kitchen, *Harper's New Monthly Magazine,* 1896

Cattle pouring into the Kansas City stockyards

addition to concentration, deeply affected the fortunes of many communities. They considered economic growth through industrialization as the one sure cure of their real or imagined difficulties. Boosters in places as different as Neenah and Menasha, Wisconsin, Newburgh, New York, and Spokane, Washington, believed that metropolitan stature was but a factory or two away. But the conditions of the mid-19th century no longer prevailed. Even then, the phenomenal growth of Chicago was exceptional and there were hundreds of places that sought to be Chicago but had to settle for something less. To be

sure, Dallas–Fort Worth and Houston, Texas, were on the move as were Denver, Los Angeles, and Seattle, but they were not strong enough to challenge New York, Chicago, or Philadelphia for leadership in economic development. For the most part, those cities with the earliest start retained the lead. There were certain shifts within the major industrialized regions, as in the dramatic growth of Detroit, just as there were some additions to industrial wealth in southern California where the growth of population prompted Ford, Goodyear, Goodrich, and Firestone to establish branch manufacturing plants in Los

Angeles. Nonetheless, capital, labor, and savings tended to flow toward established growth areas, thus widening the disparities between regions and urban centers. In spite of prodigious efforts, Spokane did not rival Seattle or become the ruling city of more than the National Apple Show.

Another major tendency was the movement of industry, commercial institutions, and residences from a central city to its immediate hinterland or to smaller places fairly close. This spread urban services and prosperity into those areas, just as it also brought problems in its wake. The shunting of heavy industry from St. Louis to East St. Louis and other nearby Illinois towns, prompted by the availability on the east side of the Mississippi of cheap land and cheap coal, did little to improve the quality of life in St. Louis while it created industrial towns fully as dismal as Gary, Indiana or the towns within the Pittsburgh district.

Some smaller and previously nonindustrial places managed to create impressive industrial sectors. There was a certain risk involved since the advantages offered by such locations were frequently the availability of a particular natural resource, often a fuel, and a supply of cheap labor. The towns of southeastern Kansas—Coffeyville, Independence, Pittsburg, Fredonia, and others, all with under 20,000 people—exploited the discovery of natural gas to develop a minerals-industry complex that placed the region in the front ranks in the production of cement, glass, brick and tile, and smelted zinc. But success was brief. Natural gas was exhausted, ending the fuel-cost advantages. Glass manufacturers lacked the financial ability to keep up with technological developments, while zinc smelters decided that more economies resulted from the location of smelters close to the consumer rather than to the ore. Between 1890 and 1920, the urban population of the nine-county region rose from 17.5 to 44 percent of the total population. But between 1910 and

1920, large pieces of the industrial base disappeared, leaving empty factories, unused railroad spurs, and a surplus industrial labor force.

Industrialism was America's "Pandora's Box." While it brought higher wages, improved working conditions, shorter hours, and, in general, an improving standard of living, it left behind many workers and communities. Not all regions possessed the prerequisites for industrialization. Some were forced out of the main current of national life while industrializing regions soon discovered the serious problems and maladjustments that accompanied the process. While rising numbers of Americans earned more money than ever before, moved into better housing, and possessed as necessities items unknown to their parents, other Americans were thrust into urban ghettos or factory towns. Scraping along from "hand to mouth," possessed of low-paying jobs that could be arbitrarily terminated without notice, they met with much frustration in their efforts to share in the opportunities inherent in a dynamic society.

One of the persistent difficulties of the time was the entrance of immigrants into the industrial sector as the least skilled and cheapest form of labor. The confrontation between newly arrived southern and eastern European immigrants and the modern factory system led to inevitable tensions between nonindustrial work habits and the demands of factory discipline. Employers or supervisors complained frequently about worker inefficiency, absenteeism, malingering, and the persistence of cultural traits that conflicted with modern notions of good working habits. The Traces, Williamses, and Markoviches were accustomed to the rhythms of the seasons, not the ticking of the clock. On the farm, they worked long summer days and short winter ones. The industrial discipline substituted the clock for nature's time schedule, demanding a set workday throughout the year. The factory ignored culture and religion, although the workers did not. Many workers clung to national and religious holidays, absenting themselves from the workplace to celebrate. Serbian wedding celebrations lasted a number of days, and Mihailo Markovich preferred to drink and dance rather than work. Unknowingly, he was resisting not only the demands of industrial discipline but also assimilation into the new society. Cut off from the pleasures and social life of the middle classes, Mihailo and other industrial workers salvaged what they could of their old ways at home.

Factories displayed little concern for the needs of workers. Layoffs were a fact of industrial life, particularly in the seasonal industries. In 1900, the census estimated that 11 percent of all working males had experienced three or more months of unemployment during the preceding year, and, in 1905, information gathered from 216,000 firms indicated that 29 percent operated fewer than 270 days annually. Those who did work had long hours and low pay. In 1905, when a minimally adequate standard of living demanded a wage ranging from $800 annually in New York City to $600 in smaller cities, census estimates indicate that 58 percent of all wage workers earned less than $11 weekly when employed. In the steel industry, employing 172,706 men for 12 hours daily, six days per week, one half of the workers including Mihailo Markovich who earned 15 cents an hour as a rigger at Crucible Steel in 1912, earned less than $12 weekly. Markovich and other workers knew they were being exploited and resisted when they could, usually unsuccessfully since labor organizations were weak compared with the power of management and government. In Stanko Simich's mining village of Primrose, in the lead and zinc mining and milling communities of southeastern Kansas and southwestern Missouri, townspeople frequently did unite with the workers in their struggles with the owners.

Midland did not, for its local authorities were representatives of Crucible's management.

Mihailo Markovich rented a company house that absorbed 42 percent of his annual income. Markovich's house was adequate in size, containing six rooms, and well constructed. Other workers living in Hunkyville in South Gary, Indiana (a U.S. Steel town), Sonoratown in Los Angeles, or East Topeka, Kansas, were less fortunate in their dwellings, which lacked the most rudimentary sanitary facilities and were frequently overcrowded. Income determined the housing choices available to workers. A skilled craftsman such as Andrew Bassano earned enough to enable him to move, in 1919, from his fifth-floor flat to a more attractive apartment at 140th Street and Amsterdam Avenue. Markovich had narrower options. In Midland, the "cake eaters"—the Serbian name for the Anglo-Saxons—lived below Sixth Street. The "bean and sauerkraut eaters"—the Anglo name for the Serbs—lived above Sixth Street in a less-attractive part of town. Mihailo was able, somehow, to purchase his home from Crucible in 1914 and still send money to his mother in Serbia. The financial pinch must have been extremely tight in the Markovich household.

Communities did little to buffer either the workers against the industrial system or the

Wife of general manager of Crucible Steel lighting the new blast furnace in 1906

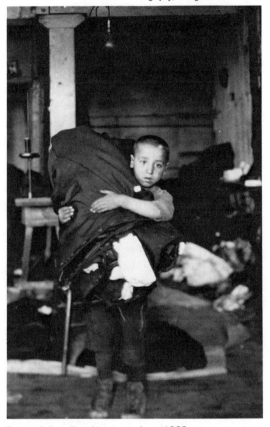

Boy with bundle of homework, c. 1909

middle or upper classes from the rude shock of industrialization. The immigrant and the unemployed, as well as the employed and the affluent, were left largely on their own. For many families, such freedom meant not only wives and mothers working but children as well, the larger number of low-paying and dead-end jobs. Contemporary studies demonstrated that the difference for many families between poverty and bare subsistence depended upon the sums brought home by children. In Providence, Rhode Island, 20,563 females, or 31 percent of all women over 10 years of age, were employed in 1900. Of that number, 31 percent were engaged in personal or domestic service (waitresses, maids, cleaning women). Foreign-born white females filled two thirds of those jobs. In Evansville, 20 percent of all females were employed in 1910 and 23 percent in 1920. While black females made up 7 percent of the female population, they supplied 14 percent of the women workers, over 90 percent of whom were servants, waitresses, and laundresses.

The government declined to check or reverse these conditions. And many Americans did not wish it to! Industrial growth continued unchecked except by periodic fluctuations of the economy. Power remained in private hands. Midland and its residents exerted no more leverage against Crucible Steel than did Howell against the Louisville & Nashville Railroad. The strengths present within the Markovich and Trace families were forged by themselves in a difficult environment.

FAMILIES IN COMMUNITIES

Social worker Sophonisba Breckinridge, among others, observed that the family was the primary agent of social life and the key to social stability. She and others were unduly apprehensive over what they saw. Marked family instability was emphasized, attested to by divorce and desertion rates, and attributed to the decay of family authority caused by the cult of individualism and democratic theories of liberty and equality. The weakening of religious standards, the assertion of female equality, the dilution of paternal authority, and the pampering of children were all singled out as contributing factors, as were pressures generated by economic change. Rising standards of living and living costs, widening job opportunities for women, a wage and salary-oriented economy, the difficulties of urban living were all suggested as explanations for a declining marriage rate, the postponement of marriage, and the declining birth rate.

The ratio of divorces to marriage did rise alarmingly from an average of one divorce to 16 marriages in the period 1887–1907, to 1 : 14 in 1900–10, and 1 : 7 in 1920. But divorce, made easier as states tended to increase the number of grounds for which they allowed it, was, because of its cost, largely a middle and upper-class device rather than a lower or working-class one. Birth rates (the number of live births per 1,000 women 15 to 44 years of age) did decline, but more rapidly for whites than for nonwhites, for the native born than the foreign born, for the urban dweller than the rural, and for the more affluent than the poor. Still, the number of babies born rose slowly each year, except for a brief decline during World War I, to a peak in 1921. Men and women were marrying at an earlier age, but while waiting longer than their parents had to have a first child, completed their smaller families at a younger age.

Many discussions of the changing nature of the "American family" measured the changes against a historical, ideal family, a self-contained unit, self-sufficient and isolated. The Traces who remained in Wayne County, Tennessee, approached this ideal but they were hardly typical in 1900. As the way of life achieved by American families became inseparable from the capacity of the breadwinner to make his living, the workplace and work tools little affected family life except on the farm. By 1900, most Americans were dependent upon wages and salaries. The insecurity of such an earning position was intensified by periodic fluctuations in the economy. Many social changes—in the status of women and children, in sexual attitudes, in the size of families, in the choice of a home—were related to wage or salary dependence.

As communities grew, they became more difficult to cope with. Presumably, they made certain needed services available to all of their residents. Some functions, such as police and

fire protection, were defined responsibilities of a municipality while others, such as housing, were indirectly affected by the action or inaction of communities in related areas of responsibility. For most families, income determined where and how they lived and, frequently, whether services were available and, if not, whether they could be obtained privately. If Andrew Bassano wished to bathe or shower, he had to go to the municipal baths, as there was not a single bath in his tenement. Mrs. John King Van Rennsalaer enjoyed a bath and powder room twice the size of the Bassano apartment.

In the great and not-so-great cities, accommodations of all kinds lagged behind population growth. Between 1910 and 1920, servicing the needs of the 480 new families who moved into the city annually sorely tested Evansville. Realtors and home builders in New York thrived on the estimated 750 newlyweds who each week sought homes in the rapid-transit suburbs around Manhattan. Within the city the competition for living space was even more intense. While some could debate the relative advantages and disadvantages of suburban places in terms of how much time they wished to travel to and from work, the Bassano's major concern was with which floor of the tenement they could afford and whether windows were necessary in each room.

In larger urban places neither the supply of housing nor its quality have ever been adequate to meet demand. In Chicago, the number of dwelling units constructed between 1910 and 1920 just managed to keep pace with the increase in population, but, as in New York, the number of rooms per apartment unit constructed declined swiftly. By 1900, Manhattan contained over 42,000 tenements, each housing as many as 10 to 20 families in three or four-room apartments, in which 1.5 million people lived. More than one half of these apartments contained one or more windowless rooms and even in the newer tenements built around an air shaft, the light and air penetrating the apartments were minimal. For such places, in which most immigrant families lived, landlords received from $4 to $5 per room per month. New York State's Tenement House Law of 1901 prevented some of the structural and sanitary inadequacies from appearing in new construction, but much of the damage had already been done.

The appearance of rows upon rows of tenements was unique to eastern industrial cities. In most cities, the typical home was considerably smaller, although not necessarily a single-family dwelling. A housing survey in Pittsburgh pointed out what was already known in New York, Cincinnati, Cleveland, or St. Louis—that low-income families frequently lived in the most squalid conditions: population outran the supply of houses; everything suitable was turned into dwellings; and many were no more adequate than New York's tenements. Studies of Springfield, Illinois, and Providence, Rhode Island, noted with alarm that tenement-type dwellings were spreading into single-family house neighborhoods, and in other places, single-family dwellings frequently housed more than one family. Commonly, working-class families took in boarders, who were often kin. Mihailo Markovich took in lodgers in Midland and, as one after another of John O'Reilly's siblings arrived in the United States, they normally found their first home with a brother or sister. The additional income was welcomed, and, in a closely knit family like the O'Reillys, it was pleasant, as well, to have family around.

Lawrence Veiller, noted housing reformer at the turn of the century, believed that the strength of American institutions depended upon a single family living in a single house. Why this was true was never spelled out by Veiller or other urban reformers beyond vague assumptions that home ownership promoted active democratic citizenship and that, in a nation based on the sanctity of private property, everyone should own some. Implicit, however, was the belief that, if every family owned its home, then all would act like Americans—that is, as Veiller wished them to act. Little progress was made between 1900 and 1920 in fulfilling this goal.

During that period, the number of owner-occupied homes remained constant at about 45 percent, and fully one half of these were farm homes. In these years, the five-year average of residential construction starts revealed a decline in single-family starts. While the foreign born displayed a somewhat greater tendency than native-born whites to own rather than rent, nationally the tendency was toward increasing rentals in multiple-family units. While no place approached New York, where 24 percent of the population lived in dwellings with 11 families or more, reports from many places indicated a rising proportion of families living in three to nine-family units.

It was too expensive for most Americans to own their homes. A small house of four rooms, in 1916, cost between $1,600 and $2,000 plus the lot. Most workers could not finance such a venture unless, as many social workers observed critically of the immigrants, everyone in the family worked and virtually the entire income went into land contracts or installment payments carrying exorbitant interest charges. Most workers, by the age of 30, were trapped in their jobs with but slim chances for significant upward mobility. Home ownership, given the uncertainties of industrial employment, was a high-risk undertaking. Not until the depression of the 1930s threatened to bring mortgage foreclosure to millions did the U.S. government create agencies to protect and encourage home ownership.

Providing housing for its residents was not a community responsibility. Guaranteeing that housing met certain minimum standards was assumed as a duty in some communities during the initial decades of the 20th century

70

but not in others. All communities, except perhaps for the smallest and most isolated of villages, functioned to some degree to protect the health of their inhabitants. By this time, most communities of some size had public-health departments whose major responsibilities were the abatement of serious health-endangering nuisances and the prevention of the spread of communicable diseases. Many towns without such departments operated within the field by providing water, sanitation, and sewage systems. Unfortunately, except in a few places, municipal governments did not efficiently use the scientific and technological knowlege that existed in dealing

with the microscopic organisms that periodically swept through massed urban populations in the form of cholera and typhoid epidemics.

The major problem was to prevent the contamination of the local water supply by germs contained in human wastes. Sewage was frequently dumped or flowed without treatment into the very waters that furnished, again without treatment, the local drinking supply. Such conditions in Newburgh, New York, earned it the title, "typhoid city." Large cities such as Chicago, New York, Pittsburgh, Boston, New Orleans, and Providence expended hundreds of millions of dollars in con-

Library of Congress

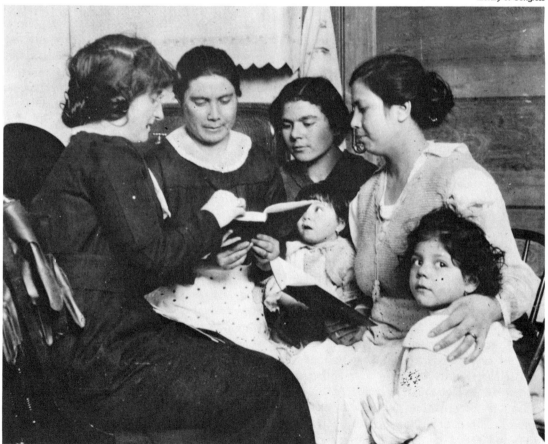

Teaching hygiene (along with English) to Italian immigrants in Gloversville, New York

structing new sewage systems, sewage treatment plants, and systems conveying pure water to its residents. By 1910, some 10 million urban people were drinking pure water and suffering much less severely from typhoid. In Midland, the steel company, owner of the water company, built a filtration plant in 1916. Most towns, however, did not provide pure water until the 1920s and 1930s. Millions of rural residents were generally left to fend for themselves in matters of public health.

Lack of public-health services took its toll on some groups more than others. Infant mortality, high throughout the nation, was twice as high in 1915 for black children under one year of age as for white children, and there was almost twice the chance that a black mother would die while giving birth as that a white mother would. Estimates from the nation's communities confirmed this statistical differential for age groups up to 12 and 15 years of age. Immigrant populations, along with Negroes, were among those with the highest death rates. A survey of 370 working immigrant mothers in New York City in 1914 revealed that 25 percent of all children born to them died in the first year.

Tuberculosis and influenza were the most serious of the death-dealing communicable diseases against which public-health services contended. In 1918, influenza spread throughout the world, killing an estimated 500,000 in the United States alone. Efforts to combat this disease made little progress, except insofar as improved standards of living increased general resistance, until the discovery of penicillin in the late 1930s. The fight against tuberculosis was also in its infancy even though Robert Koch isolated the germ in 1882 and Louis Pasteur developed the process of pasteurization of milk in 1885. In many, if not most, communities little control was exercised over the quality of milk or other foods. Topekans drank uninspected milk and, in its two poorest wards, twice as many died

from tuberculosis as in the other wards while four times as many Negroes perished from the disease as whites. In a New York study of working mothers, 35 percent of the husbands had been killed or incapacitated by the disease.

Municipalities were reluctant to raise tax monies for use in upgrading public health or other services. A few larger cities and a few rural areas employed public-health nurses in the schools, while in other places associations of volunteer visiting nurses or other philanthropic organizations devoted themselves to health problems. Hospitals and doctors in most cities clustered near the more affluent residential areas leaving poor districts without convenient medical facilities. Private citizens were responsible for the protection of their health. Medical services were available to those who could pay, but many Americans lacked the wherewithal to do much more than bury their dead.

Other municipal services, such as gas, electricity, fire protection, and police security, generally expanded at a slower pace than local needs required. In the 19th century, many communities had awarded gas, electric, and street-railway franchises to private corporations. Much dissatisfaction over both service and rates fostered a movement in various places, politically potent into the 1920s, to bring the utilities and transport systems under some form of municipal ownership. By the 1920s, some cities had managed to do this to some of the utilities, and several states had organized regulatory agencies to oversee the operation and rate-fixing practices of the utility corporations. However, the power of the utility interests, consolidated during the early 20th century into giant holding companies, frequently exceeded that of a single municipality, while regulatory commissions (when not hampered by courts) might be more representative of private than public interests. Individuals found it difficult to obtain redress against service failures and rate inequities.

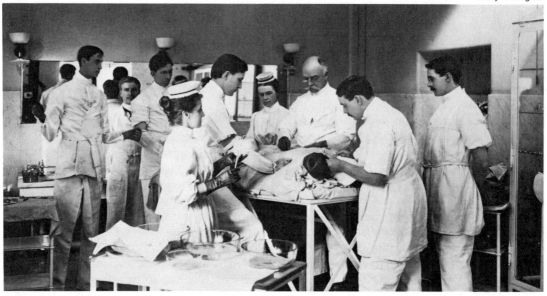

Roosevelt Hospital, New York City, near the Bassanos but far beyond their means, *c.* 1900

Electric lines under private control were extended more rapidly into middle and upper-class areas than into working-class neighborhoods, while most rural Americans were without electricity until the federal government's rural electrification program was initiated during the 1930s.

By and large, municipal services suffered from serious underfunding. City departments in most places, whether managed by elected officials or experts, could do little if financial resources were small. As a result, as late as 1915, few policemen in the nation earned over $1,000 annually. Evansville's per capita expenditures for all government purposes, 59 cents, ranked lowest of the eight cities closest in population. In 1905, for all cities with populations between 50,000 and 100,000, the average per capita expenditure was only 92 cents. Minimal revenues provided minimal services.

In the lexicon of municipal responsibilities, none would rank higher in American eyes than the provision of public-school education for all children. By the mid-19th century an ideology had developed that inseparably coupled public schools with the maintenance and continued vitality of democratic institutions. Schools, it was assumed, were to reinforce basic American moral values, provide training in citizenship, inculcate a love of country in its future citizens, serve as the nursery from which leaders would emerge who would guarantee continued economic growth, teach respect for private property and authority and conformity to social tradition, nurture the imaginative faculties, and, among other purposes, provide a basic command of certain subject areas. Underlying all of this was the still more basic belief that access to social, economic, and cultural opportunities depended upon the widespread availability of formal education. Responsibility for fulfilling these difficult—and occasionally contradictory—goals, rested, by 1900, in the hands of local boards of education and their employees, the professional educators.

Great strides were made between 1900

and 1920 in bringing more children into the public school systems. For the 5 to 17-year-old age group, public-school enrollments rose from 15.5 million in 1900 to 21.5 million in 1920, representing 78 percent of that group compared with 72 percent in 1900. School enrollments in elementary schools went up more rapidly for nonwhites than for whites. High-school enrollments quadrupled by 1920, surpassing 2 million. By 1920, 17 percent of all 17-year-olds were high-school graduates, compared with 6 percent in 1900. Rising enrollments at all levels were reflected in increasing expenditures for public education. Expenditures, at $215 million in 1900, doubled during the following decade, reaching $426 million, and then, during the next 10 years, pushed to and over $1 billion. During the entire period, local taxation was the source for about 65 percent of the funds and the proportionate share of state aid remained stable.

Certain parts of the nation advanced more rapidly than others. Achievements in the South were quite modest because a good portion of limited tax monies went into the creation of a rigidly segregated school system. Most of the increase in expenditures occurred in major urban centers while educational facilities for rural youth lagged behind, more so in the South than in the North and West. In growing cities, population pressure led directly to overcrowding and deteriorating facilities. In many rural areas, depopulation stimulated school consolidation, a trend that was reinforced by the belief of public-school administrators that unified school districts diminished costs and improved education. The positive correlation between social-class position and educational attainment was also recognized—and had been since the mid-19th century. Since those responsible for the schools were overwhelmingly middle class, improvements in physical plant and instruction were primarily available to and designed for middle-class children and schools in

middle-class areas were superior to those in lower-class districts. The five Butler boys and their wealthy contemporaries attended private schools; everyone else was dependent upon the public or parochial schools.

Not all middle-class children were well served since demand for more education, particularly through high school and beyond, outstripped the financial resources of most families. The Hart family, for instance, reasonably prosperous farmers in southeastern Kansas, sent to high school only the last two of six children born between 1903 and 1915. Although many jobs were still available to those without high-school diplomas, job prerequisites were changing swiftly and new jobs related to such industries as automotive and petrochemicals demanded considerably more technical and scientific training than was normally available in a high-school curriculum. Studies demonstrated that the career aspirations of middle-class youth were rising. In a Springfield, Illinois, survey of 650 13-year-olds, 90 percent aspired to high school—only one half would enter—and 25 percent desired a college education—only 3 percent would enroll as college freshmen.

Not all lower-class children were ill served, but many were, particularly if they were of recent immigrant origin or black or rural. States and municipalities did little to upgrade education for poorer children beyond the enactment of compulsory education laws, which, if enforced rigorously, frequently caused financial hardship in many families. Such laws, regarded by many ethnics as a direct attack on their culture, echoed the general belief among educators that equality of educational opportunity meant providing the same opportunities for all. Few recognized that the typical school program was more appropriate for some pupils than for others.

Much depended upon the parents. Neither Andrew nor Rose Bassano kept close tabs on the school performance of their eight children. But they did recognize the value of an education. All but the two oldest boys completed high school. The two oldest dropped out in their junior years, much later than the norm in many municipalities. The general pattern showed that most children remained in school until their 13th birthday. Thereafter, the dropout rate accelerated: 25 percent left before age 14; 50 percent before age 15; and 9 of 10 before age 17. Boys dropped out at an earlier age and in larger numbers than did girls. In working-class neighborhoods, as many as one third of the boys quit before age 12, thus failing to complete primary school. Most left school in order to find employment and with the approval of parents who saw no concrete connection between schooling and job opportunities. Up to a certain point, they were correct. The job histories of children completing seven or eight grades differed only marginally from the experience of children leaving during grades one through five. The presence or absence of high schools made little difference to the inhabitants of many poor neighborhoods since school curricula were neither designed to meet the needs of poor children, the vast majority of whom would only complete elementary school, nor to cope with the problems of newly urbanized residents, both native and foreign.

As in other social areas, communities frequently relied on private educational and philanthropical agencies to provide services that could only be effectively procured through community efforts. Gains made in the education of blacks were the result of private black efforts in association with foundations and, in northern cities, of adult education courses conducted by settlement houses. Charitable societies such as the Chicago School Aid Federation and the Children's Aid Society of New York undertook to provide clothing for school children who would not otherwise enroll. But these efforts were no substitute for public commitment.

Rural youth also dropped out of schools at an early age. Neither Ben Trace nor Austin Hart completed the fifth grade. As in urban areas, girls were more likely to continue their schooling. All of the Gale girls graduated from high school; none of their brothers even attended. Rural schools found it difficult to relate to the agricultural way of life or to arouse citizen interest. New educational techniques and programs, making their way slowly into urban schools, were largely absent in rural systems. Rural educators criticized the smallness of many local district units as the cause for the meagerness of school appropriations which made it extremely difficult to hire and keep good teachers. Many educators, favoring consolidation as a remedy, believed that rural schools isolated children from the values of the larger society. But schoolmen calling for such reform were ignorant of or insensitive to the place of the country school in the rural community. In many areas, the school was the basic unit of the social system, and its closing left those places without that institution around which they had originally formed.

While there was no conclusive evidence from testing that rural sixth graders were less informed than their peers in the cities, some initiative was taken to make country schools relate more closely to the rural life of its pupils. The Smith-Hughes Act of 1917 provided federal funds to rural high schools for the development of agricultural vocational and home-economics programs. This was the logical extension of legislation passed in 1914, which offered federal monies for agricultural extension and demonstration work in the states. Overall progress was slow, however, for educators estimated that less than 10 percent of rural scholars advanced beyond elementary school.

School systems and families shared the responsibility of preparing children to enter into the life of the community and into the broader national culture. But this proved extraordinarily difficult where the families themselves were foreign born or, if native born, recently removed from a slow-moving rural environment. Large city systems were particularly hard pressed to absorb the children of the foreign born. A large proportion arrived as adults and many were illiterate in their own languages. In 1910, of some 193,000 arrivals from southern Italy—the largest single group—173,000 were over 14 years old and, of those, 90,000 were unable to read or write Italian. Among the Poles, 119,000 of 128,000 newcomers were at least 14 years old and 41,000 of these were illiterate. Of the major arriving peoples, Jews had the lowest illiteracy rates, but this amounted to one of every four who were over 14 years of age.

In certain districts in the larger cities, heavy ethnic populations overwhelmed the schools. Efforts to train children for a civic life derived from the American experience—in its broadest meaning, Americanization—proved irrelevant to many, while the families tried desperately to retain their own language, traditions, and values. Instead of mediating between the families and the new society, too many schools adopted an adversary approach, believing it their role to combat the old in the name of the new. Teachers in the schools in Midland, however, did not push any harder to instill American values among their heavily ethnic student body than did teachers in Fredonia.

Time, of course, eased much of the difficulty. The children ultimately learned English, even if many adults did not. Mihailo Markovich learned enough English to get by, and, while Maria never bothered, all of the children completed high school. Stanko and Sasha Simich did not learn English but the children did. The reluctance of American society to accept the immigrants as social equals barred the older generation from total cultural inte-

A Red Cross worker in Westerly, Rhode Island, helping a recently naturalized man arrange to bring his wife and four children from Lithuania

gration, thus justifying the retention of many old ways. Second-generation Markovich and Simich children used Serbian as the language of the home. Anna Markovich, at one point in her youth ashamed of her ethnicity, ultimately came to value her origins and took pride in speaking Serbian in public.

Schools and other formal institutions controlled by the community provided but one dimension of the social experience for American families. While American cities were relatively inactive through the early 20th century in providing their residents with organized sociocultural activities, Americans had long since been accustomed to devising their own. In virtually all communities, a range of informal associations dispensed amusement and enlightenment to their members. Churches, political and occupational groups, and cultural and social clubs vied with the family and kinship and friendship groups for attention and membership. So, too, did commercial recreational facilities, notably amusement parks, vaudeville, and the moving-picture theaters. Most people, however, did not belong to a formal organization. Their personal relationships were limited to the immediate family, relatives, and a handful of neighbors or co-workers, and their contacts in other spheres rarely went beyond those necessary to earn a living, conduct business, and have a beer or see a show.

People join groups to obtain satisfaction. Middle and upper-income social organizations were often intended to be exclusive, to keep undesirables out, and to further the status ambitions of the members. In residential communities such as Webster Groves, Missouri, Montclair, New Jersey, and Fairfield, Alabama, golf courses and country clubs became more common during and after World War I. Membership in these clubs provided social focus and status for the middle classes. The upper classes derived status satisfaction from a select list of private schools, residential neighborhoods, churches, and social clubs.

The Butlers, for instance, developed a Harvard cult. Cities developed hierarchies of men's clubs from the most prestigious—the Westmoreland Club in Wilkes Barre, the Columbia Club in Indianapolis, the Maryland Club in Baltimore—to the least. The men who gathered daily at the Philadelphia Club, founded in 1834, were more concerned over American victory against a crack English polo team or the defeat of the German yacht in the Kaiserlinker Cup races than were the Howell, Indiana, railroadmen who gathered daily at the local pool hall to play penny-a-point rummy.

For workers, the higher their skill level, the more concerned they were with status. Skilled glassblowers in Coffeyville and Caney, Kansas, expected deference from the less skilled and exerted economic pressure upon recalcitrants. In Howell, Indiana, the location of a railroader's home was determined by an informal but strict caste system in which engineers built on one street, conductors on another, and shop foremen on a third street. Within the Serbian National Federation Lodge, which Mihailo Markovich joined as a charter member in 1912, free and easy association prevailed among the members who were largely unskilled steel workers. Status also played a part among the ethnic groups, even when the individuals were within the same general income bracket. On some blocks in New York's West Side, Germans and Irish who had not succeeded in moving into a better district—the leftovers—clustered in certain tenements soon after Italians, Greeks, Hungarians, and others made their appearance in large numbers. The northern Italian and skilled craftsman, Andrew Bassano, felt socially superior to the southern Italians in his tenement and moved as quickly as he could.

In response to the large numbers of foreigners converging upon the cities, a variety of immigrant organizations emerged, such as churches and banks and mutual aid societies.

One of the most active and influential ethnic organizations, the Jewish Educational Alliance, operated nursery schools, cultural programs, adult evening classes, and many other activities. Its offerings, in the first decade of the new century, attracted as many as 37,000 people weekly. Yet, even if each week's participants had consisted of totally new faces, at the end of the year there would still have been Jews in New York who had not participated. In Boston and New York, the Society for the Protection of Italian Immigrants organized an immigrant home, a labor bureau, night classes, and other services that reached several tens of thousands of the 500,000 Italians passing through and living in those cities in the 1900s. Only a small proportion of newcomers were touched by these and other ethnic organizations.

Still fewer were touched by private, indigenous organizations. In the numerous detailed studies of working-class families and working women, references to Protestant churches, settlement houses, and social-service groups are rarely encountered. In city after city, Protestant churches followed their middle-class congregations to the suburbs. In Pittsburgh, 15 churches moved away from a developing working-class slum in 15 years. Once having abandoned the poor neighborhoods, they self-righteously turned on them, waging war on saloons, gambling halls, and other immoral institutions. Victory came to Protestantism in Springfield, Massachusetts, with a campaign against the red-light district leading to the removal of the red lights and the proprietresses' names from the doors. The secular organizations were irrelevant to most urbanites, while traditional Protestantism, more concerned with overseas missionary efforts and otherworldly concerns, posed a threat to the cultural identity and social patterns of city dwellers.

In Midland in 1917, the Civic Club, led by the wife of the general superintendent of Crucible Steel, attempted to keep the immigrant majority within their assigned neighborhoods by the imposition of a curfew prohibiting immigrants from entering certain residential areas after dark. While such blatant containment was not widespread, informal restrictions grounded in the limited housing choices available to the poor were common. The urban poor generally found their amusements and developed a social life within the bounds of the street or neighborhood in which they lived. Local institutions, such as the saloon, the policy or numbers shop, the immigrant churches, the juvenile gang, the pool hall, and the brothels were all social and educational institutions. At times, it seemed that everyone was on the street that served as playground, promenade, meeting place, and market. On a hot August day, activity picked up after dark as tenants fled their breezeless apartments to seek relief on the street. Care should be taken, however, to romanticize neither the process nor the place. Ethnic ghettos did contribute to the socialization and urbanization of the newcomers. Some were zones of misfortune—dreary, crowded, and disease ridden. Residents recognized this and fled as soon as they could.

In urban working-class areas, the density of residential population compelled people to have more visual contact with one another than they did in smaller towns or in the open country. But the depth of the contact in the city was not necessarily greater than elsewhere and the deepest relationships were not confined to the closest neighbors. While much depended upon the individual's own inclinations, families moved so frequently within both blocks and neighborhoods that this geographic mobility, as in residential suburbs, weakened the stability and permanence of friendship and other groups.

Churches and synagogues found it particularly difficult to keep up with their flocks. Some were extremely stable—to the present day—such as the churches serving the Croatian and Serbian peoples of Kansas City, Kansas, while others gained permanence during the 1930s. But in Spokane, Omaha, Springfield, Massachusetts, and numbers of other places, churches and synagogues were forced to move two or three times to remain physically close to their congregations. Storefront churches were common in the larger places, not only because money was lacking for a substantial edifice, but also due to the recognition that a move was probably in the offing. Country churches, too, suffered from the mobility of the rural population. Many country churches, frequently a key or the key to the existence of a community, simply passed out of existence if they happened to be located in an area that was losing population or in an area in which tenancy was increasing. In Illinois, more than 1,500 country churches were abandoned between 1890 and 1910 while elsewhere—in both city and country—the institutional church declined in effectiveness.

Religious institutions were central in the lives of many, but, like the schools, they were not notably successful in preparing their people for the world around them. Ethnic and sectarian loyalties weakened attempts at merger, religious conservatism was not appealing to the young, and the temptations of the secular world competed vigorously with the proscriptions of the churches. Roman Catholicism was better able to minimize these weaknesses than Protestantism or Judaism since its rigidly hierarchical structure, its bureaucratic centralization, and its control over the salvation of the souls of its adherents gave it power to withstand fragmentation and punish dissidence. Nonetheless, Croatians, Italians, and other southern and eastern European Catholics were not always content with the Irish-Catholic dominance of the American Church.

In the United States, general institutions such as churches were losing their hold over the routine life of Americans. Specific local institutions were not sponsored by communities, while special-interest organizations, such as labor unions and farm societies, operated under many disabilities or served the interests of but a fraction of the potential constituency. Andrew Bassano's abiding loyalty to the Terrazzo and Tile Workers' Union, Meyer Miller's activities in New York's apparel unions, formed through Jewish initiative, Stanko Simich's commitment to the United Mine Workers, the sudden eruption of great strikes—anthracite miners in 1903, steelworkers in 1919—should not obscure the lack of union affiliation for most workers. Similarly, farm lobbying organizations and cooperatives were important to those few farmers who belonged to them. The Harts in Kansas appreciated agricultural-extension demonstrations of new farming techniques but were suspicious of the political maneuvering of Society of Equity and Farm Bureau representatives. Labor unions, fighting for economic security, achieved success in Springfield, Massachusetts, but failed in Topeka where the railroads, supported in their efforts by the community, broke the shop unions. The temper of the nation was more accurately plumbed in Topeka than in Springfield.

American municipalities, between 1900 and 1920, only indifferently provided the basic needs of their inhabitants. The common refrain of dozens of social surveys of American communities, from Newburgh, New York, to Stillwater, Minnesota, and Topeka, Kansas, bore this out. So, too, did conditions in the communities in which our families lived. Traditional concepts of the limits of community responsibility and faith in the ability of the free-market economy to provide at least something for everyone were strong restraints on municipal action. Even when they did move gingerly to regulate certain activities, they were competing with basic cultural imperatives which normally forced the best-intentioned officials to back off from rigorous enforcement.

Yet this was the age of "progressive" reform during which, as has been suggested, fundamental political changes occurred in municipal, state, and national government. But nothing fundamental changed in the operation of the governments of Midland, Fredonia, or Waynesboro. Crucible Steel's representatives controlled Midland's borough council while the company owned most of the land in the borough. In Fredonia and Waynesboro and their counties, Republican ascendancy was shared by a small group of men who regularly held municipal or county office. In those places and others, the governments did little more than they had at their founding. Private enterprise remained responsible for most of what happened. Thus, the direction and nature of expansion in Coffeyville, Kansas, was determined by railroad and business interests willing to extend utility and transportation services and to subdivide local real estate. A similar process shaped Evansville and Los Angeles.

Virtually all white adult citizens had the vote by 1920, but very few had power. Faith in the power of the ballot blinded Americans to the fact that those with economic power used it to serve their own purposes. Perhaps Americans could not cope with their real powerlessness, and so they grasped more strongly the faith that power was shared through democratic processes. Mihailo Markovich and Ben Trace were more sophisticated politically than most middle-class Americans with much more education. Workers knew who had power. Andrew Bassano witnessed the political bosses shaking down subway construction workers. Ben and Mihailo recognized power in the person of the shop foreman. This was a power that could be and was used arbitrarily to destroy lives. What was the ballot next to this?

While municipal reformers, including a relatively new group of city planners, tinkered with the structure of government, municipal blight spread. Deterioration impinged on all urban classes. The poor suffered most of all, but skilled workers and the middle classes were hardly immune. A relatively large income was required for suburban living, larger than most enjoyed. Families simply moved into different blocks or residential districts that were a little farther away from the deteriorating urban zones. The trip to work consumed a little more time, the rent was higher for a somewhat more commodious apartment, and the neighborhood more respectable—for the time being, distance protected.

The economic growth of the cities worked against the best interest of many residents. Low-wage industries encroached on residential districts, while railroad and surface transport and then automobiles created massive congestion in the CBD. Employment opportunities attracted workers to whom city life appeared to offer more promise than rural life had. Exploiting the surplus labor thus generated, employers underpaid and overworked laborers, forcing them into substandard environments that municipalities did nothing to remedy. City growth meant progress, and progress was an American dream. Municipal governments, creatures of the beneficiaries of growth, could hardly be expected to control or direct expansion or even to soften its impact. So, from 1900 to 1920 and thereafter, the zones of fortune and misfortune spread in American towns and cities.

SUGGESTIONS FOR FURTHER READING

Among the studies which were most helpful in the preparation of this chapter are Wilbert L. Anderson, *The Country Town: A Study of Rural Evolution* (1906); Otho G. Cartwright, *The Middle West Side: A Historical Sketch* (1914); John G. Clark, *Towns and Minerals in Southeastern Kansas: A Study in Regional Industrialization* (1970); Lawrence A. Cremin, *The Transformation of the School: Progressivism in American Education, 1877–1957* (1961); Charles J. Galpin, *Rural Social*

Problems (1924); Thomas J. Jones, *The Sociology of a New York City Block* (1904); John H. Kolb, *Rural Primary Groups: A Study of Agricultural Neighborhoods* (1921); Sir Horace Plunkett, *The Rural Life Problems in the United States: Notes of an Irish Observer* (1910); Paul U. Kellogg, ed., *The Pittsburgh Survey* (6 vols., 1909–14); Graham R. Taylor, *Satellite Cities: A Study of Industrial Suburbs* (1915); and U.S. Country Life Commission, *Report of the Country Life Commission* (1909). Other contemporary accounts and analyses of value include Jacob Riis, *How the Other Half Lives* (1890); Henry D. Sheldon, *Student Life and Customs* (1901); Edith Allen, *Mechanical Devices in the Home* (1922); Lincoln Steffens, *The Shame of the Cities* (1904); and Jane Addams, *Twenty Years at Hull House* (1910).

In addition to chapters in scholarly and popular histories of American cities, refer to such topical works as Robert Dykstra, *The Cattle Towns* (1968); Merle Curti, *The Making of an American Community: A Case Study of Democracy in a Frontier County* (1959); Stanley Buder, *Pullman: An Experiment in Industrial Order and Community Planning, 1880–1930* (1967); Howard Chudacoff, *Mobile Americans: Residential and Social Mobility in Omaha, 1880–1920* (1972); Lewis Atherton, *Main Street on the Middle Border* (1954); Sidney Goldstein, *Patterns of Mobility, 1910–1950: The Norristown Study* (1958); Sam Bass Warner, Jr., *Streetcar Suburbs: The Process of Growth in Boston, 1870–1900* (1962); John A. Miller, *Fares Please: From Horsecars to Streamliners* (1941); and George W. Pierson, *The Moving American* (1973).

For urban architecture and technology, *see* Carl W. Condit, *The Rise of the Skyscraper* (1952); Hugh Morrison, *Louis Sullivan: A Prophet of Modern Architecture* (1935); Christopher Tunnard and Henry H. Reed, *American Skyline* (1955); and Carl W. Condit, *The Railroad and the City: A Technological and Urbanistic History of Cincinnati* (1977). Two fascinating books on this theme are Leo Marx, *The Machine in the Garden: Technology and the Pastoral Ideal in America* (1964); and Siegfried Giedion, *Mechanization Takes Command: A Contribution to Anonymous History* (1948).

Helpful studies of labor and industrialization begin with Herbert G. Gutman, *Work, Culture, and Society in Industrializing America: Essays in American Working-Class and Social History* (1976). See also Bruno Ramirez, *When Workers Fight: The Politics of Industrial Relations in the Progressive Era, 1898–1916* (1978); Gerald N. Grob, *Workers and Utopia* (1961); Graham Adams, Jr., *Age of Industrial Violence, 1910–1915* (1966); and Milton Meltzer, *Bread—And Roses: The Struggle of American Labor in the Progressive Era, 1865–1915* (1977).

Treatments of black migration and race relations are Gilbert Osofsky, *Harlem: The Making of A Ghetto* (1966); Allan H. Spear, *Black Chicago: The Making of a Negro Ghetto, 1890–1920* (1967); David M. Katzman, *Before the Ghetto: Black Detroit in the Nineteenth Century* (1973); and Kenneth L. Kusmer, *A Ghetto Takes Shape: Black Cleveland 1870–1930*. The anthologies by August Meier, John M. Bracey, Jr., and Elliot M. Rudwick, *The Rise of the Ghetto* (1971), and Hollis Lynch, *The Black Urban Condition: A Documentary History* (1971) offer useful perspectives on this period.

Works on urban social issues include, in addition to books mentioned in Chapter 3, Roy Lubove, *The Progressive and the Slums: Tenement House Reform in New York City, 1890–1917* (1962); Allen F. Davis, *Spearheads for Reform: The Social Settlements and the Progressive Movement* (1967); Barbara Rosencrantz, *Public Health and the State: Changing Views in Massachusetts, 1842–1936* (1972); Thomas L. Philpott, *The Slum and the Ghetto: Neighborhood Deterioration and Middle Class Reform, Chicago, 1880–1930* (1978); Roy Lubove, *The Urban Community: Housing and Planning in the Progressive Era* (1967); George Rosen, *From Medical Police to Social Medicine* (1974); John D. Thompson, *The Hospital* (1975); Jerold S. Auerbach, *Unequal Justice: Lawyers and Social Change in America* (1976); and Stephen Ambrose, ed., *Institutions in Modern America* (1970).

3 | The New Century

THE MACHINE AGE

The signal came at 1:04 P.M. With it, the crowd cheered, bells rang, a hundred flags unfurled, a torrent of water cascaded down terraced slopes into a lagoon, John Philip Sousa struck up the band, machinery whirred, and the greatest exposition in the world's history was opened to the public. The St. Louis World's Fair, after that dramatic opening on April 30, 1904, received over 19 million visitors, among them Henry Brauer and his family. Aware that the nation's county fair deserved, indeed required attractions befitting the achievements and richness of the patron, the fair organizers had transformed two square miles into a wonderland. They built 1,576 new buildings covering 300 acres for the occasion, arranged for 55,000 individual displays, allotted two miles of frontage to amusements, and billed the whole thing as "the epitome of the world's progress and man's best achievements."

Visitors to the world's fair had every reason to be proud of America. Science and abundant resources combined with the profit motive had produced a new world of things which would have left their grandfathers gaping. They paused inside the doors of Festival Hall, the fair's centerpiece, to marvel at the world's largest pipe organ and then to look back down the steps at the fountain gushing 130 million gallons of water a day (enough for a city of 500,000 people). They paraded through the Palaces of Education, Art, and Liberal Arts, noting the Greek-inspired architecture and the sparkling gondolas on the adjacent lagoons. But the sights that fired their imaginations were those in the Palaces of Agriculture, Transportation, Machinery, Mines and Metallurgy, and Manufactures. These were the temples of labor-saving, profit-increasing, comfort-yielding things. The Palace of Mines and Metallurgy, featuring demonstrations of steel making, wire and tube drawing, and ore reduction, promised an

Stereograph view of the St. Louis World's Fair, 1904

abundance of stronger, inexpensive metal from which to make all these magnificent things. The Palace of Electricity showed the application of that "subtle fluid" to signals, alarms, railroads, wireless telegraphy, and telephones. In other exhibits, flush toilets, electric-lighting apparatus, processed food (frozen, compressed into tablets, and solder-sealed into metal tins) offered visitors a vision of opulence soon to come. For those with the stamina to walk nine miles through aisles of the Palace of Agriculture, the threshers, mowers, diggers, grinders, cutters, windmills, and a vast miscellany of machines impelled by wind, water, steam, and electricity augured a bright future for farming. A display of 160 steam, electric, and gasoline-powered automobiles, the fair brochure announced, showed "the remarkable possibilities of this new means of travel."

The awesome Palace of Machinery contained exhibits of the most modern means of generating, transmitting, and applying power. Under 13 acres of roof, cranes, water pumps,

conveyors, hydraulic rams, and steam hammers crowded against marvelous new types of engines. There were stationary engines, portable engines, rotary engines, reciprocating engines, turbine engines, engines that generated power from coal, gas, petroleum, alcohol, compressed air, and carbonic-acid gas. "In this giant workshop," the fair's official historian wrote, "there is the incessant sound of titanic hammer, roar of furnace, buzz of plane, whirr of wheel, swish of blow, and the composite hum of a thousand machines musical with song of industry and inspiring with hallelujahs of human progress." Fair goers, shouting to make themselves heard above the racket, surely agreed.

Americans looked to the future with confidence that application of science and intellect guaranteed constant improvement of their lot. They inclined to define improvement in material terms and they were eager to encourage and financially reward the producers of beneficial material things. The organizers of the World's Fair manifested this American spirit by awarding $200,000 in prizes for a balloon race and airship construction. "Through the stimulus given to the art through rewards," they explained, "there is reason to hope, aye, to believe that ability to sail the seas of the skies is near at hand." It was indeed. That December, at an isolated sand flat near Kitty Hawk, North Carolina, the bicycle mechanics Wilbur and Orville Wright flew an airplane for 27 seconds.

The widespread optimism dominated a setting that, in many ways, should have discouraged it. The St. Louis World's Fair, the very "epitome of . . . man's best achievements," had been scheduled to open on April 30, 1903, the centennial day of the purchase of the Louisiana Territory. The buildings and grounds simply were not completed on time and the opening had to be postponed a year. When opening day did come, the President of the United States, Theodore Roosevelt, was scheduled to start the machines and open the exhibits, via a telegraph signal, precisely at noon immediately following the dedicatory

ceremonies. A few minutes before noon, fair officials, noting that President Roosevelt's message would interrupt the uncompleted speechmaking, sidetracked the signal from the White House and turned back the fairground clocks. The crowd milled about for nearly an hour after the last speaker sat down before someone gave the signal to begin. The 20th century was like that—full of achievement, promise, and boast, the full effect of which was marred by postponement, manipulation, and disappointment.

While the comforts and scientific marvels open to view at the world's fair were destined to bring a revolution in the way people lived, they touched the lives of very few at the time and eluded millions for more than 20 years. In 1900, less than one person in 9,000 owned an automobile, and accumulated horse manure, the rotting flesh of dead animals, and the accompanying flies and stench ranked high on the list of urban problems. By 1920, despite the innovative assembly line Henry Ford had set up for automobile manufacture

Palace of Machinery, interior view, St. Louis World's Fair, 1904

in 1908, only 11 percent of the population over 14 years old contributed to the resolution of that era's pollution problem by owning a car. Although the incandescent lamp was more than 25 years old in 1904, electric service was available only in middle-class and affluent sections of sizable cities. In the next 20 years, cities became electrified but less than one farm family in seven would have electricity. Water-pressure systems were equally distant except for mainstream urbanites. The outhouse and a weekly bath in water heated on the stove characterized the sanitary habits of all country and most city folk. As with electricity, indoor bathrooms with flush toilets were common for well-off urbanites by 1920, but at least half the families in the crowded factory districts lacked the conveniences, and as late as 1930 fewer than one farm family in six had a "modern house." And so it went down the long list of industrial gimcracks and widgets that, collectively, promised an easier and happier life. For all the slowness and uneven distribution, the vast majority never flagged or questioned the worthiness of the chase.

The technological wizardry upon which the good life depended, practically everyone admitted, was possible only because some producers were big enough to undertake the complex tasks of manufacture. The village blacksmith simply could not forge a steel bridge and women at their grandmothers' looms could not make calico for seven cents a yard. At the same time, the big, rich, and sophisticated companies that produced the coveted things alarmed average people. They feared their size would give these companies the power to dictate prices and manipulate public policies to their own ends. Workers feared that they would be powerless to control or influence their working conditions and wages. Common people feared that the corporations would drive craftsmen and small entrepreneurs out of business. It was the more

frightening because of the speed with which bigness had come to characterize business.

Between 1898 and the year of the fair, the business community underwent an unprecedented number of consolidations. The necessary conditions had been developing for years, but the lesson of the depression of 1893–96 and the widespread discovery of the advantages of the modern bureaucratic corporation seemed immediately responsible. During the downturn of the 90s, at least 70,000 businesses failed; however, profits of corporate trusts, such as those in the oil and sugar refining industries, remained impressively high. The lesson was obvious. What was required was control of the entire manufacturing process from raw material to finished product—"vertical integration," architects of the new industry termed the arrangement.

Twelve steel producers, for example, consolidated in 1901 to form U.S. Steel. Immediately that corporation owned 149 steel plants, 84 blast furnaces, 1,000 miles of railroad, 112 ore vessels on the Great Lakes, and thousands of acres of land underlaid with coal, iron ore, and limestone, which it valued at $1.4 billion. Of course, not all consolidations were as spectacular or as rapid. Crucible Steel, where Mihailo Markovich worked, achieved the goal of integration more slowly. Pittsburgh Crucible Steel Company had formed in 1900 as the result of consolidating 13 "specialty" steel companies. In 1911, Crucible purchased Midland Steel Company and acquired coal mines in Greene County, Pennsylvania. The purchase of Midland gave Crucible basic steel-making capacity, but Crucible became fully integrated only in 1929 when it acquired interest in Lake Superior iron-ore properties.

By 1904, about three fourths of the 320 largest corporations were less than five years old and controlled over 40 percent of the manufacturing capital in the United States.

Almost as awesome as the size of the manufacturing giants was the changed nature of business leadership. Investment bankers eclipsed in influence the men who knew how to make products and run factories. These bankers enjoyed instant access to the public and private pools of investment capital which had been developing since the Civil War. The expensive buildings, equipment, resource developments and distribution systems necessary for the new technology and maximum profit required their kind of money. Ownership and control thus passed to the bankers.

No name better symbolized the arrival of finance capitalism than that of J. P. Morgan. Born rich, Morgan had parlayed the family money into one of the largest fortunes in America through investments in railroad stock

Library of Congress

Characteristic pose of financier J. P. Morgan, *c.* 1910

and consolidations of lines he controlled. By the first decade of the new century, the influence of about one fourth of the money invested in American railroads belonged to Morgan. His banking house turned to promoting manufacturing corporations after the depression of the 90s, and his example brought in scores of other financiers. When J. P. Morgan and Company put money into an enterprise, Morgan and Company received seats on the board of directors. When they had a majority of votes on the board, they could bring about consolidation with other Morgan-controlled companies. Morgan's most spectacular venture was the acquisition of Andrew Carnegie's steel works and consolidation with 11 other producers to form United States Steel. In addition, Morgan had a voice in the management decisions of International Harvester, the nation's largest producer of farm machinery; General Electric, the largest maker of electrical equipment; New York Life, Mutual Life, and Equitable Life, three of the largest insurance companies; and other corporations.

To maximize profits, Morgan and other financiers delegated the business operations to a new class of professional managers whose byword was "efficiency." Following the teachings of an energetic engineer, Frederick W. Taylor, these managers talked enthusiastically about modifications of plants and workers' tasks according to the findings of time and motion studies. The idea was to maximize the productivity of every physical movement. For industrial workers, efficiency usually meant demands for a work speedup.

The consolidation movement was restrained only by the provisions (largely unenforced) of federal antitrust laws. Certainly no government body considered itself to have a mandate to guarantee workers a living wage. As we have seen in Chapter 2, municipal governments did not insist that industrial plants be situated where they did least damage to the environment. Instead, they accepted the notion that maximum growth required minimum restrictions. While there were isolated and occasionally successful efforts to curb pollution prior to World War I, more typical was the industrial experience of southeastern Kansas. By 1914, 28 zinc smelters, 25 glass plants, 15 cement plants, and dozens of clay-products plants were located in the nine-county area. Environmental impact played absolutely no role in locating them. While the towns intervened to obtain the industries, once successful, the tradition of nonintervention ruled. Economic considerations were paramount. Far from being concerned over the slag heaps, gouges in the earth, or dusty air, the municipalities sought more of the same.

The situation of industrial workers lent credence to the idea that environment changes people. Stanko Simich, Mihailo Markovich, John O'Reilly, Meyer Miller, Ben Trace, and other workers in industrial districts were good people who were dislocated and frustrated. A few never adjusted, turning instead to crime or embracing anarchistic schemes for abolishing the system that belittled them. Crime rates in America's industrial districts far surpassed those for the more pastoral places. Every industrial city had its Bandit's Roost where criminals prowled and police rarely patrolled. Most industrial workers, however, coped, and many actively sought to improve their lives. Stanko swore by the United Mine Workers and Mihailo similarly saw salvation in unionization. Meyer Miller studied socialism. But such efforts served only to further separate the workers from the Butlers, the Gales, and others of the affluent classes. As the distinctions became more and more blatant, more people at all levels began to diagnose the malfunction in the American industrial machine and to try to tinker with it.

Unions appealed to a few workers as a means of improving their lot. Between 1900

and U.S. entry into World War I in 1917, total union membership increased nearly fourfold, to about 3,000,000. Even so, unionized workers never amounted to as much as 10 percent of the American work force. Moreover, the workers who did join were overwhelmingly skilled or semiskilled, and their vision of appropriate union activity was decidedly conservative in comparison with unions in the rest of the world. The vast majority of unskilled laborers in the new consolidated mass-production industries remained outside union ranks.

Samuel Gompers, president of the American Federation of Labor, set the tone of the union movement. He wanted craftsmen of each type (as opposed to all workers in an industry) to unite. He wanted "pure and simple" unionism—which meant higher wages, shorter hours, and better working conditions obtained through collective bargaining with employers. The AFL embraced no political or social reform program. The AFL well served craftsmen such as Andrew Bassano and others in the building trades, printing, and so forth. But it shunned the unskilled line and floor workers in heavy industry. Nonetheless, the United Mine Workers, the International Ladies' Garment Workers, and the Amalgamated Clothing Workers were new industrial unions (membership open to *all* workers) that survived. They were exceptions; the large corporations were so anti-union and so powerful that most efforts to organize failed aborning.

The owners of industry held that they had the exclusive right to set wages and determine working conditions. Most of them agreed with George F. Baer, a spokesman for coal-mine owners, when he said, "The rights and interests of the laboring man will be protected and cared for—not by the labor agitators, but by the Christian men to whom God in His infinite wisdom has given the control of the property interests of this country." Such talk infuriated

Bandit's Roost, 39½ Mulberry Street, New York City, 1888

Stanko Simich and Mihailo Markovich. Experience had taught them that even if owners understood workingmen's interests, they did little to protect them. Endless talk with bosses about dangerous working conditions and low wages inevitably got nowhere. What else could they do except to attempt to change things themselves through job action—slowdowns—or unions? The men for whom George Baer spoke responded to such tactics by hiring large numbers of security guards, frequently from the Pinkerton Detective Agency, who harassed and fired the workers. Simich, basically peace loving and opposed to violence, yet hating exploitation and the armed legions of the owners more, on one occasion packed a loaded revolver to the picket lines. He fired, missed, and never forgot it. Markovich, no less fearful and brave, armed himself with a stout club when trouble brewed at Crucible Steel and management called in the scabs. Stanko and Mihailo simply did not trust the owners to act on their grievances. They recognized the gulf between their interests and those of the bosses and unionized when they could because in numbers there was strength.

The National Association of Manufacturers, hysterically anti-union, urged businesses not to recognize unions and to refuse collective bargaining. The NAM held that union tactics like the nationwide strike and especially the boycott amounted to "restraint of trade," as forbidden in the Sherman Antitrust Act. On occasion, the courts agreed. In 1902, a union of hatmakers in Danbury, Connecticut, called for a national boycott of products made by a local company. The company went to court, won damages, and sought to collect them by attaching the bank accounts of union members and initiating foreclosure proceedings against their homes. (The damages were eventually paid from national union treasuries.)

The Industrial Workers of the World (nicknamed "Wobblies") attracted a few laboring men (never more than 60,000) who believed Gomper's conservatism made him "a greasy tool of Wall Street." The IWW, formed in 1905, contended that the interests of employers and employees were incompatible and that those of the former were evil. Wobblies advocated worker control of production and condoned violence to accomplish it. Although small units cropped up in eastern factories, most members of this radical organization worked in mining, lumbering, and agricultural enterprises in the West. The union's greatest success, however, was in the eastern factory town of Lawrence, Massachusetts, and it was nonviolent. A spontaneous strike occurred in Lawrence in January 1912, when the city's textile mills cut the salaries of 30,000 workers. The IWW moved in, organized the strikers, and, largely through exposing nonviolent strikers and their children to the angry and fearful local police, were able to publicize incidents of police cruelty. Public opinion forced the operators to capitulate to strikers' demands. Despite occasional and dramatic successes, unions were pitifully weak in comparison with the power of capital and remained so until the 1930s.

As the family biographies and community studies point out, workers sought means other than unions to gain a sense of control over their lives. Centering their activities around the church and synagogue was one possibility. The absence of a church in Midland did not prevent the Markovich family from deriving comfort and direction from Serbian Orthodoxy and Serbian culture. Annie Miller successfully insisted upon maintaining a Kosher home in the face of Meyer's professed atheism. Beyond the church, there were mutual aid societies, voluntary organizations that provided sickness, injury, and death benefits as well as social activities and educational

Confrontation between troops and strikers in Lawrence, Massachusetts, 1912

services. The Millers turned to such organizations as necessity dictated. The Bassanos, more typical, had no contacts with them at all.

Andrew Bassano and Stanko Simich—recent immigrants—and Charles Gale and James Williams—old stock—neither expected nor received direct aid from government in making their way through their productive years. All of them agreed with the mainstream politicians that individuals were responsible for themselves and they accepted responsibility for their old age in the same way. Each tried to make provisions out of current income. Andrew Bassano charged room and board to his children who had jobs and set aside part of it for his retirement. When he was 60, he took the money to Italy and settled on the small family holding north of Venice where he felt at peace and where his money would last longer. The idea simply was to save as much as possible during the productive years, live as frugally as possible during the retirement years, and rely upon the grown children to make up any deficiency between assets and expenses. Bassano lived longer than he expected, and his children sent him money when he needed it. They and their generation had been taught, as Andrew's son Robert Bassano put it, that "it was considered an honor as well as a pleasure to take care of one's parents in their old age. Today's children (those of the 1980s), because of Social Security, health plans, pension plans, no longer have the responsibility of caring or sharing with their parents certain sacrifices we accepted with dignity and love." Of course, few workers were as lucky as the elder Bassano. Many moved into the home of one of the children or, as did Mihailo Markovich, brought the children back home for support and care when they became ill. Generational differences and the additional burdens on finances and time made that solution far from ideal. If family ties were weak, or there were no children, or the children were dead or impoverished, old people could be reduced to loneliness and the mercy of private charities.

Political activity offered little reward to industrial workers in the early 20th century. The government had little direct impact on their lives. They paid few taxes and received few services. The needs of industrial workers were immediate and material; their previous failures in appealing for reforms or relief made the stuff of legislative chambers seem long range, abstract, and distant. This is not to say that politics and government did not touch the lives of some. The ward politicians of the cities offered social services in the form of jobs, legal aid, food, and coal, which no one else offered. The local politician expected only votes and sometimes a little contribution when the people were working. Andrew Bassano watched Italian and Polish workers, diggers of the New York subway, form a pay line outside a nearby saloon and drop a quarter in the local boss's hat as they filed between the paymaster and the bar. The ethics of such a scene bothered the middle class more than it did the workers.

During the first two decades of the 20th century, innovations in technology and finance transformed the face and lifestyle of American cities. The symbols of relief from the daily struggle popped up everywhere—electric-power cables, pipelines for gas and water, streetcar tracks, paved streets, iron sewers, concrete and brick sidewalks, and school buildings. Even if the benefits fell unevenly, the general agreement was that the world was improving. Merchants, clerks, teachers, preachers, servicemen, lawyers, doctors, salesmen, and contractors never had so many comfortable things or so much money. And yet, city life was not what it could have been.

While the general philosophy of the era restrained city governments from regularly intervening in the community's economic and social life, city governments had limited authority to act. Cities received their authority from state governments and the rural-dominated state legislatures limited both indebtedness and tax rates. Even in matters over which cities received jurisdiction, there were frequently problems with state courts. Ordinances regulating health and social conditions, for example, often were struck down as infringements upon the freedoms of employers and landlords. Then, there was the highly visible problem of corruption. Utility and public-works franchises, contracts, and licenses at the disposal of city governments were worth the fortunes of kings, and so were the profits to be enjoyed by the firms upon which the city bestowed them. Kickbacks, bribes, shoddy construction jobs, and interruptions in utility service were the inevitable results of collusion between profit-greedy contractors and city governments controlled by cliques of self-serving politicians. The middle elements of urban society helplessly watched—at least at first—as assorted land speculators, bankers and industrialists, utility operators, and politicians grew gaudy rich and flaunted the power of their money. At the same time, the conditions in factories and across the tracks in the working districts became clearer to the middle class. Some individuals deplored the effects of corrupt city practices upon personal morality. Some feared widening class distinctions would foment workers' revolts. Some sensed an eclipse of their own social status. All these apprehensions put together portended reaction against the ethical and social consequences of the new urbanism.

FARMERS IN THE MACHINE AGE

Life improved on American farms in the first two decades of the century. While living and production expenses did go up, the prices farmers received for their products rose more. Austin Hart's father had sold wheat for 62 cents a bushel in 1900. The market price inched up to $1 by 1908, and then, with the food requirements of World War I, peaked above $2.15 with the 1919 crop. The surplus from the family farms operated by Jacob Reinhardt and William Trace similarly profited the producers. The corn the Reinhardts sold for 21 cents a bushel in 1900 was worth $1.51 in 1919. Eggs at 41 cents a dozen, beef cattle at 10 cents a pound, porkers at 13 cents a pound, and hens at $1 apiece were other examples of food for which prices had more than doubled. Although the Trace family in Tennessee, always strapped for money, was denied any improvement in lifestyle, the Reinhardts and Gales periodically found themselves with enough extra money to buy a machine or some new equipment to make life

easier. Jacob Reinhardt bought a sulky plow for $50 and a disc harrow for $25. Charles Gale replaced his old broadcast seeder with a disc drill for $60 and ordered a $40 windmill (disassembled) from the Sears, Roebuck catalog. During the years 1910–14, agricultural experts concluded, the purchasing power of the farmers equalled that of their urban counterparts. In terms of the ratio of prices received by farmers to the prices they paid for goods, the high demand for food during World War I boosted farm purchasing power another 20 percent.

Nonetheless, the Country Life Commission had reported in 1909 "serious agricultural unrest in every part of the United States, even in the most prosperous regions." Farmers had felt victimized in one way or another by big industry and big money since the burst across the country of railroad tracks just after the Civil War. The Grange, a politically moribund farmers' organization by 1900, had protested in its heyday that the freight rates enjoyed by the railroad owners established a tyranny over farmers "unequalled in any monarchy of the Old World." In the 1890s, the farmer-dominated Populist Party claimed that only industrialists profited by the nation's money system and that society was evolving two great classes—"tramps and millionaires." The Populist Party fell apart after the depression of the mid-1890s, leaving farmers more disorganized than they had been for years, at the very time that their industrial antagonists were refining the arts of collusion.

Aside from memories of depression, the feelings of farmers were conditioned as much by the *possibilities* of an even better life as by physical realities, as much by *fear* of impotence in influencing morals and decisions as by their actual strength. The industrial city generated both the possibilities and the fears. The typical farmer's list of material wants by the eve of World War I would feature electricity to power a pump and washing machine, a telephone to call the doctor or a friend, a surfaced road to make town more accessible, and more machinery to shorten time spent in the fields. The list of fears would be less precise, though it would doubtless be longer.

Farming was America's traditional occupation. Until the end of the 19th century, few people questioned the nobility of working with the soil, the inherent goodness of the simple life, and the social ethic of self-sufficiency and neighborliness which supposedly grew out of the physical setting. By 1900, only 35 percent of the people were actually cultivating the earth and raising animals (the census taker listed nearly 60 percent of Americans as "rural," but over a third lived in villages and towns of less than 2,500 and serviced the 35 percent who farmed). And, notwithstanding the best efforts of a host of rural apologists, the vocation of farming never had a worse reputation. The "best" people no longer invariably came from or defended farm life. The National Education Association attacked the emotional attachment to the little red school house and mercilessly indicted the quality of rural education. Moreover, some of America's fiction writers, caught up in the realist and naturalist literary movements, seriously undermined the agrarian myth that farmers enjoyed a special harmony with nature and possessed an extra measure of virtue. The stories of Hamlin Garland, especially, pictured haggard, dull farm men and women whose lives were characterized by loneliness, ignorance, and serial tragedy. The farmer now exhausted his body and the soil in a grisly struggle against the mortgage company, gambled life or death stakes with nature, and, symbolic of the quality of farm life, coped endlessly with steaming piles of dung.

Charles Gale and Jacob Reinhardt, whatever the tarnished reputation of their way of life, still believed that America was great because its people had been close to the soil. They may even have distrusted the habits and thinking of city folks. Certainly a new breed of rural sociologist hammered away at the evils of the urban environment and the awful consequences should the cities' multiplying hoards gain political dominance. Editors of small-town newspapers and farm magazines transmitted the message to their readers—the city was an economic trap and full of moral pitfalls, a rise to political eminence of urban boodlers and ethnic radicals could only erode the national commitment to law-abiding conduct, energetic work, and devotion to family and private property. How seriously Charles and Jacob took such preaching to heart is problematic. They were practical men busy with the daily chores and the seasonal requirements of cropping—men who worried about prices and weather, a sour milch cow, and money for a needed hay baler or thresher. They knew that by comparison to the 1890s, times were good, and they knew they were better off than the likes of William Trace who was eking out an existence on marginal land. They wished for a larger income—most people did, and do—and were vaguely discontented.

It is true that the standard against which they measured the quality of their lives was the best of city amenities and services, and they could not help a certain feeling of envy. A questionnaire sent to over half a million farmers in 1908 showed that they saw lack of organization in rural society and poor education as their greatest handicaps. The farmer was left a detached man in a society that was awed by the possibilities of collectivity. The schools did not offer practical courses to improve farm efficiency or teach the advantages and potential joy of farm life. Two to one, farmers concluded that the lack of *proper* education was responsible for youths' lack of ideals and their drift to town. Life would be more as it should be if tax systems were adjusted, absentee farming eliminated, tariffs reduced, middlemen regulated, the one-crop system abandoned where it was depleting the soil, highways expanded, hired hands dissuaded of the city's lures, health services expanded, and the seamier aspects of women's work muted by convincing husbands that their wives, too, should have labor-saving devices.

REFORM

Although vast physical and cultural distances and different occupations separated Charles Gale and Mihailo Markovich, both felt a common threat—the modern business conglomerate. The Anglo-Irish foreman at Crucible Steel could fire Mihailo at any moment, and there would be no recourse. The Chicago Board of Trade, mysteriously setting grain prices (often unconnected with actual supply and demand) similarly affected Charles' fate. Most Americans, one way or another, were affected by the giant corporations. For most people, the new business developments seemed a mixed blessing. They did not think it inconsistent to praise the technological virtuosity and crisp efficiency of the giants while lamenting their ruthless pursuit of profits and their callous social consciences. Most people could credit the corporate giants with raising, or potentially raising, the nation's standard of living while condemning them for wrenching changes in the society. For city and rural Americans alike, so much depended upon the conduct of the corporations. When the corporations proved too self-serving, when they seemed to victimize well-intentioned employees and patrons, the Reinhardts and Gales could join with the Simiches and Millers in applauding the efforts to force the corporations to respond to the public interest. These efforts brought into existence the modern regulatory capitalist system.

The public's knowledge of corporate activity and morality came from hearsay and a spate of popular monthly magazines. Technological developments in printing and papermaking, the recent improvements in the mail system, and the innovations of a number of imaginative editors and publishers put more reading material in American homes than ever before. By 1905, readers had a choice of over 6,000 magazines, the most popular of which sold for a dime (or an annual subscription of 12 issues for a dollar) and featured revelations of business and government immorality. Several of the magazines sold upwards of half a million copies a month and attracted advertising worth half a million dollars a year. Before World War I, *McClure's Magazine, Cosmopolitan Magazine, Munsey's Magazine, The American Magazine,* and *Ladies' Home Journal* brought a disturbing view of reality into thousands of middle-class homes.

The writers for the mass-circulation magazines showed a special talent for finding and describing the seamy side of American life. They seemed so preoccupied with problems and evil that President Theodore Roosevelt upbraided them. In a speech that made headlines across the country, the President compared them to the character in John Bunyon's *Pilgrim's Progress* "who could look no way but downward with the muckrake in his hand, who was offered a celestial crown for his muckrake but who would neither look up nor regard the crown he was offered, but continued to rake to himself the filth of the floor." The name "muckraker" stuck.

Muckrakers worked many fields. Ida Tarbell laid out the secrets of John D. Rockefeller's industrial empire in her "History of Standard Oil Company," a study *McClure's* ran in 18 installments. *McClure's* writer Lincoln Steffens specialized in exposing municipal graft, while his colleague, Ray Stannard Baker, stripped away the aura of nobility of purpose surrounding labor unions and later exposed Jim Crow. Other writers, intent on rousing feelings of indignant shame at the state of affairs, detailed the crimes of life-insurance companies; sounded the alarm about manipulations made possible by the spectacular concentration of money in New York; revealed the secret ingredients that "toadstool millionaires" used in their cure-all tonics, salves, and pills (usually alcohol, opium, or digitalis); and documented the presence of poisonous and disease-bearing filth (rats, excreta, tubercular animals) in processed food and medicine. David Graham Phillips launched a series in *Cosmopolitan,* titled "The Treason of the Senate," in which he showed that Senator Chauncey Depew of New York received director's fees from more than 70 companies, and that 18 other senators mentioned by name had corporate allegiances and entanglements. If one accepted the view that the corporate giants had become an enemy of the people, senators with corporate links were guilty of treason, according to Article III, Section 3 of the Constitution, for giving them "aid and comfort."

Some muckrakers examined the effects of giant industry upon the lower classes and bewailed the injustice. They wrote heartbreaking stories about "workin' kids" and "fallen women," about saloons and dives, about hideous housing and sanitary conditions, about racial animosity, about churches that abandoned the poor, and politicians who leeched off them. The emphasis was on the conditions that brought on the plight. Significantly, muckrakers' pleas for abolition of child labor, special protection of working women, prohibition of liquor, introduction of housing codes, and other "progressive" reforms to benefit the bottom of the social strata, were aimed at the middle class who were then to take action in behalf of their poorer countrymen. Like the middle class from which they came, muckrakers never fully trusted the under classes and rarely advocated sharing power with them.

More importantly, the muckraking journalists gave a troubled generation in search of explanations and solutions a blunt description of the reality of life in America. None of the standard textbooks in law, political science, ethics, economics, or history gave a clue to the existence of bribes, rebates, bought franchises, or the desperate struggle to survive in the slums. *Reality* was the journalists' "inside story." Through exposé and dramatic revelation, they served as "consciousness raising" leaders. They contributed to a sense of community simply by focusing national attention on local realities. Readers of Lincoln Steffens' articles understood that the shenanigans of streetcar promoters in St. Louis were little or no different from those in Pittsburgh, the Bronx, Kansas City, or Evansville, The writers sustained and encouraged many middle-class people who had the will and collective power to force change and convinced others, who had neither the will nor the power, that the reformers were doing needed work.

Historians have inclined to describe the variety of people who worked through government to create a world more to their liking under the collective label "Progressives." The term is imprecise and, if it suggests great cohesion, misleading because the causes for which various individuals fought were so diverse and the common denominators so few. The zealot for public regulation of the corporate giants might stand squarely opposed to women's suffrage or public-housing codes. Motives ranged from outrage at the deterioration of Christian decency to desires to impose upon more of American life and its institutions the efficiency born of technology and business cunning.

"Progressivism," then, had many faces. But two stand out. One, appearing with varying intensity now here and now there, was a local or popular manifestation of a fear of overwhelming corporate economic power. In a normally placid town like Fredonia, it surfaced briefly in a show of local support for the striking workers of the nearby cement plant, then quickly subsided. In other places, as in some Wisconsin communities, tension and conflict remained at the surface and issues were sharply defined. Among the larger cities, Toledo's Mayor, "Golden Rule" Jones, successfully but temporarily massed public support against the utilities and other special interests. But in most communities, popular clamor was conspicuously absent. Reformers in those places frequently tinkered with the structure of local government and, as in Pittsburgh, made government less representative of the whole public than it had been.

Perhaps Pittsburgh's reformers better reflect the second face of "Progressivism," which is distinguished from the first not by the arena in which it operated, but by the interests that it served. Those interests did not include the likes of Simich or even Bassano but did include America's middle and upper classes. Most leaders derived from those classes, accepted capitalism as a given, rarely toyed with alternative systems, and believed that the best prospects for the future lay not in scrapping the American way but in fixing it. Fixing it . . . but not so much that wealth and power were redistributed.

No one can say just why so many comfortable people decided at about the same time to invest part of their energies in reform. The decisions were personal. However, intellectual as well as physical developments in the first decade of the 20th century were conducive to a new activism. For some "Progressive" leaders, the repudiation of Social Darwinism removed a block to action. Social Darwinism held that meddling with social institutions deflected the evolutionary upward spiral of progress. The best of the "Progressive" leaders—Robert M. LaFollette, Jones, Senator George Norris, and Iowa Governor and Senator Albert Cummins—were not prone to intellectualizing. They were prag-

matic men guided by common sense and experience who felt that the environment was changing and could be further changed for the better by Americans. Another stream of thought, represented by Walter Rauschenbusch, a Baptist teacher at the Rochester Theological Seminary, offered devine blessing for social activism. The teachings of the Bible demanded social justice. The great question of the 20th century, Rauschenbusch wrote, was "not a matter of getting individuals to heaven, but of transforming the life on earth into the harmony of heaven."

PROGRESSIVE REFORM IN THE CITIES

City governments had been an American disgrace long before 1900. The respected English observer James Bryce had called them "the one conspicuous failure of the United States," and to Andrew D. White, President of Cornell, they were "the worst in Christendom—the most expensive, the most inefficient, and the most corrupt." The longtime inclination of indignant reformers was to expose the sins of the spoilsmen and unite to "throw the rascals out." They did in scores of cities, but the problem was in instituting changes that would prevent the rascals from coming back. City charters were granted by state governments, and state governments had to approve any subsequent changes, a difficult setup for reformers. But local pressures and the urging of the National Municipal League prompted 12 states by World War I to allow local changes without state approval.

Galveston, Texas, offered one model that appealed to reformers, the commission plan. When a tidal wave drowned one sixth of the coastal city's population and laid waste one third of its buildings, the city turned to five nonpartisan elected commissioners to run the city. They could hire and fire without regard

Galveston Texas, c. 1912, making the transition to urban center

to political allegiance, and each commissioner was responsible to the whole city.

A flood in 1913 in Dayton, Ohio, brought another model to national attention, the city manager plan. When the rescue and shelter efforts of city officials collapsed in the first hours of crisis, the managers of Dayton factories stepped in and performed the job with awesome efficiency. When the waters went down, the city set up a government, modeled on the business organization that provided the citizens their livelihood, and saved them from the flood. The city-manager plan used the corporation as a model. The stockholders, in this case the citizens, elected a board of directors—five city commissioners. The commissioners hired a manager, an expert on the details of municipal affairs. The manager was hired on the open market and had no connec-

tion with Dayton. The manager then had the corporation president's authority to run the city, hire the department heads, and demand results. The voters and commissioners held him directly responsible. The innovations of commission and commission-manager governments usually brought increased efficiency in the operation of city departments. The bookkeeping procedures were set straight; the garbage was collected regularly; police punched in and out on time clocks; and oats for the garbage-wagon horses were purchased on bids. The innovations also brought less city government responsiveness to the working class, the very people who needed expanded services the most.

In the old system, city government was usually a confederation of wards, each represented by a councilman in the city legislature. The councilmen concerned themselves with the needs of their small constituencies, which ranged from streets and sewers to defense of the community's cultural or language differences, and even the right of wards to maintain their own elementary school boards. A councilman's visions and allegiances were narrow, rarely focusing on citywide problems. Since lower classes were most numerous in the cities, the holders of city offices were often petty entrepreneurs who had risen out of the ranks of their constituents (saloon keepers, grocers, livery-stable operators, druggists), white-collar workers (bookkeepers), and skilled and unskilled workers. All too frequently, a superstructure of boodling, manipulating politicians overlaid this representative system. The focus of moralist reformers was on the superstructure. As they achieved power and altered the structure of city government to suit their class interests, they diminished participatory democracy.

The "businessman" managers of the reformed system had no less a constituency than the ward-based machines. They found kindred spirits among the business community and middle class, and, quite naturally, they put their best efforts where their hearts were. Low-income sections of town found it more difficult to get city water and sewer lines, to obtain paved streets, and to gain a sympathetic hearing for other neighborhood problems. The emphasis of "business" government on the special interests of the industrial and commercial sector was strengthened by its ties with affluent and by the at-large system of representation.

In 1907 and 1908, Pittsburgh was the setting for the most comprehensive social survey of an American community ever undertaken. The survey director, Paul U. Kellogg, emphasized that Pittsburgh was selected, not because of its uniqueness, but because it was so typically, so "rampantly" American. Subsequent surveys and contemporary studies of other American communities, in addition to the more recent studies of Pittsburgh, support the conclusion that the second face of "Progressivism," class conscious and elitist, was far more in evidence than the first, more populistic, face.

In Pittsburgh, the names of 65 percent of the members of the two organizations most active in the cause of municipal reform appeared in upper-class directories which listed only 2 percent of the city's families. Some 52 percent of them were bankers and corporation officials or their wives. The membership list approached a *Who's Who* of 14 large banks, Westinghouse Electric, U.S. Steel, Pittsburgh Plate Glass, Jones and Laughlin Steel, J. H. Heinz, Pittsburgh Coal Company, the Pennsylvania Railroad, and lesser companies. It was not that the plutocrats of Pittsburgh were incensed at the corruption of the local government or even that they wished to institute businesslike efficiency. It was, rather, that the old system no longer met their needs, no longer seemed capable of response to their own expanded sense of civic responsibility.

Industrialists and bankers, managers, engineers, sales chiefs, and all their lackeys, were believers in rationalizing and systematizing modern life. City governments composed of squabbling, narrow-visioned, and unenlightened ward politicians could never rise to an overview of the totality of urban life and its problems, and could never implement solutions consistent with broad, citywide needs. The bulk of Pittsburgh's reformers, by 1910, had wider visions than were prevalent during the 19th century. Their plants were in town and they lived in the suburbs. Their cultural institutions (like symphonies and museums) required citywide interest, and their desire to improve the environment and make the city more comfortable involved them in matters of health, education, and planning that transcended ward boundaries. They demanded a city government with perspectives similar to their own. They believed the ward system blocked the realization of their ideas of orderly, more rewarding urban life.

Urban reformers often spoke of "more democracy" and included provisions in new charters for party primary elections, the initiative, referendum, and recall. The latter three innovations involved so much effort and time that citizens rarely used them. The primary did eliminate the crudest practices of old-fashioned bosses and political kingmakers. It did not, however, ensure more democracy, if democracy is defined as equitable representation of all levels of the social strata. When Pittsburgh received its new charter in 1911, the representatives from each of the wards (a council of 27) were replaced by a council of 9, each elected by the city as a whole. In effect, this eliminated the local saloon keeper or druggist while selecting candidates acceptable to the elite. Upper-class money bought convincing publicity in every ward while high status had an appeal of its own to many poorer aspirants to social mobility.

Many of the changes that occurred at local and state levels during the "Progressive Era" were analogous to the changes in city governments. They resulted from problems left in the wake of an industrial-financial system hellbent for maximum profits, security, and growth. They were inspired by a clouded mix of middle-class indignation at the world they had lost and upper-class aspirations for a world they wanted—with a tinge of agitation from a working class against the world they felt oppressed them. They brought structural changes that left the pressing social problems of the day unresolved.

Many Americans believed that a cure could be achieved by the adoption of more democratic devices. However, they overlooked or chose to ignore the possibility that rigid class consciouness, racial intolerance, and an imbalanced distribution of wealth and power would still exclude masses of people from full participation in the system. Ballot-box democracy did not get at the roots of the problem. Still, by World War I, 22 states had adopted the democratic devices of the initiative and referendum. Every state had primary elections for at least some offices. The constitutional requirement that each state legislature elect the state's U.S. senators had been subverted by schemes for legislative rubber stamping of statewide senatorial elections in 29 states by 1912, the year Congress submitted the 17th amendment (for popular election of senators) to the states. By 1915, the men in 11 states (all western) voted for women's suffrage, and more than half a dozen others permitted women to vote in school-board elections. The model of reform came from Wisconsin. Robert M. LaFollette, governor from 1900 to 1906, fostered laws to give the state railroad commission effective power to regulate, to adopt the direct primary, and to tax corporations and personal incomes. These and other Wisconsin measures designed to purify state government, became known as "the Wisconsin idea."

The amount and quality of welfare legislation varied from state to state, depending upon the local mix of "modern" businessmen, the organizational skills of the moralists, and the activism of workers. Child labor enraged so many Americans that every state passed laws dictating the minimum age for labor—usually 12 years old, but as high as 16 in some states. Most states, after a Supreme Court opinion in 1908, passed laws to "protect" working women by limiting the hours they could work. Nearly half the states voted subsistence pensions to women with dependent children. City building codes and sanitation standards generally stiffened, benefiting some urban dwellers. Much of the legislation in behalf of the poor, as well as the attitudes of people who urged it and administered it, had a paternalistic, lady-bountiful quality. Moreover, the responsible officials rarely enforced this new legislation with enthusiasm.

Americans dealt first and most directly at the local level with the changes and problems brought by technology and industrial-financial consolidations. Collectively, budgets of state and local governments were more than twice that of the federal government. Moreover, there was a tradition of distrust of centralized government power and an emphasis on local authority. Nonetheless, the changes and the implications of new developments so permeated national life and were so far beyond the powers of local or state governments to resolve that many came to advocate vigorous involvement by the federal government. Between the turn of the century and the entry of the United States into World War I, the federal government used the commerce clause and general welfare clause of the Constitution to expand its regulatory powers. At the same time, the office of president drastically changed. Most 19th century presidents had been content to enforce the laws made by Congress, as the Constitution required. Theodore Roosevelt (1901–09), William Howard Taft (1909–13), and Woodrow Wilson (1913–21) transformed the presidency into a policy *making* branch and by their activism made the federal government's presence more real in individual lives.

NATIONAL POLITICS

For the families portrayed in this book, with the possible exception of the Butlers, national politics at the turn of the century was in the same category as spectator sports. The excited banter around the stove in the Howell poolroom or at the curb in front of the Bassanos' tenement could as well have been prompted by a horse race as a national election, except that words like "corruption," "favoritism," "neglect," and "erosion of the national character" occasionally rose above the din. Certainly no one felt his personal commitment or conviction made any real difference. And for all the talk about the "right" to participate, a low percentage determined the results. Of course, only the women of Wyoming, Colorado, Utah, and Idaho—less than 175,000 out of a national female population of about 38 million—had the right to vote in presidential elections. Nearly all black males in the South were disfranchised or intimidated so they would not vote. The people of America's colonies (Philippines, Puerto Rico, Guam, and Samoa) had no franchise. Of over 21 million males of voting age, some 14 million actually went to the polls in 1900 to choose between William McKinley and William Jennings Bryan—a very high proportion by 20th century standards. The ballots of slightly more than 7 million men made William McKinley president of 84 million people under the American flag.

Although politics never seemed very personal, and it was easy to become cynical about the hallowed principle of majority rule, anxiety born of the evolving complexity of life made Americans long for a leader who could cope and inspire them. William McKinley, representative of the genteel manners and political permissiveness of the 19th century, was no such man. His vice president, Theodore Roosevelt, was. And after the Polish immigrant Leon Czolgosz moved through a presidential receiving line at the Pan American Exposition in Buffalo, New York and shot McKinley point blank in the pancreas with a .32 caliber revolver, Theodore Roosevelt became president. TR was far from the "average" man. His family was "old wealth"—Dutchmen of commerce and large estates who came to the United States in 1644. They took a patriarchal interest in politics, lived in town houses and on estates, educated their children through tutors and private schools, and inevitably sent the males to Harvard.

TR set tough goals for himself, perhaps as

psychological compensation for feelings of inadequacy born of his frailty and poor eyesight as a child. At age 23, he wandered into the Republican headquarters in New York City and signed on. "I intended to be a member of the governing class," he explained bluntly, and he saw in the Republican party the means to his end. He won a seat in the state legislature in 1881 and created an immediate commotion by seeking to impeach a state judge. The issue centered on the judge's conspiracy with "malefactors of great wealth" to bilk the public in a railroad scheme. Thus began TR's rise to national prominence. The route was through a stint of ranching in the Dakotas, and the offices of Civil Service Commissioner, Police Commissioner of New York City, and Assistant Secretary of the Navy. Roosevelt's habit of pushing himself to bold action became his hallmark. He believed his own character had been hardened in the fires of struggle, and he projected that principle to the nation. He admonished Americans that they had become softly civilized when the only true course was to retain "pioneer virtues." Bringing back virtue was the task of the Republican party.

In 1898, the war with Spain made him a national hero as leader of the Rough Riders. TR rode down the hills of Cuba and into the governor's mansion in Albany, New York. Theodore Roosevelt's future might have been very different had he not pushed the old-guard leaders of his party. Picqued that the popular governor had unpredictably proposed a tax on corporation franchises, the state bosses decided to "reward" him by nominating him for vice president at the party convention in 1900. One out-of-state party boss, powerless to stop the nomination of the popular hero, complained that only one life stood between America's highest office and "that damned cowboy."

TR perceived that bigness was not an undesirable characteristic of a business or a union if it followed a course that did not harm the community. When business acted contrary to the public interest, government should intervene. Thus, for TR, government was both the partner and policeman of business. The crucial questions for the elite interested in such matters were what specific actions "harmed" the community; what, after all, was the national interest; and precisely how should government go about the business of intervention without exceeding the limitations placed upon it by the Constitution and without stunting the growth and dulling the innovative spirit of the financial-industrial community?

Theodore Roosevelt turned out to be less assertive than his actions made him seem at the time. He seemed so confident and blunt, so clear about what was right and wrong. During the term he inherited from McKinley, TR gave the impression that he was about the business of effectively "policing" the business beat and doing it without acrimonious disputes with his conservative brethren in Congress. By focusing on "regulating the trusts," he had picked the one issue that most reformers could rally around. By selecting blatant cases, he obscured and postponed resolution of more subtle issues.

In 1902, Roosevelt instructed the Department of Justice to file suit against the Northern Securities Company, a mammoth formed in 1901 that combined the Great Northern Railroad properties of J. P. Morgan and James J. Hill with Edward H. Harriman's Union Pacific. Northern Securities controlled virtually all of the transportation in the western half of the nation. The Supreme Court found Northern Securities guilty of restraint of trade and ordered its dissolution. As a result of the case, there was no immediate free competition among carriers where lines were close, and no end to discriminatory rates against the short-haul shipper or those in the mountains and prairies where one line offered the only possible route for freight. Actual control of the railroads remained in the hands of the Morgan-Hill combination. But the decision was widely applauded for it appeared that "the malefactors of greath wealth," so long convicted in the minds of moralists of foul play and flaunting the law, at long last had been brought to rein by the national government.

In the second newsmaking event, TR leaped into a labor dispute between anthracite coal-mine owners (some 70 percent of which were railroad companies) and 50,000 United Mine Workers. The miners, having received only a 10 percent raise since 1880, needed more money. They worked unreasonably long hours in dangerous conditions and had to pay for various types of equipment (including explosives). Management could not understand why anyone who did not own the mines should be given any say whatsoever in the way the mines were run—and that included in establishing wage rates. As the winter of 1902 approached, with homes, factories, and transportation systems dependent upon coal for over 90 percent of their fuel, the miners struck and the nation faced an emergency.

Roosevelt called leaders of labor and management to the White House (an unprecedented step) and proposed a scheme for arbitration. When the owners balked, the president announced that a winter without hard coal would endanger the national welfare, and he let it be known that the government might sequester the mines if the owners persisted in their arrogance. After some maneuvering to save face, the strike issues went to an arbitration board, which, in due course, awarded a 10 percent pay increase and a shorter working day (but denied union recognition)—and the miners went back to work.

Roosevelt's action in Northern Securities and the 1902 coal strike made him seem a champion of national interest in what was

Theodore Roosevelt speaking to college students in Evanston, Illinois, 1903

evidently a jungle struggle between national interest and private corporate gain. If the Traces, Williamses, Gales, and Bassanos did not think in terms of such principles, they understood that the federal government was responsible for ensuring there was enough coal to heat the parlor and boil the coffee.

The tough questions for Theodore Roosevelt and his contemporaries remained. Precisely what were the obligations of business enterprise to workers, to consumers, to the government? What were the "proper" relationships of workers, consumers, and government to business? If business defaulted in its obligations (once they were defined) what, exactly, should be done, by whom, and by what right? TR postured confidently. In truth, neither he nor the majority of reformers clearly perceived the answers.

Theodore Roosevelt, on one side, tried to "bust" the corporations that most conspicuously controlled their markets. This meant government regulation and oversight. Roosevelt's trustbusting was much more spectacular than it was effective. The mood of the courts upon which the outcome of the cases depended was cautious and the laws under which Roosevelt's attorney general prosecuted were vague in the extreme. Certainly TR did not want to regulate corporate life. Such an undertaking would have required him to define "national interest" and then to make specific proposals to protect and further it. He knew full well the Congress and the people they represented would never be able to work out and agree upon a usable definition of national interest.

TR had a conception of the national interest that included a conventional view of public morality, an unconventional view of America's role in the world (see Chapter 4), and an acceptance of the prevailing class and caste systems that defined personal worth, set limits on mobility, and diluted the effects of democratic government. Powerful national corporations fit well into his world view but mass democracy did not. Corporations must not step out of line, must use power with some restraint, as gentlemen use power, but otherwise must not weaken American growth and expansion. Stanko Simich had a much different, a simpler, view of America. He acted out his belief that the people should rule the interests.

The course of reform was never straight. The author Upton Sinclair liked to take credit for the Meat Inspection Act (1906). Sinclair intended his novel (The Jungle), about the miserable life of workers in the Chicago stockyards, to sensitize his readers to the evils of capitalism and inspire sympathy for socialism. The main character slogged all day through blood, guts, and excrement, some of which slopped onto consumer-bound meats.

He saw flesh of diseased animals treated with chemicals, and saw rats and a workman fall into the lard vats—only to be processed with the hot fat. The Jungle became an immediate best-seller and it produced an outcry for federal meat inspection laws. Senator Albert Beveridge took up leadership of the cause and the Congress shortly agreed on an inspection law. Sinclair exclaimed: "I aimed for the public's heart, and by accident I hit it in the stomach."

The reform was a dubious victory for the champions of hygienically processed meat. The meat packers wanted change. What with federal price fixing and antitrust suits against Armour and Swift (the industry leaders), and the revelations of Sinclair, other journalistic muckrakers, and a team of federal investigators, the packers were anxious to change their villainous image. Moreover, the uproar threatened their European trade. The packers wanted sufficient regulation to quiet the customers, but no more. Lobbyists for the packers saw to it that specific procedural changes in the slaughterhouses were minimized. They also ensured that inspectors were paid by the federal government. Under this arrangement, the thoroughness of the inspections was directly dependent upon the amount of federal government funding. A stingy congressional appropriation would mean fewer inspectors to oversee the operation. In any case, only meat that moved in interstate commerce was inspected. Packers also blocked the proposal to date canned meat. The result? The packers had what they wanted—an improved image. Consumers had more assurance that they were not being poisoned. But the people championed by Upton Sinclair, the workers, were not greatly affected. It was still possible for bits of an overshoe to turn up in the breakfast sausage.

The Pure Food and Drug Act (1906) was the same kind of mixed blessing. Progressive moralists in women's clubs, state food de-

Armour & Company, beef-knocking pens, Chicago

partments, and the young American Medical Association deluged Congress with information on adulterated foods and ineffective packaged medicines that claimed to cure everything from snake bite to syphilis. The law to remedy this went through Congress on the heels of the Meat Inspection Act and brought similarly mild standards and penalties. The maximum fine was $300 and, for more than 25 years, the average fine was about one fifth of that.

Even TR's strong exertions in behalf of resource conservation were not a simple decision to preserve the nation's inheritance.

Roosevelt had championed the Newlands Act (1902), which set aside some of the federal receipts from western land sales for dams and reclamation. He closed more than 17 million acres of government land to developers who wanted to exploit its coal, oil, timber, and mineral resources. The president had also proceeded vigorously against stockmen who were ruining national grazing land by running too many animals on it. Fear that something irreplaceable would be lost was part of it, to be sure; but the agitations of a new breed of government bureaucrat—advocates of scientific management and anxious for their own

Theodore Roosevelt and one of his victims, a bull rhino, claimed while on safari in Africa

empires—were part of it, too. And so was the support of a few large corporations already involved in resource extraction who expected to have some influence with government conservationists and who understood that observation of conservation codes would mean higher initial costs for potential competitors and tend to discourage them.

TR talked endlessly about what was *right* with his country and refused to see the power of concentrated corporate capital as more than a surface blemish. While in office, his interventions were cautious, though accompanied by great ballyhoo. His rhetoric seemed straightforward and proud and tough to people burdened with hucksters, promoters, and silver-tongued confidence men. Above all else, TR was "decent" as the Butler family understood that word. George Butler conceded that the president's hyperactivity made him a little odd by the standards of demeanor accepted by Boston's best people, but he clearly had their interests at heart.

TR saw to it that William Howard Taft, his Secretary of War, inherited his mantle in the Republican party and that he was elected president in 1908. Taft, however, could not and would not generate the aura of activism in the name of decency that TR expected. Taft was impeccably honest and well intentioned. He could be affable, and his 300-pound body offered new material for joksters. He believed in change and initiated more antitrust suits against the industrial giants than had TR. Taft lost ground because his soul mates were conservatives; most reformers impressed him as impetuous, and they made him nervous.

Taft was not a man for the times. Deep down he distrusted the masses and feared reform. Thus, he opposed primary elections and the right of the electorate to recall officials. When reformers protested loudly against the Payne-Aldrich tariff of 1909, a muddled law in which rates seemed to change according to the effectiveness of lobbyists and the power of some legislators to protect local industries, Taft defended it as "the best tariff bill that the Republican party ever passed."

These complex machinations and the rhetoric swirled above the heads of most Americans and had no real meaning in their lives. William and Millie Trace did not understand the tariff at all. Management of the steel and coal industries tried to convince Mihailo Markovich and Stanko Simich that a higher tax on foreign-made structural steel would deter potential customers from purchasing it and ensure continuation of their wages and full-time jobs. Other people argued that, since American mills already undersold imported steel, the new tariff would simply allow the owners to raise their prices. Any effort to convince Rose Bassano that the Republican tariff would lower the price of shoes for her children fell on deaf ears. Only George Butler's adrenalin flowed with mention of the tariff. A good part of the family wealth came from the sale of lumber and pulp wood to feed the insatiable appetite of the East Coast for paper. The $6.10 tariff levied on every ton of Canadian wood gave Stetson, Butler and Company just that much advantage. All of George Butler's sons understood that their social clubs, the servants, travel, their whole lifestyle benefited from "good Republican protectionism."

To the accusation that the desire of American industrialists for profits had received precedence over "the rights of the ultimate consumer" (meaning the choice of buying the best product for the money in a truly competitive marketplace), the president snapped: "If the country desires free trade, and wishes the manufacturers all over the country to go out of business, and to have cheaper prices at the expense of the sacrifice of many of our manufacturing interests, then it ought to say so and put the Democratic party in power."

Taft lost "Progressive" sympathy almost completely when he fired Gifford Pinchot, the conservation-oriented Chief Forester appointed by TR, and failed to join the reform element in an attempt to unseat the old guard Speaker of the House of Representatives, Joseph G. Cannon. Taft had good reasons for his positions, but he handled the situations badly, and left his opponents with the impression that his true disposition was reactionary.

Insurgent Republicans flocked to TR to protest Taft's failures and to plead that the former president run for president again in 1912. Roosevelt merely needed to be asked, because, despite all his attempts to sympathize with his old friend's problems, TR could not forgive the president for a lengthening list of small actions that seemed to repudiate the precedents of 1901–09. Roosevelt entered the primary races in states that had them. Taft countered by putting his supporters in tight control of the committees of the Republican National Convention. This strategy assured the quick nomination of Taft as the Republican candidate. Roosevelt's supporters walked out, reconvened a few weeks later with a motley assortment of allies, and formed the Progressive Party with TR as its candidate.

Roosevelt had to be a little uncomfortable. He had always been a careful and cautious reformer, ever mindful of the virtues of hard work, individual initiative, competition, and private enterprise. Now, zealots and dreamers joined estranged Republicans. Together these assorted malcontents wrote a party platform that listed the specific, unfinished business of bringing order and justice to industrial America. If elected, Progressives would work for: direct primaries, initiative, referendum, and recall; women's suffrage; recording and publication of all congressional votes; prohibition of court injunctions against labor unions; laws to increase safety; and unemployment and old-age insurance. The platform vaguely proposed an end to trustbusting and proposed "a strong Federal commission of high standing, which shall maintain permanent and active supervision over industrial corporations."

While the issue of reform—how much and what kind—produced an organizational hemorrhage in the Republican Party, the Democratic party struggled with the same kind of internal disorder. Delegates to the nominating convention in Baltimore sweated out 46 indecisive ballots before Woodrow Wilson, Governor of New Jersey and former President of Princeton University, finally won. Of all the Democratic aspirants, Wilson had the best chance of stealing some of TR's thunder and winning public confidence as the guardian of national morality. The reform faction that won control and nominated Wilson provided a platform incorporating modest promises for change.

Wilson tried to articulate an alternative to TR's scheme for reforms. Yet there was little substantive difference between TR's "New Nationalism" and Wilson's "New Freedom." Roosevelt recognized that "the concentration of modern business, in some degree, is both inevitable and necessary for national and international business efficiency." Wilson paraphrased him: "I dare say we shall never return to the old order of individual competition, and that the organization of business upon a great scale of cooperation is, up to a point, itself normal and inevitable." TR cautioned that "there should be no penalizing of business merely because of its size." If a corporation grew by "the legitimate processes of business, by economy, by efficiency," said Wilson, "I am not afraid of it, no matter how big it grows." TR hammered at the need to recognize the reality of corporate combination and to regulate it. Wilson talked about preserving and regulating competition. The difference was mostly in the words, as someone called to Wilson's attention. Wilson responded bluntly that "when I sit down and compare my views with those of a Progressive Republican, I can't see what the difference is,

THE "OPEN ROAD"

"I suppose you know the force that is behind the new party that has recently been formed—the so-called Progressive party. It is a force of discontent with the regular parties of the United States.   It is the feeling that men have gone into blind alleys and come out often enough, and that they propose to find an open road for themselves."—WOODROW WILSON

From the *Journal* (Boston)

A romantic cartoon about the Progressive Party seen by the Butlers and Gus O'Reilly in the *Boston Journal*

except that he has a sort of pious feeling about the doctrine of protection which I have never felt."

So far as national politics interested Americans in 1912, the excitement pretty much ended with the conventions. In the Butler house, the high point was the nomination of

Taft—decent and not at all odd. TR's separate candidacy, splitting the Republican Party and giving the edge to Wilson, seemed such a shame. Charles Gale and Jacob Reinhardt, mildly disconcerted at the Republic split, had nothing against Wilson save his party affiliation. Although Socialist candidate Eugene V.

Debs promised workers a new day, and Mihailo Markovich, Stanko Simich, and Andrew Bassano much admired him, they vacillated between Roosevelt and Wilson. Woodrow Wilson, it turned out, was a master of platitudes and evasion, endorsing both states' rights and additional federal powers. More attention getting than anything new anyone said was the incident in Milwaukee when someone shot at TR during a speech and grazed his chest. Characteristically, the former president finished speaking, poking the air with his bloody handkerchief in cadence.

If many Americans believed with Roosevelt that they were at Armageddon or with Taft that the direct government proposed by Wilson and TR threatened national stability, others obviously did not believe they could do much about it at the polling places. On election day, fewer than 14 million of the approximately 24 million native-born or naturalized males over 21 who could have registered and voted took the trouble. Eugene Debs, the Socialist party candidate, won 6 percent, Taft won 23 percent, TR 27 percent, and Wilson 42 percent of the vote. Thomas Woodrow Wilson, undoubtedly a loser had it not been for the Republican split, had more support than his 6 million popular votes indicated. Since both he and Roosevelt appealed to the reform-conscious public, the 69 percent of the vote they polled together could be interpreted as a mandate for action.

The new president, born in Virginia, was the son of a Presbyterian minister. He had trod the path of academe for 24 years, teaching at Bryn Mawr and, in 1890, joining the staff of Princeton. Wilson's first big break came in 1902 when he was named President of Princeton. Eight years later, he became Governor of New Jersey.

Wilson's distinguishing characteristic was his commitment to "moral" conduct. He could always be counted upon to insist, "I must do what is right!" He packed too much Calvinistic baggage, bestowed upon him by his father: God had a plan for the universe and He used men to make it work. God's men knew good and bad, right and wrong when they saw it and knew what to do. Wilson *knew* he was God's man. And still, in coping with day-to-day problems, he lacked self-confidence. When strongly opposed, his inclination was to quit, and he fell perilously near the clutches of the "blue devils" of abject depression. His strong sense of religiously inspired mission seemed to compensate for his low self-esteem.

Wilson started his stewardship with the conviction that the modern world was plagued by special privilege and artificial advantages that smothered the competitive spirit. His pledge was that, "Every man who wants an opportunity and has the energy to seize it is going to have a chance." High tariffs constituted an artificial advantage for American manufacturers in the marketplace; therefore, Wilson called for reduction. The concentration of money in Wall Street enabled a few men to manipulate the national economy; therefore, Wilson proposed a law to give the government more control. Big business had devised "impediments" to competition and "illegitimate" kinds of control over the market; therefore, Wilson asked for legislation that would enumerate the sins and dictate the retribution.

A burst of presidential energy, the support of rural people whose interest dictated the most competition possible among consumer products, and the passionate arguments of mobilized Progressives that the tariff was "the mother of trusts" forced early congressional action on the first element of Wilson's three-point program. When the Underwood-Simmons tariff (1913) came to Wilson's desk for his signature, he delighted that he had brought about the first substantial tariff reduction since the Civil War. And among the witnesses of the happy moment were those who rejoiced at an amendment that created the present-day graduated income tax. These achievements inevitably fell short of the marks set by purists. The Underwood tariff modestly reduced the average duty on imported products. The prices of foreign products would be closer to those produced domestically, but home industry still had a large advantage. Congress tacked on the income-tax plan to make up for the money the government would lose by lowering the tariff. Neither the tariff losses nor the income-tax proceeds amounted to very much. Business continued about an usual.

Wilson's proposal for banking reform emerged in law as the Federal Reserve Act. Essentially, the struggle developed into a fight among bankers. Eastern and Wall Street banking interests wanted a centralized banking system that would run through the board of directors. Southern and Western banking interests, anxious to increase the amount of money in their areas and decrease their dependency upon expensive eastern money, wanted a decentralized system run by a board of presidentially appointed directors. Wilson yielded to the Southern and Western wings of his party. Those desiring a publicly owned and controlled system opposed Wilson's bill, as did conservatives.

The Federal Reserve Act gave something to everyone. A Federal Reserve Board in Washington, appointed by the president, made general policy. In theory, it orchestrated the economy by loosening and tightening credit. New Federal Reserve Banks in 12 Federal Reserve Districts offered the desired services to local banks and exercised limited autonomy in setting credit policy. The existence of 12 districts also ensured the participation of financiers outside of New York. The results of reform were hardly dramatic. The connection between the Federal Reserve Board decisions and the tempo of the economy was obscure. Moreover, New York

bankers quickly came to dominate both the board in Washington and the operation of the system.

Woodrow Wilson asked Congress for legislation to deal with corporate bigness. If the representatives of the people could articulate the rights of the players and the rules of the competitive game, they could identify the infractions, anticipate the subtle infringements, and enumerate commensurate penalties. The Clayton Antitrust Bill was an attempt at Wilson's request. Amendments and inability to agree on all but the most innocuous portions demonstrated the futility of the effort. Some union leaders did call the Clayton Act "Labor's Magna Carta" because it limited restraining orders and injunctions against labor to cases where irreparable damage to property was involved and because it excluded unions from the scope of antitrust laws on grounds that "the labor of a human being is not a commodity or an article of commerce." Otherwise, the bill prohibited price discriminations and interlocking directorates which diminished fair trade or created monopoly.

With the failure of Congress to provide an adequate regulatory law, Wilson turned to a device that had been evolving since the turn of the century, the regulatory commission. In the form of the Federal Trade Commission, this innovation fulfilled the need for change, but it left the most difficult question unresolved. By using the device of the regulatory commission to cope with the problems posed by modern business, Congress could set forth general principles and provide for presidential appointment of "experts," who constituted the commissions, to apply those principles. The history of the nation's most famous regulatory agency, the Interstate Commerce Commission (in existence since 1887), illustrated both the advantages and risks.

At the time that Congress established the ICC, a loud segment of farmers and small shippers insisted that railroads leeched away their profits and destroyed their competitive position by charging discriminatory rates to move their produce. In their defense, railroads contended that different rates resulted from the cost differentials of transporting various commodities and that, considering their investment, rates were reasonable.

To avoid mastering the complexities of railroad rate making itself, Congress turned the problem over to a commission (the ICC) with power to invalidate discriminatory rates. Periodically, new laws strengthened the ICC. By 1913, the agency could set maximum rates and command statistics from railroads, which more clearly showed the relationships between rates, investment, and profits. The expert members of the ICC, however, came mostly from the managerial staffs of the railroads and they guarded railroad interests.

The Federal Trade Commission, formed to oversee business practices and trade standards, consisted of businessmen who never functioned consistently as a brake upon the desires of industrial captains. After World War II, the FTC had a reputation as one of those havens where old politicians were sent as a reward for faithful service—to wile away their last years in decorous inactivity.

The regulatory commission allowed Congress to incorporate the lowest common denominator into law and shunt to experts the problems that were too intricate for the representatives of the public. By doing so, they imposed a measure of order and predictability upon business life that America in an age of galloping disorder and change sorely wanted. The commissions gave the members of the business establishment and their major customers a forum to air their problems and an opportunity for direct contact with the men who would make decisions important to their livelihood. But as for the public interest under such an arrangement, historian Otis Graham succinctly wrote that there was no agreement on what had become of it or into whose hands it had been delivered.

Of the three Progressive Era presidents, Woodrow Wilson most clearly voiced his opinion that many current ideas simply were outside the bounds of possibility, if not of propriety. He told one group of petitioners: "It is plain that you would have to go much further than most interpretations of the Constitution would allow, if you were to give government control over child labor in the country." Wilson, like TR, did change while in the White House. After 1914, he accepted a great deal of special-interest legislation. He signed, for example, the Keating-Owens Act, which forbade the sale in interstate commerce of products made by children. He also signed a law that defined the working day of railroad

A classic depiction of child labor is Jacob Riis's photograph of a 12-year-old pulling threads in a sweatshop c. 1889

workers as eight hours, a law that established workmen's compensation, a farm loan act, and a federal highway law (mostly of benefit to farmers). Just why Wilson changed has mystified historians. Most seem to believe that he concluded he would lose the election in 1916 if he did not.

The federal government, in the years between 1900 and the First World War, preoccupied itself with perfecting "the system," and that meant mostly financial-industrial matters. Many reformers talked about social justice and the quality of American life. That so little came of it is testimony to their ideological restraints and the power of the opposition. However sympathetic an individual might be to the problems of the working people or the farmers, their environment, and their attempts to improve it, the greater commitment was to free enterprise.

SUGGESTIONS FOR FURTHER READING

The scholarly literature dealing with aspects of the Progressive Era is enormous and new studies of the how, who, what, and why of Progressivism continue to appear. Still an excellent starting point is the classic treatment of life in these years, Mark Sullivan's *Our Times* (6 vols., 1926–35). See also *The Good Years* by Walter Lord (1960); Gilbert Ostrander, *American Civilization in the First Machine Age, 1890–1940* (1970); Harold U. Faulkner, *The Quest for Social Justice, 1898–1914* (1931); George E. Mowry, *The Era of Theodore Roosevelt, 1900–1912* (1958); and Otis L. Graham, Jr., *The Great Campaigns: Reform and War in America, 1900–1928* (1971). More analytical works include Richard Hofstadter's *The Age of Reform: From Bryan to F.D.R.* (1955); Robert H. Wiebe's *The Search for Order* (1966); *The Triumph of Conservatism* by Gabriel Kolko (1967); Samuel P. Hays, *The Response to Industrialism, 1885–1914* (1957); and David Noble's *The Progressive Mind, 1870–1917* (1969).

Works that emphasize the organizational and broad economic dimension of Progressivism include Samuel P. Hays, *Conservation and the Gospel of Efficiency* (1959); Robert Wiebe, *Businessmen and Reform* (1962); and Jerry Israel, ed., *Building the Organizational Society* (1972). On the conservation issue, see Alpheus T. Mason's *Bureaucracy Convicts Itself: The Ballinger-Pinchot Controversy of 1910* (1941); and the more recent book by James Pennick, *Progressive Politics and Conservation: The Ballinger-Pinchot Affair* (1968). Case studies of the organizational component include: Gerald D. Nash, *State Government and Economic Development: A History of Administrative Policies in California, 1859–1933* (1964); Stanley P. Caine, *The Myth of a Progressive Reform: Railroad Regulation in Wisconsin, 1903–1910* (1970); and William Graebner, *Coal-Mining Safety in the Progressive Period: The Political Economy of Reform* (1976). Related works include Paul T. Ringenbach, *Tramps and Reformers, 1873–1916* (1973); John Tripple, *The Capitalist Revolution: A History of American Social Thought, 1890–1919* (1970); Stephen E. Ambrose, ed., *Institutions in Modern America;* Louis Filler, *The Muckrakers: Crusade for American Liberalism* (1961); and David M. Chalmers, *The Social and Political Ideas of the Muckrakers* (1964).

The most influential study of Progressivism at the state level, at least until the appearance of David Thelen's instant classic, *The New Citizenship: Origins of Progressivism in Wisconsin, 1885–1900* (1972), was *The California Progressives* (1951) by George E. Mowry. Also useful in the older tradition are Russell B. Nye, *Midwestern Progressive Politics* (1959); C. Vann Woodward's *Origins of the New South, 1877–1913* (1951); Hoyt Warner, *Progressivism in Ohio, 1897–1919* (1964); Sheldon Hackney, *Populism to Progressivism in Alabama* (1969); Richard Abrams, *Conservatism in a Progressive Era: Massachusetts Politics, 1900–1912* (1964); and Robert S. LaForte, *Leaders of Reform: Progressive Republicans in Kansas, 1900–1916* (1974). Studies reflecting the assumptions of the new political history include John D. Buenker, *Urban Liberalism and Progressive Reform* (1973); Lewis L. Gould, *Reform and Regulation: American Politics, 1900–1916* (1978).

Urban Progressivism is treated in numerous studies: Bruce M. Stave, ed., *Urban Bosses, Machines, and Progressive Reformers* (1972); John M. Allswang, *A House for All Peoples: Ethnic*

Politics in Chicago, 1890–1936 (1971); Zane L. Miller, *Boss Cox's Cincinnati: Urban Politics in the Progressive Era* (1968); Melvin G. Holli, *Reform in Detroit: Hazen S. Pingree and Urban Politics* (1969); Theodore F. Lowi, *At the Pleasure of the Mayor: Patronage and Power in New York City* (1964); Joel A. Tarr, *A Study in Boss Politics: William Lorimer of Chicago* (1971); and that fascinating account by a fighter for urban reform, Frederick C. Howe's *The Confessions of a Reformer* (1967). See also *Yankee Reformers in an Urban Age* (1954) by Arthur Mann; John G. Sproat, *The Best Men: Liberal Reformers in the Gilded Age* (1968); and Gerald W. McFarland, *Mugwumps, Morals and Politics, 1884–1920* (1975).

Interest groups and special issues are the subject of such works as Robert H. Bremner, *From the Depths: The Discovery of Poverty in the United States* (1956); Roy Lubove, *The Progressives and the Slums* (1962); Marc Karson, *American Labor Unions and Politics, 1900–1918* (1958); Irwin Yellowitz, *Labor and the Progressive Movement in New York State, 1898–1916* (1965); Allen F. Davis's very influential *Spearheads for Reform: The Social Settlements and the Progressive Movement, 1890–1914* (1967); Oscar E. Anderson, Jr., *The Health of a Nation: Harvey W. Wiley and the Fight for Pure Food* (1958); James Harvey Young, *The Toadstool Millionaires: A Social History of Patent Medicines in America before Federal Regulation* (1961); and David Musto, *The American Disease: Origins of Narcotic Control* (1973). For prohibition, see Joseph R. Gusfeld, *Symbolic Crusade: Status Politics and the American Temperance Movement* (1963); James Timberlake, *Prohibition and the Progressive Movement, 1900–1920* (1970); and Lewis Gould, *Progressives and Prohibitionists: Texas Democrats and the Wilson Era* (1973). Works on women in the Progressive Era include William L. O'Neill, *Everyone was Brave: The Rise and Fall of Feminism in America* (1969); Aileen Kraditor, *The Ideas of the Woman Suffrage Movement* (1965); June Sochen, *The New Woman: Feminism in Greenwich Village, 1910–1920* (1972); and the general study by Lois Banner, *Women in Modern America: A Brief History* (1974). William O'Neill, *Divorce in the Pro-*

gressive Era (1967); and David M. Kennedy, *Birth Control in America: The Career of Margaret Sanger* (1970) treat important issues.

The problem of race and the Progressive reform impulse is complex and not well understood. Helpful studies are C. Vann Woodward, *The Strange Career of Jim Crow* (1969, rev. ed.); Charles E. Wynes, *Race Relations in Virginia, 1870–1902* (1961); Gary B. Nash and Richard Weiss, eds., *The Great Fear: Race in the Mind of America* (1970); Jack T. Kirby, *Darkness at the Dawning: Race and Reform in the Progressive South* (1972); Allan H. Spear, *Black Chicago: The Making of a Negro Ghetto, 1890–1920* (1967); David M. Katzman, *Before the Ghetto: Black Detroit in the Nineteenth Century* (1971). Also useful are August Meier, *Negro Thought in America, 1880–1915* (1963); Robert L. Allen, *Reluctant Reformers: Racism and Social Reform Movements in the United States* (1974); Rayford W. Logan, *The Negro in American Life and Thought: The Nadir, 1877–1901* (1954); and Charles F. Kellogg's excellent *NAACP: A History of the National Association for the Advancement of Colored People* (1967). Essential reading is W.E.B. DuBois, *The Souls of Black Folk* (1903).

Biographies and biographically oriented works include Francis L. Broderick's *W.E.B. Dubois: Negro Leader in a Time of Crisis* (1959); Elliott M. Rudwick's *W.E.B. Dubois: Propagandist of the Negro Protest* (1960); Samuel R. Spencer, Jr., *Booker T. Washington and the Negro's Place in American Life* (1955); Allen F. Davis, *American Heroine: Life and Legacy of Jane Addams* (1973); Jack Tager, *The Intellectual as Reformer: Brand Whitlock and the Progressive Movement* (1968); William H. Harbaugh, *Power and Responsibility: The Life and Times of Theodore Roosevelt* (1961); John M. Blum, *The Republican Roosevelt* (1954); Henry F. Pringle, *Life and Times of William Howard Taft* (2 vols., 1939); and the superb work by Edmund Morris, *The Rise of Theodore Roosevelt* (1979). For other figures, see David P. Thelen, *Robert M. La Follette and the Insurgent Spirit* (1976); Justin Kaplan, *Lincoln Steffens* (1974); and Robert C. Twombly, *Frank Lloyd Wright* (1973).

4 | Becoming a World Power

AMERICA'S CHANGING INTERNATIONAL ROLE

On June 28, 1914, a young Bosnian student assassinated Austrian Archduke Franz Ferdinand and his wife in Sarajevo. Within weeks, a peace of 40 years duration among the major powers of Europe was shattered. On August 2, 1914, Germany declared war on Russia, France joined its Russian ally, and in a few days the British joined in. With the exception of Italy, which chose to remain neutral, the Great Powers succumbed to the pressure of alliances and nationalistic pride, and that impossible event, a general war, spread across the continent of Europe.

Americans responded to the grim news from Europe by thanking God for geography and the wisdom of the founding fathers. "I thank heaven for the Atlantic Ocean," wrote the United States ambassador in London. "Thank God," *World's Work* commented,

"our policy of friendship to all and entangling alliances with none was made for us by wise men a hundred years ago. . . . May we in wisdom and humility learn as much from it as did they!" That Europe had finally fallen into the dark pit American leaders had predicted for a century and a half was not of serious import for the American people. In Evansville, Indiana, for example, a minor depression in the summer of 1914 pushed war into a position of second importance. If they thought about foreign affairs, most Hoosiers looked toward Mexico where American troops had occupied Vera Cruz, and Generalissimo Victoriano Huerta's little-loved regime was about to collapse. They doubtless agreed with the *Evansville Journal-News* that the European war signaled "death and disaster unparalleled, unprecedented, and immeasurable"; still, it little affected their own lives.

In Evansville, the *Courier*, the *Press*, and the German-language newspaper, the *Demo-*

113

krat, carried reports of the war under three-column headlines. Will Trace's son, Ben, only occasionally glanced at newspapers. Word about Europe's lapse into insanity reached Waynesboro, Tennessee, on August 4 in a brief, error-filled story in the *Wayne County News.* Will Trace heard about it when he drove into Waynesboro for provisions. He decided it was no business of his or any other American—a sentiment reinforced by talks with friends on the courthouse square and at Harkins' general store. Will returned to preparations for harvesting his tobacco crop. There seemed no reason for the Traces or for most other old-stock Americans to pay any attention to events in Europe. Even George Butler and his boys, who were worried about friends in various European countries they had visited, believed the war would last only a few weeks and would not affect their lives. There were, of course, some qualifications to this "business as usual" attitude, and these were to become more and more important.

Among the families with ties to Europe, the response was somewhat different. Andrew Bassano and his family worried about Italy's possible involvement in the war, especially since Andrew's mother had recently returned to the family home and she was located squarely in the path any invading armies would use. The Miller family in Providence feared for the safety of their many relatives in western Russia. But while Jewish immigrant newspapers hotly protested Russian participation, believing that Russian advances would mean greater persecution of Jews in Central Europe, the Millers were so immersed in the daily challenge of surviving in this strange new environment that they did little more than worry. The Markoviches in Midland were much concerned about the fate of Serbia and their relatives and friends. The war was a reality to them from the first, for they knew where Sarajevo was and that Serbians in Bosnia were conscripted into the Austro-Hungarian

army, overtaxed, and otherwise oppressed. This war was, however, far away, and they were fighting, like the Millers, a battle for survival. They could do little but wait for letters from home, talk with Serbian friends about the evil of the Central Powers, and send occasional packages of food and clothing to Mihailo's family.

Nonetheless, from the time the Austrians decided to punish Serbia, the overwhelming majority of Americans gave their sympathy to Britain and its allies. One clearly distinguishable reason was the autocratic nature of the governments of Austria and Germany. Most newspaper editors, the opinion makers of the middle class and would-be middle class, blamed the institution of monarchy, with its attendant militarism and secret diplomacy, for the war. Prussian (German) militarism—particularly its prototype, Kaiser Wilhelm—came in for special criticism. With his spiked helmet, army cloak, upturned mustache, sword, boots, spurs, and grim visage, the Kaiser personified the American conception of a Prussian warlord. High as this first crest of anti-German feeling rose, however, it did not carry with it any discernible demand for action.

The Reinhardts watched with alarm as their English-speaking neighbors voiced increasing hostility to Germany—and to German culture. During the first months of the war, two assumptions shielded the German community from the worst of popular hostility. One was that Germany would be defeated, and the other was that the conflict itself would be short. As well, politicians held anti-German sentiment in check by courting the German vote in the important local, state, and congressional elections of 1914. But even more important was the challenge of making a satisfactory living and coping with the daily problems of family life.

President Wilson and his advisers shared the convictions espoused by neighborhood generals about the European war. They also believed that it was no business of the United States. Wilson was largely indifferent to European problems, much preferring to grapple with the issues of domestic reform for which he had campaigned in 1912. He and other Americans directly concerned with the conduct of diplomacy trusted in the traditions that had served America so well and which, they believed, were still pertinent. Over the years, the principles of foreign policy had been amazingly consistent: the search for a diplomatic strategy that would protect the national interest, ensure independence, ward off threats to domestic stability, provide for expansion, ensure maximum commercial opportunity in world markets, and do all these things while satisfying deep-seated convictions about America's moral superiority. Moreover, the means by which American objectives—isolation (in its peculiar 19th century sense), neutrality, domination of the Western Hemisphere, territorial and commercial expansion, and a quite remarkable talent for fishing in troubled waters—were to be realized also were relatively constant in importance.

What had changed were the attitudes of American leaders and diplomats, backed by public opinion, toward the global role of the United States. Disinterest in the world was replaced by significant, if sporadic, obsession with events outside America's boundaries. While the influence of public opinion was essentially passive, it established parameters for the activities of groups and individuals who did possess an abiding interest in foreign affairs. The transformation of American foreign policy in the years before 1900 expanded the limits of permissible action in recognition of America's changed status, of its economic strength, and of its burgeoning naval power.

The gradual modification of old assumptions about America's role in the world was reflected in the increasingly expansionist nature of national ambitions during the late 19th century. America's empire had moved abroad—to Alaska and Hawaii—until by 1900, the Stars and Stripes waved in the breezes of Manila in the Philippines and San Juan, Puerto Rico, and American hegemony was recognized in Cuba and asserted throughout Central America. Among the foremost of the proponents of what came to be known as the "Large Policy" were Henry Cabot Lodge, senator from Massachusetts, and Theodore Roosevelt. Sharing wealth, social position, and a faith in the superiority of American civilization, these men energetically preached imperialism. For Lodge and TR the intellectual foundation for their exalted national vision was Social Darwinism. In distorting Darwin's biological theory, Lodge and others were able to convince themselves that the Anglo-Saxons were the "fittest" of all people. As Lodge then reasoned: "The great nations are rapidly absorbing for their future expansion and their present defense all of the waste places of the earth. It is a movement which makes for civilization and the advancement of the race. As one of the great nations of the world, the United States must not fall out of the line of march."

In common with his older expansionist colleagues, TR was greatly influenced by the theories of Alfred Thayer Mahan, author of *The Influence of Sea Power Upon History* (1890) and promoter of a large U.S. navy. The foundations of greatness, he said, parroting the writings of Mahan, consisted of a flourishing commerce, a large merchant marine to carry it, a strong and modern navy to protect it, and colonies to serve as bases and coaling stations.

The strategic goals of proponents of the "Large Policy" thus necessitated a flourishing trade. Others—business leaders, industrial magnates, and journalists—also clamored for a huge expansion of commerce, but as an end in itself. They faced and feared the simple fact that, because of ever-improving efficiency, America's farms and factories possessed the ability to produce far more than the internal market could absorb. The prospect of a glut of goods and produce led naturally to interest in selling surpluses abroad, establishing entrepôts throughout the world as distribution points, and guaranteeing a foreign market by obtaining far-flung colonies. The vastness of the potential Asian market—a will-of-the-wisp beckoning Americans since the men of Salem sent the first U.S. ships to Canton in the 18th century—was the focus for this interest.

Foreign trade represented only a small proportion of the U.S. gross national product in these years; however, it was extremely important for certain sectors of the economy. Wheat sales to foreign countries accounted for 30 to 40 percent of growers' gross income by the 1880s, and the significance of foreign markets for the agricultural sector in general remained relatively constant. Similarly, companies such as Hercules Buggy Works in Evansville, Midland Steel and Iron (Crucible Steel), and Detroit's burgeoning manufacturing concerns, as well as such giants as Standard Oil and Carnegie Steel, were becoming more and more involved with foreign trade and investment. The established trading partners of the United States were Canada, Great Britain, France, and Germany (see Table 4–1).

Desire to export Christianity was another powerful motive for expansion. American missionaries were found in Africa, the Middle East, India, South Asia, and a few Protestants even tried to break the Catholic domination of Latin America. They carried their special denominational messages and, coincidentally, the benefits of Western civilization. Though largely sincere and altruistic, these missionaries were the shock troops of a blatant cultural imperialism. The American Protestant missionary effort focused on China and the prospect of saving the same 400 million souls that American textile manufacturers wished to outfit in cotton underwear. Fifteen hundred servants of the Lord worked the Chinese vineyard at the century's end. By 1905, 3,000 of America's 3,800 missionaries were at work in China. These people, mostly Methodists, Baptists, Congregationalists, and Presbyterians, experienced great difficulties both with the Imperial Chinese government and with foreign powers to which the Chinese had granted special rights and "spheres of influence." The missionaries and the organizations at home that supported them naturally pressed the United States government for protection.

Expansionism, the national turmoil caused by the depression years of the 1890s, and the announcement that there no longer existed a frontier to sustain growth all converged upon Americans simultaneously. The exhaustion of old possibilities produced what Richard Hofstadter has called a "psychic crisis," one that led the American people to accept the

TABLE 4–1

Value of U.S. Exports of Merchandise by Country, 1880–1920 (in millions)

	Canada	Mexico	U.K.	France	Germany	China	Japan	Africa	Total
1880	29	8	454	100	57	1	3	5	836
1890	40	13	448	50	86	3	5	5	858
1900	95	35	534	83	187	15	29	19	1,394
1910	216	58	506	118	250	16	22	19	1,745
1920	912	208	1,825	676	311	146	378	166	8,228

Large Policy, with its central element of expansionism, as a quick remedy for their afflictions.

An opportunity for action came in Cuba when that Spanish colony, just 90 miles from Florida, made a bid for independence. The precipitating event occurred on February 15, 1898, when the *U.S.S. Maine,* at anchor in the blue waters of Havana harbor, exploded and sank with the loss of 260 American lives. An American investigation blamed the tragedy on an "explosion of a submarine mine, which caused the partial explosion of two or more forward magazines," but failed to identify the perpetrator. Few doubted that the explosion was the result of Spanish perfidy. Responding to the cry, "Remember the *Maine,*" popular opinion swung dramatically in favor of intervention. President McKinley tried to head off the stampede of Congress, the public, and assorted newspapers toward war. He proved unsuccessful, for the idea of

war with Spain (a cruel, monarchical, and *weak* power) to secure independence for Cuba (deserving, if illiterate and inferior people), and to spread the American eagle's wings proved irresistible.

Cuba fell to American forces after a few days fighting, and the neighboring Spanish colony of Puerto Rico capitulated almost without incident. The U.S. Navy blasted Spain's Atlantic battle fleet in several engagements and capped the war at sea with the stupendous victory of Commodore George Dewey over a Spanish flotilla in the Philippines, in which not one American was killed. When the U.S. Army moved in, however, they found the Spanish more cooperative than the natives. Walter Trace had left his father's farm for Nashville to enlist on April 22, 1898, 11 days after McKinley requested authority to send American forces to Cuba. Walter found himself in the Philippines, fighting not the hated Spanish but Filipino "insur-

Regulars in the trenches during the war against the Philippine insurgents, *c.* 1900

rectionists." He was awarded the Silver Cross, one of two given out in the Philippine insurrection, for his military exploits and did not return home for almost 11 years.

A treaty of peace, signed in Paris in October 1898 and ratified in February 1899, freed Cuba and forced Spain to cede Puerto Rico, Guam, and the entire Philippines to the United States. Thus, the United States broke away from the tradition of noninvolvement. It was now an imperial nation with far-flung colonies in the Pacific; it now controlled the Caribbean. It appeared that the "Large Policy" advocated by Roosevelt, Mahan, Lodge, and others was reaching fruition. Nonetheless, there were dissenters. Many Americans had been shocked and embarrassed by the jingoistic craze that had swept over the country. The Senate approved the Treaty of Paris by the margin of only one vote. The settlement generated powerful anti-imperialist, anti-expansionist views. Their ranks included representatives of all parties and factions, reformers of every kind, distinguished intellectuals, scientists—and even steel magnate Andrew Carnegie and labor organizer Samuel Gompers put aside their differences to participate in the fight.

The arguments of the anti-imperialists were as diverse as their motives, but they stressed a number of basic issues: constitutionality, democracy, morality, tradition. Senator George F. Hoar asked whether Congress had the authority to conquer and govern alien peoples; and did it possess a moral right to do so against their will? William Graham Sumner warned that imperialism would harm American institutions and democracy. Although the anti-imperialists lost the treaty fight, it is arguable that their campaign, in conjunction with the three-year jungle war required to subjugate the Filipinos and the disillusionment that accompanied America's brief exposure to power politics, succeeded in damping down

popular enthusiasm for the "great game" of empire.

Theodore Roosevelt, McKinley's successor after the latter's assassination on March 12, 1901, hugely enjoyed the game of power politics and endeavored to secure the geopolitical aims he and his friends had spelled out a decade previously. During TR's incumbency, U.S. marines landed in Latin America to ensure regional stability, mediated the settlement of the Russo-Japanese War, tried to meddle in European politics, and rattled the national saber in the Kaiser's face when Germany threatened intervention in the American hemisphere. Preeminently, however, these activities reflected the rhetorical activism of President Roosevelt and did not commit the nation to much. The pendulum of public interest had swung quickly and the numerous diplomatic episodes of his administration were set against a backdrop of popular indifference and anxiety. Perhaps only TR's decision to build an American-controlled canal across the Isthmus of Panama obtained broad support. Otherwise, the public viewed TR's maneuvers as not quite respectable but understandable and momentarily diverting actions to be expected from the man who was so full of physical courage, moral fervor—or frenzy—and zeal to fell lions, discover rivers, bust trusts, simplify spelling, and expose nature fakirs.

Only when an issue of foreign affairs intruded on domestic arrangements did the public take notice. One such intrusion occurred in 1906 when a decision of the San Francisco school board provoked a full-blown diplomatic crisis and focused the country's attention on prevailing views of racial equality. In October 1906, the San Francisco school board approved a resolution that required the segregation of Japanese pupils (93 in all) in a special school. The decision, for which the flimsiest of reasons were given, reflected the growing anti-Japanese sentiment in San

President Roosevelt visiting the Panama Canal during construction, 1906. The canal was completed in 1914

Francisco and all California. This hostility stemmed both from the supposed economic threat posed by Japanese immigration and racial antagonism. The issue was the more sensitive because the Japanese population in California was growing so rapidly. (See Table 4-2).

Yoshisuke Kurihara, who was living in Sacramento in 1907, learned of the school board's decision through friends. They told him that it stemmed from the sexual paranoia of the Anglo children's parents. (There were about eight Japanese males in California for each Japanese female.) By that time, Yoshisuke had encountered enough discrimination to be aware of the intensity of white antagonism. He recalled many years later:

> While walking on K Street from the Depot toward the Japanese district, suddenly a fairly well dressed person came and kicked me in the stomach for no reason whatever. . . . In this same city of Sacramento, as my friend and I were walking in the residential district a short distance away from the Japanese center, something came whizzing by, and then another and another. We noticed they were rocks being thrown at us by a number of youngsters. As we went toward them, the boys ran and hid. Feeling perplexed, I asked my friend, "Why do they attack us in such a manner?" He answered, "It's discrimination." No such thing ever happened where I came from. It was disgusting. I felt homesick for my good old native land, Hawaii.

Anti-Japanese sentiment had mounted swiftly after 1905, when immigration from Japan and Hawaii increased rapidly. Japanese truck

Table 4-2
California Japanese Population, 1900–1920

	Foreign born	Native born	Total
1900	10,008	143	10,151
1910	38,184	3,172	41,356
1920	51,138	20,814	71,952

farmers had demonstrated amazing success and were well on their way toward the control of production of certain vegetable crops. White Californians viewed such success as a direct threat to their own enterprises. The California legislature had voted unanimously for exclusion of Japanese, and individuals and assorted organizations began to boycott Japanese business. As elsewhere, California's racial nervousness soon expanded to include all foreigners, and congressmen from the Pacific Coast gave strident support to proposals for total restriction of immigration.

Already outraged by instances of boycotts and discrimination against Japanese residing in California, the government of Japan issued a strong protest when word of the San Francisco insult reached Tokyo. Anti-American riots in many Japanese cities accompanied a call for military measures. The *Japan Weekly Mail* editorialized:

> Stand up Japanese nation! Our countrymen have been humiliated on the other side of the Pacific. Our poor boys and girls have been expelled from the public schools by rascals of the United States, cruel and merciless demons. At this time, we should be ready to give a blow to the United States. Yes, we should be ready to strike the Devil's head with an iron hammer.

American opinion staunchly supported the San Francisco school board; however, the president, who shared his countrymen's anxieties about the Japanese menace, was forced to consider the effects of Japanese hostility on national security. As TR wrote to his son, "The infernal fools in California and especially in San Francisco insult the Japanese recklessly and in the event of war it will be the nation as a whole which will pay the consequence." A war scare developed in 1907, and only TR's personal intervention defused it. Though legally powerless, President Roosevelt used political pressure to convince the San Francisco school board to rescind the segregation order. Soon after, in February

1908, he obtained a promise from the Japanese government to "regulate" the influx of Japanese nationals to the United States. (Japan agreed to issue passports only to former residents of America or to relatives of those already present.) This arrangement, termed the "Gentlemen's Agreement," brought a temporary solution, but it did not dissipate hatred of Yoshisuke Kurihara and his compatriots. Employers discriminated against both native-born and foreign-born Japanese while county tax boards unfairly assessed Japanese property. TR satisfied his own bellicosity by sending the "Great White Fleet," 16 U.S. battleships and auxiliary vessels, on a world cruise. A principal aim of this "goodwill mission" was to impress the Japanese with America's naval might, though this backfired, since the fleet was grimy and badly in need of overhaul by the time it reached Japan in October 1908, and it compared unfavorably with the more modern Japanese navy.

At the time the rambunctious Teddy Roosevelt left office, public interest in world affairs still moved in the same streams (though their courses had been greatly enlarged) as it had a decade or more earlier. Meddling in Asia was accepted so long as no large-scale commitment of American power was required. The same could be said for relations with Europe. Toward Latin America there was widespread agreement that the United States must maintain a position of paramount power and influence. American policy in the two decades after the Spanish-American War represented, at the highest level, determination that America's hemispheric domination be made forever secure. The isthmian canal had been constructed under American auspices and the Stars and Stripes flew over Panama. Central America and the Caribbean were havens for American investment while protectorates and strategically located naval bases had been secured. The United States earned the respect of Latins, and in the process their fear and hatred.

Mostly, though, Americans considered these activities irrelevant. American participation in international conferences to limit armaments, to substitute arbitration for the use of force in settling international disputes, to codify the rules of war so that belligerents would fight fairly and respect neutral rights appealed to some Americans and even generated some enthusiasm among intellectuals. The visible expression of such attitudes was the growth of an American peace movement. Though peace societies enjoyed a long and flourishing tradition in the United States, the new century found them stronger than ever. At one peace congress in Boston in 1904, 3,000 delegates representing 200 organizations (churches, women's clubs, boards of trade, labor unions) hailed the coming of the millennium. Three years later, the American Peace Society convened its first national meeting in New York. In attendance were thousands of peace advocates, including 10 mayors, 19 congressmen, 4 supreme court justices, 2 presidential candidates, 30 labor leaders, 40 bishops, and 60 newspaper editors. At the APS's meeting in 1911, equally well attended, President Taft sanctified its cause by giving the major address. Robert Butler was an active member of the Boston Chapter of APS for some years. The highwater mark of the prewar crusade for peace came in 1910–11 with, first, the creation of the Carnegie Endowment for International Peace, financed by a $10,000,000 gift from Andrew Carnegie, and then secondly, in 1911, with the establishment of the World Peace Foundation by a Boston publisher who donated $1,000,000. Money made the peace movement even more respectable, especially when it came from hardheaded businesspeople.

In America and other enlightened nations, it seemed that peace was at hand. Despite the frantic warnings of men such as Theodore Roosevelt that the peace crusade was a dangerous illusion and that only military preparedness could prevent wars, despite the best-selling melodramas of Homer Lea, who described imaginary Japanese and German invasions of the United States, the public and politial leaders preferred to bask in a euphoric climate of optimism and ignorance. Ignoring nationalism and runaway militarism, they insisted, as a senator observed in 1909, that the prospects of the United States becoming involved in a war are "as chimerical and unlikely as a descent on our coasts of an army from the moon." When the European war erupted, the public continued to believe that it would not, could not, touch America.

That the United States could avoid all involvement was, of course, an illusion—one that produced bitter fruit. The *Evansville Demokrat* lavished banner headlines on June 28, 1914, on "German Day," the city's annual celebration of German culture. Reporting that the festival's cost of $1,063.45 had been met through record Bierstube sales, the *Demokrat* pledged that 1915 would witness an even greater celebration. The paper devoted only four lines to the assassination of Archduke Franz Ferdinand.

Popular songs reflected the national mood. On vaudeville stages—the liveliest form of contemporary entertainment—headliners such as Nora Bayes, Sophie Tucker, and Trixie Friganza belted out "Don't Take My Darling Boy Away," and pleaded "I didn't raise my boy to be a soldier." Tumultuous applause rewarded the purveyors of such sentiments, as it did President Wilson's confident statement: "It is entirely within our own choice what [the war's] effects on us will be." The president's own conviction was that the nation should hold itself "ready to play a part of impartial mediation and speak counsels of peace." To do that, the president counseled, both the government and the people would

need to remain "impartial in thought as well as in action." While recognizing that few Americans would heed a call for absolute impartiality, President Wilson did believe that formal neutrality could and would be maintained. Polls and other evidence suggest that, at the beginning of the European war, the vast majority of Americans, whatever their ethnic and national background, favored neutrality and manifested detachment from the conflict.

It was true that almost every American had some attachment to the Old World. Of a population of some 92 million, 32 million were either foreign born or had at least one parent born abroad. Almost all native-born Americans possessed affinity—ethnic, familial, cultural, social, economic—with one or another of the contending nations. Still, sympathy did not equate with desire for American participation. A metamorphosis in attitudes was necessary for that, and, though perhaps underway already in the summer of 1914, three years of agonizing changes were required for it to attain final form. The causes of this metamorphosis were essentially threefold: the conversion of vague popular sympathy for one or the other side into open, rancorous partisanship; the economic stake of the United States in the conflict; and the interpretation applied by President Wilson and others in his administration to basic American interests.

The first of these causes of changed attitudes existed because of the "hyphenate" influence in American politics and diplomacy. Mihailo Markovich, Serbian-American, and Andrew Bassano, Italian-American, were hyphenated Americans. Traditional wisdom was that the experience of life in America—the melting pot—would transform hyphenates and their children into loyal citizens, Americans. And the majority believed that those cultural ties and special qualities that were not destroyed in the melting pot were innocent and, indeed, diverting additions to American culture. But in the months following the outbreak of war, hyphenate groups attempted to influence national policy and this suggested that alien ideas and attachments had survived their immersion in American life.

In 1915, a storm of nationalistic and nativist fury broke unexpectedly over the heads of German-Americans. They were considered the most assimilable of all immigrants, and they were confident of their status, well organized, and determined to press their case. In the winter of 1914–15, the German-American Alliance launched a nationwide campaign to win sympathy for Imperial Germany, raise relief funds for their brethren, prevent the Allies from floating war loans in the United States, and, most importantly, pressure the Wilson administration into imposing a total embargo on munitions shipments to the warring powers. The alliance organized rallies, purchased newspaper advertisements, and circulated petitions demanding absolute neutrality.

In the anxiety and confusion of 1914–15, such blatant partisanship appeared "un-American," even treasonable. The *New York Times* charged that a Washington, D.C., conference of German-American leaders opposed to arms shipments to Britain had committed treason. In early February, newspapers carried stories of attempted sabotage of American industries by German agents. Thereafter, plots to smuggle bombs onto U.S. ships and to cripple American factories periodically came to light, heightening suspicion of the German-American community's motives. Public opinion shifted dramatically against Germany with the sinking of the *Lusitania* on May 7, 1915. Torpedoed by a German U-boat in the Irish Sea, this British passenger liner (which was carrying munitions) sank within 20 minutes, drowning 1,198 men, women, and children—including 128 Americans. This tragedy was an inevitable result of the German government's establishment, in February 1915, of a "war zone" around the British Isles in which any ships, neutral or allied, would be sunk without warning. The *Lusitania* was a victim of the German desire to starve the British Isles into submission. Though this policy was logical and perhaps strategically correct, Americans viewed the *Lusitania* only in terms of traditional international law—and, thus, as an attack on American lives and honor. The enormity of this German act far overshadowed the seizure of American ships and cargoes by British war vessels. With superior maritime strength, Britain pressed the blockade of its enemies with less viciousness than was true of the German counterblockade, which relied largely on U-boats.

The growing anti-German hysteria only gradually affected families such as the Reinhardts. In Evansville, German-American groups participated in relief activities for German soldiers. By March 1915, 30 sewing clubs under chairwoman Frieda Lauenstein, wife of the *Evansville Demokrat* editor, had organized to make garments for the wounded. Mathilde Reinhardt took part, explaining that it was the same sort of work she had done for "the poor people" of San Francisco when an earthquake leveled that city in 1906. "To us this was no different." For the Reinhardts' English-speaking neighbors, there was a difference. Sewing clothing for wounded German soldiers, speaking in defense of Germany, opposing loans and munitions sales to the Allies amounted to giving "aid and comfort" (words of the Constitution defining treason) to a foreign power. Instances of overt anti-German hostility were rare in Evansville before 1917, though there was occasional hooliganism at German-American meetings and vandalism at such places as the First Street Market, where the Reinhardts and other German-American farm families sold their eggs, apples, potatoes, and other produce.

For many months the Reinhardts ignored

the war. The years 1915–17 were prosperous and mostly satisfying ones for them. Their almost total self-sufficiency in food and the sharply rising prices realized for corn, wheat, and rye permitted the purchase of more land, farm machinery, and, in 1917, a Model-T Ford. All the while, though, the nativist-nationalist tide mounted in Evansville and throughout the country. Old-stock residents began demanding that German-Americans (and other hyphenates) abandon practices and customs basic to their cultural identity. The use of German in public was one example. The Reinhardts' fire-insurance policy, which in 1915, they held with the *Feuer Unterstutzungs-Verein von Perry Township,* was converted into a policy with the "Fire Protective Association." Vanderburgh County Schools soon abolished German-language teaching and, immediately after America's entry in the war, St. Paul's German services stopped. In May 1917, a mob of angry citizens compelled the editor of the *Demokrat* to cease publication. Jacob and Mathilde Reinhardt and their neighbors mostly acquiesced to the pressures for Americanization. Still trusting in the long acceptance of German-Americans in Evansville (after all, Mayor Benjamin Bosse was of German origin) and in their stable economic status, they believed that the political system would protect citizens such as themselves. As late as January 1917, Jacob signed a petition sent by the Benevolent Society of Perry Township to the Vanderburgh County State Assembly-man, which urged a vote against statewide Prohibition, women's suffrage, and a proposed constitutional convention. These measures struck directly at German customs. The petition read:

> We believe in temperance in all forms of life, but are opposed to prohibition in any form, because prohibition is dangerous to any commonwealth. We are opposed against a new constitutional convention, because the voters of our state decreed by a majority of over 120,000 votes that the state does not want the constitution changed . . . We are opposed to Woman Suffrage, because we hold the mission of our mothers too sacred and because our mothers, wives, and sisters do not want woman suffrage.

Such hopes proved unfounded, for the war converted xenophobic anxieties into a crusade against everyone and everything not safely American.

Not just German-Americans, but almost every other immigrant group was assaulted. All hyphenated Americans came under scrutiny from those concerned about patriotism and divided loyalties. The Irish found themselves under suspicion because of their attacks on Great Britain, a nation to which most Americans imputed only good and generous motives. John O'Reilly had never supported the radical Irish nationalist groups, the Fenians and Clan-na-Gael, and only a few of his friends and relatives were members of the moderate United Irish League of America. To be an Irish policeman in Boston demanded loyalty to the Chief, the Police Commissioner, and to the political machine. Not much allegiance was left to be given to abstractions such as Boston, the United States, or the nebulous ideal of an independent Ireland. Yet the war, which revived again the age-old revolutionary axiom "England's difficulty in Ireland's opportunity," produced a resurgence of interest in the cause of Irish independence. John and the majority of Irish-Americans did not believe Germany was a proper champion for Ireland, and most concluded that neutrality was the wisest course for America, but they found irresistible the opportunity to lambast Britain and British policy.

The Easter Rebellion of 1916 in Dublin proved a watershed for John O'Reilly and millions of other Irish-Americans. Although many Irish spokesmen condemned the uprising as poorly planned and "a needless letting of good Irish blood," they were shocked and enraged by the brutal manner in which the British crushed the revolt. The chief beneficiary of British repression was the recently formed Friends of Irish Freedom, an organization whose announced goal was national independence for Ireland. This organization quickly developed into the largest and most effective of all the Irish-American pressure groups. John O'Reilly began to contribute to the FOIF and to debate strategy with his friends after he learned that his 18-year-old brother, Peter, had been jailed by the British authorities in Dublin for possession of explosives. He stopped short, however, of abandoning his primary allegiance. Despite President Wilson's rebuff of Irish nationalist hopes, his exploitation of the hyphenate issue, and the blandishments of Republican standard-bearers, O'Reilly and Boston's Irish voted overwhelmingly for Wilson in the 1916 election.

The vast majority of immigrants found themselves somewhere in the limbo inhabited by the Reinhardts, O'Reillys, Millers, Bassanos, and Markoviches. Jacob and Mathilde Reinhardt, who thought of themselves as good Americans, learned that the definition of "American" was not immutable but depended upon prevailing whim. John O'Reilly discovered that America sometimes demanded more than family tradition, church, and conscience told him to give. Annie Miller continued to drop pennies into her collection box for Zionism, but much more went to help her son Jack pursue his studies at Brown University. The threat of "divided loyalties" had no large meaning for the vast majority of immigrants (or for native-born Americans, for that matter), who simply desired to get on with the business of living.

Nevertheless, immigration restriction had come up again almost immediately after Wilson's election in 1912, but other matters postponed consideration of the question by

Congress until 1914. A bill was introduced in the House of Representatives that revived the restrictionist language of earlier attempts, in particular the requirement of a literacy test, and added eugenic and political grounds for restriction. Support for restriction came principally from the South and West, with the Midwest split, and the urban-immigrant centers of the North strongly opposed. Notably, almost all industrial magnates, eager to maintain the flow of cheap labor from Europe, lobbied against passage. Senate and House passage of the bill was followed by Wilson's veto, which the House failed to override by four votes. America's doors still stood open, though, ironically, the war prevented anyone from entering.

The doors slammed shut in February 1917 when Congress once again passed a comprehensive immigration restriction bill. Again, Wilson vetoed it, but this time antihyphenate sentiment, combined with fear of revolutionary ideas espoused by immigrants and a conviction that if barriers were not raised the country would be deluged by immigrants once the war ended, led to overturning of the president's veto. The law was based on the original recommendations of the Immigration Commission Report of 1911. It excluded adult immigrants (with some exceptions) "unable to read a simple passage in some language." Also denied entrance were "persons of constitutional psychopathic inferiority," chronic alcoholics, "vagrants," and, of course, alien radicals. Since 65 percent of immigrants from southern and eastern Europe were illiterate as compared with a miniscule number from the "Anglo-Saxon" nations, the law was patently discriminatory. The leaders of the Immigration Restriction League, to which George Butler belonged, held a victory dinner at Boston's Union Club and discussed further measures, but they and the American people agreed that the immediate danger of a foreign influx at war's end had been averted. Within months, the United States was engaged in a kind of reverse immigration, the dispatch of an army of young men, including thousands of hyphenate Americans, to fight in Europe.

Antihyphenate hostility was not the major cause of America's entry into the war, but the suspicion and hostility engendered by the nativist-nationalist reaction contributed to the decision for war. Growing sympathy for the Allies also played a significant role. In particular, relations between the United States and Great Britain reached a level of cordiality unimaginable a few years before. By 1914, the major points at issue between the two nations had been settled largely through British concessions. After the war began, the British government set in motion an efficient, clever propaganda machine that exploited all the historic ties between America and Great Britain, to convert sympathy into outright partisanship for the Allied cause.

Then there was the economic factor. President Wilson knew that the policy of absolute impartiality which he publicly proclaimed was impossible because America's economy was deeply intertwined with the economies of the Allies. While both sides were eager to purchase war goods from the United States, only the Allies had the ability to transport them. Paying for the goods was the Allied problem. Wilson, at the insistence of his pacifistically inclined Secretary of State, William Jennings Bryan, initially opposed private loans to the Allied governments. Pressure from the business community quickly brought about a reversal of this policy. By 1915, the ban on loans was amended to permit "long-term" credits and, in August, when the Allies confessed that any further war purchases were impossible without a $500 million loan, the Bryan policy was abandoned. That opened the floodgates. By April 1917, the Allies had obtained some $2.3 billion in loans from the American financial community. (In contrast, loans to Germany totaled only $27 million.) These funds purchased rolled steel from Crucible Steel and assured Mihailo Markovich steady employment, gunpowder from the huge DuPont chemical complex where Andrew Bassano worked, small arms from Colt, Remington, and Winchester, and shipload after shipload of wheat. Allied war orders were placed in 32 states, and, through subcontracts and service charges, benefited the entire country. Mid-1915 found the United States wallowing in a tremendous boom initiated and partly fueled by the orders pouring forth from the Allied purchasing missions.

Mihailo Markovich, Andrew Bassano, Charles Gale, Ben Trace, and other Americans engaged in producing and transporting the myriad items called for in these contracts knew where the goods were going and, probably, who was responsible for fattening their pay envelopes, but it is likely that very few Americans understood the stake in an Allied victory thus engendered. J. P. Morgan and his colleagues understood, of course, that repayment of these loans by the Allies depended upon an Allied victory, and they became strong partisans of the Allied cause.

Whether the war loans ultimately forced the Wilson administration to decide for war, as some historians argued in the 1930s, is doubtful. It appears that the president was influenced in this matter, as in almost all others regarding the American position toward the belligerent powers, by a narrow and obsolete view of neutral rights, which served the purposes of the Allies far more than those of their opponents. When Germany reacted to Wilson's definition of neutrality by unleashing its submarines to stop the flow of American goods to its enemies, Wilson took it as a direct assault on national honor. A confusion of neutral rights with defense of American sovereignty against German aggression meshed well with the pro-Allied convictions that came to dominate the president's cabinet after

"Europe, 1916," appeared in *The Masses* in 1916

Bryan's resignation. The president's earlier conviction that America was "too proud to fight" had been forgotten.

The convergence of principle, honor, sentiment, and practical economic considerations found concrete expression in the preparedness movement, the campaign for national defense that burgeoned in 1915–16. Advocates of preparedness, such as Theodore Roosevelt, Augustus P. Gardiner, and Henry Cabot Lodge, were also fervent proponents of immigration restriction. Indeed, the preparedness movement aggravated anti-German feelings because it raised the specter of foreign aggression but also because it was easier to talk about domestic threats to security than to discuss seriously a possible enemy invasion of the United States. Until autumn 1915, President Wilson resisted pressures for expansion of the armed forces. Then he jumped aboard the bandwagon and in December requested an increase from 105,029 to 219,665 men in the regular army and funds to build ten battleships and 16 cruisers. By summer 1916, citizen soldiers, members of a variety of semiofficial military organizations, were packing valises and cleaning hunting rifles in preparation for two weeks of close order drill and bayonet practice. It should be noted that this furor for "playing soldier" attracted predominantly upper and middle class New England participants. Robert Butler, his father, and numerous other relatives, joined a Back Bay chapter of one of these organizations and tramped off to Plattsburg, New York, for training. Mihailo Markovich and Charles Gale were largely indifferent to the preparedness crusades. Indeed, Indiana's National Guard ordered the Evansville company disbanded in early 1916 because of declining interest and poor organization and discipline.

Wilson was renominated in 1916 by a Democratic convention which lapsed into frenzy at the keynote speaker's characterization of the president: "He kept us out of war." In part because of the image as peace-keeper—and prospective peacemaker—which he quietly encouraged, Wilson won a close election over the Republican candidate, Charles Evans Hughes. Though Wilson gained only a bare majority in the electoral college, his popular-vote margin was impressive. The Democrats also won control of Congress, helped by versions of the "He kept us out of the war" slogan such as Indiana's "the Nation is out of War, the State is out of Debt, the Democrats did it." Any suggestion that the country would repudiate the first two parts of this boast within six months would have been greeted with derision.

The president returned to his earlier hope of sponsoring a negotiated peace—"a peace without victory"—between the belligerents. But as each side still believed that it would emerge victorious, each side ignored Wilson's efforts. In the end, the various pressures propelling America toward the abyss proved irresistible. More and more, the domestic anxieties that had spawned the nativist-nationalist upsurge focused on Germany, compelling President Wilson to adopt a harsh stance toward the "creatures of passion, disloyalty, and anarchy" at home and the violators of common justice and international law elsewhere in the world. More and more, informed opinion was openly championing the Allies, even advocating American participa-

tion in the war if that were necessary to ensure Allied victory. The president found his freedom to act restricted, not least because of his rigid commitment to an outmoded code of neutral rights. Military stalemate in Europe threatened to push the German government into a renewal of unrestricted submarine warfare, and that, because of the identification of the unhindered access of Americans to the war zone with the nation's honor, would mean war.

AMERICA ENTERS THE WAR

On January 31, 1917, Berlin announced the resumption of unrestricted submarine warfare. This act, decided upon after agonizing debate within the German government, triggered a sequence of events leading toward America's entry. Faced with the awful consequences of his policy, the president procrastinated for two months. Meanwhile, public opinion, spurred by inflammatory disclosures such as the Zimmerman telegram, a message from the German foreign minister to his representative in Mexico City proposing an alliance and promising the return to Mexico of the territory lost in 1848, became increasingly bellicose. The president, though outraged by this example of German treachery, still balked at war; instead, he asked Congress for authority to arm American merchant ships. Armed neutrality would prove, he hoped, a viable alternative to war. But, as Henry Cabot Lodge observed with considerable satisfaction, the president and the nation were "in the grip of events." On March 14, an American tanker was sunk. Four days later, three freighters were torpedoed with the loss of six American lives. On March 21, seven more Americans were killed at sea. That same day, the president issued a call for Congress to meet in special session. At 7:30 P.M. on April

2, 1917, President Wilson stepped forward to address a joint session of Congress. He condemned Germany's policy of unrestricted submarine warfare for its "reckless lack of compassion or principle," as "war against all nations." The president proclaimed: "There is one choice we cannot make, we are incapable of making. We will not choose the path of submission." Then, speaking slowly and with great solemnity, he requested his rapt audience to issue a declaration of war against the "Government of the German Empire." After returning to the White House, Wilson broke down and wept. Two days later, the Senate voted 82-6 in favor of war and, at 3:00 A.M. on April 6, the House passed the resolution by a vote of 373-50. That day the country woke to find itself at war.

America's greatest contribution to the Allied cause, since they were already receiving funds and munitions, was the infusion of fresh, able men to reinvigorate French and British armies worn down by three years of trench warfare. Delivering this contribution required unprecendented efforts by the national government.

The nation's regular army in peacetime had consisted of 80,000 officers and men plus some 130,000 part-time soldiers organized in National Guard and militia units. The best estimate was that 1,000,000 American troops would be needed in Europe. Thus, the regular

Wilson delivering his war message to Congress, April 2, 1917

army and National Guard had to serve as a cadre, to knead and shape the raw dough of an enormous citizen army. Volunteers would not be sufficient. The first step was to obtain approval for an organized system of conscription. One senator warned Secretary of War Newton D. Baker, former mayor of Cleveland, "You will have the streets of our cities running with blood, if you attempt a draft of men." Nevertheless, Baker went ahead. A sweeping publicity campaign was undertaken to spur enlistment and also to sell the draft to the public.

The procedures worked remarkably well. In Evansville, Midland, Detroit, New York, and elsewhere American males between the ages of 21 and 31 reported to their local election polling places and filled out registration forms. Each received a number. A lottery would decide the sequence of numbers on the draft list. The process was carried out entirely by civilians. Governors, mayors, and sheriffs issued registration, and draft boards, staffed by local citizens, dealt with deferments.

Arrangements were made in great secrecy, while Baker waited for Congress to exhaust its emotional attachment to voluntarism and enact a conscription law. June 5 was the day set for registration. To everyone's surprise, it took place without incident. A total of 9,600,000 men completed the forms. In Howell, Ben Trace walked over to Daniel Wertz School to register. On July 20, when a blindfolded Secretary Baker pulled numbered slips out of a large glass bowl, Ben and 686,999 other Americans learned they had been selected for military service. Gus O'Reilly was drafted; Mihailo Markovich was also drafted but was informed, when he reported for enlistment, that he was deferred because of his family obligation. Jack Miller joined an ROTC detachment at Brown. Yoshisuke Kurihara had volunteered in late April. Robert Butler, whose military experience consisted of three weeks at Plattsburg,

was commissioned a captain in the army. His brother Eliott joined the medical corps, and another brother enlisted in the navy.

Ben and his fellows were informed that they were to report for duty in eight days. Ben laughed at this information for there were almost no facilities for training the nearly 700,000 young men who had been called into military service. Establishment of the camps in which young men were to be converted into professional soldiers was a War Department responsibility. Adopting a pattern that was to be typical of America's wartime mobilization, the army called on the just-created Emergency Construction Committee of the General Munitions Board. Its chief was W. A. Starrett, a famous builder who had volunteered to serve for "a dollar a year" and expenses. Starrett pulled together a legion of architects, city planners, and engineers for the monumental task.

Construction of the camps presented staggering problems. A single camp designed to accommodate 30,000 men, required 120 barracks plus administration buildings, post exchange, quartermaster depot, kitchens, showers, latrines, laundries, hospitals, and recreation halls. Also needed were water, electricity, and gas services, and 25 to 30 miles of hard surface roads. These facilities were largely completed in three months, an incredible feat. In early July, a civilian army of 50,000 carpenters and 150,000 other workers began to drive nails and saw 450,000,000 board feet of wood. The key element in the construction program was typically American: standardization. "Every stick and board, every type of building, every window sash and ventilator will be turned out to the same measurements." This, of course, resulted in enormous profits for a few large companies. Actual construction was done by local contractors who were allowed a profit of only 3 percent. If everything needed was on hand and if the work force cooperated, a barracks could be erected in less than two hours. However, those conditions rarely prevailed. The target date for 80 percent completion of the cantonments was September 8, but only one facility, Camp Taylor in Kentucky, was that far along on the magic day. Most were not finished until October, and the job of furnishing them took even longer. Until then, draftees bunked in tents, as their brethren in National Guard and officer-training camps had been doing since early summer.

After reporting for service on September 15, Ben Trace underwent basic training at Camp Leonard Wood, a new army facility in the backwoods of central Missouri. He trained with the 42nd Division, an Ohio National Guard unit that included recruits from Indiana and Michigan as well as Ohio. For two months, the 42nd lived in tents, bathed in cattle tanks, and ate at rough board tables. "Everywhere was a bedlam of hammering, shouting, and choking dust," Ben later told his children. Full uniforms for the entire division arrived only one week before training was to end. Ben drilled and practiced marksmanship with an obsolete Krag. Springfield rifles were not issued to his unit until late October, sent direct from the factory, still smeared with cosmoline and packed in huge, coffin-shaped boxes.

Gradually, Camp Leonard Wood took on a military appearance and so did its inhabitants. "It is fall-in, fall-out, from the minute you climb out of the dear old bed at 6:45 until taps at 9:45," one of Ben Trace's comrades wrote back home. Ben and most other draftees adjusted with surprising ease, for this regimented life was not, after all, very different than their civilian careers. The strict routine was described in a marching song adopted by the 77th Division.

> Oh, the army, the army, the democratic army!
>   They clothe you and they feed you
> Because the army needs you. Hash for
>   breakfast,

Benjamin Trace, United States Army, before shipping to France

> Beans for dinner, stew for suppertime.
> Thirty dollars every month, deducting
>   twenty-nine.
>   Oh, the army, the army, the democratic
>   army!
> The Jews, the Wops, and the Dutch and Irish
>   cops,
>   They're all in the army now!

It was a cosmopolitan force, especially in those camps where draftees from urban centers were thrown together with farm boys. For some, basic training offered the first close contact with different ethnic groups. Yoshisuke Kurihara, who had enlisted on a whim while visiting relatives in Ann Arbor, Michigan, found himself in training with national guardsmen from the lumber towns of Michigan's Upper Peninsula, swarthy Italians and Poles from Detroit, and tradesmen's sons from small towns everywhere in Michigan. Yoshisuke was often the butt of racial jokes but finished training with his company. Then, to his disappointment, he was assigned to an ambulance unit in the Medical Corps. Japanese, he was informed, did not make good doughboys, the common term for combat infantrymen.

The training Ben, Gus, and Yoshisuke received was businesslike and thorough. They dug mock trenches and strung ugly strands of barbed wire on top. They practiced hour after hour with Springfield rifles and grenades, and they lunged interminably with bayonets at dummies hanging from gallowlike supports. By year's end, they looked and acted like professionals, but the Army General Staff knew the test would come in France and was deeply worried. So further training was laid on, while the American Expeditionary Force's equipment (especially ordnance, which was still in short supply) was manufactured.

Boredom set in and with its fights and minor rebellions. The War Department's response was to supply the bases with bowling alleys, movie theaters, pool halls, and "day rooms" with victrolas, magazines, games, and ample supplies of stationery. The Red Cross, Salvation Army, YMCA, and other organizations opened canteens and sponsored baseball leagues, boxing tournaments, and dances. Many young men from the slums and the backwoods found Army life more appealing than what they left at home. Ben Trace played second base for the company ball team and spent many off-duty hours in the camp pool hall. Unlike many of his friends, who lived from one weekend pass to the next,

Ben rarely visited the bordello–honky tonk town that had sprung up outside the camp gates. He was not prudish, but he wanted to save as much of his pay as possible, and he had a healthy fear of venereal disease. Besides, whoring around had an awkward aftermath for an enlisted man. Army regulations required that every soldier returning to camp after sexual intercourse report immediately to a prophylaxis station. The penalty for noncompliance was stiff. So Ben, and for different reasons, Yoshisuke Kurihara, mostly remained in camp. Gus O'Reilly and Robert Butler, both of whom trained in New England, used their liberties for brief visits to Boston. Gus was homesick through basic training and actually began to look forward to the journey to France as relief from the torture of being so close to home and friends.

The first American troops landed in France in September 1917. By October 24, a battalion of the First Division had slipped into the trenches. Then, casualties. On November 2, three Americans fell victim to a German raiding party, their throats cut and bodies mutilated. One of the dead was James Gresham of Evansville. The city went into mourning and local patriots arranged a public subscription to build a new home for his parents. Although 50,000 Americans were arriving weekly in France by late autumn 1917, it would be spring before the American Expeditionary Force (AEF) could play an important role. The early calculations regarding the time required to train and equip the troops had rested on wishful thinking. While Ben, Gus, Yoshisuke, and their comrades drilled, General John J. Pershing, commander of the U.S. forces in France, beat back repeated efforts by the French and British to use American soldiers as replacements in their own decimated units. Pershing's position, supported by the president and public opinion, was that American troops would go into battle only under the U.S. flag, would take commands only from

American officers, and would have their own front and important military objectives. In the end, American troops made their presence felt far earlier than the German High Command had anticipated.

In late March 1918, just two weeks after Ben Trace and the 42nd Division landed at Le Havre, the Germans launched a tremendous offensive. Bolstered by reinforcements from the Eastern Front and driven by awareness of the buildup of American forces in France, Germany attempted to split the French and British armies, drive to the sea, and force a settlement before the Americans were strong enough to stop them. This offensive almost succeeded and the German drive on Amiens, in the Somme sector, halted only when Pershing threw in his untested divisions. They acquitted themselves brilliantly. In hand-to-hand combat, a French observer attested, these fresh-faced Americans killed or captured at a ratio of three to one.

On May 28, for the first time, American troops took the offensive, attacking and seizing Cantigny, at the spearhead of the German salient in northcentral France. In the last German offensive in June, which reached the river Marne at Chateau Thierry only 50 miles from Paris, the Americans turned the tide. While the French government prepared to flee to Bordeaux, units of the U.S. 3rd Division, the 2nd Division, and marine outfits joined the battle. They held and then advanced. The situation changed when American soldiers and marines took the vital terrain of Belleau Woods—though at enormous cost. This was not the critical battle of the war, but it demonstrated to both sides that Germany probably would be defeated. The Germans had lost precious time, the initiative, and, perhaps most importantly, confidence in their military superiority. By mid-July, the AEF was ready to contribute fully to a major offensive. Allied commanders assigned the U.S. Army a front of its own, one that expanded as the

drive toward German frontiers gathered momentum. Brutal fighting took place as Allied forces ground forward. Especially bloody was the battle of the Meuse-Argonne, which was preeminently American and which lasted from September 28 until early November. Afflicted by bad weather, poor planning, and supply foul-ups, the Americans made slow progress and suffered over 120,000 casualties. Gus O'Reilly, by this time a gunnery corporal, served with an artillery unit in the Meuse-Argonne battle. His unit fired its 75 millimeter howitzer (obtained from the French) almost continuously for weeks. Yoshisuke Kurihara, who was with the Medical Corps, drove an ambulance in the same area. Ben Trace, fighting with an infantry squad in this battle, was caught in a mustard-gas barrage and was evacuated to a field hospital. Ben was still recovering on November 11, when Germany, facing military collapse and political chaos, signed an armistice.

In all, some 2 million American troops served in France, and 53,000 died in battle. Compared with the human catastrophes among the other belligerents (65 million bore arms on both sides, and some 10 million were killed), the losses of the United States were small. However, the presence of the AEF had ensured Allied victory and ranked in importance with the tremendous material aid which America's farms and factories delivered to the Allies. Before the conflict ended, black doughboys assigned to the docks were unloading 20,000 tons of supplies per day. In this mountain of material, for example, were 5,400,000 gas masks, 2,278,000 steel helmets, 9,500,000 overcoats, 22,000,000 blankets, and 85,000,000 undershirts. These items had been ordered, manufactured, and shipped in the incredibly brief period of 18 months.

The miracle of American war production astounded the world, especially the Germans. The achievement was not without cost. With little concern for the consequences, the American government and leaders of finance and industry entered into a new and remarkably intimate relationship. Even though experience had shown that prewar attempts to regulate business largely represented victories for the regulated, government and business had remained adversaries with neither admitting subservience. War brought the two together in ways that changed American economic life. Once the United States entered the war, Wilson asked the business-financial community to rally around. Of necessity, he had accepted the assumptions of his Advisory Council on National Defense. The federal government did not possess the expertise to directly control the entire economy, and it would not obtain maximum effort from either producers or labor if it had tried to do so. The way to maximum production was through voluntary cooperation coordinated from the top. The solution to the demand for produc-

tion was, as a contemporary slogan said, "Business as Before—Only More." No responsible person thought otherwise.

The Wilson administration created a multitude of boards, bureaus, and commissions to oversee the production effort. A *Washington Star* headline, "Ten Thousand New Clerical Workers Expected This Summer," gave a hint of the dimensions of government's growth. Policy and planning slots, the really powerful positions, went to the top management talent of Wall Street banking houses, the Union Pacific and other railroads, Sears, Roebuck, International Harvester, U.S. Steel—a galaxy of respected firms. The mission of these managers, many of whom came to Washington as "dollar-a-year" men on leave from their jobs, was to apply their technical knowledge to obtain production efficiency rather than profits. Businessmen turned bureaucrats soon occupied important positions on the General Munitions Board, a special agency given

Military uniforms appeared everywhere. Boy Scouts, Midland, Pennsylvania, c. World War I

broad, if hazy, powers over purchase and allocation of wartime contracts. From that vantage, they came to dominate the war effort.

The war agencies effected the increased production—and also spiralling inflation. Business profits trebled. Even after paying heavy taxes in 1917, oil companies realized average profits equal to 21 percent of invested capital, and steel producers wallowed in profits that ranged from 30 to 300 percent.

During the winter of 1917–18, the coldest in Weather Bureau records, it became clear that the railroads, the most important and vulnerable link in the production-distribution chain, were failing to meet their wartime responsibilities. Ghastly foul-ups occurred. For example, General Pershing, nervously waiting in France for guns and supplies, learned he had been shipped lawn mowers and obstetrical instruments. Shortages of food and, in particular, coal became desperate as the weather worsened. People froze, and some war plants closed down. Obsolete stock and the labor shortage partly explained railroad inadequacies, but the arrogance and conservatism of the railroad magnates also affected operations. In December 1917, the president stepped in and nationalized the nation's railroads for the duration of the war. Since some steel mills and other vital plants periodically defied the government's program and war production schedules lagged, Wilson took a further step in March 1918. He appointed Bernard Baruch, the self-made millionaire who was known as "the wizard of Wall Street," Chairman of the War Industries Board (WIB) and gave him power (if necessary by coercion) to move the nation, at long last, onto a war footing. The WIB halted production of nonessentials, such as construction of movie theaters and use of metal stays in women's corsets (saving enough steel to build two warships). The United States ultimately met and exceeded its production commitments.

Baruch and the other dollar-a-year men did not completely absorb or outmaneuver all "regular" government officials, and the latter continued the struggle to control America's giant corporations. Congress passed an excess profits tax; the administration coerced some industries into accepting the eight-hour day and the formation of unions; and the threat of outright seizure by the federal government, so bluntly applied to the railroads, extracted grudging cooperation from most industrialists. Actually, there were many advantages, business leaders discovered, to this 1917–18 style of planned economy. Because government offered a guaranteed market, there was steady production, the future was predictable, and cutthroat competition, expensive and risky, was abolished by government order. As a result, profits were more than gratifying. Indeed, the system was too beneficial to give up when peace came. The domination of national life by business that characterized the 1920s was greatly accelerated by the drive for production of tools with which to "Hang the Kaiser" in 1917.

To ensure that American troops and their allies had sufficient food, Wilson relied again upon voluntarism, augmented by the appointment of a federal overseer with broad powers. The government asked people to conserve food and to grow as much as possible themselves. Hundreds of thousands—some said millions—of patriots dutifully turned their backyards, lawns, and vacant lots into victory gardens. This program produced a significant amount of fresh vegetables (though almost nothing to meet the critical need for fats and oils); more importantly, it gave the public a sense of personal participation in the war effort. It symbolized the faith of most middle-class Americans in voluntary methods—and the administration's faith in propaganda and the use of mass psychology to ensure popular support.

The president called upon another self-made man, millionaire engineer Herbert Hoover, to head the food program. Hoover's title was food coordinator, which conveyed the widespread belief that organizational tricks—efficiency—could solve any problem. His responsibilities included watching over the production and distribution of essential crops, efforts to foster the consumption of perishable foods (thus permitting export of flour, beans, and other imperishable items), keeping a lid on food prices, and ensuring that the American people—those who could afford it at least—obtained a nutritionally balanced diet. Hoover accomplished these goals without compulsory rationing and the wage and price controls familiar to a later generation of Americans; however, the brevity of the crisis and the exceptional agricultural conditions that prevailed largely explain his success.

Producing munitions and saving goods for shipment to the Allies were meaningless if the government lacked the ability to pay for them. To finance the war, the president turned to his son-in-law, Secretary of the Treasury William McAdoo. His was perhaps the most challenging task of all, for the costs of the war, both direct expenditures by the government and public loans to the Allies for their purchases in the United States, promised to be astronomical. For the first time, public officials threw off the word *billions* without gulping in awe. The federal budget had been $1.5 billion in 1915; it was $35 billion in 1918. Tax revenues, including the miniscule amounts realized from the new federal income tax, did not even approach the government's enormous bills. McAdoo broke precedent by the decision to fund a large part of this debt by public subscription, that is, by asking Americans to purchase government bonds at 3.5 percent annual interest. Raising of money for the war would be a patriotic crusade, put over by the power of modern advertising. The Treasury set the goal of the first loan campaign—which some unknown genius dubbed the Liberty Loan—at $2,000,000,000. A worried people responded with $3,035,228,850. Subsequent Liberty Loan drives netted $16,950,000,000. The appeal of patriotism and McAdoo's promotional methods proved irresistible. His lieutenants and a legion of patriotic orators spread across the country, addressing Liberty Bond rallies and whipping up popular enthusiasm. They convinced bankers to make the bonds available at tellers windows. They encouraged chambers of commerce, fraternal groups, and many other organizations to train their members as salespeople and pay for publicity. Teachers sold 25-cent stamps for pasting in special "Liberty Books" which, when filled, could be redeemed for a bond. "Lick a Stamp, and Lick the Kaiser," a popular lunchroom slogan urged youngsters, who dutifully brought their quarters to school or were subjected to ridicule by teachers and fellow students. The bond-drive promoters splashed similar slogans across the country via billboards, theater announcements, and public appearances by Broadway stars. Often, strong-arm techniques and pressure for conformity resulted in bond purchases by many who could not afford them. As a gunnery corporal, Gus O'Reilly received $36 a month. With this princely sum, he sent $15 home and purchased three $5 Liberty Bonds, leaving him $6 for spending money.

In the bond drives and other programs, the effectiveness of popular mobilization through advertising appeared irrefutable. The chief advocate of these techniques (which some termed information, others propaganda) was George Creel, a former newspaper reporter. Creel persuaded the president to create an agency to "sell the war," to make every American participate fully in the war effort. This was, he believed, "a plain publicity proposition, a vast enterprise in salesmanship, the world's greatest adventure in advertising." He soon found himself director of the Committee on Public Information, charged with

Children taking part in the Fourth Liberty Loan Drive, Washington, D.C., 1918

the task of generating public support for the war and assorted other activities. The Creel Committee racked up an impressive record but also an unsavory one, by stimulating antihyphenate hostility and bigotry.

Ordinary people in Midland, New York, Fredonia, Evansville, and Detroit, were largely bystanders, daily watching the panorama of wartime decisions flow by. However much America's participation in the war affected their lives, the most obvious effect of war was economic. All the families described in this book, except perhaps that of Will Trace isolated in the Tennessee backwoods, benefited from the war boom. They worked regularly, earned more, and, despite ferocious inflation and occasional shortages, lived better.

Andrew Bassano left his job with the Wrigley family to work at the huge DuPont munitions complex in Dover, Delaware. Placed at a station on a huge, noisy assembly line, Andrew capped rifle cartridges eight hours a day, six days a week. He hated every minute of it, because he believed, as a craftsman, that the work was beneath his dignity and because he was separated from his family, still living in New York City. Still, he was making 70 cents an hour and was able to put something into savings, including two $50 Liberty Bonds.

When danger on the seas and lack of ships effectively ended the immigration of foreign laborers, and when the pressure of war orders began to break down the pattern of low wages and periodic layoffs, life improved for the Markovich family. At the Midland mill, which struggled to meet the huge demands of armaments factories for rolled steel, Mihailo and his friends became valued commodities. Soon, Mihailo was bringing home $20 to $25 a week. He built a two-room addition to the house, joined a Serbian Club, and permitted his wife to contribute each week to St. Stanislaus Church in Aliquippa.

Farmers such as the Gales and Reinhardts found their real income climbing almost daily. Both grew most of their own food and raised cash crops that were desperately needed for the war effort. Both decided to take advantage of the agricultural boom to expand their operations. Jacob Reinhardt bought more land, a small tractor, and added two outbuildings and a machinery shed. After the fall harvest in 1917, he paid cash for a Model-T Ford. The Gales made similar improvements, though the astonishing jump in land prices compelled Charles to take out a loan to buy 60 acres south of Fredonia.

Yoshisuke Kurihara's family moved from Fresno to San Francisco while he was serving in France. Leasing a small grocery store in the Japanese district, they also prospered, though twice shop windows were broken by drunken sailors invading the Japanese community for a night of fun, and their insurance was canceled. The Meyer Millers benefited economically, though the effects were less because of Meyer's continued poor health. In September 1917, Meyer's family rejoined him in New York, and the two oldest girls, Betty and Rose, found jobs at the Bulova Company packaging military chronometers.

James Williams and his brother, Henry, also benefited from the war boom, which concentrated in Detroit more than any other city. The federal government turned to Detroit to build the mechanized equipment, especially internal combustion engines, needed for modern war. By mid-1917, Henry Ford (who had proclaimed during his campaign for peace in 1915 that he would burn down his factory rather than manufacture instruments of war) had received orders for 20,000 tractors, 16,000 tanks, and 1,200 subchasers. To fill these orders. Ford constructed the world's largest factory at River Rouge just outside Detroit. The federal government paid the $10 million cost of connecting this complex with Lake Erie and, in the bargain, gave Detroit a ready-made port. Ford's competitors also prospered. General Motors' work force, some 10,000 in 1912, reached 50,000 by 1918. Ford's labor force rose from 32,000 in 1916 to 48,000 in 1918. Still, once the war began, the labor market was tight. Wages rose dramatically—$5 to $6 to $7 a day—and the steady work and high pay produced a great migration of workers from other states, especially blacks from the Deep South. Housing of some kind had to be provided for these new citizens, and the Williams brothers cashed in, building cheap houses on land they owned near the factory section and bidding for cement work in the black ghetto. By 1918, they had attained as much security as northern blacks could expect.

For the Williamses and the others, making a livelihood took precedence over Liberty Bond rallies, parades, theater going—all those activities designed to foster a sense of public involvement in the war. They were, of course, affected by the superpatriotism of the war years: one of Meyer Miller's friends was arrested as a dangerous radical; the Reinhardts found themselves cut off from the larger society of Evansville. Popular hostility caused the dissolution of the *Turnverein* and the Perry Township *Volksbund*. In fall 1917, German was dropped from the curriculum at White Elementary and Reitz High School. The Reinhardts witnessed the public embarrassment of Friedrich Lauenstein who, after having his newspaper shut down, was compelled to become a bond salesperson.

These and myriad other examples of war

hysteria (sauerkraut renamed "liberty cabbage") might be related, but their immediate significance to our families was minor, while long-range effects, such as the loss of cultural identity, were either missed or considered as virtues.

What mattered to most families was not so much what the national government did but, rather, what it did not do. In its frantic drive for production of war material, the Wilson administration failed to prevent or even to slow a rampant inflation that eroded the economic advances of the war years. According to the primitive indexes then published, the cost of living almost doubled between 1914 and 1920. This meant in real terms that American families paid 10 cents per pound for flour (4 cents more than in 1914), 39 cents for a pound of round steak as contrasted with 23 cents per pound five years before, and 55 cents for a pound of bacon (up from 27 cents per pound in 1914). Butter cost 68 cents per pound slab (36 cents in 1914), and housewives were dazed by the jump in costs of staples such as milk (from 9 to 17 cents a quart), potatoes (18 cents for 10 pounds in 1914, 38 cents in 1919), and eggs (from 35 to 62 cents a dozen).

Instead of dealing with inflation or making more than a minimal effort to ease the impact of population growth in communities with war plants, the government occupied itself with writing a peace settlement. Woodrow Wilson turned from critical domestic problems to the flashy and dramatic challenges of big-time diplomacy. Wilson laid out the principles he believed must govern the peacemakers on January 8, 1918. His "Fourteen Points," as the address became known, called for open diplomacy, freedom of the seas, removal of barriers to international trade, reduction of armaments, self-determination for national minorities, specific boundary adjustments for France, Italy, and several Eastern European countries, independence for Poland, and a league of nations to enforce the peace and serve as an international forum for resolution of future disputes. The last point, Wilson asserted confidently, was the key, the *sine qua non* for creation of a viable international society and for American participation in that system. Woodrow Wilson was to pursue his plan for lasting peace with single-minded zeal.

The president faced difficulties. The leaders of Britain, France, and Russia already had arranged for peace through secret treaties and agreements that would strip their enemies of their empires and crush their war making capacity. Those objectives, not Wilson's "peace without victory," would guarantee lasting peace. Few Americans shared the president's vision of a future world, but Wilson refused to listen. When both Austria and Germany expressed interest in an armistice on the basis of the Fourteen points, the Allies were caught between acceptance of Wilson's plan or an open break with the United States. Georges Clemenceau of France bespoke the skepticism and resentment of Allied leaders: "I am sick of hearing about Wilson's Fourteen Points he said. "God Almighty was satisfied with only ten." Nonetheless, the American president's peace program, backed by his enormous popularity, had to be considered.

The German High Command signed a military truce with the Allied forces on November 11, 1918. President Wilson then took the unprecedented action of coming in person to Paris to preside at the peace conference which opened on January 12, 1919. Wilson was not entirely unaware of the opposition he faced. He realized he would have to make concessions to the ancient prejudices of his colleagues, and that local antagonisms might render the initial settlement inadequate. But he was convinced that these posed only temporary impediments so long as the League of Nations, the final and essential principle in his Fourteen Points, was made an integral part of the peace treaties.

PEACE

Coming to Paris in the guise of a missionary, President Wilson brought the Word, the covenant of a League of Nations he himself had drafted. Wilson's League, consisting of a world assembly and a council controlled by the major victorious powers, embodied the principle of collective security, the idea that a threat to the security of one nation represented a threat to all nations. Retaliation against aggressors was provided for by the use of economic sanctions, the cutting off of all trade with the aggressor nation, and, as a last resort, the cooperative use of military force by League members. If the system worked as President Wilson hoped, the old balance-of-power arrangements, so dangerous and so futile, would be rendered obsolete.

That this "noble dream" was not realized was as much the fault of Woodrow Wilson as

National Archives

Wilson, with French President Raymond Poincaré, waving to adoring crowds on his arrival in Paris in January 1919

it was the fault of chauvinistic attitudes among world leaders and their countrymen. If Wilson did not win the support of other national leaders, neither did he mobilize American political support—particularly that of the Senate which would have to ratify any treaty. Instead, his egotism and fanaticism alienated powerful Americans, while his desire to obtain a commitment of European leaders to the League led him to accept compromises that may have guaranteed another war 20 years later. Germany was stripped of its colonies, made to admit responsibility for the war, forced to pay reparations, and watch powerlessly as two new nations, Czechoslovakia and Poland, seized German lands and France occupied part of Germany itself. Wilson's obsession with the League drove him to accept deals which turned into mockery the goals of a just peace, of national self-determination, and of open diplomacy.

Even if Wilson's parliament of man had acquired sufficient wisdom to accomplish this monumental task, too many people were unwilling to wait for their particular cause to be considered. Back home, John and Gus O'Reilly were boiling mad about Wilson's failure to force the British to give independence to Ireland. Mihailo Markovich was baffled by the ruling that Serbia be amalgamated with several other Slavic peoples—including even the despised Croats—in some new state that was given the name of Yugoslavia. Jacob and Mathilde Reinhardt talked with their neighbors about the president's promise of a fair peace for Germany. How did that square with this "Article 231," which forced Germany and Austria to admit they had started the war? Moreover, the question regarding self-government was being violated in Russia where British, French, and American troops occupied Russian ports, refused to recognize the Bolshevik regime, and denied Russia a place at the peace table.

Opinions such as these might not count, but others, politically powerful, were concerned about the peace treaties and Wilson's League covenant. Senator Henry Cabot Lodge, who hated Wilson and considered his League of Nations a threat to America's independence, was especially active. By the time President Wilson became aware of the opposition at home and interrupted his work in Paris for a brief trip to Washington to deal with it, Lodge was able to present him with a statement signed by 37 senators (more than enough to prevent ratification) to the effect that Wilson's draft treaty was unacceptable. Wilson grudgingly agreed to a number of changes, mainly striking from the League's purview such potentially embarassing topics as the United States' self-appointed guardianship over Latin America and American immigration policy. When he returned to Paris, other nations demanded changes, many of which were inconsistent with the high principles of the Fourteen Points. Still, he obtained approval of a League covenant essentially intact, and he set sail for America determined to ram it through the Senate. While most Americans worried about high prices, coal shortages, and domestic violence, the president, his supporters, and their political opponents engaged in a titanic struggle over the peace treaties. A few senators, mostly Midwesterners, were "irreconcilables," who opposed the League idea and rejected American participation under any circumstances. Most opponents were "reservationists," men who followed Senator Lodge's position that the United States might safely ratify the treaty if some 14 reservations were appended. Most importantly, America must reserve its right to withdraw from any League activity at any time, the right to decide whether any matter was inappropriate for consideration by the League, and the requirement that no American troops be used in support of any League decision without prior authorization by a joint resolution of Congress.

At this point the president balked. He believed that tacking on reservations implied a less than total commitment by the United States and set a bad example for other nations. Believing that his logic was unimpeachable and that popular morality and concern for international justice mirrored his own views, President Wilson determined to bludgeon his opponents into acceptance of the League covenant by arousing public opinion. It would "break the heart of the world if the United States does not ratify this treaty," he proclaimed. He set out in early September 1919 on an 8,000 mile speaking tour to rally the American people behind the League. Apparently, Wilson thought he could obtain a vote of confidence and force the rascals in the Senate into cooperating with him.

The president pushed himself so hard that his health broke. Compelled to cancel the last segment of his tour and to return to Washington, he then suffered a brain hemorrhage. He was never to recover completely from this stroke. While he lay paralyzed, the Senate backed away from the League of Nations. Wilson—or persons in his entourage—never gave up. Word went out from the White House, presumably from Mrs. Wilson, that no compromise, no reservations, would be acceptable. The Senate thrice voted to ratify the treaty—twice with reservations and once with none—but the treaty never obtained the necessary two-thirds majority. Wilson was left with the hope that he would recover sufficiently to run again for president in 1920 or, failing that, that the Democratic nominee would make the election a referendum on the League. In either circumstance, he believed, the American people would respond to the call. That may have been Wilson's final and greatest miscalculation.

The struggle over the League took place against a backdrop of popular indifference. Americans simply had other problems to worry about. In the final weeks of the war, an influenza epidemic spread over the country, bringing tragedy to more American families than had all the Kaiser's legions. More than

20 million people were stricken with the Spanish flu. The disease spread like wildfire, felling old, young, strong, and feeble. It began with dizziness, aches, and, for the lucky ones, climaxed with a racking cough and four or five days of high fever. For others, influenza progressed into pneumonia and death by suffocation.

No one understood exactly how to treat the flu or how it spread. The best medical opinion held that soldiers originally had brought the germ back from Europe and had spread it by kissing and handshaking. "There is a great deal of kissing," lamented the chief of Kansas City's Health Department. "If a ban should be placed on it, there would be less influenza." He settled for closing the city's schools, movies, and churches, forbidding meetings of more than 20 people, and for

Masked New York City sanitation worker during the influenza epidemic of 1918. The New York Health Board urged: "Better be ridiculous than dead"

identifying any place refusing compliance with big yellow stickers, "Unfit for Human Habitation." Frightened citizens stayed indoors, seeking to avoid exposure to the dread disease. By November 1918, whole cities were paralyzed. Police, firemen, and transportation workers lay coughing in their beds. In Philadelphia on one day in mid-October, 650 died. Ben Trace, who mustered out of the army and returned to Evansville just in time to contract the disease, was nursed back to health by his roommate's sister. He married Anna Lee Bonham seven months later. The Reinhardts lost an infant daughter. Almost everyone saw relatives or close friends cough their lives away. Before it ended, the influenza pandemic spread to every continent and killed more than 21 million persons. Only the bubonic plague of the 6th century and the 14th century Black Death had claimed more lives. Indeed, it is possible that influenza, which killed at least 548,000 Americans—10 times as many as died in France—affected American life more than any event occurring during the war.

In the wake of the influenza epidemic came chaos, violence, and fear. Not that the disruptions of 1918–19 affected every American directly, but they hit closer to home than did maneuvers in the mud and mist of Flanders or the diplomatic minuets being danced in Paris. People who had agonized about a possible revolt of the masses during the heyday of Progressivism now had reason to believe their prophecies were being confirmed. Once industrialists lost the argument that demands for more money by their workers was disloyal, talk of strikes echoed in every union hall. By any accounting, wages had not kept up with increased productivity or living costs. By November 1919, over a million workers had thrown up picket lines. Employers, though flushed with wartime profits, determined to hold firm, fearing that any concessions would only encourage labor and lend support to

A special camp for influenza-stricken soldiers on the grounds of the Correy Hill Hospital, not far from the Butler home in Brookline

union organizers. The steel industry, in particular, was a target of union activity and, in response, a campaign by management to brand efforts by workers to organize as "un-American" and communist inspired. Strikes, lockouts, shootings, and bombings swept over the country. In Boston, even the police proved susceptible, deciding to organize a union. When the commissioner suspended the organizers in September 1919, a large part of the police force walked out. Widespread looting resulted, and the governor called out the state guard. Governor Calvin Coolidge instantly became a national hero for lecturing the striking policemen that there was "no right to strike against the public safety by anybody, anywhere, anytime." John O'Reilly, whose friends were enthusiastic supporters of the strike, reluctantly turned in his night stick and uniform and joined the picket line. The step so depressed him, however, that he never entirely recovered self-respect.

Coincidentally with the strikes, race riots further eroded the "peace" that had been promised. Overt racial violence revealed only the surface part of bitterness and hostility. Following "the war to save democracy," white Americans were no more inclined to accept any change in traditional patterns of segregation than they had been before the war. But black soldiers who had served in France (in segregated units) came home transformed, having been exposed to a white society that treated them fairly. Many had saved a little money, and friends and relatives had been well paid for working in war plants. They found adjustment to the old patterns of life, the ancient humiliations, difficult. As war plants shut down to retool for civilian production, blacks in industrial cities seemed always to be the first fired, and when factories reopened they hired returning white veterans first. Moreover, competition for housing increased with demobilization, and poorer whites became resentful of the expanding black populations in northern cities. Rents everywhere skyrocketed, but whites blamed blacks and vice versa. Tensions erupted into rioting in East St. Louis in 1917 and now, with the nation caught in an economic downturn, clashes occurred in numerous places. In Chicago, the stoning death of a black teenager swimming at a white beach quickly exploded into a full-scale riot. When it ended in late July, after state militia units had been called in, 23 blacks and 15 whites had died, and 342 blacks and 178 whites had been injured. The report of the Chicago Commission on Race Relations (1922) listed a number of causes for the riot: black migration, competition for industrial jobs, the housing conflict, discrimination in public places, and, also, the growing recourse to violence everywhere in America. The report was fair but it changed nothing.

"Once unleash this people in war and they will forget there is such a thing as justice and tolerance," Woodrow Wilson had predicted in 1915. The violence of the immediate postwar years seemed to fulfill his prophecy. The apparent success of Communism in Russia, unsuccessful revolutions in Hungary, Ger-

U.S. War Department General Staff, National Archives

Chicago's Federal Building, wrecked by a bomb explosion, 1918

many, and Italy, and the strikes and industrial violence in Europe and at home, heightened and confirmed the fears of some of the more affluent that the working classes were rising against the system. To be sure, revolutionary activity in the United States did escalate during these years when compared with prewar days. Workers, while more militant, still acted within the parameters established by Samuel Gompers: to strike for higher pay, shorter hours, and better working conditions—bread-and-butter unionism. The assertion by management, most of it designed to destroy industrial unionism, that labor was going (or had gone) communist and that the United States was being pushed toward a violent revolution was simply not true. None of our families and very few Americans felt strongly enough about the "pie in the sky by and by" offers to man barricades. A few, however—the Millers and Markoviches—did know revolutionaries, men who wanted to overthrow an oppressive capitalist system.

The emotions churned up by the war, already focusing on hyphenate groups, were easily converted into distrust and fear of ethnic radical activity. When someone mailed three dozen bombs to prominent businesspeople and politicians, the public, unsure about the right to strike and unnerved by the violence that accompanied many strikes, reacted hysterically. The federal government's actions increased the tension.

Attorney General A. Mitchell Palmer gave encouragement to the view that riots, strikes, dispatch of bombs through the mail, anarchism, and communism all were somehow related. Seizing upon the widespread strikes and labor violence (a general strike in Seattle, the much-publicized Boston police strike, a steel strike in September 1919, and UMW-led walkouts in the bituminous coal industry), Palmer launched a carefully prepared attack on "radicals," who were mostly recent immigrants. Palmer himself led troops into the coal fields. After an apparent attempt on his life on

Armistice Day 1919 (which failed when a man blew himself up outside Palmer's home), the Department of Justice began to compile dossiers on "undesirable" radicals. Then, on January 2, 1920, federal agents raided the meeting places of alleged radical groups, arresting over 4,000 people in 32 cities. Palmer's men often neglected to obtain proper search warrants and violated the civil rights of prisoners in the interim between arrest and trial. When the cases came to court, evidence of subversion against the United States seemed less important than being foreign or radical. A large number of people were deported, many to the Soviet Union, as undesirable aliens. A "red" menace never actually existed, though Palmer and many others persuaded themselves that it did, and their fears produced the "Red Scare" of 1919.

The strikes, outbreaks of racial violence, and resurgent nativism struck a nation already reeling from the influenza epidemic, coal shortages, runaway food prices, and other dislocations. Just these issues—inflation, shortages, war profiteering, and fear of radicalism—had been featured in the congressional elections of 1918. President Wilson, who was then in the midst of preparations for his journey to the peace conference in Paris, had called upon the American people to make this election a mandate for his peace program. Those of our families who voted had other things on their minds. The outcome, with Republicans gaining majorities in both houses of Congress, was not so much a repudiation of Wilson's policies (the League of Nations idea obtained wide popular support until the fall of 1919) but an expression of general dissatisfaction with the domestic economic situation. Once the boys had returned home, our families and most Americans asked to be left alone, to assimilate the changes they had undergone, and to work out for themselves satisfying lives. To that search, government contributed in 1919—as in 1914—very little.

SUGGESTIONS FOR FURTHER READING

Reading about Progressivism and the presidency of Woodrow Wilson still begins with Arthur S. Link, *Woodrow Wilson and the Progressive Era* (1954). Link's mammoth biography of Wilson is now almost completed, and the second and fifth volumes focus especially on domestic issues. See also Henry F. May, *The End of American Innocence, 1912-1917* (1959). Other helpful works on Wilson are Arthur Walworth, *Woodrow Wilson* (1958); John M. Blum, *Woodrow Wilson and the Politics of Morality* (1956); and Alexander L. and Juliette George, *Woodrow Wilson and Colonel House: A Personality Study* (1956). Many of the works cited in the previous chapter cover the themes considered here. Special studies include James E. Anderson, *The Emergence of the Modern Regulatory State* (1962); John M. Blum, *Joe Tumulty and the Wilson Era* (1951); Richard M. Lowitt, *George Norris* (3 vols., 1963-78); Milo J. Pusey, *Charles Evans Hughes* (1951); Walter Lippman, *Public Opinion* (1922); and William C. Widenor, *Henry Cabot Lodge and the Search for an American Foreign Policy* (1980).

United States foreign policy before 1914, especially the issues of economic expansion and ideology, is explored in such works as Ernest R. May's *American Imperialism* (1968); George F. Kennan's imaginative treatise, *American Diplomacy 1900-1950* (1950); the relevant chapters in the excellent work by Thomas G. Paterson et al., *American Foreign Policy: A History* (1977); *Politics, Strategy, and American Diplomacy: Studies in Foreign Policy 1873-1917* (1966), by John A. S. Grenville and George B. Young; and Walter LeFeber's challenging *The New Empire: An Interpretation of American Expansion, 1860-1898*. On the Spanish American War and America's reaction, see Walter Millis, *The Martial Spirit* (1936); Frank Freidel, *The Splendid Little War* (1958); Robert L. Beisner, *Twelve Against Empire: The Anti-Imperialists, 1898-1900* (1968); Leon Wolff's *Little Brown Brother* (1961); Peter Stanley, *A Nation in the Making: The Philippines and the United States, 1899-1921* (1974); Charles H. Brown, *The Correspondent's War* (1967); and E. Berkeley Tompkins, *Anti-Imperialism in the United States: The Great Debate, 1890-1920* (1970). The peace movement is studied in Sondra R. Herman, *Eleven Against War: Studies in American Internationalist Thought, 1898-1921* (1969); Warren F. Kuehl, *Seeking World Order: The United States and International Organization to 1920* (1969); Calvin Davis, *The United States and the First Hague Peace Conference* (1962); C. Roland Marchand, *The American Peace Movement and Social Reform, 1898-1918* (1972); John W. Chambers, ed., *The Eagle and the Dove: The American Peace Movement and United States Foreign Policy, 1900-1921* (1976); David Patterson, *Toward a Warless World: The Travail of the American Peace Movement, 1887-1914* (1976); and the superb recent synthesis by Charles DeBenedetti, *The Peace Reform in American History* (1980). The "Open Door" is analyzed in such special studies as Thomas J. McCormick's *China Market* (1967); Paul A. Varg, *The Making of a Myth: The United States and China, 1897-1912* (1968); Marilyn Young, *The Rhetoric of Empire: American China Policy, 1895-1901* (1968); Jerry Israel, *Progressivism and the Open Door: American and China, 1897-1912* (1971); and Michael Hunt, *Frontier Defense and the Open Door: Manchuria in Chinese-American Relations, 1895-1911* (1973). See also Akira Iriye, *Across the Pacific: An Inner History of American-East Asian Relations* (1969); and A. Whitney Griswold's *The Far Eastern Policy of the United States* (1938). United States–Latin American relations are treated in Dana G. Munro, *Intervention and Dollar Diplomacy in the Caribbean, 1900-1921* (1964); Lester Langley, *Struggle for the American Mediterranean* (1976); Walter LaFeber, *The Panama Canal: The Crisis in Historical Perspective* (1978); David McCullough's superbly written *The Path Between the Seas: The Creation of the Panama Canal, 1870-1914* (1977); and Robert Quirk's *An Affair of Honor* (1962). Presidential diplomacy is considered in Howard Beale, *Theodore Roosevelt and the Rise of America to World Power* (1956); Raymond Esthus, *Theodore Roosevelt and the International Rivalries* (1970); Eugene P. Trani, *The Portsmouth Peace Conference* (1969); Walter and Marie Scholes, *The Foreign Policies of the Taft Administration* (1970); Arthur Link, *Wilson the Diplomatist* (rev. ed., 1978); and N. Gordon Levin, Jr., *Woodrow Wilson and World Politics: America's Response to War and Revolution* (1968). Also useful are Bradford Perkins, *The Great Rapprochement: England and the United States, 1895-1914* (1968); the essays on Mahan, TR, Straight, and Wilson in Frank J. Merli and Theodore A. Wilson, eds., *Makers of American Diplomacy* (1975); Richard D. Challener, *Admirals, Generals, and American Foreign Policy, 1898-1914* (1973); Robert P. Schulzinger, *The Making of the Diplomatic Mind: The Training, Outlook, and Style of U.S. Foreign Service Officers, 1908-1939* (1975); and Benjamin F. Cooling, *Gray Steel and Blue Water Navy: The Formative Years of America's Military-Industrial Complex, 1881-1917* (1979).

Any investigation of the intertwining of immigration, popular attitudes, and national policy must begin with John Higham's *Strangers in the Land* (1955). Also of interest are Philip Taylor, *The Distant Magnet* (1971); Louis L. Gerson, *The Hyphenate in Recent American Politics and Diplomacy* (1964); Roger Daniels, *The Politics of Prejudice: The Anti-Japanese Movement in California and the Struggle for Japanese Exclusion* (1962); William Preston, Jr., *Aliens and Dissenters: Federal Suppression of Radicals, 1903-1933* (1963); Gerd Korman, *Industrialization, Immigration, and Americanization* (1967); and Ralph A. Stone, *The Irreconcilables: The Fight Against the League of Nations* (1970).

A few of the slithering heap of books treating aspects of America's entry into the First World War are Ernest R. May, *The World War and American Isolation* (1959); H. C. Peterson, *Propaganda for War: The Campaign Against American Neutrality, 1914-1917* (1939); Ross Gregory, *The Origins of American Intervention in the First World War* (1971); Warren I. Cohen, *The American Revisionists: The Lessons of Intervention in World War I* (1967); John M. Cooper, Jr., *The Vanity of Power: American Isolationism and the First World War, 1914-1917* (1969); Barbara Tuchmann, *The Zimmerman Telegram* (1958); Thomas A. Bailey and Paul Ryan, *The Lusitania Disaster* (1975); Patrick Devlin, *Too Proud to Fight: Woodrow Wilson's Neutrality* (1975); John G. Clifford, *The Citizen Soldiers: The Plattsburg Training Camp Movement, 1913-1920* (1972); and Daniel Smith, *Robert Lansing and American Neutrality, 1914-1917* (1958). The conduct of American diplomacy after U.S. entry is treated in Lawrence P. Gelfand, *The Inquiry: American Preparations for Peace,*

1917-1919 (1963); Arno J. Mayer, *Politics and Diplomacy of Peacemaking* (1968); Thomas A. Bailey, *Woodrow Wilson and the Lost Peace* (1944); Carl P. Parrini, *Heir to Empire: United States Economic Diplomacy, 1916-1923* (1969); the study by Levin cited above; Arthur Walworth, *America's Moment: 1918* (1977); and Charles L. Mee, Jr., *The End of Order: Versailles, 1919* (1980). Military operations are covered in Edward M. Coffman, *The War to End All Wars: The American Military Experience in World War I* (1968); David F. Trask, *The United States in the Supreme War Council* (1961); and Lawrence Stallings, *The Doughboys: The Story of the AEF, 1917-1918* (1963). Also see John Toland, *No Man's Land: 1918, The Last Year of the Great War* (1980); A. E. Barbeau and Florette Hari, *Unknown Soldiers: Black American Troops in World War One* (1974); and Harvey A. DeWeerd, *President Wilson Fights His War* (1968).

David M. Kennedy, *Over Here: The American Home Front in World War I* (1980) is a persuasive and comprehensive treatment of domestic history during the First World War. Also of interest are William C. Mullendore, *History of the United States Food Administration, 1917-1919* (1941); James R. Mock and Cedric Larson, *Words that Won the War* (1939); Russell Weigley, *The American Way of War* (1973); George T. Blakey, *Historians on the Home Front* (1970); Carol S. Gruber, *Mars and Minerva: World War I and the Uses of Higher Learning in America* (1975); Robert D. Cuff, *The War Industries Board: Business-Government Relations During World War I* (1973); David F. Noble, *America by Design* (1977); John W. Chambers, *Draftees or Volunteers* (1975); Seward W. Livermore, *Politics is Adjourned: Woodrow Wilson and the War Congress, 1916-1918* (1966); Horace C. Peterson and Gilbert C. Fite, *Opponents of War, 1917-1919* (1957); and the previously cited *Our Times*. Problems of the war and immediate aftermath are treated in Robert K. Murray, *The Red Scare* (1955); David Brody, *Labor in Crisis: The Steel Strike of 1919* (1965); William Tuttle, Jr., *Race Riot: Chicago in the Red Summer of 1919* (1968); James R. Mock and Evangeline Thurber, *Report on Demobilization* (1944); John D. Hicks, *Rehearsal for Disaster: The Boom and Collapse of 1919-1920* (1961); and Burl Noggle, *Into the Twenties* (1974).

San Francisco
(Berkeley)
19

Fresno
20–22
Dinuba

Los Angeles
62–65

11–
Rop
8–10
New Albany

Fred

Sherr
7

E
74 Hawki
75 Tyler

74   Kos
Marlin ● ● (Sh
Gr
72–

81
Laredo

78–80
Los Eb

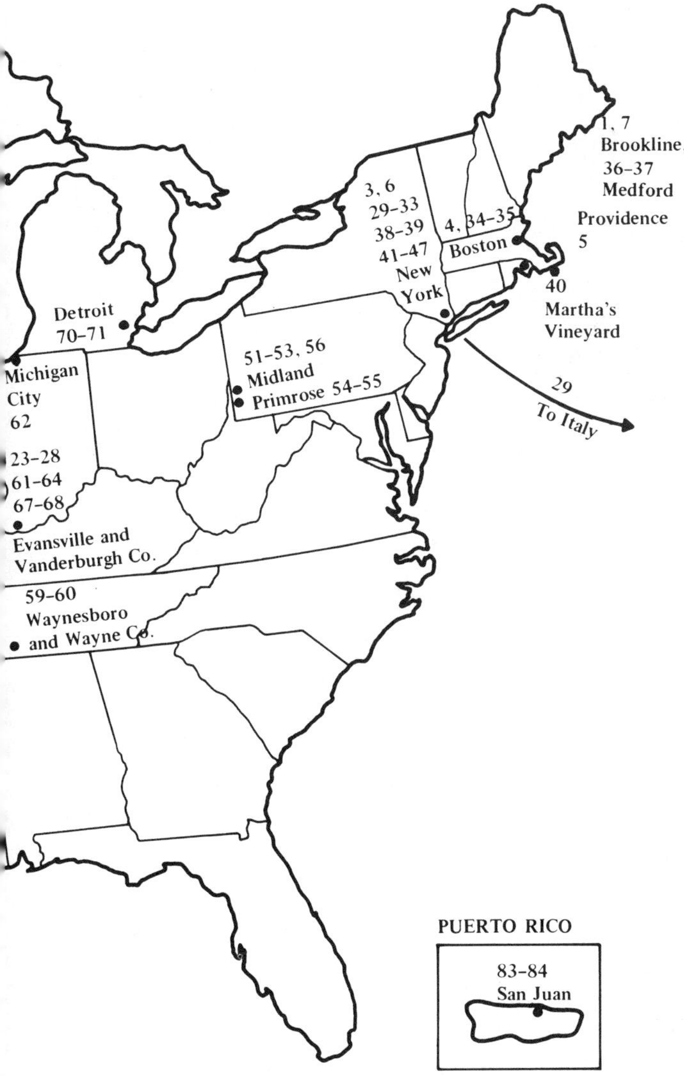

PART **2**
1920–1945

1, 7
Brookline,
36–37
Medford

Providence
5

3, 6
29–33
38–39
41–47
New
York

4, 34–35
Boston

40
Martha's
Vineyard

Detroit
70–71

Michigan
City
62

51–53, 56
Midland
Primrose 54–55

29
To Italy

23–28
61–64
67–68

Evansville and
Vanderburgh Co.

59–60
Waynesboro
and Wayne Co.

PUERTO RICO

83–84
San Juan

5 | The Second Generation

INTRODUCTION

By 1920, few families could live the independent existences for which Ben Trace, Mihailo Markovich, Charles Gale, and others strove. Only a favored few in the complex industrial-urban system that had spread its dominion over almost all aspects of life by the 1920s could hope to be totally self-reliant. Young Robert Butler, returning from duty with the American occupation forces in Germany in August 1919, confronted real options: family business, another fling in the groves of academe, law school, and even a life of total leisure. Following a series of bicycle trips around New England, canoeing in Maine, and parties without end, Bobby Butler abandoned pleasure for a hard bench in Harvard Law School. Perhaps not even he possessed true freedom. The grim observation of Charles Dickens in 1840—that a worker with an income of 20 shillings and expenses of 19

shillings, six pence considered himself wealthy, while one with wages of 19 and 6 and expenses of 20 shillings faced the poorhouse and oblivion—was applicable to the vast majority of Americans in 1920.

The treadmill of getting and spending occupied the attention of the families as it had always done, though the mechanisms changed greatly. During the years 1920 to 1940, American families confronted forces they only vaguely comprehended, but which increasingly dictated their choices, their styles of life, even their dreams. Economic "adjustments" that were glibly accepted as natural phenomena during the 1920s and as maladjustments of the capitalist economic system during the 1930s affected their lives in innumerable ways. For the Bassanos, Markoviches, Traces, Millers, and the farm families in particular, wage and price shifts had direct and traumatic consequences. In the spring-summer of 1920, Rose Bassano was angered by food prices, which seemed to be higher every time she walked into her grocers. "Flour at 41 cents for a five pound bag, bacon at 55 cents a pound, sugar at 97 cents, eggs at 70 cents a dozen and not very big ones either. I couldn't pay such prices. Some things soon became cheaper but it certainly hurt us, what with Mr. Bassano's pay packet so often empty during that time." The "prosperity" of the 1920s, a reality for the O'Reillys, was essentially illusory for working-class Americans. The depression was to be, for many, nightmare.

Not just economic security but something even more important, psychological security—the feeling of control over the inner rhythm of one's life—was jeopardized. The families would find the interwar period a time of wrenching change and ambivalence, reflecting both achievement and deep-seated frustration. The greatest achievement, perhaps, was survival. Numerous children were born while the lives of some were saddened by the death of several infants and a number of adults. Some of the families expanded their participation in their communities; others remained aloof, perhaps even alienated, from society. In like measure, the families and millions of others experienced the birth, nurture, and often death of dreams for a full life.

Some of the ambitions—for the next generation, at least—would be realized. Overcoming the failures of the system in which they were enmeshed, Will Trace, Andrew Bassano, Mihailo Markovich, Annie Miller, and the others offered relative abundance and social mobility to their children as their chief legacy. But unending toil and sacrifice proved insufficient to ensure that the next generation thought and acted and wanted as had its parents. It may not be an exaggeration to assert that the similarities of thought and outlook among native-born and immigrant Americans who attained adulthood before 1920 were far greater than similarities be-

tween them and their children. This mirrored the increasing homogenization of American life produced by economic circumstances and social stratification. Even more, however, it reflected the diffusion of authority within the family unit and a partial loss of control to outside institutions.

Though the family and the home remained the spiritual, psychological, and physical center of life in America, its predominance was increasingly challenged. The shift toward specialized occupations unrelated to the family, reduction of the family's role in the socialization of children and the growth of the school's role, declining reliance on kin for assistance in time of crisis, increasing geographical mobility, and the effects of leisure combined to further weaken the hold of the family and the home. No one conceived of these changes in apocalyptic terms. There was no muttering: "What shall it profit a man to gain the whole world and lose his own soul." The changes were small and gradual—Robert Bassano's decision to marry a non-Italian, the role of Jerry Trace's math teacher as an authority figure, the need for the Miller girls to work to support their ailing father—in the context of the lives of the families. But if largely unplanned, they nonetheless were incremental and eventually disruptive. Taken together, the changes distorted the inner rhythm at the core of each family's security and introduced discordancies that denied tranquility to the older generation. Like good soldiers, they stepped in cadence to the drumbeat of change. Like good American soldiers, they questioned the necessity of the trip.

THE TRACES OF EVANSVILLE, INDIANA

By 1920, the Traces from Wayne County, Tennessee, formed a sizable group within the working-class, railroad-service community of

Howell, on the west side of Evansville, Indiana. Kate Trace Wolfe, her husband, and four children lived in a huge Victorian house on Ewing Street. Ben Trace, newly married, had rented a small house on Glendale, less than three blocks from his sister's home. In fall 1919, Walter Trace abandoned the effort to scratch a decent living from the small, worn-out farm he owned outside Waynesboro and brought his family to Evansville. Walter bought a five-room house in Howell, and he

Ben Trace, home from the railroad yards, 1920s

found work as a mechanic's assistant in the L&N shops. The youngest brother, McKinley Trace, still lived in the boarding house on Front Street, some four blocks from his kin, in which he and Ben had stayed since coming to Howell.

All the Traces, except perhaps for Kate, believed that the move to Howell was temporary. When the good times returned, when enough money had been saved to buy a decent-sized farm—located on rich bottom land rather than on the scrub pine, gully-washed land on which most of their other kin were forced to live—they intended to go back to Wayne County, much as immigrants from southern and eastern Europe dreamed of a triumphant return to their native villages. In 1929, Walter would go back—not in triumph but in need. Never able to gain the necessary seniority to win steady employment, he took the depression as a personal failure and returned to the family farm. Ben and McKinley stayed. Ben talked and planned for the time of his return until the obligations of a growing family snuffed out the dream and he discarded it. McKinley kept the dream alive by pickling it in the cheap booze he bought in the speakeasies and poolrooms along Front Street. Neither brother admitted, even to himself, that Evansville, rather than Wayne County, was and forever would be home. If nothing else, death would call them back to the red clay of the Trace family cemetery.

There, in Wayne County, little had changed. Until his death in 1925, Will Trace doggedly worked in his tobacco and corn fields. The family gathered—for the last time—for Will's burial in the hill cemetery near Topsy. Millie then lived with her daughter, Sally, until the former's death in 1934. Another son, Tom, took over the family farm. As late as the mid-1930s there were fewer than two-dozen tractors in the entire county and almost no paved roads. The agricultural depression of the 1920s and the economic cataclysm of the 1930s had little direct effect on the Traces. Credit became dearer, commodity prices even lower, but that meant simply that their "marginal" existence was rendered still more precarious. By 1935, some change was discernible as federal programs—AAA, FERA, then the CCC and WPA—reached into southwestern Tennessee, but none of the Traces became in any way involved in such activities.

After his discharge from the Army, Ben Trace returned to Evansville, confident that the goal of a decent farm back home would shortly be realized. He had saved several hundred dollars from his service pay, was to receive a sizable discharge bonus, and had returned to his job with the L&N Railroad to find that his pay envelope had grown much larger. Marriage to Anna Lee Bonham appeared to be a positive step toward a goal they both desired: the ownership of a productive farm. With Ben working steadily and bringing home $20 to $24 almost every week, financial security seemed assured. Rent for the four-room house to which Ben brought Anna after their wedding at her parents' home was only $15 per month. The newlyweds rarely spent more than $10 per week for food and other household expenses. Ben neither smoked nor drank, he walked to work (the house was less than a block from the tracks leading into the L&N yards), and the couple's social life consisted of visits with kin. Matters did not work out as Ben had anticipated, however. Almost from the day of his wedding, there was only enough money to scrape by and sometimes not even that.

It might be argued, as Ben later came to believe, that forces beyond his control conspired to strip him of economic independence. The inflation of the immediate postwar years, the financial difficulties experienced by the L&N, the severe recession of 1921-22—all struck directly at Ben's savings. Most

Anna Trace, 1920s

damaging were the bitter strikes of 1919-20. Labor activism produced outbreaks of violence in the L&N yards and caused work stoppages for weeks. Ben was, at best, a passive supporter of the strikers; he worried about his empty pay packets and the struggle to keep the rent paid and food in the house. After the strike was settled, Ben worked irregularly for the L&N, averaging only eight months of full-time work each year from 1920 to 1927.

Even more important was the way in which Ben and Anna Trace managed their affairs during these first years. For they took on obligations—children, material possessions—which placed far greater restrictions upon them than did the "goddamned system" Ben was wont to blame. The choices that lay before them were not premeditated; they and most of their contemporaries moved within a larger stream that led without challenge to marriage and family.

Americans subscribed to the belief that marriage and family life best organized and gave meaning to individual existence. During the 1920s, the marriage rate remained relatively stable, declined sharply during 1930–32, and then gained steadily until 1940. The institution of marriage, however, was caught between powerful, conflicting forces in American society. Though retaining its dominant role as the vehicle for sexual expression and social organization, its functions and standing continued to be modified. Monogamous, legally contracted marriage was traditionally the accepted state for the satisfaction of sexual needs, procreation, psychological equilibrium, and as an efficient division of labor. Important attributes of marriage were its high status, patriarchical orientation, stress on permanence, emphasis on mutual affection—at least in the beginning—and free choice of spouses. Increasingly in the United States, romantic love and the notion that matrimony would (or should) automatically guarantee self-fulfillment became integral, and for many, all-important conditions of marriage.

At the same time, the forces of industrialization and urbanization were striking directly at the traditional economic rationale of marriage—as a cooperative enterprise in which the partners divided work and had clearly defined responsibilities. As families moved from farms to factories, from self-sufficiency to wage and salary dependency, the husband typically acquired sole responsibility for his family's welfare while the wife was relegated to a dronelike status. But this transformation of economic roles did not produce any clear, lasting definition of the appropriate roles for marital partners. Job insecurity often mocked the husband's ability to fulfill the role of provider, and the system offered females *potential* economic independence. Since the mid-19th century, halting steps were taken to eradicate the legal inequalities with which women had been burdened. The rights of wives to hold property, and to carry on businesses and earn wages for their own benefit had been recognized. However, attitudes regarding appropriate female roles (within and outside marriage) changed only very slowly. Logic dictated one course, but the weight of socioreligious dogma pointed to traditional arrangements—male supremacy, belief in feminine weakness—as the only way to marital bliss. The result was confusion and growing frustration.

In the interwar years, certain effects of this continuing confusion became clear. The majority of marital relationships more nearly approached a partnership, with the husband retaining male supremacy, economic and other, and the wife assuming the roles of child rearer, consumer, and companion. Families typically became smaller, because of economic pressures, social prescription, and growing awareness of contraceptive techniques. The divorce rate shot up markedly and permanent separation for those who could not seek divorce was increasing even faster. Many believed these trends proved that "marriage is no longer a . . . lifelong state but a union existing during the pleasure of the parties," and considered it a harbinger of the imminent collapse of civilization. The idea of "companionate marriage," contracted "for the purpose of a legalized intimate comradeship of a man and a woman without the obligations of parenthood," was widely pub-

156

licized. For many, such a relationship, offering "love" (sex plus mutual affection) and also the opportunity for individual growth, promised to reconcile the institution of marriage with the demands of modern life.

Companionate marriages might be permissible for F. Scott Fitzgerald's characters (or for Fitzgerald and his wife Zelda), but most Americans still sought to establish and maintain marriages that conformed with their own experiences. Ben and Anna Lee Trace's marriage exemplified the difficult and frustrating problems this effort could generate. Ben accepted as his right the position of patriarch, but his was abstract dominance. He abdicated to Anna Lee responsibility for everything con-

The "smart set," a *Harper's Bazaar* portrayal of the cultural/sexual revolution of the 1920s

cerning the home (management of the family's finances, discipline of the children, scheduling shared activities) and retreated to his gardening and beekeeping. He asserted this abstract authority only sporadically, when Anna Lee overextended the family's credit at Koressel's Grocery or when one of the kids directly challenged a maternal decision. Ben gave little time to the children. After arriving home at 3:30, grease and soot covered, he usually worked in the garden or his basement workshop until supper. "My daddy never taught his kids," Ben's eldest explained. "He showed us how by doing things himself and then silently going his own way. He didn't coddle us. He didn't play games with us, carrying out this buddy-buddy stuff." Awkward at showing emotion, Ben assumed—as had his father—that the effort he expended to feed and house his family was sufficient proof of his concern. The older boys learned quickly to conceal their emotions under a facade of self-reliance. Jacqueline felt keenly the lack of intimacy with her father. By the mid-1920s, after their first three children were born (Ben, Jr. in 1921, Jerry Conrad in 1924, and Wilma Jacqueline in 1926), Ben and Anna Lee had abandoned their yearnings for romantic love and self-fulfillment and had accepted the gray sameness of their marriage, the prosaic discussions of family activities and problems as the measure of male-female relationships. The marriage lasted because Ben and Anna Lee could not imagine anything better; however, in their case, familiarity bred not contempt but a comfortable tolerance.

For Ben, marriage provided stability, good southern cooking, and convenient sex. Sex had been vitally important in Ben's expectations regarding marriage. Both Ben and Anna, products of farms, were fully knowledgeable about the mechanics of reproduction, but neither had received any practical advice about the opposite sex's physiological and psychological needs (except for whis-

pered: "Nice girls don't enjoy doin' it, Ben, so don't expect too much," and to Anna Lee, "It will be painful and disgusting, but it's your duty.") As with most Americans of their generation, Ben and Anna Lee's sexual knowledge was a confusion of folk tales, moral strictures, and misconceptions. Satisfaction of male needs was natural (if not carried to excess), but strong female responses were abnormal; masturbation weakened the body and could produce boils, blood disorders, and even insanity; menstruation was enervating and repulsive and women suffering "the curse" were to avoid physical activity and public exposure. Sex, though necessary for the perpetuation of the species, was embarrassing and somehow tainted. Explicit discussion of sexual matters was taboo in most homes. A few progressive educators introduced children to the "biological, physiological, and ethical aspects" of sex; but not until the late 1930s did colleges begin to offer courses in marriage and sex education. Ben Trace merely informed his sons: "Don't believe everything you hear in the street or the toilets at school." Jacqueline did not receive even this advice from her mother. That Ben continued to use Anna Lee as a sexual partner was witnessed by the birth of two more children: William J. (1929) and Theodore Allen (1940). Anna Lee never complained but neither was she able to enjoy the sex act. Indeed, revulsion (and perhaps her own frustration) may have caused Anna Lee's rapid slide into obesity. By her 35th birthday, she was carrying 215 pounds on a 5 foot, 1 inch frame. Not many years later, Ben's demands ceased. The Traces had developed their own version of companionate marriage.

An intelligent, strong-willed woman, Anna Lee nonetheless was required by her circumstances and upbringing to repress her own needs and to seek fulfillment through serving others. Having discovered that marriage did not ensure "happiness," she endeavored to offer it to her husband and children and then share in their bliss. Anna Lee kept a spotless house and the boys and Jacqueline carefully groomed, satisfying their every whim, and yearning after the newest household gadgetry. Within the narrow limits imposed by the family's purchasing power and Anna Lee's scanty information about fads and fashions (she almost never read women's magazines and only occasionally the fashion pages in the *Evansville Sunday Press)*, she pursued the acquisition of "things" as guarantors of happiness as avidly as the ideal consumer in *Good Housekeeping* and *Cosmopolitan*. The result was that phenomenon of American culture which Philip Wylie christened "momism" a few years later. Anna Lee Trace appeared to be a warm, yielding marshmallow but at the core was resilient steel. The outpouring of love was so overwhelming, the sacrifices their mother made for them so enormous, that the children experienced great difficulty asserting their independence. Only later would they learn that Anna Lee's willingness to give, everlastingly give, produced obligations, binding them and, in turn, their spouses and their children.

Long before Anna Lee's petit figure disappeared in mounds of fried chicken, baking-powder biscuits, and milk gravy, she and Ben had come to terms with their situation. After the birth of their second son, Ben used the money that had been set aside for a Wayne County farm to buy a five-room house across the street from their rented quarters. The Traces' new home, for which Ben paid $3,200, boasted two bedrooms, living room, sitting room (which was converted into a third bedroom when Jacqueline was born), kitchen, and bath with built-in plumbing, though not hot water. It spread across two lots, and Ben immediately put in a huge garden. There was a small garage and a chicken house at the back of the property. The house was considered quite modern, with electric

The Trace home

lights and a coal furnace, and even a goldfish pond in the backyard.

Anna Lee loved her home and began immediately to fill it with furniture, knicknacks, and kitchen gadgets. Ben soon came to hate it, for the financial obligations pushed him to the brink (and several times over the edge) of insolvency. He worked irregularly for the L&N throughout the 1920s. He struggled to supplement his income by planting a large garden (which supplied the family and brought in extra money), raising chickens and rabbits, and by keeping bees (selling the honey to a local bakery). "Many early memories relate to the struggle for money and the big fun on payday when mom and dad came home from cashing the check and brought in the huge sack of groceries," Jerry Trace later recalled. Ben could never get ahead, and when the depression hit Evansville, the Traces faced very difficult times. Ben was laid off for three long periods (1931, 1933–34, and 1938–39). During the first two periods, the family moved to a friend's farm in Union Township, renting the house on Glendale in order to continue the payments. Even this stopgap failed in January 1934, and the home was saved only when Ben obtained refinancing from the Home Owner's Loan Corporation, which enabled him to postpone payments on principal and interest for five years. The family gradually recovered a measure of financial stability. Ben returned to work full-time with the L&N and the boys, all of whom held after-school jobs, helped to pay the bills at Koressel's Grocery.

Despite the grim problems they faced during the depression, Ben and Anna were determined that their children take advantage of the educational opportunities available to them in Evansville. All five eventually earned high-school diplomas. Ben, Jr., an honor student and editor of the Reitz High School *Mirror,* graduated in 1939. Fully intending to enter Evansville College when he had enough money, he found work at Hoosier Cardinal Corporation. That year, Jerry, also an outstanding student, was named to the all-city football team as a sophomore. He played baseball and was on the track squad while working at a Thom McCann shoe store most afternoons. The next year, Jacqueline entered Reitz, leaving only Bill, a fifth grader, at Daniel Wertz Elementary School. School attendance was difficult for the Trace children both physically (a three-mile walk each way) and economically, but they never questioned their parents' wishes in this matter.

The world of school and its myriad activities—sports, clubs, and social events—was alien to Ben and Anna, and this served to increase the distance between them and their children. However, they accepted it as inevitable and even desirable. By the time a fifth child, Theodore "Teddy" Allen, was born in September 1940, the Traces were solidly rooted in Evansville. However, they were no more active in the community than they had been in 1920. Their life was circumscribed by work and visits with kin, and their economic situation was hardly less tenuous. (Ben earned $955 in 1939). But the children were healthy and moving up the ladder of education. For them, a bright future beckoned and

that, for Ben and Anna, offered sufficient compensation for the failed dreams and difficulties they themselves had experienced.

THE MILLERS OF NEW YORK CITY

The apartment into which Meyer and Annie Miller, their son, and four unmarried daughters moved in April 1920, seemed the epitome of comfort. In contrast with the cramped, antiquated quarters the family had inhabited for five years in Providence, their new home, in a modern tenement at Franklin Place and 170th Street in the West Bronx, boasted two bedrooms, a separate bathroom and kitchen, steam heat, *and* electric lighting. It was in a neighborhood that was 85 percent Jewish and thus offered the amenities— kosher grocery, bakery, and butcher shop; orthodox synagogues and *cheder;* bathhouses and bookstores—which Meyer and Annie considered essential for a decent life.

Meyer and Annie Miller were comfortable in this environment, surrounded by familiar sights, sounds, and smells. They were fortunate in other ways. Many Americans were living in inadequate, overcrowded, and unsafe quarters. In 1932, a presidential commission found that one of six dwellings in urban centers was unsafe or "unfit for habitation" and that one of every six families in America's cities lived in overcrowded conditions. Rural Americans faced even worse problems, for one of every two dwellings in rural areas required major repairs or was unfit. The 1940 census reported that, in New York City alone, there were 236,000 occupied apartments without tub or shower, 190,000 without indoor toilets, 6,700 without gas or electricity, and 244,000 without hot water.

Such conditions generated high disease and death rates (especially infant mortality), and increased crime and delinquency, and

psychological problems. While upper middle-class reformers bemoaned the unfortunate weakening of patriotism and self-reliance
that attended the trend toward renting
domiciles, they should have been more concerned about the harmful effects that attended the overcrowding of families without
proper sanitary facilities, ventilation, and lighting, whether the family rented or owned its
place of residence. The correlation was strong
between inadequate housing and infant mortality, for instance. A federal children's bureau
survey of eight cities revealed that the infant
death rate nearly doubled when the ratio of
people per room increased from one to two
and, when more than two persons inhabited a
room, it jumped 50 percent. Similarly, statistics on crime demonstrated a firm connection
between juvenile delinquency and overcrowded housing conditions. The problem of
inadequate housing became widely known
after the First World War, but its solution was
left in the hands of the private construction
industry. In the meantime, millions of families
existed in squalor.

The Millers were lucky, for they possessed
sufficient resources to rent acceptable housing
for themselves. Their fine new apartment was
a staggering $50 per month, almost half of the
family's combined incomes. The Millers had
now won through to financial stability and
even such an extravagance as this could be
afforded. Jack Miller, who graduated from
New York University with a degree in accounting in 1919, had found a position as
bookkeeper in an automotive-parts business.
His mother and father, who had sacrificed so
much to send Jack through high school and
college, anticipated that their only son would
contribute a large part of his income to the
family. The eldest daughter, Pauline, had
married a Jewish immigrant in 1916 and was
living on Martha's Vineyard where her husband had launched a grocery business with
his brothers. Betty and Rose, the next two

daughters, had left school and had found
steady jobs. Both continued to live at home.
Betty worked on the assembly line of the
Bulova Watch Company factory in Brooklyn
while Rose obtained a job with the Arrow
Manufacturing Company, a watch and jew-
elry-case manufacturer partly owned by
Bulova. Since the Arrow factory was in
Hoboken, New Jersey, Rose commuted six
days a week from the Bronx. Betty and Rose
turned over their wages to the family, keeping
only carfare and a few dollars for "incidentals." The two youngest girls, Billie (12) and
Bertha (9), were attending elementary school,
and the family hoped that they would be able
to earn high-school diplomas.

Unfortunately, Meyer Miller's health, never
robust, began to fail shortly after the family's
move to Franklin Avenue. In November
1920, Meyer was involved in a freak accident
(his leg was caught in a pressing machine) in
the belt factory where he then worked. He
never recovered full use of the leg and found
it difficult to work regularly. "I can never remember my father working at all," his
youngest daughter said later. Then, in 1925,
Meyer suffered a collapsed lung. The children
accepted the obligation of supporting their increasingly feeble father.

The Millers did not have a family physician.

Bertha Miller, left, and sixth grade chums on Franklin
Avenue, Bronx, 1923

Illnesses and wounds, even serious ones, were normally the province of Annie and knowledgeable neighborhood women. The injury to Meyer's leg had been treated in a neighborhood clinic, and when he became ill in 1925, the family insisted he see one of the doctors there. The doctor recommended surgery, but Meyer refused to enter a hospital, preferring to live with but one lung than to risk dying under a surgeon's knife. (A glance at the survival rate of postoperative patients in even the best hospitals suggests that Meyer may have been wise.) Then, in spring 1929, Meyer began to lose weight rapidly and to manifest an intermittent high fever. When Annie confessed that he was passing blood, the children insisted that Meyer enter the new Jewish hospital on 162nd Street for a thorough checkup. Tests revealed that Meyer had cancer of the lower intestine. It appeared hopeless, but the consulting physician suggested that a colostomy, a radically new surgical procedure in which the cancerous tissue was removed and an external shunt for waste was created, would extend Meyer's life. The family gave approval, and, on July 3, 1929, Meyer underwent the operation, the fifth colostomy performed in the United States. The doctor promised that if Meyer lived five years, he would be entirely cured. Almost exactly five years later, during which time he was almost totally bedridden, Meyer Miller died. The Miller family was able to provide the best medical care then available for Meyer, though the effort exhausted the family's savings (some $8,000 in 1929). No medical insurance, private or public, eased their financial burden.

Meyer Miller's illness was not untypical of the dealings most Americans had with doctors and hospitals in the two decades prior to the Second World War. Modern health care was in its infancy in these decades. The world of well-trained doctors and modern hospitals was open, with some few exceptions, only to well-to-do Americans. Specialized medical care was tremendously expensive because there were so few specialists and also because the referral rate was so low. People refused to enter hospitals because of the expense and because they feared what would happen to them. Those who could preferred to go to general practitioners (GPs) who delivered medical services at a very reasonable cost. Unhappily, the number of physicians increased only 7.2 percent in the period 1921–40, a time when the American population increased 20 percent. In one way, the Millers and others who lived in medium and large cities were fortunate, for the doctor-patient ratio was far better in urban than in rural areas. In 1930, 44 percent of all physicians practiced in places with 100,000 or more people, and the shift of medical expertise to cities occurred rapidly. Not just doctors but also medical facilities were concentrated in urban centers.

For many families, the most direct (and often most traumatic) contact with the medical profession was the experience of childbirth. During the 1920s and 1930s the participation of a physician in the delivery of babies grew steadily, and it became more and more typical for babies to be delivered in hospitals—again except in rural areas. While the trend toward reliance upon professionals in childbirth certainly was a major cause of the drop in infant mortality rates (from 99 per 1,000 births in 1915 to 65 in 1930 to 51 in 1940), medicine remained an inexact science and the impersonality of hospital procedures undoubtedly persuaded many mothers and fathers to avoid further contact with the medical profession. In particular, the archaic and often dangerous gynecological procedures followed by many doctors (and the sexist repugnance regarding childbirth they reflected) repelled many women and killed others. A pioneer in the study of childbirth and maternal mortality, Dorothy Reed Mendenhall, found that, in 1912, the death rate for mothers was three times as great for hospital deliveries as for deliveries at home—or even for deliveries in vehicles en route to the hospital. These problems were corrected, but it was a slow process, for the medical profession rejected outside efforts to improve medical training and hospital procedures. The essential problem regarding improvement of health care for families in America was one of broadening the definition of a satisfactory standard of living and then of democratizing the delivery of medical care. For this, awareness was needed that such factors as proper dietary practices (especially for children), adequate housing, and recreational opportunities directly affected the health of individuals and family units. An acceptable number of physicians and medical facilities for all classes of Americans was required; but, as well, the public had to be educated to use these services and to understand that good health was largely the product of a physical, nutritional, and psychological balance. Strides were being made, such as the clinic system and the housing codes enacted in New York; however, the mortality and morbidity rates remained shockingly high.

Meyer Miller's experience in one of these clinics convinced him that he never would regain his health. During the years of enforced idleness, Meyer turned again to the scholarly endeavors he had pursued as a young rabbinical student in Russia. He contented himself with the newspapers, socialist tracts, and historical works supplied by relatives and friends. The family's economic survival was assured, he thought. Life, if tragically unfair to the laboring classes, was bearable, and frankly, Meyer much preferred the world of reading and political debates to the demeaning work he had performed since coming to America. Thus, Annie Miller was left with total responsibility for the children, the family's finances, housing—all the difficult decisions that daily intruded on the Millers and other Americans. She worked to ensure that the family remained together. With the exception of Jack, whose marriage in 1925 to Rose Neuman, a well-educated girl from a German, Reform Jewish background, imposed awkward social barriers between him and his family, the Miller children maintained their ties to family and heritage after reaching adulthood.

The strongest element in this continuing solidarity was the emphasis Annie placed on Judaism as the core of the family's being. Even though Meyer vehemently proclaimed atheistic views, Annie insisted on maintaining a Jewish home. In fact, there was no basic conflict here, for Jewishness did not necessarily entail, even to Annie, acceptance of Jewish religious views. While the children were growing up, Annie attended synagogue in a storefront on the major Jewish holidays. She observed Sabbath rules against work and travel, and she scrupulously followed kosher dietary laws. Annie contributed regularly to Jewish charities: orphan asylums, old-age homes, and the Jewish National Fund. She remained a passionate Zionist. Her daughters were baffled by this attitude until the blatant antisemitism in Nazi Germany during the 1930s caused them (and most American Jews) to reevaluate their own status. The children were not required to adhere to Annie's strict Judaism, but they were expected to think of themselves as Jews, both in origin and in outlook if not in formal adherence to Jewish religious doctrines. Jack had attended *cheder* and had undergone the *bar mitzvah* ritual, but none of his sisters received formal Jewish education outside the home. The neighborhood reinforced the family's consciousness of themselves as Jews. The people with whom Meyer and Annie and their children lived and worked were almost without exception Jewish.

Annie's days were taken up with housework and cooking. The apartment contained few appliances. The Millers purchased their first electric refrigerator in 1928, and Annie was given an electric iron for her birthday in 1930. They did not own a radio until 1935. Jack gave his parents a victrola in the mid-20s and gradually, via gifts, a small collection of records—mostly Yiddish songs and a few classical selections—was acquired. However, until Meyer's death, he and Annie occupied themselves most evenings with card games, usually 500 rummy. Once a year, the entire family attended the Yiddish theater. The children were permitted to go to movies, but neither Meyer nor Annie ever saw a motion picture. No one in the family drove. There was no reason, since a car was both impossibly expensive and unnecessary. When, occasionally the family visited Meyer's sisters in Brooklyn, they used public transportation.

After her husband's death, Annie Miller became even more preoccupied with the daily routine of taking care of her home and watching over her children—those still at home and those living nearby. As with Anna Lee Trace and Charlotte Bassano, but unlike Chloe Gale, Annie increasingly submerged her own individuality in the blossoming lives of her children, vicariously sharing their triumphs and failures and devoting her great strength of will to the cause of offering them psychological and real sustenance. In return, she expected loyalty, respect, and continuing interest on her children's part. Jack failed her, seduced from his responsibilities by his wife and her uppity relatives. Pauline, though physically distant, was a "good" daughter, and the four younger girls did everything a mother could ask.

In 1940, Rose and Billie were still living at home, and Betty and Bertha lived within three blocks of their mother's apartment. Rose, who never married, worked for Arrow Manufacturing Company for 16 years. Then, in 1934, she became a supervisor for a new company, Braun and Crystal, which also manufactured watch and jewelry boxes. Rose never missed a day of work even during the depths of the depression, and she continued to give most of her pay—some $35 per week by the late 1930s—to her mother. Billie had graduated from Morris High School in 1926. She found work with Columbia Pictures as a secretary in 1928, and for the next eight years she was employed by a number of theatrical agents and booking offices, changing employers as better jobs were offered to her. Except for a four-year stint as a secretary with a Philadelphia booking agency, Billie lived with her parents and contributed her paycheck to the family. When she returned to New York in 1936 for a position with Billy Shaw's theatrical agency, she moved back into her mother's apartment.

The two daughters who did strike out on their own, Betty and Bertha, remained close. Betty worked for the Bulova Watch Company until 1929, when she married Al Goldberg, a native New Yorker who had worked for Ford Motor Company in Detroit and then returned to New York. Annie did not wholly approve of Betty's husband, who possessed only a grade-school education and no trade, but he proved a loyal and responsible son-in-law. Through the 1930s, Al worked in a Manhattan restaurant, providing a shaky livelihood for Betty and their two children. Happily, the Goldbergs located in the Bronx, first near Van Courtlandt Park and then, in 1935, in a small apartment just three blocks from the Millers.

The youngest daughter, Bertha, graduated from high school in 1928 and worked for her brother while taking business courses at City College. Following her recovery from a bungled appendectomy, Bertha found a place in the purchasing department at Columbia Pictures. She received $18, working nine to six weekdays and a half day on Saturday until 1936 when Columbia shifted to the five-day week. By that time, Bertha had met and married Henry Gishman, an aspiring composer

Bertha Miller, 1933, at her desk in Columbia Pictures offices

and pianist. Though he was from a wealthy Russian Jewish family—his father was a successful musician—Bertha's husband got along well with his mother-in-law and the other Millers. Annie worried that Henry Gishman, as a musician, would be unable to support her daughter. Indeed, the Gishmans' finances were precarious, particularly after Bertha became pregnant in 1938 and quit her job. Henry, who was frequently unemployed, pieced together occasional tours with George Gershwin and jobs with the studio orchestras for radio shows ("Hit Parade," "Fred Allen," and "Dr. I.Q."). He also wrote popular songs. After his son Michael was born, Henry decided to abandon the uncertain future of a performing musician and found a steady job with Broadcast Music Incorporated, a music-licensing agency that represented song writers and publishers. He established his family in a roomy (two-bedroom) apartment on Jerome Avenue, less than two blocks from his mother-in-law's home.

By June 1940, the Millers again were able to proclaim their financial independence and solidarity. Annie and her two married daughters packed up children, bedding, and household utensils and set out for a summer home the Millers, Goldbergs, and Gishmans had rented in Belmar, New Jersey, one of the few shore communities that did not bar Jews. The husbands came down on weekends, and Rose and Billie spent their vacations at the Millers' beach house. Here, in the fresh air, surrounded by growing things and laughing children, Annie could immerse herself, without any hindrance, in the matriarchal role she so enjoyed. Enclosed in the isolation and familial unity of Belmar, it seemed that the Millers had achieved economic self-sufficiency without sacrificing family-ethnic ties.

THE MARKOVICHES OF MIDLAND, PENNSYLVANIA

Crucible Steel dominated Midland during the interwar years as it had since the town's formation. The Markoviches and virtually every other family in Midland were dependent upon Crucible for jobs, housing (the Markoviches were among the few home-owners in the Serbian population), and water. Crucible's control of land and jobs allowed it to establish social patterns and political structures, since Midland's tax base rested almost entirely upon Crucible's physical assets. The distance from the western edge of Midland (a few blocks from the Markovich home) to the town's easternmost limits was not more than two miles. But to Mihailo and his friends in 1920, it was still a continent, for, by custom, they were prohibited from entering the "cake eaters" domain. Crucible acted paternalistically—and not infrequently oppressively—toward its workers and dominated the political life of the community. Nonetheless, Mihailo and Maria Markovich created a family lifestyle that, while never independent of the constraints imposed by Crucible's power, did provide a remarkable degree of satisfaction and self-fulfillment.

The domination over Midland by Crucible and its native-born and educated, Protestant elite was most obvious in the factory itself. Although Mihailo Markovich had worked steadily for Crucible since he arrived in Midland and by 1920 had reached the position of crane operator, he could never be sure that he would be admitted when he joined the line outside the factory gates each morning at 6:30 A.M. Job insecurity and discrimination because of his ethnic origins were a way of life for Mihailo. (His stepson, George, found it necessary to change his name to Miller in order to be considered for a job at Crucible.) All the foremen were English-speaking natives. They mocked the inability of Crucible's immigrant workers to decipher written work rules and assignment sheets. They possessed the authority to hire or fire workers at will. Some would issue "pink slips" for minor infractions. Many expected workers to offer kickbacks—gifts of liquor, food, even money—in return for their jobs. When Serbian workers celebrated national holidays, these foremen often would crash the parties, guzzling homemade brandy and grabbing handfuls of cigars. In March 1927, on the feast day of St. Peter, Mihailo, who fiercely resented such invasions of his home, threw out a drunken cake eater who had spilled a pitcher of beer over Maria's treasured lace tablecloth. He was thereafter marked as a troublemaker. Two weeks later, when an inexperienced truck driver backed into Mihailo's crane, he was called into the office and informed by the plant superintendent, who could not hide his embarrassment, that he was fired. After working for 2 years with a construction company, Mihailo returned to Crucible, but he had lost 14 years seniority and was made a "chipper," one of the most demanding and low-paying

jobs in the mill. Crucible operated at less than half of capacity during the depression, so Mihailo worked irregularly until 1938, when foreign orders began to arrive and when the CIO finally succeeded in organizing Crucible Steel. For these years, the money Maria earned ($1.25 per day) doing housework and the small amounts contributed by boarders kept the family afloat.

Mihailo's difficulties with the Anglo foremen at Crucible reflected the experiences of many industrial workers during these decades. For blue and most white-collar workers, a job was not one's right but a gift to be bestowed or withheld at the employer's whim. Authoritarianism, frequent layoffs, long hours, often dangerous and always noisy and dirty work conditions were almost universal, even where unionization had occurred. The steel industry, in particular, was notorious for exploiting workers, controlling their lives, and preventing organization. The company town, common in the iron and steel industries, served to isolate workers and further their dependence on the corporation. With schools and police the instruments of the company, independent action by workers was difficult and risky at best.

Mihailo's day began at 5:30 A.M. Monday through Saturday, for he had to be at the Crucible gate for check in at 6:30. The next five hours found him submerged in a maelstrom of sound and heat, the screech of chipping tools, conveyer belts, and presses so loud that conversation with fellow workers, forbidden according to the English-language notices posted in the work area, was impossible anyway. When the noon whistle blew, Mihailo was grimy, sweat soaked, and bruised, but as the plant offered only toilets and a few open pipes for washing, he usually took his lunch pail out into the yard without washing up. After gobbling the sandwiches or *piroshkii* Maria had made, he stretched out, talking with fellow Serbians or watching one of the ongoing card games. At five minutes before one o'clock, the whistle sounded again, warning everyone to be back at their places by 1:00 precisely or face "disciplinary action." A favorite pastime was to bet on which of the group of men who drank their lunches at the taverns across from the plant would lose the race back to work that day. At 6:00 the whistle blew again, announcing that yet another 10-hour day was over, and Mihailo put down his chipping tools, grabbed his lunch box and coat, and trudged out the gate toward home. So it went day after day. Mihailo and his co-workers almost never complained about the system or the work itself. Constant, grinding toil was, after all, a fact of life. They objected only to the inequities, to the precariousness of employment, not to the job itself.

Frequent unemployment and the daily presence of large numbers of jobless at the factory gates weighed heavily on blue-collar workers. For most workers, it meant diminished individual resistance to management demands; increased powerlessness flowed from their insecurity. Only collective action could provide any protection, and thus workers looked to unions, to collective action not only for higher wages and job security, but also as a check to unilateral managerial control of the work itself. Unions protected workers by demanding safety standards, reasonable hours, rest periods, and so forth. Although overt labor-management conflict and tension increased, as manifested by strikes, lockouts, and work slowdowns, management began to lose its unchecked power over the workers.

The tensions produced by economic insecurity and persistent discrimination might have become intolerable but for the support and sense of identity the Markoviches received from Midland's Serbian community. Family life was largely organized around meetings of Serbian organizations, daily visits to Mihailo's favorite Serbian tavern, and family outings, Mihailo had joined Lodge 35 of the Serbian Benevolent Society in 1912 and served as secretary, treasurer, and in various other offices. Maria was an active member of the Circle of Serbian Sisters. Though neither ever learned more than a smattering of English, they found this only a minor obstacle. Maria knew enough to understand the simple instructions of the "American" women whose homes she cleaned. Otherwise, her world was entirely Serbian: she shopped in Serbian stores, gossiped daily with friends (some of whom came from villages close to her own place of birth), and led her family through a calendar of social and religious events that precisely followed traditional celebrations in the old country. There was no Serbian church in Midland—a lack which Maria and her friends were determined to correct—so the Markoviches attended Orthodox services two or three times a year in Aliquippa. For Maria and even more for Mihailo, except for work, life in Midland brought acceptance and, eventually, recognition as elders in the Serbian community.

As with many immigrant families, the Markoviches were subjected to the stresses of dual loyalties. Practical considerations and a maturing sense of commitment to the United States prompted Mihailo to attend night classes in English and citizenship at Midland High School beginning in 1922. These skills enabled Mihailo to read the increasing quantities of printed materials Crucible distributed to its work force and gave him more confidence when speaking with his shift bosses. While Mihailo was proud of his new knowledge (he feared the citizenship examination and remained a resident alien for another 18 years), he and Maria were also proud of their origins. They were determined to pass along Serbian traditions and cultural heritage to the children. Mihailo maintained contact with his relatives in Primjsle, sending money and clothing to his mother and sisters whenever possible; and he kept up with political conditions in Yugoslavia via the Serbian language newspaper, *Srbobran,* published in Pittsburgh.

The elder Markoviches found themselves pulled by the old and the new. Their customs and associations reenforced their ethnic and religious cultural traditions while work, school, and commitment to their new land pulled them in the opposite direction. Sometimes, of course, there was no contradiction; membership in the Serbian Benevolent Society or Circle of Serbian Sisters did not conflict with English night school or joining a union. Major problems, however, did arise. What language, for example, should be used at home? The Serbian of the parents or the English of the school children? More and more, English predominated, but it never won out completely. The result was adaptation, a tense compromise between total Americanization and adherence to tradition.

For the Markovich children, of course, school and, later, work pushed them toward more complete conformity. All the children attended an elementary school exclusively for immigrants on First Street. From the seventh grade on, they went to the same school as English-speaking children—Lincoln Junior-Senior High. The three oldest, Mihailo's stepchildren, did not finish high school; the two boys, Michael and Paul, went to work "because of the rough times," and, at 15, Amelia ran away to marry an Italian miner. The four younger children—Miles (1912), Anna (1918), Sophia (1921), and Maria (1923)— did earn high-school diplomas, and two went on to college. Miles was an excellent student and also played on the Lincoln High football team. Following graduation in 1930, Miles received a partial scholarship to Geneva College from the Beaver County Women's Club—the first given to any Midland student. His parents offered encouragement but could

not provide any help. Miles, who wished to become a doctor, worked as a laboratory assistant and at other part-time jobs to pay his way through Geneva. He finished in 1934 and, lacking the funds for medical school, went to the Kirksville School of Osteopathy and Surgery, from which he graduated in 1938.

The Markovich children participated in numerous school-related activities, even though the "American" kids controlled the most prestigious clubs and organizations. Anna joined the Girl Scouts (and thus ventured into the better section of Midland for the first time). She resented the occasional mockery of her name and the smart-aleck comments about Bohunks and Wops, but her parents "taught their children kindness and respect toward others and never to be ashamed of our heritage." An outstanding student, Anna pursued a college preparatory program in high school, even though college was simply not possible for a second child and a female at that. "I really enjoyed going to high school," she later recalled. "I was a serious student and worked hard. Upon graduation I was proud to learn that I had two scholarships offered to me which, unfortunately, I couldn't accept. They weren't full scholarships and, since my parents were not able to contribute towards continued education, I had to decline the offer." While Anna enjoyed high school and was a member of the Latin Club, Varsity Chorus, and Tri-Hi-Y (which encouraged "school spirit," especially at athletic events, the one community activity uniting all elements in Midland), she and her younger sisters also were deeply involved with activities sponsored by the Serbian community. Anna and Sophia faithfully attended the weekly sessions of the Serbian school, which had been established in 1930 to teach Serbian language, literature, and history to the younger, American-born Serbians. Both were charter members of the Lazo Kostich Singing Society, organized in 1936, and Anna was named a member of the committee to apply for a charter from the Serbian Singing Federation and to plan a Bingo night to raise funds for the club. Mihailo and Maria were deeply proud of their talented offspring and grateful that the girls, at least, were maintaining an interest in Serbian culture. "You good American girl. You good Serb. That good together," Mihailo told Anna at her high-school graduation in June 1936.

Since Miles had established an osteopathic practice in New Carlisle, Ohio, and Sophia wished to pursue nurse's training in Pittsburgh, Anna assumed the role of family manager. Giving up any hope of college for herself, she got a job at Woolworth's 5 & 10 and a weekend position with the Midland newspaper. Living at home, Anna became immersed in the doings of the singing society, serving as an officer and attending state and regional competitions. Then, in August 1939, while collecting news items for the *Courier,* Anna met Michael Simich, a dark-haired young Serbian who recently had come to Midland to work at Crucible Steel. Soon "Mike" Simich had joined the Lazo Kostich Singing Society, was taking Anna to the movies every Saturday night, and was a regular guest at the Markoviches for Sunday dinner. Mihailo questioned Anna's beau closely about his background, prospects, and intentions. In June 1940, he gave his approval for Anna and Michael to announce their engagement.

Michael Simich was the second youngest son of Stanko Simich, a recently deceased coal miner from Serbia and Washington County, Pennsylvania. The Simiches had always been desperately poor, living in a tumbledown company house in Primrose on the tiny wages Stanko earned. However, five of the seven surviving Simich children, including Mike, had graduated from high school. Stanko had suffered a stroke in 1935 and,

receiving no pension for his 20 years of employment with Carnegie Coal Company, had to rely on his children for support. Several of the boys went into the mines, but Mike learned from relatives that Crucible Steel in Midland was hiring unskilled laborers. In autumn 1936, he went to work for Crucible for $3.68 per day. Forty years later, he remembered that occasion vividly: "Men were just milling around near the hiring gate. Then foremen from various divisions came out and asked if there was anyone who could do various kinds of jobs—weld, puddle, scarf, etc. The foremen just picked out several at random and had them come in for physicals. I soon learned to raise my hand when any job was mentioned, and one day I was lucky enough to be picked." A few months later, however, Mike was laid off with no assurance that he would be notified or rehired if the same opening became available. Discouraged, he returned to Primrose, to find his brothers out of work and one sister supporting the family. Mike moved to Midland permanently in 1937. He hired on again at Crucible and roomed with relatives.

Mike became a "chipper," like Mihailo before him. But the job had changed considerably. Mike used a compressed-air hammer to chisel imperfections off of the burning steel ingots. Mihailo, in the 1920s, had used a heavy, one-hand sledge. Mechanization increased production but it also increased the hazards the workers encountered. The air hammer was used with less finesse, so that more imperfections remained on the ingots. Also, the chipper was less able to control the direction of the flying pieces of superheated metal chipped from the ingot. However, through an incentive system, Mike could earn up to $10 per eight-hour day—when he worked.

The employment situation and the plant environment improved greatly once the Steel Workers Organizing Committee forced Crucible Steel to admit the United Steel Workers–CIO. Mike immediately joined the union—as did Mihailo—and recruited several of his fellow workers. Mike, Mihailo, and other Serbians who had prayed for the unionization of Crucible now believed they had job security. The war orders deluging Crucible were largely responsible for the steady work they enjoyed after 1939. Just as important was the knowledge that the absolute power previously enjoyed by plant bosses was crumbling, and that a few Serbians were being named to supervisory positions at Crucible.

On February 21, 1940, after several false starts, Mihailo Markovich became a naturalized citizen in ceremonies at the town hall, and that fall he marched into the First Street School to vote for the reelection of Franklin D. Roosevelt, "because he was for unions and the workingman." This personal declaration of independence soon was followed by another, the shredding of the mortgage on the Markovich home. These were happy times. The Markoviches were healthy and holding respectable jobs, Mihailo's eldest daughter was betrothed to a sober, responsible young Serb, and the Lincoln High Leopards seemed destined for an undefeated season and yet another Pennsylvania state championship. The only flaw was the maelstrom which threatened to engulf his native land; but Serbia (Mihailo could never think of his country as Yugoslavia) was far away in distance and memory now. He worried greatly, awaiting each letter from his family, but he did not think America, his country, could or should become involved.

THE O'REILLYS OF MEDFORD, MASSACHUSETTS

John O'Reilly never recovered from the shock of his dismissal from the Boston Police Department following the abortive police strike of 1919. He refused to turn in his uniform and badge, and persisted in appeals to the police commissioner and Governor Coolidge for reinstatement. When a new police force was recruited (almost entirely from outside Boston) and his petitions were repeatedly denied, John O'Reilly withdrew inside himself, refusing even to read the stories about the police's inept attempts to enforce the Volstead Act. He spent most of his time at a speakeasy (formerly the Rose of Tralee Pub) around the corner from his home at 1411 Burke Street, Brighton, drinking Cuban rum smuggled into Boston from ships anchored beyond the seven-mile limit. His health began to fail, and in 1923 he suffered a stroke. He died at home on January 4, 1924, leaving his widow, May Quinn O'Reilly and four daughters almost destitute except for a $1,000 insurance policy from the Police Benefit Association.

During the years of John O'Reilly's emotional depression and terminal illness, his brother Augustus (Gus) O'Reilly assumed responsibility for the family's welfare. Gus O'Reilly was a "go getter," a young man with considerable ambitions and equal determination. With his older brother's help, Gus had attended business college in Boston and earned a degree in accounting. Following army service in France, he obtained a job with Weston Thurston, a wholesale meat company with offices in Faneuil Hall Market. Already married and the father of one daughter (Jeanne, born in 1918), Gus at first had difficulty making his salary of $15 per week cover living expenses. However, within a year he was earning $35 per week plus a New Year's bonus of $300. Friendly and knowledgeable, he soon won a reputation as one of Weston Thurston's top salesmen, and his salary rose accordingly. In 1925, after Gus had established John's family in a comfortable apartment in South Boston and had arranged for

The new Faneuil Hall Market, Boston, where Gus O'Reilly worked

May O'Reilly's unmarried brother to come to live with them, Gus accepted a position with a large meat-packing firm, Kingan and Company of Indianapolis, Indiana, as a route salesman. Traveling to retail stores in the greater Boston area, Gus hawked Kingan hams, bacon, and pork products. He was paid a munificent $45 per week (increased to $55 in 1928) and a yearly bonus—sometimes nearly a thousand dollars—based on commissions. Only 32, Gus O'Reilly had achieved a degree of economic security unimaginable to his parents and the brothers and sisters still living in County Cork.

It is true that Gus O'Reilly's income placed him in the top half of all Americans in 1920 and in the highest 30 percent after his transfer to Kingan and Company in 1925. However, the margin between relative affluence and persistent financial insecurity for Gus, as for most Americans, was extremely narrow. Al-

most no attention was given to family financial management in schools or anywhere else. Careful management of family finances was absolutely essential, and Gus, because of his training in bookkeeping but also because he was determined to escape the penury and consequent helplessness that typified life in Ireland and life among the first generations of Irish in the United States, proved a wizard at financial management.

Every penny of income was accounted for and, whenever possible, used to produce more. In 1922, Gus withdrew his savings ($3,600) and purchased a house in a new development on the outskirts of Medford, Massachusetts, a small city just north of Boston. The new home, a large, frame house skirted by porches that faced broad lawns and a playground across the street, offered shelter for Gus, his wife Margaret, their daughter Jeanne, and the five children born there:

Elinor (1923), John (1925), William (1926), Allan (1928), and Denyse (1931). It also provided a steady rental income. The O'Reillys occupied a seven-room apartment on the second floor and rented out the six rooms on the ground floor, more than covering the mortgage payment, taxes, and insurance. Gus paid $9,000 for the house in 1922; he added a two-car garage in 1930 (cost: $750) and finished off the attic for $250 in 1934. Each apartment had a white, paneled dining room, living room with fireplace, hot-water heat, and electric lights and outlets in every room. In 1960, Gus sold the house for $25,000. He recently estimated its present value at $75,000.

The O'Reillys availed themselves of normal pleasures and equipped their home with the appliances and electric gadgets so popular among middle-class American families in the 1920s and 1930s. Gus replaced the original oil-burning stove with a "white gas" range when that marvel of design became available. The old Eddy ice chest was banished when the O'Reillys gave themselves a Frigidaire electric refrigerator for Christmas 1935. Several radios were bought in the late 1920s, and the family regularly went to the movies and to band concerts in Boston. They "managed" almost every summer, following Gus's promotion, to rent a house in the New Hampshire mountains or at the seashore, "so the children could hike or swim." Gus never purchased a car himself, but he had the use of a company Ford for family outings.

Their comfortable lifestyle was undergirded by an annual income of approximately $3,800 ($3,200 from salary and bonuses, $600 from rent). From this amount, Gus housed, fed, and clothed a family of eight, paid doctor's bills, made several improvements in his home, kept up two life insurance policies, held out funds for the family's vacations, and set aside at least $1,000 each year in savings for his children's college educa-

tions. Of course, Gus was fortunate because he was not laid off once during these two decades (the wholesale meat business was slowed but not destroyed by the depression). As well, neither he nor any of his family suffered a serious, costly illness, and, except for occasional packets of clothing and food sent to relatives in Ireland and the brief period when he assumed financial responsibility for John O'Reilly's family, he did not have to provide for aged or indigent kin. If one looks at consumption expenditures for typical families, however, the extent of Gus's accomplishment is clear.

For the years 1918–20, when Gus was just beginning his career in sales and earning roughly $1,100 per annum, average expenditures for a family of four, with income of $1,070 after taxes, were:

Food	$456.00
Alcoholic beverages	7.00
Tobacco	14.00
Housing	150.00
Household expenses	14.00
Fuel, light, refrigeration	64.00
Furnishings, etc.	43.00
Clothing	156.00
Transportation:	
Auto	4.00
Other	18.00
Medical Care	46.00
Personal Care	11.00
Recreation	15.00
Reading	8.00
Education	3.00
Miscellaneous	7.00

This information and that which follows is taken from *The Statistical History of the United States* (Stamford, Conn., 1965). It is drawn from data collected by the Bureau of Labor Statistics, U.S. Department of Labor.

Total expenses: $1016.00; difference between income and expenditures: $54.00. For the years 1934–36, when Gus was bringing home something over $3,000 per year and taking care of eight persons, the average expenditures for a family of four, with an income of $2,867 after taxes, were:

Food and alcoholic beverages	$837.00
Tobacco	58.00
Fuel, light, refrigeration	131.00
Household operation	119.00
Housing	370.00
Furnishings and equipment	83.00
Clothing	388.00
Transportation:	
Auto	197.00
Other	78.00
Medical Care	109.00
Personal Care	59.00
Recreation	88.00
Reading	31.00
Education	17.00
Miscellaneous	25.00

The family's total expenditures were $2,590.00, thus producing an excess of income over expenses of $277.00. One might observe that for such a family, *provided that income was not disrupted,* the depression had very little impact, indeed, it may well have eased the financial struggle because of deflation. It is also obvious from a comparison of these tables that the pattern of expenditures had shifted considerably from 1920 to 1936, reflecting greater emphasis on possessions, mobility, and satisfaction of personal cravings.

Gus O'Reilly proved a better manager than the average head of household in his income bracket for several reasons. First, he kept tight control of the purse strings, giving Margaret a specified amount each week for food and incidentals, personally approving all other purchases, however small, and providing an allowance (50¢ for the girls, 75¢ for the boys) for each child until they entered high school when they were expected to earn their own pocket money. Second, it appears that the "consumption revolution," which is often identified with the 1920s, hardly touched the O'Reillys. Perhaps because neither Gus nor Margaret read the glossy magazines with their hard-sell "buy this and keep up with the Joneses" messages, the O'Reillys simply were not interested in acquiring possessions for

their own sake. More likely, Gus was too busy with his work and Margaret too involved with raising six children to pant after the latest rage in coffee pots, patio furniture, and high-style, six-cylinder Chevrolet automobiles. Finally, Gus was adamantly opposed to buying anything on credit. The notion of obtaining things and paying for them on the installment plan, a practice that first became prevalent during these decades, struck him as blatantly uneconomical and somehow immoral. This approach to family finances carried Gus and his family through the depression with very little difficulty. They continued to spend summers in the country. There was money to send Elinor and Jeanne, following their graduation from Medford High School, to the prestigious Chamberlain School in Boston, where they studied merchandising, interior decorating, and period furniture at a cost of $350 per year. As well, Gus financed John's education at Boston College (tuition: $300) until the war intervened.

There were hidden costs. Gus O'Reilly was deeply committed to his work and consequently saw little of his children from infancy to adolescence. The burden of child rearing rested with Margaret. Further, Gus's work and his commitment to a personal version of the American dream meant that he abandoned the Irish cultural and religious heritage. None of Gus and Margaret's children thought of themselves as Irish, though their parents held many of the attributes of "lace curtain Irish" families. The O'Reillys, after a time, saw very little of their relatives. When his younger brother, Peter, came to the United States in 1924, Gus did find him a temporary job at Weston Thurston, but they saw little of each other after Peter moved to New York. Even relations with May, John's widow, and her family declined after a time to sending of birthday gifts and occasional dinners. Margaret did insist that the children be confirmed into the Roman Catholic faith and that they attend mass regularly, though Gus went only on Christmas, Ash Wednesday, and Easter. He joined the American Legion and was active for some years. Margaret was a faithful member of the Medford Women's Club. A poignant example of Gus's eagerness to shed his Irish origins and to Americanize is his description of occasional family outings into Boston, "a city steeped in history. We'd take the children to the old Granary buying ground, Lexington and Concord, old North Church, and the State House, a fine example of Bulfinch architecture. Louisburg Square on Christmas Eve was a sight to see. The fine old houses with every window to the third floor lighted with real candles. Carollers stopping at each house to sing. The throngs that listened were quiet and beautifully behaved."

THE REINHARDTS OF EVANSVILLE, INDIANA

Jacob and Mathilde Reinhardt's fourth child was born on June 5, 1926, in Mathilde's parents' home, with Dr. Tweedall, the family physician, in attendance. There were no complications at the birth of Kars Kenneth Reinhardt (named after his paternal uncle, a popular cartoonist for the *Evansville Courier*), but his arrival did force the Reinhardts to decide, reluctantly, to find a home of their own. The little house on Red Bank Road which Mathilde's father had built in 1910 simply was too small for Henry and Ruth Brauer, their unmarried daughter Freida, and Mathilde Brauer Reinhardt, her husband Jacob, and their children: Raymond (1917), Hilda (1918), Regina (1920), and little Karl. Although Mathilde, extremely loyal to and protective of her aging parents, was disturbed about leaving the only home she had known, something had to be done. Not only were the two girls sleeping on cots in their aunt's room and nine-year-old Ray in the musty, cramped

attic, but the "old fashioned" attitudes toward children held by grandpa and grandma Brauer—particularly their stubborn insistence on speaking only German—was, Mathilde and Jacob believed, harming their children.

After a long search, Jacob found a six-acre plot of land on Middle Mount Vernon Road, some two miles east of the Brauers and just a few hundred yards from White School, where the three oldest children were already enrolled. A house on the property was not large (two rooms and kitchen downstairs, three bedrooms upstairs) but it was quite modern, boasting indoor plumbing, electricity, and a coal-fired furnace. Some outbuildings—a summer kitchen, coal shed, split-rail corn crib, and a small barn—already existed, and there was sufficient room to build storage sheds for

Jacob and Mathilde Reinhardt, *c.* 1920

the farm implements Jacob was acquiring. Jacob and Mathilde raised the $3,500 purchase price, and the Reinhardts moved to their new home in March 1927.

The Reinhardts found a place of their own (the one in which they still live) because of a desire to give their children a modern, comfortable environment, privacy, and proximity to school. Like the vast majority of Americans, Jacob and Mathilde gave central place to the "proper" development of their children. The emphasis on offspring, which has perhaps come to dominate American values in the 20th century, is a recent phenomenon. Until recently, there was little recognition of "childhood" or "adolescence" as separate or unique stages of life; children were simply miniature adults. Why this changed, why child rearing came to occupy such an important and tension-producing role in family life, is still being debated, though shifting economic circumstances affecting the structure and values of the family played a large part. These economic factors gave rise to greater expectations, if not for oneself then for the next generation, as we have seen with the Ben Trace family; they also could produce tremendous anxiety, for the attainment of social and economic goals seemed to demand rejection of traditional values and their replacement by patterns of conduct more meaningful to a society based upon the presumption of social and geographical mobility, rapid change, and weakening of kinship and community ties.

The home (defined as the family) was universally upheld as the most satisfactory environment (some experts, citing studies that children languished and died in foster-care institutions, asserted it was the *only* environment) for the rearing of children. "Even well ordered institutions are no substitute for the regularity and discipline of the everyday household. It is in the home that the proper training and discipline must be taught. Regu-

lar sleep, regular feeding, regular play, and regular family life is indispensable," wrote Sophonisba Breckinridge in 1919.

What went on in those homes to influence the development of children in "right" directions—beyond provision of a routine, love, and discipline—was not spelled out. Some studies recommended the use of the family as a socializing agency to teach both individuality and adaptation to group life. However, families such as the Traces, Reinhardts, Markoviches, Gales, and O'Reillys basically tended to stress the values, behavior patterns, and authority of the parents and then hope for the best. For certain types of families in which a strong sense of identity based upon social or ethnic consciousness was present—such as the Markoviches, Millers, and Butlers—acceptance of parents as "role models" occurred almost automatically. For many families, perhaps the majority, parental authority and values clashed with authority figures outside the home, especially the school. "Why, even my youngster in kindergarten is telling us where to get off," wrote Jacob Reinhardt to his brother. "He won't eat white bread because he says they tell him at kindergarten that brown is more healthy." Attitudes imbibed at school—on nutrition, personal hygiene, discipline, career goals, and so forth—often contradicted views presented at home, and thus confused the child and irritated its parents. This situation could produce frustration on both sides, with children, especially after they reached adolescence, desiring to adopt standards of appearance, recreational activities, and a standard of living totally contrary to the experience of their parents and beyond their parents' ability to provide. A constant theme among lower and middle-class parents—the Traces, Millers, Markoviches, and Bassanos, for example—was their frustration at not being able to "do better" for their children.

The Reinhardts escaped these frustrations and, perhaps, many of the other problems because their occupation, farming, involved the entire family. They were a very close family, one united by the needs and demands of the farm. Although Jacob and Mathilde did not assume that all their children eventually would become or marry farmers, the daily routine of farm life demanded that the children give first allegiance to the home and thus to the farm. Everyone, regardless of age and sex, had chores, and they did them with little complaint. Neither Jacob nor Mathilde believed in corporal punishment. Occasionally, Jacob might raise his voice if a child rebelled or, very rarely, tweak the ear of a disobedient youngster. Although the Reinhardt children enjoyed and did extremely well in school (first White Elementary School and then Reitz High School), they were not much involved in school activities—essentially because of the obligations at home—and certainly were not seduced away from primary loyalty to the family by school. Ray, the oldest, did not speak English when he first enrolled at White School in 1923, and he devoted his free time to hunting rather than sports or school-sponsored activities. Hilda and Regina did join a few clubs at Reitz, and when Regina entered Evansville College's nursing program

The Reinhardt children with Model-T Ford, *c.* 1924

in 1938, she did join a sorority; however, both girls continued to live at home and to emphasize family as opposed to school or other social events. For the Reinhardt children, there was not much time for anything outside the home, even if they had desired to escape the authority of their parents. It was a narrow, uneventful life in many ways, but it was comfortable and secure. Not until the next generation of Reinhardts faced the challenges of child rearing in the 1950s and 1960s would they encounter the uncertainties and frustrations many of their counterparts faced during the years between the First and Second World Wars.

In part because of the contributions of his children (Ray was driving a tractor 10 hours a day during planting season by his 10th birthday), Jacob Reinhardt did reasonably well at farming through the difficult decades of the 1920s, and the family survived the 1930s with its holdings intact. For many years, Jacob earned extra money by operating a thresher in partnership with his brother, Kenneth. Though no one in southern Indiana became wealthy from farming in these years, the Reinhardts were sufficiently prosperous that they invested $2,000 in utility company bonds in 1925; $5,000 in the Loew's Victory Theater in 1927 (for which they received 6 percent interest and free movie tickets, which no one in the family ever claimed); and even took a flyer on a scheme by a Perry Township inventor to develop a soil pulverizing plow, investing and losing $1,400 in 1930. The difficult times of the 1930s did not perceptibly change their style of life. "We just had to work harder and watch our pennies more closely," Mathilde later recalled. She and Jacob did fear that they might not be able to pay their taxes and would lose their land, and they shared the prevailing anxiety about their children's futures. But the Reinhardts had sources of income not available to many. When wheat and corn prices collapsed, Mathilde and the children expanded the family's vegetable gardens, and Jacob sold produce from his truck in Howell and on the west side of Evansville, earning enough to pay for schoolbooks, dry goods, and the necessities ordered out of the Sears, Roebuck catalog. Mathilde made the family's clothing, except for overalls, Sunday outfits, and such items as shoes. The family did not buy much, because they did not need much. An Airline radio from Sears to hear "Amos and Andy" was a big purchase for the home. Neither the living room nor the parlor was furnished until the war brought a tide of prosperity.

Given the family's commitment to the farm and the never-ending chores that accompanied farming, it is not surprising that the Reinhardts took little interest in social affairs outside a small circle of relatives and close

Son and father, the Reinhardts planting corn, c. 1930

friends. They continued to attend St. Paul's Church and went to church suppers and picnics, though neither Jacob nor Mathilde took an active role in church affairs. Jacob was a member of the Perry Township Volunteer Fire Department and the Farm Bureau, and was an energetic Republican. Mathilde was very active in the White School PTA while the older children were going there and served as an officer of the Farm Bureau Association for several years. Neither Jacob nor Mathilde had time for hobbies, though she did belong to a local sewing club (successor to the *Frauenverein,* which had disbanded in 1918), but she quit in disgust in 1940, because the women played "clabber"—a regional variation of the card game euchre—rather than sewing.

Life for the Reinhardts throughout these two decades was comparatively tranquil and uncomplicated. Adjustments were required, to be sure. The tight-knit German community in which Jacob and Mathilde had grown up, and the value system it represented, was fraying year by year under the pressure of external hostility and internal lack of interest in German customs. The Reinhardts accepted the necessity to conform for themselves and especially for their children. They both were ardent advocates of the use of English at school and at home and spoke German only when visiting the Brauers. However, they were also bitter about past and present persecution of Germans, "as good Americans as those English in Evansville," and resented the pressures that caused many Germans to change their names and to repudiate their heritage. But if they lost, they also gained, for by 1940 the children—Ray, a Reitz graduate engaged in farming with his father; Hilda, holding a good job with the A.A.A. in Evansville; Regina, an honor student at Evansville College; Karl, a 4-H member and junior varsity football player; and Phyllis, a healthy four-year-old—confirmed by their present accom-

plishments and ambitions that the years of effort and adjustment had been worthwhile.

THE GALES OF NEW ALBANY, KANSAS

Martha Isabelle Gale's sixth birthday, August 13, 1925, was the occasion for a grand birthday party. Her parents invited all six of Martha's friends from the primary class at New Albany Methodist Church, there were buckets of home-churned ice cream and devil's food cake, and her mother allowed Martha to wear the crinkly white dress and patent leather slippers that had been bought for the first day of school to begin in early September. But Martha remembered this birthday as a sad day too, for Priscilla Fields, her closest friend, had pushed her down and said: "My mommy says your mommy and daddy are uppity. They won't let you go to school with me. You have to go to school in Fredonia. I hope the car goes in a ditch and you're tardy and the principal spanks you the very first day." When Martha went to her mother to have her tears dried and her dress brushed off, she asked why she couldn't go to school with Prissy and the other kids. She long remembered her mother's sad, frowning face and the words, "It's for the best, Martha. We're only thinking of you." How could it be for the best, if she could not see her friends and had to go with her older brother and sisters to the strange, big school in Fredonia?

The decision of Charles and Chloe Gale to have their youngest child begin school in Fredonia (and to transfer Billy and Anna Ruth) rather than send them to the old two-room New Albany elementary school their four other children had attended reflected their unhappiness with the poor instruction offered there. It also conveyed their dissatisfaction with the continuing decline of the tiny community of New Albany, in which Charles and

The old two-room elementary school at New Albany, Kansas

Chloe Gale claimed positions of social and intellectual leadership. By the mid 1920s, the formerly prosperous town was almost abandoned. Its bank, drugstore, lumberyard, the ornate five-room hotel down the street from the Gale home, and four of its five churches had been closed. The town's only doctor moved to Fredonia in 1924. Only the school, the Methodist Church (served by a circuit-riding minister), and a tiny general store remained open. Chloe Gale, a longtime member of the New Albany School Board, had fought for a bond issue to construct a new school building with up-to-date facilities, laboratories, a gymnasium, and a music hall. If a new school were built, she hoped that outlying communities would send their pupils to New Albany, competent teachers could be attracted and kept, and the school might serve as a focus for revival of New Albany itself. The school board rejected the plan, asserting that taxes were too high already and, besides, what was wrong with the present school? It taught farm children all they needed to know: the basics of reading, writing, and ciphering. What use was chemistry, or "home economics," or music appreciation to a farmer or a farmer's wife?

The Gales were not sure what the answer to that question was, but they did know that they wanted something more for their children, the choice of careers that a good education could provide. They shared this viewpoint with millions of Americans, for whom education was the key to progress and self-fulfillment. Some Americans always had believed in the efficacy of education, and by the First World War the vast majority were persuaded that education, at least through high school, was a *sine qua non* of upward mobility. The percentage of American children ages 5 to 17 in public day schools rose from 72.4 in 1900 to 77.8 in 1920 and 85.3 in 1940. The number of students enrolled in public secondary schools jumped from 519,251 in 1900, to 2,200,389 in 1920, and 6,601,444 in 1940, and high-school graduates as a percentage of 17-year-olds in the total population soared: from 6.4 percent in 1900, to 16.8 percent in 1920, and 50.8 percent in 1940. From 1910 to 1928, the number of college students tripled.

The "selling" of American education was extremely impressive, but the system and the assumptions that supported it did not at first match the exorbitant promises. Much of the attention given pedagogical changes derived from the proposals of "progressive" educators, most notably John Dewey and his disciples. Dewey, in his major works, *The School and Society* (1899) and *Democracy and Education* (1916), insisted that education be an instrument of social progress, that it relate to the everyday needs of citizens in an urban, industrial, and democratic society, and that it inculcate values found to be appropriate for successful adjustment to modern life. Much that progressive educators advocated was admirable and long overdue: de-emphasis of rote learning and reform of teaching methods, introduction of practical subjects into the curriculum, awareness and encouragement of individual differences and interests. But the movement failed to achieve the revolution

The founder of the progressive education movement, John Dewey

within the classroom that had been trumpeted, foundering on the gut issues of *what* values for *what* kind of society should be taught—issues not susceptible to the "scientific" (largely statistical) investigations of which progressive educators were so enamored.

Nonetheless, the ideas of progressive educators in conjunction with the professionalization of education (especially teacher training), and the revolution in transportation and distribution of income did change the interior landscape of America's schools. The most noticeable change was the growing power of the school to shape values, its importance for the "socialization" of the child.

Partly this was intentional; but even more importantly, rapidly growing numbers of American children spent the bulk of their waking hours in these education factories, imbibing—whatever their economic status— similar information and attitudes, and, because of rapid communication and transportation, everywhere embracing the same fads and fantasies.

There existed dramatic differences, of course, between schools and the curricula they implemented. The prep schools John Butler, Jr. attended contrasted painfully with the tiny school in New Albany and even more sharply with Sylvia Hunt's improvised classroom in Kosse, Texas to be discussed later. The facilities and outlook of American schools varied tremendously, and thus their products, the adolescents forced into a hostile world, also differed greatly. It was these differences that obsessed Chloe Gale, and she willingly paid the $21 per semester for each child to insure that each received the educational advantages which the Fredonia school offered. In 1929, the New Albany school closed. Construction of a consolidated school was begun, only to be halted when the depression hit Wilson County. For many years thereafter, all children from outlying communities were bused into Fredonia.

Martha came to enjoy going to school in Fredonia, and with her mother's encouragement seized upon every possible cultural opportunity. In high school, she played the violin in the school orchestra, was president of the pep club, and a loyal member of the Girl's Reserve, a school-sponsored religious group. For Martha, in contrast with Regina Reinhardt, school and family were synonymous. The Gales supported their children's extracurricular interests, excusing them from chores at home and contributing time and money to school affairs.

Fortunately, Charles Gale was sufficiently prosperous throughout the 1920s and into

Fredonia High School

the depression years not to require the help of his children. The Gale farm totaled about 130 acres of crop land (usually planted in corn and wheat alternated with alfalfa) and 200 acres of pasture on which Charles grazed cattle himself or which he leased to others. Charles and Chloe were not wealthy but, like the Reinhardts, had enough to be comfortable and help their friends and relatives when necessary. Charles was a modern farmer, both in the techniques he employed and the attitudes he espoused. A founding member of the Wilson County Farm Bureau, he kept up with the agricultural advances described in *Capper's Farmer* and USDA publications. He was a Democrat in a strongly Republican county, a supporter of the farm program of President Roosevelt and Secretary of Agriculture Henry A. Wallace. Charles became extremely active in such New Deal agencies as the Wilson County Agricultural Adjustment Administration Committee, which set local acreage allotments, served on the National Reemployment Service Committee for Wilson County, and helped establish a Civilian Conservation Corps camp near Neodesha.

Chloe Gale was the first president of the "ladies unit" of the Farm Bureau, organized

in 1922, and wholeheartedly approved her husband's liberal efforts. However, she devoted most of her time to campaigns to improve the lot of farm wives in the area. Convinced that farm life must offer women something more than mind-dulling drudgery, Chloe initiated a variety of social and cultural activities designed to offer local women leisure as well as some intellectual stimulation. All through these decades, the *Wilson County Citizen* carried notices of the forthcoming "ladies study group," or Better Business Builders, or the New Albany Library Association (funded briefly by the Works Progress Administration) to meet at the home of Mr. and Mrs. C. E. Gale. Interspersed with these announcements were equally numerous items about Mrs. Gale's recent visit to "the Tipica orchestra concert at Chanute," her attendance at plays, lectures, and card parties. The Gales could legitimately claim a position of cultural leadership in their community. They read books, lots of them, from Zane Grey through the Harvard Classics. Chloe subscribed to the Book-of-the-Month Club, and she took such magazines as the *Delineator, Pathfinder,* and *McCall's.* At the same time, they were great fans of Fredonia High football and basketball, and the entire family enjoyed radio comedy shows ("Lum and Abner" was a favorite) and soap operas. On most Saturday evenings, the children—and sometimes Charles and Chloe—went into Fredonia to a movie or a dance. On other weekend nights—the Gales' home was thrown open to the children and their friends, with cards, group sings, and parlor games especially popular during the depression.

It was not an impossible distance from such an environment to anywhere one wished to go—or so Chloe and Charles hoped. The older children took the giant step out of Wilson County into the larger world. Charles, Jr. went to Kansas State University, graduating in 1932 with a degree in agricultural economics.

He found employment with the Department of Agriculture, first in Washington and then in drought-stricken Oklahoma. Mary, the oldest girl, attended the University of Wisconsin and became a social worker on a Menominee Indian Reservation. Anna Ruth graduated from Fredonia High School in 1931 and four years later, entered nurse's training in Oregon. The youngest child, Martha Isabelle, popular and musically gifted, long had dreamed of going to the Kansas City Conservatory and training to become a music teacher. But just before she enrolled for her senior year of high school, army worms devastated the Gale's crops. That disaster, added to the poor harvests of the drought years, wiped out the family's margin of security. There would not be enough money to send Martha Isabelle to college. She worked for some months at the Fredonia Telephone Company and then, disconsolate over the disintegration of her dreams, suffered a nervous breakdown. During the next two years, Martha Isabelle visited Kansas City several times; however she went, not to the conservatory, but to the University of Kansas Medical Center for treatment. Her recovery resulted more from the support of parents and friends than the psychiatric counseling she received. In particular, a young man from Roper, Austin Hart, helped Martha Isabelle to shake off her depression by visiting week nights and taking her to movies and ball games in Fredonia almost every weekend. Martha had known Austin for 10 years, since he began to play baseball on the diamond her father had built behind the Gales' home. Now she came to see Austin, who was working on his father's 300-acre farm, differently. In August 1940, Martha made her last visit to the K.U. Medical Center and, shortly after, Mr. and Mrs. C. E. Gale announced their daughter's engagement to Austin Hart. A "winter wedding" was planned only to be postponed when Austin learned that he had been drafted into the United States Army.

THE HUNTS OF KOSSE, TEXAS

By the end of the First World War, James and Henry Williams were doing extremely well. Their cement-contracting business was on a solid footing, and, by plowing much of the profits into purchase of house lots in the black section of Detroit, the brothers had acquired more security than most blacks in America could expect. However, the Williams brothers realized that this hard-earned independence was transitory. Lacking true equality and, because of their rootless existence, lacking the web of kin relationships that sustained blacks in the South, any minor legal problem—an uneven concrete floor or a minor accident to a white worker involving the Williams' equipment—could easily wipe them out. As well, both James, now 50, and Henry, 48, were tired, their bodies and energies depleted by the long years of toil. For years they had thought of selling the business and their properties, converting the proceeds to cash, and then retiring to some small, predominantly black community out west (where they heard prejudice against blacks was least prevalent). The family down home in Mississippi had broken up and scattered, and James and Henry kept in touch only with a much-younger sister, Hanna.

We have no further knowledge of the Williams brothers. Perhaps they made it to the West, or perhaps they were caught in the depression of 1920–21 and wiped out. But we do know that before they disappeared from our view their parents had died and that, in 1920 or 1921, Hanna, too, died leaving a baby daughter, Lila Williams. The Williams brothers arranged with relatives—James and Sylvia Hunt—to receive and care for their little niece. James, a part-time Baptist preacher and farmer, and Sylvia, a school teacher, lived in Shady Grove, an all-black community on the eastern edge of Kosse, Texas. Lila was adopted by the Hunts (giving a sister to the two boys, James C. and Roy) and grew up in that central Texas community of 600 people.

The black population of Limestone County, in which Kosse is located, comprised 25 to 30 percent of the total population through the interwar years. Kosse's population consisted of 350 whites, largely in and around the center of the small place, 175 blacks, and 75 Mexican-Americans. Most of the blacks lived in Shady Grove and sharecropped land in the immediate vicinity. The Mexicans were scattered in crude shacks in town and along the railroad tracks to the south, where the cotton gin was located.

James and Sylvia Hunt were leaders in Shady Grove and the chief mediators between the black croppers and the ruling white establishment in Kosse. James preached at the Kosse Calvary Baptist Church and at other black churches in the area, and also owned 40 acres, planted in cotton, just each of Shady Grove. Sylvia, who had received some normal-school training at Jarvis Christian College, an all-black school in East Texas, was upset at the absence of a black grade school in Kosse and prevailed upon her husband to move into Kosse during the mid-1920s so that she might start a school. Thereafter, James leased his land, found additional preaching dates, and did other odd jobs to support his family.

The Hunts moved into a large house, well constructed and recently remodeled, two doors from Calvary Baptist Church and close to the main street. (Any part of Kosse was but a stone's throw from the rest of the community.) This home, which they occupied for 20 years, had indoor plumbing, electricity, a pasture, and a corral for horses and several milk cows. James was quite handy and maintained the home nicely, repainting every five years—a necessity in that flat, dry, and windy clime—and keeping the front yard well covered with flowers and shrubs. The boys roomed together and Lila, queen of the house, enjoyed her own room. Lila, in later years, remembered that they played with white and Mexican children but never at the same time. Her impressions, after many years, was that the blacks were slightly above the Mexicans in the pecking order of the community.

The white establishment did nothing to obstruct Sylvia's plans to open a school for black children. Neither did the town provide any aid. Throughout the rural South, most black schools within the segregated system had primitive facilities. Whether motivated by beliefs of black inferiority or by fears that education would stimulate black dissatisfaction with their subordinate position, rural Southerners had little interest in providing schools for blacks. Many of the black schools came from black initiative with construction funding provided by private sources, such as the Rosenwald Foundation of Chicago. When Sylvia sought to open the Kosse black school, she had to obtain permission, not from the school district since she had no intention to seek accreditation, but from the town council and, specifically, from the councilman who acted as fire marshall. Permission was granted to use the Baptist Church as the schoolhouse and, on September 14, 1925, Sylvia opened the doors of her school to a class of 32 black children ranging in age from 6 to 19. During the winter months, it was not unusual for a few adults to take their turns at the three Rs, and from time to time James served as guest lecturer.

No tuition was charged and Sylvia received no salary. The first supplies were paid for by the Hunts, but thereafter the parents were asked to contribute what they could. Still, it was a hand-to-mouth operation. Sylvia despaired from time to time when funds nearly ran out, but the parents always came through with something. Still, the black children of Kosse were better served by Sylvia's makeshift school than were most black children in other parts of the South.

In 1931, when Lila was 12 and had finished six grades in "Mrs. Hunt's school," Sylvia decided that her daughter, an outstanding student, should go to junior high school and high school. This required sending her to live with a widowed aunt, James's sister, in Marlin, Texas, some 12 miles away. She graduated from George Washington Carver High School in Marlin in 1938 (with a straight-A record) and, after lengthy family debates on the best post-secondary institu-

tion, her parents enrolled Lila at Jarvis Christian College. Her brothers, who went to work after high school, offered to help pay Lila's tuition and expenses, and her parents, proud of their bright daughter, helped as well.

The Hunts were less fortunate with James C. and Roy. Neither liked school and were far behind their sister in achievement when she moved to Marlin. Still, they might have made it but the impact of the depression struck tiny Kosse in the early 1930s and destroyed the

Library of Congress

A Farm Security Administration photograph of an Alabama sharecropper, 1937

black community in Shady Grove and the school that it supported. Sharecroppers were the most expendable factor of production in the calculus of the landowner. Farms were abandoned, sharecroppers became migrants, and the press of hard times forced James C. and Roy into a shrinking farm-labor market in order to contribute something to a much-depleted family income. So they labored, along with their father and mother, until James C. was drafted and Roy enlisted in the early years of World War II. As for Kosse, it too persisted—persists—but was never even granted the luxury of a "Last Picture Show."

Louis G. Gropper

Growing up the youngest child by some 20 years in a black sharecropping family near Bonham, Fannin County, Texas, made things somewhat easier for Louis Gropper; but "easier" was relative only to the difficulties experienced by his parents and eight brothers and sisters. Louis's father, Dennis, was an illiterate and unskilled but proud man. During the course of his life he drifted from seasonal jobs as a cotton picker and construction laborer and in and out of sharecropping. When Louis was born in 1918, Dennis Gropper was eking out a precarious existence as a cropper on a farm outside of Bonham. A good part of the family income was contributed by Lottie Gropper, Louis's mother, who could always find work as a domestic servant.

All but one sister had left the Bonham home when Louis came along, but brothers and sisters drifted back home from time to time, embittered men and women who cursed the whites and their power and warned young Louis never to trust any white. These warnings were burned indelibly into the youngster's mind and were confirmed from time to time when news of white violence toward local Negroes spread quickly, by word of mouth, from one black family to another.

None of the Gropper children had advanced beyond the fourth grade and they never attended the same rundown black school for two consecutive years. Lottie determined that these would be different for Louis and insisted that Dennis find jobs within the Bonham school district. Thus Louis graduated from Bonham's public school and was boarded out at a sister's in Sherman where he attended high school. He then enrolled at Texas College in Tyler on a football scholarship. Louis was an outstanding tackle and student, majoring in education and economics with minors in natural science and physical education. Upon graduation in 1941, he wrote 54 applications for teaching positions. Two schools accorded him interviews but hired persons with experience. Shortly thereafter, after failing his army physical because of a pierced eardrum, he found himself odd-jobbing it in Gainesville, Texas. There he met Lila Hunt who was in her first year of teaching. Lila and Louis were married in 1943.

THE BASSANOS OF NEW YORK CITY

Many Italian immigrants to America came with the idea of saving money and returning home. And many succeeded. Perhaps as many as 35 percent of the Italians reaching the United States between 1880 and 1910 went back to Italy, a much higher proportion than found among the other major ethnic groups. Those Italians arriving after 1910 tended to remain or retire to Italy in their old age. But many, almost 600,000 Italian-born immigrants living in the United States in 1940, had never applied for citizenship papers. They kept their options open. Andrew Bassano was one who returned, as his mother had before him.

Andrew's sojourn in the United States ended on May 7, 1936, when he boarded a liner at New York's 18th Street Pier, waved goodbye to his eight children and numerous grandchildren, and headed into the Atlantic toward a retirement on the family farm in Udine Province. Following Rose's death in 1924, Andrew had saved every penny and his children had contributed to a fund for their father's eventual retirement in Italy. "I will never be a burden to my children in my old age," Andrew had always insisted. Without a pension and realizing that his savings would not last long in America, he retired in 1936 and purchased his steamboat ticket for

Andrew Bassano shortly before retiring to Italy

Genoa. His children saw this independent man only one more time, when, after the Second World War, the children pooled their savings to pay his air fare for a brief visit to America.

Andrew Bassano took back to Italy 37 years of memories, the last 17 of which mixed happiness and sadness in equal proportions. Except for Rose's sudden passing, the 1920s had been good years. Established in his profession, Andrew had more jobs than he could handle during the great construction boom that swept New York and the country during this decade. Terrazzo flooring, a strong, easily maintained surface, was in demand. Almost every new office building, insurance company, and bank installed terrazzo floors, and Andrew did the work in many of them, earning $66 for an eight-hour, five-day week. As a skilled building craftsman, especially one in a highly skilled and creative role, Bassano worked under conditions radically different than those of factory or mill workers. Basically, he controlled his own work; he provided his own tools, and he determined how the work should be done and at what pace. With a strong union that scheduled the jobs and served as liaison between members and the contractors who employed them, the workers' independence was guaranteed. The union was local, exclusive (only northern Italians were permitted in through the 1930s), and very effective because of the complex nature of the terrazzo-tile mason's craft.

Even with eight children, Andrew was able to put away a large part of his weekly pay, for living expenses were low. The Bassanos occupied the four-room apartment at 140th Street and Amsterdam Avenue until 1929, when they moved to a larger apartment, costing $35 monthly, at 200th Street, in that northern section of Manhattan called Inwood. Food was a major part of the family's budget, and there was little left for "luxuries" such as a radio or movies or new shoes. One son later described his youth:

We grew up in a happy household, never lacked direction or responsibility. We all lived together, played together, fought together. We all had chores to perform and without pay. The older children had to take care of the younger ones. Very few luxuries. We shared toys, we spun tops, we played jacks, we jumped rope, we shared hobbies, we wore hand-me-down clothes."

During their mother's long illness, the children still at home, ranging from 8 to 20 years in age, took total responsibility for running the household. Every summer from 1923, when Rose first suffered the excruciating pain of a gall bladder attack, the younger children, Louis (1911), Robert (1912), and Lawrence (1915) were sent to board with farm families in New Jersey and Long Island. Catherine and Beatrice, both with full-time jobs, kept house until they married and left home in the mid-1930s. As with many other working-class families in which the earnings of the children provided a margin of financial security and allowed the occasional purchase of goods and even homes, all the Bassano children contributed to the family treasury. This money became extremely important after 1929, for Andrew never again worked steadily. For Robert Bassano, the depression years "don't stand out particularly in my mind since I was just starting my job. Most of my brothers and sisters also had jobs so they were not any worse off than in the 20s." Three of the older sons, Phillip, Alfred, and Vincent, went to Peter Cooper Vocational School but found jobs in nonmanual occupations. Each gave his father $15 monthly for room and board and the retirement fund, and even Bob, the second youngest, contributed 50 percent of the wages he earned as a delivery boy for Giuseppe Selantano, owner of a neighborhood Italian grocery on Dyckman Street. (Years later, Bob's son worked for Mr. Selantano.)

The elder Bassanos had little interest in further education for their children. A good job, Andrew believed, was sufficient. Neither Catherine nor Beatrice finished high school, but the three younger boys, reflecting the family's improved economic status, completed four years at George Washington High. Only Lawrence, the youngest, went to college, earning a B.S. in accounting through night-school courses. The Bassano children tolerated school but, like many urban children, took almost no part in school-related activities. Their world was the block on which they lived. Athletic teams, for instance, were organized on a block-by-block basis, and there was a social club that sponsored dances, held raffles for group projects, and enforced on all the kids from 3 to 17 the elaborate rules devised to ensure efficient use of neighborhood facilities.

The social and athletic pursuits that occupied Bob and Larry Bassano's free moments represented an urban, working-class solution to the need for recreation. Park facilities were distant, and there was no money for equipment. So the streets were utilized for everything—stickball, roller hockey, football—and equipment was improvised—broomsticks for bats, newspapers, tightly rolled and tied, for a football. Such improvisation was typical in working and lower-class areas around the country even though the games might be different. The well-to-do played these and other sports too, but with standard equipment. Bob Bassano (or Miles Markovich) never held a tennis racquet or golf club, never set foot on a sailing vessel or mounted a horse. Such pursuits were too expensive for the Bassano or Markovich children and inaccessible to many middle-class families.

During the 1920s, the pursuit of leisure accelerated greatly among all classes. With most Americans possessing blocks of free time, an industry arose that hawked "leisure" as a product. Millions who had never seen vaudeville or traveling theatre groups went to the movies to watch Mary Pickford or Douglas

Fairbanks. Indeed films virtually destroyed those institutions except in the largest cities.

In combination with movies and radio, "automobility" diminished such traditional leisure pursuits as clubs and lodges, lectures, gardening, and walking or bicycling. In addition, by 1940, some 28.5 million families had at least one radio, which brought the world into the front parlor. During the depression, radio provided the major—if not only—form of entertainment to millions of economically pinched Americans. However, a majority of Americans still were without cars in 1940, including the Millers, Markoviches (and Simiches), and Bassanos. Social dancing rose in popularity, but there was a definite hierarchy of dance events, from the cheap "five-cents-a-dance" emporia that sprang up in Springfield, Ohio, Newburgh, New York, and other cities, to the traditional debutante balls. Manners and mores were intimately involved. Springfield's matrons deplored the holding of school dances in hotels at the same time that the school board prohibited dancing in the schools. Social drinking also became more popular, even during prohibition. Prohibition did indeed deny to millions of workers the pleasures of a pail of beer, but for those with the cash, speakeasies continued to provide booze. Mixed drinks, Scotch, and aperitifs flowed at middle and upper-class parties while 3.2 beer and illegal wine became the staples at working-class gatherings.

In sport, college football enjoyed golden years in the 1920s, producing such great stars as Red Grange of Illinois and the Four Horsemen of Notre Dame. The National Football League was established in 1920. Football really came into its own when the ball, cantaloupe-shaped in the 1920s, was redesigned for throwing in 1934. The forward pass revolutionized the game, just as Sid Luckman of the Chicago Bears and Sammy Baugh of the Washington Redskins rewrote the book on quarterbacking. Still, college and professional football appealed mostly to the middle class.

Baseball's appeal reached further into the class system for support, particularly when the games were broadcast over the radio. The 1920s were truly great years for baseball, despite the eruption of the 1919 Chicago

Crucible plant baseball team, Midland, 1925

"Black" Sox scandal. The star system made Babe Ruth and Ty Cobb household words, and the efficient organization of the minor leagues ensured a constant flow of talent into the majors. Baseball's success was epitomized by the completion of the Yankee Stadium in 1927 and the performance of the 27 Yankees, considered by connoisseurs as the premier team of all time. Most ball players came from lower-class backgrounds. Very few—Lou Gehrig was an exception—had more than a high-school education. Much the same was true for boxing, another sport that radio popularized. World heavyweight champion Joe Louis was a source of great pride to blacks just as Barney Ross, an outstanding lightweight, was to Jews.

Americans turned out in incredible numbers for sporting events, both amateur and professional. Owners of baseball teams learned soon enough to charge different prices for different seats, and by the mid-1920s, the crowds at ball games were divided between the more sedate and nattily dressed box-seat fans and the raucous crowds of beer drinkers that populated the center-field bleachers. The sports craze continued through the 1930s. Few high-school football coaches were fired, and most schools maintained full schedules in major sports during the depression. Though gate receipts for professional sports declined somewhat, interest became obsessive for many. Before marrying, Charlotte and Bob Bassano attended many a Giants game at the Polo Grounds. Once the Giants' road trips were broadcast, Charlotte could always be found by the family's enormous Motorola radio, keeping score.

Robert Bassano was the only one of Andrew and Rose's children to remain in the old neighborhood. He graduated from George Washington High School in June 1929, having taken a general business course. He was eager to start work and finally, after a six-month search, he found employment as a messenger boy in the Wall Street offices of the Manhattan (later Chase Manhattan) Bank. It meant long hours for low pay ($22 a week), but it was a job and a white-collar job to boot, with the opportunity for advancement. Besides, Bob Bassano was eager to get married to a girl he had met at a neighborhood dance during his senior year. Charlotte Bauss, the only child of a third-generation German family, had also attended George Washington High and had found employment at a Woolworth's store near the school. She and Bob Bassano originally had agreed on a long engagement, until they had a financial cushion, but the worsening of the depression in 1930 suggested that conditions would not improve for a long time, so why wait? Moreover, neither family expressed concern over differences in religion or ethnic background. Both families believed in the melting pot and looked to ethnic mixing, if they thought about it at all, as a positive step. In these second and third generations, as was not true of the more ethnocentric Markoviches and Millers, there was little tension between ethnic traditions and culture and the larger society. Bob and Charlotte were married in St. Mark's Lutheran Church in Manhattan in March 1931.

The newlyweds found an apartment at the corner of Nagel and Dyckman Streets, just across the street from Bob's father and not far from Charlotte's parents. Their new home, for which they paid $30 per month rent, comprised three rooms. In the 1930s, Inwood was an area of comfortable low and middle-income housing, bounded on two sides by parks and wooded sections and offering all necessary services for young families such as the Bassanos. The neighborhood in which they lived was primarily Irish Catholic and Jewish, though sizable groups of Poles and other east Europeans, Italians, and a scattering of Anglo-Saxons were located close by. Dyckman Street, the main shopping area for Inwood, was then crowded with stores of

The Bassano's Hillside Avenue apartment building and elevated tracks of the IRT to the left

of the block society. His father earned a promotion to cashier at Chase Manhattan in 1937 (at a time when hundreds of employees were being released), and the Bassanos might have moved to a better apartment in a more expensive neighborhood. They never considered doing so for their life, their friends, everything they needed and enjoyed was to be found in Inwood.

THE TRACES OF NOWHERE AND LOS ANGELES, CALIFORNIA

On June 4, 1923, the St. Louis, Missouri police arrested McKinley Trace and charged him with aggravated assault, malicious destruction of property, and public drunkenness. "Kenny," Will Trace's youngest son, had been picked up by police responding to a riot call, staggering drunkenly out of a speakeasy frequented by railroaders. Later it was learned that Kenny had started a fight and had cut a man seriously with a broken whiskey bottle. He was booked and thrown into the drunk tank, while the authorities telegraphed his brother, Ben Trace, whose address was in Kenny's wallet, and the Evansville, Indiana police. No reply was received from Ben; however, information from the authorities in Evansville revealed that McKinley Trace had a lengthy record, with four "drunk and disorderly" convictions and two arrests, not prosecuted, for assault and battery. At a preliminary hearing 10 days later, confronted by his battered, heavily bandaged victim and the angry owner of the speakeasy, Kenny Trace pleaded guilty to all charges. He was sentenced to 12 months labor at the State Work Farm, Springfield, Missouri.

The year Kenny Trace spent in a Missouri prison was the turning point of his life. As one of some 600 inmates, he was stripped of iden-

every description and thronged with shoppers from a dozen countries and speaking as many languages. The merchants lived in the neighborhood, and there existed a community of interest between store-owners, inhabitants, and neighborhood churches and social clubs.

Not only was Nagel and Dyckman Street a good place to live—convenient to the subway and thus 30 minutes from Bob Bassano's work, a few steps for Charlotte to the stores where she shopped daily—but Inwood was also a wonderful place for the children who flooded its streets and occupied the stoops that fronted every apartment building. Robert Bassano, Jr. (Robbie) was born at St. Elizabeth's Hospital on Mother Cabrini Boulevard on July 18, 1936. Though Robbie was Robert and Charlotte's only child, he never lacked for playmates, for things to do. From the time he learned to walk, Robbie lived in the street outside, accepted as a prospective member of the block's gang, named the Satans, and watched over by older children. When he grew older, every afternoon after P.S. 152 released the neighborhood children, there were games—marbles, stickball, ring-o-leevio—explorations of the cliffs and lush woods of Fort Tryon and Inwood Hill Parks and the Cloisters, and the security

tity, self-confidence, and dignity. Forced to work in the prison's fields from dawn until dark, forgotten by his relatives in Evansville and Waynesboro, brutalized by guards and by fellow inmates who confiscated his small earnings and forced him into homosexual activities, Kenny emerged in July 1924 a changed, beaten man. The robust good looks and loud, confident talk remained, but the personality beneath, already crippled by self-indulgence and insecurity, was mortally wounded.

Kenny Trace had come to Evansville, Indiana in 1914 with his brother Ben, swearing that he would make it big and then return to Tennessee, marry the prettiest girl in Wayne County, buy the biggest farm, and enjoy the good life. He was then 17, the youngest and favorite child of Will and Millie Trace, protected and indulged by his numerous brothers and sisters. At first, it appeared that Kenny might make good his boasts. Much more outgoing and clever than Ben, with whom he roomed when they arrived in Evansville, Kenny talked his way into an office job at the L&N repair shops in Howell. But he quickly acquired a taste for the all-night poker available in the back room of the Front Street pool hall, the moonshine liquor sold in the alley, and the company of women who congregated in the Howell Cafe next door. Especially while Ben was in the Army, they helped Kenny overcome the homesickness and depression that made a hell of his tiny, colorless room and boring job. By the time Ben returned, Kenny had been arrested twice for public drunkenness and was deeply in debt. The brothers quarreled and Ben moved out, shouting that Kenny had disgraced the family and would end up a worthless bum. Over the next five years, Kenny Trace set out, as if to confirm his brother's bitter prophecy. His drinking became so noticeable that he was transferred from the front office to a position as brakeman on the L&N's Evansville to St. Louis freight. He became involved in a number of scrapes, each time avoiding criminal prosecution—until the fracas in St. Louis.

Kenny returned to Evansville in later summer 1924, determined to stay away from liquor and find a steady job. In the isolated hills of Wayne County, Kenny might have been embraced and protected by kin. But in Howell, ex-mountaineers, now solidly middle class in moral attitudes, if not in income, viewed him as a pariah. Family and friends interpreted his lawlessness as proof of deeply rooted personal defects. This attitude reflected those of the law-abiding majority in America who believed that the commission of a criminal act was de facto evidence of character deficiencies. This view lingered into the 20th century although reformers had been stressing environmental factors for several decades.

Research by psychologists and sociologists, beginning in the early 20th century, did offer serious challenges to the prevailing wisdom, for numerous scholars asserted that not heredity but environmental factors—economic deprivation, the hostility and alienation generated by slum life, social disorganization—chiefly were responsible for crime. This argument was brilliantly propounded by Emile Durkheim who stressed the importance of *anomie* in understanding the incidence of crime. The theory stressed the frustration and resentment, frequently expressed through socially deviant behavior, that might be felt by people unable to achieve aspirations—wealth, social position—encouraged and valued by the culture. A few criminologists delved into possible means for resolving the frustrations, usually economic in nature, that pushed individuals toward crime, but, with the exception of such works as John Landesco's *Organized Crime in Chicago* (1929) and Frederic M. Thrasher's *The Gang* (1936), research increasingly focused on juvenile delinquency and related problems. Ignorant of such studies, many Americans continued to ascribe criminal acts, at least the organized aspects such as racketeering, prostitution, the liquor traffic, and gambling, to the proclivities of depraved (rather than deprived) racial and ethnic minorities. The tendency of blacks to engage in crime was explained in these terms; and in the 1920s the acts of well-organized gangs (such as the Al Capone mob) were treated as a continuation of the "well-known appeal of crime to Italians," stretching from the stories of the Black Hand to the emergence of the Mafia myth. Perhaps the popular explanation was most relevant to Kenny Trace's career. His frustrations were no greater than his brother Ben's, his chances no less. Kenny was of weaker stuff than Ben who survived and prospered modestly in the new urban environment.

Good intentions did not long survive such pressures. Kenny began to drink heavily and to spend most weekends in the drunk cell of the city jail across from the courthouse. He lost job after job. In January 1925, during the period of high determination to become a solid citizen, he had married Velma Milton, a 19-year-old bar girl with whom he had been living and had made pregnant. Kenny's new wife had learned that an alcoholic dentist on West Franklin Street offered after-hours abortions. Kenny tried to obtain the $90 fee from friends, but his credit was nil. So, one Friday night in May 1925, he robbed a roadhouse on St. Joseph's Avenue. Two days later, before Velma visited the abortionist, Kenny was arrested, charged with grand theft, assault with a deadly weapon (he had waved a knife at the cashier), and conspiracy to procure an illegal operation. He was convicted and, without having seen his baby son, Calvin, joined the 96,000 other Americans then incarcerated in state and federal prisons. (The number of prisoners—and of crimes committed— mounted steadily from the mid-1920s to 1940, when 154,446 convicts were in state

prisons and 19,260 in federal custody.) Help- less, bewildered Kenny Trace, viewed as a hardened criminal because of his record, was sentenced to a three- to five-year term in the Indiana State Penitentiary at Michigan City.

Abandoned by her bumbling husband and saddled with a squalling baby (the care of which she knew almost nothing about), Velma Trace scrawled a letter to her parents, who had moved from Evansville to Los Angeles in 1923, begging their forgiveness and pleading for train fare to California. Al- though Velma had left home at 14 when her father had learned she had slept with men for money, her parents, concerned about their first grandchild, sent the fare. For three years, until Kenny traced her down, Velma lived with her parents, using their home as a base for a career as a waitress and B-girl. Following his release from prison in 1929, even more demoralized and disoriented, Kenny decided once again to go straight. When his brother and sister refused even to see him, he jumped a freight lumbering west from Howell, cutting all ties to the past.

A new life in sunny California, the ambition of millions of Americans in these years, for a time appeared to be coming true for Kenny Trace. Velma agreed to take him back, his son soon accepted him as a "daytime" daddy, and his father-in-law found work for him as a rough carpenter in the San Fernando Valley. This time Kenny stayed on the wagon for al- most three years. It became increasingly dif- ficult as carpentry jobs became scarce and as Velma's contempt for him was made clear by her return to part-time prostitution. He tum- bled off in March 1933, when Velma an- nounced she was pregnant again. He never climbed out of the bottle again. For two years, Kenny drifted around southern California, sometimes sleeping on the beach, but more often in alleyways, freight cars, and the drunk tank, while Velma pursued him with a sum- mons for nonsupport of herself and their two sons—the youngest, Franklin, born in late 1933. In October 1935, he was committed to the California State Hospital for the Criminally Insane and Habitual Alcoholics. Eight months later, on June 8, 1936, Kenny died from a massive kidney failure. He left a penknife (a gift from his father on his 12th birthday), a battered wallet containing a picture of Calvin, his brother Ben's address as next of kin, and a membership card in the Brotherhood of Railway Workers. When notified of her husband's death, Velma Trace, then subsisting on welfare, occasional tricks, and a part-time job in a tavern, told the coroner she could not afford a funeral or a cemetery plot. McKinley Trace was buried at public expense in the potter's field just south of the highway linking Glendale and Los Angeles. Calvin, 10 years old at this time, was already a truancy case and his future looked bleak, while Franklin, at 3, fell more and more under the care of his grandparents.

THE BUTLERS OF BROOKLINE AND BOSTON, MASSACHUSETTS

The annual reunion of the Butler brothers, traditionally held on June 1, their mother's birthday, was successfully arranged in 1924. Not lack of interest—the Butlers remained intensely loyal and affectionate toward each other and the families visited frequently—but the press of professional obligations had prevented any full reunion for some years. During the war, Roger and then Robert had been absent from Boston. By the time they were discharged from service, Eliott was away in San Francisco, having accepted a residency in thoracic surgery at the University of California Medical School. Now he had returned to Boston as surgeon-in-chief at Peter Bent Brigham Hospital, and the annual excuse for horseplay, family gossip, and reminiscing could re-

sume. This time the five brothers—John, a stockbroker in Boston, Eliott, Roger, just married to a fertilizer heiress from an old Massachusetts family, George, a banker in New York City, and Robert, a junior member of a distinguished Boston legal firm—convened at John's summer place in Beverly on the Massachusetts North Shore. John Butler had just added a new wing to this house, which he mysteriously described as "absolutely fitting" for the brothers' annual reunion.

When all his brothers had arrived at Beverly and had been furnished drinks, John escorted them through to the new wing, threw open its doors, and gleefully watched his brothers' expressions shift from polite interest to amazement to something akin to awe. "It's Porc, it's all Porc," Robert shouted in delight. The two-room suite, which John proudly termed his "sanctum," was filled with evocations of Porcellian, the exclusive senior club to which all five brothers had belonged at Harvard and which still occupied a central place in their social and professional lives. "To be a Butler and to have been to Harvard without having been elected to the Porcellian Club," an English writer who, as a boy, lived with the John Butlers during the Second World War once remarked, "was nearly as bad as having been sent down from Oxford for 'gross and continued immorality.' " John's study was crammed with momentos, pictures, and athletic trophies from undergraduate days at Harvard. Even more significant, pigs, the Porcellian Club emblem, were everywhere. There was a pig doorknocker, a pig doormat, pig salt cellars, pig footrests. The wine glasses and cutlery bore a piggish design, the curtains were ablaze with pigs, and they festooned the bath towels and even John's hairbrush. This obsession with all things Porcellian, seemingly so juvenile, captured the outlook of the Butlers, George and all his sons, regarding the familiar world in which they worked and played. Porcellian was a sign of their acceptance into Boston's upper class, a continuing source of reinforcement for the values special to that class, and to them, and proof of their permanence and stability.

Participation in activities outside one's family and kinship group was hardly a unique attribute of the Butlers and their class, though the importance John Butler and his brothers attached to such associations was decidedly atypical. Americans had always taken part in formal or informal associations with others, and their tendency to be "joiners" was observed by Alexis de Tocqueville, among many other foreign visitors. The 1920s, however, witnessed an enormous expansion of America's associational enthusiasms, particularly within the middle and upper classes, along with increasing stratification and exclusivity within these groupings. Babbitt was not every American, nor was the urge to join, to boost one's community and express civic pride, justifiably condemned out of hand as "Babbittry." Boomerism had a long tradition and was firmly rooted in the belief that general economic growth brought improved standards of living.

The principal association for most Americans remained organized religion: church attendance itself, or a youth, men's, or ladies' study group, or church-related social organizations such as the Methodist Youth Fellowship to which Jerry Trace belonged, and the Holy Rosary Society which enrolled Margaret O'Reilly. But organizations derived from school, work, and recreational pursuits became very important during these years. As joiners, however, not all Americans were alike. The Butlers and the Gales derived greater status satisfaction and economic gains from their memberships than the Markoviches who sought cultural identity, familiar sights and sounds in a cold environment. The Bassanos, Millers, and Traces, although not joiners, belonged to unions, burial societies, or other beneficiary societies, thus collectively

seeking security against powerful natural and economic forces. By the 1920s, the programs of the older ethnic associations reflected middle-class preferences, while the needs of the laboring poor were inadequately met by general charities or primitive public-service agencies. The laboring poor and almost poor—Ben Trace for one—had neither the time, money, nor inclination to run off to a lodge meeting after work. Other than religious groups, their wives never joined formal organizations, either. The Butlers' private Boston clubs, in one sense, were similar to the Serbian societies in Midland. But other associations were exclusively middle and upper class: country clubs, civic and business groups, and reform societies. In smaller cities and towns, businessmen joined together to boost their town and increase local pride. In larger cities, families such as the Butlers worked in associations to shape economic and political life and to satisfy their sense of obligation and stewardship. Thus, some of their associational activities were far removed from the experiences of other families. Cost was a key factor, but an adequate income did not turn Gus O'Reilly into a joiner. It did postpone the building of a Serbian church in Midland until after World War II.

One activity in which all Americans took part involved the getting and spending of money. The position of the Butlers, though on a different plane from that of the majority, was still vulnerable; although several of the brothers prospered even during the depression, one, apparently possessing economic security in 1929, was almost destroyed by the crash. Because of business reverses (largely caused by the shift in lumbering to the Pacific Northwest), Stetson Butler and Company was on the verge of receivership by the recession of 1920–21. George C. Butler's sons, George and Robert, arranged for sale of the business a few years later to its largest competitor. After six years of golfing, fishing, and traveling,

George Butler died suddenly in May 1927, at the Heath Street house, leaving some property in Brookline and Maine and a few thousand dollars to each of his sons. Their major inheritance, however, was the Butler name, education, and upper-class ties.

The eldest son, John, was by that time well established, a member of Lee, Higginson and Company, Boston's leading stock brokerage. Married in 1910 to the daughter of a New York congressman from a patrician family, John Butler led a very social, very comfortable existence with his wife and their five children. They moved to New York in 1928 in order that John test himself in the big time of Wall Street. He did extremely well until the crash. They traveled between a town house in New York (a five-floor brownstone on East 80th Street staffed by two nurses, a governess, two maids, a chauffeur, and an Irish cook), the summer place at Beverly (which had been given as a wedding present to John's wife, Rossalyn, by a disappointed beau), and their yacht, the *Helianthus* (crewed year round by a crusty Maine captain and a Chinese cook). The children attended exclusive day schools and prep schools, traveled to Europe, and engaged in a busy social life in both Boston and New York. But John Butler was not as secure as appearances suggested, and the stock market crash hurt him badly. "From then on," his second daughter recalled 40 years later, "my father spent less and less time at home and more time at his club. There were drinking episodes and heated discussions with my mother late into the night over priorities and ways to economize." They sold the yacht and the Beverly house. One by one, the servants disappeared. There was still enough money to send John, Jr. to Harvard, but that proved a disappointment for he was thrown out in 1938, during his sophomore year. His father, unable to deal with the changed circumstances and relegated to a job as a front man,

a party giver for his firm, became a hopeless alcoholic by 1940.

Eliott's career was much more even and successful. Having acquired excellent training at Harvard and California, he became known as an outstanding surgeon (he co-authored a textbook with the great Harvey Cushing) and headed Peter Bent Brigham Hospital for many years. His family life was dull but stable. Two of his sons eventually graduated from Harvard and made Procellian—a source of great family rejoicing. George, the most "un-Butlerish" of the brothers, ironically, was the most successful in economic terms. He became President of the Baltimore Bank, after having worked for many years for Guaranty Trust in New York City. He married a Boston girl from an "old bean" family and they produced four children, all of whom attended boarding schools in the Boston area. The only complete failure, Roger, enjoyed incredible success at marrying rich women but not much at holding on to their money. Fondly described as a "n'er-do-well" by his brothers, Roger was conned into a series of disastrous get-rich-quick schemes. His four children grew up to despise their irresponsible father and to blame their own difficulties—which were substantial—on him. One, however, Roger, Jr., was early identified as the "standard bearer" for the next generation of Butlers. An outstanding student and athlete at Harvard and member of Porcellian, Roger, Jr. was the pride and joy of his Uncle Robert.

The youngest of the Butler boys, Robert, justified his life on the basis of the associational endeavors he pursued. After military service, Robert dashed through Harvard Law School and into a firm specializing in corporate and tax law, Herrick, Smith, Donald & Farley, with offices on State Street. Robert's brother, George, was a partner and all five of the firm's founders were Harvard-Porcellian. By the time of Franklin Roosevelt's election, Robert Butler was himself a partner, director of numerous companies, and highly regarded for his knowledge of family and corporate trusts. Once the New Deal was launched, he made skillful use of this knowledge in negotiations with the National Recovery Administration.

One of Robert Butler's major responsibilities at Herrick, Smith, Donald & Farley was advising wealthy old Bostonians, most usually widows, as to appropriate disposition of their estates. Invariably he persuaded these clients to include sizable bequests to his favorite charities—the Boston Symphony, Peter Bent Brigham Hospital, and the Harvard Medical Center. More strongly than any of his brothers, Robert was driven by the ideal of stewardship practiced by the Butlers' flinty ancestors. The impulse to do "good works," which dominated his life, was perhaps a substitute for the sexual and social release he missed by never marrying, an acceptable outlet for his driving energy; but it nonetheless exerted great influence over Robert Butler's career.

By the late 1920s, when he moved from the Butler home on Heath Street—which Eliott's growing family could better use—to a spartan apartment in the Somerset Club, Robert's life had assumed definite shape. A demon for work (his office was universally known as "Hurricane Corner"), he customarily spent 16 to 18 hours each day on legal matters, family business, and his philanthropies. He took all his meals in the dining hall of the Somerset Club or with friends. In 1934, Robert did buy a country place at Harvard, Massachusetts, but used it only rarely. His life was family, work, and increasingly, the social and cultural improvement of Boston.

To his musical and medical charitable work, Robert added involvement in the Community Fund, an association of organized charities that swept over America (as did the Community Chest, Red Feather

Drive, and so forth) in the 1920s. In 1937, he served as the general chairman of the second annual Community Fund Campaign of Greater Boston. In 1940, Robert Butler was selected as national chairman of the Chest and Council Organization of America and spent considerable time presiding over board meetings and addressing "kickoff" rallies across the country. These efforts made Robert a well-known figure throughout Boston. As well, he had long been an active, though discreet, member of the "liberal" wing of the Republican Party in Massachusetts. He was especially interested in bridging the chasm between Republicans and ethnic groups in Boston and Massachusetts politics. In September 1940, Robert was asked by Mayor Maurice Tobin, a young Irishman with whom Robert had worked in the Community Fund, to become Boston Corporation Counsel. It was unusual for a Harvard-educated, traditional Republican such as Robert Butler to be offered such a politically powerful office, but it was still more novel for one to accept. "I could hear the bell ringing once more the call to duty," Robert later explained. It was fateful, for the political path embarked upon in 1940 soon led him far afield from his quiet rooms at the Somerset Club and the charities he so fiercely guarded. But that was more the world's decision than it was his own choice.

SUGGESTIONS FOR FURTHER READING

Especially useful in the drafting of this chapter were such miscellaneous works as Oscar E. Anderson, *The Health of a Nation* (1958); Robert C. Angell, *The Family Encounters the Depression* (1936); Glen H. Elder, Jr., *Children of the Great Depression: A Study in Social Structure and Personality* (1974); Bird T. Baldwin et al., *Farm Children: An Investigation of Rural Child Life in Selected Areas of Iowa* (1930); Daniel I. Boorstin, *The Americans: The Democratic Experience*

(1973); Alfred Kinsey et al., *Sexual Behavior in the Human Male* (1948) and *Sexual Behavior in the Human Female* (1953); Ruth Lindquist, *The Family in the Present Social Order: A Study of American Families* (1931); and President's Research Committee on Recent Social Trends, *Recent Social Trends* (2 vols., 1933). Also very helpful were Irving Bernstein's superb study, *The Lean Years: A History of the American Worker, 1920–1933* (1966); Arthur Knight's fascinating survey of motion picture history, *The Liveliest Art* (1957); and Studs Terkel's *Hard Times* (1970), an oral history of the depression experience.

Many of the "family history" studies cited in the list of readings for Chapter 1 are relevant here. Also see Andrew Billingsley, *Black Families in White America* (1968); Gunnar Myrdal's classic, *An American Dilemma* (2 vols., 1944); and the Lynds works on "Middletown" cited elsewhere. Louis Adamic, *My America* (1938); Margaret Mead, *Blackberry Winter: My Earlier Years* (1972); and August Derleth, *Village Year: A Sac Prairie Journal* (1941) are three memoirs of the time which deserve particular notice. Philip Wylie's *A Generation of Vipers* (1942) is a warped, fascinating document.

Works on women's history include William H. Chafe, *The American Woman: Her Changing Social, Economic, and Political Roles, 1920–1970* (1972); Anne Firor Scott, *The Southern Lady: From Pedestal to Politics* (1970); Stanley J. Leites, *The Woman Citizen: Social Feminism in the 1920s* (1963); Mary Anderson, *Woman at Work* (1951); Leslie W. Tentler, *Wage-earning Women: Indus-trial Work and Family Life in the United States, 1900–1930* (1979); Winifred D. Wandersee, *Women's Work and Family Values, 1920–1940* (1981); Susan Ware, *Beyond Suffrage: Women in the New Deal* (1980); and Molly Haskell, *From Reverence to Rape: The Treatment of Women in the Movies* (1974). Other studies of film history are Robert Sklar's comprehensive *Movie-made America* (1976); Martha Wolfenstein and Nathan Leites, *Movies: A Psychological Study* (1953); and Andrew Bergman, *We're in the Money: Depression America and Its Films* (1971). Useful treatments of culture include Roderick Nash, *The Nervous Generation: American Thought, 1917–1930* (1970); Carolyn Ware, *Greenwich Village, 1920–1933* (1973); Elizabeth Stevenson, *Babbitts and Bohemians: The American 1920s* (1967); Loren Baritz, *The Culture of the Twenties* (1970); and J. C. Furnas, *Great Times: Social History of the United States, 1914–1929* (1974); along with the books listed in the appendixes to Chapters 6 and 7. Nathan G. Hale's *Freud and the Americans* (1971); Robert Elias, *Entangling Alliances with None: An Essay on the Individual in the American Twenties* (1977); Ronald C. Tobey, *The American Ideology of National Science* (1971); William E. Akin, *Technocracy and the American Dream* (1977) treat important themes. For advertising and magazine journalism, see Stuart Ewen, *Captains of Consciousness* (1975) and Theodore B. Peterson, *Magazines in the Twentieth Century* (1964). Donald Meyer's critique of Dale Carnegie and the organizational ethic, *The Positive Thinkers* (1965), is excellent.

6 | Prosperity and Modernity, 1920-1932

PROGRESS AND POVERTY

At last in the 1920s, the promises of the St. Louis Exposition of 1904 seemed to come to fruition. The marvels found in 1904 in the Palaces of Agriculture, Transportation, Machinery, Mines and Metallurgy, and Manufactures had become commonplace in factories, farms, and homes. Increasing productivity brought greater national wealth, and most people remembered the decade for its prosperity and gaiety. Much of this bright image, though, was formed by sharp contrast with the dismal years of depression that followed. Frederick Lewis Allen, an editor of *Harper's Magazine,* fathered the pulp novel and screen image of the 1920s when, in 1931, he nostalgically recalled the boom years in a best-selling book, *Only Yesterday.* However, not all Americans shared the better life and the fun Allen described. Old troubles remained, sometimes with new consequences, as economic and social forces worked their way with the way Americans lived—be it in Kosse, Texas; Evansville, Indiana; or Boston, Massachusetts.

The boom of the twenties started with a bust. As the nation converted from war to peace, it experienced a sharp depression (1920–21), brought on in part by the withdrawal of the federal government from its wartime role of big spender. Between February 1920 and April 1921, the index of factory production dropped by one third; factory employment dropped by more than 40 percent between its high in June 1920 and its low in July 1921. Prices fell 45 percent. According to neoclassical economists, it would all work out for the best, and indeed the course of this brief depression seemed to confirm what they had been saying about the regularity of the business cycle. Businesses reduced costs, cut inventories, and liquidated debts. Eight percent fewer businesses were in existence in

1921 than in 1919. Mihailo Markovich and Ben Trace, both laid off during those years, were the human victims of this cycle. Mihailo was convinced that Crucible's cutbacks were premeditated, designed to reconstitute a pool of surplus labor that allowed the firm to break unions and pay low wages. The ruthless readjustment, accompanied by the hardship of unemployment (a decade of underemployment for Ben) and the grimness of deflation produced a turnabout in the economy. By the end of 1921, recovery had begun. Prosperity roared in, bringing with it the first consumer age in the United States.

By whatever indicators one might choose, the 1920s seemed unprecedented as a time of progress—an era in which prosperity reached more Americans than ever before. For once it seemed an adequate supply of comfortable housing might be available. The rate at which new dwellings were constructed in the 1920s prompted optimistic projections of an early solution to the perennial housing problem. Before the 1920s, the highest number of new homes and apartments to be built in any year had been 507,000 in 1905. From 1922 through 1929, that total was surpassed in each year, with a high of 937,000 new units in 1925. And the new homes and apartments were modern. In 1920 fewer than half of urban and nonfarm rural dwellings (47.4 percent) and only 1.6 percent of farm homes had electrical service. While the Reinhardts enjoyed the miracles of electricity in their home and the Gales ran a gasoline engine to generate power for farm use, their farms were among the fortunate few that had electricity. Electric lines were run to both the Gale and Hart farms in the 1930s, but the Traces of Tennessee were without service until after World War II. With electricity came new appliances, and by 1930, 5 percent of American families had replaced iceboxes with electric refrigerators. By the late 1920s, many apartments in New York, including the Nagel

Avenue apartment of the Bassanos, came furnished with a refrigerator and stove. Between 1920 and 1930, the number of telephones in service increased from some 13 million to 20 million. James Hart and Charles Gale came to depend upon the phone in running their farms. The sharp rise in automobile registrations, from 8 million in 1920 to more than 23 million in 1930, further reflected a consumer-oriented society.

This broad expansion of inventions and innovations geared to the consumer was bound to make some highly visable changes in American life. Not only was it obvious that Americans as a group were better housed than ever before, it was also clear they had never been more mobile. Automobile production was accompanied by an unprecedented flurry of building new roads and paving old ones. Public transportation improved as bus lines took up the slack created by the decline of interurbans. Consumer air travel began in 1926, and by 1929 four companies boasted a total commercial squadron of 83 airplanes. In bridging space, these improvements in transportation reduced the vastness of the United States. They cut travel time, made available inaccessible areas, and helped destroy many of the last remnants of localism. An invention that further reduced the vastness of the country and muted local peculiarities was the radio.

The commercial exploitation of Marconi's wireless was an inevitable result of America's business orientation. While the government controlled the use of radio during World War I, several large corporations achieved control over all of the principal patents, and this eventually served to guarantee private rather than public control. In other nations, public control evolved. The first commercial radio station, KDKA of Pittsburgh, went on the air in November 1920, broadcasting the Harding-Cox election returns, phonograph records, and live music. Just 10 years later, there were 618 radio stations in operation throughout the United States, and their broadcasts were received by radio sets in an estimated 14 million homes.

Radio transcended time and space and placed millions of Americans at an event at the time it was happening. It informed illiterates, it entertained people in their own homes, and it accelerated the process of making Americans more spectators than participants.

Radio broadcasting companies easily justified private development of the air waves. Commercial sponsorship of air time created "free radio"—education and entertainment without direct cost to the consumer. Furthermore, advertisements were considered to have no less value than news reports. With

large corporations increasingly dominating the production of consumer goods and relying heavily on the idea that people would buy brands whose names they recognized, businesses used radio to inform consumers about their new and old products. In the sense that it explained what was available in the market places, radio could be seen as an educational medium.

If radio brought everyday events into American homes, it also made events and people larger than life. No doubt the reputations of the great sports heroes of the 1920s—baseball's Babe Ruth, football's Red Grange, golf's Bobby Jones, tennis' Bill Tilden, and others—and the "hero of the century," Charles Lindbergh, were due in large measure to radio. Sports broadcasting be-

Library of Congress

By 1929, programs were being broadcast from remote locations such as the kitchen of Chicago's Sherman Hotel shown in this photo of a WLS radio feature

came a staple and the airwaves were filled with play-by-play descriptions of football and baseball games and boxing matches. In the process, interest in sporting events increased and attendance grew rapidly during the 1920s. Radio emphasized the big games and the big matches, to the neglect of smaller and local ones. Also, radio sportscasters highlighted the star player's importance at the expense of the other players. Still, by World War II, local radio stations carried the play-by-play of the local "fives," "nines," and "elevens." Years later, the Bassanos, Harts, and nearly all of the other families recalled events of the era that radio covered as if they had been present at the occasion itself.

Inventions and innovation improved the quality of life in the United States. Automobiles not only bettered travel and enhanced leisure activities but saved lives by transporting the sick, while telephone communication could summon medical care. Consumer items such as the electric refrigerator were not merely luxuries. In 1927, General Electric published *Electric Refrigerator Menus and Recipes,* dedicated "To the MODERN AMERICAN HOMEMAKER," which stated: "The owning of such a refrigerator is a form of health and happiness insurance which every homemaker in America should have the privilege of enjoying." An electric refrigerator made it possible to store perishable food longer because the low temperature retarded the multiplication of harmful bacteria. It freed the Bassanos and Millers from shopping daily for food.

The great changes that occurred in the 1920s were not all accidental. Many Americans recognized their own role in bringing them about and, at times, even congratulated themselves for creating this "new era." Perhaps the best illustration of public self-congratulation occurred when aviator Charles Lindbergh made the first solo airplane flight across the Atlantic. Since 1919, there had been a standing prize of $25,000 to the first individual to cross the Atlantic Ocean in either direction between the United States and Europe. In 1927, several fliers raced to claim the prize. While Lindbergh worked on the West Coast building his aircraft, all his principal American rivals crashed during test flights. On May 8, the French aces Francois Nungesser and Charles Coli departed from Paris. The world awaited progress reports and news of their arrival. It soon became apparent that they had met disaster over the Atlantic. At this point, Lindbergh claimed center stage. He flew to St. Louis, setting a new American distance record for the journey. He then proceeded to Roosevelt Field, in Mineola, Long Island. When weather conditions were right, Lindbergh set out across the Atlantic in the *Spirit of St. Louis.* Thirty three and one-half hours later, he arrived safely in Paris. The welcoming crowds were so great that Lindbergh described the reception as "the most dangerous part of the whole flight." Here the story might have ended. Instead, it was just the beginning.

In June, Lindbergh returned to the United States as a conquering hero, celebrated as the "Lone Eagle." The National Geographic Society awarded him a medal inscribed: "Courage, when it goes alone, has ever caught men's imaginations." Broadcasters and journalists talked of the hero who had come out of the West, who had single-handedly conquered a "new frontier," the last frontier. Yet, as historian John William Ward has noted, Lindbergh did not view his feat as one man alone. Lindbergh's own description of the flight was titled *We* (1927), and, in 1953 in his book, *The Spirit of St. Louis,* Lindbergh never said "I," but always "we." When some people emphasized Lindbergh's role, the aviator complained, "You fellows have not said enough about that wonderful motor." President Calvin Coolidge understood this well when he told Lindbergh: "We are proud that

Lindbergh speaking before a huge crowd gathered at
the Washington monument to celebrate his return,
June 11, 1927

in every particular this silent partner represented American genius and industry. I am told that more than one hundred separate companies furnished materials, parts or services in its construction."

What America was celebrating was the cooperative effort of the man and the machine. It was not only a triumph of courage, of man against the elements in an epic battle, but also a triumph of modern engineering. By lionizing the flight, Americans were honoring themselves more than Lindbergh, celebrating the engineering of modern life which had brought not only the *Spirit of St. Louis* across the Atlantic Ocean, but had placed automobiles on roads, electricity in homes, prosperity in American life.

THE BUSINESS
OF BUSINESS

Underlying all of this was a basic shift in the way people thought about themselves in relation to their environment. The change was rooted in the 19th century but culminated in the 1920s. The environment seemed more controllable; life appeared liberated from environmental constraints. Having long since begun to regulate life by artificial conventions such as the clock, now, in the 1920s, a totally man-made environment seemed possible. Business leaders, professionals, and planners felt that they had the proper tools, knowledge, and wisdom to construct a humane environment, to regulate nature, and to build monuments far surpassing any natural ones, in short, to rationally create a more perfect society, polity, and economy.

This changing attitude was especially apparent among those concerned with urban life. At the turn of the century, sociologists at the University of Chicago were pioneering in the study of the city and human ecology. Led by Robert E. Park and Ernest W. Burgess, they sought to discover "natural laws" of urban development. Implicit in this search was the view that contemporary urban problems could be solved by manipulating the environment of the city. This helped boost urban planners and political reformers in the 1920s. One group sought control over the pattern of people in space, the other sought control of the distribution of power in communities. Both approached their concerns as "exact sciences": planners referred to their methods as social engineering; political scientists called theirs scientific government. Planners moved away from the 19th century approach which had made aesthetic concerns paramount. Furthermore, they rejected local planning in favor of regional planning in order to gain greater command of the environment. Rather than tinkering with individual houses, men such as C. S. Stein sought instead to develop "New Towns." Some few experimental communities were launched, mostly through federal programs during the 1930s. For the most part, such ideas as regional planning, garden apartments, or New Towns remained just that—ideas.

Similarly, political scientists continued to seek changes in the political environment through nonpartisan city manager or city commission forms of government. As in the pre–World War I period, advocates of "scientific government" viewed the political environment as corrupt and wished to remove city government from the ordinary political process. The solution lay in business management. Despite the publicity given to these forms of municipal government, only one third of cities with populations of over 5,000 had adopted them by 1930. All cities of over 500,000 retained the mayor-council system as did over 70 percent of the places containing between 5,000 and 10,000 inhabitants. By the 1920s, business administration had become a science, with businessmen trained in schools of business and management to govern large corporations. Thus, city managers could be trained as the counterparts of businessmen in the public sector. In the 1920s, this comparison was an apt one, for no discipline seemed to have changed so much as the old dismal science, economics, and what was seen as its applied aspect, the science of business.

More than anything else, the 1920s reflected a business civilization. Businessmen and economists claimed credit for the prosperity of the "new era." Businessmen, not engineers, received credit for the 102-story Empire State Building in New York City. Just as architects developed new methods to build taller and taller buildings, so, too, did businessmen and economists feel they commanded new financial and managerial tools that would create and ensure prosperity in the 1920s. The steel frame of business was

the corporate structure. During the 1920s, the modern corporation matured. By 1930, the 200 largest corporations had assets of $81 billion, approximately one half of all corporate assets in the United States. And these corporations tended to be monopolies or oligopo-

Library of Congress

The Empire State Building, New York City, symbol of an age

lies; they operated in situations where they either controlled the market by themselves or in combination with a few other giant firms. Before World War I, many people would have been frightened by such developments, but in the 1920s business spokesmen found acceptance for their argument that this concentraton of power was beneficial. The economy was in the hands of a small number of corporations, which in turn meant control by a small group of well-trained men. The result was believed to be permanent prosperity since the economy was freed from dependence on the blind economic forces that had ruled in the past.

This new confidence in businessmen arose from the changing profile of the corporate manager in the 1920s. Corporation management had changed radically since the 19th century. Initially, corporations were run by inventors, entrepreneurs, investors, or capitalists—men with the ability to invent things or to organize firms but with little knowledge of managing a corporation. The railroads pioneered the development of a professional bureaucracy, and a half-century later nearly all corporations were in the hands of trained managers. These organization men were the secret of success of the early conglomerates—firms such as General Motors and General Foods. The value of a professional management attuned to shifts in consumer preferences, indeed prepared to stimulate tastes, and supported by fiscal experts and corporate decentralization was demonstrated by the great number of people who switched from the black boxlike Model-T Ford to the more streamlined and colorful General Motors products. Henry Ford never quite learned that consumers must be given a choice and that his organization must be modernized.

With market power concentrated, stock ownership dispersed, and government refraining from antitrust action, there was no check on the power of corporations other than the consciences of the managers. Men such as Owen Young, president of General Electric, saw themselves as carrying a heavy burden of responsibility toward their shareholders, customers, workers, and the American consumer. In retrospect, it is clear that, for many businesses, this attitude reflected not only a rationalization of their extraordinary power,

Courtesy of General Motors Corporation

Compare this 1929 model Chevrolet with the Model-T Ford shown in Chapter 5

but also a sincere desire on the part of management to serve. The clearest sign of the latter was the maturation of welfare capitalism during the 1920s.

For the employer, welfare capitalism assumed that the interests of employers and employees, on labor and capital were identical. Its roots were in the late 19th century, influenced strongly by early attempts at industrial paternalism (as in the development of Pullman, Illinois, by George Pullman), by scientific management, and by anti-union sentiment. When Gerard Swope became president of General Electric in 1922, he propagated the gospel of welfare capitalism. In informal talks with plant managers, he told them that they were to be concerned with production, costs, *and* relations with workers. Workers were not to be considered as machinery. He reminded the managers that, while their basic job was to maximize output, one way to increase production was to gain the cooperation of workers by according them better treatment. As in other areas of the 1920s, this arena became dominated by professionals. The industrial-relations movement arose, with personnel managers trained to deal with workers. Although only a relatively small number of workers worked in firms that introduced welfare capitalism, in those firms, progressive managers sought to increase production by raising the satisfaction of workers. They introduced welfare plans: stock purchasing plans in which the firms would add to the employee's contribution, group insurance, and interest-on-savings plans. U.S. Steel introduced a medical program, Crucible Steel a credit union. Those who saw no fault with the system heralded the achievement of industrial harmony. In 1929, a director of the United States Chamber of Commerce said: "We are acquiring a new industrial philosophy . . . that the fundamental of decent and right conduct laid down by Jesus of Nazareth constitutes the soundest, most sen-

sible, and workable economic system possible to devise." At the same time, welfare capitalism had as a prime motive the obstruction of unionization. Firms such as U.S. Steel saw no conflict between welfare capitalism and an internal anti-union spy system, layoffs, and tightly controlled company towns.

Nothing seemed to confirm the era's optimism and promise more than the stock market. During the 1920s, the value of shares of stock traded on stock markets experienced a spectacular rise. Although to many, such as John Butler, the market represented a speculative game, a form of gambling where one wagered that stock would rise, most contemporary observers reported that stock markets reflected the economy. The purchase of stock represented more than merely finding an adequate investment for excess savings; it represented an investment in the new era and in America itself. Moreover, as more Americans saved money and invested in stocks, they contributed to a "revolutionary" new kind of industrial democracy—in a painless fashion, businessmen argued, ownership of the means of production was being transferred from the hands of a wealthy few to all of the American people through the dispersion of ownership of corporate stock. While AT&T reported proudly at the end of the decade that it had 600,000 stockholders, in fact, 210,000 owned five shares or fewer.

Contributing to faith in the new era was a general confidence in the politics of the 1920s, the politics of moderation. The presidential election of 1920 between Senator Warren G. Harding, Republican from Ohio, and James Cox represented a victory for moderation. Although the Democrats attempted to make Wilsonian idealism and the League of Nations the basic campaign issue, no clear-cut issues emerged in Harding's landslide victory. In his inaugural address, Harding promised a path of moderation to the American people, calling for "Not heroics, but

Ohioans campaigned for Warren G. Harding in 1920

healing; not nostrums, but normalcy." Accordingly, Harding began no crusades, and his accomplishments as president were limited—a Bureau of the Budget in 1921, the Washington Peace Treaty, debt reduction, and economy in government.

Harding's name was to become synonymous with scandal, yet history students of recent generations have been more concerned than were the people of the 1920s. Neither the whispers of a presidential mistress nor the accusations of corruption did him much harm. And then came "Teapot Dome." This episode involved the transfer of Navy Department oil reserves at Teapot Dome, Wyoming, to the Interior Department which, in turn, leased them to the Mammoth Oil Company. Accusations were made that former Secretary of the Interior Albert Fall had been bribed by Harry F. Sinclair of

Mammoth, and that Attorney General Harry Daugherty had failed to investigate the charges when they were brought to him. Eventually Fall was jailed for accepting a bribe, while Sinclair was jailed for refusing to testify and for contempt of court. Further scandals in the Office of the Alien Property Custodian and unproven accusations of graft in the Bureau of Internal Revenue further tarnished the reputation of the Harding administration. Perhaps because both major parties were tainted by Teapot Dome—Democrats as well as Republicans had been named in the investigations—the incumbent Republicans survived the scandal. In 1924, the country rejected the alternatives offered by the Democrats under John W. Davis and the Progressive Party headed by Robert LaFollette and Burton K. Wheeler.

The Republican presidential candidate,

Calvin Coolidge—who had succeeded to the presidency after Harding's death in 1923—offered reliability. Moderation was the guidepost of both his personal and political life. Like his predecessor, and unlike his progressive opponents in the 1924 campaign, Calvin Coolidge never sought problems. Donald McCoy, Coolidge's biographer, has summed up Coolidge's life succinctly: "The lesson of Calvin Coolidge is that of a man bred and trained to avoid the daring." By avoiding risks and problems, Coolidge managed to restore public confidence in the White House. With the new prosperity, few people seemed to ask more of Washington, D.C., than to allow free reign to business.

Those who were most receptive were upper-class families such as the Butlers and middle-class families such as the O'Reillys. John Butler and his family shared royally in the business and financial profits of the era. In 1928 he became senior partner in a leading Wall Street investment banking firm, and his world was that of town houses and summer estates, a retinue of domestics, of Rolls Royces and 58-foot yachts. The Butlers were solidly Republican. Robert, then a "comer" among Boston's corporate lawyers, held no animus against John Davis save his party affiliation. But he could not understand why LaFollette gained almost 5 million votes when the country was moving along so smoothly. On a more modest scale, but nonetheless successful, Gus O'Reilly advanced himself and his family out of the insecure world of the working man and into the more economically stable world of the middle class. The O'Reillys achieved prosperity and security, a house in Medford, and summers in New Hampshire or at the seashore. This apparently produced a minor conflict for Gus. He could not clearly recall how he cast his vote in 1924. He remembered harboring some bitterness toward Coolidge, whom he held responsible for his brother John's dismissal from

the police force and subsequent death. Still he might have voted for Coolidge because, as a meat salesman, he opposed lowering tariffs on foreign meats. Democrats, as Gus clearly remembered, were unsound on the tariff. Since he was not a drinking man, Prohibition aroused little resentment in him. Among working-class families, the Traces felt secure enough to purchase a house while the Millers and Bassanos achieved collective economic security. While the margin between security and crisis was narrow, these families did not view politics as a realistic device for widening the margin. None seem to have been interested enough to vote until the 1930s. Their daily struggle to remain solvent and raise their children absorbed most of their energy. In addition, newspapers and magazines moved further away from their 19th century role as political organs and radio aroused greater interest in sports and other entertainment than in political events. Ben Trace complained about the system but also believed it was far beyond his power to influence.

F. Scott Fitzgerald was as much the literary chronicler of the era as Frederick Lewis Allen was its historian. Widely read in novels and in such magazines as the *Saturday Evening Post,* Fitzgerald offered a romantic environment in which his characters were concerned more with themselves than with the larger world around them. While recent literary criticism suggests that Fitzgerald consciously portrayed a moral wasteland, the stage on which his characters performed in novels such as *This Side of Paradise* and *The Great Gatsby* confirmed Allen's view of the 1920s. It was a stage filled with parties and elegant automobiles and suburban estates. Sinclair Lewis and other writers explored the era at a much deeper critical level. Whereas Fitzgerald evoked the mood of Allen's 1920s, Lewis, in *Babbitt* and *Main Street,* probed beneath the surface, and implicitly criticized what he found. The progress of the 1920s, according to Lewis, was just a veneer; prosperity had not brought an improvement in the moral quality of American life. However, if some people were troubled by inner doubts and problems raised by Lewis and others, most were convinced that all was right with America.

The image of prosperity was not limited just to those who had shared in the bounty before World War I. Increasingly a new, stable working class was being forged, one with a middle-class style of life. Building-trades workers, white-collar workers, and mobile ethnic families were building new lives in which they, too, participated in the modern society of the 1920s.

While the total number of gainfully employed workers rose from 42.4 million in 1920 to 48.8 million in 1930, an increase of 15 percent, the number of nonmanual workers—professionals, wholesale, and retail dealers, other proprietors, and clerks and kindred workers—increased from 10.5 to 14.5 million—38 percent. "During the 20s," historian Irving Bernstein has noted in *The Lean Years,* "the American worker on an increasing scale took off his overalls and put on a white shirt and necktie." Many Americans in the 20th century considered themselves truly successful when they shifted from blue to white-collar work, and the 1920s were a decade of great "success" for many American families, the Gus O'Reillys among them. While Andrew Bassano did not sport a necktie at work, his sons did. The four oldest boys all launched white-collar careers during the 1920s, and the two youngest, Robert and Lawrence, followed suit during the 1930s. White-collar work also brought different identities and outlooks as well as material rewards. Greater stability of employment, higher wages, and increased fringe benefits might be accompanied by a stronger desire to assimilate, to gain acceptance in the larger society. Jack Miller was following this course. Re-

spectability and social presence were of far greater importance to white-collar workers than to manual laborers, and thus such shifts could affect home life as well. That it did can be seen in the growth of second-generation ethnic neighborhoods removed from the old immigrant portal areas. Mobile second-generation Jewish-Americans, Italian-Americans— the Millers and Bassanos, for instance—and others left the Lower East Sides and Little Italies of their parents and cousins to settle in new apartment buildings along the public transportation routes. The neighborhoods were clearly ethnic in character but far removed from the ghettolike settlements that new immigrants had found. They often changed denominations in religion and began to lose fluency in their parents' native language.

Many factory and building-trades workers also participated in the increased prosperity and experienced a sense of success. Between 1919 and 1929, the output per man-hour in manufacturing increased 72 percent. The pre–World War I trend away from skilled handwork to greater mass production accelerated. The classic symbol of this was the automobile assembly line in which the men remained stationary while the partially assembled car or truck moved past them. The speed of the line determined the number of autos produced per hour; during the 1920s, the line moved increasingly faster. In other industries, the construction of modern plants, such as Crucible Steel's new mill, introduced new, labor-saving devices and greater rationalization of work tasks, thereby increasing productivity. Even in the more traditional craft industries, such as Andrew Bassano's tile and terrazzo work, productivity increased. Although Bassano laid tiles as he always had, improved scaffolding, new mortar mixes, and precut tiles increased his output per hour.

Unionized workers achieved greater income and, through union-provided benefits, more security than did other workers. Railway Brotherhood membership, however, did little to alleviate the impact of the frequent layoffs that sapped the economic strength of Ben Trace and his family. While assured that he, rather than some nonunion individual, would be called back when there was work, Ben was still forced to manage on a much reduced income. Seasonal employment caused similar difficulties for members of building-trades unions. The craft-dominated American Federation of Labor experienced a membership decline. The AFL unions lost ground because they had little interest in enrolling the unorganized, because skilled artisan jobs declined, and because they failed to maintain strength among those brought into the unions during World War I when the government facilitated union membership to avoid strikes.

WEAKNESSES IN THE SYSTEM

As most working-class families could attest—and many farm families and white-collar families as well—there were serious problems in the economy. Interpreting them as the persistence of problems from the prewar era, the oracles of the new era expected that most would be solved in due time. First, they could point to the jarring impact of the great strikes of 1919, tell with satisfaction of the route of organized labor, and hold out the promise of greater gains through corporate welfare capitalism. No matter that the strikes had broken the likes of John O'Reilly and left Mihailo Markovich at the total mercy of his employers. As for the depression of 1921 in which unemployment affected more than 5 million workers, it was explained as a natural postwar fluctuation in the business cycle. That Ben Trace's small dreams of returning to a farm in the hills of Tennessee were shattered

was of little moment. After all, the quick recovery following the depression and the brevity of recessions in 1924 and 1927 seemed to prove that business was in firm control of the economy. The Gales and Harts in central Kansas were not so sure of this when they looked at agricultural commodity prices and the prices they had to pay for goods and services. For the Hunts and their sharecropping friends in Texas, assurances that the tools were available to prevent the kind of depressions and panics that had regularly plagued America fell on deaf ears. They were too poor to worry about depressions.

While dissent and disruption were apparent in American society, faith in modern America was also strong. Neither Ben Trace nor Mihailo Markovich was a fit target for radicalism. Ben berated the system but had fought for it and was proud to be an American. Mihailo thought of himself as a Serbian-American and, while he was strongly committed to unionism, did not view it as a device to radicalize his country. Stanko Simich had faced the coal miners' goons, but they were cancers in the system, aberrations that did not reflect the America in which Stanko believed. As with the economy, so, too, were the causes of dissent viewed as susceptible to the healing of time. Suppression of radicalism during World War I and the ensuing Red Scare combined with the extreme Americanization programs during these periods left radical movements of the 1920s in disarray. The four-time Socialist candidate for president, Eugene V. Debs, was still in prison in 1921, and the only visible activity of the left was the industrial union movement, a relatively weak contingent within organized labor. The 19th amendment—women's suffrage, which went into effect on August 26, 1920—had no significant effect on American voting patterns as women seemed to vote as men did. It did, however, further diffuse radicalism as the women's movement declined in strength. A small group of women continued fighting on the political front for equality through the Women's Party and other organizations, while others, such as Margaret Sanger, focused on individual liberation by establishing birth-control clinics. Crusading reform, however, was more of an irritant to Americans than it had been earlier in the century. Even reform-oriented Progressivism would carry little weight in the 1920s. The insurgent Progressive political ticket of LaFollette and Wheeler trailed far behind the two major parties in 1924 with only 13 electoral votes (LaFollette's Wisconsin) and 17 percent of the total vote.

The salient public issues were ones that had been opened before—immigration restriction, evolution versus the Bible, white-black relations. Underlying these issues were tensions created by the 1920s as well as ones inherited from the prewar era. The spread of communications—radio, national magazines, improved roads—intensified the urban content of small-town life and challenged traditional values. On the other hand, the migration of nearly 20 million Americans from farm and village to cities brought the urban-rural conflict into urban areas. Immigrants experienced similar tensions between their adherence to cultural traditions and the demands of modern society. In the 1920s, however, with immigration slowed to a trickle, ethnic communities lost the cultural protection provided by the constant infusion of new arrivals, and thus the more acculturated second generation assumed leadership. Mass production and the more rationalized organization of work also changed life; the all–northern Italian tile-and-terrazzo workers' union, of which Andrew Bassano was president, became an anachronism as large-scale factories employing thousands of workers abandoned ethnically homogeneous work forces. More than ever,

workers were expected to adapt to impersonal jobs and abandon old cultural traditions. While they tended to adapt and conform, it was not without tension and resistance.

Old-stock Americans blamed immigrants for many social ills—the strikes of 1919 and other disruptions of "industrial peace," subversion during World War I, and a lowering of the standard of living of all Americans. The Anglo-Saxon and northern European "racial" groups had forged a democratic society in the new world, they argued, and now the race that had sustained this experiment was threatened by "mongrelization." Maintaining American society required the preservation of the race, and it was this theory that found currency in the immigration acts of the 1920s. The permanent immigration restriction act, the National Origins Act of 1924, which superseded the Emergency Quota Act of 1921, restricted annual immigration to the United States to 2 percent of the immigrant population of each group in the United States in 1890. The formula was designed to exclude the mass of immigrants that had arrived after 1890, the period of greatest migration from eastern, central and southern Europe. Western Hemisphere countries were excluded from the quota system, but the prohibition against any Japanese immigration made the exclusion of Orientals virtually complete.

American racism also found expression in the 20th century revival of the Ku Klux Klan. Organized at Stone Mountain, Georgia, in 1915 by a former Methodist minister, William J. Simmons, the Klan dedicated itself to white Protestant supremacy. It spread rapidly in the early 20s, rising from 5,000 members in 1920 to an estimated 5 million in 1925. Its strength was not only in the South and Southwest—in Oklahoma, Texas, and Louisiana—but also in Indiana, New Jersey, Kansas, and other states. The Klan appealed to native-born

Americans disturbed by what they perceived as attacks on their traditional values—whether social, racial, industrial, or theological. Evansville, Indiana, with a large Catholic population, an influx of rural migrants, and a rapidly industrializing economy, became a Klan stronghold even though its Negro and foreign population was very small. Klan-backed candidates narrowly lost the governorship of Kansas but captured those in Oregon and Indiana before the movement collapsed beneath a series of scandals that unmasked the Klan organization. If the Klan as an organization was discredited, its racial philosophy remained intact.

Although the Klan was anti-Catholic and anti-Semitic, its most intense phobia was reserved for blacks. Black migration, dating from World War I, continued during the 1920s with a steady stream of rural blacks from the Deep South resettling in the cities of the North. Black communities in the nation's largest cities became black metropolises, literally black cities within cities. Black met white on the job, in the streets, in parks, and occasionally in residential neighborhoods. The result was an attempt, in many areas, to limit and control blacks much as they had been segregated and discriminated against in the South. This was heightened, though not caused, by the presence of millions of Southern white migrants in the cities of the North. The race riots of World War I, the Chicago race riot of 1919 that left 38 dead, the bombings and violence designed to enforce residential segregation in Chicago and other cities, city ordinances in Indianapolis and elsewhere which gave residential segregation legal sanction, and, generally, the rigid application of Jim Crow customs throughout the North all served to control blacks. The northern Klan was one agency of control.

A Ku Klux Klan rally in Beckley, West Virginia, 1924

At the same time some blacks, mostly in Northern cities, were less willing to accommodate themselves to an inferior position. A substantial legal assault on segregation had begun with the founding of the National Association for the Advancement of Colored People in 1910, and with W.E.B. DuBois as editor of its monthly organ, *The Crisis,* outrages against blacks were widely exposed and publicized. Out of World War I came a new black militancy and a strong resolve not to be intimidated. When labor friction and the stoning of a black teenager by white bathers at a Lake Michigan beach resulted in the Chicago race riot in 1919, blacks defended themselves and fought back. In Detroit, in 1926, when a white mob stormed the house of Dr. Ossian Sweet, a black dentist who had moved into a virtually all-white neighborhood, Sweet and his family resisted the assault. Marcus Garvey's United Negro Improvement Association, best known for advocating the return of blacks to Africa, also addressed itself to the plight of working-class blacks. Garvey stressed race pride and self-awareness, and although he was opposed by most black leaders and eventually convicted of fraud, his was a theme which black intellectuals could share, as well. The Harlem Renaissance—the 1920s flowering of black artistic creativity—expressively presented black self-awareness and pride.

Most blacks seem to have assumed an accommodative posture. The Hunts sought small gains within the caste society of Kosse. They moved quietly, using acceptable procedures, to establish their school. However much Sylvia and James must have been frustrated and deeply embittered, they did not lash out at the system. That could only bring disaster. The Hunts recognized the presence of a racist force, prepared to beat, expel, or even lynch, should they go beyond caste boundaries. These and other problems, however, were not seen as incurable. Middle and upper-class Americans, when they recognized them, generally believed that education eventually would solve the social problems. They also recognized some of the more blatant economic problems but placed their faith in the economy of the new era to resolve those issues.

But not all in American society shared this optimism. The 1920s were prosperous for the largest producers of food and fiber and for dairy and truck farmers in the urban hinterlands. For the majority of American farmers, the 1920s brought recession or depression. Throughout the period, a steady stream of Americans abandoned their farms; the Department of Agriculture estimated that more than 19 million rural farm dwellers entered the cities. Seito Kurihara, an alien and prohibited from purchasing land in California, moved from one leased vegetable farm to another, planting some 20 acres and barely making a living. Many other tenant farmers moved frequently. These migrations, to the city and from farm to farm, reflected, in part, the failure of farmers to share in the prosperity of the times.

Farmers never recovered from the depression of 1920–21. Depression lingered because of changes that occurred during World War I. Spurred on by the demands of the war, farmers rapidly increased production by using land that formerly lay fallow, by more intensely using their existing cultivated acres, and by the acquisition of a great deal of new tractor-powered machinery. Prices were at an all-time high during the war, and farmers went deeply into debt to finance this expansion. But the boom in prices and land values broke for farmers in 1920 when they shouldered a heavy debt borrowed at inflationary levels and when European agriculture recovered. Thereafter, farm income dropped more severely than did costs, while taxes and the cost of freight, handling, and selling, packaging and processing all rose sharply. Thus, less and less of the market price of foodstuffs was returned to the farmer. Yet the needs of small farmers were greater than ever.

Productivity increased rapidly while the available markets expanded only slightly, and American farmers encountered greater international competition. The greatest factor in increased production was mechanization, and, to a lesser extent, the discovery by farmers of chemical fertilizers. Between 1920 and 1929, the number of horses and mules on American farms declined by nearly 6 million, or 23 percent, while the number of tractors rose 247 percent to 853,000 in 1929. The use of combines for wheat and the widespread use of trucks also aided increased productivity. At the same time, European agriculture had recovered from the devastation of war, and Canada, Argentina, and Australia became major agricultural competitors, especially in wheat and beef. It seemed the only way to cope with declining prices and debts was to increase yields, a feat which required more land and more machines which, in turn, required greater borrowing. But many farmers found credit even more difficult to acquire in the 1920s since land values and prices had declined and farm-credit institutions were also changing. More than 5,000 banks closed in the 1920s, and the overwhelming majority of them were in small market villages and towns. Many farmers were compelled to seek credit from larger urban banks with less liberal lending policies and little interest in agriculture. The Federal Farm Loan system had less money available because of the sharp rise in foreclosures and the heavy lending of the wartime period. Most farmers found mortgage

J. W. McManigal from Grant Heilman Photography

The boundless expanse of Kansas wheat land

renewals difficult to obtain, and many had to accept the high interest rates demanded by tractor and implement dealers. Corn farmers were relatively better off than wheat growers. The former faced less international competition and were not so highly mechanized as the latter. The equipment used in the corn belt was less expensive than the costly combines required on the thousand-acre farms becoming common in California and the western Great Plains.

Cotton suffered more than wheat farming. Indeed, cotton acreage in the Old South declined, with the slack taken up by the expansion of cotton acreage in Texas. The boll weevil, soil depletion, the sharp drop in prices, and the increased transportation costs took a great toll. The farmers in the Deep South were in the most desperate straits because a majority were sharecroppers without the resources to weather the crisis.

Federal programs, which made agricultural credit more accessible or encouraged the formation of cooperatives, were of limited use to a minority of farmers. Even more radical programs, such as the price support features of the McNary-Haugen bills, none of which were enacted, would theoretically have benefited only a minority of the larger commercial farmers. While neither the Gales nor the Reinhardts made use of available federal credit, they did use the growing body of agricultural knowledge disseminated by the Department of Agriculture, agricultural extension agents, and agricultural colleges. Such technical knowledge was not used by either the Traces in Tennessee or the Hunts in Texas. The debate over the proper federal role in agriculture, the controversy precipitated by McNary-Haugenism, and some of the programs of the later Hoover years did influence the agricultural programs of the New Deal. But while the New Deal programs added an essential element of local participation, they were no more all-inclusive in coverage than

earlier policies had been. Expanded participation was not a result of extended coverage but of greater crisis among middle-class commercial farmers such as the Gales and Reinhardts.

Appalachian and New England mill workers also found themselves in trying circumstances. The textile industry was the lifeblood of the Piedmont region that stretched south from Washington, D.C. to Atlanta—and cities such as Lynchburg, Greensboro, Gastonia, and Spartanburg became known as mill towns. About 60 percent of the nation's textiles were produced in the region where 100,000 workers were employed in North Carolina; 70,000 in South Carolina, and 25,000 in Tennessee, Forsaking New England, the mills had moved south in search of low wages and nonunion labor.

By the 1920s, however, the industry was in poor health. The fluctuating price of cotton had taken its toll on the industry. Changing fashions such as shorter skirts reduced the demand. The Southern textile industry was cotton based and it faced increasing competition in the 1920s from imported goods—silk—and from the new "miracle" fabric, rayon. By 1924, the Southern textile industry was in a serious depression. In the late 1920s, less than one half of the Southern mills paid dividends, and many others were in bankruptcy.

To compete with each other and foreign producers, the mills cut wages. Workers lucky enough to maintain their jobs worked longer hours for less pay than they would receive in any other manufacturing industry. Workers were also subject to the stretchout—the mill equivalent of speedup. In the stretchout, workers were required to work more machines without additional pay. Thus, the textile workers paid the cost of the effort to revive the industry, and they were least able to bear the cost.

It would have been difficult to convince a textile worker that the 1920s were a decade of prosperity. A full turn (regular workweek) in Southern mills ranged from 66 to 74 hours per week, for a salary less than half that of New England mill workers. In 1928, an average full week's work paid $12.83 in the Carolinas, Georgia, and Alabama. Workers in these areas were powerless to change their way of life. They were predominantly of Anglo-Saxon stock (blacks were barred and few immigrants came), formerly tenant farmers and mountain people who were no longer able to eke out a living from the land. As Irving Bernstein has noted, they were "industrial nomads," moving from one mill to another as the only way to protest their wretched conditions. Even more than the Markoviches and Simiches in the steel and coal towns, the textile operatives lived in communities owned and regulated by the mill owners. Everything in their villages was controlled by management, from work to school. Employment was based on the entire family, which workers from a traditional agricultural background accepted as natural. The level of wages was so low that it was impossible to support a family on a single income, and the entire family was compelled to enter the mill. Children were of special value because many jobs required extreme dexterity of hand and keenness of sight, skills of the young more than the old. Children, not the mills, assumed the burden of supporting those unemployed. With unemployment so high in the region, workers could easily be replaced, and they were.

The conditions experienced by farmers, mine and mill workers, urban blacks, Southern sharecroppers, and older factory workers reflected the great paradox of the 1920s poverty amidst prosperity, insecurity amidst abundance. It could even touch factory workers in the boom industries of the decade, as Robert and Helen Lynd discovered in *Middletown*. In their study of Muncie, Indiana (representative of Middletown and Every-

town, U.S.A.), the Lynds found that two thirds of the business group in the city never faced unemployment. The working class, however, lived continually with the prospect of unemployment because plant and shop shutdowns or layoffs were common. In 1923, for instance, one Muncie machine shop employed 68 percent fewer workers than it had at its peak. Another leading plant had a "normal" work force of 1,000 workers, and only 250 were employed at the time of interview in 1924. In that instance, the bosses thought of 550 men as their regular employees; the rest of the jobs would be filled by "floaters." Employment among the seven leading plants in the city showed wide variations between 1920 and 1925. In comparing the high and low points of employment, the Lynds found that, at the low point in December 1924, 50 percent of the workers were laid off. The disastrous effects of this on workers and their families can be seen in the Lynds' sample of 165 workers in the first nine months of 1924, the worst period of unemployment. Sixty-two percent of the men had lost time during the nine months; 43 percent had been unemployed at least one month. Ben Trace experienced similar circumstances when he averaged only eight months' full-time work each year during the 1920s in Evansville's L&N shops.

Work, and hence income and wealth, was unevenly distributed. A Brookings Institution study published in 1934, *America's Capacity to Consume*, revealed the pattern of this maldistribution of income (see Table 6–1). Twelve million families in 1929, or 42 percent of all families, had an annual income less than $1,500, and collectively they shared 13 percent of the total family income. At the other end of the scale, one fifth of one percent of all families, or 73,000 families, had the same share of income as the 12 million families. The top 1.2 percent of families in income

Table 6-1
Family Income, 1929

Income class (in dollars)	Percent of families	Cumulative percent of families	Percent of income	Cumulative percent of income
Under 500	7.65	7.65	.02	.02
500–1,000	13.82	21.47	3.79	3.76
1,000–1,500	20.94	42.41	9.33	13.09
1,500–2,000	17.11	59.53	10.59	23.68
2,000–2,500	11.63	71.19	9.28	32.96
2,500–3,000	7.24	78.42	7.05	40.01
3,000–3,500	5.27	83.69	6.07	46.07
3,500–5,000	8.10	91.79	11.91	57.99
5,000–10,000	5.91	97.70	14.03	72.02
10,000–50,000	2.07	99.77	13.20	85.21
Over 50,000	.23	100.00	14.79	100.00

(those above $15,000) had the same total combined income as 59.5 percent of families (those below $2,000).

Assessments of the 1920s vary widely. The great discrepancy among the differing views was partially caused by the attention given to the New York Stock Exchange and its spiraling inflated prices during the decade. The stock exchange was widely interpreted as an indicator of the health of the economy and society. Furthermore, many business and government leaders argued that investment in stock shares—participation in the ownership of corporations in the American economy—represented not just faith in the performance of an individual corporation but also faith in the structure of the United States itself. Thus stocks at their peak sold at multiples of earnings approaching 100-fold because purchasers expected a return in future growth and price rises, not in dividends. At another level, the stock market offered to all a potentially easy path to wealth. As the great bull market surged to astronomical levels in 1928 and 1929, business leaders such as John J. Raskob of General Motors argued that anyone could become wealthy by steadily investing savings in stock purchases. He projected the recent rise in stock prices into the future and predicted that riches would thus be within the reach of anyone who saved money.

DEPRESSION

In the fall of 1929, the bubble burst. Stock prices tumbled. A decline in stock prices began toward the end of September, but it was not recognized at the time. When the market collapsed on October 29—Black Tuesday—nearly everyone from coast to coast knew. As prices plunged, the volume of shares exchanged was so great that the stock ticker recording transactions operated two-and-one-half hours after closing to record all of the trading. The great bull market was dead. Indeed, the stock market crash symbolized the end of an era.

Believing firmly in the new economic era, however, business and government leaders still forecast continued prosperity. On December 10, 1929, Charles Schwab of the Bethlehem Steel Corporation said: "Never before has American business been as firmly entrenched for prosperity as it is today." Some even welcomed the market crash: "Viewed in the longer perspective," wrote the editor of the *Survey* of the Guaranty Trust Company of New York, "the collapse of the inflated price structure may be correctly regarded as a favorable development from the point of view of general business." But it was neither favorable nor temporary, and stock prices continued to decline over the next three years.

The collapse of the bull market revealed that speculation and manipulation had been the engine of stock-price inflation. The rise and fall of the market was a classic "bubble"—built on hot air, it must eventually burst. Later congressional investigations would reveal how insiders manipulated stock transactions and corporations to drive up prices and how widespread was the purchase of stock on margin—borrowed money— rather than through the investment of savings. Basically, many of the transactions in the stock market were motivated not by a desire to invest but instead by a very simple expectation that what was bought today could be sold tomorrow at a higher price.

Far more serious than the collapse of price levels on the stock market itself, the crash would eventually lead to the shattering of economic confidence that had dominated the 1920s. Probably the greatest effect of the crash was psychological. By 1930, business leaders themselves were beginning to doubt their first optimistic reactions, for the crash had inaugurated a period of pessimism among business leaders as their confidence slowly eroded. As a result, managers began to reduce production and lay off workers. The crash itself had probably discouraged consumer demand somewhat, while diminished business confidence coupled with layoffs led to further consumer retrenchment. Thus the spiral of declining demand and production and increasing unemployment began. The stock-market crash did not of itself cause this spiral; indeed it was more an indicator than a cause. Although Americans had not known it at the time, the United States already had been headed toward a depression by the time of the great crash in the fall of 1929.

Despite assurances to the contrary by the captains of business and by the White House, the economy of the United States in 1929 was not fundamentally sound. During the 1920s, the corporate structure and banking system had been weak, a fact obscured by the great growth in the gross national product and enormous expansion of credit. When credit began to contract in the early part of 1929, the stock-market crash accelerated contraction, and banks and businesses that could not borrow as usual began to fold like a house of cards. The most serious weakness in the economy, however, was the maldistribution of income. Too many people lacked the money to buy the basic necessities of life. The prosperity of the 1920s, to a great extent, was built on the small number of American families, such as the Butlers and O'Reillys, who enjoyed the lion's share of the nation's income. By 1929, as a group, they had bought most of the new homes and automobiles, electric refrigerators, and other new inventions that they intended to purchase; thereafter, they would be buying mostly for replacement. And after the stock market crash, with pessimism growing, they further curtailed their spending.

Given the maldistribution of income and the cyclical instability in a free-market economy, the depression was inevitable. In retrospect, it is clear that a number of deflationary forces appeared in the spring of 1929 that set the depression in motion. Most significantly, consumer purchases fell off at the same time that residential construction waned. Moreover, credit began to contract. Then the crash accelerated all of these trends. Thus all of these factors were present in 1929 to cause the depression. The recession in 1924 had been brief because a decline in consumption expenditures had been offset by expansion in the petroleum, rubber, and electrical industries but most notably by a great boom in construction. Three years later, a slowdown was precipitated because more homes had been built than people could afford to buy and by a decline in automobile production from 4.3 million in 1926 to 3.4 million in 1927. But recovery came quickly as foreign trade expanded, as construction revived, particularly public utilities and federal public works, and as auto production rose again. In 1929, no factors intervened to offset reduced consumption and a precipitate decline in construction, which combined to seriously limit investment opportunities. An unprecedented depression began.

The Great Depression lasted until 1941, when World War II brought economic recovery to the United States. Gross national product shrunk sharply, reflecting both the deflation and the shutdown of industrial plants (see Table 6-2). Official unemployment reached such high levels that, in 1933, one of every four workers was unemployed (see Table 6-3).

From 1929 to 1932, the economy shrunk at virtually every point. Twenty percent of the banks closed and those that remained open commanded little faith from depositors. Charles Gale and James Hart could no longer secure quick credit and had to cut back their trading ventures. Stores facing Fredonia's square closed as they did on main streets across the nation. A drastic decline in the output of basic industries inevitably accompanied

Table 6-2
U.S. Gross National Product, 1929–1945

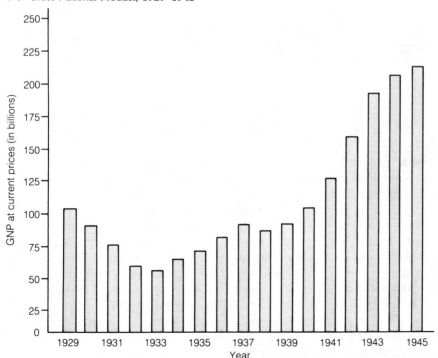

Table 6-3

Unemployment in the United States, 1929–1941

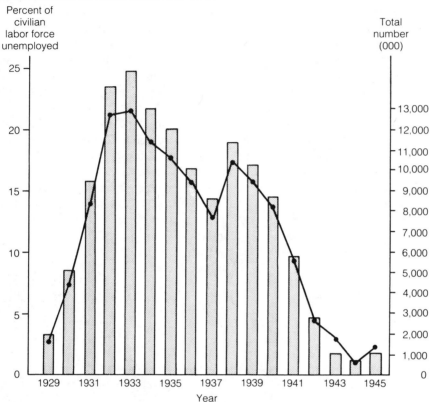

contracting retail sales. With no demand for the construction of new buildings, the production of bricks dropped by 83 percent between 1929 and 1933. A dozen or more brick and tile plants in southeastern Kansas closed and threw several hundred men on the job market. Automobile production declined by 65 percent, depriving Crucible Steel, as well as the glass, paint, and rubber industries, of a major portion of their business. Other industries suffered similar setbacks: production dropped by 65 percent in cement (also causing additional unemployment in southeastern Kansas), by 59 percent in iron and steel, by 60 percent in lumber, and by 56 percent in furniture. Lumber and furniture had provided

the Louisville & Nashville Railroad with a good part of its inbound and outbound freight. With the decrease in freight loadings, Ben Trace's tenuous position became desperate. Layoffs stretched out over longer periods of time.

As industries were selectively affected by the depression, so too were different groups in society. A study of Philadelphia in April 1931 revealed that the younger and elderly workers suffered the most. Unemployment among those 16 through 25 in age was 34.7 percent; among those 66 years and older, 34.4 percent; whereas the average unemployment for all ages was 25.5 percent. The study found another 13.8 percent employed only part time. Blacks and women tended to bear more of the burden of unemployment than others. In 1931, for instance, blacks comprised 38 percent of the population in Memphis and 75 percent of those out of work, and in Chicago, 4 percent of the population and 16 percent of the unemployed. With most black women employed as domestics—the most expendable of household expenses for many families—unemployment among black women soared. In January 1931, the percentage of black female unemployed reached 75 in Detroit, 58 in Chicago, 55 in Cleveland, 51 in Pittsburgh, 48 in St. Louis, and 46 in Houston.

The servants released by the John Butler family or the workers laid off by Crucible and the other unemployed millions had to rely on local resources for relief. Local governments did what they could, but tax collections diminished as the economy worsened. Cities borrowed not only to provide minimum humanitarian relief but to meet their own payrolls. In 1932, Chicago could no longer meet its regular payroll and had to issue notes in anticipation of taxes in order to pay teachers. By 1933, 1,300 local governmental units had defaulted on their bonds—the equivalent of bankruptcy. This group included 644 cities and towns, 303 counties, and 300 school districts. Although only three states defaulted—Arkansas, Louisiana, and

Unemployed men line up outside a Chicago soup kitchen opened in 1931 by Al Capone

220

South Carolina—many more were unable to borrow additional funds because they verged on bankruptcy.

The major task of aiding the unemployed fell to private charities and benevolent institutions. By 1932, they were in no better financial condition than local governments were. Welfare agencies borrowed on future income and even then fell far short of being able to handle their case load. In a number of cities, churches established soup kitchens to feed the hungry, but by 1932 most had collapsed financially or resorted to doling out meals.

Economic conditions produced sporadic acts of desperation. Mobs stormed groceries in Oklahoma City, Minneapolis, and St. Paul in January and February of 1931. Meanwhile,

millions turned to the open road, tramping from one town to the next in search of work, food, and shelter. Boy and girl tramps as well as adults became common sights at rail junctions, as Austin Hart recalled. Local governments and charities offered to share their meager resources in exchange for a pledge that the tramps would move on to the next town before another night fell. In some cities, the homeless constructed shanty towns, which the newspapers dubbed "Hoovervilles," from scrap lumber. During the spring and early summer of 1932, homeless veterans formed an "army" that descended on Washington, D.C. to lobby for the immediate payment of World War I veterans bonus certificates. Some 17,000 veterans camped in

Veterans in the Bonus Army encampment, Washington, D.C., June 1932

Washington and lobbied the halls of Congress. After the defeat of the measure in the Senate, the government offered to pay fares home for the veterans. Many left, but others had no place else to go. When President Hoover ordered district police to evict the men, two veterans and two policemen were killed. Federal troops, using tanks, completed the rout of the veterans.

The use of federal troops was a desperate measure by the government, but reflected fears that a revolution might be brewing. The food riots, the millions on the road, the "invasion" of Washington by the so-called Bonus Army were ominous developments. Acts of desperation in the agricultural sector seemed to confirm the worst fears, even though they were only occasional and confined to a few areas. Prices tumbled sharply after 1929, and farmers were faced with a great surplus as they were unable to sell part of their crops and produce. In addition, many farmers were losing money on every bushel they sold; bankruptcy was just around the corner. In some areas of the country, farmers turned to radical measures as they had during previous economic upheavals. Acts of rural resistance heightened in 1932. Foreclosure was the worst thing that a farmer could experience, and it was predictable that farmers would be most militant in thwarting mortgage foreclosures. Penny sales or Sears, Roebuck auctions became common in farm communities. At penny sales, neighbors would intimidate serious bidders at public auctions forced by foreclosures. A neighbor would buy the farm for one penny and return it to the original owner. When a stranger or serious bidder attended the sale, he might find himself surrounded by strong-arm farmers hinting that the auction was a closed affair. Courts tended to side with the farmers; the Nebraska Supreme Court ruled that the amount of a bid could not justify a court in refusing confirmation of a sale.

In the summer of 1932, Milo Reno formed the Farm Holiday Association to withhold produce from market until prices rose. In Iowa and Nebraska, members of the association coerced other farmers to support the action. And when some sought to take food to market, the militants blockaded roads, punctured tires with pitchforks, and fought sheriff's escorts. In Nebraska, they waylaid a freight train and scattered the shipment of cattle. In Wisconsin, they dumped milk on the roadsides.

Fostering organized farm action, as well as desperate acts by workers, was the perceived inaction of the central government in Washington. Most Americans had expected little directly from the federal government, but it soon became apparent that neither voluntary associations nor state and local governments had the resources to alleviate conditions for their unemployed constituents. The Millers and Bassanos saw despair growing among their neighbors in New York City who could not find jobs, and soon realized that the problems were national in scope. All the Miller daughters remembered men milling around street corners, trading rumors of jobs and frightened of another day without work. By 1931, Governor Franklin D. Roosevelt of New York had aroused the political awareness of the Millers, and they looked to Washington for initiative. Although Meyer Miller's fatal illness took most of their energies, the children discussed politics and their disenchantment with what they perceived as an inactive and unconcerned president. Letters to and from Pauline in New England mentioned nonfamily affairs for the first time as they shared news of friends out of work and suggestions for federal action. It was not so much the administration of Herbert Hoover that placed Washington at center stage but the expectations of a citizenry ridden by desperation and also the financial poverty of local governments and voluntary associations.

Upon entering the White House in 1929,

Herbert Hoover seemed to reverse the trend of mediocrity and the commonplace associated with Warren G. Harding and Calvin Coolidge and to offer the promise of raising the presidency to a level associated with Theodore Roosevelt and Woodrow Wilson. Rarely, it had seemed in 1928 and 1929, did an individual have so much to offer to the presidency. Hoover personified the self-made man. Born in West Branch, Iowa, a graduate of Stanford University, he became a famous mining engineer on an international scale, surveying properties and organizing mining companies throughout the world. During and after World War I, he retired from business and devoted his time to public affairs. As organizer for relief for Belgium and then later War Food Administrator in the Wilson Ad-

ministration, his name became a household word. Mentioned prominently by both parties for the presidential nomination in 1920, Hoover endorsed Harding after the conventions and was rewarded with appointment as Secretary of Commerce. His achievements in reorganizing the Commerce Department, improving economic information, and creating the Federal Radio Commission to regulate radio contrasted favorably with the ordinary accomplishments of other cabinet secretaries under Harding and Coolidge.

In 1928, Hoover received the Republican nomination for the presidency. He had a reputation for his capacity to grapple with tough problems and as an efficient, able administrator and organizer. His defects were deemed unimportant, but from a political and

Library of Congress

President Herbert Hoover addresses the "prosperity conference" in August 1932

psychological viewpoint they would prove disastrous during the depression; he was shy, formal, reserved, and solemn in manner.

Overall, Herbert Hoover's policy in reaction to the depression was guided by three principles: his inability to recognize the level of severity of the depression, his emphasis on external causes, and his reliance on voluntarism to relieve the social and economic suffering. Although, by comparison with past administrations during depressions, Hoover was an activist, still he opposed interjecting the federal government as the prime economic mover and dispenser of relief. He never lost his faith in limited government and in privatism. Accepting premises that greatly appealed to Robert Butler, he placed greater faith in the individual than in collective action, and the state represented collective action. Also, he favored voluntary as opposed to compulsory (state) action in the belief that the former was not only more efficient in safeguarding liberty, but also because of the ostensible moral benefits to the volunteer. Because of this failure to comprehend fully the real causes or to appreciate the severity of the depression. Hoover never realized, until it was too late, the inadequacies of voluntarism. His programs for halting unemployment— conferences with businessmen and such voluntary agencies as the President's Organization for Unemployment Relief (with the unfortunate acronym of POUR, pronounced "poor")—and providing relief through voluntary agencies were a total failure. Local resources were not available in the extraordinary quantity needed. But the failure was not Hoover's alone; it was also the failure of American business and social institutions.

The positive steps taken by the Hoover administration were too little, too late. Though reluctantly, Hoover accepted a deficit budget. Moreover, he initiated an expanded program of public works, although, as a fiscal conservative, he emphasized pay-as-you-go

projects. His most important program was in reinvigorating the capital structure of large banks and other corporations. After the failure of his National Credit Corporation, Hoover accepted the creation of the Reconstruction Finance Corporation to lend money to corporations. But his support was lukewarm since he feared the centralization of power in Washington, and in July 1932, he vetoed the extension of RFC to other areas of the economy. His support of RFC and his opposition to federal financing of direct relief efforts, (as in his opposition to the Emergency Relief Act of 1932, which Congress passed over his veto) stamped his program as relief for ailing corporations but not for people in need of food and shelter. And Hoover's problems were magnified by the image he projected; he appeared aloof and distant, isolated in the White House. Opponents damned his lack of concern.

By 1932, it seemed certain that any Democrat would be able to defeat Hoover, because the election would be virtually a referendum on his presidency. Hoover ran against the governor of New York State, Franklin Delano Roosevelt. After a lackluster campaign in which neither candidate promised any dramatic shifts in government policy, except for Roosevelt's pledge to end Prohibition, Roosevelt swamped Hoover in the election. Following the election, however, conditions worsened and the period between the election of Roosevelt in November 1932 and his inauguration in March 1933 was the lowest ebb of the depression. Not only did the loss of confidence in the economic system increase, but skepticism grew as to whether or not the inauguration would ever take place in March. On Christmas Eve 1932, Rexford Tugwell, one of Roosevelt's closest advisers, wrote in his diary: "No one can live and work in New York this winter without a profound sense of uneasiness."

The depression left most Americans with

an amorphous sense of resentment. There was no real focus for their desperation, anger, frustration, or desire to end the unemployment and hunger. Andrew Bassano did not seek scapegoats. He knew the connection between the construction industry and his paycheck. Knowing this, he began to prepare for his retirement in Italy. While president of his union, he did what he could to secure work for union members, striking in one instance over the employment of German terrazzo workers recruited from abroad. Some accepted Hoover's arguments and blamed the world economy, which was similarly depressed. Most probably blamed themselves for failing to be exempt from the widespread unemployment and distress. "After all," they might reason, "other people *were* working, and if only I had not dropped out of school, or not changed jobs, or . . . I might not now be unemployed." Workers such as Mihailo Markovich and Ben Trace were in familiar circumstances; they were accustomed to both the short and long-range fluctuations in the business cycle, and they were probably less upset at their distress than would be middle-class families who had never expected such deprivation and were facing these conditions for the first time in their lives.

One group which could be blamed for the conditions, however, was businessmen. After all, they had taken credit for the prosperity of the 1920s. In the spring of 1932, Hoover encouraged a congressional investigation into Wall Street, and his critics charged that he was looking for scapegoats because his own policies were failing. The congressional hearings, led by the Committee Counsel Ferdinand Pecora, revealed the abuses and manipulation in the great bull market of the late 1920s. It also revealed that some Wall Street leaders had made millions of dollars during the crash by selling short and by other specialized transactions. The hearings seemed to document the lack of social responsibility of bankers and businessmen.

The persistence of the depression raised old questions, not merely about business leadership, but about American capitalism itself. The contradictions in the economy of the 1920s had not been clear at the time, but during the early 1930s they seemed glaring. The presence of great abundance amidst widespread poverty seemed to be an insoluble riddle. In 1932, while the jobless were unable to buy clothing, farmers could not market 13 million bales of cotton. While children went barefoot or stuffed their shoes with cardboard or newspapers, the shoe factories in Massachusetts were closed for half of the year. But the militancy and radicalism of 1931 and 1932 did not seem to be building; instead, despair was growing. Rather than the winds of revolution from the left, there was an increasing loss of faith in the democratic process itself—the kind of drifting that had brought totalitarianism in Germany and Italy.

There were numerous suggestions for abandoning the traditional American political and economic systems. Some critics suggested suspending the system of checks and balances in the government and installing a leader with dictatorial powers. Others proposed the creation of an economic council that would govern through edicts, bypassing Congress. *Barron's,* a conservative financial weekly, editorialized that dictators in peacetime were "quite contrary to the spirit of American institutions and all that"; yet "a genial and lighthearted dictator might be a relief. . . . So we return repeatedly to the thought," *Barron's* concluded, "that a mild species of dictatorship will help us over the roughest spots in the road ahead."

Meanwhile, bank failures reached epidemic proportions. On February 14, 1933, the governor of Michigan declared an eight-day bank holiday—a euphemism for closing the banks to protect them from depositor runs. The governor had been forced into this action by the failure of the two largest banks in the state, the Union Guardian Trust and the

First National Bank, both of Detroit. With the banks closed, checks were worthless. Businesses did not have enough money to pay their employees, so there was little incentive for people to work. Nobody wished to take a check since it was not known whether or not it could ever be cashed. Under the bank holiday, many people reverted to the simplest of economic systems: barter. They exchanged goods with one another and with shopkeepers. In some towns, the chambers of commerce sponsored "trade dollars" as substitute currency to circulate until banks reopened, if they ever would, when the currency could be redeemed.

President Hoover and President-elect Roosevelt declined to cooperate to soothe public fears. Hoover, responding to a request by Great Britain and France to postpone payment on World War I debts, invited Roosevelt to join him in a common position. More concerned with the domestic economy than with the international gold standard, Roosevelt and his advisers refused to be drawn into the issue, especially since they saw few economic benefits but great potential

FDR's inauguration, March 4, 1933

political liability. In February, as the economy mired down, Hoover again attempted to persuade Roosevelt—this time by trying to induce the incoming president to carry on attempts to balance the budget and maintain the gold standard. Neither man performed well and the government was paralyzed.

In the week prior to the inauguration, during Hoover's last days in office, everything appeared to collapse. On March 1, the governors of Kentucky and Tennessee declared bank holidays; that night, California, Louisiana, Alabama, and Oklahoma followed the same course. By March 4—inaugural day—38 states had bank holidays. Shortly before dawn on the fourth, Governors Herbert Lehman of New York and Harry Horner of Illinois suspended bank operations in their states. The president of the New York Stock Exchange followed by suspending trading. New York City's other commodity markets also closed their doors, while the Chicago Board of Trade shut down on a normal business day for the first time since 1848. Factories across the nation turned dark and quiet, and little money circulated in the market places. The American economy virtually had ground to a halt. And on that day, Franklin Delano Roosevelt became President of the United States.

Roosevelt had a great deal to offer, and he exploited his advantages. He entered the White House following two successful terms as an efficient, progressive governor of the state of New York. He was a professional politician. Having served in the New York State Senate before the war, having run unsuccessfully in the New York Senate primary as a Wilsonian Democrat, he then had moved to Washington as the new Roosevelt in the Navy Department. In 1920, he ran unsuccessfully for vice president on the ticket of James Cox. Polio interrupted his political career in the 1920s, and he remained above the Democratic Party's internal struggles. His political involvement was kept alive during years of intense physical therapy by his wife, Eleanor Roosevelt, and his political advisor, Louis Howe.

Roosevelt also projected himself as the man of the people; yet, unlike the self-made Hoover, Roosevelt came from an upper-class family and grew up amidst manorial splendor. A distant cousin of Theodore Roosevelt, he followed his cousin through Harvard with "gentleman's Cs." He never had to work for a living but was financially dependent upon his mother since he did not inherit the bulk of Roosevelt money until near the end of his service as president. Nonetheless, family money freed him to make politics his life work. And he had an enthusiasm and personal enjoyment of politics few presidents could match. Campaigns invigorated him, political manipulations delighted him.

Politics, and not ideology, motivated Franklin Roosevelt. He saw his own role as a broker for the interchange of programs and ideas, and in fulfilling that role he would at times commit his administration to opposing policies. FDR distrusted rigid intellectual systems and was skeptical about utopian programs, though willing to give their advocates a hearing. Instead, this New York patrician liked experimentation and viewed himself as a tinkerer. Once, when a well-meaning friend told FDR that the New Deal was analogous to a great painting and, therefore, like a great artist completing his best work, he should add the final touches to perfect it and then offer the masterpiece to posterity, the president snorted: "There 'ain't no such thing' as a masterpiece of permanence in the art of living or the art of government. That type of art catches a mood, fits the method of expression into the emotions of the day and mingles oil with watercolors, and steel engraving with dry point." FDR had none of the fears about the centralization of power or the primary of individualism and voluntary action which had paralyzed Hoover and other presidents. At the heart of his policies was simple, strong humanitarianism. As Frances Perkins, his Secretary of Labor, summed up: "The intellectual and spiritual climate was Roosevelt's general attitude that the *people mattered.*" FDR's program largely consisted of determination to convey this concern to the American people, to show them that government could be used for the betterment of their lives. This determination infused the new president's every word on a cold, gray inauguration day, March 4, 1933, as it was to dominate the hectic months that followed.

SUGGESTIONS FOR FURTHER READING

There are quite a few brief surveys of the 1920s. See especially Frederick Lewis Allen's fascinating potpourri, *Only Yesterday* (1931); George Soule, *The Prosperity Decade* (1947); William E. Leuctenburg's, *The Perils of Prosperity* (1958); and Roderick Nash's *The Nervous Generation* (1970). For the depression years, see William Leuchtenburg, *Franklin D. Roosevelt and the New Deal* (1963); Broadus Mitchell, *Depression Decade* (1947); William Manchester, *The Dream and the Deal* (1977); Carolyn Bird, *The Invisible Scar* (1966); George Wolfskill, *Happy Days Are Here Again!* (1974); and Frederick Lewis Allen, *Since Yesterday: The Thirties in America* (1941). An excellent brief treatment of the interwar period is Donald R. McCoy's, *Coming of Age: The United States During the 1920s and 1930s* (1973).

Studies of political issues and personalities include Robert K. Murray, *The Harding Era* (1969); Eugene P. Trani and David L. Wilson, *The Presidency of Warren Harding* (1977); Burl Noggle, *Into the Twenties* (1974); Wesley M. Bagby, *The Road to Normalcy* (1962); Donald R. McCoy, *Calvin Coolidge: The Quiet President* (1967); David P. Thelen, *Robert M. LaFollette and the Insurgent Spirit* (1974); Lawrence W. Levine, *Defender of the Faith: William J. Bryan, 1915–1925* (1965); and Matthew and Hanna Josephson, *Al Smith*

(1970). Norman H. Clark's *Deliver Us From Evil* (1976) is an excellent study of prohibition. Other works on social/political issues are Kenneth T. Jackson, *The Ku Klux Klan in the City* (1967); Charles Alexander, *The Ku Klux Klan in the Southwest* (1965); Roberta S. Fuerlicht, *Justice Crucified: The Story of Sacco and Vanzetti* (1977); Ray Ginger's study of the Scopes Trial, *Six Days or Forever?* (1958); and Norman F. Furniss's analysis of religious ferment, *The Fundamentalist Controversy, 1918–1931* (1954). William Allen White's biography of Coolidge, *A Puritan in Babylon* (1938) and his *Autobiography* (1944), along with Otis L. Graham's, *An Encore for Reform* (1967), and Leroy Ashby's, *The Spearless Leader: Senator Borah and the Progressive Movement in the 1920s* (1972), chronicle the demise of Progressivism. See also David Burner, *The Politics of Provincialism* (1967)—for Democratic party politics; Theodore Draper, *The Roots of American Communism* (1959); Frank Freidel, *Franklin D. Roosevelt: The Ordeal* (1954); and James Weinstein, *Ambiguous Legacy: The Left in American Politics* (1975). Also interesting are Robert F. Himmelgerg, *The Origins of the National Recovery Administration: Business, Government, and the Trade Association Issue, 1921–1933* (1976); James W. Prothro, *The Dollar Decade: Business Ideals in the 1920s* (1954); Paul A. Carter, *Another Part of the Twenties* (1977); the final section of Alfred D. Chandler's masterful work, *The Visible Hand* (1977); Malcolm Cowley's bitter cultural critique, *Exile's Return* (1934); Eric Barnouw, *A Tower in Babel: A History of Broadcasting in the United States to 1933* (1966); and James J. Flink, *The Car Culture* (1975).

Studies of groups left untouched by "New Era" prosperity include St. Clair Drake and Horace Cayton, *Black Metropolis* (1945); Kenneth Kusmer, *A Ghetto Takes Shape: Black Cleveland, 1870–1930* (1975); Nathan I. Huggins, *Harlem Renaissance* (1971); Edward D. Cronin, *Black Moses: The Story of Marchus Garvey and the Universal Negro Improvement Association* (1955); David L. Lewis, *When Harlem Was in Vogue* (1981); and Paul Oliver, *The Story of the Blues* (1969). Also useful are Theodore Saloutos and John D. Hicks, *Twentieth Century Populism: Agricultural Discontent in the Middle West* (1951); Bernstein's and Brody's studies of labor; Loren

Reid, *Finally It's Friday: School and Work in Mid-America,* 1921–1933 (1981); and Clarke A. Chambers, *Seedtime of Reform* (1963).

John Galbraith's *The Great Crash* (1972) remains a most perceptive analysis of the onset of the depression. Other good surveys are Peter Fearon, *The Origins and Nature of the Great Slump 1929–1932* (1979); Robert Gordon, *Economic Instability and Growth: The American Record* (1974); the challenging work, *Did Monetary Forces Cause the Great Depression?* (1976) by Peter Temin; Charles P. Kindleberger's concise review of international conditions and effects, *The World in Depression, 1929–1939* (1973); and Gordon Thomas and Max Morgan-Witts, *The Day the Bubble Burst* (1979).

The Hoover administration is treated in Albert U. Romasco, *The Poverty of Abundance: Hoover, the Nation, and Depression* (1965); Ellis Hawley et al., *Herbert Hoover and the Crisis of American Capitalism* (1973); and Lester V. Chandler, *America's Great Depression* (1970). Three excellent biographical studies are Joan Hoff Wilson, *Herbert Hoover: Forgotten Progressive* (1975); David Burner, *Herbert Hoover: A Public Life* (1979); and William A. Williams, *Some Recent Presidents* (1976). Roger Daniels, *The Bonus March* (1971) is excellent.

7 | A New Deal

THE PEOPLE'S GOVERNMENT

It was not so much an explicit program but the "spirit" of the New Deal that rallied the American people in the spring and summer of 1933. Franklin Roosevelt assumed the presidency at a critical juncture. Though he and the country faced enormous problems, the opportunity for constructive solutions was great. When FDR intoned the presidential oath on March 4, 1933, more Americans than ever before were willing to admit that individual initiatives, voluntarism, and local action were inadequate to deal with their personal and collective dilemmas. The public and Congress were united in begging the executive branch for action of any kind to resolve this crisis. President Franklin Roosevelt reacted brilliantly to this clamoring consensus. In his inaugural address, Roosevelt set the tone, saying he would request from Congress "broad executive power to wage a war against the emergency, as great as the power that would be given to me if we were in fact invaded by a foreign foe." The recourse to the analogue of war was a carefully planned and hugely successful appeal to emotion. Though doubtful on logical and historical grounds, Roosevelt's assertion that he headed a war government whose opponent—never identified—used economic rather than military weapons brought together Americans as diverse as the Reinhardts, Bassanos, Hunts, Butlers, and Harts, persuading them and the vast majority of Americans that the New Deal, whatever that might be, was necessary and patriotically justifiable. Clearly, the wartime atmosphere so skillfully maintained by FDR during these first months was largely responsible for pulling the American people out of despair and setting in motion the great psychological victories of the early New Deal.

The promise of action was immediately followed by action itself. The day after his inauguration, President Roosevelt called Congress into special session. In rapid order, he submitted 15 special messages and Congress produced 15 laws, all of which greatly expanded the power of the federal government over the individual lives of Americans. One hundred days after it first convened, an exhausted Congress dispatched a final sheaf of bills to the White House and adjourned for the summer. As the president signed the last bill, he commented: "More history is being made here today than in any one day of our national life." Oklahoma Senator Thomas Gore's interjection, "During all time!" expressed the sentiments of his colleagues and the public.

The flood of laws, decisions, and statements pouring out from Washington left the country gasping. Gus O'Reilly followed events in Washington through the *Boston Globe,* attempting to sort out what was being done. He read about Congress as "the Hill," the professors and professed intellectuals in Roosevelt's inner circle as "the Brain Trust," and the various efforts to stimulate spending as "pump priming." But Gus was unable to identify a clear philosophy or coherent program undergirding the outpouring of legislation and executive decrees. The president and his aides spoke confidently of their intention to provide relief for the suffering, to spark full economic recovery, and to reform the system itself. But did "relief" mean only that government would feed hungry people, or did it portend some effort to elevate "victims" (of the depression and of industrial poverty) to the standard of living enjoyed by middle-class Americans? Did "recovery" imply restoration of conditions as they existed before the great crash, or did New Dealers envision some other golden mean? Did "reform" mean laws to enable government to act more quickly and powerfully in monetary and financial matters, or was there some unspoken scheme to re-

structure American society? Some people feared that New Deal laws might set the country irretrievably on the road to communism. Others feared that White House proposals concealed a plan to establish Roosevelt as the first American dictator. Most people were uncertain about where they were being led. Gus O'Reilly himself soon became disenchanted with the administration's deficit-spending theories. Most of the families did not connect the costly New Deal programs with their taxes—which, except for those of the Butlers, Reinhardts, and Gales, were minimal.

Roosevelt had no clear vision, no grand design for America 2 years or 20 years hence. One reason he never tried to describe precisely the kind of America that "ought to be" was that the nation in 1933, as it had been in 1916, was too diverse to come to agreement on any but vague and platitudinous goals. More important, the 26th president of the United States did not think in terms of coherent systems, of the national interest as something susceptible of precise definition. Although various advisers did produce quite specific ideas about what the national interest required and detailed schemes for their implementation, the president's preference was to make decisions as problems presented themselves. He was willing to try any experiment that seemed reasonable. The "Roosevelt revolution" stemmed not from actions taken but from the fact of action and from pressures that made Washington, D.C., and one particular address, 1600 Pennsylvania Avenue, the hub of American society. FDR and his advisers did not possess all the answers, nor did they ask all of the right questions. They did, however, possess the ability to obtain information, dredged up and summarized for them by a vast army of government employees. And even though knowledge of the problems besieging America did not automatically produce solutions to those problems, it offered more data about the

Men out of work, New York City docks, 1934

structure of American society and conditions of life than anyone would have imagined was possible previously. *That* was of revolutionary import.

The public's impression of the frantic happenings in Washington was decidedly different. It seemed the nation's capital was being overrun by zealots, all propounding world-saving schemes. Of course, not all the traditionalists in Congress and the federal bureaucracy had fled, and they persisted in arguing that capitalism was a self-correcting mechanism. Against these proponents of patience and passivity, however, mustered a growing army that advocated tinkering with the system. Some groups concentrated on the monetary system, other groups armed to "bust the trusts," and still others preached comprehensive economic planning. On the fringes were those demanding the nationalization of large industries. Mostly college professors, young lawyers, and persons who had been alienated by the do-nothing politics of the 1920s, these groups appeared to the traditionalists (and some liberals) as harbingers of socialism. Not just intellectuals, but leaders of almost every important interest group descended on Washington, clogging the corridors of federal buildings.

It was, without question, a bizarre, exciting time to be in the capital. On the first day of the special session of Congress, Speaker of the House Henry Rainey read aloud a bill sent up by the White House that gave the president greater control over the flow of money and prescribed procedures for reopening stable banks and reorganizing weak banking institutions. Congressmen who never saw the bill (because the printer did not have time to make copies) shouted "Vote! Vote!" when colleagues rose to comment. Within an hour, the bill was approved and presented to the Senate. There its stay was similarly brief. That evening, Franklin Roosevelt signed the Emergency Banking Act into law.

The weeks that followed brought bold headlines and accounts of new legislation and chaotic jockeying for influence and power. At first, it appeared the president intended to balance the budget. On March 20, Congress passed his Economy Act, which cut the salaries of government workers and pared down federal pensions. But the next day Roosevelt asked Congress to set up a costly Civilian Conservation Corps (CCC) intended to enlist unemployed young men and set them to work restoring forests and controlling erosion, to appropriate half a billion dollars to the states for welfare programs, and to authorize a $3 billion, job-creating public-works program.

As Congress took up the CCC proposal, the press reported that "men wearing wide brimmed hats and thick sole shoes of the timberlands flocked into Washington." When the welfare proposal came up in the form of the Federal Emergency Relief Act, the halls of government filled with grim-faced state bureaucrats, socialists, representatives of the unemployed, and labor leaders. Consideration of the National Industry Recovery Act, of which the public-works proposal was a part, eventually brought herds of lawyers, contractors, and managers who crowded anterooms and corridors waiting to make their case to someone they considered influential. The bankers and brokers maintained a permanent delegation, very adept at verbal hand wringing, while Congress followed the president's advice and abandoned the gold standard (April 19), abrogated the gold clause in public and private contracts (June 5), and imposed a degree of control over the stock market in the Truth in Securities Act (May 27). A series of farm bills, which greatly interested Charles Gale and Jacob Reinhardt (who took diametrically opposed positions) and Gus O'Reilly (who was worried about the supply and price of meat), occupied a great deal of newspaper space. The Agricultural Adjustment Act (May 12), the Emergency Farm Mortgage Act (May 12), and the Farm Credit Act (June 16) reflected the views of Henry A. Wallace, Secretary of Agriculture.

Gus O'Reilly took note of the statement by William Cardinal O'Connell, dean of the Roman Catholic hierarchy in America, that "President Roosevelt is a God-sent man, the very essence of democracy." And when the president signed away 12 years of Prohibition, others read with approval of Mrs. Roosevelt's intention to serve beer in the White House. Still, the impression of bedlam persisted. During one week in May, in addition to the jostling zealots and the smooth lobbyists, Washington witnessed the arrival of

8,000 veterans who camped along the Potomac and prepared to demonstrate against the cuts in their pensions. At the same time, 2,000 out-of-towners—mostly black—arrived by car, truck, and freight train to march on the White House with a petition demanding release of the "Scottsboro boys" (11 black youths accused of raping two white girls on a freight train going through Alabama). Both groups roundly booed the authorities when their cases were rejected.

All the while, the legislation machine ground onward. The Tennessee Valley Authority Act (May 18) empowered the government to generate electricity and to "develop" the entire watershed of the Tennessee River. The Wayne County Traces took note of Roosevelt's explanation that the electricity bill at his resort home in Georgia was based on a kilowatt hour rate four times the rate he paid in Hyde Park, New York. The government needed a generating facility to use as a "yardstick" to determine whether and how much private utilities were gouging the public. Even more importantly, subsidiary programs of TVA would raise living standards in one of the nation's pockets of dire poverty. The Home Owners Loan Act (June 13) injected the government directly into loans to homeowners, albeit only after they had defaulted on commercial mortgages. A bill sponsored by Senator Hugo Black proposed to reduce the workweek to 30 hours nationally by prohibiting the movement through interstate commerce of all products made by laborers who worked more than five, six-hour days. Roosevelt's advisers convinced him that, rather than sharing the existing work (or unemployment), the answer to unemployment lay in creating new jobs. To increase industrial output required planning at the top. Word of FDR's supposed conversion to the planning approach drew a new legion of industrialists and economists to Washington—to stop the 30-hour bill and have a say in any

program for industrial recovery. A page or two beyond accounts of these events, the *Boston Globe* carried the advertisements of a downtown department store offering men's suits (with two pair of pants) for $20, and a local car dealer offering Chevrolet's Standard Six Coach for $455. The question posed by Gus O'Reilly and all those who had jobs was: What would controlled production do to those prices?

As never before, the outcome depended on one man, the crippled, aristocratic, supremely self-confident Franklin D. Roosevelt, and his ability to convince his countrymen that he would end this national paralysis. Charles Gale remembered sitting by his big Silvertone radio whenever the president was about to speak "over the air." Across the country, in the millions of homes (more than 60 percent of the total) with electric or battery-powered radios, other Americans patiently waited for the tubes to warm up, and then usually someone deftly adjusted the antennae and twiddled the knobs to tune out static. By the time President Roosevelt was cued to speak, 60 million listeners gathered around. In these "fireside chats," as FDR called his radio speeches, he set out to assure people that his experimentation was in their best interests and that nothing was taking place in Washington that was too complex for them to understand. The president could hardly pass himself off as "just plain folks," as an average man among average men. His muted oratorical delivery and failure to pronounce *rs* at the end of words, if nothing else, marked him as an eastern aristocrat. Still, there was something about that warm, smooth voice that invited trust. Overcoming the depression "is your problem as well as mine" was his sincere appeal for support. "Together we cannot fail," was his confident conclusion. He salted his speeches with personal references: "You and I know," "Feel free to criticize; tell me how the work can be done better," and "I think it will interest you if I tell you what we are going to do." FDR spat out words like "chiseler" and "shirker," bragged about programs that would make "dirt fly," confessed to an "old-fashioned country philosophy," and spoke reverently of "material and spiritual improvements" that were yet to come "through the instrumentality of the democratic form of government." The effects were astonishing. For millions, the strength to recover personal self-confidence and faith in a better tomorrow came directly from the genial, sincere man in the White House.

Although the president's talks and newspaper coverage of the New Deal often portrayed the administration's efforts as piecemeal attempts to alleviate the desperate pains of hard times, FDR and his brain trust did soon reach a consensus about the basic causes of the depression, and they worked out a rough list of priorities, as well. Like Herbert Hoover before him, FDR considered the depression largely a loss of confidence in the future by those people who made the American economy move. But unlike Hoover, FDR prescribed massive government intervention in the economy to generate an atmosphere that would revive confidence and speed the flow of money. Thus, legislation designed to bolster the agricultural and industrial sectors, upon which prosperity appeared to depend, overshadowed all else in importance.

When New Deal planners gathered to devise a scheme for restoring confidence in the business community, they shared few common ideas about the role business should play in postdepression America. Behind the president's overly simple assurances and the confused press accounts of their work, the planners divided into essentially three groups: one group envisaged a system in which businesspeople devised a plan for cooperation and order, one that guaranteed every member a fair profit; a second group, accept-

ing the inevitability of business combination, argued that business was too important to leave to businesspeople alone. They preferred a centralized planning structure in which the important decisions resulted from the joint efforts of businesspeople, labor leaders, and representatives of consumer groups. The group that tugged in yet a third direction remained convinced that decisions made independently by individual businesspeople, influenced by the pressures of an impersonal marketplace and in pursuit of their own self-interest, resulted in the greatest social good.

Faced with the necessity of "doing something," these men drafted a law, the National Industrial Recovery Act (NIRA), which was a mixture of all three positions and which spawned the Public Works Administration (PWA) and the National Recovery Administration (NRA). PWA was intended to pump money into the economy through a massive public-works program (federal buildings, bridges, dams, roads). The NRA would organize business so that potential profits were not lost through cutthroat competition. General Hugh Johnson, a tough ex-cavalry officer and member of the War Industries Board during World War I, was chosen to administer NRA. Johnson presided over the next-to-impossible task of devising "codes of fair competition" for each important industry. He began by asking everyone to accept a "blanket" code: no child labor, a minimum wage of $12 for a 40-hour week, the right of labor to organize and bargain collectively, and display of the NRA emblem to show compliance. He then called in representatives of each industry to help draw up codes reflecting each industry's peculiar requirements. Robert Butler became the representative of a few small textile manufacturers in New England and a smaller group of oilcloth raincoat producers. Butler and other representatives of industry found the NRA staff sympathetic. They obtained for their clients a large measure of freedom to fix prices and to diminish competition. Eventually, NRA and industry spokesmen wrote some 600 codes, and a business system evolved that was largely self-policed.

While details of the codes differed from industry to industry, all emphasized industrial order and higher profits. Section 7(a) of the National Industrial Recovery Act, which some union spokesmen termed "labor's bill of rights," mandated that each firm signing a code guarantee workers the right to organize and bargain collectively. Adherence to this principle varied widely, as Mihailo Markovich was quite aware. Almost all codes prohibited selling below cost; most contained mechanisms for setting minimum retail prices; some fixed prices explicitly; some assigned production quotas to individual producers; and others prescribed regulations and hours for operation of plants. According to procedures built in by the code makers, questions of compliance, interpretation, and exemption were to be dealt with by "code authorities"—in almost all cases committees of businesspeople.

Without question, goods and services produced under the NRA codes would cost consumers more. It fell to Hugh Johnson to convince the American people that paying higher prices for Swan's Down cake flour, Servel refrigerators, and Buster Brown shoes was a patriotic act. He organized a brigade of "four-minute speakers" to exhort any audience willing to listen and sponsored hundreds of rallies and parades. As part of the effort to familiarize the public with the NRA emblem—a Blue Eagle with industrial gear in one claw and lightning bolts in the other, and the motto: "We Do Our Part"—Johnson enlisted comely girls in bathing suits to parade emblem-splashed sandwich boards before newsreel cameras. Local leaders were enlisted to drum up business and consumer support. Hundreds of articles flowed from Johnson's office to newspapers and magazines, carrying

Cartoon by Clifford Berryman, November 1933, offering an optimistic view of the NRA

the simple message that every person who purchased products made under NRA auspices contributed to ending the depression—and implying that those who did not cooperate were slackers or worse. By all accounts, it was the greatest propaganda campaign since World War I, and, as with the war effort, the commitment of consumers and producers to voluntary compliance would determine the fate of NRA.

Across the mall from NRA headquarters, lights burned late in the Department of Agriculture. Secretary Henry A. Wallace and a band of commodity experts, lawyers, and farm-organization leaders were grappling with the other basic problem confronting the New Deal, the plight of American agriculture. The economic crisis of 1929–33 had intensified farmers' troubles, for the agricultural sector had been mired in a depression since 1920. The new administration quickly acted to dampen the hostility caused by foreclosures and sheriff's sales. In March, Roosevelt gave responsibility for agricultural financing to the

Farm Credit Administration, and, shortly thereafter, Congress approved the Emergency Farm Mortgage Act, which made available loans to those whose farms were in jeopardy. Later, the Frazier-Lemke Farm Bankruptcy Act (passed in June 1934, but declared unconstitutional in 1935) returned foreclosed properties to their owners and provided federally guaranteed repurchase loans. These measures, though necessary and extremely popular, did not meet the problems that had led to the wholesale confiscation of fertile farms.

The farmer was not forgotten by the New Deal. New Dealers called for restoration of agriculture to its rightful place in American society, maintaining that the family farm was essential to the preservation of society. Both Secretary Wallace and the president were undiluted romantics about the superiority of rural life. Wallace was a respected agricultural economist, geneticist, son of Harding's Secretary of Agriculture, and editor of *Wallace's Farmer.* But what could he do to ensure that the Gales and Reinhardts (and the Traces and Hunts, too) would receive a decent return on their invested capital and labor, enabling them to stay on the land?

During the 1920s, the McNary-Haugen plan, which was meant to raise prices on agricultural commodities at home by dumping surpluses abroad, passed Congress only to face two presidential vetoes. Wallace, an early proponent of such a plan, had rejected the approach by 1933. He and others realized that an increase in prices without production controls would simply stimulate farm productivity and drive prices down again. Thus, Wallace and his advisers, including representatives of the Farm Bureau Federation and the National Grange (which spoke for the larger farmers), decided to try to reduce production first.

The Agricultural Adjustment Act, passed in May 1933, embodied the ideas of production controls, marketing agreements, and authorization for export subsidies. Its central component was the so-called "domestic allotment plan," which set up a system giving federal payments to farmers who agreed to restrict their production of certain basic crops. The anticipated result was a new equilibrium between supply and demand. The AAA (both the act and the Agricultural Adjustment Administration it created) had the general aim of raising the purchasing power of farm income to an equitable level, defined in the act as that balance—parity—that had existed during the prosperous years, 1909–14.

Secretary Wallace and his lieutenants were empowered to use assorted means to accomplish this aim: payments for voluntary crop restriction by farmers, production quotas, commodity loans, and marketing agreements. The staples covered by "Triple A" authority were wheat, corn, cotton, tobacco, rice, milk, and hogs at first, with sugar and cattle being added later. Thus, Charles Gale as a participant in the Wilson County Crop Allotment Committee, withdrew from production 46 acres that had been planted in corn and wheat the previous season. He received a lump sum payment of $1,210 for not growing corn and wheat on his land, and he could look forward to considerably better prices for the corn and wheat he did plant at the next harvest. Large numbers of farmers agreed with Charles Gale and trooped into local extension offices and courthouses to sign up. Unfortunately, the crop-restriction program would not have immediate results, since the AAA went into effect after most farmers had planted crops for the fall of 1933 harvest. Secretary Wallace, to dramatize the necessity for production controls, arranged for the purchase and plowing under of one fourth of the cotton crop, some 10 million acres, and authorized the purchase by AAA of some 6 million newly farrowed pigs, to be slaughtered and distributed to the needy. The latter act, though eminently logical, produced a barrage of criticism, ranging from emotional denunciations of Wallace as "the assassin of little pigs" to warnings that the Roosevelt administration was pursuing a policy of scarcity which would provoke hungry people into riots or rebellion. To the argument that farmers should grow more because so many urbanites were hungry, Wallace retorted: "Agriculture cannot survive in a capitalistic society as a philanthropic enterprise."

By harvest time 1933, which coincided roughly with completion of the NRA's code-making campaign with major industries, it was becoming obvious that neither NRA nor AAA was having the immediate, sweeping economic effects that had been projected. In the first months of NRA's existence (July to November 1933), industrial production declined 30 percent while prices rose—in some industries, like textiles, over 13 percent. Industrialists had taken advantage of NRA's machinery for raising and fixing prices; then they had cut production, laid off workers, and dumped the surpluses in their bulging warehouses on the market at the higher prices. Further, many businesspeople deliberately circumvented the guarantee of unionization by setting up company-controlled unions, firing organizers and refusing to bargain with unions. A wave of strikes that swept the country, with the union recognition as the major issue, made the problem embarrassingly visible.

It was also becoming painfully clear that codes best served the larger firms. Crucible could profit within an industry-wide code because of the high price of its specialty steels, even though the hours provisions required the company to employ as many men to operate 7 open-hearth furnaces as had formerly operated all 12. Many of Evansville's industries were so small and marginally efficient that they could not adjust to the wages and hours set up in the codes. A number of small

furniture factories, collectively employing some 2,500 workers, made kitchen and dining-room chairs for contract buyers such as department stores and mail-order houses. To adopt the industry code of 34 cents per hour for a 44-hour week would mean a 40 percent pay boost for many Evansville woodworkers. Of course, the factories could increase the price of the furniture to meet the added expense, but if the furniture did not sell immediately, the factories did not have the reserves to keep going. Similarly, the bituminous coal of Vanderburgh County lay in thinner veins and graded lower in quality than coal in the Appalachian fields. If they had to pay miners $4.57 a day as prescribed in the code written by the owners of the richest, most efficient mines, so claimed the Southern Indiana Coal Producers Association, they would make no profit at all. These dilemmas cropped up across the country when businesses attempted to honestly follow the NRA guidelines.

During the summer, after the plowing up of so many crops and the killing of 6 million baby pigs, farm prices did rise significantly. Cotton farmers fared best, collectively taking in half again as much money as they had during the previous year, but this was partly the result of a bumper crop caused by heavy fertilizing of their remaining land. Overall, American farm income increased 20 percent. But a rise of 20 percent over the ruinously low level of the previous year was hardly cause for jubilation. More importantly, purchasing power increased little because NRA codes had raised the prices of the items farmers had to buy.

The uneven distribution of benefits stood out as the most visible problem at the end of the AAA's first season. The AAA subsidy system proved ill suited to small, diversified farms. Crop allotments, even in combination with subsidy payments, offered too little total income. Families such as the Reinhardts, who tried to retain the traditional complement of cows, chickens, hogs, sheep, and to grow the corn, wheat, oats, and hay to feed them, discovered that participating in AAA programs meant splitting fields and erecting temporary fences (AAA prohibited grazing on land it rented) and running the risk of too little yield from the remainder to support their livestock. The Traces and many of their hill neighbors

were untouched by AAA. Their cash crop, tobacco, was one of the major staples covered by the program, but only a small proportion of Wayne County farmers signed up, and those were owners of large bottom-land tracts.

The worst injustice of AAA resulted from the failure to deal with the problem of farm tenancy. Landless farmers, who constituted

A dispossessed sharecropper and his family heading west from Idabel, Oklahoma

over 40 percent of the farm population and operated over half of the nation's farm land, were demonstrably second-class citizens. In the South, where 64 percent of the tenants lived, observed one presidential investigating committee, many endured "a standard of living below any level of decency." Approximately one third as many tenants as owners had water piped to their homes, and one fourth as many had electric lighting. About 25 percent of tenants had never been to school. The value of all farm equipment owned by the "average" southern tenant was only $126, while America's "average" owner-operator amassed tools worth $544. Tenant families in Mississippi (where they comprised 70 percent of the farmers) lost about 14 days a year to malaria attacks, and more than one person in four suffered from hookworm. An examination of 33,000 black croppers revealed that one in five had syphilis or gonorrhea. And when life's veil of pain lifted, the nation's tenant families paid an average of $35 for last rites; land-owning families absorbed such solace as a $217 funeral could buy.

Although the Hunts of Shady Grove, Texas, owned their land, most of the people they knew, and more than 80 percent of all black farm families in the South, did not. These people quickly learned that AAA's intention to "relieve the existing national emergency by increasing agricultural purchasing power" implied no commitment to give priority (or even equity) to those in greatest need. No one doubted that black farm families in the South were the most impoverished group in the nation. Various surveys in the early 1930s computed the income of black sharecroppers at between $100 and $295 a year. AAA contracts for $7 to $20 for each acre of cotton not grown paid benefits only to the landowners. Later instructions advised owners to share payments with tenants according to the interest of each in the crop, but AAA never forced the distribution. The

cotton program for the next year, 1934–35, contained a complex provision for payment to tenants. When all the computations had been made, tenants on cotton farms received one ninth of the government payment. After the checks had been mailed out, however, a government investigation in Alabama revealed that nearly half the landlords had devised ways to capture a portion of the AAA money received by their croppers.

Tenants on the Great Plains, most of them white, knew equally hard times. Landowners sometimes transformed their AAA payments into down payments on huge tractors and harvesting equipment. The owner could rent as much land as possible to the AAA and, with his new equipment and the help of a day laborer or two, tend farms that formerly occupied several tenant families. Moreover, the weather, beginning in 1934, turned to drought that parched the crops and winds that stripped away the top soil and carried it away in great, brown billowing clouds. When thousands of Kansas, Oklahoma, and Arkansas tenants found themselves in a "dust bowl" or "tractored off" the land, they spontaneously formed tattered cavalcades and fled. Lines of dilapidated automobiles, overhung with mattresses, chamberpots, cardboard suitcases, whatever could be tied down, chugged off powdery dust roads and onto main highways. Mostly they headed west, as did the Joad family of John Steinbeck's famous depression novel, *The Grapes of Wrath,* lured by rumors of jobs in the orchards and vegetable fields of California, the fabled warm winters, and like Kenny Trace, the belief that in the West lay opportunity.

Big business and big agriculture benefited most from NRA and AAA. General prosperity had not returned and FDR blamed that fact on the "economic royalists" who "ratholed" their profits when they well knew that the public interest required spending. Charging betrayal, he replaced NRA chief Hugh Johnson with a tough, five-man board that began to

Dust storm in western Kansas, 3 P.M. April 1935

pare away the powers of business-dominated code authorities. By mid-1934, the honeymoon of business and government was at an end. Some of the nation's richest families set up the "American Liberty League" and dedicated it to the defeat of Franklin D. Roosevelt and his radical horde. A similar but more gradual alienation occurred between Secretary Wallace and the powerful farm organizations. By 1936, Roosevelt could say of both big business and big farmers: "They are unanimous in their hate for me and I *welcome* their hatred." For once, he was wholly sincere.

Government's failure to bring swift recovery via cooperation with the "haves" by no means reduced the Roosevelt administration to despair. FDR shifted attention to programs in behalf of the middle and bottom levels of the economic pyramid. He favored increasing the purchasing power of consumers. More important, to provide what FDR called "the more abundant life," the New Deal went beyond the tradition of negative regulation and into the realm of positive welfare for all citizens. What was sought included: decent working conditions, access to reasonably priced food and energy, the opportunity to live in a decent apartment or to buy a house, some kind of dignified aid in the event of unemployment, and a financial subsidy for the years of retirement. Although a number of bureaucratic creations during the first 100 days were imbued with this spirit, Roosevelt engineered his most pervasive social reforms in 1934 and 1935.

No part of this attempt to bring recovery by increasing consumer income (and, incidentally, to solidify political support among the middle and lower classes) received greater attention than the relief programs. Not since the Freedmen's Bureau dispersed rations to displaced whites and ex-slaves at the end of the Civil War had the federal government spent money on personal relief. The relief agencies created between 1933 and 1935—the Federal Emergency Relief Administration (FERA) and the Civil Works Agency (CWA)—though assisting millions of Americans, had been conceived as temporary and suffered from serious defects. In May 1935, Congress approved the president's plan for yet a third relief agency, the Works Progress Administration (WPA). The WPA lasted—albeit with a name change to Work Projects Administration in 1939 and considerable interference from Congress—until 1943. The proliferation of acronyms that made up the "New Deal alphabet soup" was confusing, but it is worth remembering that FERA, CWA, and WPA created and confirmed a commitment by the federal government to individual well-being. Most of the $15 billion spent by these agencies did find its way into the pockets of individuals who otherwise might not have survived.

Harry L. Hopkins, FDR's chief adviser on welfare programs, held as his first premise that 13 million jobless Americans were "unemployed through no fault of their own." Until a reviving free-enterprise system restored their opportunities to work, government had a responsibility to help them. The American minister of relief understood those ingrained attitudes that held that asking for public assistance marked the applicant as too lazy or too stupid to hold a job and testified to his personal failure. Therefore, Hopkins proposed that all able applicants perform "useful work" in return for their government checks. Before the depression ended, millions of individuals had undertaken activities that included digging sewers, building roads and sidewalks, organizing courthouse records, stuffing mattresses, painting murals, staging plays and concerts, counting hogs and cattle, and building airports.

A behind-the-scenes dispute between old and new philosophies of social work and shifting political assessments, together with optimism that the emergency would soon end, explained the course of the New Deal's relief programs. Primarily to ensure its passage by Congress, the FERA was decentralized. Each county (there were over 3,000 in the United States) had a welfare board or office charged with investigating and "certifying" individuals who confessed they were destitute and requested assistance. Each office imposed its own criteria to determine who needed help. When FERA sent money to the states, it sent along "guidelines" for spending it. These guidelines, of course, called for creation of "useful" work projects. Failure to comply could mean the end of federal aid, but Harry Hopkins realized that cutting off federal funds would hurt needy reliefers rather than obstinate bureaucrats. Local relief boards made Hopkins furious with their subjective distinctions between the "deserving poor" and the "lazy poor." Many states conducted expensive investigations to determine who were "proper persons, physically, mentally, and morally." Most states also required one year's

Job applicants waiting outside the FERA office in New Orleans, October 1935

continuous residence. As a result, thousands of migrant workers were unable to qualify until FERA established a special fund for them. WPA abolished this account, and, thereafter, migratory workers mostly fended for themselves.

In order to circumvent such regulations and to ensure that useful work was performed by reliefers, Hopkins urged on FDR the scheme that became the Civil Works Ad-

ministration. CWA, which employed 4 million people during the winter of 1933–34, operated directly from Hopkins' office. The CWA stipulated only that the applicant be unemployed to obtain aid. Hopkins desired to create enough different projects to permit people to work at their usual occupations. He arranged to pay reliefers the going minimum wage (considerably above the subsistence wage of FERA). These efforts took place amidst increasingly loud and outraged protests: "Government is competing with private enterprise." "The scheme is socialistic." "Roosevelt is buying votes in the next election." Some workers, in fact, saw no difference between working for CWA and private enterprise and demanded collective bargaining, sick pay, and vacation time as CWA "employees." Such problems and the staggering $900 million cost prompted FDR to abandon CWA. In May 1935, WPA, a typical New Deal compromise, was born. County welfare boards certified eligibility, each state's governor appointed a WPA administrator who handled personnel and payroll, and a national WPA office approved the work projects and supplied some of the supervisors. FDR's preference for decentralized activity was satisfied, local politicos were given a say (which translated into a certain amount of support for the program in Congress), and Harry Hopkins was permitted to carry forward his ideas about the administration of relief.

While the relief programs of the New Deal did constitute a commitment to aid individual citizens in distress, they were more a commitment to a principle and to the citizenry at large. Because of the differences in FERA, CWA, and WPA and the way thousands of communities interpreted them, there continued to be individual cases of suffering and anxiety. Some 9 million Americans applied for CWA's 4 million jobs, and WPA never had sufficient funds to employ everyone the local welfare boards certified as destitute and able to work.

New Deal relief programs, running counter to conventional self-help assumptions in certain respects, supported those assumptions in others. The retention of traditional procedures for determining who was eligible for relief by requiring that recipients submit to a means test and sign a statement admitting destitution—a Pauper's Oath—kept many people from applying. Typical instructions issued by

county and city relief boards read: "No case may be accepted for relief, even though there is no income from a job, if the applicant has assets in the form of cash savings, stocks and bonds, insurance or real property which can be converted into cash." For a family on home relief (as opposed to work relief where payments were fixed and a good deal higher), investigators referred to a schedule that set out the amount required for subsistence. After subtracting occasional income and potential cash from the sale of property, the investigator computed the family's "budget deficiency." The relief office then paid the deficit. So far as we know, Velma Trace was the only individual from among our families who received relief. Mihailo Markovich worked too frequently and, in any event, asserted that he would have starved before accepting charity. If Annie Miller's family had not supported her, she would have been eligible, after intensive investigation, for a monthly payment of $22.50.

As business support for New Deal projects continued to wane (the NAM had been critical from the beginning; the Liberty League was formed in 1934; and the U.S. Chamber of Commerce defected in early 1935), Roosevelt pushed through Congress projects designed to sustain the working class. Like the NRA and AAA, each reflected compromises between different, often contradictory, views. As well, they constituted responses to specific problems rather than parts of a comprehensive program. Taken together, these new additions to the New Deal potpourri did bring government closer to individual lives.

The HOLC of the 100 days already had saved the home of Ben and Anna Trace. Now, in 1934, Ben was covered by the new Railroad Retirement Act. He would pay a small percentage of his wages into a fund; the railroad would contribute double that amount. When he retired after 30 years, and if he and Anna could keep their health, Ben figured he would have enough income to be independent of his children. James Hart had no intention of giving up his farm, although he admitted that low prices, the drought, and the poor returns on his trading deals had kept him in a state of constant worry. But should the worst happen, the Frazier-Lemke Bankruptcy Act protected him against foreclosure. In Kansas, Kentucky, and elsewhere, cooperatives financed by the Rural Electrification Administration (1935) were stringing electricity lines along rural roads. The Gales invited REA linemen to camp on their farm when their trucks rolled into New Albany. Next day, Chloe Gale took sandwiches and cold drinks to the men engaged in setting the poles and stretching the lines that would bring the prom-

ises of the St. Louis World's Fair of 1904 to the rural neighborhoods of Wilson County, Kansas. Mihailo Markovich, Betty and Rose Miller, Gus O'Reilly, and Robert Bassano carried their new Social Security cards. Farmers Reinhardt, Gale, and Hart, railroad man Ben Trace, and James Hunt, dayworker and preacher, were all ineligible. Banks in Evansville, Fredonia, Midland, Boston, and the Bronx began to display the placard "Member FDIC" (Federal Deposit Insurance Corporation), the government's program guaranteeing deposits in case of bank failure. Two million jobs for young people were made available through the National Youth Administration (1935), and local projects were started in Fredonia and Waynesboro. Good

An REA crew stringing lines not far from the Gales home in New Albany, Kansas

credit risks such as Robert Bassano and Gus O'Reilly stood to gain, should they decide to move, from the Federal Housing Administration. This agency provided federal guarantees (up to a maximum of $5,400) for private loans for remodeling or construction of new homes. The closer relationship was not all one way. In 1937, Jack Miller, his accounting business prospering, became the first in his family to pay income tax. This achievement placed him with Robert Butler, Gus O'Reilly, Jacob Reinhardt, Charles Gale, and James Hunt.

The capstones of this evolving welfare state were the Social Security Act and the National Labor Relations Act, popularly known as the "Wagner Act" after Senator Robert Wagner, its chief sponsor. These efforts affected an impressive number of people at the time and were to have even larger importance in the future. New Dealers began to work seriously on the idea of social insurance in June 1934, although the idea had been pushed by reformers since the turn of the century. At one point FDR told Secretary of Labor Frances Perkins, "Everybody ought to be in on it . . . From the cradle to the grave they ought to be in a social insurance system." The Social Security (formally Old Age Survivors Deposit Insurance) law which Congress approved in August 1935 amounted to considerably less.

The new agency operated 10 distinct programs: old-age insurance, unemployment compensation, old-age assistance (welfare payments), aid to the blind, aid to dependent children, maternal and child health services, services for crippled children, child-welfare services, public-health services, and vocational rehabilitation. Except for old-age insurance, all of the programs were administered by the states. Financial contributions were required from the states, and the federal government contributed only to approved plans. But federal standards were low, and financially harassed states funded them in a niggardly fashion. Payments varied from district to district. They were lowest in the rural South and highest in New York City. Advance was spotty. While 45 states had aid-to-dependent-children laws by the end of 1937, only 29 state legislatures actually funded the programs. Mike Simich received unemployment compensation from Pennsylvania in 1938, but unemployed workers in 16 other states had no such program to turn to. By 1937, 36 states administered old-age assistance plans. Although the federal government required that each state must guarantee the elderly "a reasonable subsistence compatible with decency and health," in 1939 the average payment was $29 monthly. Since old-age insurance payments did not begin until 1942, even for those who qualified, the dependent aged had little choice but to turn to the old-age assistance programs.

Some progress was made through federal grants-in-aid to upgrade and extend the coverage of public-health services in the states. More public-health nurses appeared in rural counties, and prenatal clinics were established in urban areas. But the inclusion in the report the President's Committee on Economic Security (the body that drafted the legislation) sent to Congress of a discussion of national health insurance so aroused the American Medical Association that a special meeting of its house of delegates was called. The delegates adopted resolutions opposing health insurance and federally supported maternal and child-health services.

For a worker making Mihailo Markovich's salary of $2,000 a year, the monthly retirement check from old-age insurance would amount to a little less than $21. Some of the money would be deducted from Mihailo's wages. The idea of noncontributory retirement payments was never seriously discussed. Mihailo's contribution to the fund would be 1 percent of the first $3,000 of income in 1936, 2 percent in 1937, and 3 percent in 1938. Farmers, agricultural workers, casual laborers, and domestic servants—poor people who most needed help—did not qualify. Social Security hardly provided the degree of protection against the "hazards and vicissitudes of life" that Roosevelt had proclaimed, but it did offer, as he said, "some measure of protection for the average citizen." And there was, now that the logjam had broken, always the chance of later expansion. American workers regularly thanked the New Deal for its labor legislation by x-ing the block printed next to the Democratic rooster on the election ballots.

After the Supreme Court struck down the NRA, with its guarantees to labor, in 1935, New York Senator Robert Wagner pushed through a stronger law. The National Labor Relations Act expressly affirmed workers' rights to organize and forbade employer interference. Thenceforth it was unlawful for an employer unfairly to prevent union activity in his shop, to influence unions through contributions, to discriminate in hiring according to the applicant's attitude to or membership in the union, or to refuse to bargain with union representatives. Notably, the law placed no restraints on unions. Roosevelt had not been enthusiastic about such a drastic law at first but was persuaded that only through such federal assistance could labor meet management on anything like equal terms. A short time later, an investigation showed that since the passage of NIRA, corporations had hired some 3,871 agents from four "protection agencies" to infiltrate and block union activities, and that a reputable firm like Youngstown Sheet and Tube Company (not alone in such tactics) had prepared to meet the demands of labor by acquiring 8 machine guns, 369 rifles, 190 shotguns, 450 revolvers, and 109 gas guns. Because of the threats of labor violence, even those Americans who worried vaguely about "the right of a man to run his business any way he sees fit" found it easier to accept the Wagner Act. The result was the rapid spread of mass unionism in nearly all major industries.

REDEFINING THE NEW DEAL

The social conscience of Roosevelt and his brain trust, pressures from the grass roots, together with the political necessity of winning and holding a constituency after so much of the business community had been alienated, all contributed to policies that came to define the New Deal. There was yet another powerful influence: the need to head off charismatic men who offered other deals. The challenge did not come so much from the "out" political party, or from the communists, or from the extreme right, although all these elements increased in strength as the depression lingered on. The New Deal's main competition came from a retired doctor, a parish priest, and a country boy who became a United States Senator—humanitarians and good capitalists all.

In September 1933, Dr. Francis E. Townsend was 66 years old and semiretired in Long Beach, California. One morning while shaving he turned to see through his bathroom window three elderly women amid the garbage cans in the alley. The sight of these women "stooped with great age, bending over the barrels, clawing into the contents," Townsend said, so enraged him that he determined "to shout till the whole country hears!" Francis Townsend believed that government owed a decent living to the elderly, and he lost no time in offering a simple plan. Government should pay every person over 60 years of age $200 each month with the proviso that he or she spend the money in 30 days. The plan would give dignity to old people and the money they spent would revive the economy. The doctor claimed that a federal sales tax could raise the necessary funds.

Using the ballyhoo tactics of a California

The Tenino, Washington, Townsend Club headquarters which was still flourishing in 1939

real estate promoter and a national magazine, and charging only 25 cents for initiation and 10 cents for dues, Townsend rushed to establish a nationwide organization. Elderly persons mostly lower middle-class whites, joined in droves. By late 1935, Townsend claimed approximately 8 million members in 7,000 clubs, including one in Fredonia. The political potential of the Townsend clubs, based on the real needs of silver-haired grandmothers and gnarled grandfathers, was explosive. When the Townsend plan was first voted upon in the House of Representatives in 1934, nearly 200 members failed to vote. For a time, those members of Congress who had publicly opposed the plan were threatened with crushing defeat in the 1936 elections.

An old peoples' crusade never fully materialized. Some labeled Townsend a "charlatan and a quack." Others pointed out the fantastic expense. There were at least 12 million people over 60 years of age in 1935 so the

cost would be $2.4 billion monthly. But Townsend's shaky grasp of economics, evidence of corruption in some Townsend clubs, and his citation for contempt of Congress in 1936 did not completely destroy the movement. Several states, including Ohio and Colorado, adopted versions—much scaled down in payments—of the plan. In 1939, over 50 Representatives and two Senators testified in its support. In various forms, the essence of the plan was reintroduced during and after the war. At the least, the Townsend plan stimulated a genuine concern for the problems of the aged.

Huey Long represented a far more serious threat to the established order. The "Louisiana Kingfish" claimed only 6 million adherents, but he was a creative, seasoned politician. Certainly, President Roosevelt feared Long more than any other potential opponent, for he spoke to the deep frustrations and anger, the yearnings for easy solutions to the complexities of modern life, that affected vast numbers of Americans.

Huey Long's political rise differed little from countless other chronicles of political success, except that the depression propelled him out of the backwaters and into the mainstream. Born on a farm scratched from the pine woods of Louisiana, he had worked his way through college and Tulane Law School. He entered politics at 25, and a series of carefully planned campaigns (featuring loud, populist-style attacks on the corporations that dominated Louisiana) took Long to the governorship in 1928 and to the United States Senate in 1930. By 1932, Huey Long held the state of Louisiana in the palm of his hand.

By the standards of mainstream politics, Huey Long was an uncivilized, unethical rabble-rouser, ambitious only for power. He was all that, but Huey Long was also sensitive to the frustrations of the poor, rural South that had spawned him. He could turn on and off at will the goddamit-redneck-sapsucker vernacular of the small-town general store, but Long's audiences *believed* when he voiced their long-festering questions: What services did 2 percent of the people provide that entitled them to 70 percent of the wealth? Why was it acceptable for the few to live in luxury while the many scrabbled for life's bare necessities? Governor Long quickly cowed the Louisiana legislature and set out to give his fellow rednecks their due. Within months, the state was alive with highway and school construction, work on new hospitals and insane asylums—all paid for by heavy taxes on the large corporations and the rich.

Though he had supported FDR, Long soon became disillusioned with Roosevelt and the New Deal. In February 1934, Huey Long went on national radio to offer his solution to the depression. Concentration of wealth was the problem, and the "Share Our Wealth" program was the solution. Under the motto "Every Man a King," Long's Share Our Wealth Society promised *every* family in the country a "homestead" of $5,000, enough in those days for "a house, an automobile, a radio, and the ordinary conveniences." It promised a guaranteed annual income of between $2,000 and $3,000 and an "adequate" old-age pension. Share Our Wealth stood for free college education for bright young people, a 30-hour workweek, and an 11-month work year. For farmers, the plan promised that government would raise and stabilize prices by buying and storing surpluses. To pay for everything, government would adjust the tax laws to confiscate all family fortunes in excess of $5 million and all family income over $1 million a year.

Spokesmen for the New Deal countered Long weakly, declaring that Long's program (like Townsend's) was economically unsound and attempting to frighten Americans with vague charges that Share Our Wealth would lead to fascism. But they did not answer Long's basic criticism: that the depression re-

mained and that maldistribution of income persisted. Ben Trace found Long's message so appealing that he joined the Howell Share Our Wealth chapter, Ben's first and last political act. Millions of others did likewise as Long's popularity spread like wildfire. Local chapters of the society numbered 27,000 and reached every state by 1935. A worried FDR began to consider Long a legitimate presidential contender. But Long's political power was not to be tested in a national election. On September 8, 1935, a disgruntled physician stepped from behind a pillar outside the governor's office in Baton Rouge and shot Long in the stomach. Huey Long died two days later, and after his death the Share Our Wealth movement slowly dissolved.

It was ironic that the person who informed President Roosevelt of Long's death was the New Deal's third maverick opponent, the nation's then most famous clergyman, Father Charles E. Coughlin. "Hey, your boyfriend is dead," Coughlin announced when the president greeted him, having invited him to Hyde Park to talk over his growing hostility to the New Deal. The priest and the president parted six hours later, having resolved nothing.

From his base, the Shrine of the Little Flower in Royal Oak, Michigan, Coughlin broadcast a popular children's program during the 1920s. Then he abruptly abandoned Bible stories for political commentary, and became famous as "the radio priest." He had been an enthusiastic supporter of FDR (he coined the phrase "Roosevelt or ruin") and for a time was a regular White House visitor. But, like Townsend and Long, he gradually decided that the New Deal was merely a slicked-up version of the same old game. His Sunday afternoon broadcasts began to carry ever shriller denunciations of administration policies as too little too late. Coughlin's pet theory was the monetization of silver. There simply was not enough gold in the world, he thundered repeatedly over the airwaves, to make it the basis for real prosperity. In November 1934, Father Coughlin announced the formation of the National Union of Social Justice with its mishmash of social welfare proposals, monetary experiments, anticommunism, anti-Semitism, and religious enthusiasm—based, he said, on the admonitions of papal encyclicals. Surveys revealed that between 30 and 50 million listeners were tuning in on Coughlin's weekly broadcast, although none of our families recalls listening to him regularly. He was forced to hire 200 clerks to handle his correspondence, and the National Union of Social Justice soon boasted 5 million members. After a final break with FDR in the fall of 1935, Coughlin, who was searching for some means to retain his huge following, drifted toward direct involvement in the political arena.

The following summer, Coughlin formed a loose alliance with Townsend and Gerald L. K. Smith, a rabidly anti-Semitic preacher who had inherited the disintergrating Share Our Wealth movement. The three men, who met only once for a few minutes, discovered that they had in common only bitter resentment of President Roosevelt and the New Deal. Nonetheless, Townsend and Smith agreed to support the Union Party, which Coughlin had organized to stand against FDR, and its candidate, Representative William "Liberty Bell" Lemke of North Dakota. This decision to field a third party exploiting the groundswell of hostility and intolerance spawned by the depression came too late; Lemke received fewer than 900,000 votes in the 1936 presidential election.

It turned out that neither the political mavericks nor the loyal opposition stirred the voters. When all the ballots were counted, the Republican candidate, Governor Alfred M. Landon of Kansas, had won only two states—Maine and Vermont—and the Republicans had suffered the greatest defeat in the history of presidential elections. Though

he could not vote, Mihailo Markovich was pleased that Midland and Beaver County, which had gone for Hoover in 1932, turned out nearly two to one for Roosevelt. The Midland precinct where Mihailo and most Serbians resided endorsed the president by an eight to one margin. All of our families, with the exception of faithful Republicans Robert Butler and the Reinhardts, voted for Roosevelt. Ben and Anna Lee Trace did not choose to vote, while James and Sylvia Hunt would have endangered their lives had they voted. It should be noted that Democratic ascendancy in Washington did not automatically translate into sweeps of county courthouses. As a rule, those who considered themselves Republicans remained loyal to the local ticket. Thus, the familiar Republican organization that the Markoviches so disliked in Beaver County, Pennsylvania, and James Hart had supported in Wilson County, Kansas, survived—weakened and chastened, to be sure, by the Democratic landslide in presidential and Congressional races.

Gus O'Reilly and Charles Gale were at their radios the night of October 31, 1936, when Franklin Roosevelt spoke at New York's Madison Square Garden and laid out what he would do if reelected. After berating the "economic royalists" for their betrayal and greed, the president promised to continue and expand his efforts in the field of social welfare. He reeled off a long list: improved working conditions, collective bargaining, cheaper electricity, better and less expensive transportation, lower interest rates, elimination of slums, reduction of farm tenancy, useful work for the needy unemployed, educational assistance to young people, consumer protection, better old-age insurance, and unemployment compensation. "For all these, and a multitude of things like them," he said with passion, "we have only just begun to fight." After his resounding victory, the president returned in his inaugural address to the theme of expanded social-welfare programs. One statement stood out: "I see one-third of a nation ill-housed, ill-clad, ill-nourished." The rest was a promise to correct that condition.

The reform phase of the New Deal, however, was already over. During the next four years, Roosevelt made three grave mistakes that eroded his popular support and so strengthened a coalition of opponents in Congress that they were able to block additional sweeping initiatives. The first mistake was FDR's challenge to the decisions of the Supreme Court. The second, the decision to cut off pump-priming programs, prompted a serious recession. The third was his attempt to "purge" his opponents from Congress. In addition, Europe and the Far East were falling into war. Roosevelt's belief that the United States had a stake in the outcome diverted attention from domestic problems.

From the beginning, the architects of the New Deal worried about the Supreme Court's reaction to the expanded authority of the federal government. While the Trace and Gale children listened, high-school civics teachers in Evansville and Fredonia chorused that the expansion of federal power was rationalized under the clauses of the Constitution which gave the federal government the power to "regulate commerce among the several states," "provide for the general welfare," and make such laws "as are necessary and proper" to carry out other mandated duties. But exactly what these phrases intended was a matter for the nine justices of the Supreme Court to decide. By late 1936, the trend of their thinking had become clear. The Court seemed determined to dismantle the New Deal. Virtually all of our families were directly affected when, in the spring of 1935, the Court unleashed a crippling barrage of legal decisions that voided the Railroad Retirement Act, the Frazier-Lemke Farm Mortgage Act, and the National Industrial Recovery Act. On January 3, 1936, it declared the AAA unconstitutional. Cases challenging the validity of the Wagner Act and Social Security decisions waited to be heard. The decisions roused Roosevelt to fury. He accused the Court of choosing "a horse-and-buggy definition of interstate commerce" and the remainder of the Constitution. Congress revised most of the laws or extracted and repassed their important provisions to get around the Court's objections, but FDR wanted to stop its obstructionism.

Two weeks after his inauguration in February 1937, the president asked Congress to permit him to appoint one additional justice to the Supreme Court for every justice on the Court who was over 70 years old (the maximum increase would be six). He justified the proposal on grounds that the work load of the modern court was so much heavier than in former years that old men simply could not stand the pace. While there was some truth in the argument, the plan was a transparent device to appoint enough new, sympathetic justices to save the Roosevelt version of the welfare state. The shrillness of the cries against "court packing," as opponents called the scheme, surprised Roosevelt, since reformers had ralied against the Court for 30 years and many members of Congress had introduced constitutional amendments to alter the Court structure. Many New Dealers (in and out of Congress) rose to declare that Roosevelt had gone too far. His enemies insisted that he was trying to seize control of the judicial branch, thereby destroying the American system of checks and balances and preparing the way for dictatorship. The president erred in thinking that his countrymen, who shared his disgust with recent decisions of the Court, stood ready to alter the institution. The Supreme Court was shrouded in myth. In simplest terms, Americans revered the Court because Americans revered the Constitution; justices were seen as holy men.

One of Roosevelt's arguments for court re-

Clifford Berryman's cartoon about the court-packing fight

form was that new laws—which the old men would doubtless declare unconstitutional—were needed to protect a coming tide of prosperity. All the indicators were right. By spring 1937, the charts of government statisticians showed production at the 1929 level, and total profits and wages closing in on the figures of Hoover's only good year. Roosevelt had never liked deficit spending and was eager to balance the budget so as to stop the steady rise in the national debt. His advisers, as on almost every other issue, proposed contradictory courses of action. At this point, however, the jockeying for influence found financially conservative Secretary of the Treasury Henry Morgenthau in closest proximity to the presidential ear and able to silence the competition. In June 1937, Roosevelt proclaimed that Dr. New Deal soon would prescribe taking off "the bandages and throwing away the crutches." The patient was cured.

Funds for the construction projects of the Public Works Administration were shut off. Other presidential orders resulted in the firing of half of the 2.5 million WPA workers and reduced the federal grants to home-relief programs. Five million people were eliminated from federal assistance programs in 1937. The consequences were most alarming. Between July 1937 and May 1938, the index of industrial production dropped from 117 to 76, the wholesale price index from 88 to 78, and farm prices from 123 to 92. Employment in manufacturing was down more than 20 percent. Not only had the patient failed to walk without support, he had collapsed. Only by restoring relief and public works ($3.75 billion in 1938) was the economy buttressed. Although the public did not adopt the political equivalent of suing the attending physician for malpractice, it never had the same confidence in Dr. New Deal again.

The New Deal did not stall completely. Two measures enacted in 1937, the Farm Security Administration (FSA) and the United States Housing Act, promised to help some of those neglected by earlier New Deal remedies. FSA was intended to place marginal and tenant farmers on productive land, but was never adequately funded. The Housing Act created the U.S. Housing Authority as the agency to oversee slum clearance and provide low-cost public housing for the poor. Opposition to the concept of public housing guaranteed that accomplishments would be minimal. At best, the Housing Act committed the federal government to action in the field and provided a legal precedent for the future. A third measure, the Fair Labor Standards Act (1938), did establish minimum wages for certain industries, and a second AAA (1938) created a modified program for dealing with low farm prices and surplus crops.

Perhaps the most successful program emanating from the "last-gasp" reform phase dealt with commercial agriculture. In February 1938, Congress approved a new Agricultural Adjustment Act, which emphasized soil conservation rather than crop restrictions in order to satisfy the Supreme Court's objections. This "Second AAA" embodied a dramatic shift in attitude from a policy of planned scarcity back to the economics of abundance. Secretary Wallace was responsible for its central component, the concept of an "ever normal granary" (an idea he had borrowed from Confucius and justified through Biblical examples). The federal government undertook to maintain price levels for staple crops in "fat" years (through parity payments and crop-storage loans) and also to ensure against inadequate supplies of cotton, tobacco, wheat, corn, and rice during "lean" years. The scheme cost very little, produced significant stabilization of commodity prices until the war intruded, and received an overwhelming endorsement by farmers such as the Gales and Reinhardts.

The second AAA was, frankly, an admission that the future of American agriculture lay with big commercial farming, though other features dealt with the problems of small farmers and tenants. Another innovation, given surprisingly little attention, was the Food Stamp Plan, which distributed certain surplus commodities to the urban poor. Velma Trace, for example, used the book of "food stamps" given her by the Los Angeles Welfare Agency to get $1.50 worth of staple foods for each $1 she spent at the local grocer from her relief check. She had no idea that the Food Stamp Plan was part of an enormous effort to rationalize the agricultural production and distribution system. Anything that helped stretch her relief check was accepted, no questions asked.

The New Deal also suffered disturbing defeats. Congress killed outright a scheme to create seven regional development projects patterned on the TVA. A tax-reform law, which opponents charged was designed to "soak the rich" and advocates claimed would redistribute wealth, emerged from the congressional meat grinder a pale shadow of its original self. A bill to reorganize the bureaus of the executive branch came up three times in 1937 and 1938. It was thrice defeated, with opponents purporting to see an analogy to the court-packing misadventure and proclaiming executive reorganization would make FDR a dictator.

Angered by opposition within his own party and concerned about the future of the New Deal in the Democratic Party, FDR sought to purge conservatives in the 1938 primaries. Although all but one of his opponents won renomination, FDR gave political notice that he intended to remain a strong force in party politics to insure that the directions of the New Deal would continue. In the general elections, the Republicans restored some of the two-party balance in Congress, replacing seven Democratic senators and 80 representatives. The New Deal came under stronger attack from Republicans and conservatives, but it was not systematically destroyed as some had feared.

A DEMOCRATIC CULTURE

Not all the depression's drama occurred in the halls of federal offices and the headquarters of various interest groups. If one judged by some of the cocktail parties in the elegant town houses of Washington's Georgetown section, the depression saved American civilization. There, a cluster of intellectuals, many of whom had disassociated themselves from what poet Ezra Pound had labeled the "botched" society of the 20s, at first were entranced with the possibilities of the New Deal. The gods of materialism no longer held power, and for the first time in the 20th century government invited men of ideas, sensitive men, into its inner sanctums. From their ghettos in New Haven, Cambridge, San Francisco, Greenwich Village, the Left Bank of Paris, and outposts in Ann Arbor, Atlanta, and Albuquerque, intellectuals had converged on Washington to take part in the work of reconstruction. Some found jobs in the proliferating new federal agencies. Certain of the most creative proved temperamentally unsuited to bureaucratic routine and swiftly departed. Those who could adjust settled down to long struggles to liberalize trade, plan regional development, protect civil liberties, and raise the artistic consciousness of the citizenry.

Intellectuals inside and out of government treated the problems around them as uniquely American. Where "gaping primates" and "boobs" had stood a decade before, most now perceived a hardy, virtuous proletariat that possessed laudable ability to endure adversity and determination to overcome it. These changed feelings sparked a quest to "rediscover America," to revitalize and unify those marvelously diverse, if presently insensitive, people. Government was to be their chosen instrument.

A popular syllogism among New Deal intellectuals contended that the United States had long since established the principle of political democracy, that the New Deal was bringing about economic democracy, and that the ultimate perfection of the system demanded cultural democracy—a truly native version of the arts which all Americans understood and appreciated. Franklin Roosevelt never voiced such an argument, but he did believe in fostering the arts. His motives were patrician and paternalistic. At home and at Groton and Harvard, he had been taught that exposure to the arts enriched one's life; the tradition of his class included patronage of artists. When Roosevelt spoke of government's responsibility to provide the people with "a more abundant life," he certainly had in mind cerebral as well as material betterment. It remained for the intellectuals to find a way to carry on the program of cultural improvement (which Congress would never pay for) through the programs for increasing material abundance (which Congress would pay for).

Pressed by outsiders and the president's known desire to "do something for the arts," the Treasury Department (which built and maintained post offices and other federal buildings) in late 1933 set up a small Section of Fine Arts to place murals in hundreds of new government buildings. Sensitive to the times, its director, Edward Bruce, insisted that the subject of each decoration be a part of "the American scene." Bruce liked art, he said, which gave him the same feeling he had when he smelled a sound ear of corn. He wanted paintings in the post offices that reminded people of the countryside around

them and that made them feel "a little better" when they left the building than when they entered. The Section of Fine Arts alienated some artists with its dictation of subject and style, but "post-office art" (some 1,200 murals altogether, including one each in Midland and Fredonia) furthered the trend toward veneration of things uniquely American: muscular farmers and their weathered wives, livestock, fierce Indians and indolent cowboys, strength, purpose, and vibrant colors.

When projects for the WPA were being devised, intellectuals in residence saw to the inclusion of four small programs to develop and disseminate the native heritage: the Federal Art Project, the Federal Music Project, the Federal Theatre Project, and the Federal Writers Project. During the next eight years, these projects took in about 40,000 destitute artists—people whose skills might otherwise have atrophied—and encouraged them to further the spirit of cultural nationalism. Although the WPA imposed almost no requirements of subject and style on these reliefers,

A set of murals, "Evolution of Western Civilization," by Michael Newell, for Evander Childs High School in New York City. A similar mural, featuring heavy-muscled men and women, sharp definitions, and historical motifs characteristic of the regionalist school, was installed in Evansville's T. J. Reitz High School in 1938

TO PLAN IS TO DESIGN

A Federal Art Project–sponsored class in costume design at the Walker Art Center in Minneapolis

interpretations of the American scene showed up in most of the work produced under its auspices.

The Federal Writers Project, except for an anthology called *American Stuff,* did not compete with "creative" literature. Rather, writers' teams in each state turned out state "guidebooks." For about $2.50, motorists could purchase explanations of the scenes just beyond the windshield as they traveled main highways. The guidebooks also contained detailed essays on the state's towns, government, history, and cultural achievements. From these collective research efforts grew the philosophy that history is the story of los-

ers as well as winners. The guidebooks offered anecdotes about men and women whose greatness died aborning, designated the sites of local "follies" and catastrophes, laid out the local legends and folk wisdom— all dimensions of the American scene.

The Federal Art Project yielded 2,566 murals, 17,744 pieces of sculpture, 108,099 paintings, and 240,000 copies of 11,285 original designs by graphic artists. Featuring local scenes and events (or, rather, artistic views thereof), most of this art went up to public view in high schools, community centers, hospitals, and government offices. During Jerry Trace's sophomore year, an enormous mural depicting some mythical battle between bronzed savages and flinty settlers appeared in the main hall of Reitz High School in Evansville. It was still there, grimy but powerful, when his brother Ted graduated in 1958. For the Traces and most other Reitz students, the mural was the first "hand painted" picture they had ever seen. Not all of them became lovers of art because of its presence, but it did spark in some the curiosity to see more art.

The Federal Theatre gave many depression-generation Americans their first glimpses of live actors, employing some 13,000 performers. Some 60 percent of its performances were presented in communities that had not previously hosted professional theatrical productions, and in many other communities the population had not seen a professional troupe since the early 1900s. Federal Theatre's repertoire included Shakespeare and other classics, but most of the dramas were by American playwrights. The Theatre Project also developed a reputation for supporting plays projecting radical political messages. Sinclair Lewis' *It Can't Happen Here,* a diatribe against ultraconservatism and fascism, did not play well in Boston—or Evansville—or Washington, D.C. In several "Living Newspaper" sketches (a newsreel on stage), prominent U.S. Senators considered themselves "held up to opprobrium." Congress abolished the Federal Theatre Project in 1939.

The New Deal cultural projects, unprecedented in American history, ultimately failed to meet the hopes of its advocates for cultural democracy and of a small but loud group of radicals who demanded the American people's "cultural rights." Probably the main reason was the inflexible rules of the relief organization they were required to follow. Actors, painters, and poets were treated no differently than unemployed bricklayers and accountants. The state investigated and certified as penniless all applicants. The pre-

rogatives of hiring and firing fell to the state WPA organization (under the state governor), and the law required state legislatures to contribute financially to individual projects. Only technical direction and control over standards came from Washington. Creativity and bureaucracy proved to be incompatable. Even had the problems of inflexible procedures and elitism been resolved, maximum effects demanded an equitable, nationwide distribution of artistic production. Unfortunately, approximately 40 percent of the painters and sculptors lived in New York City and most of the rest were located in half a dozen large metropolitan areas. Statistics revealed an analogous concentration of actors, writers, and musicians. Thus, the move to democratize culture had its greatest effects in places where the arts already were strongest.

Aside from isolated events—the coming to town of a Federal Theatre Project troupe, organization of an exhibit of the daubings of local artists at the Community Center or a neighborhood church—our families found "culture" where they had always found it—in the downtown movie houses, on the book and magazine racks of the corner drugstore, emanating from their radio sets every evening. To almost all (only Chloe Gale and Robert Butler, and perhaps Sylvia Hunt, were exceptions) culture did not mean solemn gawking at still lifes or listening enraptured to the complexities of a symphonic composition; rather, it was entertainment, a means of release for a brief space from the trials of daily life. Although the concern with escape during the 1930s, as exemplified in the lavish musicals of Busby Berkley, romantic films (Clark Gable's and Claudette Colbert's *It Happened One Night,* for example), the raft of gangster pictures, and the huge popularity of radio comedy, has perhaps been exaggerated, it is clear that the trend toward a standardized popular culture, which had accelerated during the 1920s, continued and intensified during

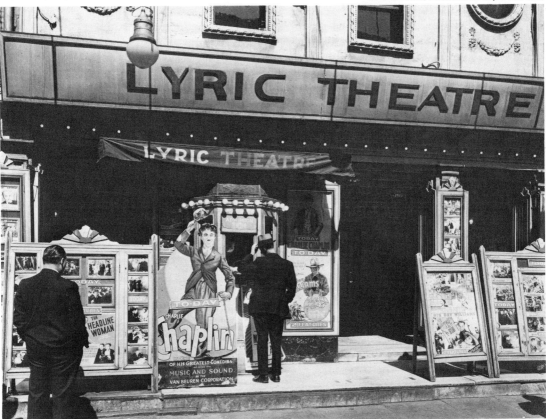

Lyric movie theatre on New York's Third Avenue

the depression. Their motives may have differed greatly, but it is significant that the Gales, Traces, Bassanos, Hunts, Markoviches, and O'Reillys were doing, seeing, reading, and hearing the same things almost every day of every week of the year. Social changes no one really understood flowed from the communications revolution, a technological breakthrough that compressed time and space, and knocked down economic barriers.

At the time of the 1929 crash, only slightly more than a third of the American people lived in homes in which the family budget could absorb the $100 average cost of a radio. By 1935, the radio industry had developed new production techniques, and General Electric was advertising sets "from $19.95." Five years later, 86 percent of the population resided in homes containing radios. Equally significant, the creation of national syndicates among broadcast stations brought a high proportion of the same programs, music, and commercial messages into 28 million homes.

The crash had caught the motion-picture industry in a state of transition, vulnerable to economic disaster. The "talkies," which first appeared in 1928, required total re-equipment and the development of new technique—and new stars. Once the novelty wore off (the first sound films were only filmed stage plays), audiences showed only moderate enthusiasm for talking pictures. Nearly a third of the nation's movie houses had closed down by Franklin Roosevelt's inauguration day. By the mid-1930s, however, mobile cameras, microphones, and other new inventions for fully integrating sound with action brought the movies bounding back. For 25 cents (10 cents for children), Americans could buy the latest celluloid dream, and by the end of the decade they bought about one each week. Families such as the Gishmans and the Bassanos went twice weekly. Not only did the fantasies on the screen offer relief from the hard times, but also lucky ticket holders could win dishes, glasses, towels, and pots. The distribution companies adopted a profit-generating plan of block booking whereby movie houses had to take features in groups of 50 (each group contained only a few first-rate attractions). The system frustrated both local exhibitors and guardians of taste (though the motion picture industry did impose self-censorship as partial compensation). Thus, more Americans than ever were going to the movies, and they were everywhere seeing the same films.

The reading material offered during the depression came, as well, from fewer sources. Newspapers consolidated. The weaker national magazines went bankrupt, and those that survived owed much of their success to the expanded space devoted to advertising, pictures, sports news, and "women's features." The *Saturday Evening Post* and *Collier's,* the leading mass-readership magazines, shared newsstand and coffee table space with the decade's two phenomenal successes, *Reader's Digest* and *Life.* The *Digest,* which consisted largely of articles reprinted from other magazines, manifested a philosophy described as "a tidy compound of two ageless aphorisms: 'Money isn't everything' and

'What does it matter as long as you've got your health.'" *Life,* which first appeared in 1936, rapidly became the most successful weekly magazine in publishing history. It offered news and education through pictures, and it related to the widespread desire to "see things as they are," to get at the "real America."

It was, and is, difficult to assess the effects of increased exposure to the media upon attitudes and behavior. According to contemporary studies, radio had become "a modern substitute for the hearthside," and in order to retain that honored place, radio programmers scrupulously avoided issues that might challenge "those attitudes fundamental in the great American home." Radio does appear to have exerted a strongly conservative influence.

The movies played a different role, perhaps because movies were enjoyed outside the home, thus providing a means of escape from familial restraints. Whatever the moralistic concerns of filmmakers or their commitment to film as art, their survival depended upon the box office. Sex and violence appealed to audiences. Voluptuous Mae West, who contended she served a social need by making sex humorous, found herself in constant trouble with guardians of morality. When screen shootouts between gangsters and "G-men" in which the gangsters won brought threats of federal censorship legislation, the studios arranged for the "good guys" to win. Extravaganzas also were popular. The dream factory that was Hollywood retreated to sumptuous boudoir sets, tuxedoed heroes, and gossamer-gowned heroines descending spiraling staircases onto endless, shimmering stages. The influence of Hollywood stars and radio performers as "role models" (to use contemporary jargon) was seemingly unlimited. Their clothing styles sparked national fads, and their speech mannerisms and preferences in food, music, and secondary sex

The sultry Marlene Dietrich in a February 1933 advertisement. Ads such as this one often promised more than the film delivered, especially after the Legion of Decency campaign to clean up Hollywood began

characteristics were dutifully copied by adolescents everywhere. The line from Rudy Vallee, Russ Columbo and Frank Sinatra to Elvis Presley and Bruce Springsteen was straight and true. One producer said the movie-going public had the mentality of a 12-year-old child, insisting as it did on "life as it ain't." The Roman Catholic hierarchy worried so much about Hollywood that, in 1934, it began to review films and to forbid the faithful, "on pain of sin," to see the movies it deemed unacceptable. Whether the movies undermined the teachings of the home, schools, and church worried most parents, but they and their children continued to line

up for Friday night double features and Saturday matinees.

Occasionally, someone agonized that the media were distorting basic values and that they were "commercializing" America by making people worry about bad breath or pressuring them to buy the latest kitchen gadget. Certainly their ability to impress and persuade was considerable. Not until 40 years later, with the revival of the feminist movement, were other effects of advertising's power acknowledged. For example, a November 1936 ad for a popular soap carried the message that little boys who become frightened and run are sissies, little girls can-

Newsstand, 32nd Street and 3rd Avenue, New York City, 1935

not run as fast as little boys, good little girls know about washing clothes, women are humiliated who fail to meet consumer standards, and superior knowledge of women's work brings little girls rewards. Charlotte Bassano and Anna Trace might have thought it silly to become so upset about a gray sheet or to give a little girl roller skates for telling about Fels-Naptha, but the advertisement conveyed powerful attitudes about the way things were and ought to be.

The new and old forms of communication were invited and intruded themselves into the lives of this depression generation as never before. They explicated high and low culture, incredible banalities, the vibrant power of the nation's diversity, and crass commercialism—often all at the same time. The depression also stimulated a revival of "traditional" leisure activities—picnics, church suppers, hayrides, card parties, and dances—and for all our families the most common entertainment, visiting kin. It may be that the depression produced a marked increase in "neighborliness," a closer rapport within families and between people enduring similar privations. Sentiments such as "We're all in the same boat" and "We don't have much, but you're welcome to share what we have" *were* often heard in bingo parlors, union halls, synagogues, and crossroads gas stations. Looking back, the families who remained together recall the spirit of community, the warm friendships, the openness and trust that prevailed. Ironically, if they did exist, those values were to be victims of the return of good times. It was the organized, externalized forms of leisure and communication that defined the future.

THE WORLD INTRUDES

One evening in November 1938, Robbie Bassano's occasional baby-sitter brought his two-year-old charge home from an afternoon in the park. Five minutes later, Charlotte Bassano ordered Robbie's friend and protector out of the apartment. In attempting to explain a fight on the block, the neighbor boy had called his antagonist of the moment "a damned Jew bastard." Charlotte had been shocked, for the neighborhood always had been ethnically mixed and, if like tended to seek like, there was also a practical toleration of other, different peoples. She later learned that the neighborhood kids had become resentful of a recent influx of "foreign" Jews into the Inwood school district. These newly arrived Jewish children threatened the neighborhood order. They worked too hard in school, talked and acted differently, were too clanish. Their fathers worked as subway conductors and shoe salesmen, but many previously had been doctors, scientists, and teachers, and they put on airs.

Bob and Charlotte Bassano understood that these newcomers had been forced to flee Nazi Germany. They, themselves, were worried about the safety of Andrew Bassano, who had recently retired to the family land in northern Italy. They often had seen film clips of the Nazi leader, Adolf Hitler, at the movies, in "The News of the World," and had listened to kids booing and heiling as Hitler spoke. Nothing in Europe seemed certain. Thus, international problems touched the Bassano household in a direct, important way. The same was true of the Markoviches who agonized over newspaper stories about events in Yugoslavia and fearfully awaited the next letter from their relatives; the Millers, who had relatives but also a personal and psychological stake, as Jews, in the holocaust that was about to engulf European Jewry; and the Butlers, who had many friends and business ties in France and Great Britain and a great understanding of and interest in the issues.

For the rest, however, the problems of Europe and Asia might as well have been taking place on the moon. The American public was apathetic toward world problems in the years after 1920. Most Americans in the 1920s and 1930s had returned to an independent, quasi-isolationist stance. A majority had come to believe that U.S. entry into the Great War had been engineered by bankers and munitions manufacturers, a view confirmed by congressional investigations such as that of the Nye Munitions Committee (1934). Besides, the greatest threat to domestic security in the 1930s was the depression, not rearmament in Europe. In February 1937, 95 percent of a Gallup poll sample stated that the United States should stay out of any future general war.

Thus Americans watched indifferently while Europe and the world slid toward the abyss. Peace in Europe and the Far East deteriorated steadily through the 1930s. In 1931, Japan pushed into north China and set up the puppet state of Manchukuo. Through the 1930s, Japan's military command, "wild, runaway, half-insane men" Secretary of State Cordell Hull termed them, gained in prestige and power. Japanese spokesmen argued that Japan deserved recognition of its status as a great power. During the late 19th century, the Western nations had acquired the colonies and spheres of influence that were the hallmarks of that status. Now they denied Japan's right to these accoutrements. One exasperated Japanese diplomat charged that the Western powers had taught Japan the game of international poker, but when Japan began to demonstrate considerable skill, they "pronounced the game immoral, and took up contract bridge." American newspaper readers, if they made it to the editorial pages, learned to scoff at the divinity of the Japanese Emperor, to respect the nation's military prowess, and to think of "sneakiness" as a national trait.

In 1933, Adolf Hitler took office in Germany. A man with illusions of grandeur and psychological abnormalities, he preached that Germany had been "stabbed in the back" by politicians at the end of the Great War and that Germany must regain her place in the sun. Two years later, Italian dictator Benito Mussolini launched a campaign to create a second Roman Empire. Ethiopia, the first victim, brought the case of Italian aggression before the League of Nations. League members dithered over whether to impose total economic sanctions upon Italy—and decided against it. The United States responded by passing a neutrality law. The United States would not export munitions to belligerents, and forsaking one of the principles so sacred to Woodrow Wilson, Americans traveling on ships of belligerent registry would do so at their own risk.

In 1936, the Spanish Civil War erupted. The right-wing Falangists enlisted aid from Italy and Germany, and the left received support from the Soviet Union. The United States responded by passing another neutrality law, adding a proviso that Americans could not make loans to belligerent nations. In 1937, Hitler "annulled" obligations imposed on Germany by the victors of the First World War and explicitly repudiated the "war-guilt clause" of the Versailles Treaty. Soon thereafter, he sent German troops into the Rhineland and claimed territory the treaty had specified would be demilitarized. The European powers dithered. The United States passed another neutrality act, this one reaffirming the provisions of the previous acts but, as an added safeguard, imposing the "cash and carry" principle. As Bernard Baruch succinctly explained: "We will sell to any belligerent anything except lethal weapons, but the terms are 'cash on the barrelhead and come and get it.'" An editorial in the *Midland Weekly News* proclaimed "The Second World War seems to be 'just around the corner.'" Too bad for silly Europe.

In 1937, also, Japan and China stumbled

While the world stumbled toward war, Americans such as the Reinhardts and Traces contended with problems closer to home, such as the disastrous Ohio River flood of 1937. The half-submerged house in this photo was the home of a neighbor of the Reinhardts and the future brother-in-law of Bill Trace

into a full-scale war. In December, three Standard-Vacuum Oil Company tankers and the U.S. gunboat *Panay,* steaming slowly up the Yangtze River 27 miles north of Nanking, were bombed by pilots of the Japanese Air Force. Four British vessels were also hit. Three men died, the *Panay* sank, and two of the tankers burned. The Japanese government apologized for the "accident" and paid $2,214,007 indemnities, over half of which went to Standard Oil.

In 1938, Hitler levied a 1 billion mark fine against German Jews when a Jew assassinated a minor diplomat. Jews were barred from practicing law, from retail trade, from high schools and universities, and Jewish property was to be "transferred to German hands." Synagogues and Jewish property were put to the torch. Franklin Roosevelt admitted: "I myself could scarcely believe that such things could occur in the 20th century." He recalled the American ambassador from Berlin for consultation.

Earlier in the year, Hitler had forced the union of Austria with Germany. "Watch out for Czechoslovakia," Mike Simich read in the *Weekly News.* Sure enough, at a meeting with Europe's leaders in Munich, Hitler won back the part of Czechoslovakia that had been

German before World War I. Japan now controlled more than half of Chinese territory and over 200 million Chinese. The Japanese government told the Western powers that the "open door" in China could no longer be maintained because of the chaotic conditions there. The Tokyo government informed the Japanese people that thenceforth metals, fuel, and fibers would be rationed; it ordered the use of rat skins in the manufacturing of leather and decreed a shorter match to save wood.

In 1939, Hitler absorbed the rest of Czechoslovakia. He demanded that Poland return former German territory. On being refused, he formed a nonaggression pact with the Soviet Union, and then, on September 1, at 3:00 A.M., a phone call from Ambassador William Bullitt in Paris roused Franklin Roosevelt from sleep: "Mr. President, several German divisions are deep in Polish territory. . . . There are reports of bombers over the city of Warsaw." "Well, Bill," came the response, "it has come at last. God help us all." Within the week, all Europe was at war.

The U.S. response to the tragic events in Europe and the Far East before 1939 may, in hindsight, seem blind to have missed early opportunities to head off the war. FDR did not possess sufficiently strong convictions, neither did his constituents have a sufficiently developed and unified attitude toward foreign affairs to make the response any different. The president attempted to ignore foreign affairs until about 1937. He concentrated on domestic problems where a consensus did exist, where individuals and groups across the spectrum of American politics were begging him to act boldly. When he entered the White House, the touchstone of his beliefs was that the nation must take an active role in world affairs. But this did not prevent him from avoiding international cooperation as an answer to the depression or from acquiescing in the passage of neutrality legislation. Basically, he was inclined to become active in world affairs, but only when he sensed the people would support him. As a result, the United States swung to and fro between full participation in and boycott of the world community.

The Department of State, responsible for the nation's day-to-day confrontations with the outside world, imposed little of its collective advice or will upon FDR. The department did play a crucial part in extending recognition to the Soviet Union and in furthering the Good Neighbor Policy with Latin America. Mostly, though, FDR, who thoroughly distrusted the "striped pants boys" in the Department of State, bypassed the department on important matters. In 1937, he got around Secretary of State Cordell Hull by appointing Sumner Welles, a fellow Grotonian and Harvard man who had been a page boy at FDR's wedding, as Under Secretary of State. By the end of the decade, the department was a bureaucratic snarl, operating in an atmosphere of Byzantine intrigue, and Hull went so far as to threaten resignation "because the president very obviously seeks Sumner Welles' advice in preference to his own." Mutual lack of respect and communication between the White House and the ornate State Department offices next door deprived FDR of knowledge and advice and inhibited his ability to exercise strong leadership when he chose to do so.

In October 1937, Roosevelt suddenly sounded the alarm over the ominous situation in Europe and Asia. Using the medical metaphor, Roosevelt suggested that: "When an epidemic of physical disease starts to spread, the community approves and joins in a quarantine of the patients in order to protect the health of the community against the spread of the disease." So it was with nations. Immediately, the press clamored to know just how the disease (aggression) should be quarantined—through collective action with other nations? Asked bluntly what he meant by the passage, FDR told a reporter: "I can't

give you a clue to it. You will have to invent one." Reaction to this "trial balloon" showed Roosevelt that the public had no intention of closing ranks behind him for the purpose of "quarantining" anyone. The Gallup polls of public opinion had shown, in 1935, that 75 percent of the American people believed that Congress should get the approval of the electorate in a national vote before declaring war. A subsequent poll, in early 1937, showed that 70 percent believed it had been a mistake to enter the First World War. For the next two years, Roosevelt sent messages of encouragement, cajolery, and warning to the heads of powerful nations, many of whom recognized him as the leader of world opinion. He moved battleships and approved decisions that ultimately gave the United States unimaginable military power. Still, American public opinion did not jell on what the nation would and should do as Europe plunged headlong toward war and Japan marched deeper into China. Under these circumstances, Roosevelt was reluctant to take decisive action.

In May 1939, Roosevelt concluded that the arms embargo imposed by the neutrality laws benefitted Germany, Italy, and Japan. He called congressional leaders to the White House to ask them to repeal it. Almost immediately, Secretary Hull fell into an argument with Idaho's isolationist senator, William Borah. Dispatches from all over Europe showed that war was imminent, said Hull, and removing the arms embargo would aid Britain, France, and other friendly nations sure to be involved. "I don't give a damn about your dispatches," Borah roared, and steadfastly refused to concede the approach of war or the need to remove the embargo. As tears welled up in Hull's eyes, crusty Vice President John Nance Garner turned to Roosevelt: "Well, Captain, we may as well face the facts. You haven't got the votes, and that's all there is to it." That *was* all there was to it for the time being. Roosevelt could not override the opposition. He had to wait for events to create new pressures.

After the German Panzer divisions moved toward Warsaw scattering the Polish army, circumstances and American public opinion changed rapidly. Six months before the German invasion, Americans divided about evenly on the question of selling airplanes and other war materials to Britain and France in the event of war. When war broke out, the public overwhelmingly supported the cash sale of munitions and the 1939 version of the neutrality law allowed it.

Once Poland capitulated, the fighting died down. No one attacked during the dark winter; it was almost as if the warring nations slept, gaining strength for a hard day's work. In the dawn of spring, Germany struck with such suddenness and force that a new word, *blitzkreig* (lightning war), entered the world's languages. In April 1940, German military forces held victory parades in Copenhagen and Oslo. Just days later, they goose stepped past the seats of government in the Hague, Brussels, and Luxembourg. On June 22, German officials heaped humiliation upon defeat by requiring French leaders to sign an instrument of surrender in the same railroad car in which the Germans had signed the armistice of November 11, 1918. Just before the signing, some 300,000 British soldiers, driven to the very water's edge, had miraculously escaped annihilation. Thousands of boats, from yachts to dinghies, put out from England for the Dunkirk beaches; they took away the boys, leaving their equipment and the field to the Germans. The stunned British prepared to defend their island against what some observers expected to be the first foreign invasions since that of William the Conqueror in 1066.

In August commenced The Battle of Britain. Night after night, warning sirens howled the signal to take cover, and searchlights pierced the darkness in the direction of the droning bomber motors. Night after night, the survivors fought the bomb-ignited fires and combed the rubble for the dead. Few doubted that, after more terrorizing and softening, Germany would invade. England's doughty resistance and the skillful way in which press, radio, and movies presented the saga went far to explain the changing public opinion toward the war. Rossalyn Butler determined to show her compassion by giving a dollar to every British soldier she met on the streets of New York. Occasionally, she encountered so many as to leave her temporarily penniless. She would then offer some flabbergasted sailor the services of her beautiful daughter, Judy, to take him around the city for the evening. Few went so far as "Rossy" Butler, but most Americans responded to the British plight with deep sympathy.

Tough talk from the Japanese proved embarrassing to Seito and Tamako Kurihara and their daughter Elaine. Hollywood films were already portraying the Japanese as a devious and cruel people and the term "Nip" was occasionally flung at Elaine and her school friends. That Elaine and her family considered themselves Americans became less relevant as the Japanese talked boldly of the Greater East Asian Co-prosperity Sphere under the hegemony of Japan. The Kuriharas expected only the worst when, in September 1940, Japan signed an alliance with Germany and Italy (the Tripartite Pact).

The question was: Did United States security demand participation in the war? Orators of the "Committee to Defend America by Aiding the Allies" shouted equally positive orators of "America First" to a standoff. Advocates of preparedness demanded that the nation strengthen its military services. Arguing that there was no reason to have armed force unless you intended to use it, opponents tried to stop congressional passage of the first peacetime draft law in American history. They failed, and on October 16, 1940, Mike

Simich, Austin Hart, Bob Bassano, Louis Gropper, John Butler, Jr., and another 16 million men between the ages of 21 and 36 dutifully registered themselves with local draft boards. On October 29, the president looked on as Secretary of War Henry L. Stimson drew the number of the first draftee. In the face of the breakdown of international law and order, officials explained, the United States required an expanded army as a precautionary measure and deterrent. Some 75 percent of the people told pollsters that America should help the British; yet 85 percent indicated a desire to avoid war at all costs.

How to assist the beleaguered British and still remain technically neutral? Roosevelt knew that, under international law, private agents in a neutral country (such as the Unit-

ed States) could sell munitions to a belligerent government (such as that of Great Britain); the government of a neutral country could not. The immediate solution was for the U.S. Army to sell some of its armaments to private agents for resale to the British. The kind and volume of aid that Britain really needed for the future, however, could not be so deftly handled. In September 1940, FDR broke the neutral's code. With a German invasion expected at any time, Great Britain faced the problem of fending it off in the English Channel and convoying supply ships from the United States, all with about 100 destroyers. At the moment, the United States inventoried 240 destroyers with 57 more under construction. Roosevelt determined to make a trade: 50 destroyers of World War I vintage in exchange for leases to set up military bases in

Blindfolded Secretary of War Henry L. Stimson prepares to draw the first number in the U.S. draft lottery on October 29, 1940, as FDR watches

British-controlled Newfoundland, Bermuda, the Bahamas, Jamaica, St. Lucia, Antigua, Trinidad, and British Guiana. An Executive Agreement consummated the deal, and the ships, "more precious than rubies" in the eyes of Prime Minister Winston Churchill, steamed eastward in the service of Britannia.

During these crisis months, FDR decided to run for a third term as president. Many objected to this break with tradition, but most people accepted the argument that in such tense and uncertain times a change of leaders might lead to some fatal mistake. The Republican candidate, Wendell L. Wilkie, agreed with the idea of aid to Britain. His quarrel was with Roosevelt's failure to clear the transfer of the destroyers with Congress. That high-handed act was "the most dictatorial action ever taken by any president," he charged during the campaign. Roosevelt had found a new consensus—aid without troop commitment. People remembered the innovative way he had handled the early "war" on the depression without destroying the essence of democratic capitalism. Once more he won reelection handily.

Soon after the election, the clerk of the House assigned a number to a Roosevelt-inspired aid bill—H.R. 1776, "a veritable declaration of interdependence" the president's supporters termed it. This law empowered the president to "lend, lease, or otherwise dispose of" war materials to nations whose defense was vital to the security of the United States. Britain was running out of money, and Roosevelt wanted to avoid the "nonsense" of traditional financing. As he explained it: "Suppose my neighbor's house catches fire, and I have a length of garden hose. . . . If he can take my garden hose and connect it up with his hydrant, I may help him put out the fire. Now what do I do? I don't say to him before that operation, 'Neighbor, my garden hose cost me $15; you have to pay me $15 for it.' No! . . . I don't want $15—I want

my garden hose after the fire is over." Others saw "lend-lease" differently. Senator Robert Taft, the conservative Republican of Ohio, rejected Roosevelt's parable of the garden hose: "Lending war equipment is a good deal like lending chewing gum. You don't want it back." And "the rottenest thing that has been said in my public life" according to Roosevelt, was Senator Burton K. Wheeler's comparison of lend-lease with the AAA crop destruction of 1933: "it will plow under every fourth American boy." After three months, lend-lease passed Congress. America would become the arsenal of democracy. Everywhere people were wondering about the future. How would the foreign wars affect their lives? Austin Hart received an answer in February 1941, when the mailman brought what became the most famous form letter of his generation:

> Greetings:
> Your friends and neighbors have selected you to represent them in the Armed Forces of the United States. . . .

Austin reaffirmed his love for Martha Gale, and they decided to get married as soon as he could get leave after finishing "boot camp." On May 13, he reported to the induction station in Topeka.

SUGGESTIONS FOR FURTHER READING

Of great help in the writing of this chapter were Charles C. Alexander, *Nationalism in American Thought, 1930–1945* (1969); Barton J. Bernstein, ed., *Towards a New Past* (1968); Carolyn Bird, *The Invisible Scar* (1966); James M. Burns, *Roosevelt: The Lion and the Fox* (1963) and *Roosevelt: The Soldier of Freedom* (1970); Edward R. Ellis, *A Nation in Torment* (1972); Federal Writers' Project, *These Are Our Lives* (1939); William Leuchtenburg, *Franklin D. Roosevelt and the New Deal* (1963); Studs Terkel, *Hard Times: An Oral History of the Great Depression* (1970); and

Raymond Wolters, *Negroes and the Great Depression* (1970).

Biographies and memoirs are very important to an understanding of the New Deal. In addition to James M. Burns on FDR, see Frank Freidel's monumental, unfinished biography, *Franklin D. Roosevelt* (5 vols., 1952, 1954, 1956, 1973, 1978); Arthur M. Schlesinger, Jr., *The Age of Roosevelt* (3 vols., 1957, 1959, 1960); Tamara K. Hareven, *Eleanor Roosevelt: An American Conscience* (1968); Joseph P. Lash, *Eleanor and Franklin: The Story of Their Relationship* (1971); Rexford G. Tugwell, *In Search of Roosevelt* (1972); Charles F. Searle, *Minister of Relief: Harry Hopkins* (1963); Henry Adams, *Harry Hopkins* (1978); Robert Sherwood's classic account, *Roosevelt and Hopkins* (1950); George Martin, *Madam Secretary: Frances Perkins* (1976); John M. Blum, *From the Morgenthau Diaries* (3 vols., 1959–1967); Paul H. Douglas, *In the Fullness of Time* (1972); James A. Farley, *Jim Farley's Story* (1948); Joseph J. Huthmacher, *Senator Robert F. Wagner and the Rise of Urban Liberalism* (1968); Hugh S. Johnson, *The Blue Eagle From Egg to Earth* (1935); Matthew Josephson, *Sidney Hillman: Statesman of Labor* (1952); Arthur Krock, *Memoirs: Sixty Years on the Firing Line* (1968); Eleanor Roosevelt, *This I Remember* (1949); Samuel I. Rosenman, *Working with Roosevelt* (1952); Russell Lord, *The Wallaces of Iowa* (1947); Grace Tully, *F.D.R.: My Boss* (1949); Harold L. Ickes, *The Secret Diary of Harold L. Ickes* (3 vols., 1953–54); Donald R. McCoy, *Alf Landon* (1967); Charles J. Tull, *Father Coughlin and the New Deal* (1965); and T. Harry Williams, *Huey Long* (1969).

Studies of New Deal programs include Elliott Rosen, *Hoover, Roosevelt, and the Brains Trust* (1977); Rexford G. Tugwell, *The Brains Trust* (1968); Susan E. Kennedy, *The Banking Crisis of 1933* (1973); Thomas K. McGraw, *TVA and the Power Fight* (1971); Roy Lubove, *The Struggle for Social Security* (1968); Leonard Baker, *Back to Back: The Duel Between FDR and the Supreme Court* (1967); Ellis Hawley, *The New Deal and the Problem of Monopoly* (1966); Jane DeHart Matthews, *The Federal Theater* (1967); Richard D. McKinzie, *The New Deal for Artists* (1972); James T. Patterson, *The New Deal and the States: Federalism in Transition* (1969); and Richard

Polenberg, *Reorganizing Roosevelt's Government: The Controversy Over Executive Reorganization, 1936-1939* (1966). Reactions and responses to the New Deal are in Otis L. Graham, *Encore for Reform: The Old Progressives and the New Deal* (1967) and his *Toward a Planned Society* (1976); James T. Patterson, *Congressional Conservatism and the New Deal: The Growth of the Conservative Coalition in Congress, 1933-1939* (1967); Bruce M. Stave, *The New Deal and the Last Hurrah: Pittsburgh Machine Politics* (1970); David E. Conrad, *Forgotten Farmers: Sharecroppers in the New Deal* (1965); John L. Shover, *Cornbelt Rebellion: The Farmers Holiday Association* (1965); Van L. Perkins, *Crisis in Agriculture* (1969); Abraham Holtzman, *The Townsend Movement* (1963); George Wolfskill, *The Revolt of the Conservatives* (1974); Donald R. McCoy, *Angry Voices* (1959); Irving Bernstein, *Turbulent Years: A History of the American Worker* (1970); David H. Bennett, *Demogogues in the Depression* (1969); and Richard H. Pells, *Radical Visions and American Dreams: Culture and Social Thought in the Depression Years* (1973).

For United States diplomacy during the interwar period, a good place to begin is Arnold L. Offner, *The Causes of the Second World War* (1973). Also useful, though rather dated, are Selig Adler, *The Uncertain Giant* (1965); E. H. Carr, *The Twenty Years Crisis* (1946); and such special works as Joan Hoff Wilson, *American Business and Foreign Policy, 1920-1933* (1971); Dorothy Borg, *American Policy and the Chinese Revolution, 1925-28* (1968) and *The United States and the Far Eastern Crisis of 1935-1938* (1964); Russell D. Buhite, *Nelson T. Johnson and American Policy Toward China, 1925-1941* (1969); two fine books by Akira Iriye, *After Imperialism: The Search for a New Order in the Far East, 1921-1931* (1965) and *Across the Pacific: An Inner History of American-East Asian Relations* (1969); John DeNovo, *American Interests and Policies in the Middle East, 1900-1939* (1963); Herbert Feis, *The Diplomacy of the Dollar* (1950); Robert H. Ferrell, *American Diplomacy in the Great Depression* (1957); Robert F. Smith, *The United States and Cuba: Business and Diplomacy* (1960); Michael Hogan, *Informal Entente: Anglo-American Economy Diplomacy, 1918-1928* (1979); Harold and Margaret Sprout,

Toward a New Order of Sea Power (1940); John C. Vinson, *The Parchment Peace: The United States and the Washington Conference, 1921–22* (1955); Thomas Buckley, *The United States and the Washington Conference* (1970); and Bryce Wood, *The Making of the Good Neighbor Policy* (1961).

Investigation of New Deal diplomacy now begins with Robert Dallek's weighty *Franklin D. Roosevelt and American Foreign Policy, 1932–1945* (1979). Also helpful are James M. Burns, *Roosevelt: The Lion and the Fox* (1963); Lloyd C. Gardner, *Economic Aspects of New Deal Diplomacy* (1964); and Charles A. Beard's wrongheaded attack on FDR, *American Foreign Policy in the Making, 1932–1940* (1946). See also Beatrice B. Berle and Travis Jacobs, eds., *Navigating the Rapids* (1973)—excerpts from Adolph A. Berle's papers; Orville H. Bullit, ed., *For the President—Personal and Secret: Correspondence Between Franklin D. Roosevelt and William C. Bullitt* (1972); Hadley Cantril, ed., *Public Opinion, 1935–1946* (1951); Peter G. Filene, *Americans and the Soviet Experiment* (1967); Irwin Gellman, *Roosevelt and Batista: Good Neighbor Diplomacy in Cuba, 1933–1945* (1973); Waldo H. Heinrichs, *American Ambassador: Joseph C. Grew and the Development of the United States Diplomatic Tradition* (1966); Hugh DeSantis, *The Diplomacy of Silence: The American Foreign Service, the Soviet Union and the Cold War, 1933–1947* (1981); Richard Steward, *Trade and Hemisphere: The Good Neighbor Policy and Reciprocal Trade* (1975); Richard N. Kottman, *The North Atlantic Triangle* (1969); Martin Weil, *A Pretty Good Club: The Founding Fathers of the U.S. Foreign Service* (1978); and John E. Wiltz, *In Search of Peace: The Senate Munitions Inquiry, 1934–1936* (1963).

A few of the multitude of historical studies on the drift of America toward war are Dorothy Borg and Shumpei Okamoto, eds., *Pearl Harbor as History: Japanese-American Relations, 1931–1941* (1973); Robert J. C. Butow, *Tojo and the Coming of the War* (1961); Wayne S. Cole, *America First: The Battle Against Intervention* (1953); Raymond H. Dawson, *The Decision to Aid Russia, 1941: Foreign Policy and Domestic Politics* (1959); John P. Diggins, *Mussolini and Fascism: The View from America* (1972); Herbert Feis, *The Road to Pearl Harbor* (1964); Alton Frye, *Nazi Germany and the Western Hemisphere, 1933–1941* (1967); Geoffrey Smith, *The German-American Bund* (1977); John M. Haight, *American Aid to France, 1938–1940* (1970); Manfred Jonas, *Isolationism in America, 1935–1941* (1966); Warren F. Kimball, *The Most Unsordid Act: Lend Lease, 1939–1941* (1969); Michael Leigh, *Mobilizing Consent: Public Opinion and American Foreign Policy* (1976); Joseph Lash, *Roosevelt and Churchill, Their Wartime Friendship, 1939–1941* (1979); Francis D. Loewenheim et al., eds., *Roosevelt and Churchill: Their Secret Wartime Correspondence* (1975); Arnold A. Offner, *American Appeasement: United States Foreign Policy and Germany, 1933–1938* (1969); Stephen Pelz, *Race to Pearl Harbor: The Failure of the Second London Naval Conference and the Onset of World War II* (1974); Forrest C. Pogue, *George C. Marshall: Ordeal and Hope, 1939–1942* (1968); Basil Rauch, *Roosevelt: From Munich to Pearl Harbor* (1950); Bruce M. Russett, *No Clear and Present Danger: A Skeptical View of the U.S. Entry into World War II* (1972); Paul W. Schroeder, *The Axis Alliance and Japanese-American Relations* (1958); Richard P. Traina, *American Diplomacy and the Spanish Civil War* (1968); Theodore A. Wilson, *The First Summit: Roosevelt and Churchill at Placentia Bay, 1941* (1969); Robert Wohlstetter, *Pearl Harbor: Warning and Decision* (1962); David S. Wyman, *Paper Walls: America and the Refugee Crisis, 1938–1941* (1968); and James Leutze, *Negotiating for Supremacy* (1979).

8 | Communities, 1920–1940

RURAL COMMUNITIES

For the eldest sons of Ben Trace, living in Howell was much like living in the country. While the yards of the Louisville & Nashville were just a block from their home and smoke from Evansville's factories was visible, Ben Jr. and Jerry helped with the garden and plucked the roasting hens whose necks their mother wrung every Friday. Their father slaughtered a hog each year. Not far to the west of the house was a swampy area that filled each spring during the rainy season and in which the boys could swim or catch carp and catfish by muddying the water and clubbing the fish as they surfaced. The boys also visited their kinfolk in Tennessee. During the summers, Jerry helped with the farm, explored nearby caves that had once housed Indians, went fishing and swimming, and considered himself in paradise, though Grandpa Bonham, who

was not making a nickel on his tobacco, had another place in mind.

Most farmers would have agreed with Grandpa Bonham. While Jerry's boyhood impressions did not push him into farming, economic adversity pushed hundreds of thousands of farmers off the land. Those most likely to move had less education, were younger, and left smaller farms than those who remained. Females migrated at an earlier age, in larger proportions than males, and were more likely than males to move directly to a city rather than to a village or small town. Tenant farmers moved more frequently than owners, and in the South black tenants more frequently than white. In addition, the weakened economic position of the farm sector placed great strains on the communities that serviced the farmers who remained.

Advocates of life in the open country and small community have long engaged in a vitriolic dispute with urbanites. Urban spokesmen traced many forms of bigotry to the countryside. Country folk pointed to urban permissiveness and sheer size as root causes of immorality. Rural apologists viewed the inhabitants of concrete wastelands as crushed by alienation while pointing to the tranquility and self-fulfillment possible in rural communities. But it was only necessary to read a few stories in Hamlin Garland's *Main Travelled Roads* or some poems from Edgar Lee Master's *Spoon River Anthology* to dispel such myths.

The outside world has been a consistent factor in the life of the countryside, but at no time prior to the interwar years did the complexities of modern life send such shock waves through rural America. During the interwar years, accelerating change on the national and world scene exerted intense pressures on farm families and communities. All were shaken by the experience; 20 years of depression sapped the strength of many. The Hunt family's rural black neighborhood, Shady Grove, on the eastern edge of Kosse, Texas, was destroyed as mechanization, New Deal crop reductions, and foreclosures reduced the number of black farm operators by 65 percent between 1920 and 1940. The Hunts moved to town; their friends became migrants. Roper and New Albany, the villages in which the Harts and Gales lived, lost their small businesses as population declined and competition from larger towns took its toll. In other neighborhoods and small communities, school consolidation, the closing of country stores, the mobility of farmers, especially tenants, the erosion of ethnic allegiances among the second or third generation, and new roads and autos brought on collapse.

As a general rule, the large centers grew rapidly. Hamlets and villages within metropolitan areas increased their populations by over 50 percent between 1920 and 1940, while those outside such districts grew by 3

percent. Shady Grove disappeared. Fredonia and Neodesha, a sister town in the Neosho River Valley, distant from a major population center, both lost population during the period. Still, places with populations of under 2,500 survived these years of crisis and their populations rose slowly.

Fredonia, heavily dependent upon area farms, compensated for the decline in farm income by obtaining a greater share of what was spent. This was accomplished by offering new services—larger retail stores, automobile sales and service, a new poultry processing plant—and by capturing business that farmers had conducted elsewhere. Both Charles Gale and James Hart earned part of their living by buying and selling grain and, into the early 1930s, sold or stored their grain at elevators on the Missouri Pacific tracks in New Albany and Roper. These elevators—and many others throughout the Midwest—went out of business in the early 1930s, and the grain was taken to Fredonia. Both men financed their speculative ventures in grain, livestock, and land by simply telephoning a Fredonia bank, which then transferred the needed funds to their accounts. James Hunt received advances on his cotton at the gin mill in Kosse. Such credits were unavailable, however, to the 56 percent of Limestone County farmers who were sharecroppers.

Fredonia and other small towns also assumed social, religious, and educational functions that once had been the foundation of surrounding rural neighborhoods and villages. As the number of clubs, lodges, and churches declined in New Albany and other villages, the membership in Fredonia's organizations rose. Saturday nights in Fredonia were so wild, even during the depression, attracting shoppers, moviegoers, and Austin Hart, who felt "uncomfortable in the city," that town residents complained to the police chief about their driveways being blocked by trucks, cars, tractors, and wagons. Local merchants, however, counseled the police against stringent enforcement of parking regulations. School consolidations closed down thousands of country and village schools, adding a new dimension to town-country relations.

The maze of governments, especially in rural areas, contributed to the problem of providing adequate services during a period of depression. A majority of the 183,000 political units, including 123,000 school districts, existing in the United States in 1934 were rural. New responsibilities, overlapping jurisdictions and duplication of effort, the increasing costs of service, and, in many places, a declining and aging population sapped the ability of individual units to perform effectively. Basic tasks such as road construction and maintenance, providing good schools, pure water, sufficient hospital beds, and support to the needy became too complex and too expensive for many local governments to manage.

In New Albany, as elsewhere, property taxation was the traditional source of revenue supporting these operations. Farmers owned the most property. As tax rates rose, the added burden fell with disproportionate severity on farmers at just the time that farm income declined. Farmers leaving New Albany necessitated increasing taxes for those remaining. New Albany and other townships relinquished functions such as road building and repair to counties. But county revenues were similarly depleted and county autonomy diminished by state and federal action.

Not surprisingly, the onset of the depression and the virtual bankruptcy of numerous local units of government caused a drastic deterioration of educational, health, and welfare services. States came to the aid of localities reluctantly and with inadequate financial support partially because of simple inertia and declining revenues and partially because of laws limiting the amount of public indebtedness and the purposes for which it could be incurred. Only one source of succor remained: the federal government. Swallowing local pride and despite the fear of federal encroachment on local independence, the cry for help went out to Washington.

URBAN COMMUNITIES

Andrew Bassano enjoyed life in New York. His work took him to jobs throughout the city, giving him a mastery of the intricate mass-transport system that he had helped build. Most New Yorkers, he told his children, knew only one route, from home to work and back. Yet when asked for directions by a stranger, they never hesitated even though they might be sending the innocent visitor to Flatbush instead of Van Cortlandt Park. Not all city dwellers in New York or elsewhere were so content; indeed, some hated the congestion, dirt, noise, and vastness. Still, the urban population grew rapidly between 1920 and 1930. The depression slowed the movement to the cities and the pace of the 1920s was not matched after World War II.

The population of the United States grew by 17 million between 1920 and 1930. Of that increase, 14.8 million, or 87 percent, moved to or were born in cities. Fifty-two percent of the total population growth—involving almost 9 million people—occurred in 93 cities with populations of over 100,000. As a result of the immigration-restriction laws passed during the 1920s, most migrants now originated in rural America. Rural Southern blacks comprised a rising proportion of migrants to the cities. By 1940, the Negro population exceeded 10 percent in St. Louis, Philadelphia, Indianapolis, Cincinnati, Columbus, Newark, and Kansas City.

While New York's population increase between 1920 and 1940 exceeded the total population of all but three cities (Table 8–1), the South, Southwest, and Pacific Coast areas developed at an extraordinary pace between the world wars. The most dramatic growth

Library of Congress

The Dallas central business district, c. 1925

Library of Congress

Dallas in 1945—contrasting cultures

occurred in Texas, which experienced an urban explosion after 1920. By 1920, San Antonio, Dallas, Fort Worth, and Houston each exceeded 100,000 inhabitants and their populations doubled during the next 20 years. Houston and Dallas–Fort Worth were among the 25 largest metropolitan districts (see Table 8-2). Almost as striking as the Texas boom was the sudden rise to metropolitan stature of Florida's sunshine cities. Fueled by a raucous land boom during the 1920s

Table 8-1
Rank Order of Cities by Population, 1920–1940

1940 Rank order of cities over 400,000	1940 population (000)	1930 population (000)	1920 population (000)	1920 rank
New York City	7,455	6,930	5,620	1
Chicago	3,397	3,376	2,702	2
Philadelphia	1,931	1,951	1,824	3
Detroit	1,623	1,569	994	4
Los Angeles	1,504	1,238	577	10
Cleveland	878	900	797	5
Baltimore	859	805	734	8
St. Louis	816	822	773	6
Boston	771	781	748	7
Pittsburgh	672	670	588	9
Washington, D.C.	663	487	438	14
San Francisco	635	634	507	12
Milwaukee	587	578	457	13
Buffalo	576	573	507	11
New Orleans	496	459	387	17
Minneapolis	492	464	381	18
Cincinnati	456	451	401	16
Newark	429	442	415	15

Table 8-2
Growth of Central Cities and Metropolitan Districts, 1920–1940

Rank order by size of MD	1940		1930		1920	
	Central cities	Metro. district	Central cities	Metro. district	Central cities	Metro. district
New York City– northeastern N.J.*	8,186	11,691	7,689	10,901	6,333	7,910
Chicago	3,397	4,499	3,376	4,365	2,702	3,179
Los Angeles	1,504	2,905	1,238	2,319	577	879
Philadelphia	1,931	2,899	1,951	2,847	1,824	2,407
Boston	771	2,351	781	2,308	748	1,772
Detroit	1,623	2,296	1,569	2,105	994	1,165
Pittsburgh	672	1,994	670	1,954	588	1,208
San Francisco– Oakland	937	1,429	918	1,290	723	891
St. Louis	816	1,368	822	1,294	773	952
Cleveland	878	1,215	900	1,195	797	926
Baltimore	859	1,047	805	949	734	784
Minneapolis– St. Paul	780	911	736	832	615	629
Washington, D.C.	663	908	487	621	438	507
Buffalo-Niagra	654	858	649	821	507	603
Milwaukee	587	790	578	743	457	537
Cincinnati	456	789	451	759	401	607
Providence	254	712	253	691	238	444
Kansas City, Mo.– Kansas City, Kans.	521	634	522	608	426	477
Scranton– Wilkes Barre	227	630	230	652	212	348
New Orleans	495	540	459	495	387	398
Houston	385	510	292	339	138	168
Hartford–New Britain	235	503	232	471	197	300
Indianapolis	387	455	364	418	314	339
Seattle	368	453	366	421	315	358
Atlanta	302	442	270	371	201	249
Louisville	319	434	308	404	235	318
Albany-Troy– Schnectady†	288	432	296	425	274	274
Rochester	325	412	328	399	296	321
Birmingham	268	408	260	383	179	291
Portland, Ore.	305	406	302	479	258	300

* For each year, the population of the central city includes New York City, Newark, and Jersey City.
† For 1920, the population of the MD is the sum of the population of the three cities.

that included the construction of islands to house the villas of the super rich, Miami, Jacksonville, and Tampa–St. Petersburg grew by 160 percent during the two decades. By 1940, each of those places was central to a metropolitan area of over 200,000 people.

And then there was Los Angeles (see Table 8-2). California's population increased from 3.4 million in 1920 to 6.9 million in 1940. Twenty-seven percent of that growth occurred in Los Angeles and 60 percent in the Los Angeles metropolitan area of 1,540 square miles. Attracted by the climate and the economic opportunities accompanying the development of irrigated farming, oil discoveries, the motion-picture industry, and the expansion of manufacturing, hundreds of thousands of native-born whites abandoned Illinois, Missouri, Iowa, and New York (and, during the depression, the Plains states and Arkansas, Louisiana, and Texas) to seek the good life in Southern California.

During the interwar years, automobiles and buses, local job markets, prevailing wage structures, and other factors altered the character of the population in the central city and along the developing fringes of the city. In the central cities, the proportions of adults, females, foreign-born whites, and Negroes were higher than in fringe sections which held higher proportions of males and native-born whites. There were also wide variations between the cities themselves. The population tended to be younger in cities of more recent growth, such as Oklahoma City or Birmingham, and older in cities that enjoyed the climatic advantages of Tampa or San Diego.

A process of population selection, reflecting income and occupation, operated among cities and between cities and their surrounding areas. Within the urban milieu, it cost more to live in less crowded conditions. John Butler, Robert's eldest brother, purchased space—a 10-room brownstone house on East 80th Street—in the heart of New York. Other rich people could afford space in the posh apartment houses along Park Avenue in New York or Lake Shore Drive in Chicago. But for most, additional living space required a move out of the city. During the 1920s and even in the 1930s, increasing numbers of people with the economic wherewithal chose more open spaces. In 1930, 7.5 percent of Detroit's families—some 2,000 families listed in *Social Secretary* and earlier social registers—lived in the central city compared with 52 percent in 1910. Prosperity in the 1920s was real enough so that many thousands of

Americans and their newly acquired autos were able to imitate the elite of Detroit.

Mobility meant new opportunities for lower income groups. When Gus O'Reilly sold his two-family home in Brighton and moved to Medford, the new owner rented both apartments to working-class Irish families. An unskilled American worker followed the Bassanos into their apartment at 140th Street and Amsterdam Avenue. While there was a great building boom during the middle and late 1920s, residential construction was largely confined to housing suitable for middle-class and upper-class Americans. New housing became available to low income groups only as the more affluent—responding to a rising income and perhaps to the presence or threatened presence of undesirable racial and ethnic groups—moved into better housing in new neighborhoods within the city limits or in the suburbs. This process of succession, slowed down perceptibly by the depression, worked to change the character of older urban neighborhoods. Falling income levels in a neighborhood, the turning of previously owner-occupied homes into rental units, or the encroachment of apartments all affected the reputation of a neighborhood. Other factors, of course, also hurried the process. Increased building costs and fewer children per family resulted in the construction of apartments and single-family dwellings with fewer rooms. The movement of industry outside of the central city removed higher paying jobs beyond the physical reach of center-city residents. Combinations of these and other factors changed the character and appearance of hundreds of neighborhoods in dozens of cities.

The aggregate results of population succession and dispersal in the 30 largest metropolitan districts are summarized in Table 8-2. These districts had a growth rate twice that of the general population from 1920 to 1940 and 40 percent higher than the growth rate of all urban places. Suburban areas grew even more rapidly than the central cities. In April 1940, city officials and other luminaries in Evansville engaged in frantic discussions about the coming federal census. Fearful that the population of the city would register a decline because of widespread suburban development, the city fathers supported the immediate annexation of the suburbs. Evansville's response was not triggered by any demand from the suburbs for annexation. Neither was it based on any certainty that the delivery of full city services to the annexed areas was financially possible. Evansville reacted because "bigger is better." This rational had universal appeal.

The definition of metropolitan regions helped focus attention on the problems inherent in the concentration of population within a relatively small area which encompassed dozens or hundreds of political units. Farsighted urban analysts such as Clarence Stein and Lewis Mumford recognized the necessity of planning that reached beyond the boundary of a city to include its immediate hinterland. Few precedents for this existed prior to the 1920s, but during the decade a number of regional planning commissions were established as public agencies. In 1923 alone, agencies were created in Los Angeles, Allegheny, and Milwaukee counties. In the same year, the Regional Planning Association of America was chartered. Most of these agencies concentrated on roads, parks, and public utilities, and many were criticized for their emphasis on central-city rather than regional growth. Nonetheless, planning was increasingly adopted. By 1940, 50 of the 284 cities with populations exceeding 30,000 had adopted some kind of plan and 78 others were preparing plans.

For the most part, each community handled its separate problems and avoided cooperation with other places. If downtowns boomed, as they did in Evansville, Chicago, New York, and elsewhere, they remained un-

planned. Private capital, unwilling to finance new housing for low-income city dwellers, erected a spectacular series of skyscrapers along Michigan Boulevard in Chicago and in midtown Manhattan. In 1929 and into 1930, the Empire State Building rose one story per day. The depression made it a 102-story white elephant of unrented office space. The skyscraper boom necessitated the reconstruction of downtown municipal and utility services. The costs of street and rapid-transit reconstruction, borne by the public, were so great by 1929 that cities were unable to respond to the needs of the unemployed when the depression struck.

Still, the Bassanos thought it much fun to window-shop along New York's Fifth Avenue before heading for Macy's or Gimbels. And, if one could come up with rental money of from $6,000 to $15,000 annually, one could also live in luxury along Chicago's Lake Shore Drive or on New York's Park Avenue. Unfortunately, $6,000 was 20 percent greater than the annual income of 98 percent of American families.

ECONOMIC GROWTH IN AMERICAN COMMUNITIES

The work history of the Millers reflected the accelerated development of the national economy and the rise of new and highly specialized economic activities. During the long illness of Meyer Miller, he and Annie were supported by their children who worked at different jobs scattered about the New York metropolitan area. Rose, for example, worked for 16 years in Hoboken, New Jersey. Six days a week, she made an incredible trip. Taking the Grand Concourse and 205th Street line of the BMT subway, she transferred twice to get to Canal Street. On pleasant days, she walked crosstown to the Hoboken Ferry and floated to New Jersey, boarded a bus, and

Hoboken Ferry Terminal, 23rd Street, which Rose Miller used twice daily

finally arrived at work. On cold days, she took the Hoboken Tube at Canal Street, which rattled its way to New Jersey through a dank and musty tunnel, its walls weeping Hudson River water, which always smelled like a tomb. When Rose quit the Hoboken job and took one at Maspeth, Long Island, she shortened her trip by one hour a day.

Only in a large city could family wage earners pursue such a variety of occupations. Technology spawned new industries, new products, and new consumer demands. Motor transport, aviation, and radio brought to a culmination the establishment of a national market for standardized and branded goods such as Evansville's Servel gas refrigerators. Consumers confidence in the miracles and efficiencies of giant industry overshadowed such troublesome signs as the

gross differentials in income available to various occupational groups.

The economic change wrought by population growth and technological advance rearranged the general contours of the national economy and directly influenced the growth of communities. The two largest cities, New York and Chicago, parlayed locational advantages into diversified economic growth in manufacturing, transport, finance, and the distribution of goods and culture. Lesser cities tended to specialize in fewer economic activities: Pittsburgh in steel or Minneapolis in agribusiness. Industry also became more widely dispersed about the nation. In 1890, Los Angeles' labor force was smaller than Evansville's, but by 1929 it exceeded the work force of Pittsburgh, St. Louis, and Cleveland. However, a tendency in the direction of equalization of industry between regions did not eliminate the heavy concentration in traditional industrial regions. Twenty-one of the leading 33 industrialized areas were in the states of New York, Pennsylvania, Ohio, Massachusetts, Connecticut, and Rhode Island.

Just as major new industrial complexes appeared in Los Angeles, Houston, Tulsa, and elsewhere, industry tended to spread out within urban areas. Technological advances —high-power electric grids, trucks, airports —freeing industry from its traditional need to concentrate near river or rail transportation or a stationary power source, allowed the dispersal of industry outward from the center city, in the same general direction that population was flowing. Even though banks, department stores, and industrial headquarters continued to converge in the central business district (CBD), commercial strips, including branch operations, arose along major thoroughfares radiating out from the CBD. While New York City's share of national manufacturing diminished slightly, as did its control of banking, it retained its dominance in banking, as a headquarters of national organizations and the largest chain stores, as a style center, as the leader in professional services such as publishing, and as the new leader in radio broadcasting. In Chicago, industry expanded beyond the city limits, especially in the direction of Gary, Indiana, at the same time involving such new industrial giants as Admiral, Zenith, and Motorola. Within Chicago, commercial growth concentrated in the CBD. State Street, with 39 department stores doing 18 percent of the city's retail business in 1926, remained the premier shopping center west of the Hudson River.

The movement of industry and population toward the city's rim was quickened by the automobile and the truck. The enhanced mobility offered by motor transport allowed workers to travel miles to work and industry to locate beyond population centers. Autos rapidly became a necessity, less so in New York City, Boston, and Philadelphia perhaps, while trucks greatly extended the trade areas of cities, thus decentralizing distribution among a much larger number of smaller places. Problems accompanied the advantages. Residents of Fredonia and Evansville complained bitterly about downtown auto and truck congestion. By 1930, over 400 intersections in Chicago required policemen to operate traffic lights. The growing practice of "cruising the strip" compelled Evansville to add to its police force and the Trace boys to drive a bit more cautiously.

Cars and buses destroyed the older mass-transport systems. Electric trolleys and interurbans reached a peak of passengers served between World War I and the early 1920s. Thereafter, usage began to decline. In Los Angeles, passengers fell by 143 million between 1926 and 1933. Buses sped the Markoviches more quickly to church in Aliquippa on Sunday mornings and somewhat reduced travel time for Crucible's commuting labor force. During the 1920s, Crucible found it necessary to build parking lots as more and more workers drove to work. But, during the depression, many workers gave up their autos and took the bus to Midland. Much the same occurred in Evansville where buses completely replaced interurbans and trolleys in 1939. The bus lines went to the front gate of the factories, and route stops were frequently closer to the homes of commuters than trolley stops had been. Buses avoided serious automobile competition during the depression. Many interurban and trolley systems survived into the post World War II years, but routes were discontinued, fares increased, and rolling stock deteriorated, all further reducing the number of paying passengers hauled.

In 1920, the president of a Los Angeles interurban line declared that "the peak of the competition with the automobile . . . has been reached out there—and passed.'' Somehow he had missed the developing love affair between Americans and their cars. And this love affair was potent in its crippling impact—largely after World War II—on the central city. The auto, rather than relieving congestion, contributed to it, damaged the environment, and added to the financial distress of cities. In the 1920s and thereafter, all city planning was dominated by the presence of the lone American in his car.

Prosperity and mobility triggered a building boom during the 1920s that peaked in 1928 with $11.5 billion in new construction. Two thirds of this sum was in nonresidential construction. Residential construction was confined to units skilled workers and the middle and upper classes could afford. While 3.1 million Americans moved into new dwellings between 1923 and 1929 (six times the number for the seven years, 1930–36), housing authorities estimated that 9 to 10 million American families, one third of the total, lived in slums. Skyrocketing land values, construction costs, and American income patterns precluded the purchase of a home by most families.

During the period 1914–24, a survey of 178 cities revealed that rents rose by 85 percent. Union wage scales advanced by only 35 percent. Per capita income in 1929 was only $24 greater than it had been in 1916. Two thirds of the nonfarm families earned less than $2,500 in 1929. A minimally adequate standard of living required an annual income of at least $2,000. Most families, unable to afford better housing, were stuck where they were or, at best, able to make horizontal moves.

The housing spectrum was a wide one. Gus O'Reilly's home in Medford was worth more than 90 percent of the single and two-family dwellings in America. The Ben Traces were among the 60 percent who lived in dwellings valued at less than $5,000. Fewer than half of these dwellings were owner occupied.

With little low-cost housing constructed during the interwar years, the urban working poor remained tied to their low-paying city jobs and competed more intensively for a rising volume of bad housing. The prosperity of the 1920s created great monuments in the center of American cities—the Tribune Tower in Chicago and the new armory in Evansville—and new zones of fortune in the suburbs. But the vast wealth generated by industry failed to slow down the spread of urban zones of misfortune.

Many of the nation's largest cities experienced unprecedented economic growth during the heady days of the 1920s. Lesser cities grew too, but for the most part along traditional lines rather than through the acquisition of new industries. Cities that had been preeminent in manufacturing remained so, while cities of significance commercially, such as New Orleans, did not blossom as industrial centers. The growth in some older manufacturing centers was dramatically as in Detroit with the maturation of the automotive industry. Simultaneously, new growth centers, especially in the Southeast and Southwest and Southern California, assumed a place in the constellation of great urban areas.

By 1940, the populations of the Detroit and Los Angeles metropolitan areas were roughly equivalent (see Table 8–2), but they had arrived at their great size by different paths and were dissimilar in character. Detroit, by 1920, was primarily a manufacturing city, the automotive capital of the world. Los Angeles was not principally a manufacturing center even though much of its growth during the 1920s stemmed from the development of petrochemicals. Contributing as much as the location in Los Angeles of the movie industry and its many supporting services. A smaller proportion of the work force in Los Angeles was engaged in manufacturing than in Detroit.

Differences in the economic sector, Los

Angeles' marked climatic advantages and more recent growth, and an earlier tendency toward population deconcentration all combined to mold Los Angeles into an urban form different from that of Detroit and older American cities. Velma Trace's parents, the Miltons, had moved to Los Angeles in 1923 to escape the humidity and temperature extremes of Evansville. They lived among a population that contained a much higher proportion of native born and whites than lived in Detroit. The heavy industries of Detroit attracted the foreign born prior to World War I and blacks thereafter. The great range of occupational choices in Los Angeles prompted large numbers of women to find jobs—more socially acceptable than Velma's—while its "sun and fun" atmosphere attracted many aged. A cousin of the Gales, employed by the Santa Fe Railroad shops in Coffeyville, retired to Los Angeles in 1924 and wrote that many retired railroad workers were already out there. Tampa and St. Petersburg, on a much smaller scale, demonstrated demographic patterns similar to those in Los Angeles.

Cities in the Southeast and Southwest, during the interwar years, were the economic beneficiaries of enormous capital investment in pulp paper, rayon, petroleum refining, and heavy chemical and processing industries. Atlanta, Birmingham, Dallas, Houston, Tulsa, and Oklahoma City engaged in vigorous campaigns to attract capital investment, efforts attended by intense intercity competition. These cities offered cheaper labor than Northern cities did, and were close to rich natural resources. Birmingham threatened Pittsburgh's control of the basic steel industry. Tulsa and Oklahoma City emerged as oil capitals, competing with each other and with Denver, Kansas City, and Dallas–Fort Worth as financial centers for the lower Great Plains. By building its ship channel—lined with 65 industries by 1930—Houston became the leading cotton port and a major grain export center and petroleum refiner. Only New York

and Los Angeles surpassed Houston in quantity of foreign exports. Smaller cities, such as Evansville, participated in this growth, which contributed to a more equitable regional distribution of wealth.

Evansville emerged from World War I, according to its boosters, as an "all American" city. Conveniently ignoring the railroad strikes and other labor disturbances of the immediate post–World War I years, the chamber of commerce described the local labor force as calm, conservative, white, and native born. Reeling off other advantages—parks, schools, a college, 76 churches—the chamber sought to attract new industry and business. And, in truth, Evansville's economic base grew steadily through the 1920s even though its population rose more slowly than anticipated, from 85,000 in 1920 to 97,000 in 1940. But the steady prosperity of the 1920s brought few benefits to the Trace family. Ben was laid off more than one third of the time, as both truck and river transportation cut into the business of the L&N. While Evansville developed a diversified manufacturing sector—employing 45 percent of the labor force—dominated by automotives, appliances, furniture, and cigars, Ben risked losing a retirement pension and job seniority should he seek steadier work in industry.

Relative to its population, Evansville was as industrialized as Detroit, more so than Pittsburgh, and less dependent than either upon a single industry. Its diversified economy allowed it to weather the depression with less disruption than occurred in many other cities. In the depths of the depression, unemployment in Evansville was less severe and recovery more rapid than in many other industrial cities. Many of Evansville's industries suffered only moderate reductions in consumer demand: Ingleheart Brothers, a subsidiary of General Foods, continued to make "Swans Down Cake Flour"; La Fendrich Cigars increased production in 1933 and 1934; "Pablum," a product of Mead

Johnson, continued to pour down the throats of countless infants. To be sure, Chrysler Corporation's Plymouth plant experienced severe production cutbacks, as did Hercules, Incorporated (a subsidiary of Servel, Incorporated) in the production of truck bodies. But production expanded at Servel and Sunbeam Electric Manufacturing Company (manufacturer of Sears, Roebuck's "Coldspot" refrigerator). Both Servel and Mead Johnson maintained large research and engineering laboratories in Evansville, which added a layer of fairly high-salaried employees to the city's economy.

New industrial centers exploited new technologies to utilize new resources. Tank trucks roared down new highways carrying gasoline to tens of thousands of gas stations and other petroleum products to rayon and rubber-tire factories. Improved technologies in older industries such as steel diminished the earlier advantages of older industrial cities. Labor tranquility and lower wage scales, as in the South, added to the advantages of newer areas, while the very newness and freshness of the developing centers attracted enterprise that could locate without regard to the nearness of natural resources. All of this presented grave problems to "mature" industrial cities such as Pittsburgh.

The six-county Pittsburgh district, in which the Markoviches and Simiches lived, was ugly. Mining had destroyed much of the natural vegetation, undermined slopes, and poured polluting acids into most streams while the giant stacks of industry spewed tons of pollutants into the air. The district was overspecialized in heavy manufacturing. As population, markets, and manufacturers spread to newer areas, Pittsburgh's export specialities—metals, glass, coal—met stiff competition from producers closer to western markets. With a percentage of wage earners in metals and glass that was twice the national average from 1919 to 1939, with only one third the percentage in all other industry

groups, and with the declining dominance of coal as a fuel in industry and transportation, Pittsburgh was overconcentrated and had lost important locational advantages to competitors such as Gary, Indiana, and Birmingham, Alabama.

Pittsburgh's share of national steel and electrical machinery declined during the two decades under consideration. Unemployment approached 10 per cent in 1928 and 1929, while 50 percent of all families in the region including the Markoviches, earned less than $2,000 annually. As a result of declining economic opportunity, Pittsburgh's population increased at a slower rate between 1920 and 1940 than that of all but 9 of the 30 major urban regions.

As a result of the location of the specialty steel industry in such towns as Midland, Beaver County proved an exception to the general stagnation. Midland's population increased by only 10 percent, compared with 40 percent in the county, but employment rose by 26 percent. At the same time, neighboring Allegheny County lost over 18,000 mill workers. Lack of suitable housing, the reluctance of Crucible Steel, which owned most of the building sites, to sell or lease its property, and Standard Oil's purchase in 1928 of a site east of town for storage tanks, retarded population growth in Midland.

Crucible Steel operated at over 90 percent of capacity during the 1920s while adding two blast furnaces and completed its vertical integration through the purchase of Lake Superior iron-ore properties. Its high-alloy steels were especially suitable for agricultural-implement and automobile construction. In addition to Crucible, the MacIntosh-Hemphill plant manufactured rolling mill machinery and constructed entire steel plants in Europe and, in the mid-1930s, the USSR. Treadwell Construction Company and its subsidiary, Midland Barge Company, fabricated the metal work used on dams and locks and constructed large steel barges for domestic and foreign waterborne transport industries. Midland's economy was intimately connected with the continued industrialization of the Atlantic world.

Midland, Pittsburgh, and Detroit developed highly specialized industrial sectors. But Midland and Detroit held virtual monopolies in specialties that were not easily emulated elsewhere. While the automotive industry began to decentralize in the 1920s, Detroit still retained the bulk of production, engineering, and managerial capacity. Midland's strength lay in increasing demand for Crucible's high-quality steel and a research and development component that protected and enhanced that superiority. Midland's general grubbiness, its inadequate housing and nonexistent sewage system, the arbitrary—recall the firing of Mihailo Markovich—paternalistic, and anti-union character of Crucible's personnel policies and civic involvement were all muted to a certain extent by full employment.

When the depression struck and the unemployed crowded in search of work before the factory gates as a shift started, the connection between Midland or Evansville and the national and world economies became all too apparent. Crucible, Servel, Chrysler—such powerful forces within their communities—were themselves but tiny pieces of an enormous economic mechanism that was tragically out of whack. If they could not defend themselves against falling demand, vanishing investment capital, and other impersonal forces, how could a community . . . how could a family?

HOW COMMUNITIES SERVED THE FAMILIES

The Country Folk

The communities in which our families lived provided them with services that were unobtainable or available only at high cost through individual effort. The things the families needed, of course, varied according to location, aspirations, and other factors. So, too, was their ability to obtain them affected by their ability to pay. Everyone needs drinking water. The Gales and Harts could drill their own wells, but the Bassanos could not. Most families desired indoor plumbing. The Gales added it themselves and the Bassanos expected it to come with the apartment. But the Markoviches did not have it—neither did the Simiches in Primrose—and could not afford to install it. In some ways, the farm families, then, were less dependent upon community or public services than the city families were: less dependent but hardly independent.

At one end of the spectrum, the Tennessee Traces did not socialize much outside of the clan, made little use of Waynesboro, and remained basically unchanged by the events of the postwar years or by its material offerings—radio, tractors, electric ranges. Self-sufficient, loyal to kin, and relatively untouched by competitive values, the Tennessee Traces were largely indifferent to the cultural imperatives of an industrializing nation. At the other end of the spectrum were the socially active Gales, self-reliant but not self-sufficient, totally involved in the marketplace—along with the Harts, Reinhardts, and Hunts—seeking out new gadgetry and participating in new institutional arrangements in

Main Street, Kosse, Texas, 1975

Fredonia in the belief that such a course was both economically and culturally beneficial. If New Albany and Roper faded in significance for the Gales and Harts, Kosse remained the universe to the Hunts, offering a cotton gin, a church, and small stores.

Farm communities composed of families with relatively high incomes offered a greater variety of associational activities and provided a higher quality of services than did communities in which incomes were relatively low or farm tenancy rates were high. This was true even when the incomes of tenants and owners were comparable. Farm towns in southern Indiana and southern Illinois, an area of high tenancy, found it much more difficult to support churches, organize agricultural extension groups, or establish farmers' cooperatives than did towns in southeastern Kansas where the great majority of farms were owner occupied. Other patterns were also discovered. Foreign-born farmers or their children, if they lived in an ethnic community, were greater participators than were old-stock Americans. Farmers in the North were more active than farmers with equivalent incomes in the South.

Income was the major factor—if not all controlling—in determining the amount and quality of education that a farm child received, the adequacy of health care for the family, and the quality of housing. In the countryside, communities had little to do with housing and income was the determinant. But communities had much to do with education and health. The Gales could make choices about education that the Hunts could not because of where they lived, how much they earned, and who they were.

New Albany supported one of 105 rural school districts in Wilson County. The Gales withdrew their children from the New Albany school, enrolling them in Fredonia. The Gales' decision symbolized the growing concern of professional educators and rural residents with the quality of education in small rural schools. In 1932, 26 million children, or 21 percent of the entire population, and 82 percent of all those between the ages of 5 and 17, were attending schools. The Gale, Hart, and Reinhardt children were among 13 million rural scholars attending 211,000 rural schools. Austin Hart went to an eight-grade, one-room, one-teacher school with 30 to 40 students, located about one mile from Roper. Austin's school was but one of 190,000 one-teacher, one-room schools that taught 2.8 million pupils in 1920. By 1940, consolidation and simple abandonment had reduced the number of these schools by 60,000. There were also 23,000 two-teacher schools in 1940 teaching 1.3 million children.

Rural schools suffered from a variety of disabilities. During the 1930s, rural farm and rural nonfarm America supported over 50 percent of all school-age children with less than 20 percent of national income. While Austin Hart has fond memories of his tiny school and his schoolmarm, proponents of consolidation stoutly maintained that centralized schools offered superior education. Rural teacher salaries were lower than urban salaries; rural teachers had less professional training; per capita expenditures for rural students fell below urban figures; urban scholars, in 1931–32, were in school 25 days more than rural scholars were (an advantage only from an adult perspective); 91 percent of urban children attended school in 1935–36 compared to 83 percent of the rural kids.

Mounting costs per student, especially in school districts which were losing population, and declining farm income provided further stimulus for the consolidation of rural schools. Enabling legislation in numerous states encouraged consolidation. Between 1920 and 1928, the number of consolidated schools increased from 5,000 to 17,500. In 1928, the Roper grade school was consolidated with the Benedict school system. Austin Hart's two younger brothers moved into a new building built after the approval of a bond issue. When hard times came, farmers experienced great difficulty in paying their assessments on the new plant and compelled the school board to reduce teacher salaries and programs. The closing of Austin's old school removed the central prop of the Roper community. Depression-induced business failures and a migrating population transformed Roper into a mere collection of houses, many empty.

Comparative studies failed to identify serious differences in classroom performance between rural and urban scholars from similar socioeconomic backgrounds. That some children derived greater benefits than others from the school systems was due less to the particular system than to class or race. Kosse had no school for blacks until Sylvia Hunt established one on her own initiative. Kosse's white students were bused to the Marlin High School, but this service was not available to blacks. Sylvia's daughter, Lila, was able to continue her education only by living with an aunt in Marlin.

Black parents throughout the South—and not a few white families—confronted almost insurmountable difficulties in obtaining a basic education for their children. Few were so fortunate as Lila in having parents with the resources to guarantee an education for their children. In 17 segregated state school systems there were gross disparities between black and white education during the interwar years: with 30 percent of school enrollment, black schools received 12 percent of public school funds; salaries for black school teachers in 1935–36 averaged $510 compared with $930 for all rural teachers; 10 percent of the black high-school age population attended high school while the national average exceeded 60 percent.

School systems mirrored the wishes of controlling groups within the community. Roper, less prosperous than New Albany, provided no funds for extracurricular activities while New Albany's children enjoyed band, baseball, and other activities. As a general rule,

school districts—churches and other organizations also—with a large tenant population were less well supported than districts with a small tenant population. By 1937, 30 states had passed state equalization laws which attempted to bolster the schools of poorer communities through the infusion of state money. Gradually, state contributions became more important, totaling about 26 percent of all public school expenditures in 1934 compared with 20 percent in 1900. But the range of state aid was wide, varying from 2 percent in Kansas to 93 percent in Delaware. The depression accelerated this trend. State and federal aid kept hundreds of schools open.

Statewide performance standards accompanied state aid. Teacher certification requirements were imposed upon local schools and pressure to consolidate intensified. States also increasingly interfered in the field of subject matter and textbooks, and, at the time of World War I, passed hundreds of acts that compelled schools to teach courses promoting patriotism. Laws prohibiting the teaching of German were declared unconstitutional by the United States Supreme Court. The Evansville system, however, simply eliminated German from the curriculum, thus depriving the Reinhardt children of the opportunity to study the tongue of their parents.

State and municipal powers were also exercised in the field of public health. In April 1928, state law ensured that passersby would avoid contact with the Reinhardt home on Middle Mt. Vernon Road. Tacked up on a towering pin oak tree was a bright red sign reading: QUARANTINE. Scarlet fever, still a killer and frequently a precursor of rheumatic fever, raged through the family, affecting each of the four children. No sooner was the siege over and the sign taken down than diptheria struck and the sign went up again. Local health authorities traced the disease to the Reinhardts' well water, which was receiving seepage from an abandoned cesspool. The Reinhardts were fortunate in having children who were healthy to start with and in having a family doctor who journeyed daily from Evansville to attend the bedridden flock.

Health care for all families, but particularly for rural families, depended upon income and location. Specialists generally agreed that an annual income of $2,500 was minimally adequate to purchase necessary health care. Two thirds of America's families earned less. The interwar population rose almost three times as fast as the number of trained physicians while the latter concentrated in the largest cities. A number of states sent a few mobile clinics to remote areas, but most rural families were too isolated to receive adequate medical care. Kosse had no doctor. Roper depended upon a doctor in Benedict, but he retired in the early 1930s and no one took up the practice. New Albany also lost its physician.

The general population was healthier and lived longer than prior generations, but severe differentials between groups within the population persisted (see Table 8–3). Partially as a result of improved sanitation, water, and other public-health measures such as innoculation and vaccination, urban death rates declined more rapidly than rural death rates between 1915 and 1940. Infant mortality rates in urban places slid below the rates in rural areas in 1926 while the rates remained higher, irrespective of residence, for low-income families and blacks than for high-income families and whites. All of the

Table 8–3
Life Expectancy at Birth
(U.S. 1910, 1930)

	White		Nonwhite	
	Male	Female	Male	Female
1910	48.6	52.0	33.8	37.5
1930	59.7	63.5	47.3	49.2

Reinhardt children were born in a hospital; all of the Gale children were born at home with a physician in attendance. For the rural population, the Gales were typical. The Hunt boys in Kosse and Lila in Mississippi were born at home without medical attention. Seventeen percent of rural births were unattended in 1940 compared with less than 4 percent in cities over 10,000.

Lower-income families, black and white, rural and urban, were poorly served by the medical technology of the interwar years. Eliott Butler's skill as a brain surgeon was of little use to the general populace. The rapid growth of general hospitals still left the majority without care. Some 1,300 counties—including Wayne and Wilson—with over 17 million people had no hospital, and 780 counties were without a public health nurse. Moreover, even if small communities had a general hospital, there was a good chance that it had been judged inadequate by the American College of Surgeons. In 1939, 112 of 160 public hospitals in cities with populations under 30,000 were refused approval by that body.

Hospitals, medical skills, and health-care delivery based upon the general hospital served middle-class urban people far better than the less affluent and rural people. Private health-insurance programs such as Blue Cross and Blue Shield, which were developed during the interwar years, did not serve rural people at all. In effect, the evolving system of the 1920s almost totally ignored the daily health needs of low-income groups. As in the past, health care was a commodity to be purchased, like a new automobile, by those who could afford it. While the depression compelled some federal involvement, the strength of the medical lobby and the mores of the middle-class population completely defeated efforts to include adequate health care among the basic rights of an American citizen.

Farm families responded in divergent ways

to opportunities or lack thereof. Income, race or ethnicity, and location appear to be the best indicators for measuring the intensity of involvement and for explaining the quality and quantity of services available. While each family, farm or nonfarm, was unique, the Reinhardts, Harts, and Gales were more similar to one another than to the Tennessee Traces or the Hunts.

The City People

The urban families included two, the Millers and the Bassanos, who lived and worked in the heart of the nation's largest city; two others who lived in satellite cities within the Boston metropolitan area—the O'Reillys in Medford and the Butlers in Brookline; another, the Traces, in Evansville, Indiana; and one, the Markoviches (in the late 1930s, the young Mike Simich, also) residents of Midland, a place not much larger than Fredonia but, in appearance and milieu, a world apart. For the urbanites as for the rural folk, the degree of community involvement and the advantages derived from the community depended upon income, residence, ethnicity, and religion as well as individual preferences.

Job opportunities had attracted most of the families to the city in the first place. Except for the Butlers, the families' dependence upon weekly wages kept them there. Job insecurities also locked families into cities. Ben Trace and Mihailo Markovich were frequently unemployed during the interwar years. But where else would it be any better for an unskilled man? Both families had put down deep roots. The Markoviches never considered leaving Midland, bound to it as they were by ethnic and religious ties. The Butlers, the Bassanos, and the O'Reillys were engaged in work dependent upon the concentration of population and wealth in urban areas. While the Butlers were much more involved in the national market and to that extent could have

functioned in Chicago or San Francisco as well as in Boston, loyalty to Harvard, to Porc, to class, kept the Butlers active in and around the Bean City. To the Butlers, the O'Reillys, or the Bassanos, the precise location of the home meant less than it did to the Traces or the Markoviches. For the latter families, the neighbors, the neighborhood, proximity to work, in other words a specific location, meant everything.

The Markoviches and the Traces felt "at one" with their communities. So did the Butlers, but community for them transcended the local boundaries of Brookline. Midland's ethnic groups were rigidly segregated residentially. Denied representation on the borough council, the PTA, the school board, and other community-wide organizations, and discriminated against by the hiring and promotion practices of local employers, the ethnic groups of Midland organized rapidly. The Midland police picked on Slavic youth more than on Anglo-Saxons and that Anna's grade school was inferior to the school in east Midland did not undermine Mihailo's or Anna's affection for the place. For the Markoviches, the Serbian associations formed the bedrock of their lives. As with the Markoviches, home for the Traces meant a house in a particular community. Doubts that the Traces had regarding the inadequacy of fire protection, irritations over the lack of a sewage system and storm drains, the constant rumble and roar of the train yards just a block away did not unduly distress them. Schools and stores were close, the children were healthy and bright, the neighbors were like themselves, the garden was fruitful. They could make do.

For the O'Reillys, Medford meant less than Midland meant to the Markoviches. Medford, a residential suburb north of Cambridge and Somerville, had little industry and about one half of its labor force was engaged in professional or white-collar jobs in the Boston metropolitan area. Medford did contain a foreign-born population, 25 percent of the total in 1920 and 1930, but most were upwardly mobile Irish such as Gus. The housing stock was substantial, about one half built since 1920, including the duplex which Gus purchased in 1922. No other city in Massachusetts of over 50,000 persons had a higher percentage of homes with indoor baths and flush toilets. Medford was the Brookline of middle-income families.

Greater Boston, however, claimed much more of Gus O'Reilly's time than Medford did. Margaret was more active within Medford than her husband was. For Gus, business associations were central. Traveling daily by company car throughout the metropolitan area, he contributed to that highway congestion that Americans began to notice for the first time. Medford was fairly efficient in maintaining its roads; other communities which Gus visited periodically were less so. Traffic patterns were designed for horse and buggy. Roads were undrained and poorly surfaced. Time was money for Gus and it irked him when he encountered a washed-out city street or a jolting pothole. Massachusetts was only just beginning to plan a state system of roads. Local responsibility and reluctance to spend money for good roads, and the lack of statewide construction standards all conspired to waste Gus's time and bend his fenders. For the Bassanos and Millers, who traveled underground, cars were someone else's headache.

It was difficult for the Millers and Bassanos to feel the same sort of "at oneness" with New York that Anna Markovich felt toward Midland or the Trace brothers toward Howell. Annie and Meyer lived in a heavily Jewish neighborhood in the West Bronx, just off the Grand Concourse, yet socially distinct from the middle-class "luxury" housing on the Concourse. With Rose and Billie living at home and Betty and Bertha and their families close by, Annie and Meyer—and Annie,

widowed in 1934—did not need or wish to move around in the city. Kosher shops were close by and a great variety of stores, including Alexander's Department Store, were nearby at Fordham Road and the Concourse. While the Miller children confronted New York—the younger girls as public-school students and their older brother and sisters as working adults—the family was their community.

The Bassanos, seized by a sense of community when they moved to Inwood, better reflected the sort of community life possible for some New Yorkers. Andrew Bassano and six children (who were already married and the others ranged in age from 14 to 24) moved, in 1929, to an apartment on Hillside and Nagel Avenues at 200th (Dyckman) Street. Robert Bassano, the seventh of eight children, made his home in Inwood for the next 45 years.

At the northern tip of Manhattan, Inwood in the 1920s was a developing middle-class residential district. Over 75 percent of the apartment houses had been built since 1920. Ninety-five percent of all Inwood's families lived in buildings housing more than 20 families with the vast majority paying between $35 and $45 a month rent for apartments furnished with a refrigerator and a stove. Housing 43,000 people, 72 percent native born and 99.6 percent white, Inwood was divided into a number of block-centered neighborhoods each of which was attached to a major shopping street. Each of the area's major ethnic groups—Irish, German-Jewish, and Russian-Jewish—could be found on any block, but some blocks were more heavily one than the other. Most people moving into Inwood prior to World War II came from other New York streets, but between 1935 and 1939 at least 2,000 German-Jews, fleeing Nazi Germany, took up residence.

Inwood represented a move upward for the Bassanos and most of their neighbors.

While the Inwood Irish were generally located in the lower rental apartments and worked at unskilled jobs throughout the city, most workers were in nonmanual positions. The three new grade schools provided the best education that an urban system could offer, including rapid advancement or opportunity classes for quick learners, subject-matter grading, and a host of electives for all grades and both sexes—loom work and weaving, photography, home economics for girls and electrical wiring for the boys, and so on. A new high school, George Washington, was located high above Inwood on the site of a Revolutionary War fort, the walls of which still stood to serve hundreds of kids as they played their war games. George Washington was a general high school, but for those students with strength in science or math, Bronx High School of Science, Brooklyn Tech, or Peter Stuyvesant were available if the rugged entrance exams could be passed. The High School of Music and Art provided similar specialized training for those with talent in the arts. Catholic boys could attend Power Memorial, Cardinal Hayes, or other parochial high schools, while the girls could attend the nearby Sacred Heart of Mary or Mother Cabrini High Schools.

Bob and Charlotte remained in Inwood because it had about all the amenities that a town of 50,000 offered in addition to superior services, not the least of which was proximity to excellent health-care facilities. On Dyckman Street alone, there were five pharmacies, three optometrists and two opticians, six dentists, and six general practitioners. The Bassanos' family doctor, and their dentist lived and practiced less than 300 feet away. Jewish Memorial Hospital was a 5-minute walk and the Columbia Presbyterian Medical Center a 15-minute trolley ride away. In 1939, the threat of a smallpox outbreak took 35,000 Inwood residents, including a terrified Robbie Bassano, to Jewish Memorial for free vaccinations. Inwood had the lowest death rate and the lowest communicable disease rate in Manhattan. The infant mortality rate in Inwood was one third that of the Lower East Side and one quarter that of central Harlem. The only other densely inhabited area in New York with comparably low rates was where the Millers lived.

Bob and Charlotte's apartment contained about 400 square feet of living space. Bob puttered with fix-it-yourself tasks since the building's superintendent was neither handy nor quick to respond to a call for help when the toilet spilled over. Garbage was a particular problem. New York's enormous Department of Sanitation employed thousands of trucks to pick it up at the curb—if the "super" put the cans out on time—and hundreds of tugs and barges to haul it out into the Atlantic for dumping. Such was the journey of the Bassanos' garbage if they could get it on the dumbwaiter each separate apartment had. That was the roadblock in the system, for the super became very casual about collecting it or even ringing the buzzer, the signal for garbage-collection time. Uncollected garbage supported mice and roach families and required frequent visits by the exterminator, the "roach man."

On spring and summer evenings, many took to the streets to escape the heat of small apartments. Charlotte and Bob played canasta with neighbors at a card table set up on the sidewalk surrounded by street kids playing their noisy games and overwhelmed every three minutes by the passing of an elevated train. On Saturdays, Bob and his friends played ball while the wives watched the kids in nearby play areas. On Sundays, Bob took a 30-minute walk to the Polo Grounds to watch the New York Giants' Mel Ott blast the Bums from Brooklyn. Bob despised the Yankees and never set foot in Yankee Stadium even though it was just across the river from the Polo Grounds. Gus O'Reilly had similar feel-

The Polo Grounds, home of the New York Giants for over 50 years

ings about the powerful Yankees but for better reasons since the Boston Red Sox were so frequently their victims. Defying family tradition, Robbie Bassano became a Yankee fan. "Why watch a loser, Dad?" "Loyalty," replied Bob.

The Bassanos were further removed from decision-making institutions than the Gales were. They belonged to no church and were members of no community organizations. But this was by choice, not because Inwood lacked such organizations. Republicans and Democrats were active in the district, particularly the Democrats for La Guardia Club, which supported the Republican Mayor of New York, the "Little Flower," Fiorello La Guardia. La Guardia's following was enormous. How else could it be for the man who read newspaper comics over the radio every Sunday morning? Churches and synagogues flourished. PTAs were active at both P.S. 152 and P.S. 98, while the Inwood branch of the New York Public Library ran an exciting Great Books Club. The Catholic Youth Organization (CYO) and the Police Athletic League (PAL) kept some of the kids off the streets some of the time. A full range of organizations existed for the interested. Neighboring, informal group life and occasional visits to relatives sufficed for the Bassanos.

Bob and Charlotte, in a three-room apartment on the fourth floor that looked out on the elevated tracks of the IRT, surrounded by concrete and macadam, skeptical about the induction of Robbie into the midget wing of the Satans—a local street gang—at age six, were as much a part of their neighborhood as the Gales were part of New Albany. Discrete areas such as Inwood existed in most American cities. Brighton in South Boston (Irish), Strawberry Hill in Kansas City, Kansas (Slavic), or Howell in Evansville (old-stock working class) were of a manageable scale and they worked to break down the impersonality and frenzy of city life in the same way that rural neighborhoods and small villages and towns provided human contact for isolated farm families. Bob Bassano saw thousands of faces every day. Sweaty and with suit rumpled after the crush of a subway ride from lower Manhattan, he felt at home when he emerged from underground and encountered the familiar sights and sounds of Dyckman Street.

COMMUNITIES FACE THE DEPRESSION

The Local Response, 1929–1932

In thousands of American communities, signs of economic slowdown were visible by 1929. By 1930, depression was a reality with the unemployment level at over 4 million and rising. Yet it was only in 1931 and 1932 that citizens in Fredonia, Midland, Evansville, and elsewhere began to speak openly of hard times. Even in 1931, Evansville's mayor devoted the large part of his "state of the city" message to a description of city efforts to stamp out gambling and bootlegging. In Midland, with Crucible operating at one third of capacity in 1932, wages just slashed by 19 percent, and 1,200 Crucible workers laid off.

Rotarians applauded a speaker who described the present day as one of good fortune and bright promise. Communities refused to admit that something was wrong and getting worse. Hadn't President Hoover said that the economy was basically sound?

Americans believed that charity—relief, the dole, the handout—was degrading and destructive of character. Thus the poor and disabled were traditionally the responsibilities of their kinfolk and, only as a last resort, of private charitable agencies. A few states had passed legislation during the 1920s providing monthly allotments to dependent children and the aged or blind. Much of this legislation merely permitted counties to initiate such programs if they wished a state contribution. Most counties ignored the opportunity. Counties and municipalities were the only public agents in the field, perhaps operating an orphanage but totally ignoring those cast into poverty by unemployment. Private charitable agencies handled the employable unemployed. By 1930, even with the best of intentions, they were overwhelmed by the sheer numbers of people without work.

Most larger communities had some sort of a united organization of charitable agencies. In Evansville, the Community Welfare Association, organized in 1921, was an outgrowth of the Evansville Associated Charities. In 1933, the Community Fund was organized. Here and elsewhere, the member agencies were divided generally into two categories: character-building agencies such as the Boy Scouts, YMCA, and YWCA; and dependency agencies such as the Salvation Army, the Public Health Visiting Nurses Association, or the Family Welfare Agency. Most of the funds raised went to character-building groups catering to white, middle-class needs. Few blacks or working-class children were Boy Scouts, while YMCA facilities were largely off limits for blacks and inconvenient to the residences of other low-income children. Evansville's Community Chest, in 1930, refused to support the Phyllis Wheatley House for black girls, in operation since 1918, and used by over 200 girls each week.

At best, the dependency agencies could provide minimal relief for only small numbers of the needy. They could not create jobs or generate payrolls. They did provide some food relief, fuel for winter, clothing, and some medical attention. Robert Butler, chairman of the Greater Boston Community Chest organization and president of the national Chest and Council Organization of America during the 1930s, believed that these volunteer units should have sole responsibility for nonwork relief. He abhorred the intervention of the federal government. Even during the best of times, charitable agencies barely touched those in need. During the worst of times, with 12.8 million unemployed and millions more underemployed, Butler's conventional wisdom was sorely tested.

As the depression worsened, private and public relief agencies greatly increased their expenditures. Appropriations then dropped as funds dried up. In some cities, such as New York and Cincinnati, when private emergency funds were exhausted they were replaced by public funds. Private agencies continued to provide some nonwork relief while basic responsibility for wage (work) relief was assumed by public agencies. By 1931, some 250 cities with over 25,000 inhabitants operated work-relief programs. But the funds available were microscopic. In Cincinnati, 32,500 were unemployed while the city appropriated $2 million for work relief in 1932—averaging $57 of wage relief for each unemployed person for the entire year. Yet C. M. Bookman, Executive Director of the Cincinnati Community Chest, asserted that "unemployment relief can best be handled by local communities. . . ." In cities such as Kansas City, Missouri, St. Louis, and Chicago, work-relief programs were severely

tarnished by city council members who awarded jobs on the basis of political expediency rather than economic need.

Midland's relief needs were heavy. One third of the labor force, among whom Mihailo Markovich was included, was unemployed in 1932, and large numbers were working only part-time. No community fund existed, borough resources were rapidly depleted, and the state relief system only began operating in 1932 with very inadequate funds. The Midland Fellowship Club, a private group of Crucible executives and others, assumed responsibility for the relief effort, but during the three years, 1930–32, only $60,000 was raised and spent. The 250 Midland families without incomes in 1932 could expect no more than $80 to $100 in relief during the entire year. Only a few dozen men could hope for work relief on the town's roads.

It was the same story in Fredonia, Evansville, Philadelphia, and thousands of other places. In Vanderburgh County, relief costs rose from $244,000 in 1931 to $950,000 in 1933. A small Reconstruction Finance Corporation loan was obtained, but most funds came from contributions and taxes. In Evansville, an effort to create jobs by initiating a street-improvement program was blocked by residents of the streets involved. Many of the homeowners were unemployed and could not shoulder new tax assessments for the street work. Evansville did not operate either a private or a public work-relief program.

Rural districts were served less well than urban ones even after 1933 when large federal expenditures commenced. Many counties had no relief (welfare) system at all during the 1920s, and family and kin provided whatever relief there was. The rural nonfarm population was virtually neglected. Living in or around villages and small towns, they were ineligible for relief directed at farmers while their communities were generally too small and poor to organize much of a relief effort. Many in this group migrated to urban areas where more aid was available or went back to the farm where they hoped to be self-sufficient. If they did the latter, the migrants tended to aggravate pressures because more people, in 1931–34, moved to the country than to the city, a temporary reversal of past trends. Many farm youth who would normally have gone to cities remained on the farm and were joined there by kin and neighbors who had lost their urban jobs. Rural areas with the heaviest in-migration tended to be among the poorest farm areas in the nation.

Throughout the nation, traditional community services were emasculated and community relief efforts ground to a halt in 1932 and 1933. Unemployment and lack of purchasing power drastically reduced the amount of tax monies flowing into public coffers. By 1932, one fifth of New Jersey's communities were bankrupt. In Midland and Fredonia, smaller revenues meant retrenchment all along the lines (see Table 8–4). In 1932, Midland's Board of Education fired 6 teachers and reduced salaries by 10 percent, followed by 11 more releases and a 15 percent salary cut in 1932. In 1932 and 1933, Evansville's teachers suffered salary cuts of 19 to 45 percent. Expenditures for public education in Evansville declined by 30 percent from 1933 to 1934. Nationally, the decline amounted to 22 percent between 1930 and 1934. Expenditures for public health and other services were drastically slashed.

By late 1932, one of every six American families received some sort of public assistance, and for every person on relief another person living in extreme poverty had yet to take that step of last resort. In Seattle, 1,200 homeless men crowded into a Hooverville, were burned out twice by city authorities, and finally gained begrudging municipal suffrance to exist. Hoovervilles around the country; soup lines in the cities; the despairing faces of jobless and aimless humans crowding into the Salvation Army's evening prayer meeting, willing to hear the word of God if accompanied by a cup of broth, attested to the utter failure of the American system.

The New Deal Comes to Town

Roosevelt's terms produced legislation of immediate and long-range significance to communities. Of more immediate utility were FERA, CWA, and WPA which forged a new relationship between communities and the federal government that frequently bypassed the states. The dominant self-help, no-government-intervention philosophy of most communities quickly evaporated in their eagerness to get all the federal money they could. The press in Evansville, Midland, and Wilson County spurred on public officials in their efforts to submit applications for federal funds. The *Evansville Courier and Journal*, October 1, 1933, pointed to Green Bay, Wisconsin, the recipient of $725,000 for a new sewer system, as an example of the pos-

Table 8–4
Shrinking Revenue, Midland and Evansville, 1929–1935

	Midland school budget	Evansville revenue from property taxes
1929–30	$240,000	$1,597,432
1930–31	223,000	1,401,117
1932–33	196,000	1,351,191
1934–35	168,000	777,856

sibilities. Charles Gale, as a member of the Wilson County Emergency Relief Committee, jawboned his colleagues to get the applications flowing. They flowed. But not all were funded.

FERA proposals originated at the local level. Midland's borough council, working with the chamber of commerce, drafted a variety of proposals for public projects. The proposals were then cleared by the County Emergency Relief Committee and forwarded to the state committee. This was the bottleneck, for the states had to contribute $3 for each $1 of federal funds received. The will and ability of states to contribute varied greatly, with the result that numerous worthy proposals died in the state bureaucracy. WPA operated more speedily because the national agency appointed the state WPA administrators whereas the state governors appointed state and local FERA officials. In effect, WPA bypassed the states and dealt directly with communities.

FERA, CWA, WPA, and PWA provided work for less than one half of the jobless. But they did ease unemployment pressure and, in doing so, greatly improved the quality of life in thousands of American communities. In December 1933, Evansville's merchants attributed a 19 percent increase in retail sales to CWA programs which provided work for 4,000 persons. PWA funds, in 1934, provided 70 percent of the total cost of drainage and sewer works in Howell and other areas while FERA paid the labor costs.

Because of the degree of control each community exercised in implementing the various relief programs, results varied from place to place. The Markoviches read in the *Midland News* that the Beaver County Relief Board orchestrated work relief and direct (at home) relief not only according to the amount of money available, but also by the way they perceived local business conditions. Crucible's employment performance provided the

major criteria. In June 1933, Crucible called back 250 idle workers, including Mihailo Markovich. In response, in early autumn 1933, the relief board cut the number of families on relief from 450 to 50. But when the CWA was set up a few days later, nearly 400 people raced to sign up. CWA hired about 100 applicants, leaving the remainder to plead with the relief board for a direct relief dole or to their own devices.

CWA and WPA workers set about digging storm sewers and repaving the streets. They made 50 cents an hour and worked a 30-hour week. When CWA money ran out, about one third of the workers lost their incomes. Even with Crucible up to 75 percent of production capacity in 1935, about 11 percent of the city's employable workers remained idle. In 1935, WPA administrators offered a sizable fund for municipal improvements—if Midland matched it. The borough council held back and only reluctantly accepted WPA aid. Men were eventually assigned to build a stage and bandstand in Lincoln Park, pave more roads, paint and refurbish the schools, and seal abandoned coal mines whose seepage polluted the county's streams.

In Evansville and Vanderburgh County, fewer than one third of all applicants for FERA, CWA, and WPA jobs were ever hired. Massive cuts in WPA funds in 1937 forced hundreds back on the dole. When, in 1940, bad weather and the inability of local officials to dream up new projects combined to put over 1,000 people back on direct relief, an angry crowd, having been promised food and clothing handouts, ripped the doors off the Evansville community center.

While farmers quipped that WPA poison made varmints so lazy they could be caught by hand, they were also getting their share of the New Deal pie. Whatever the faults of AAA there was no doubt that benefit payments induced consumption by putting money into

WPA workers on Wabash Avenue, Evansville, Indiana, 1936

farmers' pockets. Increased farmer purchasing power was noticed by shopkeepers in Fredonia, Waynesboro, and Evansville as early as December 1933 and combined with FERA and CWA funds to bring the best Christmas business in four years.

Triple A revolutionized the attitudes of millions of farmers both about themselves and about the federal government and revitalized associational life in many farm communities. As a result of the decentralization of administration, farmers controlled the operation of AAA at the local level. In June and July 1933, farmers who planted certain critical crops within the same general area gathered together to discuss the formation of production associations. In Wilson County, a wheatgrowers association was organized in early August and chaired by Charles Gale who sent speakers into the county to enlist support. In a county referendum, 93 percent (about the national average of support) of the wheat growers voted to participate. A permanent Wilson

County Wheat Production Control Association was then formed from representatives elected by townships. Township committees checked on the acreage and production data for each farmer and then determined how much acreage could be planted in wheat. Each farmer then signed a contract with Triple A. James Hart was among the 7 percent of Wilson County farmers who refused to participate in the first Triple A.

Township committee notices in local papers then appeared, announcing box suppers followed by talks by the agricultural extension agent or a local progressive farmer on some pertinent topic. Some township committees organized recreational programs for children, others became involved in refurbishing school properties, and a few even tried to apply for WPA funds. Throughout the countryside, thousands of farmer committees functioned, many of which became engaged in land-use planning under the second Triple A. Both Charles Gale and Jacob Reinhardt were leaders on land-use committees. By 1940, 140,000 rural people sat on 1,200 county committees which were involved in area conservation programs, zoning, highways and roads, and property-tax assessments. These were the groups that assumed local leadership in 1941 when production controls were scrapped, and the cry went out to produce.

County seats such as Fredonia and Waynesboro benefited directly as they became the administrative centers for expanded agricultural extension services, AAA, FHA, and other New Deal agencies. Industrial or mill towns that were county seats gained in the same way as union activity increased and as state and federal offices were opened to administer work-relief projects, housing programs, or social-welfare programs.

Most relief programs were tailored to conform to the prevailing class and racial practices of local communities. In the South, there was great resistance to giving blacks federal relief. In Evansville, blacks were the last to receive work-relief assignments, the first to be released, and the last to be rehired by private employers. Few of the projects on which blacks worked were even of indirect benefit to Negro neighborhoods. As late as 1941, one third of the black work force in Evansville was still on relief. Neither were blacks eligible for the National Youth Administration (NYA) manual-training classes organized in Evansville or Midland. With labor plentiful, employers sought younger people and raised the qualifications for simple jobs beyond the reach of many who could easily perform them. A restaurant chain in Philadelphia, advertising for sandwich makers, required a bust of at least 34 inches.

For the forgotten Americans of past decades, the depression was a more severe episode of a chronic illness. For those unaccustomed to such travail, the New Deal resurrected hopes. Robert Butler, a specialist in NIRA law and NRA codes, thought that the great Blue Eagle was a form of national madness. Perhaps so, but at a critical moment it captured the enthusiasm of millions. Midland's Boy Scouts conducted a house-to-house canvass to obtain consumer pledges to patronize only stores displaying the Blue Eagle. Two hundred Fredonia women—11 percent of the female population—attended a mass meeting at the high school to pledge allegiance. Endorsement came from the Howell Ladies' Aid Society. During the summer of 1933, Evansville, Midland, Fredonia, Waynesboro, and hundreds of places larger and smaller, boasting of total local participation in the NRA, celebrated with glittering parades. Newspapers were filled with ads carrying the Blue Eagle and admonitions that "NOW IS THE TIME TO BUY." The Gales all drove into Fredonia for the Recovery Day parade in August, and the Traces and Reinhardts may even have rubbed shoulders in Evansville while watching a 100-float parade accompanied by dozens of marching groups and bands and featuring an exvaudevillian who walked the length of Main Street atop an enormous blue ball.

Hoopla was important in those days. So, too, were the wage and hour provisions of the NRA codes and the stipulations guaranteeing collective bargaining. Members of Evansville's NRA retailers' group and their employees organized boycotts and picket lines against Sears, Roebuck, A & P, Montgomery Ward's, and Krogers for ignoring agreements to close Saturday evenings and reduce weekly store hours to the 52 allowed in the NRA codes. Evansville's tranquil labor scene was momentarily interrupted by a series of strikes and organizational campaigns in its major industries. While union organization under NIRA did not proceed rapidly in Evansville or elsewhere, the labor movement had gained momentum, and it only awaited the Wagner Labor Relations Act to achieve fulfillment.

With the exception of the United Mine

Workers and a few strong craft unions, the labor movement, defeated time and time again after World War I, lay dormant. The best that employees could hope for was company unions. At Midland's Crucible Steel, the company permitted, in the 1920s, the organization of an "Employees Relief and Beneficial Association," which provided life insurance and organized athletic teams. Directors were elected annually, but Italian and Slavic directors were conspicuous by their absence. Until NRA, Crucible's management established wages, hours, working conditions, hiring, promotion, and firing policies as it saw fit. If a worker resisted, he was released, as Mihailo Markovich could attest.

Crucible complied with Section 7(a) of NIRA in July 1933. Management-imposed tranquility was shattered the following October. A strike for union recognition in neighboring Ambridge resulted in an attack upon pickets by 250 deputy sheriffs (largely American Legion members) that left 1 picket dead, 12 shot, and 50 clubbed into unconsciousness. On the same day, striking coal miners at Shippingport, just across the river from Midland, repulsed an attack by sheriffs and armed scabs. Strikes and walkouts multiplied during the next four years. The real test came with the appearance in Midland of organizers for the Steel Workers Organizing Committee (SWOC), an operational arm of the Committee for Industrial Organization (CIO).

SWOC initiated an organizational campaign at Crucible in 1937. In 1938, Crucible recognized it along with the union started under NIRA. Mike Simich, just arrived from the mines at Primrose, immediately joined SWOC and became a local organizer. He recalled the excitement and tensions of those days. Workers at Crucible knew well enough that the steel industry had been among the most anti-union industries in the nation.

Many, at first, were afraid to commit themselves to SWOC, and it was Mike's task to explain how the new Wagner Labor Act would protect them. This proved difficult, for Mike was fired as a result of his union activities, as were other organizers. This was precisely what the Wagner Act was supposed to prevent. Slowly, SWOC gained strength at the expense of the rival, company-dominated union with the help of National Labor Relations Board representatives who circulated through the area, conducting elections and seeing to it that companies bargained with the unions. Mike was rehired. Two strikes followed in 1939 and 1940, by which time war orders were coming to Crucible and the company capitulated. By this time, SWOC Local 1212 represented 95 percent of Crucible's employees.

The union meant much to Mike and his co-workers. Raises were won, hours were reduced, overtime pay was assured, paid vacations for those employed over five years were guaranteed, and personnel policies were regularized. The latter, particularly seniority rules, finally equalized conditions between native-born American and ethnic workers. Serbs were no longer bypassed when a better job became available; blacks remained at the bottom of the wage scale.

Unionization shook up Midland in many ways. Municipal employees were organized by the CIO in 1941. Perhaps more significantly, a viable two-party system emerged in Midland. Democrats cultivated the labor-ethnic vote and in 1932, while Midland went for Hoover, the normal 80 to 90 percent majorities the Republicans had enjoyed during the 1920s declined to 64 percent. (Republicans won 50.8 percent of the Beaver County vote.) Midland's voters went heavily Democratic in subsequent elections. In both 1936 and 1938, Democrats garnered 69 percent of the vote. In the western precincts, where the

Markoviches lived, Democratic majorities exceeded 80 percent. The Democrats also began to place a few people in borough offices and won control of the borough council in 1940. Democrats also made inroads in traditionally Republican Wilson County. Relying largely on the farm vote Charles Gale helped to mobilize, Democratic votes for state and federal offices increased during the 1930s while an occasional Democrat even won a county or city election. Much the same shift occurred in Evansville. By 1938, the Democrats controlled the city council, the district representative to Congress, and all four of Evansville's seats in the Indiana legislature. Midland, Fredonia, and Evansville represented the three-pronged labor-farm-urban coalition, which emerged during the depression to bring national supremacy to the Democratic Party.

In American communities, much had changed but much also remained the same. Community services were upgraded during the depression decade through the use of federal funds. In Gus O'Reilly's driving territory, streets were greatly improved by straightening, draining, and resurfacing. Fredonia received a new sewage-treatment plant, improved its water supply, and added recreational facilities to its park system. Federal funds paid for a new library in New Albany. Evansville completed its sewer system, reconstructed its streets, constructed a new vocational high school, and expanded the municipal airport. Waynesboro's children utilized a new gymnasium and community center. Midland's streets were all resurfaced, its schools completely rehabilitated, and a stage and bandstand arose in the Midland park. By 1940, WPA had erected more than 6,500 recreational buildings and had built or improved more than 40,000 athletic fields, tennis courts, and parks. Each of these communities and hundreds of others received a new post office, frequently decorated, as in Fredonia and Midland, with a WPA-sponsored mural. Kosse does not appear to have received any federal money.

But for FERA funds in 1933 and 1934, an estimated 20,000 rural schools would have closed. The PWA, WPA, and NYA contributed essential aid to the nation's entire educational system. In Wilson County alone, 147 youths were able to continue their high-school and college educations with the aid of NYA jobs. PWA money maintained and improved the physical plant while WPA funds and personnel launched school hot-lunch programs and adult and vocational education courses in both rural and urban areas. In Midland, 250 men signed up for the blueprint reading course in 1937. Blacks were ineligible. Bob Bassano took a WPA accounting course in the late 1930s.

Many considered federal programs that fostered labor organizations, salvaged public-school systems, or provided work relief for the construction of new sewers and water plants as revolutionary. Robert Butler felt that private initiative would suffice and he assured Harvard's graduating class of 1939 that equality of opportunity lived in America. "Anybody who tells you fellows that America is finished growing and doesn't offer smart young men a chance," he concluded, "grab him by the seat of the pants and throw him out the window." American Legionaires in Midland and Beaver County had done just that throughout 1938, conducting raids on and sending spies to purportedly communistic meetings, attacking the New Deal and its programs as socialistic, and speaking out enthusiastically for the democratic way of life.

But in no field of activity was the non-revolutionary, inconsistent, and middle-class orientation of the New Deal more apparent than in its approach to the quantity and quality of the nation's housing. Chronic housing

A metalworking class at Bethune-Cookman College, sponsored by the National Youth Administration

shortages experienced during the 1920s, particularly for lower income groups, worsened during the depression while the loss of jobs or income threatened with foreclosure and eviction millions of families who had undertaken the heavy costs of home ownership. New Deal housing programs dealt effectively with the threatened homeowners through HOLC, while FHA provided tangible aid to moderate-income families who wished to purchase homes. But they accomplished virtually nothing in providing either low-income urban or rural families with minimally adequate housing.

FHA and HOLC were irrelevant to those in the market for rental units. FHA, by encouraging private capital to flow toward single-family construction, may have retarded apartment-house development. Housing authorities in New York estimated that private builders could not build a modern dwelling to rent for less than $12 to $14 per room per month. Housing in Inwood, then, was profitable, and affordable for the Bassanos. But of the approximately 500,000 families living in New York's slum areas, 408,000 were paying less than $7 per month per room. Many could not even afford these small rents. The Home Relief Bureau in New York paid out, in 1935, over $31 million in rental allowances to families on relief. Efforts to compel landlords to comply with certain standards generally failed. In New York, owners of 30,000 tenements, knowing that the city could not close them down, flatly refused to comply with New York's Multiple-Dwelling Law.

Federal public-housing efforts under the direction of PWA and state-sanctioned municipal public housing hardly made a dent in meeting low-cost housing needs. The Housing Authority of PWA made 49 project allocations in 36 cities, adding a total of 21,321 living units to the nation's supply. Many states, however, passed legislation authorizing the establishment of municipal housing authorities. By 1940, only 10 states lacked such enabling legislation. Federal housing initiatives in rural areas, run by the Department of Interior, FERA, the Resettlement Administration, and FSA, while extremely controversial politically and containing good ideas, produced even fewer results.

In 1937, Congress passed the capstone of federal housing action, the United States Housing Act, which created the United States Housing Authority (USHA) as the agency responsible for low-cost public housing. The USHA, assuming the management of the PWA projects, opened its first project for occupancy in 1939, and 17 other local housing projects were occupied by spring 1940. By that time, USHA had committed $668 million to 169 communities in 29 states for the construction of 71,000 dwelling units, 13 percent in New York City. Given the enormous number of substandard units existing and requiring replacement in American cities—New York alone contained 250,000 apartments without a private toilet—to say nothing of the needs of an increasing population, the federal effort was less than adequate. Nonetheless, precedents now existed, some experience

had been gained, and hopes were aroused that the promises of the housing act would be fulfilled in the future.

Recovery

Mike Simich was rehired by Crucible on September 29, 1939, exactly one year after England's Prime Minister Chamberlain had flown to Munich to meet with Hitler and the leaders of Italy and France. With war orders coming in during the winter of 1939, Crucible had increased its production to 65 percent of capacity. Then, with Hitler's invasion of Poland on September 1, followed by declarations of war on September 3 by England and France, Crucible further expanded production, recalling Simich and several hundred others. By the end of 1939, industrial employment in Midland had reached predepression levels.

Recovery in other communities came somewhat slower. Federal expenditures for defense were under $5 billion in fiscal years 1939 and 1940 and reached $20 billion only in the last half of 1941 (compared with over $90 billion in both 1944 and 1945). In 1940, war production accounted for but 5 percent of total industrial production, rising to 15 percent by the time war was declared. Most of this was contracted out to existing plants like Crucible, which had the capability to fabricate military hardware. Enforced conversion to military production, attended by bitter intercity competition to obtain new facilities and their payrolls, began only after Pearl Harbor.

Even though Evansville's industries received contracts for military equipment and benefited from an improving market for automobiles, 9 percent of its labor force remained unemployed in 1940. While there were obvious signs that 1940 was a better year than 1939—new automobile agencies were established in Fredonia and Evansville, attendance at annual auto and home-furnishing shows was up, industrial production was about 12 percent higher—improving times did not come with a rush. But more and more, the attention of Americans was diverted from the lingering depression to the realities of Europe and Asia at war and the potential impact on their lives. That impact gained visibility when the draft board took its place in county courthouses or on main streets beside the older, somehow less relevant, offices of New Deal agencies.

When wartime mobilization swung into higher gear in 1941, many communities were already treating the depression as a bad dream. Evansville's annual report in 1941, summarizing the city's accomplishment since 1935, did not acknowledge the federal contribution to any municipal improvements. It was as if the New Deal had never existed. Houston's municipal leaders protested Roosevelt's embargo (September 1940) of scrap metal exports to Japan because Houston had become a center for this trade. News of a large Curtiss Wright propeller plant in Beaver County received front page attention in the *Midland News* in February and March 1941. If there was no joy in Midland as war became more likely, there was no gloom either. It was hard to be gloomy when, after 10 years, the expectation of paycheck following paycheck finally seemed assured. Few failed to see the connection between that paycheck and Warsaw, Rotterdam, and Coventry, but it was no less sweet for all that.

A SUMMING UP

Ten years of innovation, political controversy, sporadic violence, and hope tempered by doubt and bewilderment had carried Americans somewhat beyond the scurrying after pleasure and the indifference toward national ills that characterized the post-World War I decade. At the least, many Americans were willing to admit that such hoary values as individualism and free enterprise neither guaranteed success nor offered adequate protection against economic disaster. As individuals, Americans admitted their vulnerability. As citizens of communities, they recognized some of their collective limitations and weaknesses. The fruits of this new maturity—as well as its blind spots—were visible in their communities.

The proliferation of federal offices bespoke a blurring of the traditional lines of responsibility between different levels of government. Community autonomy was somewhat diminished by the intrusion of federal and state authority. In a field such as public health, communities that adhered to state and federal standards discovered that their responsibilities had expanded. In the areas of comprehensive city planning or rural land use, federal actions stimulated community concern. And even in a traditional bailiwick of local power like education, while the states might establish the qualifications of a teacher and interfere with curriculum, the policy decisions of local school boards remained a constant source of political controversy.

If certain aspects of community life did depart from the practices of earlier days, by and large it was accepted as an improvement. The federal presence brought public benefits, to be sure, more to some than to others. But these others were becoming more articulate, as in Midland where a branch of the NAACP was chartered in 1936. And in a general sense, citizens were more inclined to make positive demands to satisfy group or local needs. Numerous and well-attended mass meetings were convened in places such as Fredonia, Midland, and Howell, to formulate resolutions and proposals about this or that pressing issue: Charles Gale and other vocal farmers debating soil-conservation policy; Mike Simich and co-workers hammering out acceptable local grievances procedures—all attested to a more demanding citizenry.

There is much irony in this. In a way, the end of the depression came too swiftly, too completely, and was too enmeshed with violence of unprecedented magnitude. It was obvious that Americans had not resolved their own problems. Hitler, Mussolini, Stalin, Chamberlain and Tojo were much more responsible than Dr. New Deal. There were still serious doubts about the overall efficacy of the programs that had been devised. Moreover, as the war intensified, more people had more money in their pockets than ever before and while they could not spend it all at that moment, they knew the time would come. Prosperity born of war weakened the strong sense of community and interdependence that depression had called forth. But, what hindsight might describe as slippage, depression-weary Americans accepted as recovery . . . finally, recovery.

SUGGESTIONS FOR FURTHER READING

Many of the works cited in the bibliographical listing for Chapter 2 are relevant to the history of American communities, 1920-1940. In addition, *see* George E. Mowry, *The Urban Nation, 1920-1960* (1965); the first chapters of Blake McKelvey's, *The Emergence of Metropolitan America, 1915-1966* (1966); Robert E. Park et al., eds., *The City* (1925); and William H. Wilson, *Coming of Age: Urban America, 1915-1945* (1974). Specialized studies include Blaine A. Brownell, *The Urban Ethos in the South, 1920-1930* (1975); Don Kirschner, *City and Country: Rural Responses to Urbanization in the 1920s* (1970); Roy Lubove, *Community Planning in the 1920s* (1963); Thomas L. Philpott, *The Slum and the Ghetto: Neighborhood Deterioration and Middle Class Reform: Chicago, 1880-1930* (1978); Leslie W. Tentler, *Wage-Earnings Woman: Industrial Work and Family Life in the United States, 1900-1930* (1979); Deborah D. Moore, *At Home in America:*

Second Generation New York Jews (1981); Caroline F. Ware, *Greenwich Village* (1935); Harvey W. Zorbaugh, *The Gold Coast and the Slum* (1929); Park D. Goist, *From Main Street to State Street: Town, City, and Community in America* (1977); John Rae, *The Road and the Car in American Life* (1971); and Humbert S. Nelli, *The Business of Crime: Italians and Syndicate Crime in the United States* (1976).

Of particular utility in drafting this chapter were Lilian Brandt, *An Impressionistic View of the Winter of 1930-1931 in New York City* (1932); Edmund de S. Brunner and Irving Lorge, *Rural Trends in Depression Years* (1937); Carl Condit, *Chicago, 1919-1929: Building, Planning, and Urban Technology* (1973); Robert M. Fogelson, *The Fragmented Metropolis: Los Angeles, 1850-1930* (1967); Charles S. Johnson et al., *The Collapse of Farm Tenancy: Summary of Field Studies and Statistical Surveys, 1933-1935* (1935); Mirra Komarovsky, *The Unemployed Man and His Family* (1940); George A. Lundberg et al, *Leisure: A Suburban Study* (1934); Robert S. Lynd and Helen M. Lynd, *Middletown: A Study in American Culture* (1929) and *Middletown in Transition: A Study in Cultural Conflicts* (1937); Bessie A. McClenahan, *The Changing Urban Neighborhood* (1929); Roderick D. McKenzie, *The Metropolitan Community* (1933); James T. Patterson, *The New Deal and the States* (1969); and Mel Scott, *American City Planning Since 1890* (1969). See also Edmund de S. Brunner et al, *The School in American Society* (1936); C. Luther Fry, *The New and Old Immigrant on the Land: A Study of Amerization and the Rural Church* (1922); Richard Gambino, *Blood of My Blood: The Dilemma of the Italian-Americans* (1975); Wayne S. Fuller, *RFD: The Changing Face of Rural America* (1964); Clarence S. Stein, *Toward New Towns for America* (1957); and Edgar Sydenstricker, *Health and Environment* (1933).

Works treating urban and suburban issues include Edith Abbott, et al, *The Tenements of Chicago, 1908-1935* (1936); John W. Allswang, *A House for All People: Ethnic Politics in Chicago, 1890-1936* (1971); Sidney Axlerod, *Tenements and Tenants* (1972); Ronald H. Bayor, *Neighbors in Conflict: The Irish, Germans, Jews and Italians in New York City, 1929-1941* (1979); E. Digby

302

Baltzell, *Philadelphia Gentlemen: The Making of a National Upper Class* (1958); John E. Brebout and Ronald J. Grele, *Where Cities Meet: The Urbanization of New Jersey* (1964); Nelson M. Blake, *Water for the Cities: A History of the Urban Water Supply Problem in the U.S.* (1956); Lyle Dorsett, *Franklin D. Roosevelt and the City Bosses* (1977); Edward R. Ellis, *The Epic of New York City* (1966); Robert M. Fogelson, *Big-City Police* (1977); Sidney Glazer, *Detroit: A Study in Urban Development* (1965); Blake McKelvey, *Rochester: An Emerging Metropolis, 1925-1961* (1961); Howard L. Preston, *Automobile Age Atlanta: The Making of a Southern Metropolis, 1900-1935* (1978); Calvin Schmid, *Social Saga of Two Cities* [Minneapolis-St. Paul] (1937) and his *Social Trends in Seattle* (1944); Marilyn M. Sibley, *The Port of Houston: A History* (1968); Maurice R. Stein, *The Eclipse of Community* (1960); and Nathan S. Whetten and E. C. Devereux, *Studies of Suburbanization in Connecticut* (1936).

For studies which analyze changes affecting rural and small-town life, see George A. Works and Simon O. Lesser, *Rural America Today: Its Schools and Community Life* (1942); Kate Wofford, *Modern Education in the Small Rural School* (1938); James B. Allen, *The Company Town in the American West* (1966); John B. Armstrong, *Factory under the Elms: A History of Harrisville, New Hampshire* (1969); John D. Black, *The Rural Economy of New England: A Regional Study* (1950); John Dollard, *Caste and Class in a Southern Town* (1937); C. Luther Fry, *American Villagers* (1926); David R. Jenkins, *Growth and Decline of Agricultural Villages* (1940); J. H. Kolb and Edmund de S. Brunner, *A Study of Rural Society* (1946); John H. Kolb, *Emerging Rural Communities* (1959); Robert I. Kutah, *Story of a Bohemian-American Village: A Study of Social Persistence and Change* (1933); Lane W. Lancaster, *Government in Rural America* (1937); Theodore B. Manny, *Rural Municipalities* (1930); James E. Morlock, *The Evansville Story: A Cultural Interpretation* (1956); John L. Shover, *First Majority—Last Minority: The Transforming of Rural Life in America* (1976); Page Smith, *As a City Upon a Hill: The Town in American History* (1973); W. Lloyd Warner et al, *Democracy in Jonesville* (1949); James West, *Plainville, USA* (1945); Seymour L. Wolfbein, *The Decline of a Cotton Textile City: A Study of New Bedford* (1944); Tamara Hareven, *Amoskeag* (1980); and Carter G. Woodson, *The Rural Negro* (1930).

The scholarly literature on the depression's impact on American communities is immense. A few of these studies are Joseph L. Arnold, *The New Deal in the Suburbs: A History of the Greenbelt Towns Program, 1935-1954* (1971); Glen H. Beyer, *Housing and Society* (1965); Ewan Claque et al, *After the Shut Down* (1934); Paul Conkin, *Tomorrow a New World: The New Deal Community Program* (1959); Glen Elder's important work already cited; Clarence J. Enzler, *Some Social Aspects of the Depression* (1939); John D. Garwood and W. C. Testhill, *The Rural Electrification Administration: An Evaluation* (1963); Ivan G. Hosack, *Public Health in Pittsburgh, 1930-1940* (1941); Philip Klein et al, *A Social Study of Pittsburgh* (1938); Gladys L. Palmer, *The Search for Work in Philadelphia, 1932-1936* (1939); Ezra D. Sanderson, *Research Memorandum on Rural Life in the Depression* (1937); M. B. Schnapper, ed., *Public Housing in America* (1939); Charles H. Trout, *Boston, the Great Depression, and the New Deal* (1977); R. C. White and Mary K. White, *Research Memorandum on Social Aspects of Relief Policies in the Depression* (1937); and Donald Young, *Minority Peoples in the Depression* (1937).

9 | Waging World War II

The Japanese attack on Pearl Harbor on December 7, 1941, seared the memories of all who experienced it. The shocking news swept across a nation tranquilly enjoying the varied pursuits of an early Sunday in December. Elaine Kurihara watched a "mushy" romantic film in a Japanese movie house. Two time zones east, Jerry Trace sat in a friend's living room, rehashing the just-ended football season and wondering about scholarship offers. Both froze as the radio reported that swarms of Japanese war planes had bombed and strafed the U.S. naval base at Pearl Harbor, Hawaii, smashing the Pacific fleet anchored there and wrecking airfields and port facilities. Simultaneously, Secretary of State Cordell Hull was angrily dismissing the Japanese ambassador, who had arrived with a statement from his government shortly after the attack began. Patricia Butler learned about the coming of war much later. On Sunday afternoon, she attended a New York

Giants football game and, though she and her boyfriend wondered at the exodus of army and navy officers during the first half, Patricia only discovered the cause when they emerged from the Polo Grounds and heard the shouts of newsboys. All our families understood that Pearl Harbor would compel the United States to declare war against Japan. Today, those who survive dredge up memories of fear, anger, bewilderment, even jubilation when asked about the terrible day. But all mention the uncertainty that gripped them, a feeling that events suddenly and irrevocably had taken control over their lives.

By almost any standard of comparison, the Second World War affected more people in more ways than any previous conflict. Americans believed they were engaged in warding off the apocalypse and they acted on that belief. The war caused the industrialized nations to impose unprecedented controls over the lives of their citizens. And in many countries,

U.S. battleships at anchor in Pearl Harbor—from the perspective of a Japanese dive-bomber, December 7, 1941

there developed a pervasive sense of popular involvement. During the Second World War, the idea of "noncombatant" disappeared for all practical purposes. That war was a struggle between peoples and not just a contest between professional armies had been accepted in principle since the Napoleonic Era; however, World War II was the first conflict to convert the principle into reality. A tinsmith, aircraft factory worker, or farmer might live behind the battle lines, but his or her contribution to the war was deemed as important as that of the combat soldier. Thus, urban populations—in Coventry, Dresden, Hiroshima—became "legitimate" targets. But what happened in the United States? Did Mihailo Markovich, Ben Trace, and Lila Hunt Gropper, thousands of miles from the battle zones and safe from air attack, believe they lived and worked on the front lines?

For the Gishmans, Traces, Bassanos, Mar-

koviches, and all the others, there was surprisingly little immediate awareness of change. It was a bad time for some and a good time for many others. The pressures on families during the war years—military service, mothers at work, the demands of multiple jobs, repeated moves, adequate housing and the search for child care, racial tensions, and more—did add up to a social revolution; but few Americans bothered to do the arithmetic, for they perceived these problems to be temporary. At a time when the nation's leaders insisted that survival depended on winning the war, few bothered to monitor what they were doing to themselves.

Americans did assume that victory would usher in a glorious era of prosperity and technological miracles, a conviction nurtured by innumerable *Saturday Evening Post* articles and newsreel features about "houses of the future," automatic kitchens, personal autogyros, and the imminent defeat of every disease known to man. Similarly, they assumed this material prosperity would take place in a peaceful world. Many suffered periodic flashes of anxiety to be sure—fear that wartime prosperity might lapse again into depression and fear that the goal of global peace might prove illusory.

Had the federal government mobilized for war according to some rational model of what postwar America *should* be, many of the problems that plagued the United States after the war might have been avoided or controlled. Not surprisingly, Washington had neither a comprehensive plan for mobilization nor a vision of the ideal society to emerge from the war, much less any interest in linking the two questions. Past experience, the clamor to win the war whatever the cost, the peculiar administrative style of President Roosevelt, and popular apathy combined to determine America's course at home and abroad. Out of this mix came patchwork solutions to problems as they arose. Those in charge feared that to do otherwise would intensify existing divisions and deflect public attention from the goal of victory.

Reflecting the general confusion, the government's presentation of the war fused emotional appeals for sacrifice and total involvement in the "war effort" with vague promises about the better world to arise after victory. The public—certainly almost all our families—waded through the sloganeering and picked up the idea that there was a job to do and it was best done quickly and thoroughly. Compared with the experience of the other belligerents in the Second World War, the United States lagged behind in martial enthusiasm and willingness to sacrifice for the cause. Americans worried about their husbands, sons, and nephews in the service; they counted ration points and collected tinfoil. But to a degree they would have denied at the time, life went on much as usual—and,

for many, dramatically improved. Given this public passivity, the lack of direction, and the bureaucratic entanglements and waste that typified America's war effort, the successes of U.S. industrial and agricultural mobilization were truly miraculous. Happily, the Axis nations proved even less capable of fully exploiting their national resources.

THE CRITICAL PERIOD

During the months when the country drifted toward full involvement in the war, the Roosevelt administration struggled to prepare for total mobilization of the American economy. Modern war demanded much greater preparation ("lead time") than was called for by the myth of the citizen soldier who dropped his plow and picked up his musket to march to battle. The capacity for miracles of production existed, but the nation's resources were not unlimited. Converting the United States into "the arsenal of democracy," as FDR had promised in December 1940, demanded that certain vital industries return to full production, that many factories shift immediately to manufacture of the "sinews of war," and that a crash program begin for the construction of new war plants. To minimize delay and waste, the federal government assumed various degrees of responsibility for the production and allocation of scarce raw materials (aluminum, for example), assignment of skilled workers to factories converting to munitions production, and emergency financing of plant expansion. The president decided that political divisions and lagging public opinion prohibited dramatic federal initiatives—price and wage controls, a tough rationing system, and possibly even a national scheme for assigning workers to jobs—and that government "meddling" on such a grand scale would be tolerated only in wartime, if then. By spring 1941, the administration's

The Bassanos

Pearl Harbor hardly affected the Bassanos. Bob continued to make the trip downtown each day on the Seventh Avenue subway, and Charlotte attended to the housekeeping chores and child care. She maintained a routine of shopping along Dyckman Street, chatting with special friends, and going to the afternoon double feature at neighborhood theatres. Once Robbie started school, his mother rarely visited the parks. She preferred to go shopping, a serious business. Appliance and furniture purchases were postponed during the war, as the family invested its surplus income in war stamps and savings bonds. On Dyckman Street, Charlotte still enjoyed a good selection in the street's ethnic establishments: Jewish meat markets, Italian vegetable stalls, Greek, Italian, and other bakeries. A mini supermarket, Bedford's, was close by as were several small, all-purpose grocers, some in spaces no larger than Charlotte's living room. Eyeglasses at Bernstein's optometry shop, watch repairs at Oberman's Jewelry, an occasional roll of film at Rialto's camera store, a beer at Gallagher's saloon, chow mein at Lucky Lee's Chop Suey Heaven, fish cakes from Horn and Hardart's, notions from Kresge's and Woolworth's, an egg cream and the New York Daily News at Adler's candy store, and a host of other commodities could be obtained within three blocks of the Bassano apartment.

Charlotte shopped wisely and was rarely caught with insufficient ration stamps. For the most part, the family ate as it had prior to the war but used less sugar and coffee and used oleomargarine instead of butter. Their favorite grocer put scarce items away for them and gave credit in stamps as well as money. While not actually trafficking in ration stamps, he always had spares for valued customers. Other merchants did the same: Adler's saved the paper for Bob, and Mante's Bakery put away a half-dozen hard rolls every Sunday morning. It was a form of social recognition much prized by the Bassanos.

The closest Bob came to the war was drill at the National Guard Armory at 66th and Park Avenue, guard duty twice a week, and summer camp with his unit, the 7th National Guard Regiment at Camp Smith, New York. Bob and Robbie, however, followed the war with great interest. They kept a huge map of the European Theater tacked to a kitchen wall and moved colored pins as the Soviet armies moved westward and the U.S. and British forces took North Africa and invaded Sicily, and finally, the French mainland. Father and son built countless models of Japanese Zeros, Russian Stormoviches, Nazi Messerschmitts, British Hurricanes, and American P-38s. Robbie played "war" almost every day, and he and Bob made up table war games for rainy days. The entire family enjoyed the war films that flooded neighborhood movie houses.

For the Bassanos, the war remained a distant phenomenon, one experienced only through newspapers, radio, movie newsreels, and stories of friends and relatives. It is unlikely that their lifestyle would have been much different had there been no war. The Bassanos enjoyed these years.

program was stalled. Making America the arsenal of democracy could not be accomplished without full mobilization, and the country would not support mobilization until war was declared.

Although the United States pushed "nonbelligerency" to its limit during the summer and fall of 1941 (with American destroyers guarding Allied convoys, with American pilots ferrying aircraft to the Middle East and the

Soviet Union, and with increasing amounts of American-made and purchased munitions dispatched to the war zones), this grim equation prevented any rapid expansion of production. The Reinhardts, Traces, Markoviches, Bassanos, and Hunts, while fatalistically accepting the nation's eventual entry into the war, refused to think seriously about the looming conflict. It was not that they did not know what was happening. The war shouted from every newspaper and radio broadcast. One by one, the comic strip heroes of Robbie Bassano and Bill Trace—Joe Palooka, Terry and his Pirates, even Little Orphan Annie—enlisted in the struggle against international evil. Each new issue of *Saturday Evening Post, Ladies Home Journal,* and *Capper's Farmer* carried more ads proclaiming the contribution of Spam, Borg-Warner, and International Harvester to America's "preparedness" campaign. Movie marquees in Boston, Midland, Evansville, and San Francisco invited patrons to thrill at films featuring sadistic Japanese soldiers, noble, clean-cut British and Chinese heroes, and naive young Americans who realized, as the last reel began, that the battle to save democracy was everyone's fight. Americans read, listened, watched, and waited.

In this atmosphere, it was understandable that mobilization for "defense" moved forward slowly. Poor planning also slowed preparedness. The War and Navy Departments had assumed that, prior to a declaration of war, "it was unlikely that an appreciable mobilization, either in manpower or materials, could be expected." Congressional indifference also played a role. As late as March 1940, the House Appropriations Committee reduced a War Department request for replacement airplanes from 496 to 57, denied funds for an Alaskan air base, and expressed opposition to any panicky expansion of the armed forces.

The German *blitzkrieg* through the Low Countries and France in May–June 1940, ac-

complished more than all the interventionist speeches, pro-British films, and presidential prodding. Congress opened the floodgates. In May 1940, President Roosevelt requested of and received from Congress emergency defense appropriations totaling $2.1 billion. By September, another $5 billion had been appropriated. Between June 1 and December 1, 1940, the government awarded some $10.5 billion in defense contracts. A year later, defense projects engaged more than 5,600,000 workers in heavy industry.

Another result of Hitler's spectacular military successes was the passage of the first peacetime draft law. The Burke-Wadsworth Selective Service Act, approved despite vehement opposition in September 1940, provided for the registration of all men between the ages of 20 and 36. Under the direction of General Lewis B. Hershey, more than 6,000 draft boards were created. As in the First World War, these boards filled local quotas and ruled on deferments. With 16,400,000 others, Mike Simich, Austin Hart, Robert Bassano, Henry Gishman, Louis Gropper, Raymond Reinhardt, and several Butlers registered at their local courthouses. A few weeks later, President Roosevelt drew the first unlucky numbers from a revolving drum. The lottery caught Austin Hart, who was required to give one year of service "within the Western Hemisphere" to the armed forces of the United States. In August 1941, as Austin and several hundred thousand young men were making plans for their return home, Congress, by a single vote in the House, extended the term of service for six months.

Industrial mobilization and military expansion had to compete with new consumer demand resulting from the increased purchasing power of millions of American families. In 1941, the gross national product reached $125.3 billion, more than twice the annual total of the worst depression years. Industrial output bested the 1935–39 average by 66 percent. Though 4,000,000 Americans remained without jobs, all graphs curved upward. Ben Trace, Mihailo Markovich, Gus O'Reilly, and Jacob Reinhardt benefited directly from the prewar boom. As did most Americans, they yearned to spend this bounty, to splurge on the things their families had been denied. In these circumstances, businesspeople preferred to reach for the dollar they knew was there rather than bid for a defense contract that involved costly retooling, tiresome negotiations with Washington bureaucrats, and that might be canceled if the war in Europe suddenly ended. General Motors preferred to open a new Buick dealership in Fredonia rather than shift its Flint assembly plant to tank production. Similar sentiments prevailed across the country.

No one except President Roosevelt possessed sufficient authority to override the private sector's drift, and he decided to assert control cautiously. On May 26, 1940, FDR had appointed a National Defense Advisory Committee, with members drawn from business, labor, and government. Though the NDAC acquired a staff and circulated numerous "directives" and set up "priorities," it failed to accumulate enough clout to enforce its decisions. In December 1940, the president responded to clamor for unified direction of the defense program by establishing a new agency, the Office of Production Management (OPM). It might be claimed that OPM was a significant improvement, for it had only two heads: William S. Knudsen for industrial production and Sidney Hillman for manpower. However, OPM was only to "coordinate." The power to establish priorities, place orders, and allocate scarce resources remained in the possession of various government agencies. Shortly after Pearl Harbor, a White House organization chart listed 42 "executive agencies" with defense responsibilities. The situation was a nightmare of conflicting jurisdictions.

Still, much was accomplished. By spring 1941, 229 new training facilities had been started and many others, dating from the First World War, were being refurbished. Production of planes, tanks, and other weapons mounted steadily, though shortages slowed the lines and reduced stockpiles of some scarce metals below the critical margin. Most of this production came from contracts with the largest corporations in each industry, and often that meant concentration of war orders in a few regions, especially in New England and the North Atlantic states. As Harry S. Truman, who became chairman of a Senate committee investigating the national defense program, said: "There seems to be a policy in the national defense set-up to concentrate all contracts and nearly all manufacturing that has to do with the national defense in a very small area." Three giant corporations garnered 17.4 percent of all defense contracts awarded before Pearl Harbor, and 100 companies were doing 82.6 percent of war-related production as of January 1942. In Evansville, for example, total shutdown of several large companies (making refrigerators, automobiles, and furniture) resulted when the firms were unable to obtain adequate supplies of steel and other raw materials. As a result, employment in nondefense production among 21 major Evansville manufacturers fell from 10,764 in July 1941 to 6,573 in January 1942, while defense-related employment rose only from 229 to 1,235. By fall 1941, Evansville had earned the unwelcome distinction of being one of six communities suffering the most distress from the changeover to war production. Some improvement occurred when an angry delegation met with OPM representatives and Indiana congressmen in August 1941; but not until mid-1942, when Evansville factories won huge contracts for naval landing craft, shell cases, and fighters, did the city recover. It soon discovered that the difficulties associated with war "boom towns" could be equally threatening.

Relief from the stresses of partial mobilization and disunities born of uncertainty came, so prevailing myths have it, with the cleansing shock of Pearl Harbor. For President Roosevelt (and, it seems, a majority of Americans) it was as if a great weight had been removed. "They have attacked us at Pearl Harbor," FDR informed a jubilant Churchill. "We are all in the same boat now." Belying the view that America was now totally united, arguments persisted about the events leading to Pearl Harbor. To defenders of the president, that "day of infamy" proved the wisdom of his foreign policy. Roosevelt haters then and later considered Pearl Harbor as the last act in an evil plot to trick the American people into the war. A whispering campaign claimed that FDR not only knew about and welcomed the Japanese sneak attack but also that he had placed the U.S. Pacific fleet at Pearl Harbor as an easy target. One can dismiss such wild imaginings; but Pearl Harbor did paper over the conflict about America's real interests in the war.

Nor did Pearl Harbor end disputes about war mobilization and strategy. Even before America entered the war, differences had arisen over aid to China and the Soviet Union, the role of air power, and British interests in the Mediterranean. Secret discussions between U.S. and British planners in spring 1941 identified Germany as the strongest

Franklin D. Roosevelt Library

Roosevelt and Churchill talk after divine services aboard H.M.S. *Prince of Wales* during their secret meeting at Placentia Bay, Newfoundland, in August 1941

enemy and therefore assigned the European theater the highest priority. For a time, however, anger over the sneak attack caused Americans to think of Japan as the number-one enemy. Jerry Trace and many of his friends decided to enlist after attending a movie in which a heroic Marine (Robert Taylor) held off waves of fanatical Japanese soldiers. Jerry's final poem for the Reitz High School *Mirror* prior to graduation and enlist-ment in June 1942 began: "Oh, you gallant men of Wake; You the vitals of the earth did shake." Outside the metropolitan centers and west of the Appalachians, many people did not know much or care deeply about the conflict in Europe. They wanted to crush Japan and redress American honor. An opinion poll of March 1942 indicated that 70 percent of the respondents believed the Pacific war should get highest priority.

The Traces

Ben and Anna Trace hung the second of two blue stars in the front bedroom window of their home on August 22, 1942, the day their oldest son, J. R. was inducted into the Army Air Corps. (AAC). Over his parents' protests, Jerry joined the Marines in June 1942 and entered the grueling Marine training course at San Diego, California. Both sons would return from the war but profoundly changed. J. R. reported for basic training to an AAC base near Nashville, Tennessee. He made extremely high scores on the battery of intelligence and aptitude tests given all cadets, and it appeared that he would be approved for flight school. However, his drill sergeant noticed that J. R. was having difficulty keeping up with routine movements and often lost his balance. Following an exhaustive physical examination, J. R. received a medical discharge because of "an organic brain disorder—cause unknown" (later diagnosed as multiple sclerosis). Bitterly disappointed, he returned home. For the next few years, J. R. worked at Hoosier Cardinal and, refusing to see all but a few close friends, built a fantasy world in which he became a great novelist and recluse.

In contrast to J. R., Jerry had breezed through boot camp. Assigned to the new Third Marine Division, he trained as an amphibious tractor driver and shipped out for New Zealand in February 1943. His unit fought on Guadalcanal and Bougainville, took part in the mop-up of Guam (Jerry was awarded the Bronze Star for bravery), landed in the first wave at Iwo Jima, and was in Hawaii preparing for the invasion of Japan itself when the war ended. The experience of war changed him. Not just the brushes with death or the callousness he and his friends came to assume toward the Japanese, living or dead, but the often incompetent leadership, the inane orders, and boredom infused Jerry with determination to gain control of his life, if he survived the war.

Those who remained in Howell continued to live as they had. The war ensured that Ben Trace worked steadily. Though Anna Lee had some difficulties with the rationing system, the Traces lacked nothing important. Jacqueline became pregnant and then married a soldier from Fort Breckinridge whom she met at a USO dance. She went to her husband's home in Providence, R.I., but, desperately unhappy, begged to be allowed to return in June 1944. Ben finally relented and accepted his daughter and "bastard" grandson. The younger boys thought about the war in terms of scrap drives, battle maps, aircraft silhouettes, and John Wayne's and William Bendix's matinee heroism against the Japanese.

Army and Navy officers, almost all of whom had served in the Far East and appreciated the problems of fighting a determined, entrenched enemy across the vastness of Asia, suffered agonies as the Japanese swept through the southwest Pacific, crushing the American outposts of Guam and Wake Island, brushing aside Allied air and naval resistance, and landing overwhelmingly superior forces in the Philippines. Nonetheless, the policy of priority to the war in Europe was confirmed at a meeting of Roosevelt, Churchill, and their military advisers shortly after Pearl Harbor. This conference also produced the rough outlines of a strategic plan for defeating the Axis and approved the principle of unified command by setting up a Combined Chiefs of Staff Committee.

The formal manifestations of cooperation between the United States and Great Britain—and their proclaimed unity with the USSR following Germany's invasion of the Soviet Union in June 1941—belied deep and continuing disagreements within the Allied coalition. To the Soviet Union, there was one strategic goal: the opening of a "second front" in Europe as rapidly as possible to deflect German pressure on the battered Russian defenses. American planners, sympathetic to the Russian pleas for aid, also pressed for a quick, full-scale invasion of the Continent.

Influenced by memories of the bloodbath in 1914–18 and by awareness of Britain's limited resources, Prime Minister Churchill rejected the direct approach. Instead, he favored jabs at the periphery of Nazi power and intensified air attacks and blockade. Until late in the war, British leaders resisted efforts to launch a real second front. The consequences of British opposition were to be momentous, possibly delaying victory in Europe for a year or more and certainly intensifying Russian paranoia about the West's motives.

Those who have criticized the invasions of North Africa (November 1942), Sicily (July 1943), and then Italy (September 1943) as needless, wasteful diversions have bemoaned the concentration of Anglo-American power in the Mediterranean—a traditional focus of British interest—and the "malevolent" influence of Churchill over FDR. But whether President Roosevelt was gulled by the British is only partly the issue. Many months were to elapse before the United States could train and equip the huge forces required for the offensives American strategy contemplated. The period of buildup ended in summer 1943. After that, the United States took the role of senior partner, asserting American aims—sometimes with brutal frankness—over the wishes of its British ally. America gained dominance in the coalition because U.S. forces in combat in the European Theater of Operations far outstripped those of the British. Even more importantly, the Second World War was a battle of production, and the United States proved better able than its allies or its enemies to satisfy the voracious appetite of modern warfare.

In retrospect, it is easy to claim that an eventual Allied victory was ensured from the moment of America's entry into the war. The Axis powers controlled a total population of 500 million and about 3 million square miles of territory. In contrast, the Allies included 1.5 billion people with approximately 40 million square miles of territory and they possessed twice the coal and iron and 25 times as much oil. These statistics, so impressive in the abstract, were less so in reality, for they had to be converted into guns, shells, and soldiers transported safely to the war zones to reverse the early Axis victories.

The Battle of the Atlantic, a desperate struggle for control of critical sea lanes, wore on month after month, year after year. It did not provide the dramatic results of tank battles or amphibious operations. Neither side, with rare exceptions, won a clear-cut victory. The submarine that ripped apart a heavily laden

The Butlers

The Butler clan threw itself wholeheartedly into the war effort. Of the older generation, Eliot became Chief of Surgery, Supreme Headquarters Allied Expeditionary Forces, with the rank of Major General. Roger returned to active duty in the Navy, and Robert was commissioned a colonel in the U.S. Army and assigned first to the Pentagon and then to Secretary of War Stimson's staff.

Six of the next generation saw military service and two of the daughters, Patricia and Mary, joined the OSS. Most dramatic was the career of Jack Butler, John and Rossalyn's eldest. In 1940, two years after dismissal from Harvard for drunkenness and bad conduct, he joined the American Field Service Ambulance Corps. When Jack's unit was cut off during the Battle of France, he escaped to Spain, went to Rhodesia, and joined the RAF. Forced to accept a medical discharge after a crash landing, Jack entered the U.S. Army Air Corps in 1942 as an enlisted man. He was shot down over Ploesti and captured, escaped several times, and finally ended up in a maximum-security POW camp at Stettin, Poland. In spring 1945, Jack traded uniforms with a French corporal, escaped again and, pretending to be a shell-shocked labor draftee, made his way to the British lines.

The wartime experiences of Jack's sister, Patricia, were equally fantastic. A week after Pearl Harbor, Pat had become engaged to Lieutenant Robert Pick (Harvard '36), who was then going through a torpedo gunnery course. Spurning a large social wedding, they were married less than a month later. After a two-day honeymoon, Pick returned to torpedo school and then to a new destroyer, the U.S.S. *Duncan*. On October 11, 1942, the *Duncan* sank with heavy loss of life during the Battle of Savo Island in the Guadalcanal campaign. Robert Pick received a posthumous Navy Cross. Though newly widowed and pregnant, Pat applied for and received a job with the OSS since her father knew the director. After Robin Pick's birth, she went through "spy school." She was a counterintelligence agent in Madrid (posing as a U.S. Embassy secretary and dating Germans and Spanish officials) for a year, and served in London during the 1944 "blitz." She returned home in May 1945.

The Butlers who remained behind threw themselves into organizing the home front. An Englishman later wrote of Pat's mother: "It wasn't Pearl Harbor or the strategy of Churchill that brought the irresistible weight of America onto our side, it was women like Rossy Butler. . . . Agitating, canvassing their Congressmen, driving their husbands, converting waverers, making bandages and raising vast sums for British War Relief"—the chronicle was endless. Rossalyn Butler knew everything about every battle (abroad and in Washington) and she listened faithfully to the evening broadcasts from the front. Although the Butlers were not at all discomforted by shortages and rationing, she and several other family members refused to ask for the favors which their status permitted them. There was an awful row when she discovered that her husband had requested a "C" gasoline ration book (allowing unlimited mileage), and it ended only when the application was torn up. The Butler household observed "eggless Tuesdays" (with John giving up his favorite chocolate souffle) and "meatless Thursdays." And in November 1944, Rossalyn Butler made the supreme sacrifice for the cause. She voted for Franklin Roosevelt.

"Liberty" ship often never reached home. Even more often, the destroyer—such as the one on which Commander Roger Butler served—that depth-charged the attacking U-boat had to watch helplessly as sailors from sinking merchant vessels perished in icy North Atlantic waters. For those who lived, the convoys spelled misery and constant fear. Four fifths of the Allied merchant ships lost went down in the Atlantic and on the deadly Arctic run to Russia. Not until spring 1943 did the frantic effort to check the U-boats show results; however, Allied convoys, though shielded by escort carriers and destroyers, still suffered losses at war's end.

The solution to the "wolf packs" of German submarines was increased output of ships and the supplies they carried. By 1945, the United States and Great Britain, despite terrible losses, boasted more shipping than all nations claimed in 1939. During those six years, American shipyards launched more than 5,000 cargo vessels. The average time for freighter construction shrank from 30 weeks to 7, with ships constructed in standardized sections and riveted together like cars on an assembly line. Eventually, a "bridge of boats," carrying an endless stream of supplies, stretched across the Atlantic.

Allied hopes, said the British Minister of Production, Lord Beaverbrook, rested on "the immense possibilities of American industry." But, as the nation woke from the shock of Pearl Harbor, only President Roosevelt and his immediate circle appeared certain that the plant conversions and expansion, the marshalling of manpower, the distribution of raw materials could be accomplished with sufficient speed and efficiency to lay the material foundations of victory. The problems were as immense as the possibilities.

On January 16, 1942, making use of the sweeping powers just granted him by Congress, FDR created the War Production Board

(WPB), designed to exercise general direction over the war procurement and production program. The history of WPB and its head, Donald Nelson, an experienced and highly regarded Sears, Roebuck executive, in many ways encapsulates the battle for control of production. Nelson dared not assert authority over the War and Navy Departments, which operated their supply programs as private fiefdoms. When a WPB directive interfered with the production of some item ordered by the military, Army and Navy officers did not hesitate to protest directly to the White House, arguing that the war necessitated priority for military over civilian needs. The War Manpower Commission (WMC) and other agencies found they could safely ignore Nelson's rulings. Nelson's power depended on his personal relationship with FDR and the coterie of presidential intimates. His preference for persuasion rather than coercion (clearly reflected in WPB's courting of the business community with cost-plus contracts, tax advantages, and elaborate procedures for consultation) ensured that Nelson would become not the "super czar" many demanded but just another broker and conciliator of contending factions. Real authority remained with the White House.

Insiders in Washington, the old hands and the thousands of recent recruits from industry, commerce, and academic life, understood Nelson's status and the way wartime agencies operated. Robert Butler, called down from Boston to serve as Assistant Deputy Director of the Army Specialist Corps, which recruited persons with specialized training for the armed forces, later described the situation he confronted—"the many new agencies, commissions, and bureaus spawned by the New Deal; duplicating, overlapping, asserting conflicting claims, each engaged in a rough-and-tumble to survive." The Roosevelt administrative style spawned a helter-skelter approach

Evansville Shipyard during World War II. In the 30s men stood around in bread and unemployment lines; here they queue up to punch the time clock before beginning work. In compliance with the government contract, the work force was integrated.

to the problems of finance, manpower, and coordination, an emphasis on speed and heavy reliance on existing facilities and large corporations. Decisions to build new plants frequently were ill-advised. A study by the Bureau of the Budget later concluded: "Many a plant was changed over to war production when its normal product was more needed than its new product. Locomotive plants went into tank production when locomotives were more necessary—but the Tank Division did not know this. We built many new factories which we could not use and did not need." Manpower needs, with which Robert Butler dealt, posed a tremendous challenge. During the war, some 15 million civilians entered the armed services. To meet the employment demands of the defense industry some 15 mil-

lion people were added to the work force—approximately 7.5 million from the unemployment lines, 4 million teenagers, 3 million women, and more than 1 million elderly people. Nonetheless, awkward and serious shortages of skilled and unskilled workers occurred in critical industries.

The War Manpower Commission could never bring itself to coordinate the flow of labor by imposing penalties on those who left defense jobs for high-paying positions in non-critical industries. In 1943, President Roosevelt himself extended the workweek in all war plants from 40 to 48 hours and gave the WMC power to "freeze" war workers in their current jobs. Workers and prospective employers often found ways to get around the edicts. WMC's decisions to concentrate manpower in one industry while the WPB or some other agency allocated scarce raw materials to another often crippled production for weeks or months. Only in December 1944, during the Battle of the Bulge (when a last-ditch German offensive momentarily reversed the Allied advance), did Congress seriously consider a civilian conscription law patterned on the British system, which would have permitted the president to draft men and women for "essential" work. When panic over Hitler's last-gasp offensive in the Ardennes dissipated, so did the interest of Congress in compulsory labor legislation.

Few among our families paid any attention to the intricate maneuvers in Washington, believing that whether X got Y's job and whether agency A replaced commission B had nothing to do with them. But they soon felt the effects. The WPB's first act had been to ban the manufacture of automobiles and small trucks after January 31, 1942 (the prewar auto industry consumed 18 percent of the nation's steel, 14 percent of its copper, and nearly 80 percent of all rubber), and Detroit slowly obeyed. Next came a general restriction on "nonessential" production and a ban on the use of scarce and critical materials. Supplies of iron and steel for consumer goods were cut back and further residential construc-

Building LSTs, Evansville Shipyards, 1943

tion banned. By July 1942, production of consumer goods had been sliced by one third. In Evansville, Servel shut down its refrigerator assembly lines and prepared to turn out shell casings and bomber parts, and International Steel, which had been making revolving doors, accepted a large contract for airplane hangars. Similar conversions occurred in Midland, small towns outside Boston such as Medford, the plains of central Texas, and in southeast Kansas.

To ensure that the companies involved received the necessary supplies to complete construction and enter production proved too much for the WPB's voluntary allocation system. Pressure from Indiana congressmen had resulted in the establishment of a huge landing-craft production facility at Evansville. Several thousand jobs were involved. Millions of dollars would be pumped into the local economy. Mountains of cement, steel, lumber, and other items were necessary to construct the yards and the vessels. Labor was no problem, as the high wages attracted people from Illinois, Indiana, Kentucky, and Tennessee. But who was to ensure that Consolidated Cement in Fredonia would reserve so many tons of cement for shipment to Evansville? Who was to ensure that Crucible Steel would reserve so many tons of steel plate for the landing-craft program?

In November 1942, WPB adopted the Controlled Materials Plan. This scheme required government purchasing agencies to present their requirements to the appropriate WPB divisions, which then would dispense the needed quantity of scarce materials—particularly steel, copper, and aluminum—to the agencies for distribution to contractors. Since landing craft enjoyed top priority, the Navy's supply bureau had no difficulty obtaining enough steel and other materials for Missouri Bridge and Iron's shipyard at Evansville. Unfortunately, the Controlled Materials Plan did not include all scarce items (rubber, for

The Reinhardts

At first glance, the Reinhardts were little affected by the war. Ray and Karl received draft deferments while the other children continued their schooling. Jacob and Mathilde Reinhardt's wartime routine followed the even rhythm of a farm household, with only a few minor concessions to shortages. The biggest change was a dramatic increase in income from the farm, an increase directly attributable to the war-induced demand for agricultural products. Jacob's total income from all sources in 1940 was $2,150.66. For 1942, his income was $5,957.06. For 1944, it jumped to $12,507.76. For the first time since Jacob had assumed responsibility for the farm's operation, the family was receiving a reasonable return for its labor.

The Reinhardts were painfully conscious that this prosperity rested on shaky foundations. What would be done with America's incredible agricultural production once the war ended? And, of more immediate concern, who would help Jacob on the farm if Ray was drafted (as seemed likely in 1942 and again in 1943) and if Karl's naval reserve unit at Evansville College was called up? Would the Reinhardts continue to obtain the fuel, truck and tractor tires, fertilizer, and replacement parts needed to keep the farm going at full capacity? And always nagging at the Reinhardts was anxiety that anti-German sentiment would burst forth, as during the First World War, subjecting them to another round of hostility and ridicule.

instance) and it led to bitter complaints of WPB favoritism. In particular, military officials, believing that the needs of the armed forces had absolute priority, denounced the requests for civilian allocations by people such as Leon Henderson, head of the Office of Price Administration. The people at home simply had to make do.

Though demonstrably inefficient and under increasing attack, WPB and the prevailing administrative system survived until mid-1943. At this juncture, a series of interagency quarrels, personal feuds, and growing congressional hostility forced Roosevelt to make changes. He set up the Office of War Mobilization, yet another "super agency" but with expanded powers and, more important, with his close friend, James F. Byrnes, a former senator and Supreme Court justice, at its helm.

In the end, American industry rose above the difficulties caused by the initial unpre-

paredness for war, material and worker shortages, and the delays, waste, and confusion engendered by battling bureaucrats. In January 1942, FDR set production goals for that year that would have been inconceivable a few months before. The list included 60,000 airplanes, 45,000 tanks, and 20,000 antiaircraft guns. Shortly thereafter, the president announced even higher goals for 1943, more than double those for 1942 in some categories and requiring expenditures of $55 billion. Though not all targets were met, total production reached 300,000 airplanes; 86,000 tanks; 315,000 artillery pieces; 64,000 landing craft; 8,000 ships; and millions of rifles and machine guns. Equally impressive was the outpouring of commodities from America's farms. More than 1 billion bushels of wheat and 3 billion bushels of corn were harvested in 1944 and again in 1945, and total agricultural production rose by about 15 percent. During the peak year,

1944, the United States churned out war supplies at a rate almost equaling the combined output of its allies and the Axis.

LIFE ON THE HOME FRONT

Only Robert Butler and perhaps Gus O'Reilly and Charles Gale among all the family members understood the implications of the announcements about war production and appreciated the phenomenal accomplishment they represented. In homes of the Traces, Markoviches, Groppers, Bassanos, and Gishmans, the government's boasts occasionally provoked bafflement and frustration. They viewed mobilization in personal terms of the daily hunt for ration books and the waiting in line for coffee, sugar, and shoes. The Gales and Reinhardts grew much of their food but could not grow nitrate fertilizer, gasoline, or truck and tractor tires. Nonetheless, the most powerful testimony to the extraordinary American war effort was the absence of great hardship or of public awareness that production both of guns and butter (oleomargarine at least) might not be possible. Indeed, in 1943, of a sample who were asked whether the war had required "real sacrifices," 70 percent admitted it had not.

As mothers and wives of servicemen, Anna Trace, Margaret O'Reilly, Anna Simich, and Martha Hart certainly were convinced they were making "real" sacrifices. Although statistically World War II military service was much less dangerous than, say, that in the Civil War in which some 10 percent of all adult males were killed, wounded, or contracted disease (as compared with less than 2 percent in World War II), these figures offered little solace for relatives who read about the brutal fighting at Anzio and Iwo Jima or the virulent tropical diseases of the Pacific. Compounding the anxiety was the sense of separation and fear that, even should loved ones return physically unscathed, they would be permanently marked by experiences which their families never could understand.

For many others, the ever-present threat of the draft caused continuing anxiety. Soon after Pearl Harbor, Congress enacted new selective-service legislation, requiring the registration of all males between 18 and 65 and making men 20 (soon lowered to 18) to 38 liable for military service. It stipulated that all persons currently in the armed forces and all future inductees were to serve "for the duration of the emergency" plus six months. The law's sweeping provisions were tempered, however, by the policy of drafting only physically qualified men and by assigning highest priority to drafting unmarried persons, next married men without children, and only then husbands whose children were born before Pearl Harbor. There was also, as has been noted, considerable latitude for excusing men from the draft for reason of occupations essential to the war effort. Their status as family men protected Bob Bassano and Henry Gishman. Karl and Raymond Reinhardt belonged to the 2 million plus farm workers awarded occupational deferments, and Louis Gropper and Mike Simich found their jobs classified as essential war work. Mike Simich, who suffered from varicose veins, also was ruled out at first on physical grounds. He was thus one of the millions of males rejected for failing to meet physical or intellectual standards.

It proved impossible for local draft boards to reconcile national policy on deferments with the demand for production labor. Blatant inequities resulted. The Reinhardt boys, both healthy and both single, were not drafted because of their occupation and because Vanderburgh County easily met its quota with volunteers and men from Evansville. In New York and Midland, however, where occupa-

The Gishmans

At the time of Pearl Harbor, Henry Gishman was working part-time for Broadcast Music Incorporated, a music-licensing company, and was also holding down an engine-mechanic job with American Airlines. While 31, married, and the father of two children, Michael (1939) and David (1941), he considered himself "prime bait" for the draft although he worked at the airline to gain exempt status. Henry and Bertha's memories of the war are interwoven with the recurring uncertainty and emotional turmoil arising from Henry's shifting draft status. The Gishmans accepted the necessity for American participation in the war but suffered anxiety caused by the rapid changes in the definition of draft eligibility.

Henry was called up in March 1942 and was informed by the local board to get a war-related job or be drafted. After searching for several weeks, he found employment as a drill-press operator in a small shop in Manhattan. This factory, owned by two retired admirals, had a contract to make running lights for warships. Since Henry worked the night shift, he could continue 9:00 to 2:00 at BMI. Unfortunately, the shop closed in November 1943—when enough lights had been manufactured "for 10 wars"—and all 21 men on the night shift were called up. Even though Henry was the father of two pre–Pearl Harbor sons, he was ordered to report for induction on March 6, 1944. Having accepted his fate, Henry went down to his board to ask for a short postponement in order to settle his father's estate. The board (one man in his 70s, a business woman, and an attorney) gave him four days. On the day of induction, President Roosevelt announced that all men over 26 with children born before Pearl Harbor were exempt. "It saved my neck," Henry recalled. Once more, after the Battle of the Bulge, Henry was given an induction date. He had already given notice and farewell parties had been held when another change in the age limit excluded him from the draft. By then Henry had another job (inspecting cylinder heads for B-29 engines) at Wright Aeronautic Company's huge underground plant in Woodridge, N.J. It was a two-hour commute and Henry hated the job, but it paid well and was indisputably related to the war effort.

The Gishmans had moved to an apartment in Kew Garden Hills in Queens in early 1942. It was modern, with three bedrooms and space for a sleep-in maid. Despite his tangles with the draft board, Henry was earning a good income: $32 per week from Wright Aero, $56.50 weekly from BMI, and about $3,000 each year in royalties for his songs. However, the draft question and his struggle to hold down two jobs took its toll. There was little time to enjoy the good life that the Gishmans could now afford. Bertha spent much of her time with her mother, who enjoyed the children and the surcease from her anguished thoughts about the fate of relatives trapped in the vicious fighting in southern Russia. Had they already died? Or were they crammed into cattle cars on their way to Nazi death camps?

tional deferments abounded, local boards, assigned large quotas, exhausted their lists of single men and began to call up married men and even some fathers. Public protests, reflected in the demand of a hard-pressed senator that "slackers" be drafted "before American homes are broken up, before chil- dren are driven into the streets," had effect. In December 1943, Congress prohibited the induction of fathers, whatever their jobs, before childless men. That decision saved Henry Gishman but made the Reinhardts prime candidates for military service. A year later and after the Battle of the Bulge, the need for manpower reopened the question of drafting fathers and also men in the 4-F category, and only a last-minute decision by President Roosevelt prevented the conscription of those in exempted categories.

Shortly after Pearl Harbor, the federal government established 8,000 ration boards to enforce controls over essential commodities. This was a radical departure. Now the government claimed the right to determine who might buy coffee, and sugar, and T-bone steak—and tires and gasoline. Rumors about rationing of gasoline and rubber products had circulated even before the war. Charles Gale and Ben Trace had taken the precaution of purchasing full sets of new tires for the family cars, and both the Gales and the Reinhardts had filled the gasoline tanks buried next to their barns. Rubber was rationed first. The Japanese took over most of the Asian sources of raw rubber, and President Roosevelt ordered the rationing of tires

Glass drive, Evansville, 1943

to begin on January 2, 1942. Tire rationing boards received monthly quotas from the Office of Price Administration, which was responsible for controlling rents, wages, prices, and now, scarce commodities, and distributed eligibility lists for tires among the owners of the nation's 27 million automobiles. In late spring 1942, with stocks of rubber still dwindling, the president asked his fellow citizens voluntarily to turn in "old tires, old rubber raincoats, old garden hose, rubber shoes, bathing caps, gloves—whatever you have that is made of rubber." Despite the possible political dangers, he also instructed the OPA to prepare for rationing of gasoline.

Reports issued by various government agencies in 1941 and 1942 warned that America faced "military and economic collapse" because of the rubber shortage and that "gas rationing is the only way to save rubber." Some weeks after the 1942 midterm elections, the Roosevelt administration imposed full-scale rationing of gasoline. For a time, all pleasure driving was banned. Even after that drastic measure was lifted, car owners faced limited freedom of movement. Persons with jobs requiring travel essential to the war effort received "C" ration cards (allowing almost unlimited mileage); those who depended on their cars for going to and from work or for medical reasons got "B" cards; and others, who could make use of public transportation, received "A" cards. Local boards had the awkward assignment of explaining the allotment to their neighbors. The system worked well as car mileage declined by one third between 1941 and 1943. But the rubber shortage remained acute. A crash program for the production of synthetic rubber contributed to easing the crisis.

Thirteen-year-old Bill Trace, along with other members of Boy Scout Troop #52, joined enthusiastically in the campaign to collect items for the rubber scrap drive, knocking on doors around the neighborhood and hauling wagonloads of old boots and girdles (and himself throwing in the family's despised enema bottle) to the Texaco station on Broadway. He was less happy about the curb on gasoline, for the Traces got a "C" card and that meant no more driving lessons, picnics, or weekend trips to Grandfather Bonham's farm. The Reinhardts, Gales, Gishmans, and O'Reillys were satisfied with "B" allotments, and Robert Butler (who did not drive) and the Groppers, Markoviches, Bassanos, Kuriharas, and Velma Trace, none of whom owned cars, were unaffected.

All the families took an interest in the effort to ration foodstuffs and certain other products. Military requirements and pressure to preserve other materials (zinc for tin cans and rubber soles for shoes) finally forced the government to impose rationing of specified food products in March 1943. Each family received books containing different colored stamps for meat, dairy products, sugar, coffee, and so forth. Those with young children, such as the Traces, Simiches, and Groppers, obtained supplementary allowances.

The rationing system was theoretically

The O'Reillys

Government regulations affecting foodstuffs caused Gus O'Reilly considerable grief during the first part of the war. There was the uncertainty, first, about whether Washington would ration meat and, if so, what kind of controls would be adopted. Gus could not be certain that all the orders he took from markets along his route would be filled. Only twice, however, did there occur any significant shortages of meat in the Boston metropolitan area, and they resulted not from restrictive quotas but from the improper routing of refrigerated boxcars bringing beef and pork from the Midwest. By late 1943, Gus O'Reilly's business was booming in spite of rationing.

The O'Reillys had no financial problems and experienced no difficulty getting staples and even luxury items. They were able to continue the family tradition of summer vacations in the mountains, since Gus's job gave him preferred access to gasoline and tires. They worried greatly, however, about their oldest son, John, who had left Boston College in 1943 to enlist in the Army Air Corps. Only 20, John did well in flight training and later earned an assignment as navigator on one of the new B-29s. Gus and Margaret were quite alarmed when the planes first went into action, but John reassured his parents in letters, carefully worded to slip by the military censors. He also contacted them after each of his 25 bombing missions over Japan in spring 1945.

Then the O'Reillys heard nothing from their son for almost two months. John later admitted that his squadron had been brought back to Texas, where it had practiced the complex technique devised to deliver the atomc bomb. "Fortunately he was assigned to another plane on the day the bomb was dropped," Gus O'Reilly later confessed.

Since the O'Reillys will not be encountered again, a last word seems appropriate. After a short stint with the Massachusetts Office of Price Administration between 1946 and 1948, Gus opened his own meat brokerage business. By the time of his retirement in 1960, his business and other investments were worth $300,000. In 1973, Gus and Margaret moved permanently to Florida. There he played golf, visited on the phone with his six very successful children, and wrote and received endless streams of letters from his 35 grandchildren. As Margaret put it; "After 56 years of marriage, Gus and I can rest on our laurels." Gus died in his sleep in April 1979.

foolproof. Retail stores collected ration stamps from their customers and turned in the collected stamps for an equivalent amount of goods from wholesalers who, in turn, exchanged the stamps for fresh supplies from slaughterers and food processors. Shrewd operators, however, soon found the loopholes in the system, and a black market in stamps and goods flourished. People swapped stamps, slipped money to shopkeepers for extra meat (often purchased from ranchers and local slaughterhouses not covered by the government's inspection system), and bartered rationed goods. Black-market sales of tires and gasoline also became common. In 1944, one racketeer was arrested with fake coupons for 38,000 gallons of gas and 437 pairs of shoes in his possession. Our families were reluctant to take part in shady deals, though they occasionally succumbed.

Confusion within the government about the existence of shortages contributed greatly to popular cynicism. In spring 1944, the War Food Administration, assuming that the war in Europe would be over by year's end and faced with record production levels, ended rationing on veal, lamb, pork, all beef cuts except steaks and roasts, and all canned meat. American housewives went on a buying spree. Per capita meat consumption jumped to 160 pounds annually (compared with the prewar average of 126 pounds). This led to a "food crisis" in 1945, and rationing had to be reimposed. This time, Anna Trace, Charlotte Bassano, and others were much less tolerant about the restrictions.

The government's record regarding prices, wage rates, and financing of the war was considerably better. The need for rigorous price controls was generally recognized. By spring 1942, the combination of vastly increased purchasing power chasing diminished amounts of consumer goods had pushed the cost of living 15 percent above the 1939 level. The administration feared that inflation would damage the economy and erode public sup-

War-bond drive, Evansville

port for the war. Some pushed a rigid anti-inflation program—freezing prices and wages, instituting compulsory savings, restricting credit, and setting an after-tax income ceiling of $50,000. Roosevelt chose a more conservative course. Price ceilings and large increases in income and excess profits taxes were imposed, but the president approved a voluntary savings program and reliance on existing mechanisms, principally the National War Labor Board, to avoid dangerous wage hikes. As might be expected, the effects of these actions varied with the ability of pressure groups to force special concessions from the government. Nonetheless, consumer prices advanced by less than two percent between 1943 and 1945.

Most of our families found that the war permitted an improved standard of living. The Simiches and Markoviches received sizable pay raises, negotiated by the steelworkers' union and authorized by the NWLB in 1942. The application of this agreement, termed the "Little Steel Formula," to other industries worked reasonably well and did prevent disastrous inflation. The L&N pay envelope of Ben Trace contained 60 percent more in 1943 than it had in 1939 because of two hourly increases and overtime pay. Payroll withholding for federal taxes was introduced in 1943, and the following year Ben Trace paid income taxes—$37.02—for the first time. The government had reduced personal exemptions ($500 for single persons and $1,200 for married couples) and, in one stroke, made paying income tax an almost universal experience. By 1945, 50 million Americans paid federal income taxes compared with 4 million in 1939.

The enormous revenues from individual and corporate income, excise, and other taxes ($46.5 billion in 1945) defrayed nearly half of the federal government's wartime expenditures. The rest came from borrowing. During the war, some $200 billion in government bonds were sold. Louis Gropper and Mihailo Markovich, among others, helped by purchasing Series E savings bonds through payroll deductions. As in the First World War, there were repeated bond drives, each more successful than the last.

The Markoviches and Simiches

The military orders that stoked Midland's reviving prosperity also ensured permanent jobs at good pay for Mihailo Markovich and his new son-in-law, Mike Simich. Mihailo's weekly wages were double the prewar level. Mihailo had long hoped to find a larger and nicer house, but Midland suffered from a severe housing shortage during the war, so those dreams were postponed and the money saved. For the first time in his life, Mihailo enjoyed job security. Although the hostility of Crucible's management toward union activists continued unabated all through the war, the seniority system protected Mihailo and his generation of workers. But Mike, exempted from the draft because of varicose veins and because his job was essential to the war effort, remained vulnerable. When Mike was ordered to report for another physical in January 1944, the shop supervisor, who had the authority to approve occupational exemptions, asked: "Are you going to be a nice boy?" That was the last straw. Mike joined the Navy and two weeks later departed for basic training at Great Lakes Naval Station.

During Mike's absence, Anna and her baby son, Lawrence (1943), lived in an apartment next to her parents' home. She managed well on the $90 monthly dependent allotment and so was not motivated to find work. Mike was able to send home money regularly so the Simiches, too, started their first savings account and purchased war bonds. Anna continued her activities in Serbian affairs, lavished attention on Larry, and, except for the absence of Mike, lived a normal life.

Mike's life as a sailor was also routine. Following motor-mechanic schooling at Gulfport, Mississippi, Mike joined a landing ship crew at Houston, Texas. In early 1945, his ship reached Hawaii where it was to load cargo for the war zone. Mike, however, stayed behind in Honolulu in order to have leg surgery. He then joined Auxilliary Repair Ship 201 and helped to maintain the engines of the tiny, beat-up vessel (converted from one of the first LSTs built at the Evansville Shipyard) on runs from Guam to Saipan and, soon after VJ Day, to Yokohama. Mike, thoroughly bored by his duty, was discharged in February 1946, after a brief tour in Buffalo, New York. Mike was not untouched by his service experience or the war. On shore leave in Yokohama, he was shocked by the destruction and visible suffering. These sights deepened the sense of horror and loss experienced when he learned that his younger brother, Nick, had been shot down and killed on the last day of the Pacific war.

Mike and Larry Simich, December 1944

Americans could not avoid consciousness of the war, for they were assaulted from all sides by information and propaganda. Newspapers were crammed with war news and notices of bond drives, ration-point directives, and scrap drives. Almost every advertisement included some reference to the war effort. Box scores on the sports pages brought home the war because of the absence of many star players, and many of the comic strips portrayed the adventures of their heroines and heroes in action against the Axis. Billboards blazoned the need for greater sacrifice, and placards warning Americans that LOOSE LIPS SINK SHIPS and CARELESSNESS IS THE ENEMY FIFTH COLUMN adorned factory walls everywhere.

Radio and the movies became most closely associated with the effort to mobilize popular enthusiasm. Captain Midnight and Hop Harrigan, heroes of the airwaves, fought the enemy and uncovered spies. Radio brought the superpatriotic pitch of announcer Franklin McCormack into the home:

Boy: What can I do? How can I help to win the victory? I'm too young to join the Army or Navy. They won't even take me in the Home Defense Corps. . . . What can I do?

McC: Train to be an American! Follow Jack Armstrong's rules for physical fitness: (1) get plenty of fresh air, sleep, and exercise; (2) use lots of soap and water every day; and (3) eat the kind of breakfast America needs at times like these—milk, fruit, and Wheaties—Breakfast of Champions.

Boy: Okay Mr. McCormack—you've given us something to do to really help America—and you can bet we'll be ready to do our best when the time comes.

The motion-picture industry did its part by churning out dozens of films depicting the valiant struggle against Nazi cruelty and Japanese duplicity. Although the Office of War Information (OWI), the federal agency responsible for directing U.S. propaganda programs, continued to be unhappy with Hollywood's overly optimistic, distorted portrayal of the war, it was clear that the public preferred movies such as *Wake Island, Back to Bataan, Thirty Seconds Over Tokyo,* and *Lost Patrol,* featuring fresh-faced, brave American boys as the heroes, supported by the familiar squad of Irish cop, big city hustler, southern hillbilly, cowboy/farmer, and teacher/lawyer/accountant father figure. OWI complained that these movies failed to treat Allied war aims (except when a dying hero spoke of mom, apple pie, and democracy), pictured the enemy as pushovers, and ignored the contributions of America's allies. Nevertheless, going to the movies remained the most popular American pastime.

324

LSTs, built in Evansville, in the Pacific

While most Americans seemed willing to sacrifice and participate in the war effort, they did so calmly, even passively. The view that the war was simply another job worried national leaders who feared that acceptance might easily become indifference. There was a darker side, too. OWI feared, on the basis of opinion surveys, that "the American people have not been systematically made aware of possible dangers, have not been encouraged (or allowed) to become afraid." It claimed that fear and hatred did exist, and that, unless "the fear can be *harnessed,* hate *directed,*" there were grave dangers these emotions would find outlets within American society. The OWI had in mind a repetition of the 1917–19 excesses, with German-Americans, Italian-Americans, Jewish-Americans, and black Americans being victimized by the scapegoat psychology.

The most shameful episode of the war in America was the rounding up of the Japanese, citizens and resident aliens, and their forced confinement in "relocation camps." In February 1942, President Roosevelt was persuaded to empower the Secretary of War to exclude "enemy aliens" from areas vital to national security. Though the order dealt with aliens and could have been applied to Germans and Italians as well, the army acted only against the Japanese and Americans of Japanese descent. General John DeWitt, head of the Western Defense Command, proclaimed: "The Japanese race is an enemy race." Concluding that it was impossible to tell a loyal from a disloyal Japanese-American, the army decided to clear the entire coast. Beginning in June 1942, the War Relocation Authority began to transport people of Japanese birth and ancestry (ultimately 110,000 persons) to 10 hastily constructed camps in the Southwest and Mountain states. There the Japanese-Americans languished. Not until 1943 were procedures worked out to allow internees out if they could prove guaranteed employment. By the end of 1944, a total of 35,000 evacuees had left the relocation centers. By war's end, some 3,800 Japanese aliens had been repatriated and another 1,949, when permitted by law to renounce their citizenship, left for Japan.

The internment of Japanese-Americans raised critical questions about civil liberties. But because the victims were "yellow" and thus racially inferior, the American people, in general, approved the treatment meted out to them. The strain of racial hatred was an em-barrassingly obvious element in American atti-tudes toward the war. Popular hostility toward the "white" members of the Axis focused on their governments and leaders and not on the German and Italian peoples. Japan was al-ways in a different category. Hatred of all Japanese, racially expressed, was almost uni-versal. Americans viewed the Japanese as more cruel that the Germans; in a May 1945 poll, 51 percent responded that the Japanese were more cruel, 13 percent thought the Germans more barbaric. One may ask whether the atomic bomb would have been used against Nazi Germany had it been avail-able prior to Hitler's collapse.

Uncomfortably similar attitudes—based on radical grounds—cropped up regarding the status of Jews and blacks. Few of our families

---

The Traces of Los Angeles

The war influenced Velma Milton Trace's life in numerous ways, even though she was hardly aware of its existence. News of the great battles of these years filtered to Velma through offhand remarks and drunken arguments among patrons of the Los Angeles bars at which she worked. Velma was residing in East Los Angeles with her parents. Since Kenny Trace's death in 1936, she had drifted through a succession of temporary jobs and casual liaisons. Occasionally, still, she engaged in prostitution—though never as a streetwalker and only with "friends" she met in the neighborhood bars. Her parents repeatedly voiced their disapproval, but, desiring to raise Velma's youngest son, Franklin, in some approximation of a stable, Christian home, they dared not expel their daughter. Franklin, at least, would be given love, security, and an educa-tion.

It was too late to do anything for or with Calvin, Velma and Kenny's oldest son. By the time America entered the war, Calvin had been expelled from school for flagrant truancy and incorrigible behavior. A street-wise, tough-talking but intelligent young man, Calvin vacillated between a career of small-time crime with a gang of zoot-suited friends and efforts to hold down a steady job. He worked briefly at three of Los Angeles' booming war plants, but, bored stiff, quit two jobs and was fired from the other for pilfering. Calvin's grandparents openly spoke of their hope that Calvin would be drafted and reformed by military service. However, Calvin failed the physical exam when ordered for induction in September 1943. Eighteen years of inadequate food and a heart murmur placed him in the 4-F category. When his grandparents were killed in an automobile crash two months later, Calvin moved in with Velma and resumed his pursuit of the good life—flashy clothes, fast girls, drinking and gambling. Velma was usually so drunk that she knew nothing of either son's doings.

The Kuriharas

In the late morning of December 7, 1941, Elaine Kurihara was sitting with friends in a Japanese movie theatre engrossed in a film about the loves of a Samurai warrior. Suddenly the movie was stopped and the public address system boomed an announcement that the Japanese Navy had attacked Pearl Harbor. The frightened girls ran home. A few hours later, the Kuriharas were visited by two FBI agents who thumbed through Seito and Tamako Kurihara's passports, searched the house, and left after ordering the family to remain on the farm. "They were very authoritative," Elaine recalls with a shudder. "My father was so frightened by the whole thing that he took a stack of Japanese records and went far into the fields and broke them all to pieces and buried them for fear that they would be discovered." Seito Kurihara and his family, confused and apprehensive, waited almost two months before word came that they were to report to U.S. Army headquarters in Visalia for "evacuation" to an unnamed destination. A frantic rush ensued to sell the crops, equipment, and household belongings, since only a few suitcases were permitted for their journey to the internment camp. Seito received only a pittance for a lifetime's effort.

In late 1942, the Kuriharas' train, packed with Japanese-Americans from northern California and armed soldiers, reached the town of Parker, Arizona. Trucks took the evacuees out into the desert, to Gila River Relocation Center, an enormous rectangle of black, tar-papered barracks that was to be home for the next three years. The Kuriharas were assigned a 15 × 10 foot room in "B" block. The 20 families in their block shared a mess hall, recreation facilities, laundry, showers, and toilets.

At first, Seito, Tamako, and Elaine Kurihara were miserable. They missed their home and friends. They were uncomfortable among these strangers. The climate was appalling after the cool lushness of California. "We frequently had heavy, heavy dust storms." Elaine recalls, "On some occasions we could hardly see the next building during the daytime. There was absolutely nothing growing there, no greenery whatsoever to stop the sand." Gradually, however, conditions improved. Block organizations were formed, and B Block constructed a swimming pool, planted flower beds and family gardens, and sponsored weekly movies. Seito obtained work as custodian for which he received $16 per month. Tamako, who was experiencing leisure for the first time, took a class in flower arranging and learned to knit.

For Elaine, once the initial shock of dislocation subsided, the camp became bearable. There were children her own age and organized sports and classes. In September 1942, a school opened and Elaine joined the "College Bound Club" and enrolled in electives such as physics, advanced math, and English literature. To an impressionable teenager, reserved but obviously bright, the confidence and encouragement offered by a few teachers greatly influenced later memories of her life in Gila River Relocation Center. Nonetheless, Elaine felt a loss of freedom in the camp. For adults, many of whom had been stripped of property and businesses, internment was a disaster.

Elaine's uncle, Yoshisuke Kurihara, had a decidedly different reaction. Embittered by his treatment during those first panic-stricken days after Pearl Harbor ("I served in the U.S. Army and fought for democracy. I may be a Jap in feature but I am an American. Understand!"), Yoshisuke became openly hostile toward the government, camp authorities and those "spineless traitors," the leaders of the Japanese-American Cooperation League. His store had been closed in early January and he soon found himself deposited in the camp at Manzanar, California. Conditions were abominable. "After living in well-furnished homes with every modern convenience and suddenly forced to live the life of a dog is something we cannot so readily forget." Even worse, however, was the treatment he, Yoshisuke Kurihara, a citizen and veteran, was accorded. He was one of the leaders of the Manzanar riot of December 1942 and was transferred to a maximum-security camp. While in confinement, Yoshisuke decided to apply for expatriation to Japan. He renounced his United States citizenship in December 1943, and two years later joined the first contingent of voluntary deportees to sail for Japan.

Seito learned of his brother's fate from camp authorities. He, too, thought of requesting deportation, but what would he do in Japan, how could he support his family and pay the medical expenses that his worsening asthmatic condition generated? Even when friends left Gila River, beginning in 1943, for jobs in the Midwest arranged by the WRA, Seito chose to stay put. He would not risk the hostility of the white world outside until the war was over. Besides Elaine, doing well in the camp school, would earn a high-school diploma in 1945.

The Kuriharas survived internment and, because of the ambition and intelligence of Elaine, even prospered after the war. Elaine received a college degree from Ohio State University, served as an interpreter in occupied Japan, married a Japanese-American, and became a thoroughly middle-class American. Her husband, an accountant, was earning $25,000 annually in 1965. Prior to her marriage and during its early years, Elaine helped her father reestablish himself as a small farmer in California, where he died in 1959, leaving an estate of over $50,000. Elaine and her husband have completely rejected their ethnic heritage. Their children were withdrawn from Buddhist Sunday school during the 1960s and placed in a Baptist school. Elaine's mother is not allowed to speak Japanese at home. Elaine is convinced that the repudiation of Japanese cultural traits is necessary for the social development and emotional health of the children. One has to wonder whether Elaine's grandchildren will reach out for information about their Japanese origins, believing that recognition of their ethnicity will bring meaning to their lives.

read the anti-Semitic, racist harangues of pseudofascists such as Father Coughlin, Gerald B. Winrod, and Gerald L. K. Smith, but many accepted as truth the opinion that Jews were to blame for the war and that numerous blacks in America sympathized with the Japanese, champions of the "colored races." To the question, "Why do you think Hitler took away the power of the Jews in Germany?" the OWI found that only 25 percent believed Hitler acted because he hated Jews or used them as a scapegoat, but 47 percent believed it was because the Jews were too powerful. The same poll revealed that 46 percent believed Jews "have too much power and influence in America," with 40 percent rejecting this thesis, and 14 percent expressing no opinion. Henry Gishman encountered these views on the shop floor at Wright Aeronautics, where his fellow workers often spoke of their dislike at being forced to work with "kikes, niggers, and wimmen."

Black self-awareness and the portrayal of the war as a struggle against Nazi racism fostered a new sense of black militancy. Louis Gropper agreed with the *Crisis's* view: "It sounds pretty foolish to be *against* park benches marked *'Jude'* in Berlin, but to be *for* park benches marked *'Colored'* in Tallahassee, Florida." At first blacks were turned away from defense jobs in many industries. A threatened protest march on Washington in 1941, headed by A. Philip Randolph, forced President Roosevelt to issue executive order 8802 banning all racial discrimination in federal employment and in defense industries with government contracts. The number of blacks in manufacturing, transportation, and public utilities jumped from 700,000 in 1940 to almost 1,500,000 in 1944. The need for labor may have forced open the factory doors, but the pattern of segregated housing, schools, and recreation changed only slightly. Among the most revealing examples was a scene in an OWI documentary film, *War Town,* which showed a crowd of workers coming from a defense plant at quitting time and then, just outside the gates, separating into two streams: the whites going to their homes and the blacks to theirs. The federal government accepted "local standards" regarding housing and education, thus perpetuating racial segregation. Partly as a result, tensions arose in the boom towns and communities serving defense industries. Numerous episodes of racial violence occurred in 1942 and 1943, and in June 1943, a racial clash in Detroit left 25 blacks and 9 whites dead, with nearly 700 people injured. Federal troops were used to restore order, and while this and other riots (New York City in August 1943) dramatized black inequality, most Americans gave exclusive priority to winning the war.

Racial tensions also afflicted the armed services. Open clashes occurred, especially in the South where whites enforced Jim Crow and in England where white GIs attempted to establish a color line. When America entered the war, the army's policy was one of rigid segregation, the marines refused to take blacks, and blacks could enter the navy only as messmen. Only the Army Air Forces accepted blacks for combat assignments (though not as pilots) before Pearl Harbor. Change came only gradually. There was a half-hearted effort to integrate training camps in 1944, and the air corps modified its policy by creating an all-black fighter squadron. Still, the gap between American ideals and practices, poignantly expressed in a wartime poem by Staff Sergeant Bennie Mason, persisted:

I died today
In the stinking morass of a tropical jungle
I died with a bullet in my lungs.
Why did I die?
I died for the right of a man to make a decent
 living by the sweat of his brow;
I died for the right of any American child to
 grow up to be president;
I died for the right to cast a ballot that would be
 as influential as that of the mightiest in the
 land;
I died for the right to a decent education;
I died for the protection of a constitution
That guarantees all these rights
Regardless of race, color,
Or previous condition of servitude . . .
Yes, I died for all these things
And yet—I never knew them,
For I am, that is,
I was,
Colored.

Unlike the case in World War I, however, black GIs participated more broadly in the armed services although in segregated units, except in a few emergencies such as the Battle of the Bulge. Nonetheless, racism in uniform persisted. General H. H. Arnold, head of the Army Air Corps, said once that blacks could not be fighter pilots, for they could not withstand "high g forces" because of the simpler configuration of their brains. A similar point of view led to the decision of the American Red Cross to segregate blood donated by blacks.

Wartime did not seem to interfere with politics. The out-of-power Republicans increased their congressional strength in the elections of 1942. In 1944, they chose as their presidential candidate New York's young governor, Thomas E. Dewey, who had earned a national reputation as a racket-busting district attorney. The Democratic Party nominated Franklin D. Roosevelt for the fourth time. Missouri Senator Harry S. Truman replaced Vice President Henry A. Wallace, darling of the left wing but despised by big-city bosses and Southern conservatives, on the ticket. The change was considered further proof of the drift toward conservatism of the Roosevelt administration.

The 1944 campaign was notable more for what it ignored than for the issues it dealt with. The president initiated his campaign late. In early August he made a series of well-publicized "inspection trips" around the country to counter rumors about his health. Louis Gropper was in the audience when FDR, looking tired and ill, spoke at Bremerton Navy Yard. Dewey, a lacklustre campaigner, was restrained by FDR's status as commander-in-chief and the commitment to bipartisan cooperation in foreign affairs. Nonetheless, he hammered away at New Deal inefficiency, criticized the "tired old men" who surrounded Roosevelt, and promised, as had Alf Landon and Wendell Wilkie, to maintain the New Deal but at less cost to the taxpayer. Only Ben Trace, Jacob and Mathilde Reinhardt, and Robert Butler responded favorably to Dewey. The others, satisfied with Roosevelt's leadership and the Democratic New Deal, voted Democratic. With 3,300,000 servicemen voting under procedures established by Colonel Robert Butler, Roosevelt received 25.6 million votes to Dewey's 22 million, and 432 electoral votes to 99 for Dewey.

THE DRIVE FOR VICTORY

The election did not slow the war effort. Those who manned the guns, and those who manned the home front, steadily worked to-

---

The Groppers

Lila Hunt and Louis G. Gropper were married in Kosse on February 16, 1942. They had met when Louis had interviewed for a job in the school in Cartwright, Texas, at which Lila had been teaching part-time while attending Jarvis Christian College. Two days after the wedding, Louis left for a job at Bremerton Shipyard in Seattle, Washington, which a friend had arranged. Lila joined him when the school year ended. The couple set up housekeeping in one of several hundred quadriplexes provided for employees by the shipyard. These quarters, while modern, were segregated.

In simple economic terms, the war was a tremendous boon for Louis and Lila Gropper. Previously unable to find a teaching position, Louis had been drifting from job to job. Now he was employed as an apprentice electrician (his college courses in physics and electrical engineering made him the most knowledgeable worker in his section), provided with inexpensive housing, medical benefits, and earnings of $70 to $80 per week. Although Lila no longer worked and gave birth to their first child, Louis George Gropper III, in May 1943, the Groppers put more than half of Louis' weekly paycheck into war bonds and a savings account. Still, there was every likelihood that war's end would see a rapid cutback at Bremerton Navy Yard and, if so, blacks would be the first to go. Both Louis and Lila missed their families and the hot, dry climate of central Texas. And both were anxious to resume careers in teaching. The job in Seattle provided security (and a draft exemption), but for the Groppers their wartime stay in the Pacific Northwest was just an interlude.

ward victory. The "critical period" of the Second World War occurred from June 1942 to February 1943—embracing the Battles of Midway (where the Japanese Navy's momentum was halted) and Guadalcanal (where the United States took the offensive in the Pacific), Rommel's last-gasp bid for victory in the desert and the subsequent Anglo-American invasion of North Africa, and the titanic clash of German and Soviet armies amidst the rubble of Stalingrad. These battles resulted in defeats for the Axis, because of Allied superiority in forces and material, because of German and Japanese blunders, and because breaking the top German code "Enigma" gave Allied commanders foreknowledge of Axis intentions and strength. But victory awaited the total application of the human and material resources of the Allied nations.

After a slow start, military recruitment and training shifted into high gear. By January 1943, some 5,000,000 men, both volunteers and draftees, had been inducted. (The draft calls continued at high levels until after the Battle of the Bulge). In June 1945, the U.S. Army's strength stood at 8.2 million, the navy and marines totaled 3.9 million, and the Coast Guard had 250,000. The Women's Army Corps, the navy's WAVES, and the Coast Guard's SPARS accounted for another 200,000 persons. Methods for the "processing" of civilians into professional soldiers became familiar to all Americans: the herding into double lines for physicals— "Turn your head and cough; now, turn around and spread 'em"—the batter of injections, waiting for GI haircuts, receiving uniforms, bedding and weapons—"This is your weapon, it ain't a gun; it's made for killing and not for fun"—and the first encounter with the drill sergeant. Trainees were put through their paces by career personnel and then, as the influx reached mammoth proportions, by "old" soldiers such as Austin Hart.

Building on the experience of the First World War, training camps were, for the most part, carefully planned and efficiently administered. Fort Leonard Wood, Camp Lejeune, and Great Lakes Naval Station, where Austin Hart, Jerry Trace, and Mike Simich underwent basic training, lacked many of the comforts of home but offered adequate housing, hot and plentiful food, movie theaters, sports grounds, and other recreational facilities. To a man, those who went through the "boot camp" experience remember its difficulties and their accomplishments. "It made me a man," Jerry Trace later stated. They enjoyed meeting young men from other backgrounds, though the mixing of soldiers from contrasting social, economic, ethnic, and geographical backgrounds, a favorite theme of Hollywood movies, was hardly typical. And, of course, neither in training nor in combat were they thrown together with blacks.

Feeding the multitudes who flocked into and through the camps alone was a staggering task. Menus had to be devised that would maintain the energy and stamina of men convoying in the North Atlantic, engaging the Japanese in the South Pacific, and fighting the Nazis in the North African desert and on the continent of Europe. Factors such as seasonal fluctuations in supply, availability of shipping, refrigeration and storage space, and the food preferences of servicemen also were important. Even more complex was the apparatus that kept track of Mike Simich, Jerry Trace, John O'Reilly, and 15,000,000 other men and women assigned to stations throughout the world.

Most of the GIs served in the European Theatre of Operations. Prior to June 1943, almost all GIs in Europe were thrown into the Mediterranean campaigns where, as Austin Hart's brother and Jack Butler discovered, some of the bloodiest, most frustrating fighting of the war occurred. U.S. and British armies battled up the mountainous Italian peninsula, knocking Italy out of the war (September 1943) but immediately confronting determined German opposition and not capturing Rome until June 1944. Meanwhile, the trickle of U.S. forces and supplies into the British Isles became a torrent. Hundreds of thousands of Americans were camped all over England, awaiting the invasion of the Continent. On June 6, 1944, the Western Allies launched "Operation Overlord," the long-awaited and much-debated invasion of France. America and Great Britain had fulfilled their promise to remove German pressure on the Soviet Union, though the relief came much later than Moscow thought necessary. The invasion of Normandy was an amphibious operation on a colossal scale. The provision of sufficient landing craft, the vital element in Overlord, was achieved only at the last minute because of diversions to the Pacific, waste in the Italian campaign, and bureaucratic errors that stripped production priorities from Evansville and other shipyards just when landing craft were most needed.

The extravagant preparations for Overlord—typically American—stunned the British and astonished the waiting Germans. Throughout the night of June 5, 600 warships bombarded German shore defenses and 10,000 airplanes patrolled the skies over the invasion beaches. Then, at dawn, 5,000 ships carrying 200,000 men and 1,500 tanks turned toward the shores of Normandy. While the struggle to establish a beachhead was bitter, its outcome was never seriously in doubt. The breakout of the Allied armies from the Normandy beachhead, which took place in early June 1944, decided the fate of Germany. Following the rapid advance of American tank columns led by aggressive figures such as General George S. Patton, the U.S., British, Canadian, and French armies crushed German resistance in France. By early September 1944, they stood poised along Germany's western frontiers. Elsewhere, Nazi

opposition in Italy was sputtering out, and massive Soviet forces, grinding through Poland, were nearing Germany's eastern frontiers. It may be that a bold offensive aimed at the feeble line manned by demoralized German units would have ended the war in early fall 1944, as American planners had projected long before. However, General Dwight D. Eisenhower, commander of Allied forces in the west, opted for a cautious, broad-front advance. Nazi resistance stiffened and the war went on, with mounting casualties.

The important issues during the final months of the war in Europe were political not military. Would the Allied coalition withstand the stresses and temptations of victory? What future was in store for the Germans, for all the peoples of Europe? By continuing their resistance past the point of all hope, the Germans brought upon themselves much suffering. In particular, the Anglo-American bombing offensive that had been building gradually since mid-1942 now was fully unleashed. Waves of U.S. heavy bombers, escorted by P-51 "Mustangs" that swept the skies of opposition, thundered onward into Germany, attacking in broad daylight and using the misnamed technique of "precision bombing" to obliterate factories, military installations, and whole cities throughout the Reich.

Believing that a military setback would cause the British and Americans somehow to realize their true enemy was the Soviet Union, Hitler ordered a final effort to break the tightening ring of Allied armies. This was the desperate winter offensive in the Luxembourg sector of the western front, referred to as the "Battle of the Bulge" by American newspapers. The German surprise offensive dealt a stunning blow, but there was no danger that the course of the war might be changed. By throwing in hastily organized units and all available reserves, the Allies stabilized their lines and, when the weather cleared, wiped out the "bulge." In early 1945, British-

U.S. troops wading ashore at Omaha Beach, D-Day, June 6, 1944

American-French-Canadian armies in the west and Russian forces in the east moved forward to the last battle. In three months, Hitler was dead and victory in Europe had been won.

The Pacific War was preeminently an American show. Only in the China-Burma-India Theater did the struggle against Japan formally become an inter-Allied effort. Of course, China stoically resisted the Japanese onslaught for eight years, and in the climactic stages of the war, the British invaded Southeast Asia and Soviet armies marched through Manchuria. But the great battles for control of the Pacific's strategic island groups were fought almost entirely by Americans. This avoided the clashes of national interests inherent in coalition warfare; however, the rumors reaching Jerry Trace, Mike Simich, and John O'Reilly about angry arguments between army and navy chiefs suggested that interservice rivalries could be just as violent as international ones.

U.S. strategists and American marines and sailors encountered unique circumstances in the Pacific war. First, there was no battle front,

The Gales and Harts

Having wangled a three-day leave from his company commander, Austin Hart drove all night from Fort Leonard Wood, Missouri, to Fredonia in order to spend Christmas with his family. The next day, December 26, 1941, Austin and Martha Isabelle Gale were married in New Albany. He left immediately after the reception, a lavish affair held in the Gales' home, for the trip back to Fort Leonard Wood. Austin Hart, already a corporal and soon to be a sergeant, was assigned to the camp training cadre as a machine-gun instructor. He finally located a tiny apartment, a converted garage, off the post, and Martha, who had been staying with her parents, joined him in August 1942. They remained together at Fort Leonard Wood (except for two months when Martha visited her fatally ill mother and helped find a housekeeper for Charles Gale) until Austin was transferred to Camp Abbott, Oregon, in early 1944. With the European war winding down, he was posted to an automatic-weapons training unit responsible for new recruits for the Pacific Theater. Martha, now pregnant, followed her husband to Oregon and then to Fort Lewis, Washington, where the Harts remained until Austin's discharge in July 1945. Though one of Austin's brothers took part in the Anzio landings and served with Patton's Third Army and numerous friends saw action, Austin Hart never shot at the enemy. He never regretted it.

no clear line of demarcation between opposing forces; the front stretched along sea lanes and across scattered Pacific islands. The main extensions of Japanese power, which Bob and Robbie Bassano had marked on their global battle map by summer 1942, were three in number: one along the Asian coast from China through Indochina and Malaya; another from Formosa to the Philippines; and the third through the Bonin, Mariana, and Caroline Islands to New Guinea and the Solomons. These islands, only names to Jerry Trace, the Bassanos, and most Americans in 1942, were very familiar 18 months later.

Responsibility for hacking through the Japanese stranglehold on the mainland went to the Chinese, supported by Anglo-American forces in the China-Burma-India theater and U.S. air power. The strategy hammered out for seizing the other two strongholds was "island hopping." Marine and naval forces would bypass the Dutch East Indies and attack selected island fortresses, each closer to Japan. Concentration of superior sea and air power and the landing of highly trained ground forces would clear these islands of their fanatical defenders. They could then be used as staging bases for attacks on other strongholds and for air attacks against Japan itself.

Island hopping and the new techniques and weapons it demanded highlighted a second basic difference between Europe and the Pacific: the U.S. Navy ran the war against Japan. This was largely because Japan's power, except in China, depended on the confident, experienced ships of the Imperial Navy, especially its modern, swift-striking carriers. The great innovation of the Pacific conflict was the reliance of both sides on carrier-based air power. Long before December 7, 1941, experts such as the American General "Billy" Mitchell had questioned the value of battleships, arguing that these floating artillery platforms were hopelessly vulnerable to air attack. Such events as Pearl Harbor confirmed these views. When it entered the war, the United States had only seven first-line carriers, and four of these were to be lost during 1942. But by war's end, the U.S. Navy boasted 17 first-line carriers, 9 light, and 114 escort carriers. A parallel expansion of carrier aircraft occurred: the navy accepted 3,638 new planes in 1941; in 1944 the number was 30,070. The "floating airfields" formed the nucleus of the naval task forces that cleared the Japanese fleets from the Pacific.

The defeat-Germany-first strategy ensured that priority in manpower and supplies be given to operations in Europe. As late as early 1943, only about 15 percent of available Allied resources were devoted to the war against Japan. Thus, the struggle to expel the Japanese from their new empire proceeded more slowly than an abstract comparison of Japanese and American military and industrial capabilities might suggest. Such a comparison, as Jerry Trace and others will testify, did not take into account the incredible problems of U.S. forces in invading torrid and disease-ridden Pacific strongholds defended by a determined enemy.

Gradually, the weight of American power began to tell. After Guadalcanal was taken in February 1943, U.S. Marines invaded the Solomons in November 1943, army forces seized control of New Guinea, and the Aleutian Islands were retaken. By mid-1944, American forces in the Pacific, lavishly endowed with superb new equipment and possessing overwhelming naval-air superiority, were poised to breach the inner defense perimeter of Japan's empire. In a series of naval engagements and amphibious operations during the next eight months, Japanese carrier-based air power was destroyed, the Japanese fleet lost its offensive capability, and American forces seized airfields within bomber range of Japan. The Gilbert Islands, remembered for the grueling struggle for

"bloody" Tarawa, were won in January 1944. Saipan fell, at the cost of 24,000 Japanese lives, in June 1944, and that led to seizure of the Marianas and the vital bastion of Guam in July 1944. General Douglas MacArthur kept his promise to return to the Philippines in January 1945, following the decisive U.S. naval victory, the Battle of the Philippine Sea, in June 1944.

Japanese leaders recognized the war was lost but they refused to consider surrender. Their fatalism had disastrous effects. Facing starvation because of the destruction of merchant shipping by U.S. submarines and air attacks, Japan's civilian population also suffered unremitting air attacks beginning in March 1945. From the new air bases, B-29s, such as the one John O'Reilly navigated, launched crushing raids on Japan's major cities. In one raid, about half of Yokohama burned. Shortly thereafter, in March 1945, another raid by B-29s dropped incendiaries on Tokyo, causing a "fire storm" that swept through the wooden homes and factories of the Japanese capital and killed an estimated 100,000 people. In all, these attacks disrupted war production and transportation, killed 330,000, and destroyed over 2 million buildings. The Japanese doggedly fought on.

It appeared that the final act of this tragedy—the invasion of the Japanese home islands—would see much fiercer resistance than the Allies had experienced in the conquest of Germany. The struggle for Iwo Jima, a volcanic island 750 miles south of Japan, offered a foretaste of what U.S. forces might expect when they hit the beaches of the Japanese homeland. Along with thousands of fellow Marines, Jerry Trace drove his "Alligator" amphibious tractor ashore on Iwo Jima on February 19, 1945. Nearly a month later, after yard-by-yard fighting with entrenched defenders, Jerry watched as a knot of exhausted Marines 50 feet above him raised the U.S. flag on Mt. Suribachi. It had cost 20,000 American casualties to take a scrap of island measuring some two-and-one-half miles wide by five miles long. Iwo Jima, the even greater casualties suffered in the subsequent battle for Okinawa, and the resort to *kamikaze* attacks suggested that the Japanese were prepared to fight to the last ditch and the last man. U.S. military experts calculated that the invasion of Japan, scheduled for November 1945, would cost between 500,000 and 1,000,000 Allied casualties, and the war would drag on for at least another year. Not even Russia's entry would significantly alter this grim projection.

While the military and political leaders pieced together a nightmarish scenario of bloodletting to come, a group of American scientists, involved since 1942 in top-secret research on what insiders knew as the Manhattan Project, concluded their work. They had succeeded, as President Harry Truman tried to explain a few weeks later, in the "harnessing of the basic power of the universe, the force from which the Sun draws its power." They had made and tested an "atomic bomb," which concentrated the clout of 20,000 tons of TNT in one small package. They had devised formulas and techniques that, with refinement, promised bombs several hundred times more powerful than the prototype. Since military considerations dominated the thinking of Harry Truman (who had been elevated to the presidency in April 1945 when Franklin Roosevelt died suddenly), it is understandable that he would welcome a super bomb—something that might frighten the Japanese into surrender, thus saving Japanese as well as American lives.

For many of the scientists who had helped develop the atomic bomb, the test explosion at Alamogordo, New Mexico, on July 16, 1945, was much more than an illustration that Yankee ingenuity could be counted on to turn out a better mousetrap. Those who had come to believe that atomic weapons would revolutionize warfare and threaten mankind with extinction already had sent petitions up the chain of command. Some scientists warned that the unexpected use of the bomb would intensify the distrust the Soviet Union already felt toward the United States and provoke it to stand in armed defiance just at the moment of Allied victory. Some warned that using the weapon would make future control of the awful force infinitely more difficult. Some considered that using the weapon on civilians carried the idea of total war to an immoral, if logical, extreme. It put the United States on the list of people who had introduced horrible weapons for the extermination of man: the Germans who first used poison gas, the Japanese who tried biological agents, and the Huns and Mongols who had made destruction a fine art. One petition urged the United States to demonstrate the bomb on a desert or uninhabited island before lobbing it onto Japan. A poll of the atomic scientists showed that 15 percent wanted the bomb used in whatever way would bring Japanese surrender; 46 percent preferred "a military demonstration in Japan to be followed by a renewed opportunity for surrender before full use of the weapon is employed"; 26 percent wanted a desert or uninhabited island demonstration; 13 percent objected to any use of the bomb by the military. There is no evidence that Harry Truman was troubled by the divisions among the scientists who fathered the nuclear age. Their views were known to a special committee that advised him on atomic matters; the committee advised that there was no way of effectively demonstrating the bomb and it recommended targeting on Japanese cities that contained military installations. The assumptions all along had been that the bomb would be used when it was perfected. Good reasons for not using it never came from those

Hiroshima in the aftermath of the atomic bomb. The incredible devastation is apparent in this high-level aerial photograph

high in government. Moreover, Truman had come to distrust Soviet intentions, and the successful use of the bomb might bring peace before the Russians could lay claim to vast expanses of Far Eastern real estate.

On August 6, a B-29 dropped an atomic bomb on Hiroshima. Of the city's 350,000 inhabitants, 100,000 died instantly; a similar number eventually succumbed from injuries, burns, and exposure to radiation. After the blast and the fires, two thirds of Hiroshima's buildings lay in shambles. The next day, the Soviet Union entered the Pacific war. Two days after that, on August 9, a second atomic bomb (the last that would be available for several weeks) demolished Nagasaki. Emperor Hirohito told his ministers that continuing to fight "means nothing but the destruction of the whole nation" and ordered them to arrange the surrender.

WAR'S END

On August 13, when the news of VJ Day reached Midland, there were spontaneous parades and street dances, punctuated by the blasts of mill and locomotive whistles. The governor proclaimed a two-day holiday and closed all state liquor stores. In Midland, as elsewhere, the festival atmosphere quickly gave way to a quiet mood, relief, and thanksgiving that this awful war had ended. The boys would come home and life could begin anew.

While eventual victory had been apparent for a long time, no precise plans existed for postwar reconstruction. In the 1944 campaign, for instance, no discussion of these questions had taken place. References were made to the need for reform legislation (ending racial discrimination, and giving equal rights to women and protection against the insecurities of old age, unemployment, and ill health), improved housing, providing social benefits for servicemen, and the creation of a peaceful world order. Questions abounded. Would there be jobs for all? Would inflation ruin the prosperity for which they had worked so hard? Would the government help to build the millions of new dwellings so desperately needed? Charles Gale and Jacob Reinhardt were worried that the end of government food purchases for export and the armed forces would lead to huge surpluses and another agricultural depression. In Evansville, as in almost every community, committees were established to undertake "postwar planning" studies. In 1945, the editor of the *Evansville Courier* noted: "Postwar planning becomes an increasingly important subject in America. Much of this planning must originate in the grass-roots of the country—that is, in the Evansvilles, the Paducahs, the Daytons, the South Bends." After looking at local industries, employment prospects, public-improvement programs, education, social services, and housing needs, the Evansville Post-War Planning Council concluded that if the proper spirit of dedication and cooperation emerged, a bright future beckoned to Evansville and the nation. These sentiments

were echoed in Midland, Boston, Fredonia, and in the offices of the numerous government agencies that were preparing for the postwar era.

The Roosevelt administration had preferred not to confront the task of reconversion until victory was assured. Donald Nelson and others opposed delay, warning that the economy could, without planning, return to the depression level of the 1930s. Facing growing public anxiety about jobs, surpluses, and controls, the federal government claimed that it had everything under control: that controls would be gradually lifted as the war in Europe ended and the final phase of the Pacific War began; that the effects of millions of returning veterans on employment would be cushioned; and that stresses would be minimal. But the military had its way. No significant shift from military to civilian production occurred, and the United States entered the postwar era (which arrived a year before the most optimistic estimates) unprepared for peace.

A similar lack of preparation dogged those responsible for the conduct of American diplomacy. After Pearl Harbor, President Roosevelt chose not to engage in any further educational efforts about America's place in the world. He concentrated on prosecution of the war and shunted aside difficult questions such as the nature of the postwar world, the relationship between national sovereignty and a viable world peace-keeping organization, and basic conflicts between members of the Allied coalition. Most of our families has no interest in these questions, except as they affected special concerns. Bertha and Henry Gishman followed anxiously the discussions about creation of a "Jewish homeland" in Palestine for survivors of Nazi concentration camps. The Simiches and Markoviches debated the involvement of Americans, British, and Russians in the struggle between Yugoslav partisans. Rosalyn Butler, along with thousands of other women, took part in a weekly discussion group on the problems that would face both victors and vanquished once the war ended. But the majority, while desiring reassurance that the wartime cooperation between members of the Allied coalition would continue and that theirs *was* the last war to end war, were happy to leave arrangements for that bright future in the hands of FDR and the experts.

President Roosevelt did not lack awareness of the antagonisms beneath the surface of Allied cooperation; neither did he ignore entirely the factors limiting American ability to resolve these problems. But his addiction to "the vice of immediacy" led him to postpone any arrangements on postwar issues. He insisted that such questions be left to a "universal peace conference" over which he would preside at war's end. No desire "to make the world safe for democracy" was discernible in U.S. dealings with Franco's Spain, the tortured history of American relations with Vichy France and the Nationalist Chinese, and other corrupt regimes. Similarly, the unconditional surrender policy, the administration's callous policy toward small nations, and its adoption of "modern" techniques of warfare betrayed easy acceptance of the principle that might makes right. FDR was not directly responsible for all of these acts, but he set the tone: winning the war was the first and only aim.

Unknown to the public, which took the superficial congeniality of wartime "summit conferences" between Roosevelt, Churchill, and Stalin as proof that all was well, FDR's administrative style and the policy of postponement proved inadequate to the demands of coalition diplomacy and postwar planning. He retained control over all matters affecting strategy, and the confusion as to what was "diplomatic" and "military" ensured that little was done without presidential authorization.

As a concession to Secretary of State Cordell Hull, who was kept away from the summit meetings by explicit presidential order, FDR assigned to him the supervision of planning U.S. involvement in programs for the creation of global peace and prosperity: the United Nations, its Relief and Rehabilitation Administration, the European Advisory Commission, the International Bank for Reconstruction and Development, and the International Monetary Fund. The State Department constructed a magnificent system by which the wreckage of the war would be cleared away and an international order based on cooperation and justice established.

By approving these proposals, FDR committed the United States to participation in a vaguely conceived world organization, one presumably with power to maintain peace. Yet Roosevelt was prepared to bypass or ignore the United Nations or other international agencies when vital interests were at stake. The international organization he envisioned would be dominated by the four great powers who would disarm everyone but themselves and restructure the world according to a model of benevolent paternalism. Statements about the potential of the UN were so optimistic, however, that many Americans were persuaded. They certainly encouraged the emergence of a new consensus founded on popular enthusiasm, a jumble of stereotypes about other nations, and widespread ignorance. The dominant element in this consensus was faith in the American system. The enormous production coming from America's farms and factories, accomplished with so little strain and sacrifice, seemed to demonstrate the superiority of American institutions. By insisting that the wartime coalition between the United States, Britain, and the USSR reflected their basic interests, FDR contributed to these illusions. In the final weeks before his death on April 12, 1945,

FDR appeared to have awakened to the dangers facing the nation. If so, his efforts to deflate unrealistic hopes for peace came too late.

SUGGESTIONS FOR FURTHER READING

General works on the Second World War, most in paperback, include: Peter Calvocoressi and Guy Wint, *Total War* (1979); B. H. Liddell-Hart, *History of the Second World War* (1970); Basil Collier, *The Second World War: A Military History* (1967); James Jones, *WWII* (1975); A. J. P. Taylor, *The Second World War* (1978); Lucy Davidowicz, *The War Against the Jew* (1975); and Robert A. Divine, *Causes and Consequences of World War II* (1970). U.S. involvement in the war is described in Richard Lingemann, *Don't You Know There's a War On?: The American Home Front, 1941-1945* (1970); D. W. Brogan's superb *The American Character,* (1956); Geoffrey Perrett, *Days of Sadness, Years of Triumph: The American People, 1939-1945* (1973); and John M. Blum, *V Was for Victory: Politics and American Culture During World War II* (1976). See, for comparison, Angus Calder's survey of the British home front, *The People's War* (1969); and Alan S. Millward's brilliant *War, Economy, and Society, 1939-1945* (1977).

Strategy and military operations are dealt with in innumerable books. A few of the more interesting ones are Charles B. McDonald, *The War in the West* (1976); John Toland, *The Rising Sun: War in the Pacific* (1973); Barbara Tuchman, *Stilwell and the American Experience in China* (1970); Noel Barber, *A Sinister Twilight: The Fall of Singapore* (1968); William E. Brougher, *South to Bataan, North To Mukden* (1971); Don Congdon, *Combat: The War with Japan* (1962); Walter Lord, *Day of Infamy* (1967); Samuel Eliot Morison, *The War at Sea* (1969); James, Poling, *All Stations Manned: The U.S. Navy in WWII* (1971); Russell Buchanan, *The United States and World War II* (1972); John Toland, *But Not in Shame* (1961); Martin Blumenson, *Kasserine Pass* (1967) and *The Patton Papers, 1940-45* (1974); Richard Collier, *The War in the Desert* (1977); Ladislas Farago, *Patton: Ordeal and Triumph* (1964); Michael Howard, *The Mediterra-*

nean Strategy in the Second World War (1968); Martin Blumenson, *Bloody River: The Real Tragedy of the Rapido* (1970); Dan Kurzman, *The Race for Rome* (1975); Henry Adams, *The Year that Doomed the Axis* (1969); Anthony Cave Brown, *Bodyguard of Lies* (1975); Ladislas Farago, *The Tenth Fleet* (1962); David Irving, *The Destruction of Convoy PQ-17* (1968); Herbert A. Werner, *Iron Coffins* (1969); Martin Blumenson, *Eisenhower* (1972); Paul Carell, *Invasion: They're Coming!* (1963); Dan Kurzman's depiction of the Warsaw uprising, *The Bravest Battle* (1978); Dwight D. Eisenhower, *Crusade in Europe* (1948); H. Essame, *The Battle for Germany* (1969); Charles B. McDonald, *Eisenhower's Lieutenants: The Campaign in Europe, 1944-1945* (1981); Ken Hechler, *The Bridge at Remagen* (1954); S. L. A. Marshall, *Night Drop: The American Airborne Invasion of Normandy* (1962); Cornelius Ryan, *The Longest Day* (1959); *A Bridge Too Far* (1973); and *The Last Battle* (1967); John Toland, *The Last Hundred Days* (1966); J. H. Belote and William M. Belote, *Typhoon of Steel: The Battle for Okinawa* (1970); Burke Davis, *Get Yamamoto* (1969); Robert J. Donovan, *PT-109* (1961); Brian Garfield, *The Thousand Mile War* (1969); Edward P. Hoyt, *The Battle for Leyte Gulf* (1972); Richard F. Newcomb, *Iwo Jima* (1971); Martin Caidin et al, *Zero* (1956); Forrest Pogue, *George C. Marshall: Organizer of Victory, 1943-1945* (1972); Clark J. Reynolds, *Fast Carriers* (1968); S. E. Smith, *The U.S. Marines in World War II* (1969); Richard Tregaskis, *Guadalcanal Diary* (1943); William Craig, *The Fall of Japan* (1967); Ladislas Farago, *The Broken Seal* (1967); John Hersey, *Hiroshima* (1959); F. W. Winterbotham, *The Ultra Secret* (1974); William T. Y'Blood, *Red Sun Setting: The Battle of the Philippine Sea* (1980).

Some few of the accounts by "war correspondents" are Ernie Pyle, *Here is Your War* (1943); and *Brave Men* (1944); John Hersey, *Into the Valley: A Skirmish of the Marines* (1966); W. L. White, *They Were Expendable* (1942); Robert Sherrod, *Tarawa: The Story of a Battle* (1944); Theodore H. White and Annalee Jacoby, *Thunder Out of China* (1946); the several books by Quentin Reynolds; Jack Belden, *Still Time to Die* (1943); and Louis Snyder, ed., *Masterpieces of War Re-*

porting: *The Great Moments of World War II.* See also the classic study of the effects of combat, *The American Soldier: Combat and its Aftermath* (1949), by Samuel A. Stouffer et al.; and William Manchester's memoir, *Goodbye Darkness* (1980).

The air war is treated in Allen Andrews, *The Air Marshals: The Air War in Western Europe* (1970); Martin Caidin, *The Night Hamburg Died* (1960); Martin Middlebrook, *The Battle of Hamburg: Allied Bomber Forces Against a German City in 1943* (1981); Adolf Galland, *The First and the Last* (1970); Len Deighton, *Bomber* (1970); Edward Jablonski, *Air War* (4 vols., 1971–72), *Flying Fortress* (1965), and *Double Strike: The Epic Raids on Regensburg/Schweinfurt* (1974); Stanley M. Ulamoff, *Bombs Away: True Stories of Strategic Airpower from World War I to the Present* (1971); Gavin Lyall, *The War in the Air: The Royal Air Force in World War II* (1969); and Martin Caidin, *A Torch to the Enemy* (1960). A sampling of the numerous studies of wartime diplomacy are Diane S. Clemens, *Yalta* (1970); Herbert Feis, *Churchill, Roosevelt, Stalin* (1970); W. Averell Harriman and Elie Abel, *Special Envoy to Churchill and Stalin, 1941–1946* (1975); George C. Herring, *Aid to Russia, 1941–1946* (1973); Gabriel Kolko, *The Politics of War* (1968); Charles L. Mees, *Meeting at Potsdam* (1975); Raymond G. O'Connor, *Diplomacy for Victory: F.D.R. and Unconditional Surrender* (1971); Michael Schaller, *The U.S. Crusade in China, 1938–1945* (1979); Thomas M. Campbell, *America's UN Policy, 1944–1945* (1974); Martin Sherwin, *A World Destroyed: The Atomic Bomb and the Grand Alliance* (1975); Henry L. Feingold, *The Politics of Rescue: The Roosevelt Administration and the Holocaust, 1938–1945* (1970); Warren F. Kimball, *Swords or Ploughshares?: The Morgenthau Plan* (1976); Christopher Thorne, *Allies of a Kind: The United States, Britain, and the War Against Japan, 1941–1945* (1978); and Vojtech Mastny, *Moscow's Road to the Cold War* (1980).

For America's mobilization, see Bruce Catton, *The Warlords of Washington* (1948); Donald M. Nelson, *Arsenal of Democracy: The Story of American War Production* (1973); Keith L. Nelson, *The Impact of War on American Life* (1971); Francis Walton, *The Miracle of World War II*; the gen-eral surveys cited earlier; James M. Burns' *Roosevelt: Soldier of Freedom* (1972); and U.S. Bureau of the Budget, *The United States at War* (1946). Special studies include Rosalyn Baxandall et al, *America's Working Women* (1976); James Phinney Baxter, *Scientists Against Time* (1946); William H. Chafe, *The American Women* (1972); Benjamin Colby, *'Twas a Famous Victory* (1974); Richard M. Dalfiume, *Desegregation of the U.S. Armed Forces* (1969); Roger Daniels, *Concentration Camps U.S.A.: Japanese Americans and World War II* (1971); Audrie Girdner and Anne Loftis, *The Great Betrayal* (1969); Bill Hosokawa, *Nisei* (1969); David R. Ross, *Preparing for Ulysses: Politics and Veterans During World War II* (1969); Lawrence S. Wittner, *Rebels Against War: The American Peace Movement* (1969); Philip J. Funigiello, *The Challenge to Urban Liberalism: Federal-City Relations During World War II* (1978); Herman J. Somers, *The Office of War Mobilization and Reconversion* (1946); Neil A. Wynn, *The Afro-American and the Second World War* (1976); Francis Biddle, *In Brief Authority* (1962); Harvey Mansfield, *A Short History of the OPA* (1947); George Q. Flynn, *The Mess in Washington: Manpower Mobilization in World War II* (1979); and Marshall B. Clinard, *The Black Market* (1952).

The home front is dealt with, variously, in Keith Ayling, *Calling All Women* (1942); Ronald H. Bailey, *The Home Front: U.S.A.* (1977); the Blum, Lingemann, and Perrett surveys; the excellent book by Jack Goodman, *While You Were Gone* (1974); A. A. Hoehling, *Home Front, U.S.A.* (1966) and his *The Week Before Pearl Harbor* (1963); Richard Polenberg's analytical *War and Society* (1972); and Cabell Phillips, *The 1940s* (1975). See also Allan M. Winkler, *The Politics of Propaganda* (1978); Robert K. Merton, *Mass Persuasion: The Social Psychology of a War Bond Drive* (1946); Louis Adamic, *A Nation of Nations* (1945); Louis Ruchames, *Race, Jobs and Politics: The Story of FEPC* (1948); Howard Odum, *Race and Rumors of Race* (1943); Robert Shogan and Tom Craig, *The Detroit Race Riot* (1964); and Dominic J. Capeci, Jr., *The Harlem Riot of 1943* (1977). Treatment of Japanese-Americans is to be found in Roger Daniels, *Concentration Camp U.S.A.: Japanese Americans and World War II*

(1969); Bill Hosokawa, *Nisei* (1969), Audrie Gird-ner and Anne Loftis, *The Great Betrayal* (1969); Martin Grodzins, *Americans Betrayed: Politics and the Japanese Evacuation* (1949); Jacobus ten Broek, et al., *Prejudice, War and the Constitution* (1954); and Dorothy S. Thomas and Richard S. Nishimoto, *The Spoilage* (1946). Studies of the war's impact on American communities include F. Stuart Chapin, *The Impact of the War on Community Leadership and Opinion in Red Wing* [Minnesota] (1945); Ray H. Abrams, ed., *The American Family in World War II* (1943); Katherine Archibald, *Wartime Shipyard: A Study in Social Disunity* (1947); Lowell J. Carr and James E. Stermer, *Willow Run: A Study of Industrialization and Cultural Inadequacy* (1952); Robert W. Havighurst and H. G. Morgan, *The Social History of a War-Boom Community* [Seneca, Illinois] (1951); and W. Lloyd Warner et al., *Democracy in Jonesville* (1949).

Seattle
74–76

Fort Lewis
10, 13–14

To
Japan
19

45–46
San Francisco
(Berkeley)
19

Fresno
20–22
Dinuba

63–64
Los Angeles
Fullerton
22

Manzanar
19

20–22
Gila River
Relocation Center

Phoenix
68–69

Denver
68–69

15
Topeka

11–12
Roper

8–10, 13–18
New Albany

Fredo
14

16–17
Oklahoma

Gainesville
74–75
Shern

Bo

74–77
Lubbock

Levelland
74–76

28
Dallas

Tyler

Kosse
Marlin (Shad

28
Austin

Houston

81
Laredo

80–82
Sullivan

Los Ebanos
78–80

80–81
Pharr

PART **3**
1945-

East
Lansing
47-48

Detroit

3
Beverly

Boston
4-7
(Medford)
36-37
Providence

31-33
41-47
83-89
New
York

40
Martha's
Vineyard

ichigan
ity

47-49
Granville

Midland
51, 53, 56-58
Pittsburgh 58
Primrose 55

Columbus
22

Upper St.
Clair Twp.
31-33

Washington,
D.C. 7

83-84
From Puerto Rico

68-69
Louisville

nd
h Co.

Waynesboro
and Wayne Co.

rmingham
-69

74
Atlanta
(Decatur)
76-77

Tequesta
36-37

PUERTO RICO

83-84
San Juan

10 | The Third Generation

INTRODUCTION

In the decades after World War II, the experiences of the families chronicled in this book reflected transformations in the nation that some described as revolutionary and that others called moderate or gradual. Almost all of the first generation died, the second generation became aged, and the third reached adulthood and scattered across the nation. The size of families diminished sharply, and this was directly related to the improved standard of living. While families changed in those ways, some maintained old values, as well. Louis and Lila Gropper rebuilt their lives after divorce; Jerry and Peggy Trace transferred eight times in 22 years yet tried to identify with their communities; and the Gishmans and Simiches and their children maintained strong and warm ties despite the barriers of distance and vastly different experiences.

These success stories were, it must be noted, partly founded upon the economic security acquired by the great majority of Americans in the 1950s and 1960s. Three decades of broadly based prosperity, beginning with the recovery produced by the Second World War, made possible the acquisition of material possessions—single-family homes, automobiles, the latest gadgets—to a degree unimaginable before. Americans enjoyed some protection against sickness, injury, and the "accident" of unemployment and, through Social Security, protection of a sort for their old age. As well, most families gained access to cut-rate versions of the "good life" as practiced by upper-class families such as the Butlers: two weeks at Daytona Beach or Disneyland rather than summer on the Cape, admission to El Segundo Community College rather than Harvard, a Macy's copy of a Paris design rather than the original itself. Of course, many citizens, poverty-stricken blacks, whites, Indians, and others—the old, infirm, and the mentally unbalanced—had not even those options, and the likelihood of their joining the "haves" of American society now appears less certain than was the hope 25 years ago. Economic security, which Americans assumed had been won in the 1960s, turned out to be vulnerable to the "stagflation" that darkened the last years of the 1970s.

THE GISHMANS OF NEW YORK, SAN FRANCISCO, AND OVERLAND PARK, KANSAS

In 1947, Bertha and Henry Gishman moved from the Bronx to Glenoaks, a garden apartment complex near Belrose, Long Island. The move represented a compromise between Henry's wish to buy a house in a comfortable suburb and Bertha's yearning to remain in the old neighborhood close to her mother and sister. In part, they were searching for better educational opportunities for their two boys, Michael and his younger brother, David. Henry's desire for more space in an "American environment" and for more status (many of his fellow workers at BMI were moving to suburban Westchester County) was not completely fulfilled at

The Gishman boys, Glenoaks, 1949

Glenoaks. Both Henry and Bertha soon found themselves worried about the lack of Jewish institutions. So, within three years, with Henry under renewed pressure to locate in a more fashionable suburb, the Gishmans bought a home in a new section of Bayside, Queens. It was semidetached, on one twentieth of an acre of land, had three bedrooms and a modern kitchen, and cost $10,600 (financed via a 30-year FHA mortgage with 10 percent down). The neighborhood was about 75 percent Jewish.

For a time, there was a good chance that Henry would become a high executive in BMI. He had done well in the difficult field of station relations and was named production manager in 1952. But personnel changes, Henry's distaste for rock and roll (which became BMI's main emphasis in the mid-1950s), and office politics prevented any further advancement. However, he was making good money—$15,000 in 1956, plus royalties from his songs—and he submerged his frustrated ambitions in the family, benefit appearances, and planning for vacations. Nevertheless, by the mid-1960s Henry was desperately unhappy, considering his position as director of music clearance to be merely "busywork." When an old rival was named president in 1969, Henry jumped at the chance to head BMI's San Francisco office. Michael and David had left home, both—to their parents' delight—having entered college teaching, and Louise was completing a fine arts degree at Harpur College. The salary was appealing ($18,500) and, besides, Henry and Bertha had begun to actively dislike New York City. They found a pleasant townhouse in San Francisco. While the move turned out satisfactorily, the work situation did not, and Henry welcomed retirement in April 1977. He and Bertha live comfortably in San Francisco.

Henry Gishman was the first member of his family to move to the suburbs. He was also instrumental in founding a Reform Temple in the Glenoaks area, for he was unwilling to abandon entirely his ties with the past and deny awareness of their Jewishness to his children. At first, the congregation of Temple Shalom used rooms in a nearby mental hospital and then a rented storefront for religious classes and adult activities. In 1950, Temple Shalom moved into a modest, cinder-block structure designed by one of its members. Henry was its first president and the Gishmans were active in temple affairs while the boys were growing up. Michael received instruction from Shalom's rabbi until his Bar Mitzvah in 1952, but David was sent to Hebrew School three days a week. (Their sister, Louise, born in 1949 after Bertha had suffered two miscarriages, had no Jewish education.) In other ways, the contrasts between Michael and his bright younger brother caused problems. The elder Gishmans expected their older son to excel and pushed him toward a career as a doctor. They simply assumed that he and his brother and sister would go to college. For them, as for the great majority of white Americans by the 1950s, a college degree was the magic talisman that a high-school diploma had been a generation before.

For those who chose not to probe too deeply, education in post–World War II America appeared to have realized the democratic ideal of free instruction for all. Illiteracy was virtually abolished. Completion of high school became the norm, with 75 percent of all 17-year-olds earning a high school diploma by 1965. In the Deep South and Appalachia in 1960 between 10 and 12 percent of all whites 25 years and over had completed fewer than five years of schooling compared with 6 percent nationally. A large educational gap persisted between blacks and whites. While, in 1968, 75 percent of all whites between the ages of 25 and 29 years had graduated from high school, for blacks the proportion was 58 percent. Among the dom-

inant Mexican-American population in the Lower Rio Grande Valley, fewer than 50 percent of those over 24 years old in 1970 had more than an eighth grade education, and in Los Angeles over 25 percent of Mexican-American students dropped out of high school after tenth grade during the 1960s. Still, the number of high-school graduates exceeded 2.7 million in 1968 and college enrollments skyrocketed.

Post-secondary education underwent tremendous expansion and, with growth, acquired broadened responsibilities. Enrollments in institutions of higher education rose from 1.5 million in 1940 to 2.6 million in 1956, reflecting the opportunities available to veterans of World War II and the Korean conflict under the GI Bill. By 1970, enrollments approached 7 million. College study as the path to the good and full life was embraced by ever-increasing numbers, so much so that by the early 1970s graduate education came to perform the function of special training and social differentiation previously fulfilled by undergraduate education. The bachelor of arts (or science) degree meant less and less in the competition for desirable white-collar jobs. In 1950, 86 percent of all college and university degrees were bachelors, in 1970 less than 75 percent, and in 1980 only some 65 percent.

With the end of the Vietnam conflict and the persistence of recession and inflation, the consequences of educational expansion became more obvious and widely publicized, so much so that the willingness of communities, state legislatures, and the federal government to underwrite it waned. By the 1970s, critics questioned the value of general college education in an increasingly specialized world. Not all young people should be prepared to write critical analyses of *Troilus and Cressida* or to master differential equations or conjugate the verb *avoir*. College graduates had to accept jobs for which they were overtrained.

The challenging of education's function as social and economic escalator, when linked with dramatic declines in the 18–21 year age groups (resulting from the end of the postwar baby boom), appeared to guarantee hard times for America's colleges and universities. However, the entry into undergraduate and professional programs of increasing numbers of women and the reentry of those desiring to complete degrees or receive training that permitted career changes, had pushed post-secondary school enrollments over 9 million by 1980, and many administrators were becoming comfortable with a new jargon —"adult learners," "nontraditional study," "outreach." To some, John Dewey's goal of education for life would be realized by the acceptance of a national commitment to education *throughout* life.

For some years, Michael Gishman, like Robbie Bassano and Bill Trace, was victimized by the disparities between testing predictions of what he *should* do and his own inclinations and accomplishments. Reacting to parental and peer pressure, he was only a "so-so" student through high school, graduating with an 80 average. Becoming a doctor was no longer possible. Michael failed to gain admission to a free New York City college and entered Hofstra College on Long Island. Though he continued to live at home and his parents paid all his expenses at Hofstra, he was relatively independent and began to think, really for the first time, about what he wished to do with his life. During his sophomore year he decided to major in geology and thereafter did extremely well. Though field work greatly interested him, he decided to seek an academic career since the big oil companies, the most important employers of geologists, discriminated blatantly against Jews. Upon graduation in 1961, Michael was accepted for graduate study at all the major geology schools. However, perhaps reflecting

lack of confidence in his own abilities, Michael went to the University of Maine for the M.A. By now, Henry and Bertha were reconciled to Michael's choice of career and helped him out, refinancing their home to pay for two years of study at Maine.

In 1963, Michael entered the Ph.D. program in petroleum geology at Michigan State. He was financially independent, holding an assistantship, and was even able to save after his marriage to Karyl Gold, whom he had met while she was finishing a master's in social work. However, in 1968, Michael accepted a position at Denison College without having completed his Ph.D. dissertation. Karyl wanted to have a baby, and, most important, Michael was eager to discover whether he really liked teaching.

Denison was a good school and Michael and Karyl especially enjoyed the low-key atmosphere. Their first child, Kynan, was born there in 1970, and they might have remained indefinitely had not a crisis arisen over the college's treatment of black students. Michael, much to his own surprise, became the only scientist to go out on strike. This experience, a milestone in Michael's politicization, convinced him that academe was no less bureaucratic or competitive than private industry, and he felt he would be happier in the private sector, where the financial rewards were greater. Also, he later confessed, he had little motivation to finish his dissertation. Michael and his family left Denison in June 1971 and headed west, having arranged to stay with Henry and Bertha in San Francisco for a few weeks while he was sorting out job offers. But as the economy tightened, the available jobs disappeared and they lived with his parents for nine months. It was an awkward time, for Henry and Bertha were deeply unhappy about his decision to leave teaching, and Michael became frustrated and angry with his failure to find employment.

In March 1972, Michael was hired as a field geologist by one of the nation's largest engineering consulting firms and was assigned to the Kansas City office. The salary, $12,500, was considerably more than he had made in teaching. Michael did not enjoy the constant travel connected with his work, but since May 1975, he has served as administrative assistant to the president, a permanent shift to management, and is happy about his choice of career. While occasionally disturbed that his administrative duties have ruled out further work in the field and sometimes irritated by the political games that go on in the home office, he is good at what he does, enjoys the authority and the financial benefits, and prizes the stability.

Michael and Karyl like the Kansas City suburb of Overland Park, where they bought a home in 1973, and to some degree they have become involved with the Kansas City Jewish community. Previously, neither one had been much concerned about Jewishness but, reacting to the pressures of evangelical Christianity, decided that it was necessary to arrange Jewish educations for Kynan and their son Kaelen (1975). Michael was also affected by the late-blooming orthodoxy of his brother, David, a faculty member at a nearby university. By 1980, the identification of Michael and Karyl with the local Jewish social networks was well advanced.

A vast gulf had opened between the experiences of Meyer and Annie Miller and those of Michael and Karyl Gishman, a gulf largely caused by Michael's entrance into the middle-class mainstream beyond the narrow ethnic-religious world of his grandparents and by the process of education. But education, so Michael now believes, can also bridge that abyss and, by offering insights into the cultural heritage brought to America by his grandparents, aid him and his children in living with confidence and pride in a world very different—but still threatening to Jews—from that which the Millers encountered.

THE NAVAS OF HIDALGO COUNTY, TEXAS

The dry bush country of the Lower Rio Grande Valley of Texas has been home to the Nava family since the mid-19th century when the great-grandfather of Antonio Alvarez Nava (born in 1937), the present head of the clan, crossed the Rio Grande. Four generations have lived in Hidalgo County in the vicinity of what is now McAllen, never straying farther than a dozen miles from the Mexican border. The seven children of Antonio A. and Irma Flores Nava were taught that their ancestors did not come to the United States but that "Los Estados Unidos" came to them. Pride in their Hispanic heritage and in the tradition of participation by Navas in law enforcement sustain Antonio A. and his father, Antonio Luis. Whether the children of Irma and Antonio A., now all attaining adulthood, will gain strength from the family's cultural traditions is uncertain. Although Mexican-Americans are probably the least acculturated of all ethnic groups, they are exposed to powerful pressures to assimilate, pressures equal to those which confronted the Millers, O'Reillys, and Reinhardts.

For many years, the Navas remained largely insulated from these pressures. Antonio A. lived with his parents in a small frame house in the village of Los Ebanos, 50 yards from the turgid Rio Grande. Gardening and a few cattle made them self-sufficient, requiring only occasional visits to the larger towns to the north. Antonio Luis and Sophia traveled only to see relatives in Hidalgo County and across the Rio Grande in San Miguel and Reynosa, Mexico.

Antonio A.'s father rode for the United

Los Ebanos town square, 1975

Crossing to Mexico at the Los Ebanos ferry

States Mounted Border Patrol for 37 years, patrolling the same stretch of 20 miles on the lookout for diseased or stolen Mexican cattle. Antonio L.'s salary was much higher than that of most of his kin or neighbors, and his association with Anglos (even though he spoke little English until the 1950s) convinced him that his only child should go to school. School came as a rude shock to Antonio A. Frightened by his teachers who had little patience with their Spanish-speaking pupils (Texas law then required that all instruction be in English), the young Nava withdrew into himself and, although he graduated from high school at La Joya in 1955, he never mastered English. At his father's insistence, Antonio enrolled at Pan American University, Edinburg, Texas, in fall 1955. Classes and the influence of Anglo-American employers at a part-time job taught Antonio A. the necessity of good English for advancement in a world dominated by Anglos. Within a short time he lost the Spanish traces in his English.

Under the surface, however, he remains intensely proud of his Hispanic heritage, and his life reflects its values. During Antonio A.'s freshman year, he met Irma Flores, the oldest daughter of a well-off, Americanized Laredo family, and they married in June 1956. Two months later, she became pregnant. Antonio A. tried to stay in school while working to meet expenses, car payments, and medical bills, but in March 1957, shortly before his son, Antonio Avilo, was born, he quit school and found a full-time job with the Edinburg water department. Conscious of the status his father derived from his police career and of the opportunities for advancement, Antonio A. determined to seek a career in law enforcement. Through his friendship with the Edinburg Constable, he became a part-time deputy whose principal assignment was to apprehend "wetbacks" (illegal aliens) and drunken "green carders" (Mexicans with U.S. work permits) at $5 per head. Antonio made more in "commissions" than from his job as a meter reader.

As he edged closer to a full-time career in law enforcement, Antonio moved his family to Los Ebanos and pursued the traditional Mexican male role of patriarch and procreator. A daughter, Manuela, was born in 1960, followed by Eduardo (1963), Hilario (1965), Joel (1968), Sofia (1970), and Joaquin (1972). Because of religious convictions, Antonio and Irma used the rhythm method for contraception and they had a large family.

For the Navas, particularly Antonio, the children are central. He possesses strong views about child rearing and adolescent behavior. He wishes his children to be comfortable in both the Hispanic and Anglo worlds, but the atmosphere in the Nava home is wholly traditional. Irma favored using English but Antonio A. said: "I'll teach them Spanish. That's my language." Spanish is the home tongue. Thus, the children are able to receive oral traditions from their parents and grandparents—the verities of Mexican-American culture backed up with the conservative code of the Texas middle class. Antonio is opposed to intermarriage on practical grounds and, though the family only rarely attends mass, he emphasizes church teaching on birth control, the sanctity of the family, and paternal authority. He has only contempt for "modern" child rearing practices but does believe in "telling it like it is." There are only three things worth fighting for, Antonio A. has instructed his sons: the United States, the honor of a woman, and defense of the family name. Conversely, his three unforgivable sins are: theft, drugs, and homosexuality. He has been equally candid with Manuela, now 20, about sex, telling her to avoid premarital intercourse not because it is "bad" (which he admits would be stupid) but because she should be able to control her emotions until she decides that the "right boy" has been found. "If you let just anybody get with you," he tells Manuela, "you have to live with the consequences. If you find somebody good enough for you, marry him." In the era of the pill, when the "consequences" are avoidable, such strictures have lost their old power. Indeed, though the Nava children are well behaved and respectful of parental authority, they view many questions differently.

The difference between generations—generation gap—evoked to explain an enormous variety of stresses and strains in postwar American society, refers mainly to differences in attitudes and values that supposedly separate the young, especially those born during and since the war, from their elders. Polls and other studies of drug and alcohol usage and sexual behavior suggest that the magnitude of the "gap" has been exaggerated. Similarly,

most young people continue to adhere to "old-fashioned" attitudes toward work, success, and community.

Other behavior suggests a real difference between the generations. Many young people today show less compulsion to rush into marriage and a family than their parents did. Trial marriages—with no legal base—and other informal liaisons are common. Attitudes toward illegitimacy and divorce have also changed. Single mothers are more likely to keep their child than in prior decades, and women are more likely to opt for divorce in order to pursue career ambitions than to continue as frustrated housewives. Many young people seem more casual about such things as careers than their elders were when of the same age. There is less acceptance among today's children concerning the necessity of college and many are looking for work from choice rather than because of economic or intellectual deficiencies. The present generation appears less regimented than its elders were and less inclined to accept without question the prescribed sequence of going through life that ruled their parents.

Antonio A. Nava, however, sought a secure career in law enforcement. The "big break" came when the Hidalgo County sheriff hired him as night man at the jail. Then in 1964, Sheriff Vickers arranged a patrolman's job with the McAllen Police Department. Antonio A. performed superbly. It was city policy to award a day off to any officer who arrested a burglar at the scene of the crime. While still a rookie, Antonio accrued 36 extra days leave. Three years later, he was offered promotion to Hidalgo County deputy sheriff. In order to obtain necessary certification, Antonio A. completed 244 hours of instruction (including sociology, psychology, and FBI seminars) at the Texas State Police Academy. Unfortunately, in 1969 Sheriff Vickers retired and Antonio backed his chief deputy, an Anglo, against a local bartender who was supported by a Mexican-American political group. Antonio's choice lost the election, and eight months later Antonio was forced to resign.

For a short time he served as chief of police of the nearby town of Mission. Again, he clashed with a militant Mexican-American organization that was pressing for the mayor's removal. There were increasingly bitter clashes between Mexican-American groups and the mayor's defenders. The town split along ethnic lines with Antonio A. and his 14-man force caught in the middle. Antonio still remembers the taunts thrown at him: "You're a Chicano, too. You pig cop! Why are you helping these Anglo mother fuckers?" He claims to be sympathetic to many militant objectives, though he despises the word *Chicano* and does not believe the tactics of direct confrontation are relevant in the Rio Grande Valley. Nonetheless, when the militants forced out the mayor in a recall election, Antonio A. was dismissed from his position.

Three years of insecurity and work away from home followed. But in 1973 the second stroke of fortune in Antonio's life took place. Old friends recommended him for the position of chief security officer of Miller International Airport outside McAllen. It has proved to be the perfect job for Antonio A. Nava. The pay is good, he has full authority, and the routine, with new faces coming past his office all the time, is not hopelessly dull. He leaves the airport, with only rare exceptions, at 5:05 P.M. and arrives home in time to have a beer before the local news at 5:30. There is lots of time for other jobs (he is "on call" by the local Kroger store, and raises some cattle and hogs) and for his family.

The Navas have a comfortable life. Their home, though crowded now that the family has grown to nine, is pleasantly worn, and they have two cars, a pickup, a color TV, and the biggest freezer in Hidalgo County. An-

tonio A. enjoys his work, and Irma expresses contentment with her enforced domesticity. Most important, Antonio A. and Irma are proud of their success in transferring to their children the values and traditions central to their own lives. Antonio's oldest son, following a hitch in the Marine Corps, returned to McAllen and a job as an airport security officer. Manuela attended business college and has a good job. She is engaged, and Antonia A. is convinced that she has followed his advice. The other children are doing well in school, though their facility in Spanish is slipping. The poverty, conflict, and tensions pressuring Mexican-Americans do not trouble the elder Navas. They hope it will not trouble their children.

THE GROPPERS OF LUBBOCK, TEXAS, AND DECATUR, GEORGIA

The second son of Louis and Lila Hunt Gropper, Christopher James, is now living in a predominantly black, middle-class suburb of Decatur, Georgia, a city of 22,000 located within the Atlanta metropolitan area. For many of its residents Decatur (which some years ago was included in a list of America's 20 "most desirable" suburbs selected for *Better Homes and Gardens*) represents the apex of acceptance and achievement. For Chris Gropper, however, the $80,000 home he bought in 1973 and the Oldsmobile Omega and TR-3 sitting in its two-car garage are both a source of tremendous satisfaction and the cause of nagging guilt. Chris is caught, as in different ways are the Navas and Gishmans, in a conflict between immersion in the cultural milieu opened to him by economic status and the retention of traditions derived from his background and race. Chris enjoys his $34,000-a-year job in the personnel division of Avon Cosmetics. But he and his wife Jane share a strong sense of racial pride. Having renounced most of their fundamentalist Christian upbringing, they chose Swahili names for their children, Njeri (1972) and Kahre (1975). At the same time, both Chris and Jane reject the Black Muslim faith and are determined to "make it"—though on their own terms—in America.

Attitudes manifested by Chris's parents in part explain the direction of his views. Louis and Lila Gropper had returned from the West Coast with their two sons in late 1945. Following an unsatisfactory teaching job in Oklahoma and the birth of a third son, Chester, in 1947 Lila was refused admission in an Oklahoma hospital, and Louis was forced to drive her to Vernon, Texas, to obtain proper medical attention), Louis moved to Levelland, Texas, that summer, to become principal of a black, 12-grade school. Lila also obtained a teaching position.

The Groppers spent the next decade in Levelland, an agricultural service community of 8,200 in 1950 (10,000 in 1960), becoming deeply involved in the life of the black community. Its black population, 297 in 1950 and 525 in 1960, occupied a four-square-block area, with its own groceries, taverns, service stations, and specialty shops. The Groppers bought a lot in the "nice" part of the black neighborhood and erected a prefabricated two-bedroom house in 1950. The only professionals in the community were the teachers, and thus Louis and Lila quickly assumed positions of social leadership. Louis founded a local NAACP chapter and belonged to the Levelland Negro Chamber of Commerce. Chris remembers neighbors stopping by to ask "Professor" Gropper's advice about political issues. Louis took pride in his position and in his efforts to improve the educational program. By 1952, when the town's black pupils moved into a new brick and stucco facility (named George Washington Carver School by Louis), he had up-

graded the staff, obtained approval for a cafeteria and gymnasium, and built up a decent collection of books on black history and literature. Lila, however, became extremely bitter about the dual system and the great disparity in funding between the white and black schools.

Segregation ruled Levelland through the 1950s. Most stores excluded blacks, the movie theatre had a "nigger balcony," and residential segregation was rigidly enforced. The Groppers responded by avoiding situations where they and their children might encounter open prejudice. "If we aren't wanted, I'm not going to go," Louis often said. George and Chris do not recall meeting obvious racial bias until their teens. Only occasionally did the children play with whites. They attended school and church exclusively with blacks. Their parents did not consciously strive to inculcate racial awareness, but Chris remem-

First Sunday suits for Chris, Louis George, and Chester Gropper (left to right), Levelland, Texas, Mother's Day, 1950

bers their father making a black Santa Claus, taking his sons to films in Lubbock featuring black casts, and encouraging their interest in black sports figures. The family subscribed to the usual national magazines and to *The Crisis,* the *Pittsburgh Courier,* and *Jet* and *Ebony.*

The Gropper boys experienced "normal" childhoods—Little League and music lessons (both integrated), school, impromptu games with friends—but the strains resulting from their parents' effort to shelter them from raw prejudice and also financial and sexual tensions led, in 1957, to a decision by Lila to leave Louis. She found a teaching job in Lubbock and, eight months later, returned for the boys and informed Louis she was filing for divorce. There was a messy trial in which Lila, charging adultery, won custody of the children and the family's possessions. Louis later remarried, but Lila never found anyone who could meet her stiff social and intellectual standards.

After several moves, Lila rented a house from relatives near the elementary school at which she taught. George, then a high-school sophomore, understood the reasons for the breakup and adjusted quickly. He did well at Paul Laurence Dunbar High School, was the junior-class president and class valedictorian. George had been offered several scholarships but decided to enroll at Texas Tech in Lubbock when it desegregated in summer, 1961. He earned graduate degrees in history and library science, served as Director of the Regional History Collection at a major midwestern university, worked briefly for a newly elected Senator, and now is a lobbyist for a national association of realtors. The youngest son, Chester, was only 10 when his parents divorced. Protected by his brothers and doting relatives, he drifted through high school, gained a psychology degree at Howard University, spent a three-year enlistment playing trumpet with the Fifth Army Band, and is now

running a preschool program for disadvantaged children in Washington, D.C.

Chris had a more difficult time. Just entering puberty, he missed his father and blamed himself for the divorce. He was an average student at Dunbar, being much more interested in cars, sports, and girls than in school. In 1961, he found an after-school job at a local trucking company and immediately bought a chopped, lowered 1956 Ford. He followed his older brother to Texas Tech without thinking much about career goals. While working nearly full time, Chris floated through Tech (a school with fewer than 50 black students). He majored in psychology with a minor in music, but most of his energy was expended on the ROTC drill team and partying. Chris considered his selection to Tech's integrated drill team and later appointment as executive officer proof of his acceptance—and acceptability—in white society. Further, the idea of a military career, offering merit promotions, glamour, and travel, appealed to him, and he accepted a regular army commission upon graduation in 1967. Aware that he probably would be sent to Vietnam, Chris told his brother George, who urged him to sit out the war in Canada, that he believed America's presence to be necessary and that he was willing to do his duty.

Two years later, Chris returned from a 13-month tour in "Nam" embittered and hostile toward the army and United States policy. He had led a group assigned to recovering corpses from the battlefield and thus personally knew the discrepancies between the official reporting of the war and actual battlefield conditions. The large numbers of civilian deaths also affected him. Moreover, he had been exposed to radical and black-power literature and was cynical about the ideal of an equitable, integrated society. Feeling alienated from the passive atmosphere of Lubbock, Chris moved in with his older brother and got a job with a Head Start program. Chris became deeply involved with black militancy and joined a group that was raising funds to launch a chicken-raising business in Africa. His dissatisfaction was rooted in a national crisis of confidence and in personal doubts. As a young college graduate, he shared the idealistic repugnance of many of his generation toward the failed promises and blind materialism of postwar America. As a young, college-educated black, Chris concluded that the "American dream," the faith in a steady march toward economic security and integration in which his people—perhaps more than any other group—had trusted, was fraudulent or worse.

The civil rights agitation of the early 1960s, climaxed by the "March on Washington" in August 1963 and the "freedom summer" the following year, converted numerous young whites into radicals bent on destroying a complacent, corrupt society and redeeming America's commitment to all its people. Many blacks, however, rejected cooperation with white radicals or with whites of any persuasion. "What we need is black power," Stokely Carmichael proclaimed in 1966. As A. Philip Randolph and others had argued a generation earlier, blacks must go it alone—wherever it was they were going. At a basic level, however, these currents derived from a quite traditional concern—the need to define and confirm personal and group identity. The motivations of the 1960s activists and their parents, and older brothers and sisters, despite obvious differences in styles, were essentially similar. Young people were seeking to reconcile, through activism and personal redefinition, glaring contradictions and conflicting pressures: affluence and numbing poverty, an exhilarating freedom of choice and rigid limitations on individual opportunities. In the 1960s, the drive to discover one's own identity took various forms: involvement with Eastern philosophies and/or "consciousness-raising" drugs, practice of psychological techniques promising to enhance self-awareness, and reinforcement of elements of personal identity (whether sexual, racial, ethnic, religious) through group participation. The 1970s, according to pop analysts, reinforced the yearnings for self-awareness and personal gratification while weakening the individual's ties with groups and the larger society.

For blacks such as Chris Gropper, black power meant black pride, solidarity, and identity. The revival of interest in black history, both African culture and traditions and the struggle against slavery and prejudice of black men and women in America, provided important linkages with the past and gave at least partial satisfaction to many black Americans. Others, however, acted on the "lessons" taught by these portrayals of their past. Some militants determined to extract compensation for three centuries of white oppression. Some went further, deciding to withdraw from contact with whites—either by taking control of certain communities and their institutions or, as Chris Gropper and his friends preferred, by returning "home" to Africa.

Something happened to divert Chris from this journey toward complete alienation. He later admitted to his brother: "I was really off base there." One factor, certainly, was his marriage to Jane Mitchell, an old girl friend from Texas Tech with whom he had corresponded while in Vietnam. Jane came from a middle-class black home and had majored in textile design at Tech. Hardly a militant, she was ambitious and eager to build a comfortable life. She successfully urged Chris to enter a personnel management program at Atlanta University of the GI Bill. But Jane was also proud of her heritage. She and Chris wrote a marriage ceremony that featured Swahili oaths and African dress. The wedding, held in a Lubbock Methodist Church, reflected Chris and Jane's awareness of their dual identities.

It appears that the Groppers have no strong desire to resolve this duality. Chris's career is extremely promising. His company paid for several courses in management science, and he has received three promotions. Jane has a responsible and reasonably well-paying position as a dress buyer for an Atlanta department store. They have acquired an interesting circle of friends, both black and white, and state bluntly that they feel comfortable with the racial attitudes developing in the "new" South, though not with the resurgence of the Ku Klux Klan and the thunderings of radio fundamentalists against race mixing. Chris's mother (who completed a master's degree in library science at Atlanta University in 1976 and lives not far from her second son) is thrilled with the accomplishments of her children, especially the material status of Chris, and with the prospects for her grandchildren. Within the parameters set by the larger society, it is clear that Chris and Jane Gropper have built a solid, satisfying life. Those parameters, however, can either strangle or liberate.

THE BASSANOS OF INWOOD (NYC), UPPER ST. CLAIR TOWNSHIP, PENNSYLVANIA, AND ALEXANDRIA, VIRGINIA

Charlotte Bassano learned of Japan's surrender as she had learned of VE Day and the dropping of the atomic bomb, while sipping coffee with her best friends, Betty Clark and Sally Pritchard, in the small kitchen of the Nagel Avenue apartment. Relieved that the killing had stopped and the tyrant nations had been subdued, they shared anxieties about the possibilities of postwar depression and inflation. Living in rent-controlled apartments, all three feared the consequences should controls be lifted. None could afford much more

than they were paying. Even more ominous were the predictions of government economists, filtered through WOR radio and the *New York Daily News,* that peace could bring a return to the conditions of the 30s. These predictions were not realized, though neither were the extremely optimistic ones. The Bassanos and their friends did enjoy, a modest prosperity and sense of economic security for the first time in their adult lives.

Bob's career with Chase Manhattan Bank moved ahead steadily. In 1952, he became head bookkeeper, and between 1954 and 1957 he centralized the bookkeeping operation for the Chase branches in Brooklyn. Bob's wide experience with diverse phases of the bank's operations was put to use between 1958 and 1960 when he served as a full-time adviser to a firm devising a computer system for the bank's auditing program. In 1960, Chase offered Bob a vice presidency in charge of the bank's evening operations. Much to the firm's annoyance, Bob rejected the offer as he did not wish to work evening hours. For a time, it looked as if Chase would let him go. Instead, Bob was channeled into the branch system. From 1960 through 1962, Bob served as an assistant manager in a Bronx branch. He then moved to the Riverdale branch, just a 15-minute trip from home, as assistant manager. Bob was promoted to manager in 1969 and served in that position until his retirement in 1973.

The Bassanos have always been frugal, living well within their income and never going into debt during Bob's working years. From time to time Charlotte did secretarial work in downtown offices and, during the 1960s, she accumulated sufficient work time to gain eligibility for Social Security. Security for the Bassanos came through a pension and profit-sharing plan at Chase Manhattan. Bob contributed 6 percent of his base salary, matched by the bank, which was then invested by the bank in either stocks or bonds, or a mixed package. Interest from that plus his pension yields about $700 monthly in retirement. Inflation, however, caused him grave concern for the future, as it did millions of other aged people on fixed retirement incomes.

The financial effects of retirement were greatly diminished when, in 1974, Charlotte and Bob Bassano moved in with their son, Robbie, and his wife Dee. Not all sons and daughters are willing or able to form a household with their parents (indeed, it is becoming rare in the United States), but Bob and Charlotte and Dee and Robbie are a stable family unit. The arrangement was made not long after Bob's retirement, when Robbie was transferred from New York to Pittsburgh. The two couples purchased a home in Upper St. Clair Township, a suburb southwest of Pittsburgh's Golden Triangle. By this time, Robbie was well established as a federal law enforcement officer.

Robbie came to his career after a number of disappointments and false starts. A bright

The Bassanos at Robbie's graduation from NYU, June 7, 1961

but indifferent student, Robbie went through P.S. 152 and J.H.S. 52 in Inwood. In 1952, he entered Peter Stuyvesant High School. During his high-school years, Robbie played football, clarinet in the orchestra, and nurtured an ambition to go to the naval academy. Denied an appointment because of grades, he drifted into New York University, left to work for Equitable Life Insurance in 1958, tried Kings Point Merchant Marine Academy for a semester, and finally graduated from NYU in 1961 with a B.S. in education. Having no desire to teach, he entered the Marine Corps, went through Officers Candidate School, and served a three-year hitch as a second lieutenant at Camp Lejune, North Carolina. Robbie greatly enjoyed military life, and he expressed disappointment that his tours fell between Korea and Vietnam. Discharged in 1964 and at loose ends, he followed a friend's suggestion that he apply for training as a secret service officer. He began his present job, operating out of New York, in 1965.

Robbie's entry into police work coincided with a growing feeling of uneasiness on the part of his parents about their circumstances. The Bassanos were aging along with their neighborhood. If all had remained the same in Inwood, Bob and Charlotte and their friends would have been quite content to pass their retirement years strolling in Fort Tryon Park and maintaining long-standing friendships with people in the area. With Robbie grown up and gone and Bob holding a good job, the memories of the depression receded. They could afford a fuller life and took a step in that direction in 1963 by moving out of their Nagel Avenue apartment—under the shadow of the Seventh Avenue el—into a newer and more expensive apartment on the corner of Dyckman Street and Broadway. It was no larger, but it was airier, lighter, and less noisy. Moreover, it was an elevator apartment, a great blessing on Charlotte's shopping days.

Charlotte and Bob Bassano's Nagel Avenue apartment overlooking the el

Inevitably, change came to Inwood, change that the Bassanos and their friends did not like, change that at first caused resentment, then hostility, and finally fear. For the Bassanos, the security and familiarity of Inwood began to vanish when significant numbers of Puerto Ricans, other Spanish-speaking peoples, and blacks began to filter into Inwood.

Through 1950, blacks and Hispanic peoples formed under 1 percent of Inwood's population (see Table 10–1). It was an ethically mixed neighborhood in which German and east European Jews and Irish Catholics predominated. Jews owned many of the stores frequented by the Bassanos and, while they formed no close personal friendships with any Jewish families, Bob and Charlotte were not anti-Semitic and, indeed, reacted swiftly and firmly against juvenile outbursts

from Robbie who picked up the rhetoric, if not the feeling of anti-Semitism, from the Satans, the Irish Catholic gang to which he belonged. Bob and Charlotte were accustomed to a many-tongued street like Dyckman where they encountered Yiddish, German, Greek, Italian, and Slavic conversations each day. But these were hard-working people . . . and white.

Table 10–1
Racial Composition of Inwood, 1940–1970

	Total population	Blacks	Puerto Rican	Other Hispanic
1940	50,711			
1950	53,118	88	347*	
1960	51,823	1,621	1,029	
1970	47,584	3,081	2,799	5,762

* Includes Mexican, Caribbean, and other Hispanic peoples.

In 1958, blacks and Puerto Ricans first moved into Inwood in substantial numbers and by 1960 composed 5 percent of the population. While the percentage of nonwhites in Inwood remained much below that of Manhattan—about 40 percent—it caused consternation in the Bassano household and in the households of their friends. They reacted negatively to Spanish and Southern black dialects. These linguistic oddities, funny or mildly irritating at first, came to symbolize for the Bassanos the magnitude of the invasion which Inwood suffered and a seige mentality slowly captured their minds. Charlotte felt safe neither in her apartment nor on the street. Double and triple door locks, bolts and chains, and bars on windows began to appear. A gun was obtained.

The movement of minority families into Inwood—including Julio and Angelina Martinez, the next family to be discussed—was fostered initially by the construction of a massive public-housing project directly across the street from the Bassanos' Nagel Avenue apartment. By 1960, some 1,600 blacks (including the future basketball star Kareem Abdul Jabbar and his family), and 300 Puerto Ricans had moved in. At the same time, in-

Graffitti sprayed on a building near the Bassano's apartment in Inwood. Note the "Satan" sign, evidence that Robbie Bassano's old gang had survived all the changes which hit Inwood

creasing numbers of Puerto Ricans had moved into nearby blocks, particularly Post Avenue where the Clarks and the Pritchards lived.

The Bassanos date the decline of Inwood from the early 1960s and blame it on the influx of minority peoples. New survival rules were adopted by Bob and Charlotte: never venture in the parks beyond the fringes and only in daylight, only ride the subway at rush hour, do not wander in the streets after dark, bar the fire escape window, obtain full identification before unlocking the door for a stranger. Crime rates in Inwood, as around the country, did rise. Burglaries, muggings, vandalism, rape, and homicide rose to levels unheard of in Inwood. In the minds of the residents, they rose even faster than on the police blotters of the 34th Precinct.

From Robbie's desk in New York, the Bassanos received corroboration of their fears and pressure from their son to move. Robbie's contacts with the 34th Precinct and his own work convinced him that Inwood was no longer a secure place for his parents. Conversations invariably turned to mayhem in the streets, and the family became confirmed supporters of the Nixon-Agnew "law and order" program. Robbie's investigatory activities took him into many of the poorest neighborhoods in the city—South Bronx, Bedford-Stuyvesant. What he encountered there did not produce any sympathy for the residents of these zones of misfortune or any inquiry into the social causes of blight and poverty. Robbie has met some blacks whom he feels hold values similar to his own. If they do not, they are by definition inferior and not to be trusted. Robbie does not accept the idea that social decay breeds abnormal behavior. As a fact, he sees it every day, but as an explanation, it is unacceptable to him. Racial characteristics explain all.

Fear of violence and the association of violence with the influx of blacks and Puerto Ricans, Robbie's transfer to Pittsburgh, retirement, and a desire for quiet and comfort all prompted Bob and Charlotte to make the move with Dee and their son. Now living in a large suburban home south of Alexandria, Virginia (having left Upper St. Clair Township when Robbie was transferred to Washington in 1978), they no longer live in fear. But they have no more interest in Washington than they did in Pittsburgh. Bob has made the move to suburbia with little difficulty, becoming an accomplished gardener and making furniture for the house. Like his father, he possesses a craftsman's love for good material. Dee and Charlotte are bored. Dee misses her family in Brooklyn. Charlotte misses the Dyckman Street shops that she visited daily for over 30 years. Outside of Robbie's work-related acquaintances, they have made no close friendships.

Although the Bassanos now live in the suburbs, they are not suburbanites. They carried too much of New York with them. Still, they feel more secure—and happier—in their new home than they did on Dyckman Street. Sitting at the bar that Bob constructed for the family room, nursing a scotch and water, wondering if the graft on the rose bush would take, or planning to hit the big sale at the Falls Church shopping mall—all transformed Inwood, like Sequals for earlier Bassanos, into just another place name.

THE MARTINEZES OF NEW YORK

On a summer evening in 1955, the mechanics at the Consolidated Edison Company maintenance garage on West 96th Street, just off Broadway, were having trouble with a group of young Puerto Rican boys who lived on the block. A garage window had been broken by a line drive hit during a stickball game and than another errant ball had landed in the fenced-in parking area. The kids wanted the ball back and the mechanics refused to give it to them. Two of the boys climbed the fence from the 95th Street side but were caught, struggled to get away, and the uproar attracted a crowd. The mechanics, who often talked morosely about a "Spic takeover" of New York, decided to call the cops, and the crowd buzzed angrily. At that moment a youngish Puerto Rican man stepped forward and offered to pay for the window. Memories are fuzzy as to the negotiations that followed, but the kids agreed to move home plate some 30 yards further away from the shop and clean up the glass. The mechanics agreed not to call the police and to retrieve balls hit into the parking lot. During the next few weeks, the young peacemaker became friendly with several of the mechanics who, within a few months, obtained a job for him as a cleanup man in the shop. After 10 years in the city, Julio Martinez had experienced a bit of luck.

Arriving in New York in 1945, Julio was part of a large flow of Puerto Ricans to the mainland, particularly to the city of New York. Between 1950 and 1970, the number of persons of Puerto Rican birth or parentage living in New York rose from 301,000 to 812,000 or 10.3 percent of the city's population. By 1960, 96 percent lived in the boroughs of Manhattan, the Bronx, and Brooklyn. The largest concentration of Puerto Ricans in Manhattan was on the Lower East Side, near Rivington Street (where the Meyer Millers lived in 1893) and the Williamsburgh Bridge, and east of Central Park between 96th and 117th Streets, in so-called Spanish Harlem. Brooklyn's Williamsburgh district and the South Bronx were also heavily Puerto Rican.

The oldest son of a common laborer in San Juan, Puerto Rico, Julio came to New York in 1945 because he could not find work at home. Lacking a high-school education or trade and speaking little English, Julio moved in with an uncle on the Lower East Side. Never earning more than $12 to $14 weekly. Julio contributed part of his wage to his uncle, regularly sent some home, saved $1 weekly at Bowery Savings, and retained little for personal needs. His uncle's apartment was crowded with his own family of six and occasional relatives who moved up from Puerto Rico and as frequently returned. Julio's uncle pressed him to find his own place.

In 1947, Julio was hired by the Horn and Hardart restaurant near Macy's at 34th Street as a sandwich maker for $15.50 weekly. He met a salad maker, Angelina Lopes, courted and married her that same year. The couple moved in with Angelina's mother and three sisters on 96th Street. Angelina quickly became pregnant and had to quit work. A critical source of income had been lost. By 1955, the Martinezes had five children. Mrs. Lopes had died, and Julio had taken over the apartment Brothers, cousins, uncles appeared from time to time, stayed for a while and moved on. Julio looked for a better job on days off and even visited employment agencies, but they were of no help, referring him to jobs that were worse than what he had. His English was quite good by this time, but it seemed to make little difference. He faced a dead end on that summer evening when a broken window changed his life.

Julio's new job paid $23 weekly, put him on a pension track, and brought him into a union. More important, it placed him in a position to learn a trade. Over a five-year period, the shop mechanics taught Julio much about truck and auto maintenance. When one of the ranking shop mechanics accepted the position of foreman at a shop east of Bronx Park and found that an apprentice mechanic's position was open, he offered the slot to Julio. It meant an hour and a half commute to work and a four to midnight shift. It also meant a raise and a skilled job, a career. Julio grabbed it without hesitation.

Angelina adapted quickly to the new schedule. Julio was actually able to give her more help with the children—all of whom (except Pedro, the oldest) were still at home—taking them for walks in the morning and doing occasional shopping in the *bodegas* (grocery stores) on Broadway. Angelina began to put pressure on Julio to locate an apartment further uptown on a better block. On a few Sundays, the whole family took trips uptown to the Washington Heights and Inwood areas to look at possible apartments. Angelina preferred Inwood because of its parks and conveniently located schools. By 1964, Julio was ready to move. He applied for an apartment in the Dyckman Street project. He expected a promotion to Class C mechanic within a year, and in 1965, the advance came along with a notice that a four-room apartment was available in the project. Julio's trip to work would be reduced by an hour daily. But more importantly, Angelina hoped that the neighborhood would be better for the children. She was frightened about the drug scene. Both Pedro (1948) and Pasqual (1950) had experimented with heroin. The next two children, Maria (1952) and Juanita (1955), were constantly badgered on the streets by addicts and pushers. The youngest, Jaime (1955), was vulnerable to the pressure of those of his peers who used drugs. Pedro had been deeply scarred by his developing heroin dependency before he quit and used his influence with both Pasqual and Jaime to keep them away from drugs.

During the 1960s, the Martinezes and millions of other parents of all economic strata experienced drugs, through their children, for the first time. Marijuana, hallucinogens such as LSD, depressants such as heroin, and stimulants such as amphetamines made their appearances on the streets of cities and towns, in the hallways of public schools, and on college campuses. Addiction to such health and life-destroying drugs as heroin climbed at frightening rates. A good part of the soaring crime rate was attributed to junkies who turned to crime in order to pay for their habits. Many communities established drug-control centers and addiction clinics, attempting to treat as an illness what the police persisted (with the support of most Americans) in treating as a crime.

The Bassanos had been convinced that drugs and crime were the monopoly of the blacks and Puerto Ricans and that decent whites were invariably the victims. In truth, the black population committed a disproportionately high number of the city's crimes, but the overwhelming number of victims were of the same race or nationality as the criminal who acted against them. Nonetheless, the Bassanos were correct in associating the increased incidence of crime in Inwood with the influx of blacks and Spanish-speaking people.

The non-Hispanic white population of Inwood declined by some 14,000 between 1960 and 1970. Of the remaining whites, many were elderly. A much reduced white juvenile population and a greatly increased black and Hispanic juvenile population, coupled with the fact that most of the increase in crime was perpetrated by juveniles, meant that most of the crime was traceable to the new groups.

Angelina was also correct, however, for Inwood was less crime prone than the old neighborhood or lower Washington Heights and considerably less dangerous than the Bassanos believed. It was a definite improvement for the Martinezes even though, for the Bassanos, the appearance of the Martinezes and their brethren signaled deterioration. Julio enjoyed his work and had become active in the union. Angelina liked all the shops

Both the Bassanos and the Martinezes shopped along Dyckman Street

on Dyckman Street and sat with friends on the same park benches that Charlotte and her friends had frequented 25 years earlier. Pedro graduated from Bob Bassano's alma mater, George Washington High School—as did all his siblings—was drafted and served without harm in a combat infantry unit in South Vietnam. He was driving a truck for Macy's, at last report. Pasqual followed him two years later, emerged safely from service, and enrolled in the City College of New York in 1971. Maria married the owner of a small shop in 1973 and lives in Riverdale, just across the Harlem River from the northern tip of Manhattan. In 1973, Juanita married a young Puerto Rican policeman and moved to Queens, not far from New Bayside. Jaime, with a hearing defect, escaped the draft but could find work only infrequently.

The family moved out of the project in 1969. After frequent altercations with some black neighbors who, according to Julio, refused to take their children in hand, Julio found a rent-controlled apartment on Post Avenue, but not before paying a month's rent—a gift—to the building's agent and another sizable gift to the superintendent to obtain the flat. The family—and grandchildren—frequently gathered there on Sundays. When presiding over their flock, Angelina and Julio were content, but they too were becoming apprehensive about the future of Inwood.

During the 1960s, Inwood became increasingly drab. Then drabness gave way to physical decline. Alleys and backyards became junk piles. Whole squares of concrete were torn out of sidewalks. Chalked graffiti on walls and storefronts were replaced by spray-painted scrawls. In many places, it was apparent that the entries and hallways of apartment buildings had not seen a mop in months. Once grassy areas in the neighborhood's parks were overgrown with weeds and smothered in litter. School windows—those not boarded up—boasted heavy bars. Few signs of freshness or newness were to be found. Worse still, many vacant and even some fire-gutted buildings loomed over Inwood's streets.

The Martinezes often talked about moving, but Julio's income, while higher than that of most Puerto Ricans, was not great enough to provide for any real improvement in housing. Inwood began to pull in families with much lower incomes than that of the Martinezes who, unable to flee as had the Bassanos, were beginning to feel trapped. On January 14, 1978, a mysterious fire raced through the Post Avenue apartment building in which the Martinezes lived. They lost everything, and Jaime, who had returned to dealing and using drugs, was asphyxiated. The Martinez family disintegrated.

THE BUTLERS OF BOSTON, MASSACHUSETTS

On March 30, 1959, Robert Butler's last day in the White House, President Eisenhower arranged an informal ceremony to recognize his departing aide. After two terms as Secretary of the National Security Council and presidential confidant, the 64-year-old lawyer was returning to Boston and to the financial career he had interrupted to enter government service. The president presented "Bobby" Butler with the chair he had occupied at National Security Council meetings (an honor normally reserved for Cabinet members) and a gold medallion featuring Ike's portrait. It bore a card that read: "Dear Bobby—This is a poor thing as a memento of your long and brilliant service in your vitally important post in the Administration. But at least you will not forget the face of your devoted and most appreciative friend. Always, DDE." Butler was deeply touched, not least because he took the president's generous statement to reflect recognition of his contribution to public affairs despite his widely known homosexuality. The fear of "exposure" had caused Robert Butler great anguish many times during his career in Washington. Now the anxiety, the repression of his deepest feelings, the episodes of release and guilt seemed worthwhile.

Butler's long career had already won plaudits from the great military and political figures of his time. Having served under Secretary of War Stimson during World War II, he had been presented the Distinguished Service Medal and Legion of Merit by General George C. Marshall. In 1946, Butler had been named president of Boston's Old Colony Trust Company. He returned to spartan quarters at the Somerset Club and to the life of philanthropic fund-raising and family visits he so enjoyed. During the next few years, he served as chairman of the Peter Bent Brigham Hospital, an officer of Harvard Medical Center, an overseer of the Boston Symphony Orchestra, and chairman of the advisory board of the Massachusetts Public Welfare Department. During these same years, he assumed the position of patriarch of the Butler family. Of George and Mary Butler's other sons, John had become an alcoholic following financial reverses in the early 1930s and his health failed. He died in 1950. The distinguished career of Eliott Butler, a surgeon and hospital administrator, ended prematurely with his death from cancer in 1948. While very successful, George had little interest in social life, politics, and philanthropy. Roger, who had gone through two fortunes and the family's patience, lived for two decades in self-imposed exile in South Carolina until his death of heart failure compounded by alcoholism in 1965. Robert Butler had hoped that one or another of his nephews might emerge as inheritor of the Butler tradition; however, personal tragedies, financial problems, personality defects, and, in some, a most repugnant lack of ambition knocked out the various candidates as the years passed.

Never having married and not having chil-

dren of his own, Robert Butler could only observe the family's "decline" with growing frustration. He decided to reenter public life himself, perhaps to set an example for the next generation. In spring 1948, he accepted a temporary assignment in Washington, assisting Secretary of Defense James Forrestal to organize the presentation of the defense budget. Then, in 1952, he joined Eisenhower's presidential campaign. That led to a request from the president-elect to take on the reorganization and revitalization of the National Security Council. President Eisenhower relied heavily on the NSC as the forum for debates at the highest level about policies affecting the nation's security. During his two tours, 1953–55 and 1957–59, Robert Butler became privy to the Eisenhower administration's deepest secrets. The strain of this position combined with Butler's sexual frustrations to force him to return reluctantly to private life. Following compulsory retirement from Old Colony Trust in 1961, he served as U.S. representative to the Inter-American Development Bank, resumed his philanthropic activities, wrote the obligatory memoirs, and for the first time began openly to indulge the homosexual inclinations he had fought for so long.

Robert Butler's quiet but determined pursuit of homosexual liaisons soon became a topic of conversation within the circle of relatives and close friends in Boston and Washington, all of whom were aware of his sexual preferences. Their responses—varying from tolerant acceptance to alarm and violent condemnation—may be taken as revealing of the baffling range of attitudes Americans held about the issue of private morality during these decades. Attention focused on sexual manners and morals, the "right" of consenting adults to read about, observe, and take part in all varieties of sexual experience without interference by government or snooping neighbors.

The definitions of socially acceptable behavior expanded greatly after World War II. The acceptance of nudity in the cinema, unembarrassed descriptions and dissections of sex in publications ranging from *Playboy,* sex manuals, and *Cosmopolitan* to serious novels, the "coming out" of gay people and their organization into politico-educational pressure groups, and a wider toleration of premarital intercourse suggest that so-called "permissive" values had spread throughout American society. Whether the present climate represents a permanent change, or whether it is essentially an expression of the views of a liberal minority is moot. The censorship apparatus in existence at the end of World War II has withered away, although there are signs of its return. Recent Supreme Court decisions have affirmed the right of local communities to establish their own standards and have even rejected the principle that the state cannot intrude into private acts between consenting adults.

It is probable that this greater openness and tolerance toward "different" behavior patterns helped Robert Butler to come to terms with his own situation. We do not know why he suddenly began to practice homosexuality discreetly but openly in the years prior to his death in 1974. Nor do we know the actual effects of those repressed preferences upon his career. Publicly it had no apparent effects. At the least, his active public and private careers exemplified the truth that homosexuals can and do function in society. It is now recognized that sexual habits long considered debilitating and degrading are not sufficient causes for denying equal opportunities to those who engage in them.

THE REINHARDTS OF EVANSVILLE, INDIANA

Jacob Reinhardt informally retired on November 16, 1956, his 70th birthday. He turned over responsibility for farming the various parcels of land (some 600 acres) in Union and Perry Townships owned or leased in the family's name to his son, Raymond. The next week, Jacob applied for social security benefits and declared he intended to relax, do a little fishing, and watch his grandchildren grow up. In fact, however, the next decade was to be exceedingly busy. Jacob continued to work the farm on shares, and he expanded the hybrid seed corn business he had founded in 1947. But the greatest part of his energies went into political activities. Jacob had long been active in local politics, and he now became treasurer of the West Side Republican Club, a township assessor, and served two terms on the Vanderburgh County Alcoholic Beverages Commission. Only slowly failing health restricted the activities of Jacob and his wife Mathilde, who continued to garden, keep an immaculate home, and sew.

The Reinhardts were fortunate that one of their five children was interested in pursuing the vocation of farming. Raymond married a Reitz classmate and Evansville College graduate, Emmaline Bumb (who was Teddy Trace's second-grade teacher) in 1947. The newlyweds built a home on a two-acre plot next to Ray's parents. Ray Reinhardt was a "modern" farmer, one who believed agriculture was a profession. He kept up with recent improvements, invested heavily in timesaving machines, and adjusted plantings and sale of crops according to market conditions and federal agricultural policy. This demanded an enormous commitment of money (approximately $400,000 in land and equipment by 1970)—and an equally significant trust in the future. In the past few years that gamble has paid off. Steadily improving yields of corn and soybeans—and much higher prices—have produced a dramatic rise in income. Perhaps even more importantly, Ray Reinhardt's second son, Paul (1954), an honor graduate in agricultural economics from Purdue University, has returned to Evansville and the family farm. With the exception of Regina, who

Ray Reinhardt in front of a new 1971 John Deere combine

serves as the farm's administrator, none of Jacob and Mathilde's other children is directly involved with farming.

Regina Reinhardt left that world too, but she returned to it in 1956, responding to an appeal from her brothers and sisters to come back and take care of their aging parents. Regina had completed college, with majors in biology and math, in 1942. Having always been interested in the medical field, she obtained a job at St. Mary's Hospital, Evansville, as a laboratory technician. With the assistance of the hospital pathologist, Regina taught herself how to do tissue work and blood analyses. While continuing to live at home,

she worked part-time at St. Mary's and also privately for a physician. Preferring hospital work, Regina accepted the post of head laboratory technician in a Dallas, Texas, hospital. She moved to Seton Hospital in Austin in 1956 for a better salary ($500 a month), having become a registered member of the American Society of Clinical Pathologists.

Devotion to her chosen profession was outweighed finally by the urgings of her mother and sisters to return home. Since 1958, Regina Reinhardt has been, by her own description, "a jack of all trades." She handles the financial aspects of the farm, deciding what to sell and to whom; she nursed her father through two serious illnesses and stood by his bed as he slipped away, following a massive heart attack, in June 1968; and she served as companion and occasional nurse to Mathilde Reinhardt until her unexpected death from overexertion resulting from efforts to put out a kitchen grease fire in May 1975. Regina's careers, in health care, in service to her parents, and in comanaging a complex farm operation are the product of a strong and independent personality. Indifferent to the ideologies of feminism or "women's liberation" and opposed to the Equal Rights Amendment, she operates with confidence in the male-dominated world of agricultural marketing.

The effort to make women the coequals of men has had a long history in the United States, extending back to the private musings of Abigail Adams and encompassing the careers of thousands of women. After the winning of the vote in 1920, the women's movement received little public notice until Betty Friedan and other activists brought it to the surface again during the 1960s. Its new form, feminism is more basic and vital, increasingly organized and articulate, and far more all-encompassing in its range of concerns than earlier expressions had been. In its essence, feminism rejects as sexist the hallowed idea of the woman as destined to be only the love partner and the mother-housekeeper. According to feminists, emancipated women are those who reject the notion that women are confined by biology or ability to an inferior status in society. Feminism, then, struck at all culturally imposed attitudes, assumptions, and modes of behavior, including everything from compulsory home-economics courses for female public-school students to discrimination against the employment of women. The goal is the complete control by women over their bodies, minds, and personalities.

Buttressed by federal and state equal-employment-opportunity legislation, women are entering occupations long closed to them such as police work and engineering, and salary differentials between men and women for equivalent work are narrowing. There is no doubt that the adolescent female of the 1980s will enjoy much wider career choices than her mother had. Political activism among women, long led by middle-class, college-educated members of associations like the League of Women Voters, has become more widespread. While the League's fact-finding approach emphasized nonpartisanship and avoided sex-related issues, many of the new female activists are unabashedly partisan in their devotion to issues with immediate impact upon their sex. Organizationally, by the 1970s, feminism ran the gamut from the National Organization for Women (NOW), the National Women's Political Caucus, and the National Black Feminist Organization to local rape crisis centers, feminist credit unions, and feminist-lesbian groups. The new feminists are, moreover, much less naive than their foremothers who believed that the women's vote would clean up American politics. Political purity is not the issue now: instead it is power and equality—as the 1980 presidential conventions and campaigns demonstrated.

Millions of Americans, male and female, are disturbed and perhaps threatened by the new feminism. Women's groups are in the vanguard of the opposition to the Equal Rights Movement, fearing unisex public rest rooms as well as reduced alimony or child-maintenance payments. Women are severely divided over the right to abortion and public contraception clinics. To many, feminism is simply another name for sexual promiscuity. They do not accept the view that traditional sex roles have brought about female inferiority and dependency. But even while confusing feminist antisexism with immorality and the destruction of the family, many women, avowedly antifeminist, are subtly and unconsciously demanding more dignified and more equal treatment from their male partners, both in the home and on the job. Thus, feminism, by forcing Americans to confront embarrassing and culturally sensitive questions, is reducing the stigma of sex even among opponents of the movement. After a life satisfying the needs of others, Regina Reinhardt must now learn to live for herself. It is easier for her to find new sources of self-fulfillment than it was for a woman in similar circumstances 60 or even 15 years ago.

THE TRACES OF LOS ANGELES, CALIFORNIA

For 16 years, Velma Milton Trace lived in the small stucco house on Fisher Street in East Los Angeles that she had inherited on her father's death in 1944. Until 1954, Velma had done reasonably well. The house was paid for, and the utilities, food and liquor bills were easily taken care of with the salary and tips she earned as a waitress at the Redondo Bar and Grill, occasionally supplemented by bringing a drunken customer home to her bed. She rarely saw her children. Calvin, unemployed, an alcoholic himself and constantly in trouble with the police, occasionally brought his current girl friend to the house for a drink. Franklin had joined the Navy as soon as he could legally do so, and nothing more is known about him.

The tough times really began in 1956 when Velma, turning up at work drunk, lost her job. In July 1956, when every piece of furniture worth anything had been sold and her credit at nearby stores had been exhausted, she went downtown and applied for welfare assistance. This step delivered Velma Trace totally and for all time into the welfare system. She waited several hours to be interviewed by a harried social worker who quickly determined that Velma was a legitimate welfare case. While Velma had to answer the full round of questions about her habits, family life, and income potential, she was neither harassed and humiliated nor ignored.

Until the day of her death in 1960, welfare was Velma's way of life. She was more fortunate than most of the poor in America. While the number of Americans living in poverty probably runs from 25 to 30 million persons, 40 percent of whom are children under 18 years of age and 20 percent of whom are citizens over 65, less than 25 percent of the poor receive any kind of assistance from federal, state, or local agencies. The assistance given is inadequate. Aid to Families with Dependent Children (AFDC) payments, intended primarily for broken families with children, averaged $43 a month nationally in 1970 but were as low as $26 in the South. The amount of monthly relief available in the early 1970s to a family of four with no income in Mississippi was under $100 compared with more than $300 in New Jersey.

Of the relief categories, AFDC was the largest nationally and Old Age Assistance, a supplement to Social Security, with 2 million recipients in 1970, was the second largest. The rising number of AFDC cases, 635,000 families in 1950; 975,000 in 1964; 1.5 million in 1969; and almost 2 million by 1975, attested to the failure of society to distribute its enormous income with equity. Some 45 percent of all cases were located in nonurban counties while 25 percent of all AFDC cases were in Los Angeles, Wayne (Detroit), Cook (Chicago), Philadelphia, and the New York City Counties. In 1960, there were 241,000 AFDC recipients in Los Angeles County, of whom 34 percent were black. In New York, more than 50 percent of all recipients were black in the early 1970s, compared with 43 percent in 1961.

Few believe in the current welfare system—yet it perseveres. The system provided direct subsidy to the lowest-paying and most marginal cases. In the South and in large Northern cities, welfare payments were purposefully kept low so that the poor who prefer work to welfare would continue to perform the menial tasks available to them. Neither welfare nor work provide a living wage. The middle class frequently raises a clamor to cut back on the moochers by eliminating the able-bodied recipients who refused to work. There are relatively few of them, but millions exist who need, but do not receive, welfare. Yet in 1960, Louisiana arbitrarily cut some 22,000 illegitimate Negro children from the welfare rolls. In 1970, the nation paid out some $7 billion in public assistance payments to 10.4 million clients, or $675 per client. This might be balanced against $3.7 billion in direct payments to farmers, the several billions of dollars in grants to ailing aircraft and railroad companies, tax credits to home owners, oil depletion allowances, and other subsidies to the affluent.

Velma existed on welfare for over two years, receiving under $100 monthly, from which $22 was deducted for rent, food stamps, and occasional cartons of food and used clothing from private charitable organizations. What little was left went for alcohol—now usually cheap wine—to blot out the deadness of her life. She survived, however, until January 1960, when a three-day drunk financed by the sale of pop bottles and panhandling resulted in a fatal bout with pneumonia.

The welfare system that struggled with the "case" of Kenneth and Velma Trace did nothing to break the cycle of poverty and dependence. A determined effort was made to prevent Velma's children from becoming victims of the cycle. Money went for food, medical care, and education to ensure that they would not be prevented by physical or educational disabilities from claiming places in the larger society. Repeated attempts were made to push them—by persuasion and by force—to stay in school. Unfortunately, the efforts proved unsuccessful. The cycle of poverty has continued with Velma's grandchildren. Two have police records. One married at 16 and already has four children while her husband is serving a five-year term in the California State Prison at Chino. Another has been placed in a foster home. Whether the system failed because of lack of funds, lack of public sympathy, excess of bureaucracy, hereditary defects, or some combination of all these factors, there can be no disputing the fact that it did fail the Traces of Los Angeles.

THE SIMICHES OF MIDLAND, PENNSYLVANIA

In September 1972, Mihailo Markovich and his family celebrated the 60th anniversary of his arrival in Midland. He recalled the days when Crucible Steel first stoked up, teased his son-in-law, Michael Simich who was then employed in Crucible's shipping department, about his "cushy" job, and spoke proudly of his pleasure at being feted in his daughter Anna Simich's home on East Ohio Street, which even 30 years earlier would have been off limits to Serbians. The Markoviches and Simiches were now long-time, respected residents of Midland. Mihailo was honored as an elder in the Serbian community and, even though he had retired in 1955, in the USW local. While Mike Simich gradually became less active in union affairs than he had been during the exciting, strike-ridden years just preceding and following World War II, he and Anna continued to devote their spare time to the Serbian Orthodox Church and the Lazo Kostich Serbian Singing Society. Their children, Lawrence and Michele, the third gener-

Dr. Lazo Kostich Serbian Singing Society, 1961

ation to call Midland home, were away at school (Larry completing a Ph.D. in Balkan history at Indiana University and Michele, born in 1950, beginning her sophomore year at Duquesne) but often returned for visits.

The life pursued by Mihailo Markovich and the Simiches, with whom he came to live after his retirement, was placid and orderly. Every day, until shortly before his death in 1976, Mihailo walked downtown to the Serbian Club to gossip with old cronies. Mike works a variable shift at Crucible, often 3–11 P.M. for a month, two weeks of 11 P.M.–7 A.M., and a month of 7 A.M.–3 P.M. Mike accepts this helter-skelter schedule philosophically, claiming that it was better than a possible permanent assignment to the graveyard shift. Anna hates the constant changes in routine, but juggles her own schedule—shopping, social events, and meals—to accommodate Mike. There have been numerous opportunities for Mike to stabilize the family routine (and add to his own income) by joining management;

however, Mike believes that a foreman's position, with its attendant responsibilities and tensions, would separate him from his friends. In 1947, he quit Crucible for a better-paying job at a new Westinghouse plant in Beaver. Soon, he found himself involved in union activities and a three-month strike to force recognition of the union. After that, he was a "marked man" and left Westinghouse in 1952. He invested $1,500 in a flower shop in Monaca, 10 miles upriver from Midland, but quickly discovered that running a business was not for him. "Being a good businessman means making money. There is no way that one can do this without lying and cheating," Mike insisted during one conversation. A few months later, he sold out and returned to work at Crucible, having lost all his seniority and pension rights. Since then, he has been happy to remain one of the boys.

Mike Simich earns good wages. He has job security and satisfactory working conditions, but Mike does not particularly enjoy his work.

Four generations: Mihailo Markovich and Anna, Larry, and David Simich, 1973

It is a job, and everyone has to have a job. That sentiment is shared by most other members of his class and generation and by increasing numbers of the next generation. It was fashionable during the 1960s to bemoan the decline of the "work ethic," citing rising absenteeism, dropping productivity, and sloppy work habits. Much was made, for example, of the problems General Motors faced at its new, almost totally automated Vega assembly plant in Lordstown, Ohio. There, absenteeism and slowdowns—with resulting increases in defective products—were rampant. Most explanations stressed the dissatisfaction of Lordstown's workers at feeling themselves components of and controlled by a gigantic, soulless machine. However, studies such as Studs Terkel's *Working* (1974) suggest that the problems at Lordstown and

other plants have been largely due to local conditions, and that the vast majority of American workers, of whatever race, sex, age, or political orientation, remain willing to provide an honest day's work for an honest day's pay. Of course, very few blue-collar workers care for the repetitive tasks to which the assembly line chains them; but the current situation (especially where improvements in the workplace environment—periodic job reassignments, flexible hours, self-evaluation—and high pay and fringe benefits exist) suggests that the American factory system is hardly staggering toward some final collapse.

There have occurred a number of significant changes affecting the work force and the nature of work itself since the Second World War. Minimum-wage laws, the eight-hour day with extra pay for overtime, paid vacations, sick leave, health insurance, and unemployment compensation and pension systems are almost universally accepted. The catalyst of most of these improvements, unionization, is, however, no longer the central force it once was. In 1945, nearly 15 million Americans (36 percent of the nonagricultural work force) belonged to unions. But after reaching a high point of 18 million in 1958, union membership began to decline in both total numbers and in percentage of the work force. In part, this resulted from indifference toward the cause of unionization once the bread-and-butter issues championed by unions had been decided. More important was the changed composition of the work force. Automation and the declining importance of heavy industry relative to service industries reduced the number of blue-collar jobs. In 1956, for the first time, white-collar workers outnumbered blue-collar workers. By 1973, 48 percent of all workers were white collar, 35 percent blue collar, with the rest split between farmers and service workers. The proportion of women in the work force also increased. (Indeed, between 1920 and 1960, one female was employed for every male finding a job.) But, as with blacks and other minorities, women's earnings and opportunities for advancement were disproportionately lower than those of white males.

In sum, the changes of the past 30 years have both confirmed the existence of an American laboring class and strengthened its fusion—in terms of social expectations and consumption patterns—with the middle class. American workers are as politically conservative, consumption-oriented, and committed to tradition as other groups. Like Mike Simich, they wish to put in their eight hours (with occasional overtime to help pay off the new boat or color television) and then leave their job behind them to get on with the business of living. The relative unimportance of work in the total life of most Americans is perhaps the

greatest change. Only in time of crisis, such as the recession of 1978–80, does the job occupy center stage.

Certainly, Mike Simich's life revolves not around his job but around his family, home, and Midland's Serbian community. An inveterate "do-it-your-selfer," he reconstructed the house on Ohio Street with his own hands. The Simiches purchased this dilapidated former "boss's house" in 1957. Both Mike and Anna had become worried about the influx of blacks into their old neighborhood. (By 1956, when Michele began school, the area had become so rough that her father insisted on escorting her to and from Lincoln School.) Mihailo earlier had received an offer for the Pennsylvania Street house from a black church, but he had been afraid sale to "the coloreds" would anger his neighbors. Now, he arranged to sell, at a lower price and on contract, to a black steelworker.

For almost a year after their move to Ohio Street, the Simiches camped out in the basement while Mike redid most of the interior—paneling downstairs, changing the staircases, lowering the ceilings, putting in a modern kitchen and a forced-air furnace. Mike has never stopped building. In August 1974, he began to dig the foundations for a 20 × 24 concrete-block garage and finished the job 12 months later. Both Mike and Anna enjoy

The Simich home on Ohio Street, Midland

reading and watch their favorite television shows without fail, but the modern idea of leisure—as a vocation and way of life—baffles them. Leisure for this couple is the time to complete old projects and initiate new ones. The Simiches anticipate Mike's retirement, not as a withdrawal from work, but as a time for more rewarding work.

The Simiches like to travel, but when they do so it is for the purpose of visiting their children or participating in a convocation of the Serbian Federation of Church Choirs. Since 1970, Mike and Anna have traveled to Kansas City, Milwaukee, Omaha, and Chicago for conventions of Serbian singing groups. Their daughter has chosen to make a career of the continuing interest in Serbian music. As a child, Michele received *tamburitzan* (a peculiarly Serbian mixture of folk songs and dancing) lessons and became so proficient that she was offered a four-year scholarship to Duquesne and an opportunity to perform with the University Tamburitzans, an internationally known group. She has traveled with the "Tambys" all over the United States and to Europe and the Soviet Union. Michele, who married a graduate student in music education, has set up her own *tamburitzan* school. Unlike Michael Gishman, Michele and Larry Simich have used education to draw more closely to their roots. Thus, while entering the middle class, their ethnic interests have been financially rewarding and personally satisfying.

THE TRACES OF EVANSVILLE, LOUISVILLE, BIRMINGHAM, DENVER, PHOENIX, SUGAR LAND, AND KANSAS CITY

When Jerry Trace, his wife, and baby daughter returned to Evansville following his discharge from the Marines in 1946, he found his parents' house in Howell overcrowded.

Ben, Anna Lee, Bill (a high-school sophomore), J. R., Jacqueline and her child, and Teddy (a first grader) were all living at home. Within a year, Jerry purchased a house just three doors away. The decade following the war was one of unprecedented prosperity for the Traces. Largely this was because several persons contributed to the family income. Ben's salary, raised from $72 weekly to $90 in 1950, was supplemented by Jacqueline's $45 weekly, earned as a salesperson and sporadic child-support payments from her former husband, and J.R.'s monthly disability check from the Veterans Administration. (His disability, manifesting all of the symptoms of muscular dystrophy, had been ruled nonservice connected.) In July 1948, Bill, having graduated from Reitz High School, went to Montana to work on a ranch and, while there, wangled a football scholarship from Montana State College at Bozeman.

This prosperity was illusory and short-

Anna Lee Trace in the kitchen of her farm home, c. 1955

Teddy Trace, J. R., Anna Lee, and Jacqueline's child, 1947

lived. But it prompted the family to buy a sprawling house and 15 acres west of Evansville, not far from the Reinhardt farm. It was an unfortunate move. Jacqueline remarried and left Evansville. Ben suffered a mild stroke and was forced to retire early, having worked 37 years for the L&N. It proved impossible to keep up the house payments, so the Traces moved back to Howell. Thereafter, the family gradually dissolved. Ben died in 1957. Teddy went off to Indiana University on an academic scholarship the next year. Anna Lee and J.R. scraped along on a small Aid to Dependent Children payment for which she was eligible because Teddy was still a minor, on her widow's benefits from Railroad Retirement, and J.R.'s pension until 1963, when the progressive degeneration of J.R.'s muscles compelled his admission to a Veteran's Administration hospital. A few months later, Anna Lee died. Except for "Aunt Kate" Wolfe, living alone and almost blind in Howell, the Traces had departed Howell forever.

Always the most independent and ambi-

tious of Ben and Anna Lee's children, Jerry had tried repeatedly to force his parents to live within their income. Subsequent to his discharge, Jerry and two other veterans had launched a taxicab company. Using their savings and a bank loan secured by the VA, the trio persuaded the Evansville City Council to issue them 10 taxi licenses. By exploiting the general sympathy for vets (and the refusal of existing taxi companies to transport Negroes), Black and White Cab was soon doing a very good business. Jerry handled personnel and operations (and served as relief driver), for which he was paid $35 weekly. Unfortunately, when Jerry and his partners asked the city council for additional licenses in early 1947, they were turned down flat. Yellow Cab and Liberty Cab had exerted pressure, and there no longer was any interest in giving "special treatment" to veterans. A few months later, having suffered labor problems and unable to offer satisfactory service, the partners sold out to Yellow Cab. Jerry was hired as a supervisor by Yellow.

The next few years were superficially satisfying ones. Jerry Trace did well at Yellow; he was promoted to personnel manager in 1949 and to operations manager in 1952. Despite the hiatus caused by the call-up of his Marine Corps reserve unit in July 1950, and 10 months spent training amphibious-tractor drivers at Camp Pendleton, California, Jerry was earning $600 per month by 1954, double his father's income. He owned a nice home, got along reasonably well with his wife, Peggy, and worshipped his three blond daughters: Kathy, Virginia (1947), and Sally (1950). He was active in several civic organizations and, in 1955, was named president-elect of the Evansville Jaycees. But something was missing, for Jerry periodically experienced feelings of restlessness and frustration. Ambitious, fiercely competitive, and impatient of incompetence since his wartime service, he had begun attending night school at

Evansville College in 1946 with the vague aim of a degree in business administration. For 10 years, Jerry used his World War II and Korea GI benefits to finance a potpourri of courses, often attending classes three nights a week. There did not seem much reason to go on, considering his position at Yellow Cab, but he persevered.

A part of the puzzle fell into place in spring 1956, when a taxicab combine that owned companies throughout the upper South offered Jerry the managership of BeeLine Cab Company in Louisville, Kentucky. Jerry decided this was what he wanted—an opportunity to get ahead, to test his ability to handle total responsibility for a business. The emotional attachment to family and the familiar environment of his hometown had distorted his views. "If I ever wanted to progress, I'd have to move," he decided. The job offered an exciting challenge. BeeLine was the second largest cab company in Louisville, and it was riddled with inefficiency and corruption. There was a sizable increase in salary, but money was never a very important consideration for Jerry. Power, the opportunity to put into effect his own ideas, was the critical element.

This first move was nonetheless traumatic. Jerry and Peggy were desperately unhappy and homesick for some months, and he even looked into a return to his old job. Gradually they adjusted to the new situation, and a pattern of behavior was established that would be repeated in all subsequent moves. Jerry immersed himself in work, often spending 12 to 14 hours a day at the office. Many evenings he took part in conferences and meetings of civic groups. To Peggy fell responsibility for the home and children. They bought a new house (a three-bedroom rancher) in a Louisville suburb. Peggy and the girls quickly made friends in the tract and at school. Jerry never learned the names of the next-door neighbors.

For some time the BeeLine job proved interesting and rewarding. Jerry fired the inefficient personnel, negotiated a new contract with the Teamster's Union, and soon had BeeLine producing a good profit. But within two years, the position, now essentially routine, had palled, and Jerry jumped at the chance to move to Birmingham, Alabama, where another taxi operation owned by the parent corporation was in difficulty. He was earning a reputation as a troubleshooter. The Birmingham company (actually two operations: Yellow and Harlem, which served the black community and had black drivers but white supervisors) was beset with all sorts of problems—including political harassment by Birmingham Police Commissioner Eugene "Bull" Connor. Jerry straightened out the situation in eight months. Peggy and the children had just settled into the colonial-style home Jerry had purchased in the Birmingham suburb of Homewood when the family had to move back to Louisville. The parent company, faced with a financial pinch, had decided to sell most of its taxicab operations, and Jerry was reassigned to BeeLine.

By this time, Jerry had become active in the National Taxicab Owners' Association and was becoming known as a "comer" in the field. (In the cab business, in which most companies are family owned, topflight executive talent always has been at a premium.) In October 1960, Jerry accepted an offer to become general manager of Yellow Cab of Denver, Colorado. Once again he was responding to a challenge. The owner, an insurance magnate who had gained control of Denver Yellow during a protracted strike, promised Jerry complete freedom and an opportunity to buy into the company through a profit-sharing plan. For seven months, Jerry lived at the Denver YMCA until the children finished school and Peggy could move them from Louisville. He then installed his family in a new home on two acres in the Denver sub-

Jerry Trace in Denver office, 1968

urb of Arvada. They resumed the arrangements earlier established in Louisville and Birmingham. Jerry continued his six to six routine and had a radio telephone installed in his personal car so that he could monitor operations while going to and from social engagements. However, Peggy began to rebel at the task of raising alone three teenage daughters and a rambunctious son (Russell, born in 1958). Perhaps as compensation for his inattention to the children, Jerry became extremely possessive toward them, prohibiting the girls from dating, going to unchaperoned activities, and so forth. Two of the three girls married shortly after finishing high school but still are extremely dependent on their father.

Jerry remained in Denver for almost 10 years. Peggy and the kids liked the area, and he was encouraged to use company profits to buy other cab companies (Boulder and Phoenix) and to branch out into car leasing and tour operations. There was more than enough money (he earned $25,000 plus

bonuses in 1965), but eventually Jerry became frustrated by growing opposition to his schemes for expansion. On several occasions he was offered a chance to purchase Denver Yellow but could not raise the capital. In 1971, following an angry debate with the board of directors about company policy, Jerry arranged the sale of the Phoenix subsidiary to the Westgate Corporation, a California-based conglomerate. One condition of the deal was Jerry's appointment as general manager of Yellow Cab of Phoenix.

For the next seven years Jerry Trace continued to pursue "a piece of the action," a position in which he could fully exploit his experience. After receiving more than a dozen serious offers, some including part ownership, from companies around the country, he succumbed in 1974 to the promises of a young department-store heir in Houston. Once again a new challenge and the dream of founding a taxicab empire proved irresistible. Jerry and Peggy purchased a home in the exclusive Sugar Creek subdivision of Sugar Land, Texas, outside Houston. For the first time, they joined the local country club. But Peggy did not unpack her good china and crystal, for Jerry began pushing the Houston ownership to expand and put together deals for taxicab operations in Omaha, Kansas City, Washington, D.C., and Los Angeles. His bosses agreed to buy Omaha Yellow Cab but then balked.

In September 1978, at age 54, his daughters married and his youngest child entering Baylor University, Jerry Trace confronted the choice for which he had worked for 30 years. He could continue as general manager of Houston Yellow Cab, drawing a hefty salary and piling up stock options, and drifting toward a comfortable retirement. Or he could seize an opportunity provided by a squabble among the Houston owners to trade his small equity in the parent company for outright ownership (about $60,000 after subtracting a massive bank loan) of the Omaha subsidiary. Jerry Trace took the high-risk/high-yield option. He sold the house in Sugar Creek, cashed in his life insurance policies, and set out to found his empire. Eight months later, Jerry and Peggy (and various banks) owned taxicab companies in Omaha, Kansas City, Colorado Springs, and Austin and Fort Worth, Texas. In August 1981, they bought Evansville Yellow Cab. Jerry lives out of a suitcase, spending most weeks in Kansas City (where Great Western Transportation Company, Inc. rents a Levitz-furnished luxury apartment) and weekends with Peggy in Fort Worth. If the 18 hour days and the financial juggling pay off, Jerry soon will be a multimillionaire.

Jerry Trace's odyssey in which geographic mobility was a means of career advancement reflects an ancient theme in American life. Americans were perpetually on the move, going from one city to another, chasing opportunity that was more often real than illusory. Besides the seeming perpetual motion of Americans—moving from apartment to house, from one house to another, one city to another, distant one—other broad themes of motion were present after World War II. First came the steady shift from inner city to developing suburbs, and many of our families participated. Second came a continual stream of movers—from rural America (many of whom were black) into northern and western cities. Finally came the steady population shift towards the rapidly growing metropolitan regions of the South, Southwest, and West. Indeed, as population relatively stabilized in older cities such as Boston, residents moved less than their grandparents in those cities and the citizens of newer areas—Houston, Phoenix, San Jose—became the most mobile people. People moved to jobs, and the expanding economies were to be found, by the late 1970s, in a great arc stretching from Florida through Texas to California. And

those who moved tended to be better off than those who stayed put. At the same time, the price of restlessness and ambition was high. As Jerry Trace learned, it could mean almost total isolation from the community of residence. Further, separation from family cut generational and traditional ties for the children and their children. Although air travel and the telephone softened the effect, the great number of long-distance moves had a lasting impact. If a businessman drew his identity from his company, the family could become rootless in space.

THE HARTS OF NEW ALBANY, KANSAS

Austin and Martha Isabelle Hart and their baby daughter, Martha Ann, returned to Martha's home in New Albany following Austin's discharge in 1945. After a false start or two, Austin committed himself to full-time farming, and he and Martha decided to raise their family in New Albany. Four more children followed: Carol Kay (1945), Stanley Austin (1948), Clay Allen (1953), and Niles Jay (1956). For 10 years, Austin Hart maintained a precarious living by farming rented parcels of land and assisting his father-in-law. He was making good money, helped by higher grain prices during the Korean War. But every dime had to go for a new piece of machinery or as down payment for 40 acres here and there in New Albany and neighboring townships. Despite his aversion to federal involvement with agriculture, Austin enrolled in "GI School"—an agricultural management program—in 1949 for the $50 monthly government check. Although he now declares that similar courses and government activities are wasteful and harmful, this did not prevent him from participating in such federal programs as the Soil Bank and Federal Land Bank. By 1956, he had scratched together ownership of some 130 acres of land, two tractors, and assorted machinery. Though he was receiving between $6,000 and $9,000 cash income annually (which, considering capital invested and labor, worked out to something under a dollar an hour), Austin realized that only big, commercial farmers and not "small operators" like himself were making decent money from farming.

The years 1956 and 1957 brought sadness and happiness to Martha and Austin. Happiness came in the form of a sturdy boy, Niles Jay. But this event was quickly followed by the death of Austin's father, James, and then, within a year, a heart attack claimed the life of Charles Gale. Following rural tradition, Austin's mother had the body of her husband brought to their home for a wake and Methodist service. But unlike the practice common into the early 20th century, the deceased was first taken to the Fredonia funeral home for embalming and preparation. In earlier days, family and neighbors took care of nearly everything connected with death, the women washing the body and dressing it for the wake while males dug the grave on family property or in the local cemetery. Family and James' many friends sat with his widow in a very private and simple rendering of respect for the deceased. James was buried at Maple Grove Cemetery in Roper. The funeral of Charles Gale, handled entirely by the Fredonia funeral home, was more typical of practices evolved since the 1920s. Charles was buried in the Fredonia cemetery.

Americans have become increasingly separated from the reality of death. Fewer and fewer people die in the home or in the presence of their families. Death is made to appear even more unnatural in the typical funeral ceremony. Americans spend over $2 billion annually on funerals and burials, with the average cost in the range of $1,200 to $1,500. Over 60 percent of the annual revenue of the flower industry derives from funeral arrangements. A branch of the ready-to-wear clothing industry specializes in fashions for corpses, including inflatable bras. Embalming, which serves no health purpose, and prettifying the body are pushed by funeral directors along with expensive caskets, some with oil paintings in the lid and some with bed springs, services in the funeral home's chapel, and limousine service to the cemetery. Vast sums are paid to get the corpse to look natural for the open-casket service and the final parade of mourners by the loved one. To attain the natural look, morticians use waxes, dyes, cotton padding, plaster of Paris, cosmetics, rivets, and chicken wire.

Since the bereaved normally have a large sum of ready cash available through insurance or death-benefit payments, it is difficult to resist the hard sell. Americans seem to feel that simple and inexpensive funerals, including cremation, are somehow disrespectful to the dead. The National Funeral Directors' Association strenuously resisted any efforts to simplify or bypass their services. In California, association lobbyists tried unsuccessfully to run a cremation service out of business by legislation designed to make cremation more expensive. Funeral directors and cemetery owners work on the emotions of their customers—guilt, fear, love of family, need, status, and for cemetery plots, pride of ownership. In recent years, however, the hospice movement and the revival of burial societies have offered ways for the living to see the point and purpose of death.

The passing of the older Hart and Gale generation provided opportunity for Martha and Austin. James Hart left a 1,200-acre farm and other properties. The Hart children "sat down around the kitchen table and divided it up," taking equal portions with those who received the best land making cash payments to the others. Austin borrowed heavily to buy additional acreage from his father's estate.

The Hart home, formerly the Gale home

The death of Charles Gale also had a happy dimension. Since none of his children was interested in returning to New Albany, they were eager to sell their parts of the estate to Austin and Martha. By dumping the land he had just inherited and borrowing some $40,000 through the federal government and the Fredonia First National Bank, Austin was able to purchase the Gale farm outright: 530 acres, buildings and machinery, and the old house. For the first time, he and Martha had a home of their own.

With the Gale house came a position of leadership in New Albany. Martha accepted this obligation gracefully, and she took part in 4-H, the ladies' auxiliary of the Farm Bureau, and the New Albany Methodist Church. Indicative of her standing was Martha's appointment in June 1975, as New Albany's postmaster. Austin, though much less outgoing, did serve for 15 years on the district's school board. But to an even greater degree than Martha's parents had, the Harts were waging a hopeless struggle to keep alive community awareness. New Albany already had lost its economic viability; now, as the population declined and aged, its social institutions disintegrated.

The closing of the town's elementary school was the final blow. Both Austin and Martha fought against school consolidation, but they recognized—as had Martha's parents—the inadequacy of the New Albany school (20 pupils and one teacher in 1968) by sending the two youngest children—Clay and Niles—to school in Fredonia. The 4-H organization collapsed about the same time, and in 1970 the Sunday school program of the local church shut down. Thenceforth, Fredonia would be recognized as the community embracing the Harts, much as they hated to admit this fact and "cussed" its high prices and pretensions.

Despite these changes, the Hart family was happy and secure. They enjoyed a quiet but hardly isolated life. They subscribed to two newspapers, agricultural journals, and women's magazines. Since 1954, when Austin lugged home the first television set—a 17-inch Wizard purchased at Western Auto—the Harts have been avid TV watchers, from the Wichita farm report through prime-time situation comedies and Johnny Carson. And, like Martha's brothers and sisters, the Hart children have not found a rural Wilson County upbringing to be a handicap. Martha Ann married a pharmacist soon after graduation from Fredonia High in 1961. Carol Kay, who entered nurse's training in Kansas City, married a professional baseball player, now a realtor in Topeka, Kansas. The oldest son, Stanley Austin, trained as a draftsman and, following a divorce, studied electrical en-

Martha Hart's post office, New Albany, 1975

gineering at Kansas State University. His brother Niles, the youngest child, also pursued an engineering major at Kansas State and hoped to go into business with Stanley somewhere in the region. Only Clay had any interest in farming. He and his wife Mara lived in a trailer next door to the Harts. Both Clay and Mara worked in Fredonia, and Clay helped his father part-time. Having experienced the 16-hour days of a farmer, Clay found his job at the Fredonia cement plant (even at $6 per hour) frustrating and uninteresting, and he and Mara, who grew up on a nearby farm, were eager to get into full-time farming. Though Austin claimed that it was impossible for a young man to start out today in farming, he was secretly pleased about Clay's interest and talked about turning the "whole mess" over to him within a few years.

The farm produced as never before, for Austin adopted all the yield-increasing techniques. "Today a man can do three to four times as much as one man could do in 1945," he recently observed. Huge tractors dragging 12-row cultivators, "chemicals to control every type of weed known to man," and mountains of fertilizer became an integral part of his life. He scouted county and state demonstration plots for seeds. Although almost no fertilizer was used when Austin began farming, he became a convert when he saw how much better wheat did after an application of phosphate. Austin remained a strong advocate of fertilizer and herbicides, even though their cost rose enormously (nitrates from $65 a ton in 1972 to $320 a ton in 1980).

Austin's operation in 1980 was a diversified one. He believed that "Mother Nature" would ruin at least one crop each year and, if she proved kind, some stupid action by the government would knock down the prices of one or more commodities. He planted 220 acres in wheat, 107 in milo, 30 in corn, 60 in alfalfa, and 120 in soybeans. Austin has gone into and out of raising livestock—cattle, hogs,

and sheep—numerous times since the early 1950s, using the 200 acres of pasture on the Gale farm. He presently has 30 crossbred Yorkhamp-Duroc sows, producing feeder pigs.

An income of $30,000 is hardly magnificent when one considers the Harts' capital investment—$25,000 in land, $67,000 in buildings, and $100,000 in equipment—and the 16-hour days Austin puts in during the growing season. It did, however, offer considerable security in time of furiously mounting land and food prices and, ironically. Austin possesses a "hole card," a huge (one and one half million cubic feet per day) natural-gas well under land he owns near Roper. That, he believes, will ensure a comfortable retirement, whatever happens to American agriculture in coming years.

CONCLUSION

Gradually, the American family adjusted to changing social and economic conditions and attitudes. Overall, its forms and functions have not changed radically since the turn of the century. It is still too early to predict the long-range consequences of attitudinal changes that surfaced during the 1950s and 1960s. At the least, divorce is more widely accepted as a solution to marital disharmony, but this may work to strengthen the family since a wrong first choice need not mean a lifetime of failure. The geographic mobility necessitated by career choices—first male-centered but increasingly a concern among career-minded females—requires great family adaptability. But with one community so much like any other, the trials of frequent moving have been somewhat cushioned. New definitions of the roles of wives and husbands and children can both liberate and create tensions. The dominance of the male has been challenged and the individual needs of the female asserted. Parents seem to believe that their young, while doing about what they had done, do it much earlier. For young people, living together before marriage and exploring one another sexually and spiritually has become a common practice, but one not accepted too readily by parents. Still, the family remains the basic unit within which these changes are worked out. Middle-class American families have learned that economic security guarantees no solution to their problems. Many others have been denied the opportunity to learn this simple truth.

SUGGESTIONS FOR FURTHER READING

Among the most helpful books for the preparation of this chapter were Eric Barnouw, *The Image Empire: A History of Broadcasting in the United States* (1970); Daniel Bell, *The End of Ideology* (1960); Andrew Billingsley, *Black Families in White America* (1968); Ramsey Clark, *Crime in America* (1970); Glen E. Elder, Jr., *Children of the Great Depression* (1974); Hugh D. Graham and Ted R. Gurr, eds., *Violence in America: Historical and Comparative Perspectives* (1969); Leo Grebler, et al., *The Mexican-American People: The Nation's Second Largest Majority* (1970); U.S. Congress, Joint Committee on Housing, *Housing in America* (1948); Herman P. Miller, *Rich Man, Poor Man* (1971); C. Wright Mills, *The Power Elite* (1956); Robert Morgan, ed., *Sisterhood is Powerful* (1970); Richard Polenberg, *One Nation Divisible: Class, Race, and Ethnicity in the United States Since 1938* (1980); David Riesman et al., *The Lonely Crowd* (1950); Theodore Roszak, *The Making of a Counter Culture* (1969); Patricia C. Sexton, *Spanish Harlem: Anatomy of Poverty* (1966); Studs Terkel, *Working* (1974). See also Studs Turkel's most recent compilation of oral history, *American Dreams: Lost and Found* (1980); Gay Talese, *Thy Neighbor's Wife* (1979); the "how-to-do-it-Southern-style" Fox Fire *1–6*, compiled by Eliot Wigginton; Christopher Lasch, *The Culture of Narcissism* (1979); Alvin Toffler, *Future Shock (1970)*; Steward Brand, ed., *The Whole Earth Catalog* (1968); Gordon Gow, *Hollywood in the Fifties* (1971); James Gunn, *Alternative Worlds: An Illustrated History of Science Fiction* (1975); Jane O'Reilly, *The Girl I Left Behind* (1980); Ralph E. Smith, *The Subtle Revolution: Women at Work* (1980); Jo Freeman, *The Politics of Women's Liberation* (1975); and Gayle G. Yates, *What Women Want: The Ideas of the Movement* (1975).

Much of the literature on the American family referred to earlier is relevant here. Also informative are August Hollinshead, *Elmtown's Youth* (1949); William F. Whyte, *Street Corner Society* (1945); Art Gallaher, Jr., *Plainville Fifteen Years After* (1961); Frank A. Kostyn, *Shadows in the Valley: The Story of One Man's Struggle For Justice* [discrimination in the Lower Rio Grande Valley] (1970); Elliott Liebow, *Talley's Corner: A Study of Negro Streetcorner Men* (1967); Arthur J. Rubel, *Across the Tracks: Mexican-Americans in a Texas City* (1966); and Clarence Senior, *The Puerto Ricans: Strangers—Then Neighbors* (1961).

Other studies of socioeconomic, racial, and ethnic issues are Nathan Glazer and Daniel Moynihan, *Beyond the Melting Pot* (1964); Joseph P. Fitzpatrick, *Puerto Rican Americans: The Meaning of Migration to the Mainland* (1971); Celia S. Heller, *New Converts to The American Dream?: Mobility Aspirations of Young Mexican Americans* (1971); W. Lloyd Warner, *Social Class in America* (1949); William H. Whyte, *The Organization Man* (1965); John Keats, *The Crack in the Picture Window* (1957); Will Herberg, *Protestant-Catholic-Jew* (1960); Andrew M. Greeley, *Why Can't They Be Like Us?: America's White Ethnic Groups* (1975); Marshall Sklare, ed., *The Jews: Social Patterns of an American Minority Group* (1958); Stanley Lieberson, *Ethnic Patterns in American Cities* (1963); Michael N. Danielson, *The Politics of Exclusion* (1976); Michael Harrington, *The Other Americans: Poverty in the United States* (1962); Oscar Lewis, *La Vida: A Puerto Rican Family in the Culture of Poverty* (1966); John K. Galbraith, *The Affluent Society* (1958); David Potter, *People of Plenty* (1954); G. William Domhoff, *Who Rules America?* (1967); Harry Caudill, *Night Comes to the Cumberlands* (1963); Benjamin Muse, *The American Negro Revolution* (1970); Eleanor B.

Leacock, ed., *The Culture of Poverty: A Critique* (1971); and Daniel P. Moynihan, *Maximum Feasible Misunderstanding: Community Action in The War on Poverty* (1970). Refer also to the bibliographical essay for Chapters 11 and 13.

Cultural responses and tensions are treated in Morris Dickstein, *Gates of Eden: American Culture in the Sixties* (1977); Milton Viorst, *Fire in the Streets* (1979); Daniel Bell, *The Cultural Contradictions of Capitalism* (1976); and Alexander Kendrick, *The Wound Within* (1974). Also helpful are Lawrence M. Baskir and William A. Strauss, *Chance and Circumstance: The Draft, the War and the Vietnam Generation* (1978); Michael Useem, *Conscription, Protest, and Social Conflict: The Life and Death of a Draft Resistance Movement* (1973); Morton H. Halperin, et al., *The Lawless State* (1976); David Wise, *The American Police State* (1976); Christopher Lasch, *The Agony of the American Left* (1969); Kenneth Keniston, *Young Radicals* (1968); and Jerry Avorn et al., *Up Against the Ivy Wall* (1968). Ethnic and class responses are in Robert Coles and Jan Erikson, *The Middle Americans* (1973); Andrew Levison, *The Working-Class Majority* (1974); Irving Howe, ed., *The World of the Blue-Collar Worker* (1972); Louise K. Howe, ed., *The White Majority: Between Poverty and Affluence* (1970); Patricia C. Sexton and Brendan Sexton, *Blue-Collars and Hard-Hats* (1971); Michael Novak, *The Rise of the Unmeltable Ethnics* (1973); Richard Kirckus, *Pursuing the American Dream: White Ethnics and the New Populism* (1976); Perry L. Weed, *The White Ethnic Movement and Ethnic Politics* (1973); and Orlando Patterson, *Ethnic Chauvinism: The Reactionary Impulse* (1977).

For themes in the black experience, see Charles Silberman, *Crisis in Black and White* (1967); Thomas L. Blair, *Retreat to the Ghetto* (1977); Peter Goldman, *The Death and Life of Malcolm X* (1974); Stokely Carmichael and Charles V. Hamilton, *Black Power* (1967); Robert M. Fogelson, *Violence as Protest: A Study of Riots and Ghettos* (1973); David Boesel and Peter H. Rossi, eds., *Cities Under Siege: An Anatomy of the Ghetto Riots, 1964–1968* (1971); Allan P. Sindler, *Bakke, Defunis, and Minority Admissions: The Quest for Equal Opportunity* (1978); Sar A. Levitan, et al., *Still a Dream: The Changing Status of Blacks Since 1960* (1975); Dorothy K. Newman et al., *Protest, Politics, and Prosperity: Black Americans and White Institutions, 1940–1975* (1978); and William J. Wilson, *The Declining Significance of Race: Blacks and Changing American Institutions* (1978). Refer also to Matt S. Meier and Feliciano Rivera, *The Chicanos* (1972); Joan W. Moore, et al., *Mexican Americans* (1970); Oscar Handlin, *The Newcomers* [Puerto Ricans] (1962); Stuart Levine and Nancy Lurie, *The American Indian Today* (1970); Robert Burnette, *The Tortured Americans* (1971); and Vine DeLoria's *Custer Died for Your Sins* (1969).

11 | The New Industrial Society

A NEW STRUCTURE

VJ Day, August 15, 1945, was a holiday. Throughout the United States millions of men and women joined in spontaneous celebration at the announcement that Japan had accepted Allied surrender terms. Henry Gishman heard the radio bulletin, and, rather than work the night shift at Curtiss-Wright, joined the throngs of New Yorkers who packed Time Square. All through the night they danced, sang, drank, and kissed, commemorating the end of an era. Gishman vowed never to return to his war job, and, later, friends cleaned out his locker for him. Like many Americans, he now turned from war to the achievement of success and security for his family.

It was not altogether clear in 1944 and 1945 that the end of war would initiate an era of prosperity. Victory was expected to bring in its wake economic contraction as the gov-

ernment's massive purchases of war material ended. At the same time, the number of men looking for jobs would increase sharply because Mike Simich, Austin Hart, and millions of other veterans were coming home. The experiences of the recession of 1920–21 were clearly recalled by business and political leaders as the war was coming to an end. Compounding the fears of postwar recession were the memories of the 1930s. Mike and Anna Simich recalled those rocky years of frequent unemployment, and Austin Hart remembered clouds of dust and below-cost-of-production corn prices. Thus, while victory on the battlefields did produce a sense of national accomplishment, unemployment and its material and psychological effects had defined so much of the 1930s that the fear of its reappearance became a paramount issue as the war drew to a close. This concern played a major role in pushing through the various laws and amendments that became known as the GI Bill of Rights. Prior to World War II, veterans' benefits had consisted of cash bonuses or pensions for wartime service and extensive rehabilitation for the disabled. The GI Bill, however, was a comprehensive bill designed to provide welfare benefits, ease the transition back to civilian life, and compensate for lost opportunities while in service. Under this program, the Veterans Administration provided medical care and vocational rehabilitation even for nonservice connected cases. Thus, J. R. Trace, afflicted with muscular dystrophy, received some clinical treatment and passed his last days in a VA hospital even though his illness was not caused by military service. Veterans were also eligible for life insurance, home mortgages, farm or business loans from private institutions with the government insuring or guaranteeing the loan, readjustment allowances or unemployment insurance for up to 50 weeks for unemployed or underemployed veterans or those self-employed with a net income of less than $100 a month, and education and training.

The GI Bill of Rights had great impact on the postwar economy, especially in reducing the pressure to find jobs for returning veterans. Millions of veterans took advantage of the education benefits. Austin Hart drove to Independence two evenings each week during 1946 to take a specialized agricultural course taught under a GI Bill training grant. It was the presence of these men and their families on campuses throughout the United States that sparked the postwar explosion of higher education. Some were making up for time spent on battlefields instead of in classrooms; for most, however, the GI Bill provided access to educational opportunity they would not otherwise have had. Demobilization was also eased by the requirement that veterans be rehired at their old jobs. Thus, Mike Simich was rehired at Crucible Steel. For the veteran who did not wish to avail himself immediately of his educational benefit

and did not have a job to return to, unemployment insurance and veterans centers, such as the one in Midland, eased the period of readjustment. Finally, veterans received preference in the competitions for civil-service positions in federal, state, and local governments.

The voluntary withdrawal of women and older workers also eased the strain on the economy. The severe labor shortage during World War II had broken down the bar to employing women in many fields and also had attracted many women into the labor force. Although the percentage of women in the work force remained higher than it was prewar, many women chose to resume traditional roles as mothers and housewives. For a young couple such as Jerry and Peggy Trace, beginning a family was first on their personal agenda. Many Americans seemed determined to compensate for their lost opportunities, and in the decade following VJ Day there was a "baby boom." At the same time, large numbers of workers 65 years of age and older left the work force. Savings, social security, and pension plans combined to make retirement possible for blue-collar workers.

Basically, Americans bought their way out of depression in 1946 and 1947. For the first time in 15 years, many American families had the savings or credit to buy automobiles, houses, and major appliances. Consequently, consumer demand more than compensated for the reduction in government spending and far outstripped the ability of producers to meet it. New products—automobiles and refrigerators, for instance—sold at a premium as customers bid for the first durable goods off the assembly lines. Ben Trace ordered a 1946 Plymouth sedan in September 1945. Because he refused to make a gift to the salesman, he took delivery 14 months later.

Inflation, not depression, now emerged as the primary threat to economic security. Organized labor, fearful that postwar reconversion would jeopardize many of the gains made since the 1930s, lobbied forcefully for the continuation of wartime price controls. Business pressures to scrap controls were stronger. By October 1946, all major controls, except those on rents and sugar, had been abandoned. Workers found their worst fears realized—prices rose 32 percent. Real wages lagged behind the rise in prices. Although hourly wages did not drop after the war, the take-home pay of many workers declined because overtime pay and wartime bonuses disappeared. Wartime profits had been very high, and unions took the position that the corporations could pay higher wages to maintain labor's purchasing level. In Midland, Crucible Steel denied union allegations of war profiteering. In 1945 and 1946, the *Midland News* ran full-page ads, paid for by the American Iron and Steel Institute, that claimed wage increases in the steel industry would be inflationary. Labor rejected such arguments and used its only effective weapon, the strike. Steelworkers struck for four weeks, while automobile workers, electrical-equipment workers, mine workers, and railroad engineers and trainmen also formed picket lines. Government pressure forced the miners and railmen back, but workers had served notice of their determination to share in American economic growth.

The use of government power to halt strikes was exemplified by President Truman's denunciation of a threatened railway walkout in May 1946 and his demand for legislative power allowing him to draft strikers. Against this background, with business eyeing yet greater profits, consumers yearning for more manufactured comforts, and most everyone in a conservative frame of mind, Congress passed the Labor-Management Relations Act of 1947 (Taft-Hartley Act). In the eyes of union leaders as well as in the eyes of management, Taft-Hartley meant reversing the prolabor policies of the New Deal. But the

New Deal was not so easily dismantled. In fact, by passing the Employment Act of 1946, the federal government committed itself to the proposition that it was a function of government to ensure maximum employment and to generate conditions conducive to economic growth. In theory, the law recognized that the private and public sectors of the economy were neither separate nor distinct.

Probably the most important new tie between government and the private sector was the entry of government into the financing of research and development. During the war, the government had financed most research through contracts with private firms and universities. High-technology industries, so important in the prosperity of the postwar decades, continued to have their research underwritten by the federal government. Private and university research (a major industry in itself) in chemicals, petroleum, airplanes, electronics, computers, and medicine was paid for, in good part, by the government. Out of this system evolved elaborate government research institutes, such as the National Science Foundation, and independent research organizations and "think tanks" such as Stanford Research Institute and RAND. By 1955, half of the research costs of private businesses were paid for by the government, and by 1970 the federal share of the $27 billion research bill was much larger. Most corporate work focused on applied research —the perfection or protection of existing processes.

Much of the sponsored basic research was done on college campuses, as it had been during the Second World War. Thus, while the federal government did not make direct grants to education until the 1960s, it was deeply involved in financing the expansion of higher education. This complex involvement of universities in both federal and private research came at a crucial time, because the GI Bill and then postwar prosperity enormously increased the number of college and graduate students. Moreover, with industrial expansion taking place in the high-technology industries arising out of the war and government-sponsored research and development, the demand for college-educated workers far outstripped the supply.

The cold war, the Korean War, and the continued emphasis on military security were all vital in maintaining the close relationship between government and business. The atom bomb, the hydrogen bomb, jet aircraft, and radar defense systems involved billions of dollars of government research investment and hundreds of thousands of jobs. In the 1950s, new weapons systems were developed, and computers, missiles, and space technology became major industries. In the 1960s, the development of lasers and remote sensing devices resulted from war-related research. Billion-dollar industries whose only client was the American military became commonplace, and other industries found the military their most secure and steady customer.

As a result of war and defense spending, the federal government became the prime mover in the American economy. During the 1930s, President Roosevelt had used "pump priming," the injection of enormous government spending into the economy, to boost the economy. Although no American president until John F. Kennedy formally accepted the fiscal role of the government as economic prime mover, military spending served this purpose. The relative prosperity of the postwar decades rested heavily on the federal government's spending for defense.

As had the New Deal social policies, military spending increased the importance of the federal government and further increased the power of the executive branch within government. Corporations worked closely with the federal government. Lobbying and public-relations staffs in Washington, D.C.

became a vital part of the life of corporations; an influential Washington law firm on retainer was as important to most firms as their sales organization was. While legislation was still considered important, major concern focused on military contracts and other executive and administrative decisions. With single defense contracts worth billions of dollars, and with regulatory agencies assigning markets (airlines), fixing price ceilings (natural gas), or defining the legality of corporate action (selling of securities), the executive branch exerted the greatest power. The successive presidents through the 1970s accepted this responsibility willingly. During this period, the federal government tended to handle antitrust regulation through administrative agencies. Most government cases were resolved by the courts approving consent decrees worked out between the executive branch and the corporation under suit. Not until a 1960 price-fixing scandal in the electrical manufacturing industry did the government alter this policy and allow the courts to decide antitrust cases.

By the 1960s, many within and out of government had become concerned about the potential consequences of intimate military-business relationships. Dwight Eisenhower, in his farewell address upon leaving the presidency, warned against the growth of a "military-industrial complex" that could successfully pursue its own expansionist interests independent of the national interest. While the appointment of business executives to civilian Pentagon posts brought qualified administrators into government for brief tours, it also cemented military and industrial ties. On the other hand, retired Pentagon colonels and generals found ready employment in the offices of major and would-be defense contractors. The growing role of the government in the economy was neither planned nor anticipated. The idea of a mixed economy, with the federal government playing a significant role and accepting some responsibility for the health of the economy, was largely an outgrowth of the New Deal and the war.

As a result of the changed relationship between the government and private industry, and of the changes in corporations themselves, the economy began to differ sharply from prewar patterns. Size alone differentiated the economy. Gross national product (in current prices) soared, rising from $212 billion in 1945 to $398 billion in 1955, $503 billion in 1960, and $1 trillion in 1974. Through growth, mergers, and acquisitions, the nation's largest corporations kept pace with and surpassed the growth rate of the GNP. By 1965, the 500 largest industrial corporations employed 11.3 million workers, or 15.8 percent of the employed labor force. The nation's 10 largest employers had 2,592,983 workers, with General Motors leading with 734,594. By 1970, the 500 largest industrial corporations employed 20 percent of the work force and brought over 40 percent of the GNP to market.

Although the leading corporations grew to a fiscal and productive scale greater than that of most of the countries in the United Nations, the degree of monopoly in specific markets in the United States did not appreciably increase. The contemporary predominance of oligopoly, where a small number of producers dominated sales in a given market—for example, the "Big Three" automobile manufacturers—had been set by the 1920s. Instead, companies applied their resources to new markets or new products rather than fight price wars against their competitors. In most cases, corporate growth reflected keeping pace within an expanding market while acquiring or merging with unrelated firms.

By the 1960s, the economy was dominated by the conglomerate, a multi-industry firm dominant in a number of industries. Through merger and acquisition, the nation's largest corporations grew larger: between 1947 and 1968 the 200 largest manufacturing corporations increased their share of total industrial assets from 45 percent of all assets to 60.4 percent. Of the corporations on *Fortune* magazine's 1955 list of the 500 largest industrial firms, 68 were acquired by other firms by 1965. In 1961, for instance, the Ford Motor Company acquired Philco, which had sales of $400 million. Conglomerate development touched nearly every community. In Midland in 1967, Crucible Steel became part of Hunt Foods. A year later, it was sold to the growing conglomerate Colt Industries. By 1973 Colt, a firm that once concentrated on pistol manufacturing, approached $1 billion in sales. While these mergers did not directly affect the corporation's position in any given market, the sheer size of the nation's largest corporations resulted in greater concentration of economic power. Their complex structures and size made regulation by the government difficult, and their international activities were beyond the control of any single nation.

Moreover, the organization of production became more complex. Aided by new power sources, the development of computers and transistors, and greater integration, the tempo of change rapidly increased decade by decade after World War II. Industrial technology at the turn of the century had simplified the work task so that the worker used a machine, such as a die stamp to stamp out a metal piece, to perform the operation. The trend was toward the substitution of mechanical direction for human performance. While the worker might control, feed, or handle the machine, the machine performed the task itself. Thus automobile assembly plants utilized "robots," machines that stamped out parts. Cybernetics—the combining of feedback principles with automation—further heightened the tempo of change. Fully automated processes or machines that fed themselves materials, performed the task, and passed on the item were built with self-regulating devices. A machine with an electronic sensing device could be built to adjust itself automatically to changes in speed, to tool wear, or to other variables. Computers were essential for the processing of this information. Finally, cybernetics was used to turn distinct operations into one continuous production flow or into one simultaneous action performed by one machine. The printed circuit board or the transistor chip—important themselves in building more complex machines—represented the epitome of this development. Many of these innovations flowed from defense and space-related government research and development.

As a result of intensified technological change and relative affluence, shifts occurred in the location of the work task and the jobs Americans performed. The number of workers engaged in extracting raw materials and in agriculture declined sharply, manufacturing employment rose slightly but declined as a percentage of the labor force, while construction, service, and government employment absorbed the rest. Between 1945 and 1960,

the number of employees in wholesale and retail trade increased 64 percent, employees in finance, insurance, and real estate increased 57 percent, the number of service workers (excluding domestic servants) 60 percent, and the number of government employees, including teachers, 70 percent. The service sector of the economy expanded as did the number of white-collar jobs. Organized labor reflected this occupational shift, for the greatest gains in unionization were made among teachers, government employees, and clerks.

Bureaucratization and technology affected manufacturing and farm workers as well. The modern steel mills built in the early 1960s made Mike Simich's old job as a chipper superfluous. Automation and feedback principles had taken over and steel was turned out with few workers near the open hearth. Engineers stationed in front of computers provided most of the direction for the process. The General Motors Chevrolet plant at Lordstown, Ohio, a scene of much friction in the early 1970s, utilized robots on many of the tasks performed by automobile workers in other plants. While automation improved quality control and reduced costs, for workers, it further diminished their sense of participation in the production process. For Mike Simich, the farther he could get away from the open hearth the better he liked it. Of course, neither Mike nor Mihailo Markovich ever possessed the craftsman's identification with his product. By the 1970s, few Americans possessed this identification, for the vast majority of workers were no longer on the production lines.

Agriculture experienced a measure of automation and bureaucratization. Mechanization, the heavy uses of fertilizers and insecticides, and the spread of specialization and scientific farming continued at an accelerating pace. Between 1950 and 1965, crop production per acre increased nearly 50 percent.

Push-button automation in the automobile industry, 1948

More and more small and marginal farmers abandoned agriculture, while successful family farms became relatively large enterprises and corporate farms more commonplace. Tenant farming, associated with small capital investment, was slowly disappearing. Farm employment, which had involved 13 million workers in 1920, dropped to 8.4 million in 1955 and 5.6 million in 1965. Similarly the farm population declined from 32 million in 1920 to 23 million in 1950, and to 9.7 million in 1970 (see Table 13–1). In 1920, each farm worker had supplied 8.3 persons with food, whereas in 1964 each worker supplied 33.3 persons. These trends were reflected in the career choices of most of the Hart and Reinhardt children and in the increased scale of the operations carried on by those remaining on the farm.

Finally, a geographical decentralization of industry accompanied these changes in the economy. Because of the money markets and communication centers, corporate headquarters continued to be centered primarily in the New York area, and secondarily in Chicago and on the West coast, but many of the high-technology industries were widely dispersed. The South and Far West became major centers for electronics, aircraft, and space-related industries. Moreover, the trend after World War II was toward multiplant manufacturing rather than production in a single big plant. Government also played a significant role in this decentralization process. With trucking replacing railroads as the major shipper, the federally sponsored interstate highway system facilitated dispersion. At the same time, political power influenced the awarding of billions of dollars of government contracts. Senators and congressmen with high seniority ranking could get important government facilities for their districts and ensure that local private industry shared in the military and defense contracts. Most Americans benefited economically from this new, complex, ever-expanding economy in which the lines between the private and public sectors were fading.

THE SEARCH FOR ECONOMIC SECURITY

Mihailo Markovich had struggled to achieve economic security before World War I. His son-in-law, Mike Simich, searched for it following World War II. Mike stood a better chance of succeeding because the quest for security was recognized as a national goal. Mike labored within a system that accepted the notion that collective as well as individual activities were necessary to produce the good and abundant life. Mihailo had carried the entire burden himself. Mike and his generation—Austin Hart, Jerry Trace, and Henry Gishman—plus those entering the labor force for the first time later in the period—Robbie Bassano, Michele Simich—believed that most problems could be resolved if the nation developed a strong and vital economic base. Fighting no crusades except personal and family ones, they had faith that opportunity fulfilled would make reform unnecessary.

Subsequent to World War II and for the first time in the history of the nation, economic security came within the grasp of the overwhelming majority of American families. Technological, demographic, and other changes enhanced the career opportunities of millions. The managerial responsibilities of Regina Reinhardt were far more taxing than the farm-wife-mother duties that defined the life of her mother. The general stability of salaried white-collar work had been reenforced by government programs and the fringe-benefit plans of various companies. Bob Bassano's retirement depended upon such benefits. Paid vacations, health insurance, and pension programs all strengthened, at least to a degree, the economic circumstances of Ben Trace and Mihailo Markovich, in retirement, and Mike Simich, as he entered his last decade of full-time employment.

This is not to imply that all fears of economic setbacks were routed, for they were not. Automobile workers were hard hit by recession in the 1950s and by recession and foreign competition in the 1970s. During the latter period, white-collar personnel suffered serious unemployment and college graduates faced bleak employment prospects. Women and minority employees experienced the negative effects of seniority rules and prejudice, and those in retirement, such as Bob Bassano, ruefully watched as inflation eroded their retirement incomes. Depression memories may have dimmed during the booming 1950s, but new fears were manifest by the 1970s. Despite all of the protection and programs that buffered Mike Simich from total disaster, layoffs during the first months of 1980 reduced his income by 25 percent.

Government policies provided the underpinnings that blunted the depression psychology Americans carried with them into the postwar years. While some prophets of doom predicted another crash, the general consensus among economists and the public was that a crash-induced depression was virtually impossible. The economic and fiscal controls instituted during the New Deal and in the 1940s would prevent a collapse. On a more personal level, government programs such as Social Security, minimum wages, and unemployment insurance would prevent the general human suffering that made the depression intolerable. Government programs also spurred economic growth and prosperity. FHA-insured mortgages provided security to banks against loss by foreclosure and served to guarantee a steady flow of money into home mortgages, an important spur to the construction industry. Tax reductions to business through accelerated depreciation of capital expenditures (construction) in times of increased unemployment also served to

counter business contraction when an economic downturn threatened. A massive ($60 billion) interstate highway system combined with military and defense spending to fulfill the Keynesian requirement that continued government intervention in the economy would ensure prosperity. Thus, if it did nothing else, the government seemed to guarantee that the experiences of the 1930s would never be repeated again. By the early 1960s, the search for economic security seemed fulfilled.

The greatest change in American society after World War II was the attainment by the majority of a middle-class lifestyle. Their landscape had been transformed by automobiles and widespread home ownership. Credit and economic security enabled the overwhelming majority of families to participate in the consumer-oriented society. The characteristics of this lifestyle—job security, home ownership, automobiles, refrigerators, family vacations, college education for the children, television—all had been present in American society before the war. What was different now was the broadened distribution of these opportunities and consumer items. Permeating every aspect of postwar America was the automobile.

As attested to by the performance of Chrysler Corporation's Evansville plant and other automobile factories converted from munitions and tank and airplane construction to making passenger cars and trucks and buses after World War II, car sales, passenger-car registrations, and gasoline consumption climbed steadily. In 1949, car sales for the first time surpassed those of 1929 as 5.1 million automobiles were sold. Six million cars were sold in 1950 and 7.9 million in 1955. Following the recessions of the late 1950s, automobile sales declined, not making a comeback until the early 1960s. The late 60s and early 1970s recorded 8, 9, and 10 million cars sold in a single year. As sales climbed, so did automobile registrations, from 25.8 million in 1945 to 40.3 million in 1950, to 52.1 million in 1955, to 66 million in 1966, and to 92.9 million in 1971. Fuel consumption paralleled the rise in registrations rising from 19.1 billion gallons in 1945 to 47.7 billion in 1955, to 62 billion in 1962, and surpassing 100 billion in the 1970s.

To a great extent, prosperity and the automobile were interrelated. In 1971, for instance, General Motors was the largest industrial corporation in the United States with sales of $28.2 billion, a net profit after taxes of $1.9 billion, and 773,000 employees worldwide. The Ford Motor Corporation ranked third in sales volume in that year, with

a gross of $16.4 billion, and employed 433,000 workers. Chrysler, the smallest of the three big automobile manufacturers, was the nation's seventh largest manufacturing corporation with $8 billion in sales and 227,000 employees. Of the 20 largest corporations in 1971, 8 other corporations besides the Big Three primarily served cars: 7 oil companies and 1 tire manufacturer were in the top 20 corporations. By the mid-1970s, Standard Oil of New Jersey surpassed General Motors in sales volume.

New automobiles were the single most important market for rubber, steel, and glass, and billions of dollars annually were spent in the replacement-parts business. Even televi-

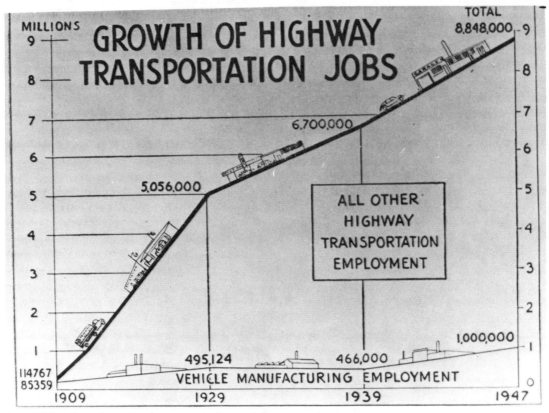

Automobile industry boosts its importance to the economy

Source: *Automobile Facts,* April 1948, p. 6.

sion depended upon the automobile dollar: in 1971, General Motors alone spent $40 million on network-television advertising alone. Ford $30 million, and Chrysler $20 million. The federal government was involved deeply. It expended $2 billion on highway construction in 1949, $3 billion in 1953, and $4 billion in 1955. And then Washington began to commit "large" sums to highway construction. In 1956, the Interstate Highway Act authorized the construction of the 42,500 mile highway system, costing an estimated $60 billion and financed through federal gasoline taxes.

Not only did automobiles offer great freedom, but the particular make and model publicized a person's position in the social order. Chrysler Corporation in the mid-1950s shifted emphasis from engineering to style, welding fins on its cars and introducing the three-year obsolescence cycle. Thereafter, the appearance of automobiles, and the status attached thereto, would be at least as important as performance.

Widespread automobile ownership facilitated the suburbanization of American life after World War II. It served as the catalyst for the new lifestyle that emerged in the 1950s and 1960s. Suburban development followed the route of the automobile, rather than that of public transportation. Indeed, major public transportation reached its height during the Second World War, and declined as the automobile gained ascendancy. Moreover, the automobile and the search for economic security represented a shift in the nature of the "American dream" in the postwar years. Much of late 19th century folklore had dealt with the rags-to-riches myth, the barefoot, impoverished boy rising to the ranks of millionaire. But the postwar dream, tempered by the leveling experiences of a nationwide depression and the change in business concentration that produced no legendary millionaires comparable to a Carnegie, Rockefeller, or Morgan, was a more modest one. Centered on the achievement of security reflected by upward mobility and material acquisitions, success meant a house in the suburbs, two cars, "better" schools, and an optimistic future.

Education promised to provide access to this more modest American dream. Indeed, a better environment for children, respresented

Courtesy of General Motors Corporation

Arguably at the zenith of the move toward bigger, heavier, more luxurious, and gaudy automobiles was the 1959 Cadillac Eldorado

by suburban surroundings and local schools, served as a magnet in attracting millions of families to suburban communities and subdivisions. For the Traces and Groppers, education promised direct monetary rewards (the more years of schooling attended, the higher the income). The Butlers and a few like them conceived of it as an investment in American society. The relationship between education, technology, and national strength was dramatized by Russia's orbiting of Sputnik (the first artificial satellite of the earth) in 1957. This event spurred greater investment in education. Sputnik led to a reevaluation of America's educational system, and this produced more money for schools, especially for programs in the sciences. Beginning with the National Defense Education Act of 1958 and continuing through the Secondary and Higher Education Act of 1965, the federal government contributed directly to public education. Local communities willingly raised their own taxes to improve schools. Public-school-pupil expenditures rose from an average of $106 per pupil in school year 1939–40 to $259 in 1949–50, to $472 in 1959–60, and to $960 in 1969–70. A great deal was expected of education both on a personal and national level.

Not all groups or units in society shared equally in this and other government programs, or in the benefits of suburbanization. But those who could share in the middle-class lifestyle fulfilled dreams far beyond those of previous generations. Jerry Trace's success, though atypical, was a model of what one could aspire toward. Few Americans earned an annual income even approaching the $45,000 Jerry received as manager of Houston's Yellow Cab Company. Given the transient nature of his career and life, many Americans might choose more permanence and less monetary success. In a sense, Bob Bassano made that choice when he turned down promotion to a nice presidency at

Chase Manhattan because it meant working nights and a radical rearrangement of the family's style of life. Too, an increased pay envelope was insufficient incentive for Mike Simich when offered a foreman's position. He preferred to stay with his friends rather than join the ranks of management. For Bob and Mike, success was not measured strictly in economic terms. Most Americans were less "successful" than Jerry Trace. Still, the Gishmans, Simiches, Bassanos, Groppers, Harts, and Navas all shared middle-class lifestyles. They bought homes—the largest single capital asset of nearly all American families—and filled them with televisions, stereos, modern kitchens, air conditioning, and electrical appliances. They bought new cars and many traveled widely. And most importantly, their children far surpassed parents' educational achievements and entered the world of white-collar work.

By 1960, more than 50 percent of American families had an income of at least $5,000 per year, and 31 percent of families had an income over $7,500 (see Table 11–1). With credit readily available and with the expectations of steady and regular employment, these families could enjoy the higher standard of living. Middle-class lifestyle was no longer the monopoly of white-collar workers. As of 1970, the income of 81 percent of American families exceeded $5,000 annually, while 69 percent of families earned over $7,000 per year. But severe inflation during the late 1960s wiped out the dollar gains of many. Those earning $5,000 annually in 1960 were on the margin of the middle class; in 1970, those earning $5,000 were poor.

As people earned more, they participated more widely in cultural affairs. Media and communications revolutionized the arts and brought to every town and city and into every home segments of a nationally shared culture. Television ownership spread most rapidly in the early 1950s, and, by 1976, 94 percent of

Table 11-1
Income by Consumer Units (families), 1935/1936–1960

	1935/1936 average		1941		1950		1960	
	Consumer units (millions)	Percent of units	Units	Percent	Units	Percent	Units	Percent
Under $2,000	29.8	77.7	24.4	58.9	11.4	23.2	7.3	13.1
$2,000–2,999	5.1	13.1	9.2	22.3	8.1	16.6	5.2	9.2
$3,000–3,999	1.7	4.4	4.1	9.8	8.6	17.6	5.9	10.6
$4,000–4,999	0.6	1.7	1.6	4.0	7.1	14.4	6.2	11.0
$5,000–7,499	0.6	1.6	1.2	2.8	8.5	17.5	13.9	24.8
$7,500–9,999	0.2	0.6	0.4	0.9	2.8	5.6	8.1	14.5
$10,000 and over............	0.3	0.9	0.5	1.3	2.5	5.1	9.6	16.8

American families had at least one television set. Primarily an entertainment medium, programming was geared to the lowest common denominator, and patrons of the "higher arts"—opera, theater, serious music—such as the Butlers decried the lowering of cultural standards. Television certainly helped to establish norms of middle-class life. Situation comedies and soap operas—the most popular TV fare—brought viewers into everyday contact with idealized middle-class environments. They helped establish aspirations and expectations that even the poorest of American families could identify with.

At the same time, the paperback revolution changed American literature. Although book clubs and inexpensive paperbound books dated from the 1920s and 1930s, they spread rapidly after World War II. Candy stores, drugstores, supermarkets, and other retail outlets became the major marketplaces for books. Authors such as Mickey Spillane, Ellery Queen, Irving Wallace, and Jacqueline Susann sold tens of millions of copies of their novels. As with Mickey Spillane, many of them featured an antihero who exemplified old-fashioned individualism in the highly complex society of the postwar years. The Bassanos, as an example, related very

strongly to the 1975 film *Death Wish* in which Charles Bronson portrayed a private citizen totally dedicated to the violent elimination of all rapists and muggers. Popular novels also began to break down traditional taboos with open descriptions and discussions of sex. Popular magazines continued this trend and *Playboy* and its host of imitators replaced all but *Readers Digest* as the nation's most widely distributed journals. Long-playing records, followed by the spread of rock and roll, altered popular music. Young people in the postwar years had both the interest in music and the money to buy records. They set the standards in popular music, which, like literature, was less inhibited and "funkier" than it had been in previous generations.

Although the "higher" arts could not compete in the marketplace with Mickey Spillane, Doris Day, Elvis Presley, and other idols of popular culture, appreciation of traditional art forms did increase. Record sales reflected the popularity of classical pianists such as Van Cliburn and Vladimir Horowitz. As symphonic music attracted a wider audience, smaller towns emulated major urban centers by organizing their own symphony orchestras. William Faulkner and Saul Bellow proved that authors could write within the old tradition of the novel and still enjoy a measure of popular acclaim. While Broadway theater and local stage productions shrunk rapidly in the 1950s and 1960s, national road companies and summer theaters blossomed.

Most importantly, however, by the 1960s there was a realization that high and popular culture were not as distinct as critics earlier had charged. Jazz music had been dismissed as an art form and its performance had been largely confined to nightclubs and bars. In the 1950s, when jazz lost its widespread popularity, college audiences kept it alive. The college-concert medium seemed to give jazz respectability and it was taken more seriously. While most listened to jazz for the sheer enjoyment, critics began to discuss, for example, the popular Modern Jazz Quartet and to compare it to chamber music groups. Similarly, after initially dismissing rock music as "trash," critics began to probe into the music of the Beatles and other groups and found much of interest. The Beatles' album "Sergeant Pepper's Lonely Hearts Club Band" received recognition as an opera in the concert context. Traditional opera was a folk medium that treated drama and satire. So, too, did "Sergeant Pepper" deal with folk themes—the contemporary problem of alienation in modern society. Matching the visual quality of Walt Disney's "Fantasia," the Beatles took their music and joy to the screen in *The Yellow Submarine* and its heroic voyage against the Blue Meanies and the world's drabness.

Each of the generations responded to its own "pop" stars. Charlotte and Bob Bassano danced to the melodies of Guy Lombardo and his Royal Canadians and listened to the crooning of the Big Three—Bing Crosby, Frank Sinatra, and Perry Como. Robbie passed through a "big band" stage with Stan Kenton and a shouting stage with Frankie Laine. Michele Simich, while never repudiating the gentle voice of Nat King Cole, also enjoyed the revival of popular folk music in the 1960s, much of it inspired by the civil-rights movement and protests against the Vietnam conflict. Pete Seeger, Joan Baez, and Peter, Paul, and Mary were among her favorites. And, in the 1960s and into the 1970s rock groups with strange names like The Who proliferated and captured Michele's attention and loyalty. Stars in other media came and went, in films and on television. Clark Gable, Betty Grable (the pinup queen of World War II GIs), and Gary Cooper gave way to the sultry Marilyn Monroe. By the 1970s, the antiheroes of literature had their screen counterparts in Dustin Hoffman and Jack Nicholson.

As tastes changed, those caught in the middle blocked their senses against the new sounds and sights, charging the newcomers with pandering to ever more crude standards of pleasure. No age group could be accused of accepting the norms of its predecessors. And while a case was made during the 1950s, stimulated by the full onslaught of prosperity, that the nation had lapsed into a dull conformity, the varieties of experience belied this. The fads of the 1950s and the images called up by such popular novels as *The Man in the Gray Flannel Suit* had their counterparts in the flippers and flappers and flagpole sitters and the celebration of success and the Babbitts of the 1920s. People in the 1950s seemed very similar to those who delighted in the marvels of the St. Louis World's Fair of 1904.

THE POLITICS OF ECONOMIC SECURITY

When Harry S. Truman assumed the office of the presidency following Roosevelt's death on April 12, 1945, he had been vice president for only three months and had little experience in his background that suited him for his new role. Having served with minor distinction as a Missouri senator since 1934, Truman was a compromise addition to the national Democratic ticket in 1944. Truman projected the image of the average man—direct and plainspoken, given to "hells" and "damns" in public. He shunned pretense and the monarchial trappings of the presidency. As an old-line politico who had lived within Kansas City's Pendergast machine for nearly two decades, he enjoyed politics and had great loyalty to the party and old friends. He faced hard decisions with decisiveness and kept a famous sign on his desk: "The Buck Stops Here." He was an avid amateur historian inclined to find "lessons" in the past which justified his own actions.

The Truman administration began as a caretaker regime trying to hold together the remnants of a New Deal under attack. Business leaders considered demobilization as an issue that could reverse what they had interpreted as the antibusiness attitude of the New Deal's last prewar years. The strikes of 1945 and 1946 further strengthened the arguments of big business, and in November 1946, the Republicans captured Congress for the first time since 1928. The Republican 80th Congress declined to enact Truman's agenda of unfinished New Deal business—aid to education, national health insurance, and civil-rights legislation. Instead, it turned to correct the imbalance that worked, in their eyes, against the private sector. The Taft-Hartley Act became law over Truman's veto, and the 80th Congress initiated what became the 22nd Amendment, limiting a president to two terms, a belated slap at Roosevelt. Other legislation cut funds for rural electric cooperatives and cut taxes. Three times Truman vetoed tax reduction bills as "soak-the-poor" measures, but the last time Congress overrode his veto.

Although they attacked New Deal social legislation and the role of big government, Republicans and conservative Democrats nonetheless accepted the basic economic and social responsibilities assumed by Washington. Except for a few diehard advocates of laissez-faire, the major division focused on the parameters of federal intervention and power. While refusing to extend government intervention in new areas such as national health insurance, Truman's opponents accepted what had already become traditional government rules.

Republican victories in 1946 and Truman's inability to carry out the unfinished business of the New Deal augered defeat for the president in the election of 1948. Even more ominous, he alienated two important sectors of the Democratic Party by his strong civil-rights and anti-Communist stands. In 1946, Truman had appointed a committee to investigate Negro civil rights following the outrageous murders of some Southern blacks. In October 1947, the President's Committee on Civil Rights issued its report, *To Secure These Rights,* which called for "the elimination of segregation, based on race, color, creed, or national origin, from American life." Truman promptly called on Congress to implement the report. His strong stand, and the adoption by the Democratic convention in 1948 of a strong civil-rights plank in the platform, precipitated the formation of a third party—the Dixiecrats, led by dissident Southerners who nominated Strom Thurmond, Governor of South Carolina, as their candidate. Further complicating the election was the candidacy of Henry A. Wallace, the last nonconsensus voice to be raised in American presidential politics until the 1960s. Wallace and a handful of supporters called for détente rather than confrontation with the Soviet Union and vigorous action to achieve social and economic justice at home. But the issues he raised were buried beneath an anti-Communist avalanche.

With the Democratic party falling apart, Governor Thomas E. Dewey, Roosevelt's opponent in 1944 and the Republican nominee again in 1948, acted as if he were

One of numerous cartoons portraying Dewey's confidence (and the pessimism of many Democrats) about the election of 1948

already the incumbent. He promised continuation of the bipartisan foreign policy but offered no domestic panaceas other than clearing up the complexities of the federal government. Truman took his case to the people, speaking at every whistle-stop and railroad crossing across the nation. He attacked the Republican 80th Congress as a "do-nothing Congress," and "the worst Congress in American history." He appealed to the non-Southern elements of the New Deal coalition, reminding farmers of Republican attempts to cut price supports, labor of the Taft-Hartley Act, Negroes of his civil-rights proposals, and urban dwellers of Republican rejection of rent controls. The Simiches,

Gishmans, Harts, and Groppers all stayed with Truman. In an election that provided hope for every underdog, Truman won despite the predictions of pollsters and newspapers, The *Chicago Tribune* actually hit the streets with the headline "Dewey Defeats Truman." Truman captured 24,179,000 votes, Dewey 21,991,000, while Thurmond received 1,176,000 and Wallace 1,157,000. In electoral votes, Truman received 303, Dewey 189, and Thurmond 39. The Democrats captured both houses of Congress.

In 1949, assuming office on his own for the first time, Truman announced his Fair Deal, pulling together his legislative proposals of the previous years into one package. Only the civil-rights proposals were totally his own; otherwise, the Fair Deal agenda promised logical extensions of the New Deal. Except for the passage of the 1949 Housing Act, the raising of the federal minimum wage to 75 cents per hour, and the extension of social security to cover 10 million more Americans, Truman was no more successful in fulfilling his program than he had been in the 80th Congress. Taft-Hartley repeal was rejected, civil-rights legislation was killed by filibustering, the American Medical Association successfully lobbied against the passage of national health insurance, and the agricultural lobby defeated reform of farm legislation.

Influential lobbies halted the Fair Deal in 1949 and 1950. After 1950, the Korean War, the cold war, McCarthyism, and Truman's declining credibility buried what remained on the domestic social agenda. Perhaps most important was the national obsession with communism. Whatever respectability the Communist party had gained in the American political spectrum during World War II was quickly dissipated immediately following the war. By 1947, anti-Communism had become the keystone of United States foreign policy. It was almost inevitable that anti-Communism would become an important plank in domestic policy as well.

Senator Joseph McCarthy of Wisconsin did not initiate concern over Communists in government. Congressman Martin Dies of Texas had pioneered in using this issue as an anti–New Deal and antilabor club. The Taft-Hartley Act had required union leaders to file affidavits that they were not Communist party members. But even New Dealers and labor leaders had initiated anti-Communist drives. In 1946, the Congress of Industrial Organizations purged leftist union leaders, and, in 1948, liberal Democrats successfully tainted Henry Wallace's campaign with charges of aiding Communist policy. Truman, calling for a purge of suspected Communists from government, had initiated security clearance programs in the federal government. Marching in step, Midland and other communities passed ordinances requiring municipal employees who were Communists to register and all employees to take a loyalty oath.

Thus, anti-Communism was already an issue when, in 1950, Senator McCarthy charged the Truman administration with harboring Communists. McCarthy took the issue and made it his own, capitalizing on popular anti-Communist feelings and the immediate concerns over the cold war, the Korean War, fears of internal subversion, conservative opposition to centralized government, and the respectability of the left in politics and labor during the New Deal. Resentment of conservative Democrats and Republicans and the senator's own talent for publicity were the driving forces behind his movement. Equally important, McCarthy gained the protection of powerful Republican leaders who saw in McCarthy a vehicle back to national political power after 20 years of Democratic control of the White House. Recklessly and without proof, McCarthy charged that subversive interests—Communists—had infiltrated government, unions, and education. McCarthyites all over the country made similar charges in their own communities, and accused leftists who would not confess to their sins found themselves blacklisted by Hollywood, universities, and businesses. The terror against the left finally ended in 1954. McCarthy fell as rapidly as he had risen. Leaders in both parties began to abandon him when they became aware that he was not particularly popular. Republicans, in particular, saw it to their advantage to reject the immoderation of McCarthy and adopt the moderate tone of the newly elected president, Dwight David Eisenhower, or the reasoned conservatism of Senator Robert Taft of Ohio. Television, too, played a role in McCarthy's demise, beginning in 1954 with the presentation of filmed broadcasts on Edward R. Murrow's "See It Now." Millions watched the live army-McCarthy hearings in which McCarthy appeared rude and ruthless and, as attorney for the army Joseph Welch asserted, lacking "all sense of decency." The opinion of political leaders and the public converged, breaking McCarthy's tenuous power and leading to his censure by the Senate in 1954.

Library of Congress

As depicted in this cartoon, by 1953, many political observers believed that McCarthy had painted himself into a corner. Hysterical anti-Communism was a destructive, negative force

The politics of McCarthyism, however, had been rewarding to the Republican Party, and when they were combined with the frustrations over the stalemated war in Korea, 1952 looked like the year that would return the Republicans to the White House. The GOP nomination of General Dwight D. Eisenhower ensured Republican victory, and Eisenhower easily defeated Governor Adlai E. Stevenson of Illinois. The New Deal coalition seemed to fall apart in the face of Eisenhower's popularity. He pulled 33.8 million votes to Stevenson's 27.3 million, and 442 electoral votes to Stevenson's 89.

No man ever entered the presidency amidst more enthusiastic acclaim than did Eisenhower. Although the campaign focused at times on "Korea, Communism, and Corruption," no magical formulas were proposed. Instead, Eisenhower's personality became the issue. His solution to the Korea stalemate was merely a pledge to visit the battlefront. Reflecting his popularity, the major campaign slogan was "I Like Ike." Eisenhower had achieved glamor as the commander of Allied forces during World War II, and was one of the few generals to emerge a national hero from a war that mostly celebrated the role of the GI. After the war he served as NATO commander with military, diplomatic, and administrative responsibilities. For several years, he served as president of Columbia University. His personal magnetism was comparable only to that of Franklin Roosevelt. Eisenhower could electrify crowds, as Michael Gishman saw in 1960 at a campaign rally at New York City's Columbus Circle. Vice President Richard Nixon addressed an indifferent and mostly Democratic gathering, but when Ike came out, the crowd responded to the president's engaging grin and confidence and roared its approval.

In obtaining the Republican nomination in 1952, the soldier-statesman had defeated the old-guard, conservative wing of the Republican Party, led by Senator Robert Taft of Ohio.

In his first speech in his campaign for the presidency, the 62-year-old contender spoke in his boyhood town of Abilene, Kansas. He talked about his parents, their honesty, courage, and integrity. In his broadcast that day from Abilene, Edward R. Murrow summed up what Eisenhower had to offer the American people: "The hallmark of this speech was restraint, coupled with a belief that the traditional virtues—thrift, honesty, and belief in God—are as essential to the country as they were when Eisenhower was a boy here." Although Eisenhower's two terms as president reflected his own style, his years in office saw the institutionalization of the New Deal. By continuing the New Deal approach in the economy and society, Eisenhower made government activism the status quo. He had the opportunity to reverse 20 years of Democratic rule, but, while altering some Democratic policies and directions, Eisenhower stayed within the parameters established by his predecessors. Fundamentally, his administration favored business and the private sector while building on New Deal policy. He sought to provide an atmosphere conducive to the search for economic security.

Eisenhower feared that high taxes and large federal budgets would inhibit economic growth by diverting capital from the private to the public sector. Within a month after his inauguration, the administration abandoned all Korean War economic controls and curtailed government manufacturing enterprises competing with the private sector. Offshore oil-land rights were given to the states as the major oil companies had requested, thus permitting private exploitation of this national resource. Moreover, the administration recognized the inflationary impact of government spending and sought to prevent the initiation of new social programs. Eisenhower opposed federal aid to education as an expensive and intrusive use of federal power and fought larger federal housing programs. Nonetheless,

the Eisenhower administration inaugurated a great road-building boom through the passage of legislation authorizing the construction of the interstate highway system and, during the recession of 1957, the administration used its fiscal powers to counter the risks of another depression.

That Eisenhower's executive style and reassuring conservatism reflected the mood of Americans was demonstrated by his second defeat of Adlai Stevenson in 1956. He swamped the Democratic nominee, receiving 35.5 million popular votes to Stevenson's 26 million, and 457 electoral votes to his opponent's 73. At the same time, the Democrats retained control of Congress, which they had won in 1954. Congress and the president seemed to work in harmony, in part because Eisenhower did not seek to dominate the Congress in the way his two predecessors had and in the way his successors would.

Eisenhower's second administration was marked by three events—Little Rock, Sputnik, and the 1957–58 recession—which would have great bearing on his last years in office, the 1960 election, and domestic and foreign policy in the 1960s. Eisenhower's broad goal of domestic harmony precluded an activist role in desegregation. The judiciary established the lead in government, and the administration did little to further integration. But in September 1957, Eisenhower was forced to act. The previously all-white Central High School in Little Rock, Arkansas was scheduled for integration by court order, and Governor Orval Faubus called out the national guard to prevent the Negro students from entering the school. A federal court ordered the guard withdrawn, but the local officials, in the face of angry white mobs taunting the blacks, barred the Negro students. The violence was an international embarrassment to the United States, and Eisenhower nationalized the guard to ensure the carrying out of the court orders. Though reluctantly,

Eisenhower had chartered a moderate path of federal enforcement of civil rights.

During this time, the United States was experiencing its most serious postwar recession, one lasting from mid-1957 through 1958. The nation had suffered a milder, briefer recession in 1953–54, following the reduction of the federal budget from Korean War levels, and Eisenhower had done little to use the federal government to stimulate the economy. In 1957–58, however, military spending was boosted and matched by large commitments of federal construction funds, notably in hospital and highway development. The recession also focused debate on the federal government's responsibility for economic growth in the private sector. Thus, in his last years in office Eisenhower had confirmed that the search for economic security had not resolved other problems. The necessity of federal action in civil rights, aid to education, and the recession of 1957–58 highlighted the problems that remained.

For all that, the years of Eisenhower's presidency were a time of comparative prosperity and satisfaction for almost all of the families in this book. Enjoying steady employment (Ben Trace, for example, worked an average of 11 months per year between 1950 and his retirement in 1956, and Mike Simich was not laid off once), they were able to buy and build and borrow as never before. In total, the families purchased 23 homes, 46 automobiles, and innumerable "consumer durables" during the decade. As well, the Harts, Groppers, and Gishmans put away money each month for their children's college education, Bob Bassano began to save for retirement, and Mike Simich launched an ambitious do-it-yourself renovation of the family home.

Though the families—when asked to analyze the most significant occurrences in their lives during this period—first mentioned the sense of economic security they enjoyed, they also listed other, equally important, if intangible matters: the absence of strife and violence, the absence of fear for the safety of relatives in the military services, the high level of public and personal morality. Few of them understood (or cared about) such issues of national importance as offshore oil, the establishment of a Council of Economic Advisers, or the National Defense Education Act. Depending on circumstance and special interests, each family member looked at national affairs from a different perspective. Mike Simich considered the Eisenhower administration's labor policy and the powerful role of businessmen proof that the government had little interest in the working man. Still, he could not but approve of Ike's tax policy and success in controlling inflation. Louis and Lila Gropper silently applauded the school desegregation decision and the sending of troops to Little Rock, but they saw no immediate benefits coming from the federal government's cautious handling of civil rights. Austin Hart accepted Soil Bank payments, while recognizing that this program, even though administered by Republicans, represented yet another temporary and partial response to the needs of farmers. The Traces and Reinhardts, affected by the economic difficulties which hit Evansville in the mid-50s, had quite a different view.

Still, the families viewed most of the activities of national government as positive and beneficial. The government received credit for the decade's general prosperity, for ensuring the safety of communities, for keeping the Communists away from American shores and sparing their sons the risk of life in foreign adventures. It informed them about child care and gave milk to needy children. Insofar as the families assigned praise or blame, "Ike" was the beneficiary. While not exhausting them with calls for social change and also not depleting their pocketbooks, Eisenhower did put across the idea that the government understood their problems and was willing to help—or to encourage them to help themselves. No more did they expect from government.

THE OUTSIDERS

Not everyone shared in the economic security of the years after World War II. Blacks formed the largest single group outside of the affluent society. Millions of black families, the majority, were still in poverty in the Jim Crow South, many of them barely scratching out a living as tenant farmers and sharecroppers. Even in the North, an effective job ceiling limited black advancement. Nonetheless, a steady stream of rural blacks migrated to the nation's cities in search of greater opportunity. In 1940, 77 percent of the black population resided in the Southern regions of the United States; by 1960, this had dropped to 60 percent. The black population in New England rose by 138 percent, in the Middle Atlantic states by 120 percent, in the North Central states by 143 percent, and on the West Coast by 613 percent. At the same time, blacks tended to be more heavily urbanized than the white population was. In 1960, 51 percent of blacks lived in central cities whereas only 30 percent of whites lived there (see Table 13–2).

While migration improved the general standard of black life since the cities offered higher wages, better health standards, and greater educational opportunity than did rural areas of the South, a comparison of black and white income reflected the degree to which blacks were outsiders in American society. The differences were startling. In 1962, 45.3 percent of all white families had an income of more than $7,000 compared with only 16.5 percent of nonwhite families (see Tables 11–2 and 13–3). And, in 1970, the median family income of whites reached $10,236 compared to $6,516 for nonwhites. The income differential of $3,720 in 1970 compared with a differential of $3,428 in 1960. Under the pressure of recession and inflation, this income gap widened.

The modern civil-rights movement, which began during World War II, had equality of opportunity as its major objective. A. Philip Randolph's threatened march on Washington in 1941 foreshadowed later developments. Randolph made his movement an all-black one, used direct action on the part of masses of black citizens, and focused on the economic problems of urban Negroes. In 1942, the Congress of Racial Equality was formed to apply the Gandhian techniques of nonviolent direct action to the struggle for racial equality, and the first sit-ins took place in Chicago dur-

Table 11-2

Percentage Distribution of White and Nonwhite Families, by Income Level, 1947–1962

Income	1947 White	1947 Nonwhite	1955 White	1955 Nonwhite	1962 White	1962 Nonwhite
Under $1,000	9.0	28.8	6.6	19.0	3.2	9.2
$1,000–1,999	14.9	33.5	8.7	20.7	5.8	16.3
$2,000–2,999	22.3	18.8	10.4	17.6	6.9	17.6
$3,000–3,999	20.8	8.4	14.3	17.2	8.2	13.5
$4,000–5,999	20.5	7.5	29.4	16.9	20.1	19.6
$6,000–6,999			9.9	4.8	10.5	7.3
$7,000–9,999	9.5	3.0	13.9	3.1	23.8	10.8
$10,000 and over	3.0	0.1	6.8	0.6	21.5	5.7

ing the war. When Martin Luther King, Jr. led the Montgomery bus boycott in 1954–55, which arose out of the impulsive decision of one Rosa Parks not to move to the back of the bus, he was building on well-established tactics.

The assault on segregated schools, which achieved legal sanction with *Brown* v. *Topeka Board of Education* in 1954, also represented the culmination of a long battle. For more than two decades, the National Association for the Advancement of Colored People (NAACP) had attacked the legality of the separate but equal doctrine. By the early 1950s, a group of cases involving different types of educational segregation had worked their way through the courts, which made it possible to directly confront school segregation. They were all decided in the *Brown* v. *Topeka Board of Education* case in May 1954. The court, under Chief Justice Earl Warren, voted unanimously to outlaw segregation. However, it moved slowly in ordering compliance. George Gropper was attending a church youth conference in El Paso when the Brown decision was announced. Discussion immediately shifted to its significance. Most believed that it would quickly bring equality of educational opportunity. Negroes did not anticipate prolonged resistance. Equally mistaken, the high court assumed that lower federal courts could easily work out integration schedules. Within communities, however, deep-rooted racial attitudes were challenged for the first time in almost a century. First in the South and then increasingly in the North, these attitudes surfaced and solidified into powerful barriers to the implementation of the decision.

That the struggle for equal opportunity should focus so heavily on education was not surprising. Black and white families looked to education as a personal means for achieving success and prosperity and also as the major route to jobs in the new industrial society.

Thus, slowly the aspirations of black citizens for equality before the law began to rise, and blacks demanded more and more.

Blacks were not the only outsiders in American society. Puerto Ricans entered the bottom of the economic ladder as had blacks and European migrants of a generation before. But in a society in which education was paramount for achieving occupational mobility, Puerto Ricans who were less fortunate than Julio Martinez found that there were few opportunities for unskilled and foreign-speaking employees.

Mexicans and Mexican-Americans were also passed by in the broadening of the middle class. In 1960, an estimated 5 million Chicanos lived in the United States, 80 percent of them in Texas, California, New Mexico, Arizona, and Colorado. Many, like the Nava family, had been citizens for generations, but others came as farm and railroad workers in the 1910s and 1920s. The wartime labor shortage, especially in agriculture, led the United States to sign a formal agreement with the Mexican government allowing Mexican workers *(braceros)* to migrate to the United States during crop seasons. The program and its successors continued until 1964. Since then, most Mexicans enter the United States illegally.

For the Mexican migrant, the United States offered hope of escaping the poverty and high unemployment rate of his homeland. Farmers and ranchers sought Mexican workers, paid them low wages, and encouraged illegal migration in order to guarantee a surplus labor supply, which further depressed wages. About 40 percent of Chicanos in the United States in the early 1970s were migrant farm workers, and they comprised about 25 percent of all migrant laborers. Confined to work in an industry with a shrinking number of jobs, they were also subjected to substandard working conditions. These workers have not been covered by the government programs that provided a secure underpinning for industrial workers. Mostly unorganized, farm workers were not even covered by federal minimum wage standards until 1966, and then coverage was extended only to employees of the largest farms (about 1 percent of the total). They were not covered by unemployment insurance, and except in California, they were not protected by workmen's compensation on an equal basis with industrial workers.

All of these factors have taken their toll on the Mexican-American communities. In 1960, probably one third of all Chicanos fell within the federal government's poverty guidelines, and this percentage increased between 1960 and 1970. In the Southwest in 1960, the median educational level of Angelos was 12.0 years, for nonwhites 9.7, and for Chicanos 8.1. In Texas, for Chicanos more than 25 years of age, the median educational attainment was 4.8 years.

As a group, blacks, Puerto Ricans, and Chicanos shared one thing in common that made their experiences radically different from those of the European migrants to America. Migration has been steady over a long period of time. While the National Origins Act of 1924 virtually halted European migration to the United States, Negro, Mexican, and Puerto Rican migrants from rural backgrounds have continued to settle in American cities and communities. Living segregated lives and suffering from low incomes and political powerlessness, these minority groups have been able to offer only minimal aid to the most recent arrivals. Moreover, each group has been characterized by the patterns, traditions, and behavior of the most recent migrants. This had been true of the European migrants as well, but in the second and third generations the stereotypes changed as migration halted. Despite the upward mobility of many black, Mexican, and Puerto Rican families, the general image of

the unskilled rural traditionalist remains the most common characterization.

Other groups and peoples—American Indians, the aged, Appalachian hill folk—have shared little of the bounty of postwar affluence. Numerous federal programs direct aid in their direction. In the case of the Indian, much of the aid was unwanted, culturally unacceptable, and viewed as conscience money. As for the other groups, while Americans know in general sense what should be done, they continued to cling to the tradition of self-sufficiency and self-help. The result has made them inconsistent and sporadic in their efforts and stingy with their dollars.

With health improvements enabling more Americans to live to their 60s and 70s, and with the decline in the birthrate in the 1960s, those 65 and older became a greater proportion of the population. By the 1970s, over 20 million Americans were retired, a condition that could mean anything from being pensioned off, to undertaking a second career, to pursuing travel and relaxation, to being tossed on the pile of human discards. Evidence from psychiatrists and geriatricians indicated that many workers had a deep inner resistance to withdrawal from work and that retirement was frequently followed by crisis, emotional upset, and sometimes even death. For millions, these were the worst days of their lives. Over 1 million were relegated to some 23,000 nursing homes, more than half of which, according to a General Accounting Office audit in 1971, were in serious violation of government standards for safety and health. Other millions, especially aged women, lived by themselves in seedy apartments or residential hotels.

THE LAST NEW DEAL

By the early 1960s, the protests of the outsiders and a vocal minority of liberal and radical insiders began to challenge the conventional belief that individualistic concentration on personal security and achievement was desirable or possible for all Americans. But most Americans were still actively engaged in searching for and consolidating economic security. And many of them, while subscribing in a general way to the belief in equality of opportunity, were—as were the Simiches—a bit disturbed over the aggressiveness of the emergent groups.

At the same time, the civil-rights movement began to confront the slow progress that had been made in integrating schools and public facilities, and in eliminating job discrimination. Nonviolent sit-ins and marches through the South enraged traditionalists not only because they threatened the social status quo but also because these activities took place in violation of local laws. Not infrequently, white fear and anger manifested itself in police brutality and mob violence. It took hundreds of U.S. marshalls and rights of violence to matriculate James Meredith at the University of Mississippi. Martin Luther King, Jr. and other civil-rights leaders, black and white, appealed to hundreds of thousands of marchers and millions of Americans through television from the steps of the Lincoln Memorial to fulfill the dreams of opportunity and equality. But violence and frustration begat more violence and Watts, a ghetto section of Los Angeles, exploded in an orgy of mass burnings by blacks in 1964, and thereafter American cities went through long, hot summers of riots in Negro ghettos. One result, widely recorded, was the backlash among whites. Families such as the Bassanos felt physically and psychologically threatened by the movement of minority groups into their neighborhoods. As their fears intensified, the issue of law and order came to challenge that of economic security as the preeminent concern in their lives.

Continued involvement in Vietnam broke the consensus on foreign policy and the cold war. Older pacifists and younger idealists challenged the U.S. interventionist role throughout the world, arguing that the United States was suppressing legitimate social revolutions. Charging that American prosperity was based on war, they challenged Americans to reconstruct their own society, to eliminate poverty and inequality at home. The movement grew largely on college campuses out of both idealism and self-interest: it was American youth who had to bear the direct physical burden of war. Radical groups, frustrated at their inability to build a popularly based movement, sought to bring the war home and directly confront the government. Peaceful marches were held in Washington and state capitols, while a small handful of radicals turned to violence to attract attention. Government buildings were bombed in the vain hope of stopping the American military machine.

At the same time that some radicals were attacking the American government, others —hippies, flower children, and Jesus freaks—rejected American values by opting out. All shared the view that American materialism had destroyed the ethereal and spiritual qualities of American life. Although they never articulated their views in the way of the antiwar movement, they challenged the value of economic security. Those who were still achieving for the first time had little patience with those who, coming from middle-class backgrounds, had the territory to advise them that material security was not worth the effort.

For some American youth, then, dissidence was expressed politically, and for a tiny minority political activity took on violent overtones. Violence on college campuses attracted the media, and college students and their institutions suffered a loss of public confidence from such exposure. Even on the campuses, only a small proportion of students engaged in public protests; most continued to work or took advantage of the hubbub to slack off. Women, however, gained visibility—some unwanted, to be sure—as leaders and protesters, thus forging the link between antiwar activities, a rising concern for civil rights, and an activist feminist movement. Still, the overwhelming majority of males registered for the draft, and if called, served, albeit with less enthusiasm than Robbie Bassano demonstrated. College enrollment protected many from the draft, so that the burden of service fell on youth in or entering the labor force. Others, mostly fleeing from the perceived sterility of college study, turned dissidence into a personal fight to free their lives from parental and institutional controls by experimenting with drugs and sex, or by going braless, or by wearing long hair. Most youth seemed less accepting of conventions than earlier generations had been; some acted in shocking ways, but it is still not clear that the youth of the 1960s became more politically sophisticated, intellectually responsive, or socially concerned adults than those of prior generations. But in ways of their own choosing, in the 1960s, they helped bring down a government, end a war, and liberalize the lifestyle of a nation.

Presidents John F. Kennedy and Lyndon B. Johnson tried to provide direction to American society. In 1960, Senator John F. Kennedy of Massachusetts narrowly defeated Vice President Richard Nixon. The two candidates had met in a series of nationally televised debates that tended to present their personalities more than an enlightened discussion of the issues. Fundamentally, Nixon was in the position of defending the Eisenhower record while Kennedy aggressively demanded a more activist administration both at home and abroad. Moreover, as candidate and later as the youngest man elected president, JFK projected an image of a youthful spirited, sophisticated president surrounded by similar people. His administration used grace and wit as a stock in trade.

Son of a self-made millionaire and strong New Dealer, the Harvard-educated John Kennedy capitalized on his war record and was elected congressman from Cambridge, Massachusetts in 1946. His career in Congress, and in the Senate (1952–60) was undistinguished. As president, most of his efforts centered on foreign policy and the cold war. The Berlin Crisis, the Bay of Pigs, the Cuban Missile Crisis, increased commitment in Vietnam and Laos, the Alliance for Progress, the Peace Corps, rationalization of the armed services, commitment to place a man on the moon, and the Test Ban Treaty were the hallmarks of his administration. Kennedy was less forceful and less successful in domestic policy. His increased military spending ended the recession that he had found upon entering office, but he never convinced his Democratic Congress to pass a sweeping tax cut to stimulate the economy. Thus, despite the strong rise in GNP, unemployment remained above 5 percent. He also used his power to force the steel companies to retreat from an announced price rise that threatened his inflation guidelines. But his major legislative requests—federal aid to education and mass transit, tax reduction, poverty program—were stalled in Congress at the time of his assassination in Dallas on November 22, 1963.

Lyndon Baines Johnson assumed the presidency amidst the shock of the assassination. His strengths and weaknesses were the very opposite of those of Kennedy. He was a master of political arts on the floor of Congress and skilled in political trading. From a poor farm background and graduate of a Texas teachers college, he lacked the style and grace of the upper-class Kennedys. He had little experience in foreign policy, and his domestic political skills ill served him in diplomacy.

In filling out Kennedy's last year of office,

Johnson traded on the shock and grief accompanying the assassination and on the skills and political influence acquired during his years in the Senate as majority leader in the 1950s. Within one year, Congress enacted aid to education, a tax cut, mass-transit funds, civil-rights legislation, and the antipoverty program. While the poverty program reflected directions Kennedy had become concerned about, especially influenced by Michael Harrington's *Other America* (an exposé of poverty in America), the program was Johnson's. In his first State of the Union address in January 1964, he declared "unconditional war on poverty." He addressed himself to those who had been outside of the economic and social mainstream of American life. The Economic Opportunity Act of 1964 that followed established the Office of Economic Opportunity as the administrative agency of a wide variety of programs: Head Start for preschool children; a work-study program for college students from low-income families; VISTA, the volunteer, domestic peace-corps program active in ghettos, on Indian reservations, and elsewhere; and the Community Action Program to inject federal assistance into poor neighborhoods while ensuring "maximum feasible participation" by the poor. The Public Works Act of 1965 added $3 billion to the war on poverty, while the Appalachian Regional Development Act of 1965 committed $1 billion to aiding that region.

The 1965 acts, though extensions of the war on poverty, were components of Johnson's "Great Society," his successor to the New Deal and the Fair Deal. Johnson's Great Society gave recognition to the challengers of consensus by describing the Great Society as a place where the "quality of . . . goals" took precedence over the "quantity of . . . goods." He envisioned abundance for all and the removal of poverty and racial injustice. The Great Society be-

came the instrument of Johnson's election to the presidency in his own right when, in 1964, he defeated Senator Barry Goldwater. Goldwater offered his own challenge to the New Deal–Fair Deal–Great Society continuum by attacking government social programs and promising to severely restrict the role of government. While Goldwater's belligerence about American military strategy in Southeast Asia accounted for Johnson's overwhelming victory, the challenger legitimized attacks on the widening federal role, which would be acted upon in President Nixon's second administration and in the administration of Gerald Ford.

Johnson and the 89th Congress enacted into law the most impressive legislative program since 1933. They extended the poverty program, created Medicare (national health insurance for the aged), rent supplements for the poor through the Housing Act of 1965, revised the immigration quota system (removing the racial and ethnic biases), initiated environmental legislation, passed aid to elementary and secondary education, and approved the Demonstration Cities program for the rebuilding of the nation's center-city areas. The legislative achievement was outstanding and gave promise of finally meeting the endemic problems of American society head-on. But something went wrong.

As the 1968 election drew close, race riots had scarred many inner-city areas, and college campuses had been politicized and become centers of antigovernment propaganda. Poverty had not been eradicated. Regional, urban, and transportation programs languished. The government offered no new solutions. And in 1968, Robert F. Kennedy, senator from New York, younger brother of the late president and a presidential hopeful himself, and Martin Luther King, Jr., Nobel Prize winner and civil-rights leader, were assassinated. The United States seemed to be falling apart.

Martin Luther King, Robert Kennedy, and President Lyndon B. Johnson at the signing ceremonies for the Civil Rights Act of 1964

Most of the trouble centered on the war in Vietnam. The critics gained strength, both popularly and within Congress itself, so that the consensus was lost. Moreover, the frustrations of supporting and fighting a war that South Vietnam was losing stirred war supporters who demanded further escalation. Johnson had argued that the United States could afford both guns and butter—to wage a war and finance domestic programs. But the programs at home were backed with inadequate resources while war expenditures began to push inflation higher and higher. Both World War II and the Korean War had been fought with price controls on the home front. In addition, backlash against race riots and social programs began to grow as the Bassanos and other conservative citizens charged that the government, rather than re-

dressing inequalities, was creating inequality by subsidizing the poor. With government policy at home and abroad under challenge from all sides, Johnson and the Great Society could only offer more of the same. The consensus in American society in the late 1940s and the 1950s precluded any dramatic new approaches to dealing with American economic, social, and diplomatic problems.

THE NEW AND THE OLD

In 1968 Richard Nixon won the presidency by appealing to diverse groups disturbed by the directions of American life in the 1960s. The Bassanos, Jerry and Peggy Trace, and the Harts all voted for Richard Nixon in 1968 because they were exceedingly disturbed over the police riot at the 1968 Democratic Convention, which they watched on television, and other "excesses" of the left. They believed that Nixon could heal America's wounds by ending divisiveness and terminating the Asian war. Nixon became a minority president when, in the three-way election, he received 43.4 percent of the vote over Vice President Hubert Humphrey's 43.3 percent and Alabama Governor George Wallace's 13.5 percent.

It is ironic that, in 1968, Nixon was the candidate of national unity. His political career had been among the most controversial of any major American politician. Born and raised in a lower middle-class California environment, Nixon, elected to the House of Representatives in 1948, catapulted to national fame in 1949 when he uncovered evidence that led to the conviction of Alger Hiss, a department of state official accused of spying for the Russians. Thereafter, his career was stormy, but he survived. In 1952, for instance, as Eisenhower's running mate, Nixon was almost dumped from the national ticket when a newspaper revealed that a group of businessmen had given him a fund to supplement his senator's income. Only a last-minute national appeal to the American people on live television convinced Eisenhower that dropping him would be a greater liability than keeping him on the ticket. In 1960, he narrowly lost the election for president to John F. Kennedy. Nixon's political survival while out of office in the 1960s, and his winning the Republican nomination in 1968, was one of the greatest political achievements in the history of the United States. In 1962, he was defeated for governor of California and retired from politics in a farewell speech that attacked the press. After moving to New York, he worked within the Republican party constructing new alliances and a grateful following. Thus, in 1968, Richard Nixon was resurrected as the unifying symbol in American life.

Once in office, he seemed no more able to unify the nation than had been his predecessor. Despite his campaign hints of a secret plan to end the war in Vietnam, American involvement continued, although with reduced involvement of American troops. He escalated mass bombing of North Vietnam and Cambodia but at the same time put greater emphasis on negotiating a truce in Paris conferences. As with Kennedy and Johnson, during his last years in office, foreign policy occupied Nixon's time.

On the domestic front, Nixon sought to dismantle some of the Great Society programs, decentralize federal power, and give freer reign to American corporations. He called this the New Federalism, and instituted revenue sharing, a program of returning money to states, counties, and municipalities with limited restrictions on its use. If those units wished to maintain local poverty programs, they could do so through revenue-sharing funds, or they could apply the money for other uses. At the same time, Nixon found that he was severely hampered in getting federal agencies to weaken regulation of business and loosen health, welfare, and safety standards. The bureaucracy, built up over 36 years of New Deal tradition and believing in what had become the traditional minimum parameters of government involvement in business and society, resisted the presidents abrogation of federal authority. Nixon's counter move, ironically, was to follow the means used by the New Deal, the Fair Deal, and the Great Society: to increase further the power of the executive within government. But whereas his predecessors had increased executive power broadly, Nixon increased the power of the White House in relation to other executive departments and agencies.

While Nixon wished to weaken federal control in many areas of the economy and society, as in business regulation and civil rights, at the same time he sanctioned and encouraged Justice Department and FBI efforts to suppress dissent. When four young people were killed by the National Guard at Kent State University in May 1970, during a protest over the sending of United States troops into Cambodia, the administration defended the necessity of protecting society against anarchy. The president used his office and administration, especially Vice President Spiro Agnew, to sow fears among middle and working-class Americans that society was on the brink of chaos. A good part of the disruption, however, would later be traced back to government agents who provoked or served as catalysts for violence.

In 1972, Senator George McGovern of South Dakota won the Democratic presidential nomination in opposition to the established party leaders. His campaign was one of protest against American policy in Southeast Asia, and he rallied blacks, the poor, and antiwar protesters behind him. This crusade of the young and poor, however, was a minority movement that lost whatever popular appeal it might have had when the Democratic vice-presidential candidate, Senator Thomas Eagleton of Missouri, was forced off the ticket following the revelation that he had received electric shock treatments for depression. McGovern appeared indecisive.

At the same time, Nixon seemed to remove from the political arena many of the issues that had so divided the nation in his first three years in office. Inflation was ended as a political issue when, in 1971, Nixon, in a reversal of policy, imposed price and wage controls. The war as an issue had lost much of its popular impact because of the withdrawal of American combat troops and Secretary of State Henry Kissinger's announcement that peace negotiations would be completed by the end of the year. Blacks had not significantly supported any Republican presidential candidate since Hoover, so Nixon's indifference on civil rights lost no votes. On the other hand, Nixon's opposition to busing to achieve integration, and his civil-rights position and nomination and appointment of Southerners to office enabled him to pick up great support in the South. Thus, in 1972, Nixon achieved a resounding electoral victory at the national level: he swept every state except Massachusetts and the District of Columbia, and his 60.8 percent of the popular vote was second only to Lyndon Johnson's 1964 total.

And then the Nixon administration collapsed. In the spring of 1974, Vice President Spiro Agnew was forced to resign from office just before he pleaded no defense to felony charges of tax evasion. By the time of Agnew's resignation, the office of the presidency itself was under fire. During the 1972 campaign, a group of men had been arrested after burglarizing Democratic National Headquarters at the Watergate housing and office complex in Washington. McGovern had been unable to make the break-in a campaign issue, but after Nixon's second inauguration and the trial of the burglars, the story slowly began to unfold. It involved more than the burglary.

What became known as the Watergate affair involved use of executive office officials to disrupt George McGovern's campaign and the secret and illegal contributions by large corporations to the president's reelection committee. Finally the "cover up" of the crimes committed became a major activity of the Nixon White House. Further revelations followed: Nixon used federal funds to develop his estates in California and Florida; he back dated a donation of his official papers to the National Archives to obtain illegal tax deductions. And then, in 1973, a Senate investigation of Watergate and its implications revealed that Nixon had tape-recorded conversations in his office and that the tapes would provide the answer as to the culpability of the president.

A number of times Nixon claimed to have honestly told all the facts, only to later contradict himself as investigators learned more about White House involvement. The Senate investigation was hampered by the president's claim that he was protecting the confidentiality of the office of the presidency by not releasing the tapes. Nixon himself released transcripts of a select group of tapes. When the president's transcripts were compared with transcripts made by the Senate committee staff after the committee and the special prosecutor had defeated the president's claims in court, it seemed that Nixon himself was a leader in the cover-up.

With the growing support of many people who had elected Nixon (including the Traces and Harts), Congress, in 1974, for the first time in a century moved toward the impeachment of a president. The issue was neither corruption in office nor the criminal acts of the president. Instead, the real issue centered on abuse of presidential power. The area of investigation by the House impeachment committee went beyond Watergate and focused on Nixon's misuse of federal investigatory powers in using White House aides as a personal police force, in misusing executive privilege to cover up crimes, and in failing to faithfully execute the laws by "impounding" properly appropriated funds. The House Judiciary Committee worked carefully to prevent the issue from becoming a partisan one, and the committee voted to send three articles of impeachment to the House floor. Further revelations about the tapes and confessions by White House aides seemed to make impeachment and removal certain. On August 8, 1974, Richard Nixon became the first president of the United States to resign.

The Bassanos were angered, and many others were saddened by Nixon's humiliating departure, but they shared the hope of millions that Gerald Ford, thrust into the presidency after serving as vice president, would restore the nation's equanimity. Ford encountered immediate difficulties. He was soundly criticized for the quick pardon he extended to Nixon. More importantly, Ford continued Nixon's approach to government, sharing as he did Nixon's distrust of bureaucracy and federal social programs. The new president gave most of his attention to foreign affairs while supporting revenue sharing and dismantling or weakening federal social legislation. Simultaneous inflation and recession proved the most difficult domestic challenge. The administration concentrated on holding down inflation even though this was accomplished only by allowing unemployment to climb to above 9 percent at its peak in the spring of 1975, the highest level since 1940. Those who had never shared in the prosperity of the 1950s and the 1960s paid the heaviest price. Unemployment among blacks was double the white rate and for black teenagers it soared to more than 40 percent. Although recession seemed to be cured by 1976, the unemployment rate remained high, affecting even white-collar workers. As the primary elections approached in the spring of 1976, Ford's record generated little enthusiasm.

At least through the primaries and the nominating conventions, the presidential campaign of 1976 illustrated in amazing detail the uncertainties and ambiguities that transfixed America in the aftermath of Vietnam and Watergate. Gerald Ford, president by accident of fate and his predecessor's arrogance, at first seemed unbeatable for the Republican nomination. But after defeating challenger Ronald Reagan, bearer of conservative hopes in several early presidential primaries, Ford stumbled. Reagan's personal appeal and the support of conservative legions in the South and West permitted Reagan to go to the Republican convention in Kansas City in mid-August less than 100 votes behind. Ford won, but the bitterness of the struggle reopened old wounds between conservatives and moderates, and between the "Eastern Establishment" and the South-West coalition.

In contrast, the Democratic nomination, against all political logic, went almost by default to a comparative newcomer to national politics, Jimmy Carter, former governor of Georgia. Mounting a campaign reminiscent of both JFK and FDR's political artistry, Carter came from almost nowhere to knock out his chief rivals in primary contests across the country. By the time the Democrats convened in New York in July, 1976, Carter had the nomination locked up. Most impressively, Jimmy Carter, peanut farmer, evangelist, and *Southerner,* had grabbed the nomination without the compromises and commitments to entrenched interests—labor, the Southern wing, blacks, and so forth—which are usually demanded. Carter thus could avoid the explicit promises to one constituency that would alienate others.

As the election itself approached, the strengths and defects of Gerald Ford and Jimmy Carter mirrored the bafflement and apathy abroad in the country. Ford had the majesty of the presidency behind him. Carter was clearly the more articulate and skillful at using the communications media. Both inveighed against "big government," waste, and corruption, and each identified himself with truth, goodness, and honor. Carter won the White House with a very small majority. He captured 297 electoral votes to Ford's 240 (one Washington State elector voted for Reagan). Carter beat Ford by 1.7 million votes out of 80 million cast. The old Democratic coalition of labor, blacks, and ethnics held together probably for the last time.

As president, Jimmy Carter remained an outsider. He distrusted the art of politics and failed to establish an effective working relationship with a Congress led by his own party. More importantly, he seemed to abandon or change policy proposals at the first sign of political opposition. At the same time, he never developed rapport with the American people. A poor public speaker, he appeared reserved and uncomfortable before large groups or on television. As a candidate, he had offered leadership; as president, that seemed to be his greatest weakness.

President Carter's domestic accomplishments were modest. He created new cabinet-level departments of Energy and Education and streamlined aspects of the civil service, but he never followed through on his promise to reorganize the federal government. He began halting steps toward an energy policy, but the government never adopted a comprehensive plan. The administration decontrolled domestic oil, created the Synthetic Fuels Corporation, provided for stockpiling oil, and made grants available to the poor and elderly to subsidize fuel purchases in the winters of 1979–80 and 1980–81. Yet after these steps, the nation was no closer to having an energy plan. Similarly, the administration responded to the threatened collapse of the Chrysler Corporation by developing and lobbying in Congress for a fed-

eral guarantee of $1.5 billion in loans to the automobile manufacturer. Yet the government offered no comprehensive plan for revitalizing American industry. Meanwhile, unemployment remained high—around 6 percent in 1978 and 1979, climbing to 7.5 percent in 1980. And, in 1979 and 1980, the nation experienced double-digit inflation. For the first time since World War I, the consumer price index rose more than 10 percent in two consecutive years. As the automobile industry had symbolized the health of the economy in much of the post–World War II United States, in the 1970s it reflected the nation's economic decline. Imported automobiles became the symbols of economy and quality, while the automobile industry and its suppliers—steel, paint, glass, and tool and die makers—all teetered on the edge of collapse. The administration, however, had no solutions.

Nothing rankled more, however, than the issue of the Iranian hostages. First, the revolution in Iran destroyed the lynch pin of American policy in the Persian Gulf, which had been based on close ties with the Shah of Iran. Then the seizure of the Teheran embassy on November 4, 1979, and the imprisonment of Americans there seemed to paralyze American power. For 444 days, newspapers, radio, and television counted the days of captivity. To many Americans, perhaps a majority, it seemed that America itself was held captive by events beyond its control in Teheran. Americans responded with flag waving and other expressions of patriotism; some groups called for an invasion of Iran while mobs attacked Iranians in Houston and other American cities. The abortive, ill-conceived attempt to free the hostages on April 25, 1980, in which eight Americans were killed, fueled American frustration. Then in its last hours, the Carter administration won agreement to free the hostages. Even this victory turned sour for Carter as the Iranians timed the captives' release to occur minutes after the new president, Ronald Reagan, took office.

The American people, believing Carter to be an uninspiring leader, rejected his reelection bid in 1980—only the second time in this century that an elected president, has lost his bid to remain in office. To a great extent, Carter's inexperience proved disastrous. He identified a host of major issues at the onset of his presidency—inflation, unemployment, government reform, energy, social welfare, education, minority and women's rights, and the environment—but failed to provide solutions, to get congressional approval, and, in some cases, to coalesce widespread support behind him. Moreover, the administration reversed itself on policy so often that it further depleted its political power and credibility with Congress.

The 1980 presidential campaign was lackluster. Ronald Reagan, former two-time governor of California and once Hollywood B-player, was the Republican standard-bearer. Drawing on his experience as governor and on his long-time career in public relations for the General Electric Company, Reagan was an articulate spokesman for traditional Republican conservatism. Handsome and appearing younger than his 69 years,

John Thoeming/Dorsey Press

Teddy Kennedy Campaigning in Homewood, Illinois, in March 1980

Reagan easily defeated a pack of younger Republican challengers who had sensed Carter's vulnerability as a candidate. Reagan chose one of his rivals, George Bush of Texas, as his running mate. Another challenger, Congressman John Anderson of Illinois, withdrew from the Republican primaries and ran as an independent presidential candidate, hoping to attract disaffected Democrats unwilling to support the more conservative Reagan. Carter and Vice President Walter Mondale won renomination after defeating a late surge by Massachusetts Senator Ted Kennedy. Although Kennedy carried primaries in a number of major, populous states, he could not overcome Carter's early lead. In the campaign, Reagan attacked Carter as a weak and vacillating leader who had left the economy in shambles and destroyed American prestige and influence abroad. Although the polls indicated a close election, neither candidate appeared to stimulate broad voter interest. The turnout of 54 percent of the eligible voters (86 million) was the lowest percentage since the 1948 presidential election.

Reagan, however, swept the election, and the magnitude of his victory exceeded the predictions of political commentators and pollsters. Reagan captured nearly 44 million votes or 50.8 percent of the total. Carter trailed far behind with 35 million votes (41 percent) while Anderson, with 5.7 million votes (6.6 percent), never seriously threatened to throw the election into the House of Representatives. Carter carried only six states plus the District of Columbia, and he lost to Reagan in the electoral college by 489 to 49 votes. Never had a sitting president received so few electoral votes, and only Hoover in 1932 had won a lower proportion of the popular vote. Equally important, the Republicans captured the Senate for the first time since 1952. The Senate Democrats, who had controlled 58 seats in the 96th Congress, became the minority party as the Republicans

swept 12 seats for a majority of 53 to 46 (with one independent) in the 1981–83 Senate. Such long-term liberal Democrats as George McGovern (South Dakota), Frank Church (Idaho), Warren Magnuson (Washington), and Birch Bayh (Indiana) lost their seats to conservative Republican challengers. Combined with the defeat or retirement of other liberal senators, the political complexion of the Senate shifted radically as the conservative wing of the Republican party took control. The Democrats retained a significantly reduced majority in the House of Representatives. Sensitive to the mood of the electorate as expressed in the November election, the House would not be an obstacle to Reagan's domestic policy, which focused on the budget process.

More than anything, economic problems dominated American concerns. The economic uncertainty of the 1970s buried the social concerns of the 1960s. Stagflation—the simultaneous presence of high inflation and declining industrial productivity accompanied by 7 percent or higher unemployment—became the major domestic problem. Economists placed most of the blame for the onset of inflation on President Lyndon Johnson's "guns and butter" policy, the expansion of both social and military spending in the late 1960s. Then, in the 1970s, the steady rise of oil prices set by the Organization of Petroleum Exporting Countries (OPEC) continually pushed costs higher in nearly every domestic industry since petroleum products were a basic ingredient not only of fuel but also of fertilizer, plastics, and hundreds of other basic commodities. The expansion of the supply of money, high interest rates, and ever-increasing prices and wages trying to catch up with cost increases all seemed to lock the United States (and other countries) into a seemingly irreversible inflationary spiral.

A stagnant economy, however, accompanied inflation. Unemployment remained at record high levels. More importantly, American productivity—the amount of goods and services produced per hour of work—declined. From World War II through the mid-1960s, productivity had increased more than 3 percent annually. Indeed, from 1960 through 1965, it rose 3.6 percent per year. But from 1966 to 1970, the increase fell to 1.5 percent annually and, from 1971 to 1975, to 1.4 percent. During Carter's presidency, it barely increased at all, averaging 0.2 percent per year, and when he left office, productivity was declining. In contrast, productivity increases in Japan hovered around the 10 percent level.

American businesspeople blamed the government for the declining productivity. Government regulations, they argued, cost billions of dollars. Safety rules, health regulations, environmental standards, and assorted government programs added tens of billions of dollars in nonproductive spending for such things as pollution controls and clerks to fill out government forms. Moreover, they claimed, government programs made it impossible for industry to raise the capital to modernize its plants and increase productivity. The high level of government spending required high rates of taxation, thus diminishing the money available for industrial investment. Moreover, government borrowing to cover large deficits competed with private industry's needs for capital. Business could not find enough money to borrow or, when it was available, found the interest rates too high to make investment profitable. Finally, business leaders claimed, government social programs removed the incentive of private individuals to save. Since the government provided security for people, they no longer had to save much money in comparison with people in other countries. But savings were the source of capital for investment. The answer: government had to encourage savings and investment in

order to increase productivity and spur economic growth. Savings were to be increased at the expense of consumption—people would consume relatively less of their income and thus save more. Thus, the revitalization of the economy would both increase productivity and reduce inflation by reducing the growth in personal consumption. And this could be done, argued a group of economists, through economic expansion stimulated by a reduction in government spending. Since the private sector would compensate for the reduction in government programs, the approach was painless in the long run. The theory behind this policy was called supply-side economics.

The result, under President Reagan in 1981, was a dramatic shift in government economic policy. Ever since the New Deal, government economic policy had focused on encouraging economic growth by supporting consumption—if people had more money, they would buy more things and industry would expand. The Reagan administration now reversed that policy. Under Reagan's budget director, former Michigan Congressman David Stockman, the administration moved quickly in 1981 to deemphasize consumption and institute supply-side economics. The federal government would slash domestic programs. A reduced federal budget would make more money available to business. By cutting taxes at the same time, especially for those in upper-income brackets, savings rather than consumption would increase. Plentiful savings would allow corporations to revitalize their plants and thus increase productivity. Increased productivity would lead to increased sales, since American industry could then successfully compete with foreign imports, as in the case of Japanese automobiles and electronic equipment. Increased sales would mean greater employment. With efficiency and sales increased, stagflation would end.

In his first year in office, Reagan concentrated on instituting supply-side economic policies. With his sweeping electoral victory in November 1980, with his solidly conservative Republican Senate, and with strong public sympathy following his recovery from an assasination attempt in April 1981, Reagan pushed through Congress sweeping budget reductions. To a great extent, Reagan's 1981–82 budget represented the repeal of Lyndon Johnson's Great Society programs. Using the budget, rather than legislative repeal, as a tool, the Reagan administration slashed federal welfare and support programs. Some programs—job training schemes, student aid, railroad subsidies, solar development, health-care subsidies—were caused to end by eventually removing all funding while others were sharply reduced. When the Democratic-led House of Representatives accepted these cuts, as well as the concomitant increase in military spending, Reagan had achieved perhaps the most dramatic shift in federal government policy since the first 100 days of the New Deal under President Franklin Roosevelt.

In many ways, Reagan's domestic and foreign policy represented a return to the Eisenhower policies of the 1950s. What the administration attacked in its extraordinary budget reductions in its first year was the body of social legislation passed during the Johnson years and expanded under Democratic Congresses under Nixon, Ford, and Carter. Like the Eisenhower Republicans, the Reaganites feared that the federal government's economic dominance inhibited initiative in the private sector. Thus, they reduced public non-military spending by more than $50 billion and sought to end or limit government regulation throughout the economy and society, believing that the latter both thwarted economic freedom and made industry less efficient.

While Reagan's supply-side economics were based on untested theory, they offered a plan of action to a nation adrift. Sensing that uncertainty and economic fears were the dominant concerns of Americans in the late 1970s and early 1980s, Reagan moved at once to confront the insecurities about the future. Time and again he quoted Franklin Delano Roosevelt in his speeches and referred to the active role of the New Deal in confronting American anxiety in the 1930s. Though the Reagan administration offered a different set of solutions, it wished to identify with the spirit of the New Deal.

Americans in the late 1970s learned that economic security was not as permanent as previously thought. In the recession of the 70s, Michael Gishman learned that lesson. Similarly, his parents, the elder Bassanos, and the Simiches faced an uneasy retirement because of the ravages of inflation. At the same time, the nation's major cities have retrenched, cutting back services, because of the economic "hard times."

For other families, the fears ran deeper. Environmental and social problems robbed economic security of its benefits. Smog enveloped cities and even small towns; oil spills marred vacation beaches. Crime and racial strife in the nation's largest cities increased the psychological costs of urban life while the decline in ready and inexpensive services affected all Americans. With higher education becoming nearly universal and expectations legitimately raised, who wants to pick up the garbage? Thus, for those better off, the progress of many workers has meant a decline in services.

Finally, there remains the larger question of the meaning of life in American society. Once earning and securing a living was so important that it overrode all other considerations. Indeed, work and identity were inseparable. For most Americans, with the 40-hour workweek universal and with the work task detached from a creative experience, work is no longer sufficient to provide a meaningful identity. Instead, workers seek escape from the monotony of industrial or bureaucratic work. The women's movement also brought discussion of sex roles. At the same time, more and more Americans wish to go beyond life in economic terms. The rise in spirituality—from interest in Eastern mysticism to attendance in churches and synagogues—became a characteristic of the 1960s and 1970s.

The United States in the 1980s was moving in uncharted directions. The confidence of the post–World War II period diminished, and in the process, the fears and anxieties led to questions not asked for generations.

SUGGESTIONS FOR FURTHER READING

Most helpful for this chapter were John Brooks, *The Great Leap* (1966); William Chafe, *The American Woman* (1972); Betty Friedan, *The Feminine Mystique* (1963); John K. Galbraith, *The New Industrial State* (1971); Eric Goldman, *Crucial Decade—And After* (1960); Alonzo L. Hamby, *Beyond the New Deal: Harry S. Truman and American Liberalism* (1973); Michael Harrington, *The Other America: Poverty in the United States* (1962); Anthony Lewis, *Portrait of a Decade* (1964); William L. O'Neill, *Coming Apart* (1973); Herbert Parmet, *Eisenhower and the American Crusades* (1972); Robert Donovan, *Conflict and Crisis: The Presidency of Harry S. Truman, 1945–1948* (1977); Theodore Sorenson, *Kennedy* (1965); and Garry Wills, *Nixon Agonistes* (1970). Also see Joseph C. Goulden, *The Best Years, 1945–1950* (1976); Geoffrey Perret, *A Dream of Greatness: The American People, 1945–1963* (1979); Howard Zinn, *Postwar America, 1945–1971* (1973); William Leuchtenburg, *A Troubled Feast* (1973); Douglas T. Miller and Marion Nowak, *The Fifties: The Way We Really Were* (1977); and Milton Viorst, *Fire in the Streets: America in the 1960s* (1980).

Biographies and memoirs include Robert H. Ferrell, ed., *Off the Record: The Private Papers of Harry S. Truman* (1980); Harry S. Truman, *Memoirs* (2 vols., 1956); Merle Miller, *Plain Speaking* (1971); James T. Patterson, *Mr. Republican: A Biography of Robert A. Taft* (1972); James F. Byrnes, *Speaking Frankly* (1947); John M. Blum, ed., *The Price of Vision: The Diary of Henry A. Wallace* (1973); Richard Rovere, *Senator Joe McCarthy* (1959); Whittaker Chambers, *Witness!* (1952); Alger Hiss, *In the Court of Public Opinion* (1957); B. J. Widick, *The UAW and Walter Reuther* (1949); Joseph Goulden, *Meany* (1970); Charles Madison, *American Labor Leaders* (1950); Alan Schaffer, *Vito Marcantonio* (1966); Norman D. Markowitz, *The Rise and Fall of the People's Century: Henry A. Wallace and American Liberalism* (1973); Peter Lyon, *Eisenhower: Portrait of a Hero* (1974); Jervis Anderson, *A. Philip Randolph* (1973); Carl T. Rowan [with Jackie Robinson], *Wait Till Next Year* (1960); Townsend Hoopes, *The Devil and John Foster Dulles* (1973); John B. Martin, *Adlai Stevenson* (1977); Patrick Anderson, *The President's Men* (1969); James M. Burns, *Kennedy* (1960); Bruce Miroff, *The Presidential Politics of John F. Kennedy* (1976); Tom Wicker, *JFK and LBJ: The Influence of Personality Upon Politics* (1968); Eric Goldman, *The Tragedy of Lyndon Johnson* (1969); Doris Kearns, *Lyndon Johnson and the American Dream* (1976); Merle Miller, *Lyndon* (1978); Ronald Steel, *Walter Lippmann and the American Century* (1981); Barry Goldwater, *Conscience of a Conservative* (1960); Arthur Schlesinger, Jr., *Robert Kennedy* (1977); Eugene McCarthy, *The Year of the People* (1969); Marshall Frady, *Wallace* (1969); Martin Luther King, Jr., *Why We Can't Wait* (1964); David Lewis, *King* (1970); Alex Haley, ed., *The Autobiography of Malcolm X* (1964); Eldridge Cleaver, *Soul on Ice* (1968); Richard Nixon, *Memoirs* (1978); Henry Kissinger, *White House Years* (1979); Bruce Mazlish, *In Search of Nixon* (1972); the memoirs and *mea culpas* by Charles Colson, H. R. Haldeman, Jeb Magruder, John Dean, Leon Jaworski, John Sirica, and other Watergate luminaries; Jimmy Carter, *Why Not the Best?* (1976); James Wooten, *Dasher* (1978); and Bob Woodward and Scott Armstrong, *The Brethren: Inside the Supreme Court* (1979).

Topics in the domestic history of the United

States, 1945–1981, are covered in Fred J. Cook, *The Warfare State* (1962); Harold G. Vatter, *The U.S. Economy in the 1950s* (1963); Barton Bernstein, ed., *Politics and Policies of the Truman Administration* (1970); Allen Matusow, *Farm Policies and Politics in the Truman Years* (1967); Richard O. Davies, *Housing Reform During the Truman Administration* (1966); Donald R. McCoy and Richard T. Ruetten, *Quest and Response: Minority Rights and the Truman Administration* (1973); Alton Lee, *Truman and Taft-Hartley* (1966); Maeva Marcus, *The Steel Seizure Case* (1978); William Berman, *The Politics of Civil Rights in the Truman Administration* (1970); Richard M. Freeland, *The Truman Doctrine and the Origins of McCarthyism* (1972); Richard J. Walton, *Henry Wallace, Harry Truman, and the Cold War* (1976); Mary Sperling McAuliffe, *Crisis on the Left* (1978); David Caute, *The Great Fear: The Anti-Communist Purge Under Truman and Eisenhower* (1978); Athan Theoharis, *Seeds of Repression: Harry S. Truman and the Origins of McCarthyism* (1970); Seymour Martin Lipset and Earl Raab, *The Politics of Unreason* (1970); Richard M. Fried, *Men Against McCarthy* (1976); Robert Griffin's study of the Senate and McCarthy, *The Politics of Fear* (1970); Alistair Cooke, *A Generation on Trial* (1950); Allen Weinstein, *Perjury: The Hiss-Chambers Case* (1978); William F. Buckley, *The Committee and its Critics* (1962); Stefan Kanfer, *A Journal of the Plague Years* (1973); and Victor Navatsky, *Naming Names* (1981). See also Arthur Schlesinger, Jr., *The Vital Center* (1949); Norman H. Nie, et al., *The Changing American Voter* (1976); Jack Bass and Walter DeVries, *The Transformation of Southern Politics* (1976); Clifton Brock, *Americans for Democratic Action* (1962); Robert Engler, *The Politics of Oil* (1962); Louis Harris, *Is There a Republican Majority?* (1954); Samuel Lubell, *Revolt of the Moderates* (1956); Emmet Hughes, *The Ordeal of Power* [an inside history of the Eisenhower presidency] (1963); I. F. Stone, *The Haunted Fifties* (1963); David Frior, *Conflict of Interest in the Eisenhower Administration* (1970); Aaron Wildavsky, *Dixon-Yates* (1962); Daisy Bates, *Long Shadow of Little Rock* (1962); August Meier and Elliott Rudwick, *Core: A Study in the Civil Rights Movement, 1942–1968*

(1973); Steven F. Lawson, *Black Ballots: Voting Rights in the South, 1944–1969* (1976); Numan V. Bartley, *The Rise of Massive Resistance: Race and Politics in the South During the 1950s* (1969); Lino S. Graglia, *Disaster by Decree: The Supreme Court Decisions on Race and the Schools* (1976); and the superb work, Richard Kluger, *Simple Justice: The History of Brown v. Board of Education* (1976). The mood of the fifties is treated in Daniel Bell, *The End of Ideology* (1960); Richard Hofstadter, *Anti-Intellectualism in American Life* (1963); Walter Gellhorn, *Security, Loyalty and Science* (1950); Michael Rouzé, *Robert Oppenheimer* (1965); James L. Clayton, ed., *The Economic Impact of the Cold War* (1970); and Theodore Caplow and Reece McGee, *The Academic Marketplace* (1958).

James Sundquist, *Politics and Policy: The Eisenhower, Kennedy and Johnson Years* (1968) is quite helpful. See also Arthur Schlesinger, Jr., *A Thousand Days* (1965); Jim F. Heath, *Decade of Disillusionment: The Kennedy-Johnson Years* (1975); the critical views by Carl Brauer, *John F. Kennedy and the Second Reconstruction* (1969), and by Victor Navasky, *Kennedy Justice* (1971); Gerald T. Dunne, *Hugo Black and the Judicial Revolution* (1977); Richard Hofstadter, *The Paranoid Style in American Politics* (1967); James Peck, *Freedom Ride* (1962); Howard Zinn, *SNCC: The New Abolitionists* (1965); James Forman, *The Making of Black Revolutionaries* (1972); and Burke Marshall, *Federalism and Civil Rights* (1964). Of the vast literature on the JFK assassination, see the descriptive treatment by William Manchester, *The Death of a President* (1967); Bradley Greenburg and Edwin B. Parker, *The Kennedy Assassination and the American Public* (1965); and Peter D. Scott, et al., *The Assassinations: Dallas and Beyond* (1976). Other useful studies of the period are Robert Sherrill, *The Accidental President* (1967); Peter Joseph, *Good Times: An Oral History of America in the Nineteen Sixties* (1974); George E. Reedy, *The Twilight of the Presidency* (1970); Theodore H. White, *The Making of the President, 1964* (1964); Sar A. Levitan and Robert Taggart, *The Promise of Greatness* (1976); Theodore R. Marmer, *The Politics of Medicare* (1972); and Abba Schwartz's biased but interesting account of immigration "reform," *The Open Society* (1968).

Changing values and protest are discussed in Joseph Kett, *Rites of Passage* (1965); Kenneth Keniston, *The Uncommitted* (1965); Theodore Roszak's already mentioned *The Making of a Counter Culture* (1969); Robert Hunter, *The Storming of the Mind* (1972); William Braden, *The Age of Aquarius* (1970); Morris Dickstein, *Gates of Eden* (1977); Charles Reich, *The Greening of America* (1970); Jack Newfield, *Bread and Roses Too* (1971); I. F. Stone, *The Killings at Kent State* (1970); Raymond Mungo, *Famous Long Ago* (1970); and Philip Slater, *The Pursuit of Loneliness* (1970). Other themes are treated in Robin Morgan, ed., *Sisterhood is Powerful* (1970); Sara Evans, *Personal Politics* [an oral history of the beginnings of the women's movement] (1979); Barbara Deckard, *The Women's Movement* (1975); Betty Gorburg, *The Changing Family* (1973); Daniel Yankelovich, *The New Morality* (1974); Peter Clecack, *Radical Paradoxes: Dilemmas of the American Left, 1945–1970* (1973); Peter Schrag, *The Decline of the Wasp* (1976); Barry Commoner, *The Closing Circle* (1971); Paul Sheperd and Daniel McKinley, eds., *The Subversive Sci-* ence [describing the ecology movement] (1969); and Paul Ehrlich, *Zero Population Growth* (1970).

The Nixon-Ford-Carter years are treated in the following: Theodore H. White, *The Making of the President 1968* (1969) and also his subsequent, though less interesting, volumes; Richard Scammon and Benjamin Wattenberg, *The Real Majority* (1970); Rowland Evans and Robert Novak, *Nixon in the White House* (1971); William Safire, *Before the Fall* (1975); Daniel Moynihan, *The Politics of a Guaranteed Income* (1973); Arthur S. Miller, *The Modern Corporate State: Private Governments and the American Constitution* (1976); Stanley Aronwitz, *False Promises: The Shaping of American Working Class Consciousness* (1974); J. Anthony Lukas, *Nightmare: The Underside of the Nixon Years* (1976); Theodore H. White, *Breach of Faith: The Fall of Richard Nixon* (1975); Robert Woodward and Carl Bernstein, *All the President's Men* (1974); Richard M. Cohen and Jules Witcover, *A Heartbeat Away: The Investigation and Resignation of Vice-President Spiro T. Agnew* (1974); Jules Witcover, *Marathon: The Pursuit of the Presidency, 1972–1976* (1977); and Leonard and Mark Silk, *The American Establishment* (1980).

12 | It's a Small World, After All

VISIONS AND REALITIES OF PEACE

A few weeks before VJ Day, bookstores began to display *An Intelligent American's Guide to the Peace.* Oversized, bound in bright orange and blue, bearing the name of former Under Secretary of State Sumner Welles as editor, the volume qualified as a "coffee-table book." Inside were essays on 80-odd countries and a powerful argument in favor of the infant United Nations as champion of lasting peace. Along with hopeful observations about Russia's evolution toward democracy and China's bright future, Welles insisted the American people must "learn to know the truth" about the world and "determine their course in that light." It was "a lamentable fact" that "to the vast majority of the people of the United States the whole problem of foreign relations has been something infinitely remote, . . . something shrouded in mystery." If, as in the past, the intelligent American left foreign affairs "to a handful of men," he would be abdicating his responsibilities for "the lives of the youth, . . . the standard of living, the economic opportunity, and the happiness of every one of us." Few people (Robert Butler was one) bought the book.

Sergeant Austin Hart, Machinist's Mate Mike Simich, Staff Sergeant Jerry Trace, and Lieutenant John O'Reilly, none of whom read this book or heard of Sumner Welles, held different views. They hardly could wait to abandon the world—at least those portions to which the war had introduced them—and go home. They believed that America had taught the forces of organized evil a lesson. Other international bullies surely would be deterred by this example and America's awesome atomic weapons.

In a few short months after Japan's surrender, the U.S. military machine was disman-

420

tled. There was simply no resisting the outcry to "bring the boys home." The plans for gradual demobilization and the program for cushioning the economic shock of industrial reconversion had to be scrapped. Morale in the armed forces deteriorated—to the point of mutiny in a few cases—when transportation bottlenecks and the rotation system kept large numbers in uniform through autumn 1945. Impatient wives and anxious mothers bombarded their congressmen with pleas and threats about the next election. Jerry Trace, who returned to Evansville in May 1946, was among the last wartime inductees to be discharged. By 1947, the American army was reduced to 1.5 million men, mainly fuzzy-cheeked boys who had never known combat.

Well before the GIs shed khaki for serge and denim, Americans were in hot pursuit of the blessings of peace—good jobs, cars, refrigerators, new homes—which a decade of depression and four years of war had denied them. They were too busy to heed President Harry S. Truman's prophetic admonition in a Navy Day speech, October 12, 1945, that it was "as important to wage peace as to wage war," even had they understood what he was talking about. Of course, the *Midland News, Evansville Press* and *San Francisco Chronicle* described collapses of governments and outbreaks of violence in Europe and Asia. Radio station WOR in New York, to which Charlotte Bassano listened, carried Edward R. Murrow's commentaries on the tragedy of war babies in Austria who were forced to rummage through garbage cans and on the growing strength of communist parties in Italy and France. Moviegoers sat through a March of Time "short" about Winston Churchill's speech at Fulton, Missouri, in which he charged Russia with lowering an "iron curtain" between its domain and the West. Newspapers, radio, and newsreels also reminded the public of America's atomic monopoly and its industrial superiority and

"remarkable" energy supplies (a third of the world's coal production, 70 percent of its oil).

While the diplomats worked out the details of the United Nations charter, public-opinion polls registered great popular enthusiasm and optimism about the future of the organization. But even before the ceremonies that inaugurated the UN in June 1945, the cooperative spirit had waned. The United States and the Soviet Union clashed over various issues, and the UN proved incapable of settling their disputes. After driving Hitler's armies from Eastern Europe, the Russians, fearing a revival of German power and suspicious of Western aims, used local Communists in Rumania, Bulgaria, Poland, Hungary, and Czechoslovakia, and the threat of the Red Army, to organize these countries as Soviet satellites. Although the United States objected that the new governments were not "democratic" (as the Soviet Union had promised in the Yalta "Declaration on Liberated Peoples") and protested the West's exclusion from political and economic decisions about Eastern Europe, the USSR went its own way. The UN also proved powerless in conflicts over Korea, Iran, Trieste, Greece, and such issues as reparations, and the Soviet obstruction of the United Nations Relief and Rehabilitation Administration (UNRRA). Disillusion occurred slowly as the many problems of the times slipped out of UN control and became subjects of bloc contention.

Americans demonstrated their preference for unilateral action by killing a UN resolution that called for world full employment and by shunting aside a proposal to create a UN army. That American officials considered the UN bankrupt was reflected in the handling of a proposal to internationalize the production of atomic materials. Although the United States enjoyed an atomic monopoly, the A-bombs of those years were too few and too puny to totally deter the Soviet Union. Thoughtful voices urged adoption of a system for the international control of atomic weapons. In March 1946, President Truman announced American was prepared to turn over its atomic secrets to a UN Atomic Energy Authority and to destroy its stockpile of atomic weapons. The UN could then oversee application of this terrible weapon to peaceful, beneficial purposes: radioactive isotopes would transform medicine; controlled explosions would dig canals and tear down mountains; and virtually unlimited quantities of power, at negligible cost, someday would revolutionize the world's standard of living. But the United States demanded that the UN would monitor all stages of atomic production through an elaborate program of on-the-spot inspections. The Soviet Union refused to accept this scheme on the grounds that UN supervision violated national sovereignty and represented blatant U.S. espionage. Russia's spokesmen at the UN insisted the Americans destroy all their atomic weapons *before* negotiations on international control. This impasse was unbreakable.

Disillusionment gradually replaced the hopes American leaders had placed in such mechanisms as the International Bank for Reconstruction and Development (IBRD) and the International Monetary Fund (IMF). At war's end, the "experts" were convinced that the nations of Europe and Asia would require about two years to rebuild their war-shattered economies. During this period, some countries would need direct aid and most would require loans for commodity purchases and economic reconstruction. Following the elimination of barriers to trade and investment, the world would commence an era of unrivaled production and consumption. But months passed and Europe's predicted recovery did not come; instead, there was stagnation, psychological demoralization, and a slide toward political chaos. At meetings of bankers and other "opinion leaders" arranged by the State Department to explain the need for U.S. economic aid (such as the

$3 billion loan to Britain in 1946), Robert Butler listened as officials described how Hitler's Ardennes offensive, the stoppage of lend-lease in summer 1945, and the A-bomb had wrecked the recovery timetable. Butler understood when told of the bureaucratic snarls that had crippled the IBRD and IMF and of the supply bottlenecks that had arisen. He knew the necessity of massive U.S. intervention to shore up foreign economies.

In approving of American aid to Europe and Asia, the Simiches, Traces, and Reinhardts were responding to the plight of starving children, not to appeals for an "open economic world" or "the convertibility of sterling." They all supported UNRRA. All of the families, except Velma Trace and Louis and Lila Gropper, gave money and clothes to CARE, the Jewish Relief Fund, American Relief for Italy, or some other charitable agency, and most took part in the voluntary food conservation campaigns of those years. In autumn 1947, 11-year-old Robbie Bassano was outraged to find the Tuesday meat loaf and Thursday fried chicken replaced by macaroni and cheese and tuna casserole. Charlotte was responding to President Truman's request to observe meatless and poultryless days and to cut down on bread and flour in order to save 100 million bushels of wheat to feed hungry Europeans. Austin Hart labeled such claims "hogwash," saying Harry Truman, himself a farm boy, knew better.

But why did the handouts go on? Why all the fuss about people who, two years after the war, were still sitting around when they could earn money for food or plant their own? The task of making people realize the full implications of America's status as economic superpower seemed hopeless. What could be done when a friend of Jacob Reinhardt, told not to expect delivery of his new John Deere tractor for at least six months because the government had forced John Deere to ship 1,200 machines to Czechoslovakia, angrily wrote Congressman William Denton that American farmers could make far better use of the tractors. In a time of political turmoil, inflation, and growing conservatism, any clash between domestic demand and other nations' needs ended in victory for the American consumer. Every decision the Truman administration made in foreign affairs antagonized powerful interest groups. All that could be done, it seemed, was to search for a "lowest common denominator," a statement of American purposes sufficiently vague and flexible to enlist wholehearted popular support.

The lowest common denominator—in the form of anticommunism—soon found the policymakers who were looking for it. Popular apathy about the crises abroad and the determined pursuit of the better life had been overlaid with increasing hostility toward the Soviet Union. The tradition of reviling "Communism" had long existed, but it now emerged as the bearer of the anxiety and dissatisfaction that afflicted Americans who wished to be left alone but feared the consequences. It appealed to many who cared little about troubles with the Soviet Union over new boundaries for Poland and Rumania, but were moved by hatred of Communists. Their fears and hatreds were reinforced when the Russians erected barricades on the railroads and highways leading to Berlin in 1948, and they cheered at the United States–British feat of dispatching waves of planes (carrying up to 13,000 tons per day) to supply the beleaguered city. They knew that Communism restricted individual choices, especially those which led to the acquisition of personal wealth

U.S. Air Force Photo

C-47s unloading supplies at Tempelhof Airfield in late 1948. After the Russians blockaded land routes to Berlin, the United States airlifted needed supplies to the besieged city

and political views. Beginning in 1947, the Truman administration exploited these feelings. When President Truman proposed to use American power to halt the spread of Communism across Europe, most Americans accepted this mission. They believed that no one would choose Communism on its merits; Europeans (and later Koreans, Cubans, and Vietnamese) were obviously compelled or duped by the Russians. Only the United States could stop this "red tide" and whatever was required to do so should be given.

By late 1947, fewer than one American in five doubted the premise that the Soviet Union was "trying to build herself up as the ruling power in the world." Only one in seven rejected the notion that "Communists would destroy the Christian religion if they could." Expressions of support for stopping the godless Russians reflected little knowledge about what President Truman and the Department of State were doing. Five months earlier, Secretary of State George C. Marshall had invited European governments to devise a plan for their economic recovery. All summer, in well-reported meetings, European leaders worked on a response to this offer. The State Department's position was that without massive U.S. aid via this "Marshall Plan," the European economy would collapse, Communists would find ready recruits, and most of continental Europe would come under Soviet control within a short time. Yet in November 1947, 4 out of ever 10 Americans had never heard of the Marshall Plan, and 40 percent of those who recognized the term did not know enough about it to have an opinion.

Most people agreed with Martha Hart that the world and the intricacies of diplomacy were too complex to understand. They accepted the government's contention that national security prevented full disclosure. Because the president knew secrets they did not, because the best and the brightest became government servants and set policy, because

both political parties agreed on foreign policy, and because what happened "across the water" had little effect upon their daily lives, they accepted the government's position.

People tended to involve themselves only when foreign policy obviously intruded on their livelihood or special prejudices. When Congress approved the Marshall Plan and committed the United States to $13 billion in foreign aid, the policy became important to certain groups. The rutabaga growers of Minnesota saw a chance to dump a bumper crop into the markets of Paris and Baden-Baden. Irish longshoremen in Boston threatened to refuse to load a single ship with Marshall Plan goods unless the government funneled a percentage of Europe-bound produce through New England ports. Openings and closings of air bases, navy yards, and defense plants directly influenced the opinions of their employees (and the people with whom they spent their wages) about the cold war. Still, politicians and diplomats tended to regard the "mass public" as a slumbering beast, potentially destructive if it were aroused.

Certain people did concern themselves with foreign policy and their views mattered. The aims of upper and middle-class activists (variously termed "opinion leaders" and "the policy elite") might be as straightforward as those of military contractors. As with Robert Butler and his friends, concern might stem from economic interests, family tradition, or a belief in their superior knowledge about such matters. Ethnic groups, too, entered the fray. Concerned about the safety of their relatives, the Markoviches and Simiches closely followed postwar events in Yugoslavia. Marshall Tito's victory and establishment of a communist regime produced strong editorials and letters to congressmen and the White House. Serbs, however, unlike Poles, Irish, and Italians, lacked both numbers and strong political organization. When the State Department gave economic aid to Tito in 1949 as a reward for his break with the USSR, protests from Midland and other Serbian communities were ignored.

The U.S. Jewish community had more success in influencing American policy. Dis-

covery of the incredible horrors of Germany's Jewish genocide shocked most Americans. Millions of Jews had been herded to their deaths in gas chambers. Hundreds of thousands more had survived a living death-

Four of the millions of Jews who did not survive the death camps

—some the victims of medical experiments, some starved to skeletons, some deranged from fear and brutality. The United States had done shamefully little before or during the war to rescue Europe's Jews; even with the revelation of Hitler's atrocities, few Americans favored offering the survivors a new life in the United States. Vast numbers remained silent because they were still anti-Semitic. The opposition of organizations such as the American Legion and the rejection by Congress of a more liberal immigration law derived from old prejudices. Nonetheless, the failure to stop the "holocaust" and refusal to take any large number of the survivors produced what might be called a national guilt complex that merged with genuine compassion.

Americans found it difficult to resist the arguments of Zionists—advocates of a home for Jews in the scriptural Holy Land—when they asked the United States to support the establishment of a Jewish homeland in British-mandated Palestine. The pitiful survivors of Hitler's concentration camps sought desperately to leave Europe, but they had no place to go. Zionists and others cited Britain's pledge for a Jewish state in Palestine, and General Eisenhower reported the great majority of Jewish "displaced persons" wished to settle in Palestine. Rose and Betty Miller, who had taken up their mother's Zionist views, worked ardently to win support for the idea of a "Jewish homeland." Henry Gishman was sensitive to the plight of the survivors but indifferent to the establishment of a Jewish state. Lobbying efforts of Jewish groups produced a torrent of letters and telegrams to the White House. As a result, President Truman badgered the British to accept large-scale Jewish immigration.

Britain took the issue to the United Nations, while Jewish refugees attempted to enter Palestine without British approval. Fighting between Jewish and Arab paramilitary groups grew while the UN debated and then approved a partition of the mandate into Jewish and Arab states. When the British withdrew on May 14, 1948, Jewish leaders in Jerusalem proclaimed the creation of the State of Israel. Eleven minutes after receiving the announcement, Truman extended "recognition" to the new nation (beating the Soviet Union by hours). Truman acted against the violent protests of his principal advisers. Middle East experts in the State Department warned repeatedly that support for a Jewish state would irreparably damage U.S.–Arab relations and open this strategic region to communist penetration. Secretary of Defense James Forrestal asserted that studies of America's oil reserves proved that without Arab oil the armed forces could not fight a major war for longer than two years. But Harry S. Truman had to consider other factors. In one stormy session with Secretary Marshall and other top advisers, he exclaimed: "I'm sorry, gentlemen, but I have to answer to hundreds of thousands who are anxious for the success of Zionism. I do not have hundreds of thousands of Arabs among my constituents." The president needed every vote he could get to win the 1948 election, and those states with large Jewish communities were especially important. Moreover, the Democratic party needed—and received—the financial support of wealthy Jews. The Millers and Gishmans rewarded Truman with their votes.

THE POLICY MAZE

By 1945, the Department of State had outgrown the gilded, high-ceilinged rooms it had occupied since the 19th century in the State-War-Navy building next door to the White House. The department gradually moved into a new, boxlike structure in "Foggy Bottom" a few blocks away. So huge and labrynthian was the building that receptionists provided callers with maps. No one seemed to know how many federal employees dealt with America's overseas business. Their numbers included not just those wandering the halls of "New State," but also people in many other federal offices. The Department of State, by the late 1940s, shared responsibility and power with at least a dozen other departments and agencies, some of which, on some issues, enjoyed greater power if not prestige than State.

A common characteristic of the individuals who presided over the sprawling foreign-affairs establishment was the belief that Americans and their elected representatives did not think deeply about foreign affairs and that the "professionals" (both appointed and elected) must be trusted. Secretary of State Dean Acheson privately launched a tirade against Congress as "too damned representative" of the people: "It is just as stupid as the people are; just as uneducated, just as selfish." This elite, however, never questioned the latent power of those whole taxes paid their salaries. Cold war warriors constantly reminded themselves of what the public and a hostile Congress had done to Woodrow Wilson.

Despite periodic agonizing about public opinion, the foreign-affairs elite devoted most attention to Congress. The democratic system required the Senate to ratify treaties and gave the House of Representatives authority to act upon the department's requests for program and operating funds. Both houses possessed extensive powers to investigate the executive agencies. As often as not since World War II, a president from one political party has had to ask a Congress dominated by the other political party for permission and money to carry out his programs in foreign policy. The adversary principle was built into the American system—in the checks of the branches each upon the others and in the scrambling for power of the political parties. Opposition by a

minority and, sometimes, by one distrustful congressman, could stop the movement of a vital program through the legislative mill.

Every postwar president has sought to prevent paralysis and the appearance of internal divisions by urging political leaders to exempt foreign policy from partisan debate. This effort, which received the dignified, if vague, lable "bipartisanship," has not always succeeded. But few have disputed the need to remove foreign affairs from politics. Dean Acheson said: "Bipartisan foreign policy is the ideal for the executive, because you cannot run this damned country under the Constitution any other way except by fixing the whole organization so it doesn't work the way it is supposed to work. Now, the way to do that is to say politics stops at the seaboard—anyone who denies that postulate is a son-of-a-bitch and a crook and not a true patriot. Now, if people will swallow that, then you're off to the races." The president and the men around him could do this because they had—or could claim to have—superior information. Congressmen could claim knowledge equal to or better than "those young smart alecks" in the Interior or Labor Departments about a Missouri dam or the Taft-Hartley Act, but only the president and a few others read all the cables describing Soviet activities; only these men were briefed by the CIA; only they, therefore, could put these bits and pieces of information into perspective.

Though the insiders were confident that they could control public opinion and train the legislative branch to respond on command, another enemy had arisen— themselves contending with each other in the game of bureaucratic politics. Rivalry between the Department of State, those components of Defense, Agriculture, Treasury, and Commerce that dealt with foreign affairs, and the mass of boards and bureaus developed an internal dynamic of its own. Battles royal ranged between second and third-echelon officials in these agencies as they fought to realize personal and organizational interests. The parochialism inherent in a bureaucratic system of fragmented power and hierarchical responsibility led men to ignore, even to sabotage, the needs of other agencies. Thus, action resulted from the pulling and hauling of men who shared power—and power (defined as the ability to influence decisions) extended deep within the government structure.

CONTAINMENT AS RHETORIC AND RELIGION

The melding of assumptions, commitments, and anxieties into what became known as "the containment consensus" took place gradually, filling the vacuum created by erosion of faith in the internationalist credo. The fusion occurred sometime between September 1946 and June 1948. Its catalyst was the idea that "the Communists" were bent on world domination. In March 1947, the Greek civil war between communist guerillas and pro-Western forces led to proclamation of the Truman Doctrine in which the president pledged "to support free peoples who are resisting attempted subjugation by armed minorities or by outside pressures." He also announced the first U.S. initiative in the cold war, a $400 million Greek-Turkish Aid Program. Belief that the Soviets had sabotaged a unified administration for Germany and the takeover of Czechoslovakia in spring 1948 contributed to this change. Much-simplified presentations of these fears appeared in newspaper editorials and the sermons of Fredonia, Evansville, and Midland ministers.

By mid-1947, the outlines of American policy were clear. The man who expressed the emerging consensus of opinion most precisely and persuasively was George F. Kennan, a career diplomat who headed the State Department's Policy Planning Staff. Famous among intellectuals for his article, "The Sources of Soviet Conduct," published anonymously in the prestigious journal, *Foreign Affairs,* in July 1947, Kennan's influence on the early development of containment was crucial and some of his views became traditional wisdom. Kennan argued that Soviet leaders were compelled to seek the expansion of Communism because, as Marxists, they believed that conflict between capitalism and socialism was inevitable and, as Russians, they distrusted "the glib persuasiveness of the outside world." Kennan concluded that the West could best deal with Russia's "expansive tendencies" through the "application of counterforce" at strategic points. A policy of "long-term, patient but firm and vigilant containment" of Communism would bring about more reasonable conduct and perhaps even the internal collapse of the Soviet dictatorship. Kennan's analysis, though superbly argued, contained numerous vague generalizations. Further, the specific goals of containment and the means to accomplish them were never satisfactorily defined. At the start, Kennan and his colleagues were reluctant to restrict their freedom of action with precise definitions. "Flexible response" was their beacon, but containment quickly acquired the status of divine writ, imposing rigidity of thought and action on its interpreters. After following the debate over the Marshall Plan for some two months in the *Wilson County Citizen,* Austin Hart gave up in disgust. The experts were welcome to conduct the cold war as they saw fit, as long as they did not weaken wheat prices or give away all the country's fertilizer. People like Austin Hart, however, did insist that the scorecard in the deadly serious game for men's hearts and minds show no new pluses for the Russians.

No one believed that people with adequate food, decent housing, and jobs would voluntarily adopt the communist system. Looking carefully at the problems afflicting Europe,

Kennan and other professionals decided that its difficulties boiled down to psychological malaise, a "crisis of self-confidence" among Europeans comparable to the American experience during the Great Depression. With returning prosperity and the comforts of life this provided, Europeans would recover faith in their leaders and in democratic-capitalist institutions. And the revival of confidence would end the threat of communist subversion. Though weighted with various other purposes, the European Recovery Plan (Marshall Plan) bespoke, more than anything else, the planners' faith in economic solutions to the menace of Communism. Congress approved some $22 billion in aid for Europe over the next four years, and the infusion of capital (much of which came back to the United States in return for such commodities as Kansas wheat and Pennsylvania coal) nourished an "economic miracle" in Western Europe. This success was precedent and justification for the massive economic aid programs of the 1950s and 1960s.

To be sure, Europeans contributed significantly to their own recovery. An important precedent was established in 1948 when Belgium, the Netherlands, and Luxembourg formed Benelux, an economic union that abolished most tariffs. This was followed, in 1950, by the European Coal and Steel Community, encompassing France, the Benelux nations, West Germany, and Italy. Finally, after many false starts, those six nations created, in 1957, the European Economic Community—the Common Market. These efforts, the withdrawal of France from NATO, and Europe's technological and industrial strength, presaged a time when Europe would envisage itself as a "third force," independent of the United States and negotiating independently with Eastern Europe and the Soviet Union.

Europe revived because its industrial infrastructure remained intact. A massive infu-

sion of money failed to save democratic capitalism in China because that nation lacked the ingredients for rapid economic development and because much of the aid was thrown away in a civil war. The United States faced three apparent options in China: withdrawal, "muddling through," or full-scale intervention. In fact, neither open abandonment of Chiang Kaishek's regime nor an imposed settlement between the Nationalists and Communists was possible. A group of congressmen, publicists, and businessmen, known as the China Lobby, campaigned ardently for aid to Chiang.

The Truman administration, though dubious about further aid, bowed to political pressures. Some $2 billion went to China between 1945 and 1949. Ignoring American calls for social reforms, the Nationalists frittered it away. Truman complained bitterly about "crooks" in Chiang's government, but the United States still preferred Chiang to a Communist takeover. When, however, the Nationalists were driven from the mainland in summer 1949, the Department of State prepared to cut ties with Chiang's remaining fiefdom of Formosa and to extend recognition to the People's Republic of China. The drift toward accommodation stopped when China and the United States involved themselves on opposite sides of the war that erupted in Korea in June 1950.

The ability of contending factions to adapt containment to special interests was clearly revealed in the fierce debate from 1948 to 1950 over military force levels and the creation of the North Atlantic Treaty Organization (NATO). The advocates of "pure" economic aid were busy with schemes to deny Western Europe to the Communists by increasing industrial productivity and encouraging European economic and political integration. Others believed that European stability rested primarily upon military strength. For a time, the purists held sway, but the other side, comprising top people from the Defense Department, numerous officials in the State Department and the Economic Cooperation Administration (ECA, the independent agency that supervised American aid), and powerful congressmen, was already preparing to take over.

State and Defense Department officials held secret talks in the Pentagon with British and Canadian representatives. When Truman signed the Economic Assistance Act of 1948, a draft defense treaty was safely locked away in the State Department. The proponents of alliance vigorously argued that the Marshall Plan were merely "fattening up Europe" and whetting Russia's insatiable appetite. But to dislodge the champions of economic aid, the alliance group needed a way to dramatize the West's military weakness. Russia's blockade of Berlin in June 1948 provided a script. Lacking sure knowledge of Soviet intentions, many Americans suspected that the blockade might initiate a full-scale westward push. The Central Intelligence Agency had to assure the president that war was not imminent.

Advocates of a military response now found willing collaborators in Europe. The blockade "scared the bejesus out of them," explained an American on the scene. On April 4, 1949, the United States and Canada joined European nations in creating the North Atlantic Treaty Organization. Despite the view of many that NATO was only to be a "symbol" of the West's unity and determination, the members immediately set about making plans for a joint defense force. George Kennan, who had described the Berlin blockade as "nothing out of the ordinary" in Russian behavior, could not understand why a new alliance was needed to meet predictable Soviet behavior. One reason was because it was easier to sell military aid—putting French pilots into U.S. F-80s and enlarging Dutch, Italian, and Belgian armies—than economic aid, which would assist European manufac-

turers in competing with American firms. When the air cleared, ECA was renamed the Mutual Security Administration. The economic internationalists had been dislodged from power. George Kennan resigned.

There was little opposition to the campaign to build up sufficient military forces to counterbalance the Red Army and its auxiliaries. The principal consequence was a new push to the arms race. Instead of accepting a "balance of terror" at a relatively low level, the United States and USSR plunged into a nightmarish contest in which "winning" meant, first, the ability to inflict the most deaths and, later, the greatest ratio of overkill, the largest bombs, and the largest number of warheads and missiles.

Military responses ended any hope for a significant thaw in the cold war and, indeed, stopped serious discussion of problems for some 20 years. It generated a world polarized between competing U.S. and Soviet camps and a strategy that envisaged decades of struggle. As the containment ideology crystallized, economic aid was converted to strategic ends, and military assistance predominated. In the first 15 years of the cold war, the United States spent approximately $100 billion for foreign aid ($500 for every American). Perhaps two thirds went for direct or indirect military aid programs.

Even technical assistance, the program Austin Hart, the Reinhardts, and Mike Simich most clearly understood since it proposed utilizing American know-how to help other peoples, was added to the list of methods for thwarting Communism. President Truman had incorporated technical assistance as point four in his 1949 inaugural address, calling for "making the benefits of our scientific advances and industrial progress available for the growth of underdeveloped areas." Once people in India, Africa, Latin America, and the Middle East grew more food, eradicated malaria, and abolished illiteracy, they would

Reflecting the shift of emphasis from diplomatic to military solutions, this cartoon suggests that Secretary of State Acheson (in the top hat) was alarmed by the change. In fact, Acheson was a dedicated "cold warrior"

be prepared to transform their societies on the American model. Although "helping people to help themselves" appealed to the strong missionary instincts of Americans, technical assistance never rivaled economic development or military schemes. The political bene-fits of introducing long-handled hoes to Middle Eastern villages and showing animated cartoons about dental hygiene seemed too gradual. As well, the elites who governed the "underdeveloped" nations demanded steel mills and airports, and they often coveted the modern military toys that accompanied nationhood. It was simpler to supply their wants—with the implicit understanding that leaders who owed their positions to U.S. support would make their countries "bastions of the free world."

Although some 70 nations and dependent territories availed themselves of American help in 1950, American foreign aid did not become a formidable instrument of counter-revolutionary policy around the world. There was not enough of it and it was maldistributed. Only a few government officials and scholars worried about communist infiltration of Latin America, France's long war with nationalists in Indochina, and stalemate in Korea. Americans were almost entirely concerned with events in Europe; more than 70 percent of foreign aid went there. The United States and its 15 NATO allies, having bound themselves to the principle "that an attack upon one shall be considered an attack upon all," were struggling to convert poorly equipped armies into an effective deterrent. They did not succeed. NATO never had enough men and modern equipment.

THE KOREAN WAR

Until 1950, the cost of containment could be measured in dollars and promises. Then a precarious peace in Korea broke down. Korea had been divided into temporary zones of Soviet and American military occupation after the Japanese forces withdrew following VJ Day. The expected unification of Korea, however, never materialized. Russian troops remained until 1949 and transferred control in the North to a cadre of Soviet-trained Korean Communists committed to unification only on their own terms. When U.S. forces withdrew the same year, they left South Korea in the hands of the anticommunist, pro-American Syngman Rhee. Rhee's dictatorial regime

embarrassed the United States. Elections held in the South in spring 1950 weakened Rhee's position and both sides stepped up guerilla raids. The North Koreans believed that a hard push would topple the Rhee regime.

When news of North Korea's attack on the south reached President Truman, the logic of containment called forth an automatic response: the North Koreans acted as Russian puppets and their attack had been ordered by Moscow; Korea was a "probing operation" by the Kremlin to test Western resolve; thus, the free world must meet force with force. Two days later, the Security Council called on United Nations members "to render every assistance" to South Korea in expelling the invaders. The Soviet Union, which doubtless would have vetoed the measure, was then boycotting the council in protest over UN refusal to seat the Peking government. U.S. naval and air units in the Far East received orders to provide "support" for the retreating South Koreans even before the UN resolution. American ground troops soon followed, and the cost of containment underwent a quantum leap.

Some disapproved of Truman's personal commitment of troops to battle, which usurped the constitutional prerogative of Congress to declare war. Other patriots objected to American troops fighting under the United Nations flag, although General Douglas MacArthur commanded the UN forces and over 90 percent of the 16-nation force was American. Still, Truman enjoyed great popularity for his bold decision to "stand up to the Communists." Except to the families and friends of the GIs ordered into Korea and the reservists and draftees called up, the war did not threaten impending disaster. During the first months of war—as UN forces retreated and then launched a counteroffensive that carried them into North Korea—Teddy Trace and George Gropper eagerly marked their National Geographic maps. Their interest waned as the Communist Chinese entered the war, drove the UN troops back across the 38th parallel, and when, following a second UN counteroffensive, the front stabilized.

President Truman had made clear that the war would be restricted to Korea, that conventional weapons only would be used, and that the objective was not total victory but negotiated settlement. Though confused by this idea of "limited war," the public accepted it. Jerry Trace had welcomed the return of his Marine reserve unit to active service in July 1950 as a part of the plan to teach the communists a lesson. But teaching amphibious tactics to green recruits bored him, and he put in for a discharge. Bill Trace was drafted a year after the front had stabilized, and soon Bill commanded a mortar platoon in Korea. In the spring of 1951, Bill had been a lackluster student at Montana State, uncertain about his future. His local Evansville selective service board had deferred him from the draft, as it routinely deferred all college men with passing grades, until graduation. Distraught after the death of a classmate, Bill left Montana State and within days received his draft notice. He graduated from Officers Candidate School at Fort Benning, Georgia, as an infan-

Bill Trace and his bride, JoAnn Houchin Trace, shortly after their honeymoon and just before he shipped out

try specialist. After a brief furlough (when he was married), he went off to the war. He accepted his fate not only because he believed men owed military service to their country, but also because refusing to serve was unthinkable. As the war dragged on, Bill began to feel that a country with the resources of the United States surely could win the war.

General MacArthur bespoke the frustration of a generation that had waged total war against Germany and Japan. He advocated bombing Chinese supply bases inside China, inviting Chiang Kaishek to launch an attack against the Peking regime, and, if necessary, using nuclear weapons. "There is no substitute for victory," MacArthur wrote a congressman. In March 1951, Truman fired MacArthur for insubordination. The general had refused to recognize that, in the atomic era, there was, as Truman insisted, "a right kind and a wrong kind of victory." The disciples of containment defined victory as denying gains to the Communists in Korea without invoking super weapons or expanding the battle zone.

Although most Americans feared nuclear war or even a land war with China, they could not easily accept battle deaths while the means to win and avoid further casualties went unused. Truman's declining popularity reflected the people's frustration. By the end of his term, less than 30 percent approved the way he had performed in office. Nevertheless, Truman had presided over the creation of a new consensus and a new world order, both of which would last until the 1970s. By 1952, nearly all Americans accepted the contention that the Soviet Union guided Communist cadres throughout the world whose purpose was the destruction of free enterprise and democratic government. They accepted the proposition that the only language the Soviets really understood was that of force.

Few anticipated that a large part of the world would rely on the United States for postwar reconstruction and defense. Few officials set out to ensure that the political and economic concessions deemed necessary for American aid would lead to massive, seemingly permanent interventions in the affairs of other nations. American influence derived from the combination, largely accidental, of wartime miscalculation, American and Soviet insecurity and aggressiveness, the eagerness of Europeans and others to look to the United States for support, and America's disposition to employ its material and technological resources instead of troops. The result of this system was a series of client states stretching from the Caribbean and Latin America through Europe to South East Asia controlled for 20 years by American economic and military aid and by the trade and investments of powerful corporations.

A NEW DEPARTURE?

The frustrated voters who elected Dwight D. Eisenhower president in November 1952 could not be sure whether or how much the diplomatic stance of the United States would change. Eisenhower promised, if elected, to go to Korea, and the electorate hoped that his experience might end the stalemated war. His reassuring, grandfatherly manner also attracted our families (all but the Groppers, Simiches, and Gishmans).

During their first months in office, Eisenhower and Secretary of State John Foster Dulles managed to unsnarl negotiations begun earlier for a truce in Korea. Using Prime Minister Jawarhal Nehru of India as an intermediary, Dulles warned the communist government that, unless some progress occurred, the United States reserved the right to use atomic weapons against North Korea and China. Negotiations resumed and, on July 26, 1953, the war in Korea ended in an armistice. Americans accepted terms that, a year earlier,

would probably have led to Truman's impeachment. The truce line approximated the original boundary at the 38th parallel. The new team had settled for containment. Eisenhower and succeeding presidents stationed 50,000 American troops in South Korea and pumped over $10 billion into the South Korean economy and army to create a counter force to the threat they perceived north of the armistice line. Lieutenant Bill Trace, wanting to go home, had no interest in the future of Korea. When he said goodbye to the platoon houseboy and the D company whores and boarded ship for San Francisco, he shut away the 18-month nightmare in a dark corner of his mind.

John Foster Dulles had not the foggiest idea what Bill Trace or others felt about the outside world. His understanding of "ordinary people" came mostly through his legal career and involvement with the World Council of Churches. If Dulles wished to find out what "people" were thinking, he dealt with a group who moved easily between business, law, government, and philanthropy and who were known as "the Eastern Establishment." Nonetheless, much of what Dulles said appealed to people about whom he was totally ignorant.

Dulles advocated basic changes in American diplomacy. The idea of containing Communism was immoral, he said, because it accepted the status quo. Right-thinking people wanted to reverse the tide, to "liberate" the "captive peoples who suffered under the yoke of communism." Bob Bassano, Jacob Reinhardt, and others were pleased by Dulles' promise to encourage resistance within the iron curtain. The Simiches remember Dulles but do not recall that he stirred up hope among Serbs in Midland that Communism would be eliminated in Yugoslavia. How could the United States government help without intervening directly in Eastern Europe? Dulles believed strongly in the power of world opinion, and of communicating truth via long-range radio and leaflets carried by balloons.

After Josef Stalin died in 1953, the Soviet Union underwent its own internal changes. This led to a loosening of the Russian grip on Eastern Europe. In Poland, a communist-nationalist faction managed to rid the cabinet of Moscow-dominated Communists. Then, in October 1956, dissident Hungarians made their move. In this case, however, people who wanted Russians out of the country took over the revolt. They rampaged through Budapest destroying symbols of Russian overlordship: flags, statues and portraits of Lenin and Stalin—and disarming the Communist police.

On hearing the news from Hungary, Dulles reportedly exclaimed: "The great monolith of communism is crumbling." He was mistaken. Nikita Khrushchev, who had emerged as the strong man in the jockeying for power after Stalin's death, might permit homegrown Communists to control the buffer states in Eastern Europe but never "anti-Soviet fascists." Americans who owned TVs watched clandestine films of Russian tanks firing on Hungarian freedom fighters who tried to stop the tanks with Molotov cocktails (gasoline-filled bottles). Radio Free Europe, a CIA–subsidized broadcasting system, beamed praise and encouragement and led Hungarian rebels to believe that help was on the way.

The convulsion in Hungary eventually cost over 35,000 lives. At one point, President Eisenhower confided to a friend: "Poor fellows . . . I wish there was some way of helping them." But Soviet-American relations already were strained to the breaking point and the Hungarian revolt coincided with inflammatory developments in the Middle East. The United States did suspend its immigration restrictions to permit entry of a large portion of the 200,000 Hungarians who fled their country. The Bassanos met some of these people as a sizable number moved into In-

wood, finding whatever jobs they could throughout the city. Bob remembers them as "heroic folk" but felt uneasy in their presence because his country had promised much and delivered nothing.

A second major change concerned military policy. Dulles, Eisenhower, and George Humphrey, the new Secretary of the Treasury, believed that the Truman interpretation of containment would bankrupt the country. Forces capable of fighting any kind of war, at any place, any time cost more than the nation should, would, or could pay. Over two years, one fourth of the Army and Navy was disbanded while the Air Force was strengthened. In the words of Secretary of Defense Charles E. Wilson, the new system delivered "more bang for the buck."

Although Eisenhower and Dulles carefully avoided saying so exactly, "massive retaliation," the administration's alternative to small wars of containment, meant that the United States might use nuclear weapons in any future conflict. If one accepted the idea that all disruptions were caused by an international Communist conspiracy masterminded from Moscow, it made good sense to bomb the Kremlin into radioactive rubble rather than waste lives and treasure struggling with the Soviet agents. Though neither "liberation" nor "massive retaliation" came to much, constant repetition of such phrases—and the creation of a sophisticated, highly visible defense system—did lull the public. Doubters had only to tour the Strategic Air Command Headquarters in Omaha or the SAC base at Salina, Kansas (just 100 miles from Fredonia), to be reassured. By 1956, a ring of bases encircled the Soviet Union, the SAC could deliver enough nuclear warheads to destroy any enemy, however powerful. Movies, plays, and books popular in the late 1950s iterated and reiterated the gigantic defensive strengths of the nation.

The policy of massive retaliation did not

B–52s on the flight line at SAC's Salina, Kansas, base

totally replace counter pressure at the periphery of the communist world, because the American people never received satisfactory evidence that Moscow controlled all the disruptions. No one could demonstrate that the North Koreans had charged across the 38th parallel on orders from Moscow. Another reason was fear of the consequences of atomic warfare. Between Eisenhower's election and his inauguration, the Atomic Energy Commission test fired a new weapon, a hydrogen bomb. The explosion was 150 times more powerful than that at Hiroshima. It disintegrated the Pacific Island of Eniwetok. Far from being comforted by this new capacity for "deterring aggression," most people realized that the Soviet Union would soon enter the hydrogen age, and that occurred in 1954.

On October 4, 1957, the USSR launched the first artificial earth satellite. A month later, the Russians orbited a 1,120 pound "Sputnik." The Sputniks had been blasted into orbit by multistaged missiles with sufficient power and accuracy to deliver a nuclear or thermonuclear payload anyplace on earth. How many nuclear weapons and missiles the Russians had and how many the United States could knock out with a defensive strike were known only to a handful. One required no inside knowledge, however, to understand that the USSR needed to be able to deliver far fewer bombs than the United States did because the U.S. landmass was so much smaller and the population so much more concentrated. The possible consequences of massive retaliation became much more immediate. The Eisenhower administration gradually turned to rebuilding for limited wars.

Man's ability to build ever more horrifying weapons forced Americans to consider the unthinkable—what would happen in a nuclear war. One study told them: a 10,000 megaton attack on the United States would leave nearly 180 million people dead. Young people such as Robbie Bassano and Michael and David Gishman watched live broadcasts of Nevada nuclear tests on the "Today Show" and read Nevil Shute's best-selling *On the Beach.* Proponents of civil defense distributed plans for home sandbag or concrete fallout shelters. The Evansville and Midland schools initiated "bomb drills" in which students filed into their shelter (usually basement hallways), sat on the floor and pulled their knees up under their chins while shielding their faces with folded arms. Sunday-school classes and persons at cocktail parties discussed whether or not to admit a neighbor to an already overcrowded bomb shelter. For a while politicians talked of an extensive national system of shelters, and Governor Nelson Rockefeller of New York promoted a state program to create shelters. Experts, however, offered conflicting opinions on their effectiveness and diplomats feared a nationwide system would lead friends and foes to believe America was preparing for nuclear war. The scare soon faded, but it left Americans with a lingering sense of vulnerability.

Intimations that the cold war involved more than the development and stockpiling of awesome new weapons everywhere intruded. Television brought news of the government's crash program to turn out more and better scientists. Americans watched confrontations between East and West over Suez, Lebanon, and Berlin. TV took them to Geneva and Paris as witnesses to "summit conferences" between a stern Ike and crude Soviet leaders. In summer 1959, there was the spectacle of Vice President Richard Nixon pulling Premier Khrushchev into the kitchen of a model home at an American exhibit in Moscow. While the cameras hummed, the premier and the vice president "debated" ways of life and national strength.

Khrushchev visited America in the fall of 1959. He argued farming techniques in Coon Rapids, Iowa, debated the merits of capitalism with the magnates of Hollywood and walked out on the filming of *Can-Can;* threatened to go home when security guards ruled out his tour of Disneyland, and delivered a nationwide television address to the American people. He seemed impressed but not overawed. People remembered Khrushchev's earlier prediction that Communism would win out over capitalism: "We will bury you." Many forgot or ignored the context of this remark, and visions of nuclear conflagration loomed. Khrushchev's return the next year to attend meetings of the United Nations intensified their fears. Ignoring UN tradition, Khrushchev responded to speeches by Secretary General Dag Hammerskjold and British Prime Minister Harold Macmillan by pounding his clenched fist and then a shoe noisily on the desk. This tantrum was shown on television and commentators speculated as to whether American power would deter this unstable man.

The capstone was a Russian disclosure on May 5, 1960, just before a heralded summit conference at Paris, that an American U-2 high-altitude spy plane had been shot down over Soviet territory. Premier Khrushchev trapped President Eisenhower into denying that the United States made such flights, and then revealed that the pilot, CIA employee Francis Gary Powers, was alive. The premier demanded an apology. The president instead claimed the right to spy on the Soviet Union and accepted personal responsibility for Powers' mission and other clandestine operations. The summit talks collapsed. The U-2 incident ended the hope for a negotiated settlement of the Berlin crisis and halted the tentative movement toward détente. It also confirmed that American leaders sanctioned unethical, illegal acts. Millions of Americans were deeply shocked.

438

A U-2, the type of spy plane which Francis Gary Powers piloted. It had been designed specifically for high-altitude photographic and electronic surveillance

Robert Butler was neither surprised nor shocked. As an officer of the National Security Council, Butler had heard about "dirty tricks" carried out by CIA "spooks." Under Director Allen Dulles, younger brother of the secretary of state, the CIA worked with rightist Iranian officers to overthrow the regime of Mohammed Mossadegh, and, in 1954, CIA agents armed right-wing dissidents and toppled Guatemala's duly elected president, Jacob Arbenz Guzman. The agency laid on a wide range of overt and covert intelligence operations, although not even Congress knew the precise number of agents or the CIA budget. In 1959, the CIA undertook the recruitment and training of a Cuban exile army to "liberate" Cuba from Fidel Castro, a leftist who had led a successful uprising against the dictatorship of Fulgencio Batista. People believed that saving the world from communism was more important than honoring the principles of fair play and nonintervention.

THE COLD WAR AT HOME

As he prepared to leave office, Dwight D. Eisenhower still spoke about America's pursuit of righteousness and the simple virtues. Though disappointed in his yearning for accommodation with the Russians (a policy he had directed personally after Dulles' death), Eisenhower saw little to regret about his administration's conduct and, neither did the electorate. The polls showed that 59 percent of the people approved Ike's stewardship. Few problems had been resolved. There was NATO's weakness and the alleged superiority of the Soviet Union in missiles. Berlin or Formosa could explode at any moment. Trouble smoldered in Cuba, Indochina, and the Middle East.

Eisenhower devoted his farewell address in January 1961 not to problems abroad but to his fear that developments *within* American society might destroy traditional American values. He warned Americans to "guard against the acquisition of unwarranted influence, whether sought or unsought, by the military-industrial complex." America had become a "warfare state," its political arrangements, social aspirations, and its very prosperity deeply intertwined with the ebb and flow of the global struggle.

What were the domestic costs of cold war? The generation of Austin Hart, Henry Gishman, and Louis Gropper contributed more than one and a half trillion dollars to a mammoth military-industrial-educational complex to produce armaments and the skills to use them. In most years after the Korean War, military expenses comprised about 10 percent of the gross national product. By the 1970s, the federal government was purchasing about 10 percent of the nation's steel production and 36 percent of durable goods for defense purposes. Almost 10 percent of the country's labor force worked for the Department of Defense, its contractors and subcontractors. The demand for weapons, troop maintenance, and foreign assistance had transformed a large segment of American business. Suppliers of defense needs did not operate in a competitive market; rather, they cooperated with a government that arranged the conditions necessary for technological virtuosity and profit.

Analysts agreed that defense dollars encouraged inflation. Defense expenditures also created more new jobs in government than in manufacturing, adversely affected the nation's balance of payments, and weakened the dollar in world money markets. There

were less obvious repercussions. Military spending acted as a substitute for the public-works projects that had characterized the New Deal. Cold war leaders discovered that military spending was an important pump-priming tool. A corollary to concentration on defense was niggardliness in other areas: urban problems, health, housing, poverty, and mass transportation. The latter *were* politically controversial and the expertise that government and industry had refined for defense was not applied to social issues.

Life for the Trace children—J.R., Jerry, Bill, Jacqueline, and Teddy—would have been very different but for the cold war. As a disabled vet, J.R. received the increased benefits provided by Congress. Korean war veterans Bill and Jerry received low-interest mortgage loans. Jacqueline's second husband (a Korea veteran) practiced law in Colorado Springs, near the huge NORAD complex, at Cheyenne Mountain. In 1962, Jacqueline, driving alone one evening, collided head-on with a truck carrying bricks to the NORAD complex. She died instantly. Teddy, then a student at Indiana University, tapped the National Defense Education Act for $2,600 to pay part of his educational expenses and to buy a ticket to his sister's funeral. After taking a degree in chemical engineering at Evansville College, Kenneth Reinhardt found work at a petrochemical works in nearby Henderson, Kentucky. When a multinational corporation bought the plant, they transferred Kenneth to Odessa, Texas, to work on the development of new explosives. Kenneth's father did not believe that his own fate was directly connected to national security. The market price of the grain produced on the Reinhardt farm, however, depended in large part upon the ability of the government to dispose of surplus. Much of this surplus grain went abroad in the form of "Food for Peace," another cold war weapon.

All of our families and most Americans

contributed to or were touched by some aspect of the cold war. Larry Simich, for example, might never have gone to graduate school had he not won a National Defense Foreign Language grant to study Serbo-Croatian and Russian.

Few communities were more than 30 miles from a defense facility. Even the highway system the families used for business and pleasure had its origins in defense planning. In many areas, the circumferential highways ("loops" and "beltways") in the interstate highway system had been sited, not to facilitate rapid transit or to avoid dissecting neighborhoods, but to speed military traffic beyond the blast area in the event of nuclear attack. Still, while Americans were constantly bombarded with reports about the relative strengths of Soviet-bloc and U.S.-bloc military forces, and while they could hardly avoid seeing physical manifestations of American military might, they did not, if they were at all similar to our families, consciously relate such information and impressions to their daily lives. As Anna Simich said: "I don't think much about things that I can't affect." Whether or not they agreed with particular U.S. policies and strategies, they did not feel that they exerted any control over the outcome.

NEW RHETORIC, OLD POLICIES

The cumulative frustrations of 15 years of cold war benefited 43-year-old John Fitzgerald Kennedy in his bid for the presidency in 1960. The Democratic candidate projected confidence and vitality. Instead of reliance on the tired formulas of the past, Kennedy promised an energetic search for new solutions. Instead of folksy virtue, he offered urbanity and sophistication. His inaugural declaration that "the torch has been passed to a new generation" appealed to young voters such as Michael Gishman and Ted Trace because it portended new presidential style and policy. Kennedy proposed: "Let us never negotiate out of fear. But let us never fear to negotiate." At the same time Kennedy pressed anticommunism. He committed his countrymen to "pay any price, bear any burden, meet any hardship . . . to assure the survival and success" of the democratic system. Yet the activism of the Kennedy years mostly passed by our families.

The USSR and the United States maintained an armed standoff, and the area of confrontation shifted to the "underdeveloped" regions. Everywhere, poorer nations stirred with demands for improved standards of living, resentment that their labor and products brought so little in the marketplace of the technologically sophisticated nations, and awareness that the competing superpowers could be lured into supporting development. Except for the festering sore of Berlin, where neither side would compromise and where the Soviets erected a concrete border wall, the most vexing problems came from outside Europe.

The foreign-affairs bureaucracy proved no more controllable to Kennedy than to his predecessors. By the 1960s, empire building and organizational rivalries had become institutionalized. Some agencies, particularly the CIA, had adopted the notion that certain programs would be kept secret even from the president. The bureaucracy scored a triumph soon after Kennedy's inauguration by obtaining his approval of a plan to depose Cuban leader Fidel Castro. Officers of the Department of State, CIA, and Department of Defense planned this drastic action because Castro apparently became a communist after he won control of the country. The three top agencies assured the president that an invasion force of CIA–trained exiles (then assembled in Guatemala) would be welcomed.

On April 17, 1961, U.S. ships carried the Cuban exiles to Cochinos Bay, the Bay of Pigs. Everything went wrong, and the chief problem was the faulty intelligence provided by the CIA. The CIA had said the landing site would be deserted. It was ablaze with the lights of workers constructing a resort. The CIA said there would be no Cuban air force in the area. The invaders suffered casualties from strafing even before they got off the beach. President Kennedy declined to commit American troops to a lost cause, and, within three days, 1,000 survivors were on their way to Cuban jails.

In October 1962, there was a second Cuban crisis. The Soviet Union was placing in Cuba ballistic missiles with the ability to hit most major U.S. cities. Kennedy declared that the United States considered this development "a deliberately provocative and unjustified change in the status quo, which cannot be accepted by this country." On October 22, a frozen television and radio audience learned that JFK had ordered Cuba "quarantined"—that the Navy would stop Soviet ships bound for Cuba and search them for missiles. The United States would consider any attack by Cuba as a Soviet act of war. Ted Trace responded to the governor's declaration of a civil-defense alert by joining friends in stockpiling canned goods and choosing a hideout in the southern Indiana hills. Robbie Bassano, just discharged from the Marines, inquired whether his reserve unit was to be activated. Disenchanted with civilian routine, he half hoped the answer would be yes.

It was one of those rare times when every citizen attempted to be informed. Behind the scenes, Kennedy and Khrushchev exchanged personal letters in which each admitted no victor could emerge from a nuclear war. The two governments negotiated on the premise that, if the Soviets removed the missiles and the UN inspected the sites, the United States would pledge not to invade Cuba. Secretary

of State Dean Rusk described the nuclear confrontation as "eyeball to eyeball," and when the Soviet ships stopped short of the quarantine line, Rusk breathed with relief, "I think the other fellow just blinked." The missiles slowly disappeared from Cuba, though there were no UN inspections and no U.S. pledge to refrain from military action. The most serious crisis of the nuclear age had passed. Discussions about arms limitation assumed a new earnestness.

When it appeared that international tensions were easing, JFK fell to an assassin's bullet in Dallas. Political leaders and the rank and file tried to give the new president, Lyndon B. Johnson, sympathetic cooperation. From Kennedy's death until mid-1966, Lyndon Johnson concentrated on domestic programs. The 90th Congress produced what many termed the most important reforms of the 20th century. But LBJ was not to enjoy or benefit from those accomplishments. Once again, foreign affairs eclipsed domestic problems.

By the mid-1960s, the idea of Communism as a worldwide movement controlled from the Soviet Union had become difficult to sustain. The rift between the Soviet Union and the People's Republic of China had widened to a chasm. The Chinese exploded an atomic bomb in 1964, and their "deterrent" was aimed as much at the Soviet Union as at the United States. The world view of America's leaders down to the late 1960s derived from memories of World War II, the sting of Communist betrayal after the war, and the experience of the Korean War. Lyndon Johnson matured in the most frigid season of the cold war. He kept the faith that "communism must be stopped," ignoring the Soviet Union's internal changes and the feuds among various communist parties. It befell Johnson to shore up the defenses against what he always considered "the international communist conspiracy." In doing so, he alienated many. The result: the end of the containment consensus.

By the time Lyndon Johnson assumed the presidency, the United States had been involved in Indochina for years, having given direct support to the French military effort since 1949, and had claimed a dominant role after the French colony's fate was decided at an international conference in Geneva in 1954. The Geneva Conference separated Indochina into the independent states of Laos, Cambodia, and two Vietnams divided at the 17th parallel. A revolutionary leader and communist, Ho Chi Minh, headed the northern provinces while Bao Dai, a French client, ruled the South. The Geneva accords stipulated that elections in 1956 were to establish a unified government for all Vietnam. To Eisenhower, Vietnam was the first tile in a row of dominoes. If the communists toppled Vietnam, Laos and Cambodia, then Malaya, Thailand, Burma, and Indonesia would fall.

To maintain a noncommunist government in the south, the United States sent money and military advisers to Ngo Dinh Diem, the strongman who deposed Bao Dai in 1955. Diem declined to hold elections in 1956 (a decision approved by the United States since evidence suggested that Ho Chi Minh would win easily), and he set out to crush his South Vietnamese opponents and North Vietnamese infiltrators. By 1960, 685 American advisers worked for Diem.

Never questioning the basic assumptions of containment, John Kennedy escalated the American commitment—a necessity, he believed, because the pace of North Vietnamese infiltration had stepped up and the South Vietnamese communists, the Viet Cong, had gained control of large areas. Kennedy used two tactics to impose stability. He sent in the Green Berets, a cadre of counterinsurgency specialists, and he withdrew support from Diem, who was embarrassing the United States by attacking Vietnamese Buddhists,

censoring the press, and jailing his enemies. Kennedy's actions encouraged military intriguers to assassinate Diem. No one emerged who could rally the South Vietnamese people.

Lyndon Johnson decided to "increase the quotient of pain" upon North Vietnam and force Ho Chi Minh to abandon the war in the south. When the president told Congress that, on August 5, 1964, North Vietnamese torpedo boats in the Gulf of Tonkin had fired on U.S. destroyers which frequently supported raids against the north, the legislators passed a resolution that gave Johnson a free hand. From that day until April 1975, no public issue absorbed more attention and more blood and treasure than the war in Vietnam. Escalation occurred in dramatic steps. Although the Gulf of Tonkin incident was largely manufactured by the White House, Johnson ordered American bombers to strike North Vietnamese military targets. During the next winter, communist forces hit the installations of U.S. military advisers. The United States then began systematic bombings in both North and South Vietnam. Stepped-up Viet Cong activity led the advisers urgently to request U.S. combat troops. The first Marines went ashore in March 1965.

Then began the skirmishes, the battles in steaming jungles where sophisticated weapons proved no more superior than old-fashioned and handmade ones. Then, too, began the long lists of casualties in the newspapers—46,500 Americans dead, 303,600 wounded. And then came the predictions of military victory next week, next month—certainly very soon.

Each delay prompted the U.S. government to commit more troops and rain more bombs on the north. By 1968, American forces in Vietnam numbered 550,000. The Pentagon met criticism with a barrage of numbers—of Viet Cong and North Vietnamese weapons captured, of dead body counts, of operations by the army of South Vietnam. This data, processed by Defense Department computers, provided the assurances of victory. For a long time, the majority of Americans accepted the declarations of imminent victory. Indeed, interest in Vietnam grew slowly. Scenes of horror and devastation, strange names and progress reports flashed across television screens and just as quickly vanished from thoughts of most Americans. Until 1966, at least, Vietnam and all the questions the conflict posed about American power and American purpose represented only a minor distraction.

President Lyndon Johnson and Americans who shared his hostility toward communism and determination to defend America's honor were angered by a minority who opposed service in Vietnam. Ironically, opposition to the war first acquired strength among students who were deferred from the draft. They thought the war immoral or saw the United States as the aggressor and thwarting the will of the Vietnamese people. Demonstrations against the war spread from campus to center city: 125,000 at a rally in New York, 30,000 in San Francisco, 220 in Midland. When, as often happened, local and federal law officers roughed up young and old marching under the banner of civil disobedience, radical

An antiwar rally in 1968, one of thousands held around the nation to demand the withdrawal of U.S. troops from Vietnam

youths took these acts as confirmation that no justice could come through the "system" as presently constituted.

Millions, including Ted Trace and Chris Gropper, joined the ranks of the disenchanted after the communist forces launched their Tet (New Year's) offensive in 1968. In spite of all the assurances of victory, the Viet Cong launched devastating attacks on 100 cities, entered 5 of the 6 largest and, most stunning of all, pushed three regiments into Saigon and barely missed seizing the U.S. embassy. Tet eventually led to a great U.S./South Vietnamese military victory, but that fact was eclipsed by its political and psychological effects. The Tet offensive was a turning point, forcing cold war warriors to wonder if victory was possible in Vietnam. These events combined with growing inflation (largely the result of Johnson's insistence on pursuing both the Great Society programs and the Vietnam war without sharp tax increases) to turn yet other groups against the war. The nation's failure to see the crisis as he did broke Lyndon Johnson, and he declined to seek reelection in 1968.

Richard Nixon won the presidency with a promise that he could "wind down the war," that there could be "peace with honor." Nixon's solution was to "Vietnamize" the war, a verbal gauchery that meant withdrawal of American troops while the United States continued to finance the war. The idea was still to stop communism, but to do so with reduced U.S. involvement. For months and months, though, high American casualties continued. Negotiations with the North Vietnamese, begun during Johnson's tenure, dragged on. The popular wave of distrust spiraled higher. How could diplomats, one heard on the college campuses, spend months arguing about the shape and seating arrangements of their negotiating table while classmates scrambled for their lives? Then, to give Henry Kissinger,

Nixon's representative, a strong bargaining position before the United States began to withdraw troops, the United States launched a massive attack on communist supply dumps in Cambodia. Many people refused to accept the Nixon rationale for the "Cambodian incursion," for the move seemed to be escalation, not withdrawal. A few of the 1,000 students at Kent State University who turned out to protest Cambodia worked themselves into a frenzy. National Guardsmen on the scene lost their nerve and opened fire. Four young people, ranging from the simply curious to advocates of a new kind of patriotism, fell dead. Within a week, more than 400 universities suspended classes in the first general student strike in American history.

Though some troops left Vietnam, the American government had too much invested to leave without some North Vietnamese quid pro quo. In particular, Nixon exploited the tremendous public concern for American prisoners of war. While the diplomats wrangled, Americans witnessed other evidence that their society was dangerously divided. In spring 1971, police arrested 7,000 antiwar demonstrators who had camped on the banks of the Potomac. It was the largest lockup ever in a single city in a single day. There were also pitched battles between "hard hats," who supported Nixon, and peace marchers. Indeed, Nixon's smashing victory in 1972 over the Democratic contender George McGovern (an advocate of complete and unconditional United States withdrawal from Vietnam) is perhaps evidence of broad support for hard-line anticommunism. Of course, McGovern's inept campaign had something to do with the outcome.

Just before the presidential election of 1972, Secretary of State Kissinger announced: "Peace is at hand." For Americans, it almost was. On January 27, 1973, the disputants signed an agreement that repatriated the prisoners, provided for an international peacekeeping force of 1,160 men, and promised total U.S. withdrawal and the right of the people of South Vietnam to determine their own future without interference.

With the Americans gone, heavy fighting resumed. "Vietnamization" had not made the fighting forces of South Vietnam into battlefield tigers. When Viet Cong and North Vietnamese forces launched a major offensive in 1974, Saigon's forces fell apart, abandoning stores of arms and equipment, including their U.S.-supplied jet fighter-bombers and tanks. In one three-week period, the northern three-quarters of South Vietnam fell. In late April 1975, with insurgent troops at the gates of Saigon, U.S. forces hastily evacuated American civilians and Vietnamese who had worked for the United States. Bill Trace was outraged by the news that the South Vietnamese stood in doorways and cheered as communist troops marched victoriously into the capital city. The vast majority of Americans accepted the end calmly, even coldly. President Gerald Ford solemnly announced: "This action closes a chapter in the American experience." With that conclusion, all could agree.

CLOSE OF THE AMERICAN CENTURY?

Gone was the sense of American omnipotence. Gone was the feeling that the United States had to be involved everywhere. In 1980, U.S. military personnel abroad totaled 489,000, sharply down from the 1,200,000 manning outposts in 1968 at the height of the Vietnam War. Much of the retrenchment had not been voluntary. Shortly after Saigon fell, Thailand ordered the United States to give up the air bases from which North Vietnam had been bombed. Greece forebade the U.S.

Navy to "homeport" destroyers at Piraeus and placed large arms orders with France. Incredibly, in January 1980, a long-time client, Pakistan, even spurned a proffered $400 million in aid as "peanuts," holding out for a more favorable deal. It appeared that former clients needed the United States less and the United States had less to offer them. Among the first acts of the Reagan administration was a campaign, orchestrated by Secretary of State Alexander Haig, to reverse this trend.

For a time, the shocks resulting from international political and economic developments became more important than bases, strategic matters, and the global communist menace. Without warning, in 1973, Americans were subjected to a series of restrictive shortages and price increases. First came the announcement that the cheap oil that had propelled a mobile, innovative, consumption-oriented society to global prominence was at an end. Although the United States still produced 40 percent of its energy requirements, it relied for the rest mainly on cheap imports from the Arab Middle East. In 1972, the Arab nations overcame decades of inertia and subservience to Western oil interests and formed the Organization of Petroleum Exporting Countries (OPEC). The Middle Eastern producers then temporarily placed an embargo on shipping their oil to nations that supported their historic enemy, Israel, and, using OPEC as a super-cartel, subsequently quadrupled the world price of oil. The comfortable, spacious Ford Country Squire station wagon Bill and Joanne Trace bought in 1971 now hulked in the driveway. During the days of "gas wars" and 24.9¢ per gallon fuel, Bill had filled its tank for less than $5. Now Bill found himself paying $13 to $15 for a full tank, and, because the car got 8 to 10 miles per gallon, feeding the monster noticeably dented the family budget. They were better off than Bob Bassano, who several times in the summer of

1973 could not buy gas. The Traces and Bassanos, like almost everyone else, blamed the Arabs.

It was one thing for Charlotte Bassano to watch grave-faced commentators on television agonize over the potential dangers in the latest nuclear disarmament proposals made to the Russians. It was quite another matter for Charlotte to return from the supermarket nearly despondent after paying $1.09 a pound for the hamburger on which, at three pounds for a dollar, she had raised a family. Inflation in construction costs and mortgage interest priced many families out of the single-family home market. These and similar problems were generated by developments beyond American shores. If one could believe the experts, the changes they imposed were irreversible. The world had entered the home, affecting the standard of living and the values of American families.

When the federal government legislated a nationwide speed limit of 55 miles per hour as a fuel-saving measure, manufacturers reported a shortage of reflective paint for modifying the signs along the highways. Austin Hart had trouble finding enough fertilizer (containing oil-derived nitrogen) for his crops. In Prairie Village, Kansas, Karyl Gishman received fewer plastic garbage bags from the city sanitation department because of shortages and rising costs. Practically every dwelling in America depended upon gas or oil for heat. Within a year, heating costs doubled, and householders lived with the warning of newly appointed presidential energy advisers that, unless they turned down thermostats and improved insulation, the day would come when some people would be without heat. Much to their dismay, the Bassanos' heating bill during their first winter in the suburbs exceeded by two times their rent on Nagel Avenue. Everything seemed to run out at once. Many states prohibited natural gas connections in new homes, while shortages appeared

in meat, coffee, printing ink, and toilet paper. By decade's end, the combination of dramatic OPEC production increases, higher profit margins resulting in ambitious domestic development and recovery efforts, and energy-conservation measures had brought about an oil glut in world markets. However, gasoline prices were hovering near $1.50 per gallon, and some forecasters were referring to "zero energy growth," a notion that appeared to worry some in the Reagan administration. Jerry Trace trusted that the free-market economy would provide adequate supplies of oil and make possible the maintenance of "traditional" living patterns. He also assumed that the federal government would cut back on its support of mass-transit systems, for otherwise, his pursuit of a Sun Belt taxicab empire was doomed to failure. The immediate steps of the Reagan administration to dismantle federally supported conservation and urban transportation programs more than justified Jerry Trace's expectations.

Except among poor families, food consumed a modest portion of American family income during the affluent 1960s. Then, in 1974, the cost of food soared. The first inclination of millions of Americans was to blame the soaring price of food on the Russians. In 1972, Russian buyers quietly contracted for one fifth (400 million bushels) of the American wheat crop. The sale depleted reserves, and the laws of supply and demand functioned automatically. Austin Hart, who sold his 1972 crop for $1.30 a bushel, pocketed $4.30 a bushel in 1974, and Anna Simich paid her part of the increase every time she bought meat or a loaf of bread. The Russian wheat deal of 1972 and subsequent Russian purchases accelerated the blurring of traditional cold war viewpoints.

Russian bureaucrats were negotiating purchases with foreign companies for some $12 billion in new factories and products. Wood, oil, coal, cotton, and metals—basic

Vanderburgh County farmers discuss farm issues, including policy with the Soviet Union, 1975

materials short in the world but abundant in Russia—were exported in unprecedented volume. In 1973 alone, there occurred a 34 percent increase in foreign trade. Allowing the Soviets to purchase the technological sophistication of American industry and the bounty of American farmland posed a new dilemma: would the acquisitions by the USSR combine with its more abundant raw materials to make it stronger than the United States and give it an edge in the continuing ideological battle around the world?

Even before the American government embargoed grain to the Soviet Union in 1979, it proved difficult to sustain the idea that Russian purchases alone forced up the price of American staples. Bad weather, richer tastes in developing countries, and the enormous population increase (at least 200,000 more every day) absorbed practically all the food

reserves of "spaceship Earth." Farmers in the U.S. Midwest, about one tenth of 1 percent of the world's population yet capable of feeding 25 percent of the world, never had experienced such demand for their products. In 1978–79, 26 percent of the feed grains, 42 percent of the soybeans, 47 percent of the rice, and 64 percent of the wheat grown by the Harts, Reinhardts, and other American farmers went abroad.

Consumers faced an era of high prices. Oil shortages doubled the cost of fertilizers in two years while increased labor and material costs pushed the price of a tractor which Jacob Reinhardt could have bought in 1955 for about $4,000 to almost $20,000. Farmers raised prices to recover their investments and maintain their profit margins. But most importantly, and regardless of the weather, production efficiency, and changed palates around the world, the increased number of mouths to be fed dictated the end of inexpensive food.

In Asia, South America, and Africa, birth rates outdistanced the land's fertility. Even though "miracle" hybrids introduced in the 1970s had produced a "green revolution" in many areas and provided the poor countries with 78 percent more grain than they had in 1950, the margin against starvation depended upon vast quantities of water and petroleum-based fertilizer and pesticides. With the advent of drought and prohibitively expensive fertilizer and equipment, a thwarted harvest could collide with a population soaring by 75 million a year. Already 10,000 people died each week from starvation, and nearly half a billion suffered some form of malnutrition. A 1976 report of the World Food Council listed 43 nations as "food priority countries," based on low per capita income, projected food deficits by 1985, extent of protein-calorie malnutrition, failure to improve domestic production of food, and balance-of-payments difficulties. The list, in order of severity of food deficiencies, was:

Extremely severe	*Very severe*	*Severe*
Bangladesh, Mali, Upper Volta, North Yemen, South Yemen, Somalia, Tanzania, Niger	Afghanistan, Benin, Cape Verde, Central African Republic, Chad, Egypt, Ethiopia, Gambia, Guinea, Guinea Bissau, Haiti, India, Indonesia, Kampuchea (Cambodia), Lesotho, Laos, Malawi, Mauritania, Nepal, Pakistan, Ruanda, Sri Lanka, Uganda	Burma, Cameroon, El Salvador, Guyana, Honduras, Kenya, Madagascar, Mozambique, Philippines, Senegal, Sierra Leone, Sudan.

Descriptions of famine conditions in several of these countries flashed across the television screens and consciousnesses of all our families during the next few years. Michael and Karyl Gishman sent a check to one of the private relief organizations. The others shook their heads and turned back to newspapers, junk food, or dozing.

Ever more, leaders of the poor countries blamed their predicament on the rich. India's minister of agriculture, Jagjivan Ram, for example, contended that centuries of exploitation by the industrial powers distorted the pattern of agriculture. Because the developed powers were the cause, they owed help in the form of huge quantities of food. Help from the food-rich nations, the argument went, should be considered as deferred compensation for the results of past exploitation. Leaders of some poor nations rejected massive birth-control campaigns because of religious and economic traditions. There were also political objections to population controls. "The large population of the Third World," the Chinese government officially proclaimed, "is an important condition for the fight against imperialism." A few people suggested that, if Americans did not give up such luxuries as spreading enough fertilizer on lawns, golf courses, and cemeteries to grow grain for 65 million people, the time might come when poor nations would plunge into famine and chaos.

Bob and Charlotte Bassano were well aware of the magnitude of the world resource problem, at least in general terms. They purposefully made their first automobile purchase a six-cylinder Ford, and they dutifully turned out unnecessary lights and kept the thermostat at 68 degrees. Americans had to practice economies other peoples took for granted. The Bassanos saved aluminum cans, glass bottles, and newspapers until their garage could hold no more. Bob used fertilizer on his lawn and garden sparingly and disliked the idea of insecticides. Yet, when he saw his neighbors fertilizing and spraying with abandon and then contrasted his results with theirs, he wondered about the sense of his own efforts at conservation. From his viewpoint, he lived a frugal life. He believed in doing his part. But, as he exclaimed, one man cannot save the world. He blamed the government for not providing direction and guffawed heartily when he read that the federal energy leaders were focusing their efforts on the elimination of the pilot light in stoves and hot-water heaters. Besides, Charlotte maintained, Americans have always come up with new machines and things to solve most problems. And she pointed to the sun and held up her hands to catch the wind.

It appeared that Jimmy Carter shared both Bob Bassano's sense of frustration with governmental red tape and waste and the mystical faith of Charlotte Bassano that Americans somehow, someway would solve their own and the world's problems. Carter brought dual beliefs to the White House—that the cold war truly had ended, and that the United

States could regain its preeminent moral, political, and economic position in the world without the trappings and obligations of empire. President Carter's "human rights" policy, his intervention in the Arab-Israeli conflict leading to the Camp David Accords of September 1978, and U.S. emphasis on improving relations with the Third World (notably, the normalization of relations with the People's Republic of China) did represent progress toward the latter goal.

Pressing hard for the further elaboration of detente between the United States and the Soviet Union, Carter demonstrated great patience in the face of Russian and Cuban intervention in Angola; Soviet meddling elsewhere in Africa, the Middle East, and Southeast Asia; the steady buildup of Soviet conventional military and naval strength; and the Russian's harsh treatment of Jews and dissidents. The Carter administration placed great hope in the "Salt II" arms-control agreement and the negotiations for a comprehensive test-ban treaty and limitation of conventional weapons which were slated to follow. However, by the time Carter and Brezhnev signed the Salt II Treaty in June 1979, detente already had unraveled, and Carter's broad-based approach to foreign affairs was hopelessly snarled.

In large part, the paralysis resulted from domestic circumstances. Carter never received popular and legislative support for his new policies of accommodation and moral leadership. Further, the belief which he and Charlotte Bassano shared in the innate superiority of American economic and political institutions was also under serious attack. Many experts acknowledged that the focus of American genius seemed to have turned away from fundamental innovation. That is, relatively less energy was being devoted to development of a late-20th-century equivalent of such revolutionary contraptions as the cotton gin, reaper, or gasoline engine. Creative energies, instead, focused upon the art

of organization and fused the talents of the brightest government officials, industrial managers, economics professors, engineers, and scientists to integrate and refine production and marketing processes. Indeed, in the 1960s, the application of this creativity in the service of large corporations led to sprawling overseas operations. By the early 1970s, over 3,500 companies each operated in at least six countries and took in over $100 million a year. The biggest of these were American. In Europe as a whole, some 15 percent of all consumer goods were being produced in American-controlled factories.

Some argued—among them President Carter—that the efficiency of multinational companies would increase production, lower costs, and mute the nationalism which had so long troubled the world. But critics charged that it was five minutes to midnight for humanity, and the huge corporations remained preoccupied with profits. Such charges were raised in the aftermath of the 1973 OPEC oil embargo, the discoveries of sales to less-developed countries of pesticides banned in the United States, and revelations that the sale of Nestle's baby formula in countries lacking modern sanitation made the product infinitely more hazardous than mothers' milk.

At first, it made no difference to Mike Simich when Colt Industries, a multinational, acquired Crucible Steel. When times began to look bad, and U.S. Steel closed 14 plants in one year, Mike wondered if Colt might decide to produce its steel abroad where labor was cheaper and abandon him and Midland. The *Midland News* asked in an editorial whether money spent abroad by Colt deprived Midland of its fullest development and whether the government should effectively control the multinational octopus. Then, in 1975 and 1976, the public learned of the corrupt practices used by Lockheed, Exxon, and other multinationals in securing contracts with foreign governments. Such revelations, involving government officials in Japan, the Netherlands, Italy, and Saudi Arabia, caused Congress to initiate investigations and brought minor crises in the nations involved. It came as a shock to many that quality and price differentials between American and foreign goods had so narrowed that the largest bribe or favor determined the selection of the supplier. What had happened to so reduce the technological superiority of the United States?

Most difficult to accept was the disappearance of America's competitive edge in various fields. The deep-seated problems of the U.S. auto and steel industries were brought into sharp focus by the 1980–81 recession. Americans were aware of the problems of the Big Three automakers, with Chrysler forced to seek a $1.5 billion federal loan guarantee to avoid bankruptcy and with Ford closing plants across the United States and avoiding financial collapse only because of the earnings from its foreign subsidiaries. But the information that, in 1980, foreign-produced cars, four fifths of them from Japan, grabbed 25 percent of the U.S. market still came as a shock. How was it possible that the Japanese, who a few decades before only exported poorly made, imitative toys and gimcracks, silk garments, and cheap china to America, were building better and cheaper cars, electronic products, and petroleum tankers? The answer increasingly emphasized the idea of "productivity"—output per person-hour. U.S. productivity since the Second World War had grown at a rate of 3 percent per year, but productivity increases dropped to 1 percent annually during 1973–78 and actually declined 2.1 percent in 1979. There were numerous villains—obsolete labor-management practices, government regulation, inflation and rising energy costs, and decline in research and development spending that led to a slowdown in technological innovation. What is certain is that Michael Gishman de-

cided to buy a Datsun station wagon in October 1980 because of appearance, mileage, cost, and because of Datsun's excellent repair service detailed in *Consumer Report*. Also known is that several good friends of Mike Simich lost their jobs when U.S. Steel closed its Youngstown, Ohio plant because of foreign competition.

The Soviet Union's invasion of Afghanistan in December 1979 delivered the knockout blow to détente, and President Carter, deeply angered and stung by the collapse of his hopes, reacted strongly. He reversed his often-stated opposition to the use of food as a weapon and suspended a 17-million-metric-ton grain sale to the Soviet Union. The Carter administration also called for a worldwide boycott of the 1980 Moscow Olympics, a move which Jerry Trace, Michael Gishman, and Larry Simich supported as effective propaganda. Carter also called for reinstitution of registration for the draft by all 18–21-year-old males, catching Rusty Trace and Eduardo Nava. Perhaps most significant, Carter asked the Senate to postpone indefinitely consideration of Salt II.

The final year of Jimmy Carter's presidency was dominated by his determined (and, ultimately, desperate) search for a solution to the Iranian hostage crisis. While that aim eluded him—Carter's successor, Ronald Reagan, received the political benefits attending the release, on January 20, 1981, of the American hostages after 444 days in captivity—Carter did preside over a rebirth of patriotism and determination in startling contrast with the national mood after Vietnam. Provoked by the violent antics of the Ayatollah Khomeini and his followers, and frustrated about the inability of the United States of America, supposedly the world's most powerful nation, to rescue American citizens from "that bunch of thugs and religious crackpots," Bob Bassano's label for the leaders of Iran's Islamic revolution, Americans of such diverse backgrounds and political views as Antonio Nava, Michael Gishman, Jerry Trace, and Regina Reinhardt expressed support for a stronger, more assertive U.S. military and diplomatic posture. By reviving the rhetoric of the cold war and by adopting a "realistic" policy toward the Soviet Union, one which required the highest priority for the defense program, President Reagan was responding to the popular mood. Whether the other component of the Reagan administration's "policy of realism," the active support of right-wing regimes against revolutionary groups as in El Salvador, would be welcomed by the American people was questionable. For the first time ever, during the spring 1981 debate over sending U.S. advisers and gunships to El Salvador, Regina Reinhardt wrote to the president to oppose "another Vietnam," and Peggy Trace and Chris Gropper joined her in this act.

During this, the first decade of America's third century of national existence, Regina, the Traces, Groppers, Harts, and all of the other families had been compelled to accept a gut-level awareness of global interdependence. Because they used more oil than America produced, and because the Arab petroleum-producing countries had discovered they could control supplies and prices to influence U.S. policy, Americans learned something about Middle East politics. Because so many automobiles and television sets came from Japan, Americans learned that such abstract notions as "comparative productivity" and the value of dollar abroad affected the cost of the good life here. That awareness could hardly be termed sophisticated. Indeed, in fall 1980, a survey of 3,000 students—presumably one of the best-informed groups—on 185 campuses found that most college students knew little about foreign affairs. Asked 101 questions about such basic concerns as the membership of OPEC, the sample (including Jerry and Peggy

Trace's son, Rusty, a Baylor senior) earned an average score of 50.2 percent. One third of the students admitted that they were not interested in what happened elsewhere in the world. Still, when foreign purchases of Kansas wheat determined whether the Harts would buy a new car and whether the Bassanos would have prime rib for Sunday dinner; when Arab financiers gained control of corporations in which the Butlers owned stock; when Vietnamese and Cuban families were brought into their communities, Americans began to understand that it was a small world, after all. What worried some was whether a little knowledge, mixed with a mood of frustration and self-doubt and with nationalistic leadership, might lead to dangerous reactions. In various arenas, the 1980s would be a pivotal decade.

SUGGESTIONS FOR FURTHER READING

Surveys of United States diplomacy include Stephen Ambrose, *Rise to Globalism: American Foreign Policy, 1938–1980* (1980); John D. Spanier, *American Foreign Policy Since World War II* (1973); Richard Barnet, *Intervention and Revolution* (1969); Walter LaFeber, *America, Russia, and the Cold War* (1976); and Thomas G. Paterson, ed., *Containment and the Cold War* (1973). Helpful "methodological" works are Ernest R. May, *"Lessons" of the Past: The Use and Misuse of History in American Foreign Policy* (1973); Graham D. Allison, *The Essence of Decision* (1971); Gabriel Almond, *The American People and Foreign Policy* (1950); Morton Halperin, *Bureaucratic Politics and Foreign Policy* (1974); John C. Donovan, *The Cold Warriors: A Policy-Making Elite* (1974); Bernard Cohen, *The Public's Impact on Foreign Policy* (1973); Robert Jervis, *Perception and Misperception in International Politics* (1976); and Robert Barnet, *The Roots of War* (1972).

Study of the early cold war begins with Daniel Yergin, *Shattered Peace: The Origins of the Cold*

War and the National Security State (1977); Thomas Paterson, *On Every Front: The Making of the Cold War* (1979); John Gaddis, *The United States and the Origins of the Cold War* (1972); and Dean G. Acheson, *Present at the Creation* (1969). See also Lyle Rose, *After Yalta* (1973); Gabriel and Joyce Kolko, *The Limits of Power* (1972); William R. Louis, *Imperialism at Bay: The United States and the Decolonization of the British Empire, 1941–45* (1978); Martin Sherwin, *A World Destroyed: The Atomic Bomb and the Grand Alliance* (1975); Gregory F. Herkin, *American Diplomacy and the Atomic Bomb, 1945–1950* (1980); Richard Hewlett and Oscar Anderson, *The New World* [on the development of the atomic bomb] (1962); William H. McNeill, *America, Britain, and Russia* (1953); and Thomas G. Paterson, *Soviet-American Confrontation.* Such works as Robert Kaiser, *Cold Winter, Cold War* (1974); John Lukacs, *Year Zero* (1978); Richard N. Gardner, *Sterling-Dollar Diplomacy* (1979, ref. ed.); E. F. Penrose, *Economic Planning for the Peace* (1953); Eugene Davidson, *The Death and Life of Germany* (1959); and Francesca Wilson, *Aftermath: France, Germany, Austria, Yugoslavia, 1945–1946* (1947); Dorothy Macardle, *Children of Europe: A Study of the Children of Liberated Countries* (1951); Jacques Vernant, *The Refugee in the Post-War World* (1953); John Backer, *The Decision to Divide Germany: American Foreign Policy in Transition* (1978); and Patricia D. Ward, *The Threat of Peace: James F. Byrnes and the CFM, 1945–46* (1979), treat the immediate aftermath. See also Robert A. Divine, *American Immigration Policy, 1924–1952* (1957), and U.S. Displaced Persons Commission, *The DP Story* (1952).

The American response is discussed in Joseph M. Jones, *The Fifteen Weeks* (1955); Thomas H. Etzold and John L. Gaddis, *Containment: Documents on American Policy and Strategy, 1945–1950* (1977); George F. Kennan, *Memoirs, 1925–1950* (1967); John Gimbel, *The Origins of the Marshall Plan* (1977); Frank Merli and Theodore A. Wilson, eds., *Makers of American Diplomacy* (1974); Charles Gati, ed., *Caging the Bear* (1974); Lynn Ethridge Davis, *The Cold War Begins: Soviet-American Conflict Over Eastern Europe* (1974); Terry H. Anderson, *The United States, Great Britain, and the Cold War,* *1944–1947* (1981); Stephen Xydis, *Greece and The Great Powers* (1963); Francis F. Lincoln, *United States' Aid to Greece, 1947–1962* (1975); Geir Lundestaad, *America, Scandinavia, and the Cold War, 1945–1949* (1980); Hadley Arkes, *Bureaucracy, the Marshall Plan, and the National Interest* (1973); and Harry B. Price, *The Marshall Plan and its Meaning* (1955). The emergence of military concerns is in Lawrence Kaplan, Search for Security: NATO and the Military Assistance Program (1980); Richard F. Haynes, *The Awesome Power: Harry S. Truman As Commander in Chief* (1973); Vincent Davis, *Postwar Defense Policy and the U.S. Navy* (1966); Warner R. Schilling et al., *Strategy, Politics, and Defense Budgets* (1962); Michael Sherry, *Preparing for the Next War: American Plans for Postwar Defense* (1977); Walter Millis, ed., *The Forrestal Diaries* (1951); and the memoirs of Acheson, Kennan, Vandenberg, and Bohlen.

U.S. interests in the third world are treated in Akira Iriye, *The Cold War in Asia* (1974); Tang Tsou, *America's Failure in China* (1963); Warren I. Cohen, *America's Response to China* (1979, rev. ed.); E. L. Kahn, Jr., *The China Hands* (1975); Ross Y. Koen, *The China Lobby* (1970); John Paton Davies, *Dragon by the Tail* (1972); David Rees, *Korea* (1964); I. F. Stone, *The Hidden History of the Korean War* (1969); Allen Whiting, *China Crosses the Yalu* (1968); Robert R. Simmons, *The Strained Alliance: Peking, Pyongyang, Moscow and the Politics of the Korean Civil War* (1975); Ronald Caridi, *The Korean War and American Politics* (1968); and Francis Heller, ed., *The Korean War: A Twenty-Five Year Perspective* (1977). See also David Green, *The Containment of Latin America* (1971); Jonathan Bingham, *Shirt-Sleeve Diplomacy* (1953); J. Fred Rippy, *Globe and Hemisphere* (1958); Bruce Kuniholm, *The Origins of the Cold War in the Near East* (1980); Michael B. Stoff, *Oil, War, and American Security* (1981); and Stephen D. Krasner, *Defending the National Interest: Raw Materials Investments and U.S. Foreign Policy* (1978).

Eisenhower foreign policy is dealt with in the studies by Parmet and Hoopes. See also Ralph Lapp, *The Weapons Culture* (1968); Adam Ulam, *The Rivals: America and Russia Since World War II* (1971); Herman Finer, *Dulles Over Suez* (1964);

Robert H. Ferrell, ed., *The Eisenhower Diaries* (1981); and Louis Gerson, *John Foster Dulles* (1967). Spooks and the secret intelligence effort are in Allen Dulles, *The Craft of Intelligence* (1963); David Wise and Thomas Ross, *The Invisible Government* (1964); the excellent book by Victor Marchetti and John D. Marks, *The CIA and the Cult of Intelligence* (1974); and Stephen Ambrose, *Ike's Spies: Eisenhower and the Espionage Establishment* (1981). For the diplomacy of the JFK years, see Roger Hilsman, *To Move a Nation* (1967); Robert McNamara, *The Essence of Security* (1968); Arthur Waskow and Stanley Newman, *America in Hiding* [on the bomb shelter mania] (1962); Karl Meyer and Tad Szulc, *The Cuban Invasion* (1962); Curtis Cate, *The Ides of August: The Berlin Wall Crisis, 1961* (1978); and three works on the Cuban missile crisis: Elie Abel, *The Missile Crisis* (1966); Robert Kennedy, *Thirteen Days* (1969); and Robert A. Divine, ed., *The Cuban Missile Crisis* (1971). Harsh assessments of JFK's diplomacy are Richard J. Walton, *Cold War and Counterrevolution* (1972); and Louise Fitzsimons, *The Kennedy Doctrine* (1972).

America in Vietnam is superbly described in George C. Herring, *America's Longest War: The United States and Vietnam, 1950–1975* (1979). See also David Halberstam, *The Best and the Brightest* (1972); Bernard Fall, *The Two Viet Nams* (1967); David Halberstam, *The Making of a Quagmire* (1965); *The Pentagon Papers* (1971); Thomas Powers, *The War at Home: Vietnam and the American People, 1964–1967* (1973); Frances Fitzgerald, *Fire in the Lake: The Vietnamese and the Americans* (1972); Guenter Levy, *America in Vietnam* (1978); Herbert Y. Schandler, *The Unmaking of a President: Lyndon Johnson and Vietnam* (1977); Allan E. Goodman, *The Lost Peace: America's Search for a Negotiated Settlement of the Vietnam War* (1978); Joseph Goldstein, et al, *The My Lai Massacre and its Cover-up: Beyond the Reach of Law* (1976); and Gloria Emerson, *Winners and Losers: Battles, Retreats, Gains, Losses and Ruins from a Long War* (1976). The last days of the U.S. presence are in Weldon Brown, *The Last Chopper: The Denouement of the American Role in Vietnam 1963–1975* (1976); John Pilzer, *The Last Day* (1976); and Frank Snepp, *Decent Interval: An Insider's Account of Saigon's Indecent End* (1977). Several first-hand accounts are valuable: Jonathan Schell, *The Village of Ben Suc* (1967); Philip Caputo, *A Rumor of War* (1977); Michael Herr, *Dispatches* (1977); and Mark Baker, *Nam: The Vietnam War in the Words of the Men and Women Who Fought There* (1981).

Other books on recent U.S. foreign policy include: Philip Geyelin, *Lyndon B. Johnson and the World* (1966); J. William Fulbright, *The Arrogance of Power* (1966); Jerome Levinson and Juan de Onis's book on the Alliance for Progress, *The Alliance That Lost its Way* (1970) Maxwell D. Taylor, *Swords and Ploughshares* (1972); Warren I. Cohen, *Dean Rusk* (1979); Tad Szulc, *The Illusion of Peace: Foreign Policy in the Nixon Years* (1978); John Stoessinger, *Kissinger: The Anguish of Power* (1976); Roger Morris, *An Uncertain Greatness: Henry Kissinger and American Foreign Policy* (1977); Henry Brandon, *The Retreat of American Power* (1974); James Fallows, *National Defense* (1981); Anthony Lake, ed., *The Legacy of Vietnam* (1976); and Earl C. Ravenal, *Never Again: Learning from America's Foreign Policy Failures* (1978).

Anna and Mike Simich always felt very much a part of Midland, but in recent years they have been dismayed by what they regard as an evaporation of the old sense of community. The Harts, the Bassanos, and other families throughout the nation experienced similar feelings. In part, their concerns stemmed from the vast physical growth which irreversibly altered the American landscape. Of even greater concern to the families, especially those in the larger cities or major metropolitan areas, were the frustrations they encountered as congestion increased, as the quality of public services declined while taxes rose, as environmental conditions deteriorated, and as perceptions about personal security convinced people that the cities were no longer safe.

Integration between communities and the national economy intensified. Communities became more vulnerable to national fluctuations. As the American population became more heavily suburbanized and urbanized, wars, recessions, inflation, and energy shortages created tensions in their communities. Suburban economic and population growth drained central cities of jobs and affluent families. Decisions made by the states and by the federal government infringed upon such traditional areas of local authority as housing, roads, education, and health. As the nation entered the last quarter of the 20th century, growth in the older and larger metropolitan centers appeared to have peaked. More Americans, frequently the children of those who had fled the cities for the suburbs, were leaving metropolitan areas to establish residences in rural areas or small towns. The flow of people to the Southwest and Far West reappeared as a significant force in the nation's development.

THE TRANSFORMATION OF RURAL AMERICA

The historic flow of Americans from countryside to city swelled to flood proportions following World War II. The farm population, forming 23 percent of the national population in 1940, fell rapidly to under 3 percent by 1979 (see Table 13-1). In 1970, under 3 million farms supplied the national output of food and fiber, 1.5 million less than accomplished this in 1950. Between 1959 and 1970, 1,000 of the 2,338 farms existing in 1959 disappeared in Antonio Nava's Hidalgo County, while the average size increased by about 100 acres. Still, about one half of all Hidalgo County farms, including Nava's, consisted of fewer than 50 acres. Like Nava, many of the owners had other full-time jobs. Far to the north, in Wilson County, Kansas, the pattern was similar. Fredonia's work force included many people who farmed during their free hours. It was becoming almost impossible to make an independent living by working "family-sized" farms. An adequate return went to those who amassed land and invested heavily in large equipment. As of the late 1970s, only 1 million of the nation's 2.8 million farms were serious producers and benefited from agricultural programs.

The difficulties of earning a living on small farms resulted in population losses in half of the nation's counties after World War II. Wilson County, Kansas, experienced decline as its population dropped from 17,930 in 1940 to 14,358 in 1970. The Harts' neighbors left. New Albany shrunk from 174 people in 1940 to fewer than 50 by 1980. In 1940, Wilson County contained 1,576 farms; in 1972, 478. The community focus of the Harts shifted almost entirely to Fredonia whose population fluctuated between 3,200 and 3,600 during this period.

Fredonia typified many small farm service centers. Such towns complained of a variety of disadvantages and pressures, but their problems were no greater than those of larger places. In fact, if they measured success in terms of population, they were progressing. Farm service towns contained some 12 percent of the nation's people in 1970 compared with about 10 percent in 1950. Since 1970, this growth has continued, consisting of not only retiring farmers from the surrounding countryside, but also migrants from metropolitan areas (see Table 13-1). Economics—employment has increased faster outside than within metropolitan areas—and attitudes—the search for a more pleasant environment—caused the move to rural

Table 13-1
Population in the United States by Place of Residence, 1940-1979 (millions)

	Metropolitan	Nonmetropolitan	Farm
1940	67	63	30
1950	85	65	23
1960	127	52	15
1970	148	54	9
1979	145	69	6

Roper, Wilson County, Kansas, 1975, a town passed by

Downtown Fredonia, Kansas, 1973

places. However, energy scarcity, especially recurrent gasoline shortages, may halt or reverse this population flow in the future.

Thirty-five years of decline in agricultural employment caused serious problems for rural America. Rural neighborhoods and their institutions—churches, schools, associations—gradually disappeared as their support evaporated. Those who stayed on had to shoulder a larger share of the costs of necessary services. With the possibility of achieving economic security in the countryside declining, many of those who remained lived on in poverty. While 30 percent of the nation's population was rural, 40 percent of the nation's poor lived in the country, and they were most prevalent in areas of rapid population decline. In vast expanses of the countryside, per capita personal income averaged about two thirds of the national average.

Not until the 1960s did substandard conditions in rural America become the target of federally funded reform programs. New Deal farm legislation and later programs such as Eisenhower's Soil Bank had aimed, with some success, at reducing the income differ-

entials between successful farmers and other Americans. In the 1960s, the Kennedy and Johnson administrations initiated regional programs such as the Appalachian Regional Commission (1965) to alleviate substantial and persistent unemployment and low family incomes. The idea was to make the regions more accessible, develop their resources, and provide alternate employment. The goals, however, were not met. Some rural political elites opposed federal programs that threatened their own interests. Others distrusted federal intervention for philosophical reasons. "We treasure our autonomy and identity," a Wilson County commissioner protested in 1972, "and fear to lose it if we rely on the federal government." More important, neither federal bureaucrats nor rural interests could agree upon the most appropriate kind of development.

Most development economists argued that the greatest number would be helped at the lowest cost by pursuing a "growth center" strategy in which communities of roughly 200,000 to 750,000 would receive the bulk of the aid monies to stimulate industrial growth, improve transportation, and so on. But in many lagging regions there were no cities of that size. The largest communities in southeastern Kansas (within the Ozarks Regional Commission's jurisdiction) were under 25,000. This issue became largely moot when the federal government's Economic Development Administration (EDA, 1965) adopted a "worst first" policy and channeled funds into areas with the least growth potential. Coupled with EDA's favoring of programs in smaller communities—between 1965 and 1968, 60 percent of public work funds was awarded to places with populations under 10,000—was the tendency to emphasize physical development, such as roads and industry, rather than human resource development such as education, health, and welfare.

Neither federal regional growth policies nor such programs of the 1970s as revenue sharing and community development were able to reverse the poor economic performance of many rural areas. Revenue-sharing funds were frequently used to postpone local tax increases rather than to address serious problems. Moreover, it was discovered in 1977 that revenue-sharing money was being sent to some 21,000 local governments that lacked even one full-time employee.

Although Fredonia served a continually diminishing farm clientele, the productive acreage in its hinterland remained nearly constant. Families like the Harts increased the size of their farms and their expendable incomes. Merchants and civic leaders in Fredonia and similar places noted that, while the absolute number of farm consumers had fallen, the amount of money spent by them had not. Still, town leaders were concerned about the future and many gave priority to diversification of the local economy, providing new jobs, and improving services.

Fredonians perceived their most serious problem as the retention of their young. Their failure to do so brought on a mounting problem of providing for their aged. The percentage of population over 65 in Fredonia increased from 17 to 25 percent between 1963 and 1975 as the percentage under 19 declined. While the proportion of aged nationally increased, it occurred less rapidly. Even more disturbing, one out of every four poor families nationally, and almost two of five in Kansas, was headed by an individual over 65. They increasingly congregated in small towns such as Fredonia. The elderly contributed little in the way of taxes while they continued to consume costly services. With the youth leaving, the inevitable question became: who would pay for services in the years to come? Small-town and rural Americans had no ready answer, but they insisted that their own

initiatives was central to a solution. They also knew that much depended upon the national economy and upon federal welfare policies. In the meantime, rural and small-town youth continued to leave, mostly for metropolitan America.

THE COMPLEXITY OF METROPOLITAN AMERICA

In 1976, most of our families lived in areas called Standard Metropolitan Statistical Areas (SMSAs) in the census and defined as a core city or group of contiguous cities (Fargo, North Dakota, and Moorhead, Minnesota; McAllen, Edinburg, and Pharr, Texas; or Kansas City, Kansas, and Kansas City, Missouri) with populations of at least 50,000, and of adjacent territory that was presumed to be functionally related and therefore interdependent. Between 1940 and 1979, the population of the nation increased by 84 million. All but 6 million persons included in this total either moved to or were born in metropolitan areas. On the eve of World War II, 67 million Americans (51 percent of the total) lived in metropolitan areas; by 1979, 145 million (70 percent) claimed metropolitan residence (see Table 13–1). Throughout the nation, though, the percentage of metropolitan population in the central city declined steadily, falling from 60 percent in 1960 to 41 percent in 1979. The South Atlantic, West South Central, Mountain, and Pacific regions, exploiting newness, climate, and economic opportunity, experienced the most rapid growth. Of the 15 fastest growing SMSAs between 1950 and 1970, six were in California, two in Arizona, and two in Florida. By the mid-1970s, even metropolitan areas were losing people. Eight of the 16 largest SMSAs have lost population since 1970 as have large suburbs in the East.

The clustering of people in numerous communities lying cheek-to-jowl in eastern New Jersey or Los Angeles County spawned a host of difficulties associated with sprawl. The multiplicity of governments within a metropolitan area was but one problem. In 1960, 18,422 local governments and special-purpose districts with the power to tax operated in the 212 SMSAs. Chicago alone sported 1,060. Initially designed to increase operating efficiency and avoid the corrupting influence of municipal governments, local water districts, airport authorities, housing authorities, hospital districts, and a dozen other types all competed for local tax dollars. These special districts frequently provided services for single communities, a water district for example, which might be managed more efficiently on a multicommunity or even multicounty basis.

The multiplicity of governments resulted partly from state indifference to housing and mass-transportation needs. It was further stimulated by federal programs dealing directly with municipalities and requiring local administrative agencies—urban-renewal agencies—to run the programs. Along with the strengthening of the city-federal bond, ineffective state governments and federal programs also fostered metropolitan and regional councils of government, some 600 of which existed in 1972. Their authority depended upon the willingness of the local governments which were members to delegate authority to the council. Some, such as the Lower Rio Grande Valley Development Council, possessed little authority to act. Others could perform specific functions in areas such as sewage and solid-waste disposal, law enforcement, and pollution control. But these councils depended almost entirely on federal grants-in-aid to support their area-wide programs. In the 1970s, revenue sharing, inflation, suburban distrust of metropolitan planning, and the absence of new federal urban initiatives combined to obstruct metropolitan planning.

THE SUBURBAN MILIEU

When the Bassanos moved to Upper St. Clair Township, southwest of Pittsburgh, in the fall of 1973, Charlotte suffered a form of culture shock. They bought their first car and she had to learn to drive. No longer could she walk down Dyckman Street and do the day's shopping. Now she had to drive to South Hills Village Shopping Center, a place she described as "shops which have access to an enclosed mall which has an upper and lower level, thereby allowing shoppers to go from one store to another without going out of doors when the weather is bad." It was all a revelation to this lifelong New Yorker who at first could not even make the local butchers understand the cut of meat she wanted. Charlotte and Bob had joined over 76 million others in suburbia.

Suburbs have existed as long as the modern city, but in 1940 only one in five Americans lived in them; by 1970, almost two in five were suburbanites. Upper St. Clair Township's population rose from 3,629 in 1950 to

The Bassano's suburban home in Upper St. Clair Township, Pennsylvania

15,411 in 1970. In the Kansas City metropolitan area, Johnson County, Kansas absorbed 160,000 people between 1950 and 1970 and grew by another 23 percent during the 1970s. The auto, rising affluence, FHA and Veterans Administration mortgage-guarantee programs, the high cost of building in the city, and the desire for a better environment all contributed to this movement.

During the immediate postwar years, the Henry Gishmans—white and with young children—were typical of the families moving to the suburbs. In 1950, there were over 600 houses for sale in the Gishmans' New Bayside neighborhood. By 1960, only 13 houses were unoccupied. In 1950, nearly one half of the residents were 18 years of age or younger while less than two percent were 65 years old or more. Many of the men, most of whom worked at nonmanual occupations in downtown Manhattan were veterans. Few women worked outside the home. When the Gishmans arrived there were no local schools, but by 1960, there were several serving a population further enlarged by the construction of more new homes. Since the 1950s, older people like the Bassanos have joined the parade to the suburbs. The population of older suburbs such as New Bayside aged because the suburbs retained many of the original home buyers. In both Upper St. Clair Township and New Bayside, the proportion of residents 18 years old and younger declined between 1960 and 1970 while the proportion of people over 65 increased.

In a critical way, the suburbs did not change between 1950 and 1970. They remained virtually segregated. Of the 76 million in the suburbs in 1970, 95 percent were white (see Table 13–2). During the 1960s, only 1.1 million blacks became suburbanites—many, such as Chris Gropper, in black suburbs—compared with 16.7 million whites. Recent trends suggest, however, that middle-class blacks are moving to the suburbs in greater

Table 13-2

Percentage of Black Population in Various Places, 1950–1970

	1950	1960	1970
U.S.	10	11	12
Metropolitan areas	9	11	12
Central cities of metropolitan areas	12	16	22
Suburbs of metropolitan areas	4	4	5

numbers. According to the Washington, D.C., Center for Metropolitan Studies, the black population in Washington suburbs rose by 110,000 between 1970 and 1974, a larger gain in four years than in the previous two decades. While fair-housing laws played a role in opening housing to blacks, more important was the rising income of middle-class Negroes who could afford better housing. In the Washington area, black affluence and legislation seemed to be overcoming traditional suburban segregation. Still, the flight of the white middle class from the central cities persisted. An estimated 600,000 whites moved out of Chicago to the suburbs during the 1970s, while the black population in the central city increased by 100,000.

Although the image of suburbia has become synonymous with conformity and uniformity, suburban lifestyles are rather diverse. There are upper, lower, and middle-class suburbs; suburbs that are distinct political entities, and suburbs that are segments of a political entity; ethnic and racial suburbs; new suburbs and old suburbs. Suburbanites in the aggregate are no more or less conformist and homogeneous in attitudes than are farmers or downtown apartment dwellers.

Jerry Trace's most recent suburban dwelling was in the relatively high-income suburb of Sugar Land, southwest of Houston, where median family income in 1970 was $11,798 (for all American families it reached $10,285 in 1971), higher than that of Chris Gropper's neighborhood by over $3,000. A few miles from Sugar Land, in Hunter's Creek Village, an incorporated city surrounded by Houston, median family income reached $29,201 in 1970, and 81 percent of all its families earned over $15,000. Hunter's Creek Village, Bethesda, Maryland, and similar places were really upper-class suburbs. Professionals were the largest single occupational group in Hunter's Creek Village and the smallest in Chris Gropper's neighborhood. Educational differentials were also significant. The median years of school completed for persons over 25 years in 1970 was 16.1 years in Hunter's Creek Village, 12 in Sugar Land, and 10.1 in Decatur.

Suburban evolution into full-service communities fostered diversity. Since the late 1950s, there has been a continuous flow of economic functions outward from the central cities to the suburbs. As suburbs emerged as major employment centers—between 1948 and 1963, the suburban share of employment in the 50 largest SMSAs rose by 10 percent, mostly at the expense of the central cities— they also declined as bedroom communities; commuting from the city to the suburbs and between suburbs increased.

By the mid-1970s, the combination of Vietnam-induced inflation and serious recession had somewhat altered suburban development. The end of World War II was followed by a great surge of home ownership with owner-occupied housing rising from 44 percent of 35 million dwelling units in 1940 to 62 percent of 53 million units in 1960, about two thirds located in suburban places. Since the mid-1960s, tougher environmental controls, shortages of power, and problems with public utilities added to the cost of a home, making it less profitable for builders to meet demand in the medium price range. Even more critical, the inflationary spiral has pushed land, material, and interest costs be-

yond the reach of many aspiring home owners. With the median price of a detached, single-family home rising from $26,000 in 1968 to over $40,000 in 1976, and $70,000 in 1979, builders turned to apartment complexes and to condominiums. In 1978, Jerry Trace sold the four-bedroom house in Sugar Creek (which had been purchased for $75,000 three years before) for $140,000. Peggy Trace dug up the six rosebushes she had planted and gave them to her daughter, Virginia. For the decade 1960–70, of 11 million new dwelling units constructed, 45 percent were multifamily dwellings compared with 10 percent in the early 1950s.

Increasing costs reshaped and slowed down suburban growth except on the urban fringe of Southwestern and Western cities. In these areas, a housing boom has produced, in former vineyards, the sprawl of San Jose, California, and, in the desert, the luxury homes of Sun City, Arizona. In the older sections of the nation, it seemed unlikely that the suburban boom of the 1950s and early 1960s would be repeated. So expensive were homes that some cities began requiring builders to price some new homes within the means of middle-class families. Called "inclusionary zoning," this idea was being tested in 1980 in Boulder, Colorado, Orange County, California, Montgomery County, Maryland, and other places. This device, in addition to the spreading practice of selling municipal bonds to provide home-purchasing money at lower than prevailing interest rates, bespoke concern over providing housing for middle-income families in an era of persistent double-digit inflation. In the meantime, the housing stock available to low-income families in major central cities continued to deteriorate and replacement building lagged far behind need.

The future of suburban development is uncertain. Dependence upon the automobile and the mobility it fostered may be reduced by persistent energy and fuel scarcities. Changing lifestyles among a growing number of young families evidenced by the declining birth rate and additional leisure time may bring more people to smaller dwellings in the city, where there are no garages to paint or property to dispose of if the marriage ends in divorce, as did one in four marriages during the early 1980s. Add to this the high cost of single-family homes, economic uncertainty, and the renewal of some city centers, and conditions promoting a gradual return to the central city might be present.

THE CENTRAL CITY

By the 1970s, downtown Omaha was empty at night. So, too, were the downtown areas of Dallas, Pittsburgh, and Kansas City. With the exception of an all-night eatery or two, one or two movie houses, and newspaper-porno magazine stores, everything was locked up. The pedestrians were hotel guests and the battalion of workers— largely black—that cleaned up the empty office buildings, banks, and stores. Few of the cars, taxis, and occasional buses seemed to be going to or coming from downtown events. In all but a few cities, downtown life had died.

The Minnesota Twins and the California Angels were at home in the suburbs. Other forms of recreation were moving out, too. The San Francisco Symphony Orchestra played in shopping centers and suburban junior-college auditoriums. Downtown retail business was severely damaged by suburban competition and the "revitalization" of downtown areas normally meant a huge convention center for outsiders rather than facilities for local residents. The flow of people and activities outward from the center altered the nature of American cities.

Between 1950 and 1970, 30 of 43 cities that lost at least 10 percent of their population

were in the Northeastern states while the West South Central, Mountain, and Pacific states contained the most rapidly growing cities. The departure of whites and the arrival of blacks and other minority peoples altered the character of inner cities. During the 1960s, the central cities of SMSAs lost over 2 million white inhabitants while gaining over 2 million Negroes (see Table 13–2). Although the rate of migration of rural Americans, black and white, into the cities peaked during the late 1950s, its consequences persisted. In 1944, 77 percent of all blacks lived in the South, in 1970, half lived in the North, mostly in places with populations of over 500,000.

Other minority groups participated in the urban flow. In New York, Julio Martinez and other Puerto Ricans and Spanish-language peoples comprised the major nonblack addition to the population. Some 70 percent of people of Puerto Rican origin in the coterminous United States lived in New York in 1970 where they formed 10 percent of the city's population—up from 8 percent in 1960. Some 80 percent of the Mexican-stock population lived in either California or Texas. Los Angeles County contained one of every five Mexican-Americans, with the highest concentration in East Los Angeles. For whites, these minority groups were the "urban problem"; for the minority groups, poor jobs, low income, wretched housing, and discrimination formed the barriers, set in place by whites, to upward mobility and a satisfactory life.

Jobs were the key to a city's viability. The nation's oldest and largest cities fared poorly when jobs moved to the suburbs along with the white population. Between 1947 and 1964, New York suffered a net loss of 204,000 industrial and tens of thousands of nonindustrial jobs. In the five years 1960–65, Philadelphia lost 4 percent of its jobs and Pittsburgh 5 percent. During the 1960s, Chicago lost 220 factories, 760 stores, and 229,000 jobs while its suburbs gained

500,000 jobs. Chicago's share of SMSA jobs declined from 78 percent in 1950 to 52 percent in 1970. An additional 200,000 jobs were lost during the 1970s.

Industrial plants had been locating beyond the central cities for over 50 years. Previously, however, gains in service-sector jobs had compensated for the loss. By the 1960s, service employment accounted for 56 percent of all jobs, but there was little room for further growth. Since 1950, 80 percent of all new jobs in the largest metropolitan areas have located in the suburbs, mostly inaccessible to inner-city residents. As in the past, the preferred jobs in the cities were dominated by whites.

For Julio Martinez, the aid extended to him by some mechanics was the turning point in his life. Few Puerto Ricans found such good jobs. A notably high proportion of Puerto Rican men did the dirty work in the city's hotels and restaurants while the women labored in the garment industry. They replaced Meyer Miller and his generation of immigrants. Occupational discrimination persisted despite equal-employment-opportunity legislation. In 1968, 47 percent of employed white men in central cities were white-collar workers compared with 21 percent for employed black males and 17 percent for Puerto Ricans in New York. Black women were more successful in entering sales, clerical, and managerial positions than were black men. From 1960 to 1968, the percentage of black women employed in those categories rose from 21 to 34.

For tens of thousands of inner-city youths, such as Jaime Martinez, entering the job market for the first time in the 1970s, daily life was drab and the future seemed bleak. As city jobs vanished, unemployment rates among minority youth soared to well over 35 percent. Most of these young people lacked experience, training, and education. Even low-paying, minimum-wage jobs were difficult to obtain.

City governments could do little to alleviate the situation. Congress, in 1973, passed the Comprehensive Employment and Training Act, (CETA), instituting a system of federally financed, locally administered, job-training and public-employment programs that included a role for private enterprise. Neither business nor government committed sufficient job positions or funds to the program. Persistent inflation, higher energy costs, periodic recessions, technological progress, all combined to retard significant increases in the kinds of jobs that inner-city youths could qualify for. As the 1970s ended, the absence of job opportunities seemed to be creating an army of young minority people who had never been employed and who seemed destined to lead street-corner lives.

Given the patterns of city employment and suburbanization, there was little likelihood that central-city housing would improve. While the Emergency Housing Act of 1975 benefited aspiring suburbanites, federal low and moderate-income housing programs had but a negligible effect on the supply. The Housing Act of 1949 projected the construction of 135,000 public housing units annually. Yet 26 years later only 700,000 had been built, 1 percent of all permanent dwellings in the country and far fewer than the number of units lost through urban renewal, highway construction, or abandonment. Between 1960 and 1970, many communities reported a worsening of conditions. New York, Los Angeles, Dallas, McAllen, and Midland all experienced accelerated deterioration. In Midland, for example, 83 percent of all housing was considered sound in 1960, in 1969, only 68 percent was so labeled. In the Simiches' old neighborhood, now predominantly black, only 39 percent of the homes were judged sound. In New York and elsewhere builders and investors viewed as unattractive the low-income housing market—and increasingly the moderate-income market—because profits were small and government regulations considered burdensome. By 1970, one out of seven families lived in a substandard dwelling.

In New York's South Bronx, likened by a visitor from the Soviet Union to a bombed city, the streets were covered with rubble and lined by hollow, abandoned tenements. Visited by President Carter in 1977 and Republican candidate Ronald Reagan in 1980, both of whom promised help to hostile audiences, the South Bronx had become the symbol of America's failing cities. Frustrated by the lack of federal attention to the area, a New York City Councilman, only partly tongue-in-cheek, applied to the Soviet Union for $5 billion in foreign aid to rebuild the neighborhood.

In 1969, one in eight families could not afford to pay the market price for standard housing. Rent subsidies and other public-housing programs reached only a fraction of those in need. Yet public-housing programs were more often opposed than supported in American communities. Fredonia consistently rejected the formation of a housing authority to provide much-needed dwellings for its aged. To receive housing at public expense seemed inequitable to millions who lived in homes obtained through FHA and VA-mortgage programs and who deducted annually the mortgage interest payments on their income-tax forms.

City transportation systems began to collapse when the federal government, in the mid-1950s, initiated construction of an immense interstate and intrametropolitan highway system. Lower suburban population densities and the one-person-to-a-car habit made it unprofitable to sustain mass-transportation systems. Most railroads abandoned passenger service while trunk lines declared bankruptcy or were sustained by federal loans. As passenger loads dropped and costs increased, city bus, subway, and elevated systems required large annual sub-

sidies. Rate increases caused patronage to drop. At the same time, auto transport was too expensive for many city dwellers.

In 1969, Joseph Alioto, Mayor of San Francisco, promised that no more freeways would be built; "San Francisco," he said, "is not going to be turned into a wasteland of freeways and garages." It was not freeway opposition, however, but the 1973 oil embargo and energy crisis that influenced gradual change in federal transportation policy. The Federal Aid Highway Act of 1973 allowed states and localities to use revenues from their share of the highway trust fund for mass transportation. This strengthened somewhat the intent of the unfunded Urban Mass Transportation Act of 1970. But as of 1980, only two new systems serving the San Francisco Bay area and the Washington, D.C. metropolitan area were fully operational.

The decline and change in central cities was the result of more than just the radiation of people outward. Cities continued to attract those who could afford luxurious apartment houses which offered total security and proximity to the intellectual or cultural offerings of the center. Upper-income groups found highly desirable such lavish complexes as the Crown Center in Kansas City or the Hancock Building in Chicago. Also in Chicago, a $170 million commercial, office, and residential complex, Water Tower Place, opened in 1976 on North Michigan Avenue. Developers in other central cities—Boston, Rochester, Los Angeles—invested immense sums in similar centers. Water Tower Place interests pointed out that 17 percent of the residents of the area earned over $50,000 annually. Two-bedroom condominiums in Water Tower Place sold for $135,000. Others warned that they created enclaves of high-income populations in the midst of unchecked urban blight. All agreed that such costly ventures were feasible only in the largest cities. Few were certain that they would restore vigor permanently to downtowns. For families such as the Bassanos and Groppers, Water Tower Place would be, at best, a tourist attraction.

In St. Louis, Baltimore, and Washington, D.C., among other cities, some professional people during the 1970s moved back from the suburbs to live in older neighborhoods. This trend was called "gentrification." Older homes on many blocks in Washington's Capitol Hill area were completely gutted, restored, and sold to high-income families. In the process, low-income families, mostly black, were compelled to move. But no new low-income housing was being built. Thus, the dispossessed were forced to seek housing in other zones of misfortune where overcrowded conditions, poor services, and high crime rates already prevailed. Gentrification, then, was not an answer to the revitalization of the inner city.

City centers, however, lost their attractiveness for most people. Residence there required incomes far higher than most middle-class Americans earned. When Austin Hart made his last trip from Fredonia to downtown Kansas City, he paid dearly to park and had

Conflicts of scale and cultural discontinuity abounded in those city centers experiencing urban renewal. This is Washington, D.C.

his hubcaps stolen. For shoppers such as Charlotte Bassano, downtown Pittsburgh or, more recently, Washington, D.C. offered far fewer attractions than nearer shopping centers did. Moreover, Charlotte and countless other suburban women were afraid to enter the downtown of any major city after dark. People other than conventioneers and workers prowled city streets after dark. Construction of blocks of office buildings, alive with people during the day but empty at night, literally took the life out of city centers.

WHO YOU ARE AND WHERE YOU LIVE MAKES A DIFFERENCE

To live in comfort in a socially and culturally homogeneous setting removed from the nuisances, disorder, and crime of the city was the post–World War II version of the American Dream for middle-Class Americans. Once there, the residents protected themselves against unwanted intrusions. They used zoning ordinances, building codes, neighborhood associations, and restrictive covenants to defend the suburb, mostly against blacks and the lower class. Before and after World War II, restrictive covenants—stipulations in deeds binding owners not to sell or lease their property to Negroes—were widely employed devices. In 1948, the Supreme Court declared them void, and suburban residents turned to other weapons, primarily zoning, to preserve homogeneity.

The original intention behind zoning, to ensure balanced community growth, was abandoned when it was used as a weapon of exclusion. Communities seeking to insulate middle and upper-class whites adopted codes requiring, for example, lot sizes of one or two acres or prohibiting multifamily dwellings, mobile homes, or industry. In the New York metropolitan area, five counties doubled their lot size requirements during the 1950s to exclude middle or low-income housing. In 1968, one fourth of all metropolitan municipalities with a population of at least 5,000 did not permit construction on lots of under one-half acre. In 1975, 99 percent of the land zoned for residential use was restricted to single-family dwellings. As suburbs rezoned for high-rent apartment complexes, they strenuously resisted low-cost public housing. In response to the Kennedy and Johnson administrations' policies of encouraging low-income housing in suburbs, communities have resorted to referenda to veto public housing. In 1971, the Supreme Court upheld this practice and President Nixon assured the suburbs that such action would not preclude further federal financial aid. But challenges to the obviously discriminatory intent of the suburbs have increased. Massachusetts, for example, recently required each town to set aside 1.5 percent of its useable land for low and moderate-income housing. Some cities in the East, beginning in the mid-1970s, filed suits in federal courts in an effort to deny federal funds to neighboring suburbs that used zoning to exclude low and moderate-income families.

However, a rash of low-income housing construction in suburbia did not occur; neither was there a notable movement of the urban poor to the countryside. For one thing, the decisions in some court cases frequently contradicted decisions in other cases. While it seemed that exclusionary zoning, that is zoning that excluded low and moderate-income housing from suburban communities, was illegal, loopholes in the decisions still allowed the suburbs, in fact, to prohibit the construction of housing for lower-income families. Open housing in suburbs and rural areas had not been achieved and, given the impact of inflation, was unlikely to be achieved in the near future.

When Julio and Angelina Martinez and

Low-income housing in Inwood, where the Martinezes lived in 1965

their seven children moved to Inwood in 1965, it was a move up. For the Bassanos, only a block away, the appearance of the Martinez family represented one more sign of decay. The Bassanos and other whites departed, fleeing a neighborhood in which the black and Hispanic population increased from 5 percent in 1960 to 24 percent in 1970. Inwood was but one of thousands of inner-city neighborhoods that experienced a radical change in population and a diminution in the quality of services. Stark differential life opportunities, rooted in unchanging income differences (see Table 13–3) distinguished the residents of Atlanta's Vine City, Los Angeles' Watts, New York's South Bronx, or West Dallas from the residents of Sugar Land, New

Table 13-3

Median Black and White Family Income in Metropolitan Areas, 1959 and 1967 (in 1967 dollars)

	Median income ($)		Differential between black and white ($)	
	1967	1959	1967	1959
Metropolitan areas				
white	8,993	7,493	3,323	3,154
black	5,670	4,339		
Central cities				
white	8,294	7,160	2,671	2,763
black	5,623	4,397		
Metropolitan areas over 1 million				
white	8,523	7,579	2,702	2,731
black	5,822	4,848		
Metropolitan areas under 1 million				
white	8,084	6,795	2,800	3,235
black	5,284	3,560		
All suburban areas				
white	9,497	7,791	3,640	3,806
black	5,857	3,985		

Bayside, Upper St. Clair Township, and even Inwood. In city after city, the spread of blighted zones such as the South Bronx proceeded as rapidly as the flight of whites and jobs to the suburbs. Federal programs failed to improve the quality of urban life, and, too often, urban renewal was Negro removal. To build Pittsburgh's Golden Triangle and Civic Arena at least 5,400 families, mostly blacks, were displaced between 1955 and 1966 while the 1,719 new dwellings constructed were almost all luxury apartments. In most cities, large and small, urban renewal well-served real estate and downtown business interests while perpetuating the zones of misfortune.

Inequities—largely with racial or ethnic dimensions—abounded within the inner city and between the inner city and the suburbs. It was no coincidence that McAllen's Mexican-American population lived in the flood-prone southern and western areas. Neither was it coincidence that, by 1970, Chicago was the nation's most racially segregated city, with 78 percent (66 percent in 1960) of all blacks living in neighborhoods that were 90 percent black. Low-income groups bore the brunt of unemployment and underemployment, lived in the inferior housing, received the worst education, and had access to the fewest health-care facilities. Optimists pointed out that a higher proportion of inner-city youth was completing high school, but the completion rate was far below that of the suburbs and it increased more slowly. Moreover, educational gains yielded fewer dollars in salaries for minorities than for whites. Central-city white males between 25 and 54 years of age with 12 years of education earned, in 1967, between $2,000 and $2,700 per year more than black males with the same schooling earned. Between 1959 and 1967, the dollar differential between white and black incomes remained virtually unchanged (see Table 13-3). But by 1979, after 12 years of recession and inflation, nonwhite families earned $7,000 less than white families. That it was blackness that made the difference was suggested by the influence that skin color had on the geographic mobility and job opportunities of Puerto Ricans and Mexican-Americans. Julio Martinez is a "white" Puerto Rican. His much darker brother-in-law, Fredrico, suffered more discrimination that Julio did. For Mexican-Americans, income disparities with other whites were basically attributable to differences in educational achievement.

In Texas, black and Mexican-American males were employed in disproportionately large numbers only in the lowest paying occupations. While blacks formed 10 percent and Mexican-Americans 15 percent of all employed males over 16 years of age, they formed 27 and 26 percent of the nonfarm laborers respectively but under 5 percent of all engineers. Still, while two Texas blacks worked for every three Mexican-Americans, there were only three black engineers for each 22 Hispanic engineers and 1 black doctor or dentist for every 6 Hispanics in those professions.

President Nixon worked energetically to terminate the urban programs of the Kennedy-Johnson years on grounds that they made conditions worse instead of better. He was correct in stating that conditions in the cities were worse than they had been in the 1950s. Federal initiative ended in 1975 when, only nine years after President Johnson had declared that the nation faced an urban crisis, policymakers in the Ford Administration announced that the urban crisis of the 1960s was over. While the median income of central-city families as a percentage of suburban income declined from 89 percent in 1960 to 79 percent in 1979, the Ford and Carter administrations and successive Democratic Congresses assigned urban problems low

priority. Americans, it would seem, were about to change the meaning of the word "crisis." This new definition guided the federal government in its reluctant response to New York's requests for guaranteed loans to bail the city out of its deep (and partly self-created) fiscal crisis. The government demanded that the city cut its basic services— health, education, welfare—before it would provide assistance. While the mayors of other large cities viewed New York's illness with foreboding, most Americans apparently preferred to let the city sink. Concurrently, the government's action to shore up homeowners and stimulate home building in the suburbs met with general approval.

Two decades of federal spending had not brought measurable relief to America's distressed cities. Some argued that the sums appropriated had been totally inadequate to the task; others argued that government spending could never resolve the problem. President Reagan adopted the latter position. As his administration began, he advocated the establishment of urban enterprise zones. Small businessmen who located in those zones and hired local workers would receive tax incentives and other indirect encouragement. It remained to be seen whether such an approach could meet the needs of inner-city neighborhoods in which one of every two adults was unemployed.

COMMUNITY ECONOMIC GROWTH IN A CHANGING WORLD

Within the setting provided by a mature and expanding industrial economy, Americans searched for economic security. Among their expectations were full employment, occupational and geographic mobility, home ownership, and increased leisure time. Within communities, the types of industry and business, where they were located, who was employed at different jobs, and various salaries or wages worked irrevocably to shape not only the physical configuration of a community but its social system as well. Crucible Steel fashioned Midland just as agriculture fashioned Fredonia and McAllen. In larger places, a similar, but less visible, process occurred.

Since 1945, industrial and service activities continued to spread more evenly throughout the nation, penetrating rural America and furthering the rise of new economic centers in the Southwest, the Far West, and other growing regions. The nation's manufacturing sector gradually decentralized, and such older industrialized states as Massachusetts and Michigan produced proportionately less of the total value of manufactured products. Simultaneously, the share of the nation's manufactured output increased in such industrializing states as Texas and California. While the 10 leading industrial centers did not change dramatically after 1947, they did produce a smaller proportion of the value added by manufacture in 1971 than they did in 1947 (see Table 13–4).[1]

The industrial mix of the leading manufacturing centers was quite varied. New York and Chicago, possessing highly diversified industrial sectors, remained the two truly national cities, although they lost some of their superiority, as in banking and credit, to regional centers. Still, both competed across the country while there was little competition within their own regions. Manufacturing in Pittsburgh and Detroit remained highly concentrated within a single industrial group.

Pittsburgh fabricated but a small portion of the steel and other metals that it produced. Instead, Pittsburgh exported the metals to Detroit and St. Louis, which produced but a small portion of the metal turned into automobiles.

Older, highly specialized, and centralized economic centers, such as Pittsburgh proved quite vulnerable to interregional competition. While the economies of cities in the Gulf States and Southern California soared during and after World War II, Pittsburgh, New England's textile cities, and other older cities experienced great difficulty in maintaining their economic strength. Not only did they frequently fall behind in their strongest sectors, but they also experienced, at best, marginal success in attracting new enterprises. With the exception of Boston, these cities were bypassed by two of postwar America's greatest industrial groups, automotive and defense-related industries.

The transportation-equipment industry was the largest industry group, producing $87 billion worth of goods in 1971, or 13 percent of the national total. The automotive industry accounted for 67 percent of this total. Each hamlet and village with its gas station and mechanic's shop formed a part of the industry. Most towns of over 2,500 had at least one automobile dealership and from there the linkages proceeded through automotive-parts stores, the glass and tire business, drive-in theaters and hamburger joints, incessant road repair and construction, police traffic duties, and on and on to the seat of the automotive empire, Detroit. Detroit alone produced over 20 percent of all motor vehicles and the industry was critical to the economies of Kansas City, Los Angeles, and St. Louis. Eighteen SMSAs accounted for 49 percent of all transportation production, with the largest share distributed within the eastern North Central states.

---

[1] VAM is considered the best measure for comparing the relative economic importance of manufacturing among industries and geographic areas. It measures the value of output less the value of the commodities consumed in production—in other words, the degree to which a raw product is transformed by the manufacturing process. Thus the VAM will be less per unit of manufactured foodstuffs than for televisions.

Table 13-4
Leading Industrial Centers by Value Added by Manufacture, 1947
and 1971

SMSA rank order by VAM in 1971	Percent national VAM in 1971	Percent national VAM in 1947	Rank in 1947
New York 8.4	12.5	1
Chicago 5.5	7.4	2
Los Angeles 4.3	3.3	5
Detroit 3.0	3.9	3
Philadelphia 2.7	3.7	4
St. Louis 1.5	1.7	9
Cleveland 1.4	2.0	7
Newark 1.4	1.0	14
Boston 1.3	1.8	8
Pittsburgh 1.2	2.3	6
San Francisco 0.9	1.4	10

The automotive industry proved vulnerable to competition from overseas. During the 1970s, foreign auto manufacturers captured an increasing share of the American market because of their product's greater fuel efficiency and, some would argue, superior construction. So severe was foreign competition that the Chrysler Motor Corporation required a federal loan of $1.5 billion to avoid bankruptcy. Sales of U.S.-made cars plunged from 9.3 million in 1978 to about 6.5 million in 1979, and the Ford Motor Company lost $2 billion in 1979. With sales declining, the auto industry closed plants and laid off almost 300,000 workers. Detroit's unemployment rate, in 1979, averaged 15 percent. Falling auto sales caused the loss of 650,000 jobs in such related industries as rubber, glass, textiles, and especially steel. In a last-ditch attempt to recapture the domestic market, the American auto industry introduced a new line of compacts in 1980 that, it was hoped, would prove competitive with VWs, Hondas, Toyotas, and Datsuns.

Steel towns in the upper Ohio River valley such as Midland, Youngstown, Ohio, and

Pittsburgh suffered grievously from the declining fortunes of the steel industry. Inflation, environmental regulations, aging plant facilities, cheaper foreign steel and shrinking foreign markets for American steel, the depressed auto industry, all contributed to severe retrenchment. U.S. Steel alone laid off 13,000 workers and closed down 13 plants in 1979. At Youngstown, all three major steel plants shut down between 1977 and 1979, throwing 13,000 people out of work and reducing the city's tax income by at least $2 million. In response to the crisis at Youngstown, the U.S. government pledged $225 million in federal loans to help create jobs for unemployed steel workers, and a coalition of Youngstown's leaders proposed a plan in which workers would buy and modernize one of the closed steel plants with the federal money. By late 1980, some 12 states were considering legislation requiring advance notice of an impending plant closing. Some of these bills would also indemnify communities for taxes lost through a plant closing.

Like the automotive and steel industries,

470

defense-related industries and the location of military bases had a profound impact on community economies after World War II. Texas, New York, and California were the greatest beneficiaries of defense spending, receiving in defense contracts 8, 9, and 24 percent respectively of all defense dollars in 1971. Three California SMSAs—Los Angeles–Long Beach, Anaheim–Garden Grove–Santa Ana, and San Jose—were awarded over 20 percent of all defense contracts in 1971, while Dallas–Fort Worth received 6 percent.

Places as small as Midland and as large as Fort Worth and Seattle alternated between despair and jubilation as the world's military establishments awarded contracts. Crucible Steel's skills in the production of titanium garnered beneficial aerospace contracts. Seattle's dependence upon Boeing brought rude shocks and severe unemployment during the late 1960s when aircraft orders declined. In Fort Worth, long a major manufacturer of military aircraft, the ups and downs of General Dynamics alternately brought prosperity and stress. In the summer of 1975, the leading air forces in the world, including the USAF, decided to adopt the new General Dynamics F-16 jet as the nucleus of their fighter force. Some $20 billion worth of fighters will have been built in Fort Worth by 1980.

The nation and the world pressed in on America's communities. In microcosm, Midland's postwar difficulties reflected the disadvantages of overspecialization as well as the degree to which external forces and events controlled its fate. Some 65 percent of Midland's workers were colleagues of Mike Simich at Crucible. The metal industries were highly reactive to changes in the national economy, although Crucible was somewhat less so because of its specialty metal expertise. In addition to providing the largest payroll for Midland, land holdings gave the company

control over residential development in the town. So new homes and jobs were at the disposal of Crucible. A serious shortage of housing and the loss of jobs since 1950 explains Midland's failure to grow from 1940 to 1960 and the population decline of 19 percent experienced in the subsequent decade.

Jobs were lost when Treadwell Construction Company closed operations following a series of damaging labor disputes. Continuing automation at Crucible eliminated more jobs. For the remaining workers, strikes and layoffs were a constant threat. Mike Simich, an ardent advocate of the United Steel Workers Union as a young man, worried that labor settlements made by Big Steel and the union did not reflect the needs of specialty steel and its employees. Moreover, over the years, coal, public utilities, and railroad strikes have all compelled Crucible to furlough hundreds of workers. Mike wondered why he should be laid off because of actions taken in the coal fields. And, in 1974–75, the decline of automobile sales caused Crucible to reduce production and lay off Mike and other personnel. Mike was happily retired when the shock of falling auto sales in 1978 and 1979 resulted in new layoffs at Crucible. Thus, crisis in the auto industry and the weakened competitive position of the steel industry in both domestic and foreign markets directly affected the future of such communities as Midland and

Looking toward Crucible Steel over the rooftops of Midland, Pennsylvania

Youngstown. So dependent were both places upon a single industry that neither could do much to buffer itself against further decline.

COMMUNITY CONTROL OF ECONOMIC GROWTH

Boosterism is an ancient tradition among American communities. A motorist approaching Anywhere, U.S.A., will pass signs reading, "Anywhere Takes Pride In Its Future," or "Anywhere, population 257 and Gro, Grow, Growing." From the early 19th century into the 1960s, towns and cities, believing that the failure to grow ultimately meant stagnation and decay, marshaled their resources to avoid the slow death of a nongrowth future. Atlanta, Houston, Kansas City, and San Jose, all boomer towns, advertised their advantages and opportunities far and wide through promotional specialists. "Goodness is bigness" and "bigger is better" summed up the prevailing philosophy.

In recent years, boosterism has given way in some places to a "stay away" or no-growth policy. Suburban and outlying areas in Chicago, Cleveland, Savannah, Denver, San Francisco, and elsewhere adopted sewer, gas and electric, and water hookup moratoria and other devices to slow down or stop growth. When Jerry Trace moved to Denver in 1960, he quickly observed the rapid growth of Boulder, a city just to the north. Connected with Denver by turnpike in the early 1950s and nestled at the foot of the Rocky Mountains with easy access to such year-round mountain resorts as Rocky Mountain National Park, Vail, Glenwood Springs, and Aspen, Boulder was a highly desirable place to live and work.

The home of the University of Colorado, Boulder, in the 1950s and 1960s, attracted other major institutions and businesses such as the Federal Bureau of Standards, Dow

Boosting unique Neodesha, Kansas, 1975

Chemicals, and Ball Brothers Glass. In 1964, IBM moved in, bringing over 3,000 employees and their families in the succeeding five years. The city's population, at 20,000 in 1950, rose to 67,000 by 1970, fueled in part by rising enrollment at the university. All of this caused a severe housing crunch and generated great opportunities for residential and commercial developers. Supported by favorable annexation and subdivision policies, builders constructed 500 to 700 apartment units and over 100 single-family houses annually between 1965 and 1970 with the peak reached in 1970 and 1971 when a total of 3,700 apartment units were completed.

Then, in the early 1970s, the city, under pressure from environmentalists and other pressure groups, undertook a reconsideration of its uncontrolled course. Following a series of well-attended public discussions on the consequences of growth, a referendum passed giving the city council a mandate to restrict expansion. Over the opposition of realtors, builders, and other businesspeople, the city doubled utility hookup fees, reduced allowable densities per building lot by 50 percent, stiffened subdivision regulations, and made annexation extremely costly and difficult. Then, in 1977, Boulder passed a growth-control ordinance that limited developers to 450 new housing starts annually. In general, the proponents of slow growth consisted of people whose income did not depend upon the local economy. Growth, however, continued during the 1970s as Boulder's population climbed to 85,000.

Boulder's Board of Realtors and its builders opposed all of these devices to retard growth, arguing that they were not causing the growth but only supplying the housing needs of new residents. Construction did decline sharply, and several major builders left the city. Boulder's efforts to protect its quality of life did not prevent it from vigorously opposing the development of a major shopping center outside of town and proposing as a substitute an unimaginative expansion of an existing in-town shopping mall. Moreover, some of the growth which would have occurred within the city merely moved into the surrounding country so that the city and its environs presented as unplanned and randomly built-up an appearance as did most other American communities of a similar size. Nevertheless, Boulder did directly confront the issue of uncontrolled growth and sought to reach solutions through democratic processes.

Other communities, too, pondered for the first time the long-term advantages of traditional economic growth. That in itself heralded a minor revolution in American attitudes. Americans, individually or collectively, had yet to exercise sufficient restraint in resource use. During the energy crunch of 1973, Los Angeles was exceptional in curbing the use of electricity. But convincing communities that both their own interests and those of the nation would be served by the adoption of resource conservation programs remained a difficult task. As both a Fredonia cement-plant worker and a Midland steel-worker expressed it, the basic issue was "dirt or work." All over the country, communities fought out that issue.

In New York, the location of a $250 million Consolidated Edison Company electric-generating station in the city—of enormous economic benefit—was blocked by the cooperation of hundreds of nonprofit organizations dedicated to the reduction of air pollution. Julio Martinez followed this controversy and could not understand why people opposed new jobs. In Midland, for 17 years, the borough evaded a state order to build a primary sewage-treatment plant while it periodically berated Crucible for smoke pollution. In Fredonia, the General Portland Cement Company (a subsidiary of U.S. Steel) refused to introduce a smoke-abatement system at its own cost. A local bond issue provided the company with part of the development expense, thereby embittering many Fredonians. Neither town had the leverage or the will to force a real confrontation. They were captives of the paymaster. Despite federal and state pollution-control laws and the Environmental Protection Agency, in Fredonia a thin, white dust continued to settle over blowing laundry and in Midland a black pall frequently shrouded the city. Dirt or work?

During the mid and late 1970s, the public became aware of even more serious environmental problems with the discovery that toxic waste dumps threatened the health of residents of various communities. Most dramatic was the revelation that near Niagra Falls, New York, the seepage of chemicals contaminated a site on which over 1,000 homes had been built. Many residents were moved at federal expense and scientific teams investigated the exceptionally high illness rates suffered by the area's inhabitants. People in dozens of other communities in New Jersey, Massachusetts, Michigan, Louisiana, and other states suddenly discovered that their water had been contaminated by chemicals. Local ordinances and state laws had failed to prevent much illegal dumping, and many called for the imposition of strict federal standards. How this could be squared with the hue and cry against "big" government was anyone's guess.

Prior to the mid-1960s, however, the quest for security through growth overrode all other considerations. When Marine Sergeant Jerry Trace returned home in 1946, he found Evansville confidently converting from war to consumer production. True, the vast landing-craft facilities of the Missouri Valley Bridge and Iron Company, employing a peak of 16,500 during the war, had been dismantled, and Republic Aviation Corporation had closed down. But Chrysler Corporation and Servel were ready to convert from the production of shell casings, tank engines, and aircraft components to cars and refrigerators. Jerry read the future as bright and, with two partners, launched the Black and White Cab Company. Evansville's adjustment to peacetime went smoothly because its industrial products were in great demand and because new firms, such as International Harvester, moved in, attracted by existing factory space and the availability of trained labor. Then came Korea and new defense contracts. Employment rose swiftly from 76,000 in 1950 to 98,000 in 1953. Few were prepared for the severity of the economic decline that followed and lingered on for a decade. After 1953, the cab business slowed down along with the rest of Evansville's economy. Viewing Evansville's future dimly by 1956, Jerry accepted a job in Louisville.

Evansville's decline was caused by forces beyond local control, although at the time labor unions bore the blame. Defense contract reductions in 1953, affecting Chrysler and Servel, forced employment down to under 80,000 by 1958 and 71,000 in 1961. But more than that, Evansville's economy depended upon a few large firms. Thirty-one percent of the labor force in 1953 worked for four companies—all of which were extremely sensitive to the shifting demands of the con-

sumer market. Between 1954 and 1959, three of the big four closed their Evansville plants. Chrysler moved to a new and larger facility in the more favorably located city of St. Louis. International Harvester's refrigerator was too expensive and inefficiently distributed. Servel's gas refrigerator could not compete with cheaper electric models. Shifting to electric appliances in 1952 and 1953, Servel products received scanty consumer acceptance. These problems were hidden through 1953 because of defense contracts. When these were lost in 1953 and 1954, Servel closed completely.

Evansville fought back successfully with local development groups such as Evansville's Future Incorporated and the Evansville Industrial Foundation. Through the late 1950s and into the 1960s, several new firms located in and around Evansville, notably Bendix-Westinghouse in town and Alcoa Aluminum about 10 miles east of the city. Finally, in 1963, employment reached the level of 1950 and the percentage of manufacturing employment to total jobs had been reduced. But the city remained highly dependent upon its industrial plant. New shifts in consumption patterns, continued national recession, or energy shortages could all breed problems for Evansville and other industrial cities.

Antonio Nava and Austin Hart lived in economically stagnant regions: Nava in the poorest metropolitan area in the nation and Hart in a nonmetropolitan region in which there was no city of 25,000 persons. In southeastern Kansas and the Lower Rio Grande Valley, a declining agricultural base was not entirely compensated for by additional industrial or service employment. The valley's problems were exacerbated by the presence of large numbers of poorly educated, unskilled, and low-paid Mexican-Americans, overwhelmingly employed as laborers in a shrinking agricultural industry. Southeastern Kansas had more industry than the valley had, but not enough to provide full-time employment for its labor force. The valley placed high hopes on tourism, but this low-paying industry did not result in significant income gains for most Mexican-Americans. In 1979, the median family income of the valley was one third the national average. Valley cities were overrun by poor Mexicans, many entering illegally, who searched for work and strained to the limit available social and community services.

Neither region possessed an urban center of great growth potential. Pittsburg, Coffeyville, and Independence in Kansas and McAllen, Pharr, and Edinburgh in Texas all had populations under 40,000, far from the 250,000 accepted by economists as the lower limit for a regional growth center. Most EDA projects in the Valley, including a $455,000 tourist center in Harlingen and grain-storage silos in Brownsville costing $638,000 were neither job producing nor of benefit to Mexican-Americans. The Ozarks Regional Commission, encompassing contiguous counties in Oklahoma, Arkansas, Missouri, and Kansas (including Wilson County), demonstrated more concern with human resource development than valley agencies had demonstrated. Job-training programs for the unemployed, emphasis on vocational education, and programs to provide training and employment for female heads of families along with day-care centers for their children, all were utilized in an effort to upgrade the quality of the labor force. But the commission was underfunded and threatened, along with the other regional commissions, with dissolution.

These regions and others—the lower Ohio Valley, most of the Appalachian Highlands, central Pennsylvania—remote from major economic centers and with underdeveloped human resources, offered locational advantages to none but the most transient and least stable businesses. Citizens in Fredonia and southeastern Kansas learned to be selective in allowing industry to locate in their communities. As a local lawyer and civic leader phrased it: "Fredonia will not encourage, will discourage, slipshod, inadequately capitalized firms. We know we can't get Dupont or GE but we will get stable firms or go without. Nor will we offer the moon to get them." But in an era characterized by a stagnant economy, rampant inflation, and energy shortages, not many communities could assume so heroic a posture. Many would take what they could attract and go to extreme lengths to keep what they had. In Hudson Falls, New York, during the mid-1970s, the fact that the local General Electric plant was contaminating the Hudson River and endangering the health of its employees did not outweigh the fact that GE employed over 1,400 workers, having an annual payroll of $14 million and paying some $1.5 million in taxes to the community. How is the public interest defined in such a case?

Most communities and groups of communities used planning and development authorities to encourage economic growth. Since they all competed for a piece of the development dollar, federal and private, they could not all be successful. Fredonia's planning commission was less active than many in competing for federal money. A few miles to the south, Neodesha actively solicited help from any and all sources. Both communities at least acted consistently and possessed an idea of what they wanted in the future. But, during the Ford and Carter administrations, there was no drive to confront and thereby shape the future. There was no energy policy, no policy to combat inflation or to relieve the human suffering caused by recession. There was no urban policy. There was bipartisan drift and formlessness.

During good times, communities could exercise certain options to guide the direction of growth. During bad times, those options vanished and community autonomy was weakened. Federal power could be used to shore up community independence, upgrade human resources, provide guidelines for future growth, and soften inequity. If those were not proper federal tasks, what were?

WHAT COMMUNITIES DO FOR OUR FAMILIES

Building on precedents set during the depression, post–World War II communities extended the range of services available to their residents. Although Americans still did not live in a society in which economic and social security extended to all, more people had access to more services than in past eras. As a provider, government did not always assume this role willingly; often it was thrust on governments at all levels because of inequities or failures in the private sector. The appearance of a health clinic in a poor neighborhood represented an extension of public service to a population that could not obtain those services, as others did, for cash on the open market. Softball fields and health clinics both might be hailed as improvements but for quite dissimilar reasons.

Most families pursued the bulk of their activities within their communities and many participated in organizations that were lively and meaningful to them. To be sure, there were places that lacked the cohesiveness that an active group life offered, and there were families who did not participate in voluntary activities. Middle-class Americans in the suburbs were more likely to participate in formal and local organizations than were those of the same class in the city itself where kinship and informal social group relations were central. Neither the middle-class Bassanos nor the working-class Martinezes in Inwood participated in neighborhood organizations, but both socialized frequently with friends and relatives. The down-and-out Traces in Los Angeles were almost totally isolated, having few friends, only occasional contact with relatives, and no formal community associations. Still, those that did participate gave vitality to associational life in communities across the country. For the upper-class Butlers, family, friends, and organizations were of great importance. A good part of Robert Butler's life was spent in community service, particularly charities. So, too, were social networks central in the lives of the Simiches and Harts and other residents of small towns. Much depended upon the income, occupation, race or ethnicity, and personal inclinations of family members. For the Simiches, ethnicity was the key.

Midland's ethnic associations grew stronger after World War II. After years of fund raising, ground was broken for St. George's Serbian Orthodox Church, which opened for worship in 1949. Under the active leadership of The Very Reverend Milorad Dobrota, who had taken up the pastorate in 1947, St. George's flourished. While Midland's younger generation was less ethnocentric than its parents had been, largely because of education, socialization, and ignorance of the mother tongue, the *Midland News'* weekly listing of club meetings attested to the strength of the ethnic groups. But Midland experienced great changes after World War II. Blacks, in 1970, constituted 20 percent of a declining population. The number of residents 18 years and younger declined by 3.5 percent during the 1960s, while people 65 years and older increased 3 percent. Longtime residents like the Simiches saw a decline in ethnic life; the growing black community, on the other hand, experienced an expansion of communal institutions.

Neither Antonio and Irma Nava nor Julio and Angelina Martinez displayed any interest in formal ethnic associations. Few were to be found in the valley and local Puerto Rican organizations became widespread only in the

1960s in parts of New York. Most of the valley's Mexican-Americans lived a rigidly segregated life, residing in poverty-stricken rural *colonias* or "across the tracks" in the small cities. Efforts to organize Mexican-Americans in the valley were singularly unsuccessful, largely because formal organizations were not a part of their pattern of life. Kin, not community, provided the most important identity, as it had with the Traces in Tennessee at the turn of the century. Moreover, Nava, sympathetic to Chicano objectives, opposed militant confrontation. "We don't need it here," he said. "We are a majority. Who are we going to demonstrate against, ourselves?" In places like Los Angeles, where Mexican-Americans are a powerless minority, there is, he says, a need "because there is no effective alternative."

Puerto Ricans such as Julio Martinez were less culturally inhibited about organization than Mexican-Americans were, but they were so dispersed through Manhattan, Brooklyn, and the Bronx that it was difficult to establish group identity. Like most Puerto Ricans, none of the Martinezes attended church. They were untouched by such service organizations as the Puerto Rican Forum, Aspira, or the Puerto Rican Family Institute. Julio was active in his union and hoped to be elected to the shop grievance committee. The union served as his window to much of the world of New York; beyond that world, little interested him.

Far west of the Hudson River, residents of Fredonia led a full associational life of both the fun and civic variety. Most Fredonians were satisfied with their town and expressed no desire to leave, even for a better job. There were dozens of groups just for women, from the informal Bid and Bye Bridge Club to the more formal Business and Professional Women's Club. The chamber of commerce numbered 188 members, or 25 percent of those males over 35 years of age. Sixty-eight percent of the families responding to a recent survey had at least one member who regularly attended at least one group or association. In addition, the proximity of kin (75 percent of respondent families had at least one child living in southeastern Kansas) and rather pleasant living conditions partially muted whatever job dissatisfactions and other grievances existed. The strength of group life in Fredonia was further enhanced as farm families became more active in local affairs because of the decay of associational life in their shrinking neighborhoods.

The nation has always had its share of public-issue-oriented organizations, but they have proliferated since the early 1960s, partly as a result of the citizen participation requirements of Great Society legislation but also as a manifestation of greater concern over pressing public issues. The establishment of an organization to integrate a neighborhood may give birth to another organization dedicated to maintaining segregation. In many cities—mostly those with over 50,000 inhabitants—neighborhood associations organized to defend the interests of a few square blocks against freeways, city garages, and other unwanted additions to the neighborhood. New York boasted a citywide Federation of Block Associations designed to aid the city's 10,000 block associations, most of them located in outlying parts of Brooklyn and Queens where voluntary associations similar to those in Fredonia flourished. In Kansas City, the Forty-Nine–Sixty-Three Neighborhood Coalition supported interracial housing and worked for the creation of a permanent, integrated, middle-class neighborhood. The enemies of such groups were frequently realtors and planners, particularly highway engineers, in municipal and state governments.

While many Americans actively engaged in community affairs, most people were without power and were uninvolved in groups that took sides on public issues. Inner-city neighborhoods were broken up by highways, as in north St. Louis and Louisville, by such enclaves of culture as New York's Lincoln Center, and by high-rise developments as in Pittsburgh. Bankers, real-estate agents, and developers induced racial turnover by means of their control of residential mortgage money and by denying credit to businesses in low-income neighborhoods, practices which were fostered by the Federal Housing Administration and the Veterans Administration. The suburbs flourished while the inner city decayed. Inner-city resistance to such developments was generally futile.

Communities that attempted to offer high standards of service to all residents flirted with insolvency. New York, for example, was forced close to bankruptcy in 1975 and was universally condemned for deficit spending. In Fredonia, a local banker and civic leader defended the concept of the balanced budget: "If we haven't got it, we don't spend it." A simple and rational philosophy—but not for New York or Detroit and, it was to be feared, not for Fredonia either. The philosophy of the welfare state imposed humane obligations upon communities to provide services whether or not they had the will or the money to pay for them.

Housing was a case in point. Fredonia's attitude was rather typical of many places. In 1971, there were only eight or nine dwellings available for a family to buy or rent. At the same time, many of the aged, who comprised 20 percent of the population, were rattling about in large homes. They expressed keen interest in the idea of a housing project for the elderly, but the chamber of commerce, the planning commission, and the city council were all opposed to such a project. They would not risk federal intrusion even for such a politically safe project as housing for the aged. Yet, at the same time, most Fredonians

admitted that inadequate housing was a serious problem.

Low-cost public housing failed to improve housing conditions. In St. Louis, Washington, D.C., New York, and other cities, public housing projects, poorly constructed and located, quickly deteriorated into new slum housing. The preamble of the National Housing Act of 1949 declared that every American should have a decent home in a suitable environment. By the mid-1970s, at least 20 million people lived in patently substandard housing. Housing units in St. Louis declined by over 15 percent during the 1970s. The partnership between government, private lending institutions, and builders, envisaged in the National Housing and Community Development Act of 1974, had not materialized.

Inadequate housing was also directly connected with health problems, many of which went unresolved because they lacked immediacy and high visibility. Sustaining interest in such issues as solid-waste disposal or the operation of the local hospital proved very difficult. Let the sanitary engineers and the doctors decide—they were the experts. All too frequently, these experts were without political power and questions were decided on other grounds than health.

Health care deteriorated and the proportion of health personnel to the total population diminished as distance from metropolitan areas increased. Fredonia's four doctors claimed they needed two additional colleagues. More fortunate than most towns of its size, Fredonia had a modern hospital, but it was as overburdened as the local doctors were. In 1970, southeastern Kansas had 73 doctors (15 over 65 years old), or 0.7 doctors per 1,000 persons. This compared with 1.4 for the total United States and 3.2 and 2.7 for the Boston and New York metropolitan areas respectively. As compared to urbanites, a significantly smaller proportion of rural inhabitants were protected by any form of health insurance, and the rural poor and the rural aged were generally uncovered. Rural states were less likely than urban states to participate, even partially, in Medicaid programs.

Doctors trained in the rural states sought their futures on the East and West Coasts. Those were doctor-rich areas. But the young doctors did not head east to heal the likes of the Martinez family. The prestigious Columbia Presbyterian Medical Center, a short subway ride from Inwood, did little to serve the increasingly Puerto Rican population that surrounded the hospital. To live in a doctor-rich area was of minimal importance to the poor of New York or Boston, particularly the black poor. The mortality rate for black infants under one year of age was 48 per 1,000 live births in Bolivar and Washington Counties, Mississippi for the five years 1965–69; for whites it was 24 per 1,000. On New York's West Side, the rate for blacks was 41, for Puerto Ricans, 30, and for whites, 18. Similar differentials existed for communicable diseases such as tuberculosis.

Angelina Martinez was surprised to find a well-baby clinic in Inwood. Puerto Ricans and blacks in New York or Mexican-Americans in the valley lacked an adequate knowledge of disease and knew less about available health facilities than the general populace knew. The poor expected more illness, expected less from health institutions, and were more likely to take a folk approach to healing than would better-educated and more affluent people. In Inwood, a comparatively greater proportion of nonwhite and Puerto Rican mothers received no prenatal care. Nonhospital births were mostly confined to blacks and Puerto Ricans, generally without a doctor in attendance and followed by little, if any, postnatal care. Infant mortality rates reflected this.

Efforts were made to bring health services closer to the needy through the location of government-subsidized health centers in poor neighborhoods and other programs, some with a rural focus. But the impact was minimal due to underfunding and the lack of commitment to them by municipal officials and local health establishments. Few doctors practiced in poor neighborhoods and most doctors were on the staffs of hospitals that did not accept public-assistance cases, including Medicaid. In most urban centers, the municipal hospitals were less adequately staffed and had poorer facilities than were available in nonpublic institutions. Urban centers were unable to finance more than minimal public health-care facilities, lacked the dollars to provide adequate housing, exercised little control over wage levels, and were vulnerable to national economic change. Rural places suffered from similar weaknesses. Communities, then, possessed but limited assets to respond effectively to critical needs.

In the field of health care, Americans knew what ought to be done and did not do it. In education, Americans did not know what to do, but did it. Most people believed that education was necessary for job security, but there was no consensus as to the content of that education or what the ultimate responsibility of schools should be. In 1945, Midland resisted a state law ordering the system to arrange for medical and dental examinations for grade schoolers. Was health an educational responsibility? In 1904, the Chicago School Aid Federation had been criticized for providing aid to the children of needy families. Seventy years later, the Welfare Fund of the Lawrence, Kansas, United School District 497, established for similar purposes, raised the same question. Was welfare, too, an educational responsibility? As school functions multiplied, criticism mounted—for the school systems could not satisfy everyone.

World War II patriotism and cold war tensions in the 1950s prompted criticism of school systems for their failure to teach the great principles for which the country stood. During the 1950s, right-wing groups attacked schools for harboring alleged communists. Other critics charged that schools failed to teach pupils how to live in a democracy and how to adjust socially through the acceptance of white, middle-class values and manners. Also present and articulate were those who would purge the schools of all instruction they defined as dirty (sex education) and unpatriotic (Marxism).

Hardly had the anticommunist mania simmered down than schools confronted the Supreme Court's decision *Brown et al.* v. *Board of Education of Topeka* (1954), which charged that separate educational facilities for blacks provided unequal education. Efforts to integrate schools led to such equally sensitive issues as busing to achieve racial balance and the decentralization of school systems. Twenty-odd years later, those newer issues often diverted attention from integration and obstructed its achievement. Suburbanites were particularly embittered and defensive for their school systems were locally controlled and the superior education available had attracted many to the suburbs in the first place. Mandated integration threatened those advantages.

Lila Gropper always had been angry about the inequities of the segregated school system. She expected much from the *Brown* decision that never transpired. True, her sons took advantage of the crumbling color line in higher education and were among the first blacks to attend Texas Tech University at Lubbock. But Lila recognized that she and her family were exceptional among blacks in having sufficient income to provide education for their children. For most blacks, as Lila and her sons maintained, the gains from integrated systems came at a frustratingly slow pace. Such progress as was made was at-

tended by great social costs. Black children who were bused to formerly all-white schools found themselves in a maelstrom; whites attempted to disrupt integration, and the irrational fury of a few led them to stone black children or to lie down in front of school buses.

Few communities experienced the violence over integration that troubled Boston in 1974, 1975, and 1976. There, a federal district court busing plan threatened to place blacks in the high schools of South Boston, one of the poorest of the city's white neighborhoods and predominantly Irish Catholic. Demonstrations for and against integration degenerated into brawls and, in the schools, order was maintained only by large numbers of police. In some areas, busing lost the support of black or other minority group parents that it once had. In Evansville, a 1968 city desegregation plan required the closing of two schools in black neighborhoods and the busing of students elsewhere. Black citizens opposed the plan arguing that the schools were important to their neighborhoods and that whites could be bused in. They charged that blacks alone bore the burden of desegregating schools. Blacks displayed increased resistance to integration plans whenever all or most of the pupils to be bused were black.

Throughout the 1970s, court-ordered busing remained the major weapon against segregated schools in Cleveland, Indianapolis, Seattle, Austin, and virtually every other big urban school district. But desegregation seemed to be a lost cause as the white population of cities continued to fall. In 1979, white students in Detroit, Chicago, and St. Louis comprised less than 20 percent of the student population. Serious resistance obstructed the busing of inner-city pupils to suburban schools. Americans were obviously reluctant to integrate their schools. This was reflected in the passage by Congress in December 1980

Police restrain a crowd of whites as black students, bused under a federally mandated plan, arrive at South Boston High School as the school year began in September 1974

of a bill (vetoed by President Carter) which would effectively kill busing as a method to obtain racial balance in the schools.

School administrators, teachers, and local citizen groups found themselves antagonists in a dispute over decentralization in which questions of performance and quality were submerged beneath a fight for control of the system. Administrators normally resisted decentralization and worked to expand their limits of authority. In Fredonia, the superintendent of United School District #387 viewed the two other school districts in the county as competitors and looked forward to the day when Fredonia would be the seat of the only county school district. He thought it ridiculous that towns had resisted school un-

ification in 1965 and 1966 out of fear that it would have killed the town. Even if the towns survived, each time a school disappeared through consolidation, local control was eroded. On the other hand, continuing local control in the face of declining enrollments could also erode the quality of education.

Midland's situation—unlike Fredonia's—supported arguments for consolidation. During the mid-1950s, 44 percent of Midland's enrollment in grades 9 through 12 came from neighboring boroughs and townships that paid Midland tuition rather than maintain their own schools. In 1952, several townships had announced plans to build a joint junior-senior high school (a project completed in 1960), which threatened Midland with the loss of tuition money. Midland, invited to join the new district, rejected the offer because it wished to remain independent. Midland's population, stable during the 1950s, then declined. While school enrollments dropped, operating budgets soared. By 1964, Midland's school board had come to regret its earlier position and attempted to initiate talks on merger. The new district rebuffed Midland largely because Midland's school population was, by 1970, over 25 percent black. The borough, once one of the wealthiest school districts in the region, was now one of the smallest and poorest, with a curriculum and plant inferior to that of surrounding districts.

Many other school districts faced analogous problems. In Inwood, the facilities available to the Martinez children at P.S. 152 and J.H.S. 52 were far inferior to those enjoyed by Robbie Bassano years earlier. Angelina and Julio Martinez lived in Inwood long enough to witness the deterioration and overcrowding of the local school buildings. Neither was aware of the efforts of the New York school system to increase the number of bilingual teachers or to open fully bilingual schools. Neither did they know that the system of community school districts, each with its own school board elected by citizens of the district, was implemented after 1969. Those districts, under the budgetary control of the Central Board of Education and bound by a citywide contract with the powerful teachers' union, faced constant pressure to adapt to population changes that involved black and Puerto Rican in-migration. Special antidrug programs, and instruction in English as a second language, prekindergarten classes, remedial reading and arithmetic, and the like, even when partially staffed by parent volunteers, were extremely expensive and required a long-term effort to yield results. Recurrent financial crises were a permanent threat to such efforts to respond to the needs of all children.

Educators in New York and elsewhere were dependent upon a public that demonstrated strong resistance to pouring further resources into schools suspected of not doing their job. Demographic changes did not help either; in the 1970s, fewer taxpayers were the parents of school-age children than had been so in the 1950s. Educators were also captives of the American educational creed that schools had to rectify social inequities and parental indifference by fostering an achievement orientation in individual students while at all costs refraining from tampering with the institutions and social attitudes that perpetuated inequality.

After World War II, community responsibilities greatly expanded as a result of the broadened scope and increasing complexity of such traditional areas of action as housing, transportation, health, education, and economic development. But in each of those areas, the freedom of communities to act or not act was gradually restricted by the imposition of state and federal standards of performance. Lack of compliance with the waste-disposal regulations of the Environmental Protection Agency could result in court suits or the withholding of federal funds. The U.S. Department of Housing and Urban Development decided where federally subsidized housing would be located. Local welfare expenditures were hedged about by state and federal controls.

Communities still wielded considerable power, but that power was not shared equally by all residents. Elected officials and administrators, civic groups, special-interest groups, and the electorate all possessed power and vied with one another in its exercise. While holding the ultimate sanction to bestow or withhold office, to pass or defeat a school bond issue, the electorate rarely initiated action and was captive to information generated by groups with vested interest in the issues at stake. From within the other power sectors, local power structures—the establishment—

emerged, possessing the capability to initiate action, to collect and disseminate or suppress information, to organize individuals or groups in their behalf, and to make decisions in the name of the public welfare.

Unorganized individuals, unless blessed with great economic strength, were without effective power in American communities. For many Americans, such as Bob Bassano and Mike Simich, noninvolvement was a matter of personal choice. Work, family, hobbies, other interests all seemed more important and less demanding than active citizenship. Both Bob and Mike were, from time to time, angered by local decisions affecting them but, believing that they were without power, felt it futile to protest.

Much depended, as it had always, on who you were, what you did, and where you lived. Robert Butler was at, or close to, the center of local and national power during his adult lifetime. He was exceptional. Most individuals were not close to power in their own communities, let alone beyond their borders. This was no less true in Fredonia or Midland than in Evansville or New York. Class and status operated in Fredonia, perhaps more sharply than it did in New York because of size. Blue-collar workers in Fredonia recognized and were resentful of existing class consciousness. A lineman for the local electric company perceived the city government as serving the purposes of the main-street merchants and bankers. He also felt socially excluded. "I've lived here all my life," he remarked, "and while I have coffee and joke with the businessmen damn near every day, I'm not good enough to be invited into their homes and my kids don't go to their parties." Informal groups and clubs also divided along class lines. The wives of workers and merchants each had their own set of organizations— Weight Watchers clubs, card groups, etc.— and there was no mixing. A local social worker explained the class system in these

words: "There is a class consciousness in Fredonia. No welfare types or poor people go to the Methodist, Presbyterian, or Episcopal churches. They go to smaller ones, Pilgrim's Holiness and the like. The establishment people shun the poor people." Establishment people made community decisions in Fredonia. Jerry Trace experienced the limits of his power in Evansville. The Groppers in Kosse lived and struggled within the confines of a white power structure.

During the decade or so following World War II, while suburbanites were castigated for conformity and other sins, they exercised more control over local government than did Americans in other types of communities. The objectives may have been exclusionist and myopic, but they suited their purposes. In hundreds of suburbs, people established governments, provided a fairly high level of services, and organized to press for or against further change. Older communities, experiencing a suburban invasion, were overwhelmed, and they had to admit the newcomers into the councils of power and provide them with police patrols, traffic signals, garbage pickup, and other services. Suburban government was viewed differently by members of different classes. High-income residents expected high-quality services whereas lower-class suburbanites tolerated or even preferred less costly government even if it meant inadequate services.

Within rural towns with a homogeneous racial and ethnic population, a small number of individuals exercised general power over most issues. In Fredonia, one or two dozen men rotated among the city council, school board, planning commission, industrial development group, and chamber of commerce committees and had a part in all decisions. This was less because of their qualifications than their availability and demonstrated willingness to donate time. One establishment member confided that the facade of unanimity presented to the public hid factional disputes over city policy based on who will gain more than whom. The planning commission was ineffective because of its large size—it had to include all the VIPs—and its inability to chart a course agreeable to all members.

Midland's politics after World War II became more complicated as increasing numbers of blacks pressed against the older ethnic groups. A Democratic-labor coalition gained control of the borough government in the early 1950s and has since dominated local elections. Slavs and Italians, once excluded, were regularly elected to public office while the chances of election for a Crucible supervisor or executive declined along with the fortunes of the Republican Party. In 1956, a black was elected to the school board, and, since the 1960s, blacks have regularly appeared on ballots and served on important local groups. But for all of this, the individuals making decisions were no better equipped to do so than they were in Fredonia. In 1960, when Midland's first borough master plan was presented to the borough council, the members viewed the criticism contained in the study as an assault on their performance. Confused about how to use it, they saw its major benefit as easing the way to state and federal money. Consequently, when a second general development plan was completed in 1972, its findings were quite similar to those of the first. Little had been done to remedy the problems uncovered 12 years earlier.

In larger places, power tended to be more diffuse and more specialized, particularly in its focus on issues affecting the fortunes of those with power. Evansville's economic crisis of the middle 1950s brought the managers and owners of Evansville's major local and national corporations—mercantile, industrial, banking, transportation—together in a loosely knit power structure, formalized in a development agency, which reversed the city's economic slide. The interests of Evans-

ville's corporate leadership were primarily economic as were the interests of elite groups such as the Allegheny Conference on Community Development (Pittsburgh), the Atlanta Forum, and the Citizens Charter Association of Dallas which resurrected the downtowns of their cities during the 1950s and 1960s. Municipal authorities rarely challenged such vast projects as Pittsburgh's Golden Triangle or Kansas City's Crown Center, tending to view a gleaming steel and glass skyline as the single measure of a city. As in Evansville, questions of housing, health, public education, and the like were of little interest to the power structure.

The power of big-city mayors has eroded since World War II. Within the context of the city-federal relationship, they have seen power shift to local development interests, the state capitol, and federal agencies. While the number of municipal employees rose from 6 million to 12 million during the 1960s, patronage powers were no longer sufficient to build old-style political machines. Powerful municipal employees' unions owed little allegiance to mayors, and more and more frequently the mayor's principal antagonists were unionized city employees. While the mayors served great economic interests, those interests did not serve the city. As corporate wealth and the middle class moved to the suburbs, the city's tax base did not expand along with costs or needs. The remaining population was poorer, requiring more from the city and paying less to it. Gestures, however nominal, toward poor minority groups aroused the ire of working-class and middle-class whites who felt neglected. City planners and other administrators intervened between elected officials and the electorate, assuming powers once held by individuals elected to office. Elected officials also lost power to special-purpose authorities which dispensed state and federal funds to build public housing, mass-transit systems, storm sewers, and waterworks. Shorn of much power, mayors still received the flack for whatever was or was not done.

Community officials, bemoaning their loss of power and wishing to recapture it, packed their public statements with homilies on political accountability and summonses to the people. But, as their responses to the first years of the Office of Economic Opportunity (OEO) and its Community Action Program (CAP) indicated, most of this was political rhetoric. The Economic Opportunity Act required citizen participation in many of its programs. CAP was designed to guarantee that the poor would participate fully in projects involving themselves and thus prod institutions serving or affecting the poor to become more responsive to their needs. Thousands of projects were launched, many originating from newly created organizations of the poor, mostly in America's inner cities but also involving American Indians and farm laborers. OEO funds were granted directly to the implementing agencies, thus bypassing municipal governments.

Local elites did not wish power to be redistributed, however minimally. Midland's borough council frowned at an NAACP march on the council in 1968. Elsewhere, in Birmingham, Alabama, authorities backed up their biases by using dogs, clubs, and cattle prods against civil-rights marchers. The steps of city halls across the nation became crowded as the aggrieved sought to assert themselves. City officials launched a drive to recapture control over the expenditure of OEO funds within their communities and thus to dull the power of the organized poor. Congress bowed to a torrent of pressure. It passed the Green Amendment in 1967, allowing local authorities to acquire control of the Community Action Programs and the $1.1 billion appropriated to them in 1968. This decision set off a scramble among local politicians eager to get a piece of the action, discouraged and confused the poor and their

advocates, encouraged the Nixon administration to proceed to strip OEO of its major responsibilities and, ultimately, to destroy it, and marked the end of an interesting, perhaps promising, experiment in the redistribution of power.

Since the demise of OEO, revenue sharing and the Housing and Community Development Act of 1974 have returned more and more authority to agencies of local government. But even with the best of intentions and the best planning, the harmful effects of inflation during the 1970s have retarded the taking of any new initiatives which would improve the quality of life for all residents. In fact, services seemed to be getting worse. Around the country, city and county roads and bridges were in ill repair. The drinking water dispensed by community systems declined in quality. In early 1981, numerous Eastern Seaboard cities declared energy or water emergencies. Sites for industrial waste disposal became more difficult to find. As, in early 1980, New York's Mayor Koch congratulated those responsible for financing the rehabilitation of the burned-out 10–20 Post Avenue building, from which the Martinezes had been driven one fearful night, he stood amid piles of uncollected garbage. Where was the money to come from to modernize such essential services?

Mike Simich was wrong to attribute excessive power to the Democratic-labor political machine in Midland. Crucible Steel ran Midland. Crucible's huge stacks manufactured the pollutants in the air that he breathed and that encrusted the home sold to him by Crucible's realty division. Crucible paid him his wages and pensioned him when he reached 65. And what was Crucible? It was not only a sprawling assortment of soot-covered buildings and heat and furnaces and cranes and track and diesels. It was also Colt Industries, Incorporated which had assumed control in 1968. And what was Colt Industries? Most Midlanders, Mike Simich included, did not know. They should know, because the future of their community depended on a single factor: how Colt Industries assessed the "profitability" of Crucible Steel. Long ago, in 1947, a steel executive spoke at a Midland Rotary meeting, warning them to go slow in trying to control smoke and water pollution. He told the Rotarians that industry *was* sensitive to community welfare but that too much pressure might interfere with productivity, compelling a reevaluation of "locational" factors. In effect, he was saying, "I have power. So don't push or I'll move 6,000 jobs someplace else." Midland and countless other communities have heeded this advice.

The uses of power within American communities have not changed dramatically since 1900 although the techniques—the arsenal of persuasion, threats, and compulsion—are more sophisticated and complex. The protagonists have both changed and remained the same. Old-style ethnic politics became a less viable force because most of the earlier ethnics were now respectable members of the middle class. However, the lower classes still existed and they received but a small share of America's abundance. Communities shared responsibility for the perpetuation of inequities with the private economic sector and with other levels of government. When such national problems as residential segregation, poor housing, inadequate educational facilities, and job discrimination were cited, the setting always was local, for that was where those conditions existed in visible and embarrassing form, where pain, suffering, and wasted lives could not be reduced to bloodless abstractions.

CONCLUSION

Considering the apparent disintegration of New York City since the spring and summer of 1976 and the only slightly less desperate plight of numerous other huge metropolitan areas, it would seem that the future of American urban life is indeed bleak. Middle-class Americans, the companies that employ them, and their tax dollars continue to flee to suburbia and the open country, leaving behind rotting city centers, violence-ridden ghettos, and disillusioned city dwellers. City after city appeared to follow the path of the "Big Apple." Inflation and other issues induce city employees to strike, schools or toll bridges close, police patrols are curtailed, another contingent of solid citizens such as the Bassanos moves out, municipal bonds go unsold, more work force cutbacks produce more strikes, and the downward spiral gains momentum.

It is understandable that the problems gnawing at America's cities should cause such alarm and doomsaying. After all, the city has dominated the stage throughout the 20th century and its threatened downfall is closely identified with dire predictions about American society. It is also understandable that the city's corporate and private residents should move to more pleasant surroundings if they are able. But the very act of moving has created problems in the recipient communities. New factories and new residents create new demands in suburban and other smaller communities. Frequently, such places are unprepared to cope with the influx and services lag behind demand. At a slower and less visible pace, the problems of the city are replicated across the land.

Some communities, in an effort to preserve natural amenities, are adopting policies that would slow or prevent growth. As a result, serious questions are raised about the right of Americans to live where they choose and the right of communities to control their futures. But most places, large or small, still wish to grow and actively seek growth-producing businesses and institutions. Many communities in America still offer comfortable living for those who can afford it. Whether they will be able to manage their growth in such a way that their citizens can still live satisfying lives is an unresolved question. To suggest an affirmative answer assumes a degree of community integration, a measure of community spirit that is difficult to develop and more difficult to sustain. As of 1981, continued fragmentation seemed more likely than the evolution of a new and dynamic sense of community purpose.

SUGGESTIONS FOR FURTHER READING

Very useful were the following: A. H. Anderson and C. J. Miller, *The Changing Role of the Small Town in Farm Areas* [a study of Adams, Nebraska] (1953); Richard F. Babcock, *The Zoning Game: Municipal Practices and Policies* (1966); Reymer Banham, *Los Angeles: The Architecture of Four Ecologies* (1974); Pierre de Vise et al., *Slum Medicine: Chicago's Apartheid Health System* (1969); Jean Gottman, *Megalopolis: The Urbanized Northeastern Seaboard of the United States* (1961); Scott Greer, *The Urbane View: Life and Politics in Metropolitan America* (1972); Chester W. Hartman, *Housing and Social Policy* (1975); Celia S. Heller, *New Converts to the American Dream?: Mobility Asperations of Young Mexican-Americans* (1971); Roscoe C. Martin, *The Cities and the Federal System* (1965); G. M. Neutze, *Economic Policy and the Size of Cities* (1967); Diane Ravitch, *The Great School Wars, New York City, 1805–1973* (1974); Gerald D. Suttles, *The Social Order of the Slum: Ethnicity and Territory in the Inner City* (1968); and Frederick M. Wirt et al., *On the City's Rim: Politics and Policy in Suburbia* (1972).

Studies of special topics include J. David Greenstone and Pavel E. Peterson, *Race and Authority in Urban Politics: Community Participation and the War on Poverty* (1976); Karl E. and A. F. Taeuber, *Negroes in Cities: Residential Segregation and Neighborhood Change* (1965); Charles Abrams, *Man's Struggle for Shelter in an Urbanizing World* (1964); Roger L. Creighton, *Urban Transportation Planning* (1970); Mario Fantini et al., *Community Control and the Urban School* (1970); Earl Finkler and David Peterson, *Non-*

Growth Planning Strategies: The Developing Power of Towns, Cities, and Regions (1974); Jonathan Friedman, *Crowding and Behavior: The Psychology of High-Density Living* (1975); George R. LaTrove, *The Politics of School Decentralization* (1973); T. F. Lord, *Decent Housing: A Promise to Keep* (1976); Richard L. Morrill and Ernst H. Wohlenberg, *The Geography of Poverty in the United States* (1971); Kenneth J. Newbeck, *Corporate Responses to Urban Crises* (1974); Francine F. Rabinowitz, *City Politics and Planning* (1969); Wallace F. Smith, *Housing for the Elderly* (1961); Stephen P. Strickland, *U.S. Health Care: What's Wrong and What's Right* (1972); Seymour I. Toll, *The Zoned American* (1969); Michael L. Vasser, *Politics and Planning: A National Study of American Planners* (1979); and James Q. Wilson, *Varieties of Police Behavior: The Management of Law and Order in Eight Communities* (1978). Also see Gary A. Tobin, ed., *The Changing Structure of the City: What Happened to the Urban Crisis?* (1979); Frances F. Piven and Richard A. Cloward, *Regulating the Poor: Functions of Public Welfare* (1971); Roger S. Albrandt, Jr., and Paul C. Brophy, *Neighborhood Revitalization* (1975); Mark H. Rose, *Interstate: Express Highway Politics, 1941–1956* (1980); and Charles R. Morris, *The Cost of Good Intentions* (1980).

Urban issues are dealt with in Howard M. Bahr, *Skid Row: An Introduction to Disaffiliation* (1973); John H. Baker, *Urban Politics in America* (1971); Robert A. Dahl, *Who Governs: Democracy and Power in an American City* (1961); Mike Royko, *Boss: Richard J. Daley of Chicago* (1971); Edward C. Banfield, *The Unheavenly City* (1968); Howard S. Becker, *Culture and Civility in San Francisco* (1971); Harry Edward Berndt, *New Rules in the Ghetto* (1977); Brian J. L. Berry, *The Human Consequences of Urbanization* (1973); Amory Bradford, *Oakland's Not for Burning* (1968); Kenneth B. Clark, *Dark Ghetto: Dilemmas of Social Power* (1965); Philip L. Clay, *Neighborhood Renewal: Middle Class Resettlement and Incumbent Upgrading in American Neighborhoods* (1979); J. Clarence Davies, III, *Neighborhood Groups and Urban Renewal* (1966); Richard O. Davies, *The Age of Asphalt: The Automobile, the Freeway, and the Condition of Metropolitan America* (1975); Daniel J. Elazar, *Cities of the Prairie: The Met-*

ropolitan Frontier and American Politics (1970); Herbert Gans, *The Urban Villagers: Group and Class in the Life of Italian Americans* (1962); Todd Getlin and Nanci Hollander, *Uptown: Poor Whites in Chicago* (1970); Scott Greer, *Urban Renewal and American Cities* (1966); Joe B. Harris, *Urban Texas* (1971); August Heckscher, *Open Spaces: The Life of American Cities* (1977); Edgar M. Hoover and Raymond Vernon, *Anatomy of a Metropolis: The New York Metropolitan Region* (1959); Larry R. Jackson and William A. Johnson, *Protest by the Poor: The Welfare Rights Movement in New York City* (1974); Jane Jacobs, *The Death and Life of Great American Cities* (1961); Suzanne Keller, *The Urban Neighborhood* (1968); Joan E. Lancourt, *Confront or Concede: The Alinsky Citizen-Action Organization* (1979); Warren Leslie, *Dallas, Public and Private: Aspects of an American City* (1964); Sar A. Levitan, *Economic Opportunity in the Ghetto* (1970); W. Lowe, *City Life* (1974); Joseph P. Lyford, *The Airtight Cage: A Study of New York's West Side* (1966); William Moore, Jr., *The Vertical Ghetto: Everyday Life in an Urban Project* (1969); Lewis Mumford, *The Urban Prospect* (1968); H. V. Savitch, *Urban Policy and the Exterior City: Federal, State, and Corporate Impacts upon Major Cities* (1979); Alvin Schorr, *Slums and Social Insecurity* (1963); Gerald D. Suttles, *The Social Construction of Communities* (1972); U.S. National Commission on Neighborhoods, *The Case for Neighborhoods: A Progress Report* (1978); Conrad Weiler, *Philadelphia: Neighborhood, Authority, and the Urban Crisis* (1973); B. J. Widick, *Detroit: City of Race and Class Violence* (1972); Paul Wilhelm and Robert Torrone, *Urban Growth* (1975); Stephen Zeverling, *Mass Transport and the Politics of Technology: A Study of BART and the San Francisco Bay Area* (1974); and David C. Perry and Alfred J. Watkins, eds., *The Rise of the Sunbelt Cities* (1977).

A few examples of the mushrooming literature on suburban problems are Bennett Berger, *Working Class Suburb* (1960); Gurney Breckenfield, *Columbia and the New Cities* (1971); William M. Dobriner, *Class in Suburbia* (1963); Scott Donaldson, *The Suburban Myth* (1969); Anthony Downs, *Opening up the Suburbs: An Urban Strategy for America* (1973); Herbert Gans, *The Levittowners: Ways of Life and Politics in a New Suburban Community* (1967); Francine Rabinowitz, *Minorities in Suburbs* (1977); Joseph T. Howell, *Hard Times on Clay Street: Portraits of Blue Collar Families* (1973); Robert Wood, *Suburbia: Its People and Their Politics* (1958); and Jon C. Teaford, *City and Suburb: The Political Fragmentation of Metropolitan America, 1850–1970* (1979).

For small towns and rural neighborhoods, see Thomas R. Ford, ed., *Rural U.S.A.: Persistence and Change* (1978); Niles M. Hansen, *Rural Poverty and the Urban Crisis: A Strategy for Regional Development* (1970); Niles M. Hansen, *The Future of Nonmetropolitan America* (1973); Otto G. Harberg, *Exploring the Small Community* (1955); Herman R. Lantz, *A Community in Search of Itself: A Case Study of Cairo, Illinois* (1972); E. E. LeMasters, *Blue-Collar Aristocrats: Life-Styles at a Working-Class Tavern* [construction workers in a Wisconsin town] (1975); Ritchie P. Lowry, *Who's Running This Town? Community Leadership and Social Change* (1962); William Madsen, *Society and Health in the Lower Rio Grande Valley* (1961); Don Martindale and R. Galen Hanson, *Small Town and the Nation: The Conflict of Local and Translocal Forces* (1969); Blaine E. Mercer, *The American Community* (1956); Bert Swanson et al., *Small Towns and Small Towners: A Framework for Survival and Growth* (1978); and Arthur L. Vidich and Joseph Bensman, *Small Town in Mass Society: Class, Power and Religion in a Rural Community* (1968).

Epilogue

Entering the 1980s, Americans confronted such apocalyptic threats as thermonuclear war, the exhaustion of vital natural resources, and disintegration of the nation's social fabric. While portents of universal disaster—the "yellow peril," collapse of the family and religious and moral values, permanent economic depression, and ecological ruin—had caused anxiety among earlier generations, America had survived them and prospered. Yet the likelihood that such dangers might overwhelm the nation was greater than it had been in earlier days. One push of a button could obliterate hundreds of millions and so contaminate the earth that few would—or would wish to—survive. The margin for error was shrinking.

Americans, most of them at least, seemed to have abandoned that unique if naive sense of self-confidence which sustained their forefathers. They had apparently joined the rest of humankind in recognizing that man-

agerial skill, technological virtuosity, and political manipulation were inadequate to the solution of *all* the problems which threatened their vision of the good life. As Americans moved into the last decades of the century, politicians certainly appeared to be more intent upon defusing a sense of crisis than in celebrating America's limitless opportunities.

Realism does offer important benefits. Too often, the faith in "America's glorious future" that sustained both political leaders and people such as the Bassanos, Kuriharas, Butlers, and Traces derived from romantic and erroneous notions about the history of their own country and the realities of world affairs. Such notions, when combined with a massive dose of "America can do anything it wants badly enough to do" spirit, tempted the United States into the quicksands of Vietnam and other adventures foreign and domestic. The limited diplomacy proclaimed by Secretary of State Kissinger and others suggested an abandonment of imperial diplomacy for more traditional, less ambitious aims. It remains to be seen whether that course will be maintained as the memory of Vietnam fades and the American people struggle with difficult problems at home.

But realism that is not founded upon a sense of the larger potential, a vision of humankind's future, is false and dangerous. For that sort of "realism" can give way to fatalism, and the healthy skepticism which accompanies it to indifference. Although collectively Americans were much more prosperous than their grandparents or parents, they were also less confident and more apathetic. The words of Paul Simon's song, "American Tune," struck a responsive chord:

> I don't know a soul who's not been battered.
> I don't have a friend who feels at ease.
> I don't know a dream that's not been shattered,
> Or driven to its knees,
> Oh, but it's all right, it's all right,
> For we've lived so well so long.
> Still, when I think of the road we're traveling on,
> I wonder what's gone wrong, I can't help it,
> I wonder what's gone wrong.[1]

The Harts, Jerry and Peggy Trace, and even that determined optimist Mike Simich, shared the anxiety about America's loss of innocence to some degree, though it certainly did not result in the "psychic paralysis" supposedly endemic. What may have resulted, however, was an acceptance of second-best solutions and second-best leadership, and the reenforcement of the traditional tendency of a broad-based electorate to ignore or react violently, as many in South Boston did, toward issues for which quick, simple solutions were not possible.

Further, the great majority of Americans appeared to be less and less able to deal with

the difficulties besetting them. A tragic paradox of 20th century life was that the achievement of material security for most accompanied, perhaps even caused, diminished autonomy for almost all. Mihailo Markovich understood the process. As an individual worker at Crucible, he had been "free" but also powerless, since his bosses refused to share their control over the work environment. Mihailo's only alternative was to organize, to rely on the collective influence of a work force prepared to withhold its labor to compel management to share power. During the first half of the 20th century, the American people followed Mihailo's example. But the more they organized to win and maintain economic security, the more necessary became the interventionist power of the state. People grumbled about the explosion of federal authority and responsibilities impinging upon families and communities, but until recently most accepted "big government" as an inevitable consequence of the drive for protection from corporate and other special interest domination. Less willingly tolerated was the growing federal involvement with such "local" concerns as the composition of school populations, the right of Mike Simich to strike, the location of low-income housing projects, or the price Ray Reinhardt obtained for his corn and soybeans. Now everyone, not just the stigmatized such as the Kuriharas and Groppers, understood the relationship between the presence or absence of government and their daily lives.

Of course, as emphasized earlier, none of our families except the Butlers ever enjoyed real power. Though most had entered the middle class by the 1950s, none had achieved complete economic security. They were aware that they had little access to the centers of power—city halls, state capitols, Detroit, Wall Street, Washington, D.C.—where the most significant decisions were made. But they had passively accepted the right and

---

[1] © 1973, Paul Simon. Used with the permission of the publisher.

superior wisdom of a small, self-perpetuating elite to decide where they should live, what cars they drove, what chemicals were added to the food they ate, whether their children would go to college or die in some unpronounceable village across the world. The events of the past decade have caused many previously trusting citizens to question the altruism and capability of elected officials and the federal bureaucracy.

The disenchantment of a majority of Americans with the direction of national life and especially the economic vise of high inflation and dwindling job opportunities brought persons and groups to power who were committed to the decentralization of political and economic institutions and to the revival of faith in individual initiative. If they are successful, Kaelen Gishman, Teddy Trace's son, Andrew, and Sofia Nava will reach adulthood in an America in which the federal government has abandoned the role of "big brother," and the needs of the aged, indigent, and others temporarily or permanently incapable of making their own way are left to the voluntary impulse or to expanded opportunities for self-sufficiency in this brave old world of free enterprise. They may also experience the replacement of their parents' fatalism and political apathy by a zealous regard for certainty in all spheres—whether that leads to the Moral Majority's smug intolerance, the rigid orthodoxy of a reborn radical political movement, or the yearning for self-destruction of Jim Jones and his followers at Jonestown.

The fourth generation of Groppers, Traces, Gishmans, and their peers will face all these and other, yet to be imagined, problems. They possess a great many advantages. Because their parents were better nourished, housed, and dressed, they are healthier and stronger. Because of the third generation's experiences—reacting to the depression mentality of their parents, experiencing less rigid family discipline—the fourth generation should be more open, self-confident, and flexible. In an era of leveling population and a stabilizing economy, they will confront challenges to family life and social relationships unique at least in this century. Still, the range of potential experience available to them is likely to continue to be narrow. Today, new fads and breakfast foods traverse the country in days. People in New York and California experience events simultaneously. First grade pupils in Fredonia follow virtually the same daily routine as those in Evansville, Midland, and Atlanta. In the face of such sameness, individuals and families strive to maintain or establish their identities so that they may cope with an increasingly collectivist world. Just as Americans painfully learned that events around the world impinged heavily upon their daily lives, so too did they learn that they were tied to one another by unbreakable bonds. The fourth generation knows that the miracle of interrelatedness hinted at in 1904 at the St. Louis World's Fair has become irreversible reality. Acting on that knowledge will prove difficult, for the appeal of simple solutions over the messy complexity of life-as-it-is, is great.

Sources

This book was not conceived as a traditional text, based on a synthesis of previously published historical works. As noted in the Preface, much of the material in each chapter was derived from interviews with the families and from research in public and local records relevant to their communities, including the U.S. Census. Most of this material is inaccessible except to researchers on the spot and its inclusion serves no valid purpose. As examples of the types of data utilized, the sections on Evansville, Indiana, and Vanderburgh County, Indiana, the home of the Trace and Reinhardt families, were based on—among other things—the following sources: Evansville Suburban and Newburgh Railway Company Archives, Indiana State University, Evansville; Evansville Chamber of Commerce, Industrial Department, *Industrial Survey of Evansville, Indiana, April 1, 1926;* R. Oleson, *Appraisal of Public Health Work in Evansville Indiana* (1926); *The Evansville Courier and Journal* (1930s); *Annual Report of the City of Evansville* (title varies), 1930–40; E. T. Attwell, *Limited Survey of Health and Allied Community Condition Relating to Colored Citizens, Evansville,* *Indiana* (1931); The Evansville City Plan Commission: *Plans for Major Streets* (1925), *The City's Appearance* (1927), *Transit Facilities* (1930); *The Evansville Survey, 1937. A Five Week Study of the Community Fund and Its Member Agencies;* Evansville Interracial Commission. Survey Committee, *Interracial Survey: A Study of Economic and Social Conditions, Educational and Social Facilities of the Negro Community* (1942); U.S. Bureau of the Census, *Population, 12th–19th Census, 1900–70;* Evansville College, *Evansville Public School Population Survey* (1946); Vanderburgh County Industrial Welfare Commission, *Public Health in Evansville and Vanderburgh County: A Study of Health Conditions* (n.p., n.d.).

Similarly, data on Fredonia, Kansas, was gleaned from the weekly *Wilson County Citizen,* a publication dating from the late 19th century, the Kansas Department of Economic Development studies, and Ozark Regional Commission contract projects. For Midland, Pennsylvania, the *Midland News* was used extensively for the mid-1920s through the early 1970s. In addition, we used, for example, Clipping File, Crucible Steel Company,

Midland Public Library; *Midland's Educational System in Its Fifteenth Year* (1956); *Midland, Pennsylvania, Research and Surveys for the Comprehensive General Plan, 1959,* prepared by Morris Knowles (1960); Pennsylvania Governors' Committee on Children and Youth, Beaver County, *Report for the White House Conferences of 1970 on Children and Youth* (n.p., n.d.); Lincoln High School Evaluation Committee, *Report* (1972); Midland Borough, Pennsylvania. *General Development Plan, 1972,* prepared by Michael Baker, Jr., Inc. (1972), and the *Census* from 1910 through 1970. Although there is no reason to provide an exhaustive list of primary data, it is important to note that students wishing to test our conclusions about families and communities against the experiences of their own localities have mountains of information available in town halls, county courthouses, and local newspapers and libraries.

As a supplement to the chapter bibliographies and the above discussion of sources, a list of contemporary novels is appended. Quite often, fictional works, many of which possess little lasting literary merit, can serve as historical documents and can evoke with remarkable effect the cultural and political milieus in which they were written.

First Generation:

Andy Adams, *The Log of a Cowboy* (1903)
Henry Adams, *Democracy* (1879)
Sherwood Anderson, *Winesburg, Ohio* (1919)
L. Frank Baum, *The Wonderful Wizard of Oz* (1900)
Edward Bellamy, *Looking Backward* (1888)
Abraham Cahan, *The Rise of David Levinsky* (1917)
Willa Cather, *O Pioneers!* (1913)
Kate Chopin, *The Awakening* (1898)
Winston Churchill, *The Crisis* (1901)
Thomas Dixon, *The Clansman* (1905)
Ignatius Donnelly, *Caesar's Column* (1891)
Ignatius Donnelly, *The Golden Bottle* (1892)
Theodore Dreiser, *Sister Carrie* (1900)
Theodore Dreiser, *The Tital* (1914)
Hamlin Garland, *A Son of the Middle Border* (1917)
Ellen Glasgow, *The Romance of a Plain Man* (1909)

Ellen Glasgow, *Life and Gabriella* (1916)
Robert Grant, *The Chippendales* (1903)
Zane Grey, *Riders of the Purple Sage* (1912)
Constance Cary Harrison, *The Anglomaniacs* (1890)
O. Henry, *Cabbages and Kings* (1904)
Edward House, *Philip Dru, Administrator* (1912)
Edgar W. Howe, *The Story of a Country Town* (1883)
William Dean Howells, *The Rise of Silas Lapham* (1885)
Sinclair Lewis, *Main Street* (1920)
Jack London, *The Iron Heel* (1908)
Frank Norris, *The Octopus* (1901)
David Graham Phillips, *The Deluge* (1905)
Ernest Poole, *The Voice of the Street* (1906)
Ole E. Rolvaag, *Giants in the Earth* (1927)
Mari Sandoz, *Old Jules* (1935)
Charles M. Sheldon, *In His Steps* (1896)
Upton Sinclair, *The Jungle* (1906)
F. Hopkinson Smith, *Kennedy Square* (1911)
Booth Tarkington, *The Magnificent Ambersons* (1918)
Lew Wallace, *Ben-Hur—A Tale of the Christ* (1880)
Edith Wharton, *The Age of Innocence* (1920)
William Allen White, *A Certain Rich Man* (1909)
Brand Whitlock, *The Thirteenth District* (1902)
Owen Wister, *The Virginian* (1902)
Harold Bell Wright, *The Shepherd of the Hills* (1907)

Second Generation:

Marquis Childs, *Washington Calling* (1936)
Clare Ogden Davis, *The Woman of It* (1929)
James T. Farrell, *Studs Lonigan* (1932)
William Faulkner, *Absalom, Absalom!* (1936)
William Faulkner, *The Sound and The Fury* (1929)
Harvey Fergusson, *Capitol Hill: A Novel of Washington Life* (1923)
F. Scott Fitzgerald, *The Great Gatsby* (1925)
F. Scott Fitzgerald, *This Side of Paradise* (1920)
Ellen Glasgow, *One Man in His Time* (1922)
Henry Hart, *The Great One: A Novel of American Life* (1934)
Sophia Kerr, *Fine to Look At* (1938)
Sinclair Lewis, *Babbitt* (1922)

Sinclair Lewis, *Dodsworth* (1929)
Sinclair Lewis, *Elmer Gantry* (1927)
Sinclair Lewis, *It Can't Happen Here* (1935)
Carson McCullers, *The Heart is a Lonely Hunter* (1940)
John O'Hara, *Appointment in Samarra* (1934)
Frederick Palmer, *So a Leader Came* (1932)
John Jos Passos, *Adventures of a Young Man* (1939)
John Jos Passos, *U.S.A.* (1937)
Richard Rodgers and Oscar Hammerstein, *Oklahoma!* (1942)
Upton Sinclair, *Oil!* (1927)
John Steinbeck, *The Grapes of Wrath* (1939)
John Steinbeck, *Tortilla Flat* (1935)
Robert Penn Warren, *All The King's Men* (1946)
Nathaniel West, *The Day of the Locust* (1939)
Edith Wharton, *The Buccaneers* (1938)
Thornton Wilder, *Our Town* (1938)
Thomas Wolfe, *Look Homeward Angel* (1929)
Richard Wright, *Native Son* (1940)

Third Generation:

Edward Albee, *Who's Afraid of Virginia Woolf?* (1961)
Nelson Algren, *The Man with the Golden Gun* (1949)
Louis Auchincloss, *The Rector of Justin* (1964)
Eugene Burdick and Harvey Wheeler, *Fail-Safe* (1962)
Truman Capote, *In Cold Blood* (1966)
Philip Caputo, *A Rumor of War* (1977)
John Cheever, *The Wapshot Chronicle* (1957)
Richard Condon, *The Manchurian Candidate* (1959)

Samuel Gould Cozzens, *By Love Possessed* (1957)
Samuel Gould Cozzens, *Guard of Honor* (1948)
Allen Drury, *Advise and Consent* (1959)
Pat Frank, *Alas, Babylon* (1959)
John Kenneth Galbraith, *The Triumph* (1965)
Robert Heinlein, *Starship Troopers* (1961) and *The Moon is a Harsh Mistress* (1964)
John Irving, *The World According to Garp* (1978)
Erica Jong, *Fear of Flying* (1974)
John Knowles, *A Separate Peace* (1959)
Fletcher Knebel and Charles W. Bailey II, *Seven Days in May* (1962)
William J. Lederer and Eugene Burdick, *The Ugly American* (1958)
Alison Lurie, *The War Between the Tates* (1974)
John P. Marquand, *Women and Thomas Harrow* (1958)
Mary McCarthy, *The Groves of Acadene* (1951)
Mary McCarthy, *The Oasis* (1949)
Arthur Miller, *Death of a Salesman* (1949)
Robin Moore, *The Green Berets* (1968)
Edwin O'Connor, *The Last Hurrah* (1956)
John O'Hara, *From the Terrace* (1958)
George Orwell, *1984: A Novel* (1949)
John Dos Passos, *Midcentury* (1961)
Ayn Rand, *The Fountainhead* (1943)
J. D. Salinger, *Catcher in the Rye* (1956)
William L. Shirer, *Stranger Come Home* (1954)
Nevil Shute, *On the Beach* (1957)
Irving Wallace, *The Man* (1964)
Tom Wicker, *The Kingpin* (1953)
Paul I. Wellman, *The Walls of Jericho* (1947)
Tennessee Williams, *Streetcar Named Desire* (1947)
Sloan Wilson, *The Man in the Gray Flannel Suit* (1954)

Genealogical and Historical Summary of Family Members

The code numbers assigned to each individual may be used to locate the places of residence

	Code number	Birth–death	Birthplace	Religion
Butler, George C.	1	1857–1927	Maine	Episcopalian
(m. 1886)				
Butler, Mary Wilson	2	? –1916	Maine	Episcopalian
Butler, John	3	1887–1950	Massachusetts	Episcopalian
Butler, Eliott	4	1887–1948	Massachusetts	Episcopalian
Butler, Roger	5	1889–1965	Massachusetts	Episcopalian
Butler, George, Jr.	6	1891–1970s	Massachusetts	Episcopalian
Butler, Robert	7	1895–1974	Massachusetts	Episcopalian
Gale, Charles Edward	8	? –1958	Kansas	Presbyterian
(m. 1901)				
Gale, Chloe Belle Packson	9	? –1943	Kansas	Presbyterian
Gale, Martha Isabelle	10	1919–living	Kansas	Presbyterian, Methodist
5 other children				
Hart, James	11	? –1956	Kansas	Methodist
(m. 1902)				
Hart, Georgia L. Story	12	? –1950	Kansas	Methodist
Hart, Austin	13	1913–living	Kansas	Methodist
Hart, Austin	See 13			
(m. 1941)				
Hart, Martha Isabelle Gale	See 10			
Hart, Martha Ann	14	1944–living	Oregon	
Hart, Carol Kay	15	1945–living	Kansas	
Hart, Stanley Austin	16	1948–living	Kansas	
Hart, Clay Allen	17	1953–living	Kansas	
Hart, Niles Jay	18	1956–living	Kansas	

on Maps I, II, and III.

Occupation	Residence(s)
Lumber business	Bangor, Me.; Brookline, Mass.
None	Bangor, Me., Brookline, Mass.
Stockbroker	Brookline, Mass.; New York City; Beverly, Mass.
Surgeon	Brookline, Mass.; Boston, Mass.
Dilettante	Brookline, Mass.; Providence, R.I.; Boston, Mass.
Banker	Brookline, Mass.; New York City; Boston, Mass.
Attorney, charities admin., presidential advisor	Brookline, Boston, Mass.; Washington, D.C.
Farmer	New Albany, Kans.
Farmer	New Albany, Kans.
Farmer, postmaster	New Albany, Kans.; Fort Lewis, Ore.; New Albany, Kans.
Farmer, land speculator	Roper, Kans.
Farmer	Roper, Kans.
Farmer	Roper; Fort Lewis, Ore.; and New Albany, Kans.
Housewife	New Albany and Fredonia, Kans.
Nurse	New Albany and Topeka, Kans.
Electrical engineer	New Albany, Kans.; Oklahoma City, Okla.
Mechanical engineer	New Albany, Kans.; Oklahoma City, Okla.
Farmer	New Albany, Kans.

Genealogical and historical summary of family members (*continued*)

	Code number	Birth– death	Birthplace	Religion
Kurihara, Yoshisuke	19	?	Japan	Buddhist
Kurihara, Seito (m. ?)	20	? –1959	Japan	Buddhist
Kurihara, Tamako	21	? –1968	Japan	Buddhist
Kurihara, Elaine	22	1926–living	Calif.	Buddhist, Baptist
Brauer, Henry (m. 1884)	23	1856–dec.	Germany	Lutheran
Brauer, Ruth Dort	24	? –dec.	Germany	Lutheran
Brauer, Mathilde	25	1894–1975	Indiana	Lutheran, Dutch Reformed
2 other daughters				
Reinhardt, Jacob (m. 1914)	26	1886–1968	Indiana	Lutheran, Dutch Reformed
Reinhardt, Mathilde Brauer	See 25			
Reinhardt, Raymond	27	1917–living	Indiana	Dutch Reformed
Reinhardt, Regina	28	1920–living	Indiana	Dutch Reformed
3 other children				
Bassano, Andrew (m. 1900)	29	1876–1958	Italy	Roman Catholic
Bassano, Rose Gondolfo	30	? –1924	New York	Roman Catholic
Bassano, Robert	31	1912–living	New York	None
7 other children				
Bassano, Robert (m. 1931)	See 31			
Bassano, Charlotte Bauss	32	1912–living	New York	None
Bassano, Robert, Jr. (Robbie)	33	1936–living	New York	None
O'Reilly, John (m. 1910)	34	1874–1924	Ireland	Roman Catholic
O'Reilly, May Quinn	35		Ireland	Roman Catholic
4 daughters				
O'Reilly, Augustus (Gus) (m. 1918)	36	1892–living	Ireland	Roman Catholic
O'Reilly, Margaret	37	? –living	Massachusetts	Roman Catholic
6 children				
Miller, Meyer (m. 1893)	38	1870–1934	Russia	Jewish
Miller, Annie Jaffee	39	1872–1950	Russia	Jewish
Miller, Pauline	40	1894–1974	New York	Jewish
Miller, Jacob (Jack)	41	1896–1972	New York	Jewish

Occupation	Residence(s)
Retail foods	Japan; Honolulu, Hawaii; San Francisco, Berkeley, Manzanar, Calif.; Japan
Farmer	Japan; Honolulu, Hawaii; Dinuba, Fresno, Calif.; Gila River Relocation Center, Ariz.; Calif.
Farmer	Same as 20
Interpreter, housewife	Dinuba, Fresno, Calif.; Gila River Relocation Center, Ariz.; Columbus, Ohio; Tokyo, Japan; Fullerton, Calif.
Farmer	Stuttgart, Germany; Spencer Co. and Vanderburgh Co., Ind.
Farmer	Vanderburgh Co., Ind.
Farmer	Vanderburgh Co., Ind.
Farmer	Vanderburgh Co., Ind.
Farmer	Vanderburgh Co., Ind.
Laboratory technician, farm manager	Vanderburgh Co. and Evansville, Ind.; Dallas and Austin, Tex.; Vanderburgh Co., Ind.
Terrazzo tile craftsman	Sequals, Italy; Paris, France; New York City; Sequals, Italy
Housewife	New York City
Banker	New York City; Upper St. Clair Township, Pa.
Clerk, secretary, housewife	Same as 31
Federal law enforcement officer	Same as 31
Railway motorman, policeman	Somerville and Boston, Mass.
Housewife	Same as 34
Wholesale meat salesman, broker	Medford, Mass.; Tequesta, Fla.
Housewife	Same as 36
Garment industry, storekeeper	Minsk, Russia; New York City; Providence, R.I.; New York City
Storekeeper, housewife	Pinsk Russia; New York City; Providence, R.I.; New York City
Salesclerk, storekeeper	New York City; Providence, R.I.; New York City; Martha's Vineyard, Mass.; Canton, Mass.
Accountant	New York City; Providence, R.I.; New York City

Genealogical and historical summary of family members (*continued*)

	Code number	Birth– death	Birthplace	Religion
Miller, Betty	42	1900–living	New York	Jewish
Miller, Rose	43	1904–1964	New York	Jewish
Miller, Matilda (Billie)	44	1908–1973	New York	Jewish
Miller, Bertha	45	1911–living	New York	Jewish
Gishman, Henry (m. 1934)	46	1912–living	New York	Jewish
Gishman, Bertha Miller	See 45			
Gishman, Michael 2 other children	47	1939–living	New York	Jewish
Gishman, Michael (m. 1965)	See 47			
Gishman, Karyl Gold	48	1942–living	Michigan	Jewish
Gishman, Kynan	49	1970–living	Ohio	Jewish
Gishman, Kaelen	50	1975–living	Kansas	Jewish
Markovich, Mihailo (m. 1912)	51	1884–living	Serbia	Serbian Orthodox
Markovich, Maria Yaich	52	? –dec.	Serbia	Serbian Orthodox
Markovich, Anna 3 other children	53	1919–living	Pennsylvania	Serbian Orthodox
Simich, Stanko (m. 1904)	54	1882–dec.	Serbia	Serbian Orthodox
Simich, Sasha Nikovic	55	1886–living	Serbia	Serbian Orthodox
Simich, Michael 6 other children	56	1919–living	Pennsylvania	Serbian Orthodox
Simich, Anna Markovich (m. 1941)	See 53			
Simich, Michael	See 56			
Simich, Lawrence	57	1943–living	Pennsylvania	Serbian Orthodox
Simich, Michele	58	1950–living	Pennsylvania	Serbian Orthodox
Trace, William (m. 1868)	59	1844–1925	Tennessee	Baptist
Trace, Millie Elizabeth	60	1851–1934	South Carolina	Baptist
Trace, Benjamin Harrison	61	1892–1957	Tennessee	Baptist
Trace, McKinley Welch	62	1893–1936	Tennessee	None
14 other children				
Trace, McKinley Welch (m. ?)	See 62			

Occupation	Residence(s)
Salesclerk, factory operative, sales clerk	New York City; Providence, R.I.; New York City
Salesclerk, factory operative, supervisor	New York City; Providence, R.I.; New York City
Secretary, booking agent	New York City; Providence, R.I.; New York City; Miami Beach, Fla.
Secretary, housewife, clerk, housewife	Providence, R.I.; New York City; San Francisco, Calif.
Pianist, composer, factory operative, music licensing	New York City; San Francisco, Calif.
Geologist	New York City; East Lansing, Mich.; Granville, O.; Overland Park, Kans.
Social worker	East Lansing, Mich.; Granville, O.; Overland Park, Kans. Granville, O.; Overland Park, Kans. Overland Park, Kans.
Steel worker	Primslje, Serbia; Western Pa.; Midland, Pa.
Boardinghouse keeper, housewife	Zagreb, Serbia, Aliquippa and Midland, Pa.
Clerk, housewife	Midland, Pa.
Coal miner	Merich, Serbia; Primrose, Pa.
Housewife	Serbia; Export and Primrose, Pa.
Steelworker	Primrose and Midland, Pa.
Historian, futurologist	Midland, Pa.; Bloomington, Ind.; Lawrence, Kans.; Tulsa, Okla.
Music education	Midland and Pittsburgh, Pa.
Farmer	Wayne Co., Tenn.
Farmer	South Carolina; Wayne Co., Tenn.
Railroad worker	Wayne Co., Tenn.; Evansville, Ind.
Unemployed, petty criminal	Wayne Co., Tenn.; Evansville, Ind.; Springfield, Mo.; Michigan City, Ind., Los Angeles, Calif.

Genealogical and historical summary of family members (*continued*)

	Code number	Birth–death	Birthplace	Religion
Trace, Velma Milton	63	1906–1960	Indiana	None
Trace, Calvin	64	1926–?	Indiana	?
Trace, Franklin	65	1933–?	California	?
Trace, Benjamin Harrison (m. 1920)	See 61			
Trace, Anna Lee Bonham	66	1902–1963	Tennessee	Baptist
Trace, Benjamin, Jr. (JR)	67	1921–1976	Indiana	None
Trace, Jerry Conrad	68	1924–living	Indiana	Methodist; Roman Catholic
3 other children				
Trace, Jerry Conrad (m. 1942)	See 68			
Trace, Peggy Reynolds 4 children	69		Indiana	Roman Catholic
Williams, James	70	1870–?	Mississippi	Unknown
Williams, Henry	71	1872–?	Mississippi	Unknown
Hunt, James (m. ?)	72	?	Unknown	Baptist
Hunt, Sylvia 2 sons	73	?	Unknown	Baptist
Hunt, Lila Williams	74	1919–living	Mississippi	Baptist
Gropper, Louis G. (m. 1942)	75	1918–living	Texas	Baptist
Gropper, Lila Williams Hunt	See 74			
Gropper, Christopher James	76	1944–living	Washington	Methodist
2 other sons				
Gropper, Christopher James (m. 1971)	See 76			
Gropper, Jane Mitchell 2 children	77	1946–living	Texas	Methodist
Nava, Antonio Luis (m. 1937)	78	1905–living	Texas	Roman Catholic
Nava, Sophia Reya	79	1908–living	Texas	Roman Catholic
Nava, Antonio A.	80	1937–living	Texas	Roman Catholic
Nava, Antonio A. (m. 1956)	See 80			
Nava, Irma Flores	81	? –living	Texas	Roman Catholic
Nava, Antonio Avilo	82	1957–living	Texas	Roman Catholic
6 other children				

Occupation	Residence(s)
Prostitute, bar waitress, unemployed	Evansville, Ind.; Los Angeles, Calif.
Petty rackets, unemployed, ?	Evansville, Ind.; Los Angeles, Calif.
U.S. Navy, ?	Los Angeles, Calif.
Domestic, housewife, parttime work	Tenn.; Evansville, Ind.
Invalid	Evansville, Ind.
Taxicab management	Evansville, Ind.; Louisville, Ky.; Birmingham, Ala.; Denver, Colo.; Phoenix, Ariz.; Sugar Land, Tex.; various.
Housewife	Same as 68
Farm tenant, bldg. contractor	Tecumseh, Miss.; Detroit, Mich.
Farm tenant, bldg. contractor	Tecumseh, Miss.; Detroit, Mich.
Farmer, preacher, handyman	Shady Grove and Kosse, Tex.
Farmer, teacher, housewife	Shady Grove and Kosse, Tex.
Housewife, teacher, librarian	Miss.; Shady Grove, Kosse, Martin, Gainesville, Tex.; Seattle, Wash.; Levelland, Lubbock, Tex.; Atlanta, Ga.
Farmer, teacher	Bonham, Sherman, Tyler, Gainesville, Tex.; Seattle, Wash.; Levelland, Lubbock, Tex.
Personnel Manager	Seattle, Wash.; Levelland, Lubbock, Tex.; Decatur, Ga.
Department store buyer	Lubbock, Tex.; Decatur, Ga.
U.S. mounted border patrol	Los Ebanos, Tex.
Housewife	Laredo, Los Ebanos, Tex.
Constable, deputy sheriff, chief airport security officer	Los Ebanos, Pharr, Sullivan City, Tex.
Housewife	Laredo, Pharr, Los Ebanos, Sullivan City, Tex.
U.S. Marine	Los Ebanos, Sullivan City, Tex.

Genealogical and historical summary of family members *(continued)*

	Code number	Birth–death	Birthplace	Religion
Martinez, Julio (m. 1947)	83	1927–living	Puerto Rico	Roman Catholic
Martinez, Angelina Lopes	84	1929–living	Puerto Rico	Roman Catholic
Martinez, Pedro	85	1948–living	New York	Roman Catholic
Martinez, Pasqual	86	1950–living	New York	Roman Catholic
Martinez, Maria	87	1952–living	New York	Roman Catholic
Martinez, Juanita	88	1955–living	New York	Roman Catholic
Martinez, Jaime	89	1955–living	New York	Roman Catholic

Occupation	Residence(s)
Sandwich maker, janitor, auto mechanic	Puerto Rico, New York City
Salad maker, housewife	Puerto Rico, New York City
Truck driver	New York City
College student	New York City
Shopkeeper	New York City
Housewife	New York City
Unemployed	New York City

Index

This book has been set VIP, in 10 and 9 point Souvenir Light, leaded 2 points. Part numbers are 18 point Souvenir Demi Bold and 48 point Souvenir Medium; part titles are 27 point Souvenir Medium. Chapter numbers are 48 point Souvenir Medium and chapter titles are 24 point Souvenir Demi Bold. The overall size of the type area is 34 by 46½ picas.